SOURCEBOOK ON OBLIGATIONS AND LEGAL REMEDIES

Geoffrey Samuel, MA, LLB, PhD (Cantab), Dr (Limburg)
Reader in Law
Lancaster University

Cavendish
Publishing
Limited

First published in Great Britain 1995 by Cavendish Publishing Limited, The Glass House, Wharton Street, London WC1X 9PX

Telephone: 0171-278 8000   Facsimile: 0171-278 8080

British Library Cataloguing in Publication Data

Samuel, Geoffrey
Sourcebook on Obligations and Legal Remedies –
(Sourcebook Series)
I Title II Series
344.2062

ISBN 1-85941 180 0

To all my friends

PREFACE

This sourcebook started life as a collection of materials for the DEA courses on the common law at Paris I and II. It is offered in this English version, in these days of research ratings, simply as an old-fashioned undergraduate teaching casebook, although it is to be hoped that there is material and comment which will be of interest to postgraduates and law teachers. Some of the comments are somewhat provocative; the purpose is simply to bring a little life to the case law and to the doctrine and to stimulate readers into responses. The aim is to get students to see that law is not just about learning and applying rules. In adopting such an approach I am deliberately adopting the methods of those teachers I found, and still find, so stimulating.

Many thanks to my colleague and friend Pierre Legrand, now Professor of Comparative Legal Culture at Tilburg University, not only for encouraging me to publish it in England, but for correcting my French in the Paris edition and giving me so many ideas with respect to comparative law. Many thanks also to Jo Reddy of Cavendish Publishing for agreeing almost at once to accept the manuscript (with major changes of course) and for being so patient both with respect to this manuscript, rewritten during the first months of my Paris appointment, and with my other commitments to Cavendish.

I should in addition like to acknowledge the great debt owed to Paris I and II for providing me with the opportunity to reflect upon the common law in the context of the civilian tradition: the many discussions with professors and students are proving most stimulating and I hope that some of this will be reflected in the notes and questions in this present collection. The law faculty at the University of Nancy also deserves thanks for giving me many opportunities over the last few years to research into, and discuss, French law, legal history and comparative law in the comfort of its town and institution. Of course I owe much to others as well – professionally to my teachers, friends and acquaintances in common law and civil law faculties who have proved so supportive, not forgetting the works of others too numerous to mention by name but hopefully reflected in the notes in this collection. Beyond the profession, my family, as usual, have been particularly, patient, not just in uprooting themselves to come to Paris for a year, but in not complaining too much about the attempts to meet deadlines. A special thanks.

Geoffrey Samuel, La Sorbonne, Spring 1995

INTRODUCTION

1 GENERAL REMARKS

In their joint statement issued in July 1993 the Law Society and the Council of Legal Education recognised the validity of the comparative, jurisprudential, historical and interdisciplinary approaches to the teaching of the foundational subjects; and in renaming Contract and Tort as Obligations I and Obligations II they seemingly went some way in injecting a comparative dimension into the common law. In addition, the statement emphasised the need for an understanding of the fundamental doctrines and principles which underpin the law together with a knowledge and appreciation of the sources, institutions, concepts and reasoning and research methods employed by lawyers. Mere knowledge of the rules is recognised as not being enough; the good jurist must be able to apply the law to the facts and to communicate the reasons for the answers arrived at, and the sources used, when it comes to problem-solving in law. In other words legal method, legal reasoning, jurisprudence and comparative law are now formally an integral part of subjects like the Law of Obligations.

All this may seem self-evident. However, it is by no means so easy to assert as a matter of form what it is to have knowledge of, say, the law of obligations since the old idea that law is a matter of learning and mechanically applying rules is no longer a viable knowledge thesis. The processes of legal reasoning and legal problem-solving are now known – thanks in part to artificial intelligence research[1] – to be much more complex and sophisticated processes. This is not to say that rules and principles are not important – knowledge of statutory rules and case law principles is undoubtedly a central aspect of learning the law. What must be emphasised is the gap between the rule and the decision: the process of moving from a legal proposition (that is a rule or principle) to an actual decision in a legal problem involves reasoning processes that need to be examined in themselves. These processes are, in other words, part of legal knowledge itself.

Traditionally, these reasoning processes have been associated with the assumption that law is a matter of propositional knowledge – that is to say that it is a subject consisting of rules and principles. And thus reasoning has, particularly on the Continent, been seen largely as a matter of mechanical application. Legal theorists have, of course, recognised a distinction between easy and hard cases: the easy case will

---

1   See generally G Samuel, *The Foundations of Legal Reasoning* (Maklu, 1994).

be one where a rule can be mechanically applied whereas the hard case will be one where the reasoner will have to undertake difficult interpretation exercises before an acceptable decision can be reached.[2] But these theorists have never questioned the assumption that law consists of rules and principles with the result that legal textbooks have on the whole been seen as being little more than descriptive works. Their role is to set out, as clearly as possible, the rules and principles of the area to which they are devoted. Sourcebooks and casebooks are, admittedly, different; their role has been to emphasise aspects of legal knowledge not to be found in the traditional textbook. And so a good casebook will invite its readers to 'brief' each case read: that is to say it will ask the reader to think not only about the rule or principle in issue but also about the interests, values, ideologies, methods and the like that each case raises. Casebooks and sourcebooks thus make good vehicles for learning to see beyond the rules.

2 SCOPE OF THE PRESENT WORK

This present work will, however, go beyond the standard sourcebooks in as much as it will explicitly devote chapters to the structure of the common law (Chapter 1) and to legal reasoning and method (Chapter 2). The aim of these chapters will be to provide a methodological context within which the details of the law of obligations can be understood; they will seek to give the reader of the contract, tort and remedies source material some further material which will explicitly help them with research and problem-solving. The point to be emphasised here is that no area of positive law can be properly understood without, first, some understanding of the mentality of the common law.

In addition to these structure and method chapters there will be a chapter devoted to the law of remedies (Chapter 3). There are a range of reasons for including such a chapter, but two are particularly important. First, the history of the law of obligations in both the common law and civil law is closely interrelated to the law of actions (ie remedies). In the Digest of Roman law[3] the title dealing specifically with the category of obligations is entitled *de obligationibus et actionibus*[4] and in the common law, before the categories of contract and tort were adopted problems were analysed via forms of action such as trespass and debt. Secondly, in English law at any rate, practising lawyers have still not escaped from

---

2   See J Bengoetxea, *The Legal Reasoning of the European Court of Justice* (Oxford, 1993), pp 184ff, 146ff.

3   A good introduction both to Roman law itself and to the Roman law of delict (tort) is to be found in Kolbert (ed), *Justinian: The Digest of Roman Law* (Penguin, 1979).

4   D.44.7.

remedies thinking: liability in contract and in tort – and even more in restitution – is often measured in relation to the existence of a cause of action and this cause of action, in turn, has been described by Diplock LJ as 'simply a factual situation the existence of which entitles one person to obtain from the court a remedy against another person'.[5] The linking of remedies to obligations has, then, not only an historical and comparative dimension, but an important practical aspect. One of the first questions that needs to be asked when 'briefing' a case is: what is the plaintiff seeking to obtain from the court? As we shall see, the law applicable to a factual situation may vary depending upon whether a plaintiff is seeking, say, damages or an injunction.

The chapters following the one on remedies will divide obligations into two broad kinds: those that are contractual (Chapters 4-6) and those arising outside of contract (Chapter 7). There is nothing inevitable about such a dichotomy and, as far as English law is concerned, it is arguable that isolating contractual obligations from the non-contractual might even be misleading since historically and conceptually compensation actions have the same remedial basis in the action of trespass. Moreover, when it comes to restitution the linking of debt to contract has caused a number of conceptual problems. Nevertheless, in both the civil and the later common law, contract has such a specific and particular history that the subject has become more than a sub-category of the law of obligations.[6] It is a fundamental legal relationship which cannot easily be abandoned in that it continues to act not just as a means of directly or indirectly transferring rights of property,[7] but as a paradigm obligation through which all other obligations often have to defer. Non-contractual obligations may be unavailable in situations where a contractual obligation governs. The distinction between contractual and non-contractual obligations continues, then, to command practical and philosophical respect and, just as important perhaps, remains a useful bridge between the English legal system and those of our continental partners.

This comparative aspect to legal knowledge has been specifically recognised by the Lord Chancellor's Advisory Committee on Legal Education and Conduct in its Consultation Document on the Initial Stage of Legal Education. Now from a comparative position the law of contract dominates the law of obligations in that it takes up most of the articles in the obligations section of the civil codes; non-contractual obligations seem by comparison an after-thought (although the case law

---

5   *Letang v Cooper* [1965] 1 QB 232, 242-243.

6   See generally J Gordley, *The Philosophical Origins of Modern Contract Doctrine* (Oxford, 1991).

7   See eg, Sale of Goods Act 1979 ss 16-18.

tells a different story). And so a work wishing to state the English law of obligations, always assuming that such a category is viable this side of the Channel, is almost forced to devote pride of place to contract. Yet contract holds a central position in the law of obligations for another reason as well. Not only does a good knowledge of contract act as an introduction to Western private law as a whole, but the subject lies at the centre of the legal system in as much as it relates, often directly, to all the other areas of private and public law. Contract is central to commercial law, property law, employment law and even administrative law and criminal law. Indeed it is important to the understanding of a number of jurisprudential and political theories. This present sourcebook in no way wishes to underestimate or diminish the importance of non-contractual obligations; the aim of the work is to provide a structural approach to the English law of obligations which reflects the category in a European rather than a strictly English context.

3 LAW OF OBLIGATIONS

In truth it is by no means easy to impose on the common law a law of obligations framework. It may seem simple enough to put the old subjects of contract and tort together under a generic heading, but it has always to be remembered that in the civil law tradition the idea of a law of obligations has had, since Roman times, a specific meaning and purpose. An obligation was not a means of making something ours or a vehicle for vindicating some right of possession or property; it was a means by which someone was obliged to do, to give or not to do something[8] and so, as Gaius points out in his *Institutes*, we cannot use an obligations remedy to get our own property back since what is already ours cannot be conveyed to us (*nec enim quod nostrum est nobis dari potest*).[9] In Roman law an obligation was defined in relation to an *actio in personam* – that is to say in terms of a personal remedy aimed at a specific and named person. This personal claim had to be distinguished from claims in respect of things; an *actio in rem* was a legal remedy that was aimed at a specific piece of property (*res*) and was used to assert either ownership (*dominium*) or a real right (*ius in re*) in a thing. This remedial dichotomy between personal and real actions in turn gave rise to a fundamental distinction in civil law thinking between the law of obligations and the law of property.[10] This distinction between property

---

8   D.44.7.3pr.
9   G.4.4.
10   H F Jolowicz, *Roman Foundations of Modern Law* (Oxford, 1957), pp 61–81.

and obligations continues to lie at the heart of the Continental civil codes and it acts as the basis for classifying legal rights. Indeed so strong is the dichotomy in German law that it is impossible to progress as a private lawyer without a thorough understanding of the difference between the relationship between person and person (obligations) and the relationship between person and thing (property). The distinction between the two relationships acts as the starting point for the whole of private law.

It is this strict separation between real and personal rights, between property and obligations, that causes the trouble for the common lawyer. Certainly the English jurist will have little difficulty in distinguishing, as a matter of form between, for instance, contract and possession or tort and ownership, but in problem-solving substance it is very easy indeed for these fundamental notions to become confused.[11] O lends goods to D and these goods are stolen by D's employee: is this a contract, tort or property problem? T steals money from P, his employer, and gambles it away at D's casino: if P sues D for the return of the stolen money, is this an action *in personam* or *in rem*? The German lawyer will want clear answers to these questions since they raise issues of basic legal science. The common lawyer, however, will be little troubled by such questions, save perhaps if the defendant is bankrupt; the common lawyer will simply think in terms of whether P has a remedy against D. From the historical position, the English forms of action, unlike those of Roman law, were little interested in conforming to the property and obligations dichotomy: to the early common lawyer all actions were a mixture of both property and obligations[12] and this has resulted in a situation where the modern law of contract and tort has to do the work of the law of property as well as the law of obligations. The torts of trespass, nuisance and conversion usually involve litigation problems arising out of the relationship between person and thing. And any problem involving damage to, or loss of, moveable property owned by one person but in the possession of another can often appear particularly complex since these facts will give rise to rights and duties arising out of contract, tort and possession (bailment).[13]

This confusion between property and obligations works against the development in English law of a category of the law of obligations in the full continental meaning of the term. Nevertheless, the notion presents common lawyers and civil lawyers with a challenge. If harmonisation of private law is to become a reality the English jurist is going to have to

---

11   See G Samuel, Property Notions in the Law of Obligations [1994] CLJ 524.

12   S C Milsom, *Historical Foundations of the Common Law* (Butterworths, 2nd ed, 1981), p 263.

13   See eg, *The Albazero* [1977] AC 774.

make some compromises at the level of legal science while the civil lawyer might have much to learn from the English emphasis on remedies which can inject into problem-solving an element of flexibility. By starting out from an injunction rather than a rigid definition of ownership the common lawyer finds it much easier to cope with changing notions of property even if it is at the price of introducing uncertainty, if not anarchy, into legal thinking. In turn a rational and structured legal science can on occasions aid problem-solving by allowing the lawyer to operate with ease at one and the same time at the level of law and fact. The relationships between person and person and between person and thing permits an ordered analysis of factual problems while at the same time facilitating with ease the application of the law.

4 LEGAL INSTITUTIONS AND LEGAL ANALYSIS

The idea that law can act at one and the same time inside and outside of the facts is the key to its success as a 'scientific' discourse. Law can, seemingly, 'explain' social facts and 'predict' what in particular circumstances ought to happen. If a coach company loses the suitcase of one of its passengers, legal discourse can explain these facts in terms of legal relationships (contract, bailment) which act as the medium for turning the factual situation into one of rights and duties; these rights and duties then become the basis for predicting what ought to happen in terms of responsibility for its loss. Thus the taking into possession of the passenger's suitcase (relationship between person and thing) gives rise to a bailment relationship which endows the passenger with certain rights and the coach company with certain duties. The passenger has the right to have his suitcase returned unless the coach company can show that it has fulfilled all its duties with respect to the thing: that is to say it can show that the case was lost through no fault on their part.[14] The key relationships here are those between passenger and suitcase, between passenger and coach company and between coach company and suitcase; and these relationships translate into rights of ownership, possession, contract and tort. Sometimes the mere relationship between person and thing can, of itself, give rise to rights and duties; thus possessory rights often follow the thing itself. If, however, instead of losing her suitcase the coach company, through the act of one of its employees, managed to injure the passenger through bad driving, then, as far as English law is concerned at any rate, merely to

---

14 *Houghland v R R Low (Luxury Coaches) Ltd* [1962] 1 QB 694.

show that the company was 'in possession' of the passenger is not enough.[15] Although the relationship is undoubtedly close enough of itself to give rise to a duty on the part of the coach company to take care of its passengers, the passenger still has to show, in addition to the relationship (duty of care), damage and fault. These latter notions are typical legal focal points: for they are notions that have meaning at one and the same time in the world of fact (broken bones, torn clothes, carelessness etc) and the world of law (tort of negligence, definitions of damage). They are, in other words, notions that operate within and without the facts.

However, even within the world of law, damage and fault cannot exist in isolation. They can only attach to things and to people. Accordingly, two other legal notions that exist inside and outside of facts are the notions of a person and a thing. This may seem too obvious to warrant attention; yet it is more sophisticated than it first appears since many 'persons' who cause or suffer damage are not real persons at all. They are organisations endowed with legal personality by the law. They are collectivities manifesting not only the characteristics of subjectivity which one normally associates with the human individual, but also their own characteristics some of which may, in turn, be imposed upon the individual human.[16] Equally there are many 'things' that are not real things in the sense that they can be touched; and so, for example, if D owes C £50,000 D has an asset that is a very real asset in terms of wealth but intangible in terms of physical existence in the real world. The result of these legal creations is that there can be, in effect, fictional people (companies) owning fictional things (debts) and it is only when lawyers are faced with certain types of criminal proceedings that the unreality of the situation has a habit of intruding. If an angry coach driver assaults one of the passengers, is it true to say that the passenger, who of course has a contract with the coach company, has been assaulted by the coach company (cf *Keppel Bus Co*, p 310)?

5 LAW OF ACTIONS

All this brings one back to remedies. For whatever the rights, duties, relations or persons in issue, the key question for the parties to any legal dispute is the nature of the legal action. Can P sue D for compensation? Can P obtain against D an order stopping him from playing his trumpet after midnight? Can P obtain restitution of property mistakenly given to

---

15   *Readhead v Midland Railway* (1869) LR 4 QB 379.
16   Cf J-P Dupuy, *Aux origines des sciences cognitives* (Éditions La Découverte, 1994), pp 174-177.

the wrong person? The granting or refusing of such actions may well, on many occasions, depend upon the rights and obligations of the parties, but these rights and obligations owe their existence to a legal structure that recognises the institutions of 'persons' and 'actions'. If P is granted an injunction against D prohibiting the latter from interfering with goods in P's possession, then the court is effectively constructing an institutional structure between 'person', 'thing' and 'action' that can act as the basis for a property 'right'. It is the action that acts as the dynamic means of constructing a relationship between person and thing (see eg *Lipkin Gorman*, p 145 and *Kingdom of Spain v Christie*, p 112). In the civil law systems on the continent this institutional role of the legal action has been suppressed by codes of rights which express the institutional structures only through written propositions (*regulae iuris* – rules and principles). For example, in the civil law, with regard to a dispute over the title to goods, one would start not with an injunction but with a definition of ownership and one would then work from there towards a court order. But in the common law one would not start out from a definition of ownership; one would start from an action for damages for wrongful interference with goods, or alternatively from an injunction, and this would lead the court towards a discussion about property rights. And, of course, if the courts grant the damages or injunction it is implying the existence of an institutional relationship between plaintiff and goods. The action remains a live institution in the common law and has not, as yet, been replaced by the notion of a right (in the continental sense of the term). However, before one can think in terms of the institutions of persons, things and actions, it is first necessary to look at the physical institutions of private law itself: that is to say it is necessary to look at the courts, judges, legislators and parties who, or which, give the law of actions its dynamic aspect.

CONTENTS

Preface   v
Introduction   vii
Table of Cases   xxi
Table of Statutes   xxxvii

1   THE STRUCTURE OF THE COMMON LAW   1
    1 INTRODUCTION   1
    2 THE ROLE OF THE COURTS   1
        (a) Trial Judge   2
        (b) Court of Appeal   4
        (c) House of Lords   7
    3 THE ROLE OF PRECEDENT   9
    4 THE ROLE OF PARLIAMENT   11
    5 THE ROLE OF INSTITUTIONS   13
        (a) The Institutional System   13
        (b) Legal Subject (*Persona*)   17
        (c) Legal Object (*Res*)   19
        (d) Legal Remedy (*Actio*)   22
    6 THE ROLE OF LEGAL CATEGORIES   27
        (a) Introduction   27
        (b) Civil and Criminal Law   30
        (c) Contract   32
        (d) Tort   33
        (e) Restitution (Unjust Enrichment)   36
        (f) Property (1): Real and Personal Property   37
        (g) Property (2): Bailment   38
        (h) Equity   41
    7 THE ROLE OF THE CATEGORIES OF PUBLIC AND
       PRIVATE LAW   43
        (a) Introduction   43
        (b) Administrative Contracts   44
        (c) Administrative Liability in Tort   46
        (d) Restitution and Public Law   54
    8 THE ROLE OF TEXTBOOKS   56
    9 THE ROLE OF FACTS   57
    10 THE ROLE OF LEGAL CONCEPTS   58

2   LEGAL METHOD AND THE COMMON LAW   61
    1 INTRODUCTION   61
    2 CAUSES OF ACTION   63
        (a) Historical Considerations: The Forms of Action   63
        (b) Modern Law: Remedies and Rights   65

3 PLEADINGS   66
4 THE LEGAL RULE   68
5 GENERAL PRINCIPLES OF LAW   69
6 LEGAL CONCEPTS   70
   (a) Normative Concepts   70
      (i) Rights   70
      (ii) Duty   73
   (b) Quasi-Normative Concepts   74
      (i) Interests   74
      (ii) Damage   74
      (iii) Interests and Damage   79
   (c) Descriptive Concepts   80
7 LAW AND FACT   81
   (a) Questions of Law and Questions of Fact   81
   (b) Establishing the Facts   82
   (c) The Legal Categorisation of the Facts   84
   (d) The Response of the Law to the Facts   85
   (e) The Reception of Facts by the Law   86
   (f) The Reception of Law by the Facts   87
   (g) The Utilisation of Facts to Determine the Law   87
8 LEGAL REASONING   88
   (a) Introduction   88
   (b) The Syllogism   91
   (c) Logic and Categorisation   92
   (d) Reasoning by Elimination   94
   (e) Mental Imagery   94
   (f) Analogy   95
   (g) Metaphor   97
   (h) The Appeal to the Facts   97
   (i) Values   98
   (j) Policy   100
   (k) Interpretation of Rights   101
   (l) Practical Reasoning   102
   (m) Symmetry   108

3   REMEDIES   111
1 INTRODUCTION   111
2 REMEDIES AND RIGHTS   117
3 REMEDIES AND INTERESTS   121
4 SELF-HELP   124
   (a) Personal Justice   124
   (b) Self-protection   125
   (c) Refusal to Pay   126

5 DEBT 130
   (a) Introduction 130
   (b) Contractual Debt 133
   (c) Debt and Damages 138
   (d) Non-contractual Debt 140
6 TRACING 140
7 SPECIFIC PERFORMANCE 154
8 RESCISSION IN EQUITY 157
9 RECTIFICATION IN EQUITY 165
10 ACCOUNT 167
11 SUBROGATION 168
12 INJUNCTION 170
   (a) The Nature of an Injunction 170
   (b) Interlocutory Injunction 171
   (c) The Role of Injunctions 175
13 DAMAGES 177
   (a) The Role of Damages 177
   (b) Contractual Liability and Damages 178
   (c) Tortious Liability and Damages 186
   (d) Exemplary Damages 188
   (e) Personal Injury 189
   (f) Fraud 190
   (g) Damages for Wrongful Interference 191
   (h) The Limitation of Liability 193

4 INTRODUCTION TO CONTRACTUAL OBLIGATIONS ... 203
1 INTRODUCTION 203
2 TYPES OF CONTRACT 204
   (a) Bilateral Contracts 204
   (b) Unilateral Contracts 205
   (c) Contract or Contracts 206
3 LEVEL OF DUTY 209
4 LAW OF PERSONS AND LAW OF PROPERTY 214
5 PROMISE AND AGREEMENT 216
6 FREEDOM OF CONTRACT 220
7 THE INTERPRETATION OF CONTRACTS 226

5 THE FORMATION OF A CONTRACT 233
1 INTRODUCTION 233
2 OFFER AND ACCEPTANCE 235
   (a) Fact and Law 235
   (b) Offers and the Consumer 236
   (c) Offers and Commerce 239

(d) The End of an Offer   241
(e) Pre-contractual Liability   241
3 CONSIDERATION   252
(a) Validity of Consideration   252
(b) Consideration and Abuse of Rights   255
(c) Third Parties   260
4 MISTAKE   261
(a) Introduction   261
(b) Liability in Contract   266
(c) Liability in Tort   268
(i) Deceit   268
(ii) Negligence   268
(iii) Statute   271
(d) Rescission in Equity   272
(e) Error *in Corpore*   275
(f) Error *in Negotio*   286
(g) Error *in Persona*   288
5 FRAUD   289
6 DURESS   290

6   NON-PERFORMANCE OF A CONTRACT   295
1 INTRODUCTION   295
2 BREACH AND NON-PERFORMANCE   296
3 THE ROLE OF FAULT   302
4 EXCLUSION AND LIMITATION CLAUSES   312
5 BREACH AND LEVEL OF DUTY   320
6 REMEDIES AND BREACH   327
(a) Self-help   327
(b) Damages   332
(c) Debt   335
7 IMPOSSIBILITY OF PERFORMANCE   338
8 CONTRACT: FINAL OBSERVATIONS   350

7   NON-CONTRACTUAL OBLIGATIONS   353
1 INTRODUCTION   353
2 DAMAGE CAUSED TO ANOTHER   358
(a) Damage   358
(b) Liability for Individual Acts   360
(c) Liability for People   362
(d) Liability for Things   373
(e) Liability for Words   387
3 ROAD ACCIDENTS   395

CONTENTS

4 QUASI CONTRACTS   403
   (a) Introduction   403
   (b) The Action for Money Had and Received   406
   (c) The Action for Money Paid   407
   (d) Quantum Meruit   409
5 UNJUST ENRICHMENT   410
6 ABUSE OF RIGHTS   413
7 FINAL OBSERVATIONS   414

APPENDIX   417
1 THE STRUCTURE OF THE COMMON LAW   417
2 LEGAL METHOD AND THE COMMON LAW   418
3 REMEDIES   419
4 NON-CONTRACTUAL OBLIGATIONS   424
5 FINAL NOTE   433

INDEX   435

TABLE OF CASES

A/S Awilco of Oslo v Fulvia SpA Di Navigazione of Cagliari; Chikuma, The [1981] 1 WLR 314 231

Abse v Smith [1986] 1 QB 536 4

Addis v Gramophone Co Ltd [1909] AC 488 189

Agip (Africa) Ltd v Jackson [1990] Ch 265 [1991] Ch 547 140-4,405

Air Canada v Secretary of State for Trade (No 2) 2 AC 394......................9

Albacruz (Cargo Owners) v Albazero (Owners) [1977] AC 774 HL 178, 429, 431

Albazero, The see Albacruz (Cargo Owners) v Albazero (Owners)

Aldora, The [1975] QB 748 ....133, 140

Allen v Jambo Holdings Ltd [1980] 2 All ER 502 CA 172

Aluminium Industrie Vaasen BV v Romalpa Aluminium Ltd [1976] 2 All ER 552..170

American Cyanamid Co v Ethicon Ltd [1975] AC 396...........................171

Anchor Brewhouse Developments v Berkley House [1987] EG 173...176

Anns v Merton London Borough Council [1978] AC 728.....................371

Anton Piller KG v Manufacturing Processes Ltd see Piller (Anton) KG v Manufacturing Processes

Archer v Brown [1985] QB 401 ....30-1, 191

Argentino, The (1888) 13 PD 191 39

Arkwright v Newbold (1881) 17 Ch D 301 268

Ashington Piggeries Ltd v Christopher Hill Ltd [1972] AC 441 206-8

Associates British Ports v Transport and General Workers Union [1989] 1 WLR 939 177

Associated Distributors Ltd v Hall [1938] 2 KB 83..............................336

Associated Japanese Bank (International) Ltd v Crédit du Nord SA [1989] 1 WLR 255 ....262, 275, 280-5

Atlas Express Ltd v Kafco (Importers and Distributors) Ltd [1989] QB 833; [1989] 3 WLR 389; [1989] 1 All ER 641 293

Attia v British Gas Plc [1988] QB 304 CA 80, 299-301, 359

Attica Sea Carriers Corp v Ferrostaal Poseidon Bulk Reederei Gmbh [1976] 1 Ll Rep 250 CA 136-7

Att-Gen v Guardian Newspapers (No 2) [1990] AC 109 HL.................168

Att-Gen v PYA Quarries [1957] 2 QB 169 123

Avon Finance Co Ltd v Bridger [1985] 2 All ER 281 CA 163, 286-7, 293

BP Exploration (Libya) Ltd v Hunt (No 2) [1979] 1 WLR 783 302

Baily v Bullock [1950] 2 All ER 1167 181

Bainbrigge v Browne (1881) 18 Ch D 188..160

Baker v Market Harborough Industrial Co-operative Society [1953] 1 WLR 1472 213

Ballard v Tomlinson (1885) 29 Ch D 115 ....375, 376

Bamford v Turnley (1862) 3 B & S 62...377

Bank of Credit and Commerce International SA v Aboody
[1990] 1 QB 923..159, 160
Bank of Montreal v Stuart [1911] AC 120..159
Banque Belge pour l'Etranger v Hambrouck [1921] 1 KB 321 141
Banque Financière de la Citie SA V Westgate Insurance Co *sub nom*
Banque Keyser Ullman v Skandia (UK) Insurance Co [1991] AC 249;
[1990] 1 QB 665 265
Banque Keyser Ullman v Skandia Insurance see Banque
Financière de la Citiè SA v Westgate Insurance Co
Barclays Bank Plc v O'Brien [1993] QB 109; [1993] 3 WLR 786;
[1992] 3 WLR 593 .... 100, 157-64, 165, 293, 294
Barher v Herbert [1911] 2 KB 633 385
Barnett v Chelsea & Kensington Hospital Management Committee
[1969] 1 QB 428..198
Bell v Lever Brothers [1932] AC 161 ....262, 264, 277-8, 282, 283, 284, 285
Benjamin v Storr (1874) LR 9 CP 400 120
Bentsen v Taylor Sons & Co (No 2) [1893] 2 QB 274.................................329
Berry v Berry [1987] Fam 1 258
Best v Samuel Fox & Co Ltd [1952] AC 716 ....35, 101, 182, 358-9
Beswick v Beswick [1968] AC 58; [1966] Ch 538 (CA)..................37, 71, 80,
86, 122, 123, 151, 154-5, 260,
261, 296, 351, 391, 413, 414

Birmingham and District Land Co v London and
North Western Ry Co (1888) 40 Ch D 268 260
Black v Yates [1991] 3 WLR 90 66
Blackpool and Fylde Aero Club Ltd v Blackpool
Borough Council [1990] 1 WLR 1195..............................46, 87, 98, 243-6,
249, 252, 351, 413
Bolton v Mahadeva [1972] 1 WLR 1009 ....126, 127, 128, 138,
227, 295, 297, 299, 349, 407, 410
Bolton v Stone [1951] AC 850 ....10, 23, 82
Bolton (HL), (Engineering) Co Ltd v T J Graham & Sons Ltd
[1956] Ch 577 18
Bone v Seale [1975] 1 All ER 787 CA...187
Borag, The see Compania Financiera 'Soleada' SA
Bourhill v Young [1943] AC 92..301
Bowmakers Ltd v Barnett Instruments Ltd [1945] KB 45 151
Bradford City Metropolitan Council v Arora
[1991] 2 QB 507 189
Bradford Corporation v Pickles [1895] AC 587 ....124, 125, 361,
395, 413, 414
Bradford Third Equitable Benefit Building Society v Borders
[1941] 2 All ER 205...265, 268, 290, 390
Brandeis Goldscmidt & Co v Western Transport [1981] QB 864...........191
Bridge v Campbell Discount Co Ltd [1962] AC 600 ....104, 335-8

Britannic Merthyr Coal Co v David [1910] AC 74....................................396
British Columbia Saw-Mill Co v Nettleship (1868) LR 3 CP 39
British Movietonews Ltd v London and District Cinemas Ltd
[1951] 1 KB 190 347
British Railways Board v Herrington [1972] AC 877 368
British Steel Corporation v Cleveland Bridge & Engineering Co Ltd
[1984] 1 All ER 504 ....250-1, 252, 409
British Transport Commission v Gourley [1956] AC 185 190
Brook's Wharf & Bull Wharf Ltd v Goodman Brothers
[1937] 1 KB 534..407-8
Broome v Cassell & Co Ltd see Cassell & Co Ltd v Broome
Brown v Boorman (1844) 11 Cl & Fin 1 324
Bryant v Herbert (1877) 3 CPD 389 ....62, 63-4, 94, 117, 132, 354, 403
Building and Civil Engineering Holidays Sceme Management Ltd v
Post Office [1966] 1 QB 247 38-9
Bumper Development Corporation v Commissioner of Police of the
Metropolis [1991] 1 WLR 1362..19
Bunge Corporation v Tradax SA [1981] 1 WLR 711...............................332
Burton v Winters [1993] 1 WLR 1077... 124, 125
Butler Machine Tool Co Ltd v Ex-Cell-O Corporation (England)
[1979] 1 WLR 401...96, 239-40
CBS Songs Ltd v Amstrad Consumer Electronics Plc
[1988] AC 1013..244
CTN Cash & Carry v Gallaher Ltd [1994] 4 All ER 714 CA 5, 21-2,
255, 290-2, 293, 412-13
Cambridge Water Co v Eastern Leather Plc [1994] 2 WLR 53 11,
92, 121, 362, 375-83, 384, 397
Canadian Pacific Railway Co v Lockhart [1942] AC 591 311
Canham v Barry (1855) 24 LJCP 100 218
Caparo Industries Plc v Dickman [1990] 2 AC 605 ....80, 96, 362, 390
Carlill v Carbolic Smoke Ball Co [1893] 1 QB 256 ....205, 206,
237-8, 239, 241, 295, 297
Cassell & Co v Broome [1972] AC 1027 ....30, 31, 36, 177, 188
Cassidy v Ministry of Health [1951] 2 KB 343.......................................213
Cattle v Stockton Waterworks Co (1875) LR 10 QB 453 ....101, 370
Caxton Publishing Co Ltd v Sutherland Publishing Co
[1939] AC 178 HL 40
Central London Property Trust Ltd v High Trees House Ltd
[1947] KB 130 ....256, 257-9, 260, 338, 413
Centrovincial Estates Plc v Merchant Investors Assurance Co Ltd (1983)
The Times 8 March 1983 CA..233
Chapman v Honig [1963] 2 QB 502 414
Charles Rickards v Oppenheim [1950] 1 KB 616 260
Chase Manhatten Bank NA v Israel-British Bank (London) Ltd [1981]
Ch 105 143

Chasemore v Richards [1843-60] All ER Rep 77; 7 HL Cas 349 124
Cheshire v Bailey [1905] 1 KB 237 39
Chikuma, The see A/S Awilco of Oslo v Fulvia SpA di Navigazione of Cagliari
China-Pacific SA v Food Corp of India, The Winson, The [1983] AC 939 409
Christie v Griggs (1809) 2 Camp 79 NP...323
Cia Sud Americana de Vapores v Shipmair BV, The Teno see Teno, The
Clarke v Dickson (1858) EB & E 148...268
Clarke v Dunraven (Earl), The Satanita [1897] AC 59 220
Clarke v Shee and Johnson (1774) 1 Cowp 197...147
Coggs v Bernard (1703) 2 Ld Raym 909 40
Coldman v Hill [1919] 1 KB 443...39, 335,
Coltman v Bibby Tankers: Derbyshire, The [1988] AC 276 12
Compania Financiera 'Soleada' SA Netherlands Antilles Ships Management Corp and Dammers and van der Heide's Shipping and Trading Co v Hamoor Tanker Corp Inc; Borag, The [1981] 1 WLR 274 197-8
Columbia Picture Industries Inc v Robinson [1987] Ch 38 173
Commissioner for Railways v Quinlan [1964] AC 1054..........................364
Conocraft Ltd v Pan-American Airways [1969] 1 QB 616........................12
Cooden Engineering Co Ltd v Stanford [1953] 1 QB 86..........................336
Cook v S [1966] 1 WLR 635..334
Cooper v Phibbs (1867) LR 2 HL 149 81
Cope v Sharpe (No 2) [1912] 1 KB 496...48
Cory v Thames Ironworks and Shipbuilding Co (1872) LR 7 CP 499.....39
Couldery v Bartram (1881) 19 Ch D 394..256
Courtney and Fairbairn Ltd v Tolaini Brothers (Hotels) Ltd [1975] 1 WLR 297 248
Cox v Phillips Industries Ltd [1976] 1 WLR 638.......................................334
Crabb v Arun District Council [1976] Ch 179 259-60
Cresswell v Sirl [1948] 1 KB 241... 48
Cuckmere Brick Co v Mutual Finance Ltd [1971] Ch 949 168
Currie v Misa (1875) LR 10 Ex 153 255
Cutter v Powell (1795) 6 Term Rep 320 126
D v National Society for the Prevention of Cruelty to Children [1978] AC 171 100
D & C Builders Ltd v Rees [1966] 2 QB 617 CA 255-7, 293
Daily Mirror Newspapers v Gardner [1968] 2 QB 762 .... 392, 393
Dakin (H) & Co Ltd v Lee [1916] 1 KB 566 127
Damon Compania Naviera SA v Hapag-Lloyd International SA: Blankenstein, The [1985] 1 WLR 435 139
Darbishire v Warren [1963] 1 WLR 1067..200

Davis Contractors Ltd v Fareham District Council
[1956] AC 696 ....45, 262-3, 283, 342-4, 345, 348, 350, 409
Davy v Spelthorne Borough Council [1984] AC 262 120
Day v McLea (1889) 22 QBD 610 257
De L'Isle (Viscount) v Times Newspapers [1988] 1 WLR 49 4
Dean v Ainley [1987] 1 WLR 1729 185-6
Derby & Co v Weldon (No 5) [1989] 1 WLR 1244 2
Derbyshire County Council v Times Newspapers
[1993] AC 534 ....52, 53, 387, 411
Derbyshire, The see Coltman v Bibby Tankers
Derry v Peek (1889) 14 App Cas 337...268
Deyong v Shenburn [1946] KB 227 364
Diamond v Campbell-Jones [1960] 1 All ER 583...................................194-6
Dick Bentley Productions Ltd v Harold Smith (Motors) Ltd
[1965] 1 WLR 623 ....264, 266-7
Dick, Re Knight v Dick [1953] Ch 343..105
Dies v British & International Mining & Finance Corporation
[1939] 1 KB 724 66
Dimskal Shipping Co SA v International Transport Worker's
Federation; Evia Luck, The [1992] 2 AC 152....................294, 395, 405
Diplock, Re Diplock v Wintle [1948] Ch 465 ....141, 143
Dominion Mosaics & Tile Ltd v Trafalgar Trucking Co Ltd
[1990] 2 All ER 246..186-7
Donoghue v Stevenson [1932] AC 562 ....33-4, 58, 69, 84, 89,
90, 91, 268, 271, 300, 361,
362, 364, 366, 383, 385, 386
Dorset Yacht Co v Home Office see Home Office v Dorset Yacht Co
Doyle v Olby (Ironmongers) Ltd [1969] 2 QB 158................................ 190-1
Drane v Evangelou [1978] 2 All ER 437.. 67
Drive Yourself Hire Co (London) Ltd v Strutt [1954] 1 QB 250 37
Dunne v North Western Gas Board [1964] 2 QB 806.........................53, 106
Dutton v Bognor Regis Urban District Council [1972] 1 QB 373 100
Dymond v Pearce and Others [1972] 1 QB 496.....................................397-9
Dyson Holdings Ltd v Fox [1976] QB 503...77
Eaglesfield v Marquis of Londonderry (1876) 4 Ch D 693.......................81
Electrochrome Ltd v Welsh Plastics Ltd [1968] 2 All ER 205..................102
Elguzouli-Daf v Commissioner of Police of the Metropolis [1995] 1 All
ER 833 CA 47
Eller v Grovecrest Investments Ltd [1994] 4 All ER 845 CA..................128
Elliott Steam Tug Co Ltd v The Shipping Controller
[1922] 1 KB 127 101
Elphick v Barnes (1880) 5 CPD 321 307
Emerald Construction Co v Lowthian [1966] 1 WLR 691.......................392
Emperor of Austria v Day (1861) 3 de GF & J 217............................114, 115

English v Dedham Vale Properties [1978] 1 All ER 382........................41-2,
168, 404, 413

Entores v Miles Far East Corporation [1955] 2 QB 327 ....241-2, 243, 247

Esso Petroleum Co Ltd v Southport Corporation [1956] AC 218; [1954] 2
QB 182 QBD; [1953] 3 WLR 773 (CA) 5, 48, 49, 67, 118-20,
121, 226, 288, 355,
361, 372, 375, 398,405

Eurymedon, The see New Zealand Shipping Co v A M
Sutterthwaite & Co

Evans v Glasgow District Council 1978 SLT 17 Outer House...............370

FA & AB Ltd v Lupton [1972] AC 634 ....91-2, 94, 234, 353

Falcke v Scottish Imperial Insurance Co (1886) 34 Ch D 234..................409

Fibrosa Spolka Akcyjna v Fairbairn Lawson Combe Barbour Ltd
[1943] AC 32..36, 130-2, 140, 403

Financings Ltd v Stimson [1962] 1 WLR 1184 ....85, 241,
264, 279-80

Fisher v Bell [1961] 1 QB 394 ....12, 30, 32, 86, 92

Fletcher v Rylands (1886) LR 1 Ex 265 ....381, 382
see also Rylands v Fletcher

Foakes v Beer (1884) 9 App Cas 605 .... 255, 256

Fothergill v Monarch Airlines Ltd [1981] AC 251 105

Francis v Cockrill (1870) LR 5 QB 501..324

Fresh Fruit Wales Ltd v Halbert The Times 29 January 1991...................78

Frost v Aylesbury Dairy Co Ltd [1905] 1 KB 608..................19-21, 210, 303

Gainsford v Carroll (1824) 107 ER 516..198, 199

General Capinpin, The see President of India v Jebsens (UK)

General Engineering Services v Kingston & St Andrews Corp
[1989] 1 WLR 69 373

George Mitchell (Chesterfield) Ltd v Finney Lock Seeds Ltd [1983]
2AC 803; [1983] QB 284 317-20

Gibbon v Mitchell [1990] 1 WLR 1304 165

Gibson v Manchester City Council [1979] 1 WLR 294; [1978]
1 WLR 520 (CA)...219-20, 235

Goldcorp Exchange Ltd, Re [1994] 3 WLR 199..............................22, 151-4

Goldman (Allan William) v Hargrave (Rupert William Edeson) [1967]
1 AC 645..367, 369, 378

Gott v Gandy (1853) 23 LJQB 1 220

Gourier v Post Office Workers [1978] AC 435 ....70, 113

Grant v Australian Knitting Mills Ltd [1936] AC 85 ....89-90, 91,324, 386

Greaves & Co Contractors Ltd v Baynham Meikle & Partners
[1975] 1 WLR 1095..209, 229, 326, 327

Green (RW) Ltd v Cade Bros Farm [1978] 1 Ll Rep 602 318

Grey v Pearson (1857) 6 HL Cas 61 346

Grist v Bailey [1967] Ch 532 ....283, 284

Groom v Crocker [1939] 1 KB 194..334

Grosvenor, Re, Peacey v Grosvenor [1944] Ch 138 104
Groves v Lord Wimbourne [1898] 2 QB 402.................................396
Hadley v Baxendale (1854) 9 Exch 341............................138, 179, 193, 194,
195, 196, 198, 334
Hall (Inspector of Taxes) v Lorimer [1992] 1 WLR 939.....................94, 96
Hamlin v Great Northern Railway Co (1856) 1 H&N 408 181
Hancock v Brazier (BW) (Anerley) [1966] 1 WLR 1317 209
Harbour Assurance Ltd v Kansa General Insurance Co [1993]
3 WLR 42 ....85, 93
Harbutts 'Plasticine' Ltd v Wayne Tank and Pump Co [1970]
1 QB 447...187
Harnett v Bond [1925] AC 669 198
Harris v Watson (1791) Peake 72...254
Haynes v Harwood [1935] 1 KB 146 ....368, 370
Heap v Ind Coope and Allsop Ltd [1940] 2 KB 476 385
Heaven v Pender (1883) 11 QBD 503...................................33, 362
Hedley Byrne & Co v Heller & Partners [1964] AC 465.................69, 102,
265, 268-71,
390, 391, 429-430
Heil v Hedges [1951] 1 TLR 512 KB 304-5
Heilbut Symons & Co v Buckleton [1913] AC 30 266
Helby v Mathews [1895] AC 471 336
Henderson v Jenkins (Henry E) & Sons and Evans [1970] AC 282 324,
399-400
Henderson v Merrett Syndicates Ltd [1994] 3 WLR 761 HL 354
Hern v Nichols (1701) 1 Salk 289 40
Heron II, The see Koufos v Czarnikow (C)
Herrington v British Railways Board see British Railways
Board Herrington
Heywood v Wellers (A Firm) [1976] QB 446 ....334-5, 359
Hickman v Peacey [1945] AC 304 2
Hill v Chief Constable of West Yorkshire [1989] AC 53 HL.................46-7
Hill v Parsons (CA) & Co Ltd [1972] 1 Ch 305 107
Hillesden Securities v Ryjack [1983] 1 WLR 959.............................192
Hobbs v London & South Western Railway Co (1875) LR QB 111 181
Hoenig v Isaacs [1952] 2 All ER 176..............................126, 127, 298
Hollywood Silver Fox Farm v Emmett [1936] 2 KB 468.................125, 413
Holmes v Hall (1704) 6 Mod Rep 161 131
Holmes v Mather (1875) LR 10 Exch 261 118
Home Office v Dorset Yacht Co [1970] AC 1004 ....29, 35, 52,
88, 91, 169, 300, 362-4,
366, 368, 371, 372, 395
Hong Kong Fir Shipping Co Ltd v Kawasaki Kishen
Kaisha Ltd [1962] 2 QB 26...327-31, 351

Hopkins v Tanqueray (1854) 139 ER 369......................216-18, 219, 266, 267
Horrocks v Lowe [1975] AC 135...387
Houghland v Low (RR) (Luxury Coaches) Ltd [1962] 1 QB 694.............viii
Howes v Bishop [1909] 2 KB 390 159
Hudson's Concrete Products Ltd v Evans (DB) (Bilston) Ltd
  SJ 281 CA 5 (1961) 105
Hughes v Metropolitan Ry Co (1877) 2 App Cas 439 256
Hyman v Nye {1881) 6 QB 685.............................73, 210, 303, 322-4
IBL Ltd v Coussens [1991] 2 All ER 133 191
Ingham v Emes [1955] 2 QB 366...305-6, 332, 351
Ingram v Little [1961] 1 QB 31 151
Inland Revenue Commissioners v Hambrook [1956] 2 QB 641...............101
Interfoto Picture Library Ltd v Stiletto Visual Programmes Ltd
  [1989] QB 433 ....222-5, 240, 413
Island Records, ex p [1978] Ch 122...70, 111
Jackson v Horizon Holidays Ltd [1975] 1 WLR 1468............. 97, 111, 117,
                                                                                      121-2, 260, 261, 334
Jackson v Union Marine Insurance Co Ltd (1873) LR 8CP 572..............329
Jacobs v Seward (1872) LR 5 App Cas 464...65
Jaggard v Sawyer [1995] 2 All ER 189...419
Janvier v Sweeney [1919] 2 KB 316..77
Jarvis v Swans Tours Ltd [1973] 1 QB 233 ....180-2, 334, 359, 383
Jasperson v Dominion Tobacco Co [1923] AC 709 392
Jones v Ffestiniog Railway Co (1868) LR3 QB 733 50
Jones v National Coal Board [1957] 2 QB 55...3
Jones v Page (1867) 15 LT 619 303
Jones (RE) Ltd v Waring & Gillow Ltd [1926] AC 670...........................131
Jorden v Money (1854) 5 HL Cas 185..258
Joeseph Constantine SS Line v Imperial Smelting Corp
  [1942] AC 154...304
Junior Books Ltd v Veitchi Co Ltd, The [1983] AC 520 371
KD, Re (a minor) [1988] AC 806...58, 71
Kelly v Solari (1841) 9 M&W 54...131
Kennedy v Panama, New Zealand, and Australian Royal Mail Co Ltd
  LR 2 QB 580 283
Keppel Bus Co Ltd v Sa'ad bin Ahmad [1974] 2 All ER 700.................19,
                                                                                      310-11, 315,
                                                                                      365, 372, 374
Khorasandijian v Bush [1993] 3 WLR 476....... 74-9, 172, 355, 360, 361, 413
King, ex p [1954] 3 All ER 897 CA 104
King v Liverpool City Council [1986] 1 WLR 890 370
King v Phillips [1953] 1 QB 429...101
Kingdom of Spain v Christie, Manson & Woods Ltd [1986]
  1 WLR 1120... 22, 66, 94, 106, 112-17, 355, 405

Kirkham v Boughey [1958] 2 QB 338 101
Knights v Wiffen (1870) LR 5 QB 660 152
Kopitoff v Wilson (1876) 1 QBD 377 11
Koufos v Czarnikow (C) [1969] 1 AC 350 196
Krell v Henry [1903] 2 KB 740...341-2
Lall v Lall [1965] 3 All ER 330 123
Lamb v Camden London Borough Council [1981] QB 625 370
Lavarack v Woods of Colchester Ltd [1967] 1 QB 278............................244
Lazenby Garages Ltd v Wright [1976] 1 WLR 459................................333-4
Leaf v International Galleries (a firm) [1950] 2 KB 86 274-5
Leigh and Sillavan Ltd v Aliakmon Shipping Co Ltd [1985] QB 350 ..371
Letang v Cooper [1965] 1 QB 232 .... 39, 65-6, 350, 416
Lewis v Averay [1972] 1 QB 198..288-9
Liesbosch Dredger Edison [1933] AC 449...196
Linden Gardens Trust v Lenesta Sludge Disposals Ltd [1994]
  AC 85..79-80, 429 431
Lipkin Gorman v Karpnale [1991] AC 548 .... 36, 70, 133,
                                                         145-50, 354, 357,
                                                         404, 405, 406, 411
Lister v Romford Ice & Cold Storage Co Ltd [1957] AC 555 169,
                                                         307-9, 332, 356, 380
Livingstone v Rawyards Coal Co (1880) 5 App Cas 25 178
Lloyd v Grace, Smith & Co [1912] AC 716..39
Lloyds Bank Ltd v Bundy [1975] QB 326 286
Lloyd's v Harper (1880) 16 Ch D 290...122
Lock International v Beswick [1989] 1 WLR 1268 Ch D.........................174
Lockett v A & M Charles Ltd [1938] 4 All ER 170 ....84, 210, 212
London, Chatham and Dover Ry v South Eastern Ry
  [1893] AC 429 CA 138, 167
Lumley v Gye (1853) 2 E & B 216 391,392
Lumley v Wagner (1852) 1 De GM & G 604 391
McCance v L & N W Ry (1861) 31 LJ Exch 65 218-19
McGhee v National Coal Board [1973] 1 WLR 1 ....82, 306
Mackintosh v Great Western Railway Co (1865) 4 Giff 683...................167
McIlkenny v Chief Constable of West Midlands [1980] 2 All
  ER 227 CA 105
McLoughlin v O'Brian [1983] AC 410..77
Mafo v Adams [1970] 1 QB 548...31
Magee v Pennine Insurance Co Ltd [1969] 2 QB 507 283
Malone v Laskey [1907] 2 KB 141 76
Mareva Compania Naviera SA v International Bulk Carriers,
  Mareva, The [1980] 1 All ER 213 CA 172
Margarine Union Gmbh v Cambay Prince Steamship Co (The Wear
  Breeze) [1969] 1 QB 219..101

Mediana, The [1900] AC 113 95-6

Merchant Prince [1892] P 179 49

Merlin v British Nuclear Fuels [1990] 2 QB 557 ....79, 387

Meux v Great Eastern Railway [1895] 2 QB 387 38

Midland Silicones v Scruttons see Scruttons v Midland Silicones

Miliangos v Frank (George) (Textiles) Ltd (No 2) [1976]
    AC 443 ....7-8, 353

Miller v Jackson [1977] QB 966 ....19, 22-6, 27, 58, 74,
                                                                    123, 176, 335, 356, 383

Ministry of Health v Simpson [1975] AC 251...150

Ministry of Housing v Sharp [1970] 2 QB 223...47

Mint v Good [1951] 1 KB 517 ....7, 355, 384-5

M'Intosh v Great Western Ry see Mackintosh v Great Western Ry

Mitchell v Ealing London Borough Council [1979] QB 1 198

Mogul SS Co v McGregor,Gow & Co [1892] AC 25...................................395

Montagu's Settlements, Re Duke of Manchester v National Westminster
    Bank [1987] Ch 264 143

Moorcock, The (1889) 14 PD 64 ....226-7, 281

Moorgate Mercantile Co Ltd v Twitchings [1962] 1 QB 701 259

Morgan v Fry The Times October 27 1966..392, 393

Morgans v Launchbury [1973] AC 127; [1971] 2 QB 245 400-2

Morris v Martin (C W) & Sons Ltd [1966] 1 QB 716 ....39-41, 41, 373

Morris v Ford Motor Co; Cameron Industrial Services (Third Party),
    Roberts (Fourth Party) [1973] 1 QB 792 ....170, 310

Morrison Steamship Co Ltd v Greystoke Castle (Cargo Owners)
    [1947] AC 265...102

Morton v Wheeler The Times 1 February 1956 CA 399

Moschi v Lep Air Services Ltd [1973] AC 331...........................32, 203, 204

Moses v Macferlan (1760) 2 Burr 1005 131

Moule v Garrett (1872) LR 7 Exch 101..407-8

Murphy v Brentwood District Council [1991] 1 AC 398.......11, 13, 55, 362

Myers (G H) & Co v Brent Cross Service Co [1934] 1 KB 46 306

National Carriers Ltd v Panalpina (Northern) Ltd [1981] AC 675 93

National Telephone Co v Baker [1893] 2 Ch 186 91

National Westminster Bank v Morgan [1985] AC 686 ....43, 291

New Zealand Shipping Co Ltd v Société des Ateliers et Chantiers de
    France [1919] AC 1...392

New Zealand Shipping Co Ltd v A M Satterthwaite & Co Ltd [1975] AC
    154 PC 103-4, 261

News of the World Ltd v Friend [1973] 1 All ER 422................................107

Nocton v Ashburton [1914] AC 932.. 268, 270

North Ocean Shipping Co Ltd v Hyundai Construction Co Ltd [1979]
    QB 705 252

Orakpo v Manson Investments Ltd [1978] AC 95..............................168, 404

Oscar Chess v Williams [1957] 1 WLR 370 266

Overseas Tankship (U K) Ltd v Miller Steamship Co Pty (The Wagon
Mound (No 2)) [1967] 1 AC 617 378-9

Overseas Tankship (U K) Ltd v Morts Dock & Engineering Co
(The Wagon Mound) [1961] AC 388..198

Overstone v Shipway [1962] 1 WLR 117..136

Owen v Tate [1975] 2 All ER 129 CA 409

Owens v Liverpool Corporation [1939] 1 KB 394..299

P (Minors)(Custody Order: Penal Notice), Re [1990] 1 WLR 613 170

Pao On v Lau Yiu Long [1980] AC 614..253

Parker v South Eastern Railway Co (1877) 2 CPD 416 223

Parry v Cleaver [1970] AC 1 HL..106

Parsons (H) (Livestock) Ltd v Uttley Ingham & Co [1978] QB 791 196,
197, 202, 212

Patel v Patel [1988] 2 FLR 179..78

Peek v Derry (1889) 14 App Cas 337; (1887) 37 Ch D 541 (CA) 390

Peek v Gurney (1873) LR 6 HL 268

Perl (P)(Exporters) Ltd v Camden London Borough Council [1984]
QB 342..368

Pharmaceutical Society of Great Britain v Boots Cash Chemist
(Southern) [1953] 1 QB 401..236

Phillips v Britannia Hygienic Laundry Co Ltd [1923] 2 KB 832 395-7

Photo Production Ltd v Securicor Transport Ltd [1980] AC 827..........170,
199, 204, 221, 240,
312-15, 372, 373

Piller (Anton) KG v Manufacturing Processes Ltd [1976]
1 All ER 779 CA 172, 173, 174

Pinnel's Case (1602) 5 Co Rep 117a..255

Pitt v PHH Asset Management Ltd [1994] 1 WLR 327 249-50

Poland v Parr (John) & Sons [1927] 1 KB 236 310

Poole v Smith's Car Sales (Balham) Ltd [1962] 1 WLR 744 ....306-7, 414

Poussard v Spiers & Pond (1876) 1 QBD 410 391

Powell v Fall (1880) 5 QBD 597 50

Powstaniec Wielkolposki, The [1989] QB 279 56

Preist v Last [1903] 2 KB 148 20

President of India v Jebsens (UK) and Others; General Capinpin,
The [1991] 1 Ll Rep 1 231

Price v Strange [1978] Ch 337..156

Printing and Numerical Registering Co v Sampson (1875) LR 19
Eq 462..69, 220

Qualcast (Wolverhampton) Ltd v Haynes [1959] AC 743 ....9-10, 81

Quinn v Leathem [1910] AC 495 392

R v Central Television Plc [1994] 3 WLR 20 CA..............71-2, 98, 105, 388

R v Leeds County Court ex p Morris [1990] 2 WLR 175 7

R v Lewisham London Borough Council ex p Shell UK [1978]
1 All ER 938 247

R v McDonald (1885) 15 QBD 323 38

R v Secretary of State for Education and Science ex p Avon County
Council (No 2) [1991] 1 QB 558 28

R v Self [1992] 1 WLR 657 ....105, 125

RCA Corporation v Pollard [1983] Ch 135 115

Radford v De Froberville [1977] 1 WLR 1262.....................................186

Raineri v Miles [1981] AC 1050..302

Rainham Chemical Works Ltd v Belvedere Fish Guano Co Ltd
[1921] 2 AC 465..381

Ramsden v Dyson (1886) LR 1 HL 129 260

Randall v Newson (1877) 2 QBD 102..20

Read v J Lyons & Co [1947] AC 156 ....8-9, 50, 53, 69, 93, 96,
108, 375, 377, 380,
381, 382, 383, 397

Readhead v Midland Railway (1869) LR 4 QB 379...............320-2, 323, 324

Reading v R [1949] 2 KB 232 43

Reardon Smith Line Ltd v Yngvar Hansen-Tangen [1976]
1 WLR 989 346

Redgrave v Hurd (1881) 20 Ch D 1.............................164-5, 202, 272-3

Reed v Dean [1949] 1 KB 188............................303-4, 341, 350, 414

Reid v Rush & Tompkins Plc [1990] 1 WLR 212.................228, 309, 356

Republic of Haiti v Duvalier [1990] 1 QB 202...............................151

Rickards v Lothian [1913] AC 263......................................377, 382

Rigby v Chief Constable of Northamptonshire [1985]
1 WLR 1242..47-52, 355

Riverplate Properties Ltd v Paul [1975] Ch 133 166

Roberts (A) & Co Ltd v Leicestershire County Council [1961]
Ch 555 165,166

Roberts Petroleum Ltd v Bernard Kelly Ltd [1983] AC 192 5-6

Roberts v Ramsbottom [1980] 1 WLR 823..400

Robinson v Harman (1848) 1 Exch 850..185

Roe v Minister of Health [1954] 2 QB 66........................212, 212-14

Romilly v Romilly [1964] P 22..161

Rookes v Barnard [1964] AC 1129................................76, 188, 257, 393

Ross v Caunters [1980] Ch 297...56, 57

Ross v Fedden (1872) 26 LT 966..401

Rover International Ltd v Canon Films Ltd [1989]
1 WLR 912 406

Rowland v Divall [1923] 2 KB 500 ....137-8, 151, 406

Rowland, Re Smith v Russell [1963] 1 Ch 1 ....62, 87-8, 94, 97, 98

Roy v Kensington and Chelsea and Westminster Family
Practitioner Committee [1992] 1 AC 624.................................44-5, 65

Ruben v Great Fingall Consolidated [1906] AC 439 41

Rutter v Palmer [1922] 2 KB 87 269

Ruxley Electronics Ltd v Forsyth [1994] 1 WLR 650 CA 184-6, 191

Rylands v Fletcher (1868) LR3 HL 330; (1866) LR1 Exch 265 48,
49-50, 50, 69, 91-2,
108, 373-4, 375, 376, 377,
378, 379, 380, 381, 382, 388

Samuels v Davis [1943] KB 526..209

Saunders v Anglia Building Society [1971] AC 1004 286

Schuler (L) A G v Wickman Machine Tools Sales Ltd [1974]
AC 235..229-31, 332

Scottish Co-operative Wholesale Society Ltd v Meyer [1959]
AC 324 335

Scruttons v Midland Silicones [1962] AC 446 39

Sedleigh-Denfield v O'Callaghan [1940] AC 880 ....119, 120, 378

Shelfer v City of London Electric Lighting Co [1895] 1 Ch 287............421

Sheikh Bros Ltd v Ochsner [1957] AC 136................................283

Shepherd (F C) & Co v Jerrom [1986] 3 All ER 589 341

Shirlaw v Southern Foundries (1926) Ltd [1939] 2 KB 206.....................281

Simpson & Co v Thomson (1877) LR 3 App Cas 279............................101

Sinclair v Brougham [1914] AC 398.....................................132,133

Siskina, The [1979] AC 210 ....75, 78

Smith v Eric Bush [1990] 1 AC 831..104, 261

Smith v Chadwick (1882) 20 Ch D 27 268

Smith v Hughes (1871) LR 6 QB 597....................................... 275-7

Smith v Littlewoods Organisation Ltd [1987] AC 241 ....10, 365-71,
372, 383

Smith and Snipes Hall Farm v River Douglas Catchment Board
[1949] 2 KB 500 37

Société Anonyme de Remorquage a Helice v Bennetts [1911]
1 KB 243 101

Solholt, The see Sotiros Shipping Inc v Schmeiet Solholt

Solle v Butcher [1950] 1 KB 671 ....263, 274,
279, 283, 284

Sotiros Shipping Inc v Schmeiet Solholt: The Solholt [1983]
1 Ll Rep 605..200, 201

Southport Corporation v Esso Petroleum Co Ltd see Esso Petroleum Co
Ltd v Southport Corporatio

Spartan Steel Alloys Ltd v Martin & Co
(Contractors) Ltd [1973] QB 27 ....58, 97, 101-2, 103,
178, 180, 186, 360

Spring v Guardian Assurance Plc [1994] 3 WLR 354 HL.................68, 389

Staffordshire Area Health Authority v South Staffordshire Waterworks
[1978] 1 WLR 1387..45, 46, 345-8

Stansbie v Troman [1948] 2 KB 48...367

State of Norway's Application Re [1987] QB 433 CA 43
State of Norway's Aplication (Nos 1 & 2) Re [1990] 1 AC 723..............28-9
Staveley Iron & Chemical Co Ltd v Jones [1956] AC 627........................372
Stears v South Essex Gas-Light & Coke Co (1861) 30 LJCP 49..............218
Stedman v Swan's Tours (1951) 95 SJ 727 CA 182
Sterman v E W & W J Moore Ltd [1970] 1 QB 596 ....66-7, 67
Stevenson v Beverley Bentinck Ltd [1976] 1 WLR 483......................214-16
Stewart v Reavell's Garage [1952] 2 QB 545 306
Stilk v Myrick (1809) 2 Camp 317.....................................252, 253, 254
Stocks v Magne Merchants Ltd [1973] 2 All ER 329............................. 95
Stoke-on-Trent City Council v W & J Wass Ltd [1988] 1 WLR 1406 70
Strand Electric and Engineering Co Ltd v Brisford Entertainments Ltd
    [1952] 2 QB 246..179, 192
Stratford (J J) & Son Ltd v Lindley [1965] AC 307............257, 392, 393, 394
Sturges v Bridgman (1879) 11 Ch D 852.. 23
Sumpter v Hedges [1898] 1 QB 673...298, 410
Surrey County Council v Bredero Homes Ltd and Mole District Council
    [1993] 1 WLR 1361 ....123, 178-80, 192, 332, 404, 407, 420
Sutcliffe v Pressdram Ltd [1991] 1 QB 153..388
Tarry v Ashton (1876) 1 QBD 314...120, 385
Taylor v Caldwell (1863) 3 B & S 826; 122 ER 309..............282, 338-40, 341,
                                                                                            342, 415
Taylor v Plumer (1815) 3 M & S 562 ....141, 146
Techno-Impex v Gebr Van Weelde Scheepvaartkantoor BV
    [1981] 1 QB 648...26, 118
Teno, The [1977] 2 Ll Rep 289 128
Tesco Supermarkets Ltd v Nattrass [1972] AC 153............................ 17-19
Thake v Maurice [1986] QB 644; [1985] 2 WLR 215 .... 214, 324-7
Thomas Bates & Son Ltd v Wyndham's (Lingerie) Ltd [1981]
    1 WLR 505.. 165-7
Thomas v Countryside Council for Wales [1994] 4 All ER
    853 ....200-01, 414
Thomas v National Union of Mineworkers (South Wales Area)
    [1976] Ch 20 ....78, 177
Thompson (WL) v Robinson (Gunmakers) Ltd [1955] Ch 177 333
Thomson (DC) & Co Ltd v Deakin [1952] Ch 646....................392, 393, 416
Thorne v Motor Traders Association [1937] AC 797..............................294
Thornton v Shoe Lane Parking Ltd [1971] 2 QB 163.............................223
Torkomian v Russell (1916) Atlantic Reporter 760................................333
Torquay Hotel Co v Cousins [1969] 2 Ch 106......................................391-4
Town Investments Ltd v Department of the Environment
    [1978] AC 359..28
Treseder-Griffin v Co-operative Insurance Society [1956] 2 QB 127 347
Turnbull & Co v Duval [1902] AC 429................................. 158, 159-60, 161

United Australia Ltd v Barclays Bank Ltd [1941] AC 1 ....130, 132, 140, 403

United Dominions Trust (Commercial) Ltd v Eagle Aircraft Services Ltd [1968] 1 WLR 74 ....204, 205

Universal Cargo Carriers Corporation v Citati (No 2) [1958] 2 QB 254 329

Vacwell Engineering Co Ltd v B D H Chemicals Ltd [1971] 1 QB 88 ....183–4, 196

Van Toll v S E Ry (1862) 31 LCJP 241...221

Vigers v Cook [1919] 2 KB 475 CA 126, 127, 296-7, 302

Viscount de L'Isle v Iimes Newspaper see De L'Isle (Viscount) v Times Newspaper

Wadsworth v Lydall [1981] 1 WLR 598.....................................138

Wagon Mound, The (No 1) [1961] see Overseas Tankship (U K) Ltd v Morts Dock & Engineering Co

Walford v Miles [1992] 2 AC 128 247-9

Wallis v Smith (1804) 1 Smith KB 346...338

Wallis, Son & Wells v Pratt & Haynes [1911] AC 394...................274

Ward v Byham [1956] 1 WLR 496 253

Ward v James [1966] 1 QB 273 ....189, 190

Ward v Tesco Stores Ltd [1976] 1 WLR 810 ....82-3, 324, 400

Warner Brothers Pictures Inc v Nelson [1937] 1 KB 209 175

Watt v Hertfordshire County Council [1954] 1 WLR 835 .... 53, 106

Watt (or Thomas) v Thomas [1947] AC 484 4-5

Watts v Morrow [1991] 1 WLR 1421 182

Weaver v Ward (1616) Hob 134...120

Weld-Blundell v Stephens [1920] AC 956 .... 367, 368

Weller & Co v Foot and Mouth Disease Research Institute [1966] 1 QB 569 102

West v Bristol Tramways Co [1908] 2 KB 14 ....50, 381

Westdeutsche Landesbank Girozentrale v Islington London Borough Council [1994] 1 WLR 938 CA....................................55-6

Wheeler v Leicester County Council [1985] AC 1054..................125

White & Carter (Councils) Ltd v McGregor [1962] AC 413 ....133-6, 136, 246, 335, 338, 414

White v Jones [1995] 1 All ER 691; [1993] 3 WLR 730 (CA)....56-7, 80, 156, 261, 357, 384, 390, 417-419, 424-432

Whittaker and Whittaker v Campbell [1984] QB 318.............92, 233-4, 289

Wilchick v Marks and Silverstone [1934] 2 KB 56 385

Wilkinson v Downton [1897] 2 QB 57 360-1

William Sindall Plc v Cambridgeshire County Council [1994] 1 WLR 1016 ....261-3, 285

Williams v Roffey & Nicholls (Contractors) Ltd [1991] 1 QB 1 ....252-4, 255, 257

Williams v Williams [1957] 1 WLR 148 253
Willis (R H) & Son v British Car Auctions [1978] 2 All ER 392 106
Wilsher v Essex Area Health Authority [1988] AC 1074....................82, 306
Winson, The see China-Pacific SA v Food Corp of India
Woodar Investment Development Ltd v Wimpey Construction UK Ltd
   [1980] 1 WLR 277 261
Wookey v Wookey: S (A Minor) Re [1991] 3 WLR 135 170
Wooldridge v Sumner [1963] 2 QB 43 84
Woolwich Equitable Building Society v Inland Revenue Commissioners
   [1993] AC 70.......................................36, 54-5, 69, 70, 133, 404, 411
Wright v British Railways Board [1983] 2 AC 773 189-90
Wringe v Cohen [1940] 1 KB 229...120, 384, 385
Wrotham Park Estate v Parkside Homes [1974] 1 WLR 798...180, 420-423
X Ltd v Morgan-Grampian (Publishers) Plc [1990] 2 WLR 421 CA 105
Young & Marten Ltd v McManus Childs Ltd [1969] 1 AC 454..............209

OTHER JURISDICTIONS

AUSTRALIA
Cameron v Campbell & Worthington (1930) SASR 402..........................333
McCrae v Commonwealth Disposals Commission (1951)
   84 CLR 377 284
Smith v Leurs [1945] CLR 256...367-8
Yerkey v Jones [1940] 63 CLR 649 161

CANADA
Mason v Risch Piano Co Ltd v Christner (1920) 48 OLR 8, 54
   DLR 653 333
Motherwell v Motherwell (1976) 73 DLR (3d) 62 76
Stewart v Hawsen (1858) 7 CP 168..333

FRANCE
Dalloz-Sirey 1965.62, Cass civ 20 October 1964 237
Jand'heur Ch reun 13 fevr 1930;DP 1930 1.57 note Ripert: S1930 1.121
   note Esmein 384

USA
Channel Home Centers, Division of Grace Retail Corporation v
   Grossman (1986) 795 F 2D 291..248
Utica City National Bank v Gunn (1918) 222 NY 204 346
Williams v State of New York (1955) 127 NE 2d 545 362

TABLE OF STATUTES

Animals Act 1971 386
  s 2 403
Chancery Amendment Act 1858.................................420-423
Common Law ProcedureAct 1854 ....63, 191, 420
Consumer Credit Act 1974 ....208, 286, 287, 338
  s 75 129
  s 100 338
Consumer Protection Act 1987 386
  ss 2-4 211
  s 5 ....99, 212
  s 6 212
County Courts Act 1984
  s 38 78
Defective Premises Act 1972 386
Domestic Violence and Matrimonial Proceedings Act 1976 78
  s 175...
Employers Liability (Defective Equipment) Act 1969 386
Factors Act 1889..215
Fatal Accidents Act 1846..359
Fatal Accidents Act 1976..360
  s 1A 183
Food Safety Act 1990 90
Gaming Act 1845
  s 18 ....146, 148
Harbour, Docks, and Piers Clauses Act 1847
  s 74 140
Hire-Purchase Act 1964
  s 27 215
  s 29 215
Insolvent Debtor's Relief
  Act 1729 128
Law of Property Act 1925
  s 56(1) 37
  s 84...421
  s 205(1)(xx) 37
Law of Property (Miscellaneous Provisions) Act 1989...........................250
Law Reform (Contributory Negligence) Act 1945 ....197, 201, 202
Law Reform (Frustrated Contracts) Act 1943 328
  s 1 349
Local Government Act 1972
  s 222 ....180, 407
  s 222(1) 74, 123
Local Government Act 1988
  s 17 ....46, 247
Misrepresentation Act 1967..181
  s 1 271
  s 2 ....30, 31, 271

s 2(1) 191, 262, 265, 272
s 2(2) 265
Moneylenders Acts 1900-1927 286
Nuclear Installation Act 1965
  s 12 79
Occupiers' Liability Act 1957 ....216, 386
Offences Against the Person Act 1861
  s 38 125
Police and Criminal Evidence Act 1984
  s 24 125
Real Property Act 1845
  s 5..37
  s 205(1)(xx) 37
Redundancy Payments Act 1965..95
Restrictive Trade Practices
  Act 1956 393
Road Traffic Act 1930 ....308, 309
Sale of Goods Act 1893 ....135, 206, 207, 208, 209,
                                             267, 282, 313, 329
  s 11(1)(c)..137, 274
  s 14 305
  s 14(1) 20
  s 16 152
  s 25(2) 215
  s 35..274, 275
  s 50 350
  s 50(2)(3) 333
Sale of Goods Act 1979..208, 216
  s 6 279
  s 13(1) 267
  s 14 ....21, 210, 228-9, 303
  s 14(3) 20, 223
  ss 16-18 21
  ss 16-20 22
  s 35 275
Supply of Goods and Services Act 1982 ....209, 210, 304, 324
  s 4 1
  s 9 210
  s 13 ....1, 21, 210, 303
Sale and Supply of Goods Act 1994
  s 2 275
Supreme Court Act 1981
  s 31(3) 123
  s 37..1, 3, 78
  s 37(1) 75, 170
  s 50 ....27, 421
Supreme Court of Judicature
  Act 1873 ....65, 128, 129, 167, 272

Supreme Court of Judicature
Act 1875..128, 129, 167, 272
Theft Act 1968 31
Torts (Interference with Goods) Act 1977 ....11, 27, 191
    s 2(1) 403
    s 2(2) 307
    s 3 191
Trade Disputes Act 1906
    s 3 393
Trade Union and Labour Relations (Consolidation) Act 1992
    s 10..19
    s 12..19
Unfair Contract Terms
    Act 1977 ....5, 216, 240, 312, 314, 317, 318, 338
    s 1..221, 315
    s 2 316
    s 2(1) 99, 221
    s 2(2) 221
    s 3..316
    s 4..316
    s 5 316
    s 13..317
Workman's Compensation
    Act 1897 53

FRANCE
Code Civil
    Arts 1102-3 204
    Art 1134 ....46, 69, 220
    Art 1150 194
    Art 1382 ....69, 109, 361, 411, 413
    Art 1384 ....69, 108, 109, 374, 383, 384, 386, 397
    Art 2279 289
New Code of Civil Procedure
    Art 31..123
Loi 5 juillet 1985 384

EUROPEAN UNION
Council Directive of 25 July 1985 212
Council Directive of 5 April 1993 93/13 EEC:l95/29 (Unfair Terms in
    Consumer Contract) 317, 338
    Art 3.1 225

CONVENTIONS
Convention for the Protection of Human Rights and Fundamental
    Freedoms (1953)..72
Convention (Draft) on Civil Liability for Damage Resulting from
    Activities Dangerous to the Environment (Strasbourg 26 January 1993)
    Art 5.1 381

CHAPTER 1

THE STRUCTURE OF THE COMMON LAW

1 INTRODUCTION

Law as a system functions at several levels. At the level of the rules themselves, the structure of the system focuses around the elements of persons, things and actions; that is to say, rules attach themselves to people,[1] to things[2] or to actions (remedies).[3] At another level, however, law functions as a political and social institution which requires it to focus around elements that stretch beyond individual persons and things to embrace the institutions of society itself. At this level law is a matter of courts, judges, legislators and parties as a class; and, before one can understand the operation of particular areas of legal rules, it is first important to have some grasp of the role of the various social and political institutions as rule and decision-makers. For between the law as social system and the law as institutional system there is the reasoning system of the politicians and jurists themselves; this latter system has its roots in both of the former systems.

2 THE ROLE OF THE COURTS

Perhaps the central social institution of the law, for the English obligations lawyer at any rate, is the court. On the continent things appear a little different since it is the legislator who has pride of place in the social and political system – and, of course, the role of Parliament as law-maker in the United Kingdom must never be underestimated. Yet the English lawyer's habit of focusing upon remedies means that it is the facts of litigation that often form the starting point for thinking about contract and tort; and litigation entails parties, lawyers and judges. What role do these judicial persons, and the social institutions in which they function, play in the development of the law of obligations?

---

1   See eg, Supply of Goods and Services Act 1982 s 13 ('the supplier').
2   See eg, Supply of Goods and Services Act 1982 s 4 ('the goods supplied ... are of merchantable quality').
3   See eg, Supreme Court Act 1981 s 37 ('grant an injunction').

(a) Trial judge

Derby & Co v Weldon (No 5) [1989] 1 WLR 1244 Chancery Division

Vinelott J: ...The function of a judge of first instance is to find the relevant facts and, with the assistance of counsel, to ascertain the law as set out in any relevant statutory provisions and in principles to be derived from the decisions of the House of Lords and the Court of Appeal, and to draw the appropriate legal consequences. It is not open to the judge in performing this primary function to consider, far less express an opinion, as to the correctness of a decision of the Court of Appeal or the House of Lords except in those rare cases where he is faced with conflicting decisions of the Court of Appeal and must choose which to follow. That does not rest solely upon the feelings of deference and respect which a judge of first instance will naturally and properly approach a decision of the Court of Appeal or the House of Lords. An opinion which the judge may entertain as to the correctness or otherwise of, for instance, the interpretation of a decision of the House of Lords by the Court of Appeal, is simply irrelevant to his primary duty which is to ascertain the statutory provisions and the principles stated in decisions that are binding on him which govern the case before him ...

Notes and questions

1. What assumptions is the judge making about what it is to have knowledge of the law? Is he suggesting that a first instance judge may have a different approach to legal knowledge than a House of Lords judge?

2. One question that will continually need to be considered throughout this sourcebook is the extent to which cases (and statutes) are objectively binding on judges. Are legal propositions really capable of governing factual situations? Are there correct and incorrect decisions in law? What is meant by a wrong decision?

Hickman v Peacey [1945] AC 304 House of Lords

Viscount Simon LC: ...[A] sharp distinction must be drawn between reaching a correct conclusion in a court of law, and establishing an absolute scientific truth. A court of law, whether it takes the form of a judge sitting alone, or sitting with the help of a jury, is not engaged in ascertaining ultimate verities: it is engaged in determining what is the proper result to be arrived at, having regard to the evidence before it. In most cases, there is a contest, and the court merely has to decide between the parties. And in reaching its conclusion, the court is greatly helped by considering upon which party rests the burden of establishing its contention. The conclusion, therefore, that the party upon which the burden rests has not proved an essential proposition, leads to the result that for the purposes of that litigation the proposition is to be rejected – a course of reasoning which could never establish a positive truth of science ...

Notes and questions

1. To what extent is Viscount Simon presenting a description of legal method different to the one presented by Vinelott J?

2. Is the role of the judge simply to decide a dispute between two parties?

3 If a plaintiff is able to establish that there is a 51% probability that the defendant's wrong caused his injury ought the plaintiff to succeed (assuming all the other requirements for a cause of action are satisfied)?

4. Is this statement authority for the proposition that a court of law is not engaged in any search for truth?

5. Can a judge take an active role in litigation?

Jones v National Coal Board [1957] 2 QB 55 Court of Appeal

Denning LJ: ... No one can doubt that the judge, in intervening as he did, was actuated by the best motives ...

Nevertheless we are quite clear that the interventions, taken together, were far more than they should have been. In the system of trial which we have evolved in this country, the judge sits to hear and determine the issues raised by the parties, not to conduct an investigation or examination on behalf of society at large, as happens, we believe, in some foreign countries. Even in England, however, a judge is not a mere umpire to answer the question "How's that?" His object, above all, is to find out the truth, and to do justice according to the law; and in the daily pursuit of it the advocate plays an honourable and necessary role ...

So firmly is all this established in our law that the judge is not allowed in a civil dispute to call a witness whom he thinks might throw some light on the facts.... So also it is for the advocates, each in his turn, to examine the witnesses, and not for the judge to take it on himself lest by so doing he appear to favour one side or the other ... The judge's part in all this is to hearken to the evidence, only himself asking questions of witnesses when it is necessary to clear up any point that has been overlooked or left obscure; to see that the advocates behave themselves seemly and keep to the rules laid down by law; to exclude irrelevancies and discourage repetition; to make sure by wise intervention that he follows the points that the advocates are making and can assess their worth; and at the end to make up his mind where the truth lies. If he goes beyond this, he drops the mantle of a judge and assumes the robe of an advocate; and the change does not become him well ...

Notes and questions

1. 'The only interest and duty of the judge is to seek to do justice in accordance with the law. The interest of the parties is to seek a favourable decision and their duty is limited to complying with the rules of the court, giving truthful testimony and refraining from taking positive steps to deceive the court' (Sir John Donaldson, *Abse v Smith* [1986] 1 QB 536). Is a judge, as Denning LJ seems to claim, under any duty to search for the truth?

2. Ought judges to have to rely upon the parties when it comes to expert witnesses, cross-examination etc, or should they be able to take a more active role?

3. Professor Jolowicz has observed how the disappearance of the jury in civil cases (defamation remains an exception) has hardly affected the procedural structure of litigation: one has to imagine that a jury still exists.[4] Why do you think the jury has largely disappeared from non-criminal cases and why do you think that its ghost remains?

4. If the judge does not represent society, who does he or she represent when conducting a case?

(b) Court of Appeal

Viscount de L'Isle v Times Newspapers [1988] 1 WLR 49 Court of Appeal

Balcombe LJ ... An appeal to the Court of Appeal is by way of rehearing: see RSC, Ord 59, r 3(1). Unlike those cases where statute limits the right of appeal to a question of law, this court in a case such as the present has the right, and indeed the duty, to review the decision of the judge at first instance both on law and on fact. In doing so, it will, of course, follow certain well-established principles. Thus it will not normally interfere with a finding of fact by the judge of first instance, where that finding depends on the credibility of a witness whom the judge has observed giving evidence. Again, an appellate court may interfere with the exercise of a discretion by a judge of first instance only if it is satisfied that the judge has erred in certain well-defined respects.... But, subject to the established limitations, this court can and should be prepared to review the decision of a judge of first instance, both as to law and as to fact ...

Watt or Thomas v Thomas [1947] AC 484 House of Lords

Viscount Simon: ... If there is no evidence to support a particular conclusion (and this is really a question of law), the appellate court will not hesitate so to decide. But if the evidence as a whole can reasonably be regarded as justifying the conclusion arrived at the trial, and especially if that conclusion has been arrived at on conflicting testimony by a tribunal which saw and heard the witnesses, the appellate court will bear in mind that it has not enjoyed this opportunity and that the view of the trial judge as to where credibility lies is entitled to great weight ... I would only add that the decision of an appellate court whether or not to reverse conclusions of fact reached by the judge at the trial must naturally be affected by the nature and circumstances of the case under consideration. What I have said applies to appeals from a judge sitting alone. Conclusions of fact embodied in the verdict of a jury cannot be subjected to the same degree of re-examination – for the course of reasoning by which the verdict has been reached is not disclosed – and consequently the verdict of a jury

---

4   'La disparition virtuelle du jury à l'ère moderne n'a guère touché les grands lignes de la procédure civile anglaise ... Autrement dit, dans ses grandes lignes la procédure anglaise est toujours fondée sur l'hypothèse d'un jury civil bien en vie.': JA Jolowicz, La réforme de la procédure civile anglaise: une dérogation au système adversatif? P Legrand jr (sous la direction de). Common Law d'un siecle l'autre, Blaise, Québec, 1992, p 237.

on fact must stand if there was any evidence to support it and if the conclusion is one at which a reasonable jury when properly directed might reasonably arrive ...

Questions

1. What is meant by a 'rehearing'?
2. Can the Court of Appeal hear witnesses? If so, could the appeal judges question these witnesses in any depth?
3. What is the role of the Court of Appeal in English law?
4. Can appeal judges decide cases on points of law not raised by the parties? What if they feel that a plaintiff has pleaded a case in the wrong sort of way? (Cf *Esso v Southport*, p 118 and *CTN Cash & Carry v Gallaher*, p 412.)

Roberts Petroleum Ltd v Bernard Kenny Ltd [1983] 2 AC 192 House of Lords

Lord Diplock: ... I do desire, however, to comment upon the use sought to be made both in this House and in the Court of Appeal of previous judgments of that court which do not appear in any series of published law reports. This is a growing practice and one which, in my view, ought to be discouraged.

Transcripts of the shorthand notes of oral judgments delivered since April 1951 by members of the Court of Appeal, nearly all extempore, have been preserved at the Royal Courts of Justice, formerly in the Bar Library but since 1978 in the Supreme Court library. For much of this period this course has been followed as respects all judgments of the civil division of the Court of Appeal, though recently some degree of selectivity has been adopted as to judgments to be indexed and incorporated in the bound volumes. Unreported judgments which have been delivered since the beginning of 1980 are now also included in the computerised data base known as Lexis and this has facilitated reference to them. Two such transcripts are referred to in the judgment of the Court of Appeal in the instant case. One of these was a case, *Hudson's Concrete Products Ltd v D B Evans (Bilston) Ltd*, to which my noble and learned friend refers, which had been the subject of a note in the *Solicitors' Journal* (1961) 105 SJ 281. The other had not been noted in any professional journal, nor had either of the two additional transcripts to which your Lordships were referred at the hearing in this House. For my part, I gained no assistance from perusal of any of these transcripts. None of them laid down a relevant principle of law that was not to be found in reported cases; the only result of referring to the transcripts was that the length of the hearing was extended unnecessarily.

This is not surprising. In a judgment, particularly one that has not been reduced into writing before delivery, a judge, whether at first instance or upon appeal, has his mind concentrated upon the particular facts of the case before him and the course which the oral argument has taken. This may have involved agreement or concessions, tacit or explicit, as to the applicable law, made by counsel for the litigating parties in what they conceived to be the interests of their respective clients in obtaining a favourable outcome of the particular case.

The primary duty of the Court of Appeal on an appeal in any case is to determine the matter actually in dispute between the parties. Such propositions of law as members of the court find necessary to state and previous authorities to which they find it convenient to refer in order to justify the disposition of the actual proceedings before them will be tailored to the facts of the particular case. Accordingly, propositions of law may well be stated in terms either more general or more specific than would have been used if he who gave the judgment had in mind somewhat different facts, or had heard a legal argument more expansive than had been necessary in order to determine the particular appeal. Even when making successive revisions of drafts of my own written speeches for delivery upon appeals to this House, which usually involve principles of law of wider application than the particular case under appeal, I often find it necessary to continue to introduce subordinate clauses supplementing, or qualifying, the simpler, and stylistically preferable, wording in which statements of law have been expressed in earlier drafts.

There are two classes of printed law reports: the two weekly series of general law reports: (a) the Weekly Law Reports of the Incorporated Council of Law Reporting, of which the more important, contained in Parts 2 and 3, are later reproduced in the Law Reports proper, together with a summary of the arguments of counsel, and (b) the All England Law Reports which report much the same cases as the former series; these do not err on the side of over-selectivity. Then there are the various series of specialised law reports which seem to have proliferated in the course of the last few decades; these may be useful in helping lawyers practising in specialised fields to predict the likely outcome of the particular case in which they are advising or instituting proceedings, by seeing how previous cases in which the facts were in various respects analogous were actually decided; but these specialised reports contain only a small minority of leading judgments in which some new principle of law of general application in the specialised field of law is authoritatively propounded, as distinct from some previously accepted principle being applied to the facts of a particular case. If a civil judgment of the Court of Appeal (which has a heavy case load and sits concurrently in several civil divisions) has not found its way into the generalised series of law reports or even into one of the specialised series, it is most unlikely to be of any assistance to your Lordships on an appeal which is sufficiently important to reach this House.

My Lords, in my opinion, the time has come when your Lordships should adopt the practice of declining to allow transcripts of unreported judgments of the Civil Division of the Court of Appeal to be cited upon the hearing of appeals to this House unless leave is given to do so; and that such leave should only be granted upon counsel's giving an assurance that the transcript contains a statement of some principle of law, relevant to an issue in the appeal to this House, that is binding upon the Court of Appeal and of which the substance, as distinct from the mere choice of phraseology, is not to be found in any judgment of that court that has appeared in one of the generalised or specialised series of reports.

Notes and questions

1. How is a law reporter to know if a case is one of principle? At the time of the giving of the judgments, did (for example) *Mint v Good* (p 384) seem an important case of principle?
2. Is an unreported case incapable of acting as a precedent?
3. '... [T]he Divisional Court ... is not called a court of appeal for in my opinion it is not such a court. It is, generally speaking, a court of review having wide powers to countermand the decisions of others no matter where those decisions emanate from, be it below the High Court or outside the courts altogether. It should therefore, in my judgment, be regarded as *sui generis*, for such it is. At times, depending on the function it is exercising, I dare say it could, practically speaking, be called a Court of Appeal, at other times clearly not. What I am confident it can never, in any circumstances, be called is a court of first instance' (Watkins LJ in *R v Leeds County Court ex p Morris* [1990] 2 WLR 175). What is the difference between a Court of Review and a Court of Appeal? Is a Divisional Court a public (rather than private) law court?
3. How does the role of the English Court of Appeal differ from the role of the French *Cour d'appel*?

(c) House of Lords

Miliangos v George Frank (Textiles) Ltd [1976] AC 443 House of Lords

Lord Wilberforce: ... The law on this topic is judge made; it has been built up over the years from case to case. It is entirely within this House's duty, in the course of administering justice, to give the law a new direction in a particular case where, on principle and in reason, it appears right to do so. I cannot accept the suggestion that because a rule is long established only legislation can change it – that may be so when the rule is so deeply entrenched that it has infected the whole legal system, or the choice of a new rule involves more far-reaching research than courts can carry out ...

Lord Simon (dissenting): ... Law is too serious a matter to be left exclusively to judges ...

[T]he training and qualification of a judge is to elucidate the problem immediately before him, so that its features stand out in stereoscopic clarity. But the beam of light which so illuminates the immediate scene seems to throw surrounding areas into greater obscurity; the whole landscape is distorted to the view. A penumbra can be apprehended, but not much beyond; so that when the searchlight shifts a quite unexpected scene may be disclosed. The very qualifications for the judicial process thus impose limitations on its use. This is why judicial advance should be gradual. 'I am not trained to see the distant scene: one step is enough for me' should be the motto on the wall opposite the judge's desk. It is, I concede, a less spectacular method of progression than somersaults and cartwheels; but it is the one best suited to the capacity and resources of a judge. We are likely to perform better the duties society impose on us if we recognise our limitations. Within the proper limits there is more than enough to be done which is of value to society ...

There are three more general questions which are raised by this important appeal.

(1) Overruling ... involves that the law must be deemed always to have been as my noble and learned friends now declare it. This may affect the vires of some rules of court; but beyond this there has been, so far as I can see, no consideration of what consequences the retrospective alteration of the law (for, let us face it, that is the reality) may have. I would be more ready to go along with my noble and learned friends if the decision had prospective effect only. One of the several reasons why radical law reform is in general more appropriately carried out by Parliament is that a statute can (and usually does) operate prospectively. I venture once again to plead that consideration should be given to the various forms of prospective overruling, such as obtain in some other common law systems.

(2) The type of law reform by judiciary which is here exemplified, and which has been exemplified in some other recent cases, is a very considerable social responsibility. Of course, no worthwhile judge is afraid of responsibility. But I presume to suggest that consideration should be given to the desirability of the Lords of Appeal sitting in banc in such circumstances – at least where the overruling of a *recent* decision of your Lordships' House is in question.

(3) The main ground of my dissent from the opinions of my noble and learned friends is that this type of issue is unsuitable for law reform by judiciary. It is the sort of case where, in my view, a wide range of advice, official especially but also commercial, is required. The training and experience of a judge is unsuitable for this type of decision-making unaided: his circumspection is too narrow; his very qualities of keen perception of his immediate problem tend to militate against sound judgment of the wider and more general issues involved. But if the courts are to undertake legislative responsibilities, something might be done to equip them better for the type of decision-making which is involved. Official advice and a balanced executive view might be made available by a law officer or his counsel acting as *amicus curiae*. I venture to suggest consideration of some such machinery.

Notes and questions

1. 'Your Lordships' task in this House is to decide particular cases between litigants and your Lordships are not called upon to rationalise the law of England. That attractive if perilous field may well be left to others to cultivate ... Arguments based on legal consistency are apt to mislead for the common law is a practical code adapted to deal with the manifold diversities of human life, and as a great American judge has reminded us, "the life of the law has not been logic; it has been experience".' (Lord Macmillan, *Read v J Lyons*

& Co [1947] AC 156.) Upon whom, then, is the task of rationalising the law of England?

2. 'In a contest purely between one litigant and another, such as the present, the task of the court is to do, and be seen to be doing, justice between the parties ... There is no higher or additional duty to ascertain some independent truth' (Lord Wilberforce in *Air Canada v Secretary of State for Trade* [1983] 2 AC 394). Is it really realistic to treat the parties in this case as ordinary litigants involved in some private dispute? Is not the House of Lords diminishing its own role?

3. What is meant by prospective overruling?

4. How can the executive make its view known in an English court?

5. How might the role of a court influence the development of the law of obligations? If the duty of a trial or an appeal judge were to change, would this, in the longer term, lead to changes in legal thinking itself?

6. Is Lord Simon saying that cases do not lay down general principles?

3 THE ROLE OF PRECEDENT

On the continent the civil codes are seen as providing both structure and stability to the law. In an uncodified system like English law this structure and stability has of course to come from elsewhere and this is the reason why precedent assumes such importance in theory if not so much in practice. It is important for law to appear as a rational discourse and part of this rationality is to be found in its apparent ability to predict as well as to explain. Precedent thus becomes part of the science of the common law; it acts as the means of analysis of past decisions and the basis for predicting future decisions. In practice the doctrine of precedent must be treated with a certain caution since the methodology of distinguishing cases can always act as a means by which inconvenient authorities can be by-passed; and when this happens the method of analysing cases needs to stretch beyond the precedent doctrine itself. One needs to look very closely at the reasoning methods used (cf Chapter 2) and the objectives (social, economic, political) of the relevant areas of law (cf eg, Chapter 7).

Qualcast (Wolverhampton) Ltd v Haynes [1959] AC 743 House of Lords

Lord Somervell: My Lords, I also would allow the appeal. In the present case the county court judge, after having found the facts, had to decide whether there was, in relation to this plaintiff, a failure by the defendants to take reasonable care for his safety. It is, I think, clear from the passage cited by my noble and learned friend that he would have found for the defendants but for some principle laid down, as he thought, by the authorities, to which he referred.

I hope it may be worth while to make one or two general observations on the effect on the precedent system of the virtual abolition of juries in negligence actions. Whether a duty of reasonable care is owed by A to B is a question of law... When negligence cases were tried with juries the judge would direct them as to the law ... The question whether on the facts in that particular case there was or was not a failure to take reasonable care was a question for the jury. There was not, and could not be, complete uniformity of standard. One jury would attribute to the reasonable man a greater degree of prescience than would another. The jury's decision did not become part of our law citable as a precedent. In those days it would only be in very exceptional circumstances that a judge's direction would be reported or be citable. So far as the law is concerned they would all be the same. Now that negligence cases are mostly tried without juries, the distinction between the functions of judge and jury is blurred. A judge naturally gives reasons for the conclusion formerly arrived at by a jury without reasons. It may sometimes be difficult to draw the line, but if the reasons given by a judge for arriving at the conclusion previously reached by a jury are to be treated as "law" and citable, the precedent system will die from a surfeit of authorities ...

Lord Denning: ... The question that did arise was this: What did reasonable care demand of the employers in this particular case? That is not a question of law at all but a question of fact. To solve it the tribunal of fact – be it judge or jury – can take into account any proposition of good sense that is relevant in the circumstances, but it must beware not to treat it as a proposition of law ...

So here, this being a case governed by the common law and not by any statute or regulation, the standard of care must be fixed by the judge as if he were a jury, without being rigidly bound by authorities. What is "a proper system of work" is a matter for evidence, not for law books. It changes as the conditions of work change. The standard goes up as men become wiser. It does not stand still as the law sometimes does.

I can well see how it came about that the county court judge made this mistake. He was presented with a number of cases in which judges of the High Court had given reasons for coming to their conclusions of fact. And those reasons seemed to him to be so expressed as to be rulings in point of law: whereas they were in truth nothing more than propositions of good sense ...

Notes and questions

1. We have already mentioned how the absent jury in private law continues to exert an influence and perhaps this case provides a good example of how the roles of judge and jury must be properly understood before one can have a proper understanding of the modern law of contract and tort. Take the tort case of *Bolton v Stone* [1951] AC 850 (read it in the law report): in the days of judge and jury, would the point in issue have been one for the judge or one for the jury? What about *Smith v Littlewoods* (p 365)?

2. Is the question of reasonable behaviour a matter of judicial intuition?

3. Is it really realistic to say that decisions of fact will not influence future cases?

4. Read *Kopitoff v Wilson* (1876) 1 QBD 377 in the law report. What was the role of a jury in a contract case?

4 THE ROLE OF PARLIAMENT

It is easy to think, given the history of the law of obligations in Western law, that it is a subject that has its source in case law and doctrine (writings of the jurists). In fact, in the civil law, it is statute (the codes) that acts as the primary source of liability and although the common law remains uncodified it is, today at any rate, impossible to ignore legislation as a major primary source. This legislation, admittedly, is dependent on the notions and classification categories developed by the judges – and so, for example, statute uses terms such as 'contract', 'trespass to goods', 'negligence', 'conversion' and the like.[5] But statute has intruded into so many particular factual areas that it has become possible to say that certain types of liability are now almost exclusively statute based. Thus liability for things (cf Chapter 7) is now a form of liability that the courts are hesitant to develop themselves; it is something they prefer to leave to Parliament.[6]

However, even where statute governs, the courts still have a major role to play in interpreting the words of the legislation and this interpretative role is as important as any caselaw analysis. Does the word 'offer' in a statute mean the same as in a contract textbook? What objects are covered by the word 'plant' in a statute dealing with safety at work? In fact the approach towards legislation is often very similar to the one adopted by the courts in interpreting wills and contracts: the point in issue is what a particular word or phrase means in the context of a particular factual situation. Statute can also exert a negative influence; in some recent cases the courts have specifically refused to develop a common law principle on the basis that the factual situation has, in general, been taken into consideration by the legislator when formulating a statute.[7] In these situations the courts often claim to be responding to the policy aspect that attaches to civil liability problems. However, the idea that the courts work in partnership with the legislator – an idea that forms part of the civil law tradition – is not something that is part of English legal history.

---

5   See eg, Torts (Interference with Goods) Act 1977; Unfair Contract Terms Act 1977.
6   See *Cambridge Water Co v Eastern Leather Plc* [1994] 2 WLR 53.
7   See eg, *Murphy v Brentwood DC* [1991] 1 AC 398.

Fisher v Bell [1961] 1 QB 394 Queen's Bench Division

Lord Parker CJ: ... The sole question is whether the exhibition of that knife in the window with the ticket constituted an offer for sale within the statute. I think that most lay people would be inclined to the view (as, indeed, I was myself when I first read these papers), that if a knife were displayed in a window like that with a price attached to it, it was nonsense to say that was not offering it for sale. The knife is there inviting people to buy it, and in ordinary language it is for sale; but any statute must be looked at in the light of the general law of the country, for Parliament must be taken to know the general law. It is clear that, according to the ordinary law of contract, the display of an article with a price on it in a shop window is merely an invitation to treat. It is in no sense an offer for sale the acceptance of which constitutes a contract. That is clearly the general law of the country ...

In those circumstances I, for my part, though I confess reluctantly, am driven to the conclusion that no offence was here committed ...

Notes and questions

1. This decision was altered by statute: did, then, the court give effect to the will of Parliament? Was it necessary to use the law of contract to decide a criminal case?

2. 'I must confess to having felt some attraction for this approach, as a matter of logic; but I have come to the conclusion that its practical consequences are such that I do not think that it can have been the intention of the legislature so to provide' (Lord Goff in *The Derbyshire* [1988] AC 276). If Lord Goff had to decide *Fisher v Bell* would he have arrived at the same conclusion as Lord Parker?

3. 'The duty of the courts is to ascertain and give effect to the will of Parliament as expressed in its enactments. In the performance of this duty the judges do not act as computers into which are fed the statute and the rules for the construction of statutes and from whom issue forth the mathematically correct answer. The interpretation of statutes is a craft as much as a science and the judges, as craftsmen, select and apply the appropriate rules as the tools of their trade. They are not legislators, but finishers, refiners and polishers of legislation which comes to them in a state requiring varying degrees of further processing' (Donaldson J, *Corocraft Ltd v Pan-American Airways* [1969] 1 QB 616). What is the difference between a craftsman and a scientist? Do they operate according to quite different theories?[8]

4. 'There may be very sound social and political reasons for imposing upon local authorities the burden of acting, in effect, as insurers ... statute may so provide. It has not done so and I do not, for my part,

---

8   Cf C Atias, *Épistémologie du droit* (Presses Universitaires de France, 1994).

think that it is right for the courts not simply to expand existing principles but to create at large new principles in order to fulfil a social need in an area of consumer protection which has already been perceived by the legislature but for which, presumably advisedly, it has not thought it necessary to provide' (Lord Oliver, *Murphy v Brentwood DC* [1991] 1 AC 398). Are these the words of a craftsman or a scientist?

5 THE ROLE OF INSTITUTIONS

The word 'institution' is generally applied to physical manifestations of the law such as courts, the police and the judiciary; but people and things are also physical manifestations of the law since, as the Romans recognised, all law is focused around *personae* and *res*. Institutions thus have a central role with respect to problem-solving in the whole of private and public law.

(a) The institutional system

Geoffrey Samuel, *The Foundations of Legal Reasoning* (Maklu, 1994), pp 171-178 (footnotes omitted)

Jacques Ellul, in a perceptive essay on the importance of Roman law, makes the point that, in addition to bequeathing the notion of the state, the concept of law and the range of judicial techniques, the Romans also provided the modern Western world with a number of legal institutions. These institutions, as others have noticed, are fundamental not just to legal thought and to legal technique, but also to the relationship between law and social reality. "Society handles the institutions of the law much in the same way as a child handles his bricks", wrote Kahn-Freund in a celebrated passage in the introduction to an English translation of Renner "It uses the same bricks all the time – or for a long time – today to build a manor house, tomorrow to build a factory, and the day after to build a railway station" he continued. And he went on to make the point, a point which he described as "Renner's positivist axiom", that "the bricks remain the same". What the lawyer does is to provide the bricks, but what society makes of these bricks "is none of the lawyer's business".

§ 1 *Definitional Problems*

Now it has to be emphasised at once that when it comes to defining a legal institution one is faced with ambiguity in that much will depend upon whether a wide or a narrow view is taken. If one takes a wide view, then the term 'institution' can embrace nearly all of the private law concepts of Roman law such as ownership, servitudes, contracts and marriage together with the courts and personnel of the law; however, if a narrow view is taken the term is restricted to a social reality around which rules form. With this narrower definition it is difficult to describe, say, a contract as a 'social reality' since it does not have the same basis in empirical reality as a person or a thing. On the other hand many legal concepts could attract the label 'institution' once a definition is framed around the idea of durability, communal organisation or social creation tending towards a common social end.

All this may seem at first sight a rather sterile debate. Yet for the epistemologist keen to gain insights into case law a narrow view of a legal institution might well prove more useful for several reasons. First, because if one restricts institution to a social reality around which rules form this will provide a model capable of acting as a meeting point for the worlds of social fact, of legal analysis and of language in general; such a model has obvious attractions for anyone searching for an ontological starting point in legal science. Secondly, because a narrower definition of institution will allow the epistemologist to see the fundamental and enduring influence of Roman law on legal analysis and legal thought in general; this influence ought never to be underestimated by anyone interested in legal knowledge and legal habits of mind. Finally, because a narrower view of legal institution will allow the epistemologist to distinguish between legal institutions, institutional relations, legal concepts and legal categories; and such distinctions, in turn, will be useful when it comes to comprehending the kind of systems that are operating within the complexities of legal reasoning, legal method and legal education.

§ 2 Gaius and the institutional system

Starting out, then, from a narrow definition of legal institution it is possible to see that the notion has its foundation in Roman legal thought and, in particular, in the *Institutiones* of Gaius "All Law", said Gaius, "relates either to persons (*personae*), to things (*res*) or to actions (*actiones*)". Now the importance of this structure, which as many have observed has left its mark on all the modern codes, is that it went much further than just conveniently classifying all the rules of private law under three headings or into three books. Each element of the tripartite classification had a meaning at one and the same time in the world of fact and the world of law. Thus the sociologist can talk of persons, things and courts as existing in the world of social fact just as the jurist can talk of legal subjects (*personae*), legal objects (*res*) and legal remedies (*actiones*) as existing in the world of law. The three terms are descriptive as well as conceptual in that they can at one and the same time be attached to 'real' and 'metaphysical' entities. Actions, admittedly, are more ambiguous in this respect since the only way they can be envisaged as existing in social reality is in terms of court buildings and legal officials; but, in tying the nature of legal claims to the processes of court procedure, the Roman jurists had a means of keeping legal 'rights' (*iura*) and legal justice (*suum cuique tribuere*: giving to each what is due) tied to objective social realities with the result that fundamental legal relations such as ownership (*dominium*) and obligations were never in need of abstract definition in terms of axiomatic propositions. In other words Roman legal thought had little need of propositional mediating concepts since they had the means of creating *iura* simply through the manipulation of apparent social entities.

Persons, things and actions are, therefore, institutions because they act as a structure capable of envisaging at one and the same time a system of legal and a system of social relations. Indeed they go further than this. In addition to acting as elements in a system of legal and social thought, the three institutions are equally capable of forming focal points in political and economic systems with the result that the moment one devises a system of juridical relations between the institutional elements one is in effect also creating a structure that has some meaning in the worlds of political, social and economic relations. Indeed, to the Marxist, legal institutions – *persona* and *res* in particular – are the basis of capitalism and economic power. "Legal institutions", writes Kahn-Freund, "can and must be understood as the tools used by society in achieving this ultimate aim" of "production" and "reproduction". This, of course, is one reason why (Roman) law has proved so central to Western social thought and Western rationality in general. "Legal analysis", observes Renner, "is of necessity determined by history", for it is history that has provided law with its "arsenal of concepts, its terminology"...

§ 4 Institution and system

It would be idle to think that this Gaian structure alone acted as the epistemological foundation of Western legal thought. It is, to use the explanation of Teubner with respect to systems theory in general, more concerned with explaining broad structural patterns rather than with providing an analysis of court decisions, statutes and the like. However, the institutional structure is, of itself, a central contribution to legal thought since it acts as the basis not only for subjects and objects around which rules are affixed ("no person shall ..."; "no vehicle heavier than five tons shall ..."), but for the elements in a system of institutional relations. Between *persona* and *res* the Roman lawyers developed the fundamental relationships of ownership (*dominium*) and possession (*possessio*); between person and person they established the "legal chain" (*vinculum iuris*) of the *obligatio*; and between *actio* and *persona* they conceived the relationship of an interest. Each of these institutions and each of these relations acted, directly or indirectly, as a classification category for a whole mass of more detailed legal propositions and judicial opinions concerning slavery, guardianship, property, succession, loss and acquisition of ownership and possession, contracts, delicts and so on. But the point is that the details within these categories were only to a limited extent defined by the institutions and institutional relations themselves; and so, as we have seen, it is quite possible to have, as between two legal systems, contrasting rules with regard to, say, the passing of property in a supermarket without the structural relationship between *personae* and *res* being in any abstract way any different. Both systems could be said to be using a model of relations based on *personae*, *res*, *obligatio* and *dominium*. What Gaius had produced, therefore, was a genuine structural model since his scheme could transcend the details of Roman law to act as an organising model for bodies of rules thrown up by societies separated from Rome by space and by time. "Having set out these grand categories", writes Villey, "it remains continually possible to modify the contents". And so, for example, one can add new types of property to the institutional category of *res* as new economic situations create new forms of wealth; equally one can add to the institution of *persona* non human legal subjects such as corporate groups, animals ('animal rights') or, indeed, even an inanimate object such as a temple.

The tripartite institutional plan is, then, as Jacques Ellul has observed, the basis for a juristic world quite separate from the world of social reality. "The law", he says, "becomes a kind of reality imposed upon the social situation, putting it into order, and ending up by becoming more 'true' than the facts". Such an abstraction is of importance to epistemology in that it immediately suggests that institutions and institutional relations function as system. Each institution as an element, and each institutional relation as a relation between elements, make sense within the Gaian scheme only by reference to the other elements and relations. However, the Gaian structure went further than this static model in that the interrelationships between the elements and relations endowed the model with a dynamic aspect; it could, so to speak, alter the very object it was attempting to describe. Legal relations could create institutions as much as institutions could create legal relations.

A good example of this dynamic ability is to be found in the notion of *persona*. Legal persons are those persons recognised in the legal scheme as being able to sue and be sued as an individual entity; and while it has to be said at once that the Roman materials on legal personality are very fragmented, a study of the *Corpus Iuris* will at least indicate that "the personality attached by the law to human beings is no less its own creation than that of so-called of 'legal' persons, and the questions at issue are closely bound up with those which concern the nature of subjective rights and the purposes for which they exist". Two important consequences flow from the recognition that the legal subject is as much a creation of law as it is of social fact. First, if a legal person is an entity capable of bringing or defending a legal *actio* in its own right, then the moment that a person – or more importantly a group of persons (*universitas*) – is granted the procedural power to bring an action in his, her or its own name this will have the effect of turning that person or group into a legal person. In other words a legal *persona* can be created indirectly simply through rules attaching to the institution of the *actio*. This point was clearly recognised by the later classical jurists and seems even to have been appreciated by Gaius himself who is recorded as observing that, in the grand plan, towns are treated as private people. Secondly, if a legal person is capable as an entity of bringing and defending legal actions, then it follows that such an entity must also be capable of having its own patrimony – its own fund of tangible and intangible assets and liabilities treated as a single whole. For any entity that can bring an *actio in personam* for a debt or for damages and an *actio in rem* for vindicating property rights must, by the sheer logic of the Gaian scheme, be capable of owing and owning. The modern commercial corporation is, then, a direct result of the dynamic qualities of the Gaian structure.

Alongside this legal personality development was an analogous development with regard to the institution of property (*res*). The starting point for the institution of a thing was the piece of tangible property which could be seen and touched (*res corporales*) and thus represented both a social fact and a legal object. However, as Gaius himself recognised, a *res* was quite capable of being conceived through the obligation relationship between *persona* and *persona*; the moment that one person owed to another person a sum of money or some other performance under a contract the debt or performance became a *res* in itself. One person could then lay claim to this *res* as if it was a form of property owned by the claimant. Accordingly a debt was, and remains today, both a creature of the law of obligations and the law of property and this duality still causes a certain conceptual confusion. In Roman law itself the conceptual confusion at the legal relation level was largely avoided at a practical level through the fundamental dichotomy in the law of actions between actions *in rem* and actions *in personam*; the form of property which a debt represented was not so much the sum of money as the entitlement to an *actio in personam*. The *res*, therefore, was the legal relation between *persona* and *actio* and not an actual right (*ius*) to the money itself. In English law one finds a similar situation with regard to debts as property in that a debt is both a personal obligation and a form of property.

However, despite the fact that the *res* is actually called a 'chose in action' in the common law, the lack of a distinction between real and personal actions in the area of moveable property has meant that English lawyers have found it difficult to avoid conceptual confusion when talking about rights to a debt. Is one asserting a property right or merely an obligational right? This is a point to which we shall return. But for the moment what needs to be emphasised is that a debt is a form of economic wealth that has been created entirely out of the Gaian system itself. It has no independent existence as a social reality and as a result was an example of a piece of property which was intangible (*res incorporales*) and existing only because of the existence of the institutional system itself. As Gaius himself put it: *Incorporales sunt quae tangi non possunt, qualia sunt ea quae iure consistunt, sicut hereditas, usufructus, obligationes quoquo modo contractae ...*

Notes and questions

1. '[L]egal rules must be grouped in organised sets which constitute the legal authority of a certain kind of social relation around a directing idea, around a common intellectual focal point. Legal institutions correspond accordingly to these organic and systematic rule sets which govern, according to a common object, a permanent and abstract manifestation of social life ... Institutions are genuine legal bodies, Ihering having written: "... the rules find in this common object their point of reunion: they surround it like muscles surround bones..."' (J-L Bergel, *Théorie générale du droit* (2nd ed, (1989), p 178). Do the rules of contract attach to the contractual relationship or to the parties to the contract?

2. English law is not based on Roman law. Does it nevertheless conform to the institutional system?

(b) Legal subject (*persona*)

Tesco Supermarkets Ltd v Nattrass [1972] AC 153 House of Lords

Lord Reid: ... I must start by considering the nature of the personality which by a fiction the law attributes to a corporation. A living person has a mind which can have knowledge or intention or be negligent and he has hands to carry out his intentions. A corporation has none of these: it must act through living persons, though not always one or the same person. Then the person who acts is not speaking or acting for the company. He is acting as the company and his mind which directs his acts is the mind of the company. There is no question of the company being vicariously liable. He is not acting as a servant, representative, agent or delegate. He is an embodiment of the company or, one could say, he hears and speaks through the persona of the company, within his appropriate sphere, and his mind is the mind of the company. If it is a guilty mind then that guilt is the guilt of the company. It must be a question of law whether, once the facts have been ascertained, a person in doing particular things is to be regarded as the company or merely as the company's servant or agent. In that case any liability of the company can only be a statutory or vicarious liability ...

17

Reference is frequently made to the judgment of Denning LJ in *H L Bolton (Engineering) Co Ltd v T J Graham & Sons Ltd*. He said:

> "A company may in many ways be likened to a human body. It has a brain and nerve centre which controls what it does. It also has hands which hold the tools and act in accordance with directions from the centre. Some of the people in the company are mere servants and agents who are nothing more than hands to do the work and cannot be said to represent the mind or will. Others are directors and managers who represent the directing mind and will of the company, and control what it does. The state of mind of these managers is the state of mind of the company and is treated by the law as such."

In that case the directors of the company only met once a year: they left the management of the business to others, and it was the intention of those managers which was imputed to the company. I think that was right. There have been attempts to apply Lord Denning's words to all servants of a company whose work is brain work, or who exercise some managerial discretion under the direction of superior officers of the company. I do not think that Lord Denning intended to refer to them. He only referred to those who "represent the directing mind and will of the company, and control what it does".

I think that is right for this reason. Normally the board of directors, the managing director and perhaps other superior officers of a company carry out the functions of management and speak and act as the company. Their subordinates do not. They carry out orders from above and it can make no difference that they are given some measure of discretion. But the board of directors may delegate some part of their functions of management giving to their delegate full discretion to act independently of instructions from them. I see no difficulty in holding that they have thereby put such a delegate in their place so that within the scope of the delegation he can act as the company. It may not always be easy to draw the line but there are cases in which the fine must be drawn. *Leonard's* case was one of them.

In some cases the phrase alter ego has been used. I think it is misleading. When dealing with a company the word alter is I think misleading. The person who speaks and acts as the company is not alter. He is identified with the company. And when dealing with an individual no other individual can be his alter ego. The other individual can be a servant, agent, delegate or representative but I know of neither principle nor authority which warrants the confusion (in the literal or original sense) of two separate individuals ...

What good purpose could be served by making an employer criminally responsible for the misdeeds of some of his servants but not for those of others? It is sometimes argued – it was argued in the present case – that making an employer criminally responsible, even when he has done all that he could to prevent an offence, affords some additional protection to the public because this will induce him to do more. But if he has done all he can how can he do more? I think that what lies behind this argument is a suspicion that magistrates too readily accept evidence that an employer has done all he can to prevent offences. But if magistrates were to accept as sufficient a paper scheme and perfunctory efforts to enforce it they would not be doing their duty – that would not be "due diligence" on the part of the employer.

Then it is said that this would involve discrimination in favour of a large employer like the appellants against a small shopkeeper. But that is not so. Mr Clement was the "opposite number" of the small shopkeeper and he was liable to prosecution in this case. The purpose of this Act must have been to penalise those at fault, not those who were in no way to blame.

The Divisional Court decided this case on a theory of delegation. In that they were following some earlier authorities. But they gave far too wide a meaning to delegation. I have said that a board of directors can delegate part of their functions of management so as to make their delegate an embodiment of the company within the sphere of the delegation. But here the board never delegated any part of their functions. They set up a chain of command through regional and district supervisors, but they remained in control. The shop managers had to obey their general directions and also take orders from their superiors. The acts or omissions of shop managers were not acts of the company itself ...

Questions

1. What if the customer in the supermarket had been injured by the carelessness of one of the employees: in what circumstances could the supermarket claim that the negligent act was not its act?

2. What if the customer had been assaulted by a supermarket employee (a) while in the store or (b) while walking home? (Cf *Keppel Bus Co*, p 310.)

3. Can a trade union own property and make contracts? Can it be sued? Can it sue? (Cf Trade Union and Labour Relations (Consolidation) Act 1992 ss 10, 12.)

4. Do legal persons have all the rights that natural persons have?

5. Can one sue a cricket club? (Cf *Miller v Jackson*, p 22.)

6. Can an inanimate object ever have legal personality? Can an animal? (Cf *Bumper Development Corporation v Metropolitan Police Commissioner* [1991] 1 WLR 1362.)

7. Is the world of law populated by individual humans or by groups of humans? Do companies actually exist? Do classes (eg consumers) exist? If so, do they have interests and rights?

(c) Legal object (*res*)

Frost v Aylesbury Dairy Co Ltd [1905] 1 KB 608 Court of Appeal

Collins MR: This is an appeal by the defendants in an action in which the plaintiff sued to recover expenses to which he was put by the illness and death of his wife, caused, as he alleged, by typhoid fever of which the infection was caught from milk supplied by the defendants. The jury found that the milk was the cause of the fever, and gave a verdict for the plaintiff, for whom judgment was entered. The first point taken is whether in point of law, on the facts as ascertained, there can be any liability on the defendants even if it is admitted that the milk was the cause of the fever, and on this it is contended for the defendants that there was no actionable wrong on their part. The point is whether the circumstances under which the milk was bought bring the case within the provisions of s 14, sub-s 1, [see now s 14(3) of the 1979 Act] of the Sale of Goods Act 1893 ... Considering the matter by steps, it appears that there was no specific evidence as to the inception of the relation of buyer and seller, because, as a matter of fact, people do not, when they want a milk supply, enter into an elaborate negotiation with the vendor of the milk. We begin the discussion with the practice followed in the dealing between two parties. The fact of the supply of the article involves a contract. That contract is for the supply of food, for no one would question that the milk was bought as an article of consumption ... [M]ilk was supplied for a purpose known to the sellers under circumstances which showed that the buyer relied on the sellers' skill or knowledge, and that the goods were of a description which it was in the course of the sellers' business to supply. The point mainly pressed upon us on behalf of the defendants was that the buyer could not be said to rely on the skill or judgment of the sellers in a case in which no amount of skill or judgment would enable them to find out the defect in the milk supplied. That amounts to a contention that a seller of goods cannot be answerable for a latent defect in them unless upon a special contract to that effect. That argument is not employed for the first time, for it was used before the Sale of Goods Act 1893, which consolidated and crystallised the law, which seems to me to be just the same under the statute as it was under the common law. The matter was specifically dealt with in the considered judgment of the Court of Appeal in *Randall v Newson*, where it was held that on the sale of an article for a specific purpose there is a warranty by the vendor that it is reasonably fit for the purpose, and that there is no exception as to latent undiscoverable defects. That was the case of a defective pole for a carriage, and the view of the Court is expressed thus: "If the subject-matter be an article or commodity to be used for a particular purpose, the thing offered or delivered must answer that description, that is to say, it must be that article or commodity, and reasonably fit for the particular purpose. The governing principle, therefore, is that the thing offered and delivered under a contract of purchase and sale must answer the description of it which is contained in words in the contract, or which would be so contained if the contract were accurately drawn out. And if that be the governing principle, there is no place in it for the suggested limitation." The suggested limitation was that the principle applied only to such defects as could be discovered by reasonable care and skill. The judgment continues:

> "If the article or commodity offered or delivered does not in fact answer the description of it in the contract, it does not do so more or less because the defect in it is patent, or latent, or discoverable."

That appears to me to be a conclusive authority on that part of the case raised on behalf of the defendants. I may, however, refer also to a matter that was dealt with in the judgment of this Court in *Preist v Last*, that a good deal of difficulty and some confusion may arise as to whether an article is sold for a particular purpose where it is capable of being used for a number of purposes. Where the thing dealt with carries in its description a limitation to a particular purpose the difficulty does not arise. In this case we begin with the purchase of milk, a commodity which carries with it a special limitation to the purpose of food. It is obvious that the obligation of the seller of food must stand in a different position from that of the seller of an article that may or may not, according to the special circumstances of the case, be used for a particular object. All the difficulty is gone when once we get in the description of the article itself the purpose for which it is to be used. That principle was applied in the case to which I have referred, which was that of the purchase of a hot-water bottle, a description which carries with it the purpose for which the article is bought. The same principle applies in this case, where it is clear that the milk was bought for a special purpose, and sold by persons who claimed and received the confidence of the purchaser in the special skill and knowledge asserted by the sellers. It seems to me to be clear that there is no legal difficulty in upholding this verdict, and that the appeal should be dismissed.

[**Mathew** and **Cozens-Hardy** LJJ were of the same opinion.]

Notes and questions

1. The sellers of the milk were strictly liable in this case because the rules regarding merchantable [now satisfactory] quality and reasonable fitness in the Sale of Goods Act focus, not on the seller, but on the object of the sale (*res*). Either the milk was fit or it was not. Had the rule been drafted differently – for example had it been drafted around the institution of the seller rather than the thing sold – the duty may well have turned out to have been different. Compare s 14 of the Sale of Goods Act 1979 with s 13 of the Supply of Goods and Services Act 1982. What if a manufacturer of a product puts a defective product onto the market: does (a) the common law and (b) statute focus upon the person or the thing?

2. Sale of goods contracts always involve persons (legal subjects) and things (legal objects) and thus a statute like the Sale of Goods Act is relevant not only to the law of obligations but also to the law of property. In Roman law, and in modern German law, the obligation and property aspects of a sale of goods transaction were always kept quite separate, but this is not true of English law which uses the contract itself as a means of passing 'property' in goods (Sale of Goods Act 1979 ss 16-18). What if the contract turns out to be defective: does this put the property title at risk? Or what if the seller goes bankrupt, or the goods are destroyed, before they have been delivered to the buyer: what kind of claim does the buyer have? Can the buyer bring an action *in rem* against the thing?

CTN Cash and Carry Ltd v Gallaher Ltd [1994] 4 All ER 714 Court of Appeal

Steyn LJ: ... On 20 November 1986 the manager of the plaintiffs' warehouse in Preston placed an order for a large consignment of cigarettes. The invoice value of the order inclusive of VAT was of the order of £17,000. By mistake an employee of the defendants put the address of the plaintiffs' warehouse in Burnley on the delivery note. On 24 November 1986 the defendants' driver delivered the goods to the plaintiffs' warehouse in Burnley. The goods were unloaded. Mr Nuttall, an assistant branch manager of the plaintiffs, signed the delivery note. Shortly afterwards, Mr Nuttall discovered that the delivery was intended for the Preston warehouse and not the Burnley warehouse. He telephoned the defendants' dispatch department about the matter. Eventually it was agreed that the defendants would arrange for the carriage of the goods from Burnley to Preston. The defendants were to undertake the carriage of the goods to Preston on 28 November 1986. Unfortunately, there was a robbery at the Burnley warehouse on the day before. The entire consignment of cigarettes was stolen ...

The question was, who should suffer the loss resulting from the theft of the goods at the Burnley warehouse? ...

Questions

1. What is your answer to this question? Is the Sale of Goods Act 1979 ss 16–20 of help?

2. Were the plaintiffs possessors of the cigarettes before they were stolen?

3. What if the cigarettes had been defective and not reasonably fit for their purpose?

In re Goldcorp Exchange Ltd [1994] 3 WLR 199 Privy Council

(See p 151)

Questions

1. Is the result of this case dependent upon the existence or non-existence of an image of a relationship between person and thing?

2. Was there ever a thing to which the plaintiffs were entitled?

(d) Legal remedy (*actio*)

Kingdom of Spain v Christie, Manson & Woods Ltd [1986] 1 WLR 1120 Chancery

(See p 112)

Miller v Jackson [1977] QB 966 Court of Appeal

Lord Denning MR: In summer time village cricket is the delight of everyone. Nearly every village has its own cricket field where the young men play and the old men watch. In the village of Lintz in County Durham they have their own ground, where they have played these last 70 years ... Yet now after these 70 years a judge of the High Court has ordered that they must not play there any more. He has issued an injunction to stop them. He has done it at the instance of a newcomer who is no lover of cricket. This newcomer has built, or has had built for him, a house on the edge of the cricket ground which four years ago was a field where cattle grazed. The animals did not mind the cricket. But now this adjoining field has been turned into a housing estate ... Now he complains that, when a batsman hits a six, the ball has been known to land in his garden or on or near his house. His wife has got so upset about it that they always go out at weekends. They do not go into the garden when cricket is being played ...

No one has been hurt at all by any of these balls, either before or after the high fence was erected. There has, however, been some damage to property, even since the high fence was erected. The cricket club have offered to remedy all the damage and pay all expenses ... But Mrs Miller and her husband have remained unmoved. Every offer by the club has been rejected. They demand the closing down of the cricket club. Nothing else will satisfy them. They have obtained legal aid to sue the cricket club.

In support of the case, the plaintiff relies on the dictum of Lord Reid in *Bolton v Stone* [1951] AC 850, 867: "if cricket cannot be played on a ground without creating a substantial risk, then it should not be played there at all." I would agree with that saying if the houses or road were there first, and the cricket ground came there second ... But I do not agree with Lord Reid's dictum when the cricket ground has been there for 70 years and the houses are newly built at the very edge of it. I recognise that the cricket club are under a duty to use all reasonable care consistently with the playing of the game of cricket, but I do not think the cricket club can be expected to give up the game of cricket altogether. After all they have their rights in their cricket ground. They have spent money, labour and love in the making of it; and they have the right to play on it as they have done for 70 years ...

If we were to approach this case with the eyes of the judges of the 19th century they would, I believe, have seen it in this way. Every time that a batsman hit a ball over the fence so that it landed in the garden, he would be guilty of a trespass ... So would the committee of the cricket club, because they would have impliedly authorised it. They cheered the batsman on. If one or two of the players went round and asked the householder if they could go into the garden to find it, the householder could deny them access ... Of course, if the householder picked up the ball himself and gave it to his son to play with, he would be liable in conversion ... Even if there was any doubt about the plaintiff's right to sue in trespass, he would have a claim in nuisance, once he proved that the balls were repeatedly coming over or under the fence and making things uncomfortable for him. To those claims, in the 19th century, either in trespass or in nuisance, the committee of the cricket club would have no answer ... It would be no good for them to say that the cricket ground was there before the house was built. The householder could rely on ... *Sturges v Bridgman* (1879) 11 Ch D 852 ...

The case here was not pleaded by either side in the formulae of the 19th century. The plaintiffs did not allege trespass ... The case was pleaded in negligence or alternatively nuisance ...

The tort of nuisance in many cases overlaps the tort of negligence ... But there is at any rate one important distinction between them. It lies in the nature of the remedy sought. Is it damages? Or an injunction? If the plaintiff seeks a remedy in damages for injury done to him or his property, he can lay his claim either in *negligence* or in *nuisance*. But, if he seeks an injunction to stop the playing of cricket altogether, I think he must make his claim in nuisance. The books are full of cases where an injunction has been granted to restrain the continuance of a nuisance. But there is no case, so far as I know, where it has been granted so as to stop a man being negligent. At any rate in a case of this kind, where an occupier of a house or land seeks to restrain his neighbour from doing something on his own land, the only appropriate cause of action, on which to base the remedy of an injunction, is nuisance ... He must have been guilty of the fault, not necessarily of negligence, but of the unreasonable use of land ...

I would, therefore, adopt this test: is the use by the cricket club of this ground for playing cricket a reasonable use of it? To my mind it is a most reasonable use ...

On taking the balance, I would give priority to the right of the cricket club to continue playing cricket on the ground, as they have done for the last 70 years. It takes precedence over the right of the newcomer to sit in his garden undisturbed. After all he bought the house four years ago in mid-summer when the cricket season was at its height. He might have guessed that there was a risk that a hit for six might possibly land on his property. If he finds that he does not like it, he ought, when cricket is played, to sit in the other side of the house or in the front garden, or go out; or take advantage of the offers the club have made to him of fitting unbreakable glass, and so forth. Or, if he does not like that, he ought to sell his house and move elsewhere. I expect there are many who would gladly buy it in order to be near the cricket field and open space. At any rate he ought not to be allowed to stop cricket being played on this ground.

This case is new. It should be approached on principles applicable to modern conditions. There is a contest here between the interest of the public at large and the interest of a private individual. The *public* interest lies in protecting the environment by preserving our playing fields in the face of mounting development, and by enabling our youth to enjoy all the benefits of outdoor games, such as cricket and football. The *private* interest lies in securing the privacy of his home and garden without intrusion or interference by anyone. In deciding between these two conflicting interests, it must be remembered that it is not a question of damages. If by a million-to-one chance a cricket ball does go out of the ground and cause damage, the cricket club will pay. There is no difficulty on that score. No, it is a question of an injunction. And in our law you will find it repeatedly affirmed that an injunction is a discretionary remedy. In a new situation like this, we have to think afresh as to how discretion should be exercised ... As between their conflicting interests, I am of opinion that the public interest should prevail over the private interest ... In my opinion the right exercise of discretion is to refuse an injunction; and, of course, to refuse damages in lieu of an injunction. Likewise as to the claim for past damages. The club were entitled to use this ground for cricket in the accustomed way. It was not a nuisance, nor was it negligence ... So if the club had put it to the test, I would have dismissed the claim for damages also. But as the club very fairly say that they are willing to pay for any damage, I am content that there should be an award of £400 to cover any past or future damage.

I would allow the appeal, accordingly.

Geoffrey Lane LJ: ... No one has yet suffered any personal injury, although Mrs. Craig at least was perhaps lucky to have avoided it. There is no doubt that damage to tiles or windows at the plaintiffs' house is inevitable if cricket goes on.

There is little doubt that if the plaintiffs were to stay in their garden whilst matches are in progress they would be in real danger of being hit ...

There is no obligation on the plaintiffs to protect themselves in their own home from the activities of the defendants. Even if there were such an obligation it would be unreasonable to expect them to live behind shutters during the summer weekends and to stay out of their garden ...

It is true that the risk must be balanced against the measures which are necessary to eliminate it and against what the defendants can do to prevent accidents from happening ... In the present case, so far from being one incident of an unprecedented nature about which complaint is being made, this is a series of incidents, or perhaps a continuing failure to prevent incidents from happening, coupled with the certainty that they are going to happen again. The risk of injury to persons and property is so great that on each occasion when a ball comes over the fence and causes damage to the plaintiffs, the defendants are guilty of negligence ...

Was there here a use by the defendants of their land involving an unreasonable interference with the plaintiffs' enjoyment of *their* land? ... A balance has to be maintained between on the one hand the rights of the individual to enjoy his house and garden without the threat of damage and on the other hand the rights of the public in general or a neighbour to engage in lawful pastimes. Difficult questions may sometimes arise when the defendants' activities are offensive to the senses, for example, by way of noise. Where, as here, the damage or potential damage is physical the answer is more simple. There is ... no excuse I can see which exonerates the defendants from liability in nuisance ... There is here a real risk of serious injury ...

I would accordingly uphold the grant of the injunction to restrain the defendants from committing nuisance. However, I would postpone the operation of the injunction for 12 months to enable the defendants to look elsewhere for an alternative pitch ...

I have not thought it necessary to embark on any discussion of the possible rights of the defendants arising from matters which were neither pleaded nor argued.

Cumming-Bruce LJ: I agree with all that Geoffrey Lane LJ has said in his ... reasoning and conclusion on the liability of the defendants in negligence and nuisance ...

The only problem that arises is whether the learned judge is shown to be wrong in deciding to grant the equitable remedy of an injunction which will necessarily have the effect that the ground which the defendants have used as a cricket ground for 70 years can no longer be used for that purpose ...

So on the facts of this case a court of equity must seek to strike a fair balance between the right of the plaintiffs to have quiet enjoyment of their house and garden ... and the opportunity of the inhabitants of the village in which they live to continue to enjoy the manly sport which constitutes a summer recreation for adults and young persons, including one would hope and expect the plaintiffs' son. It is a relevant circumstance which a court of equity should take into account that the plaintiffs decided to buy a house which in June 1972 when completion took place was obviously on the boundary of a quite small cricket ground where cricket was played at weekends and sometimes on evenings during the working week. They selected a house with the benefit of the open space beside it ... [T]hey must have realised that it was the village cricket ground, and that balls would sometimes be knocked from the wicket into their garden, or even against the fabric of the house. If they did not realise it, they should have done. As it turns out, the female plaintiff has developed a somewhat obsessive attitude to the proximity of the cricket field and the cricketers who visit her to seek to recover their cricket balls. The evidence discloses a hostility which goes beyond what is reasonable, although as the learned judge found she is reasonable in her fear that if the family use the garden while a match is in progress they will run the risk of serious injury ... It is reasonable to decide that during matches the family must keep out of the garden ...

With all respect, in my view the learned judge ... does not appear to have had regard to the interest of the inhabitants of the village as a whole. Had he done so he would in my view have been led to the conclusion that the plaintiffs having accepted the benefit of the open space marching with their land should accept the restrictions on enjoyment of their garden which they may reasonably think necessary ... There are here special circumstances which should inhibit a court of equity from granting the injunction claimed ...

Notes and questions

1. ' "Actions" do not form a part of modern civil codes, and this is not merely, as might be thought, because procedure has come to be recognised as something very different from substantive law. Though related to procedure, the subject of "actions" had never been equivalent to it ... An "action" is ..., as was a "form of action" to the Common lawyer, an instrument of attack, and the correct instrument must be chosen for the attack contemplated ... Whether, in logic, the right or the remedy comes first is not for discussion here, but if we ask the question historically, there is no doubt that in the majority of cases at Rome it was the remedy ... [T]he Roman ... thus often said "I have an action" where a modern man would be as likely to say "I have a right.' (HF Jolowicz, *Roman Foundations of Modern Law* (1957), pp 75-76, 77). Is this an accurate description of modern English law as well? Does Lord Denning nevertheless use the notion of a 'right' as an integual part of his reasoning? Or does he base his decision on the notion of an 'interest'?

2. 'It may be that, in some jurisprudential theory, it is possible to classify as a legal right some claims which will not be enforced by the court, but on a practical level the existence of a right depends upon the existence of a remedy for its infringement' (Oliver LJ, *Techno-Impex v Gebr Van Weelde* [1981] 1 QB 648). What is meant by remedy in this context – a form of action or an actual remedy such as damages or rescission? Was it the remedy of the injunction that

determined the rights? If so, what role did the cause of action in nuisance play?

3. How did Lord Denning know that the animals did not mind the cricket?

4. What if the Millers' household insurance premiums had been raised as a result of the possible danger of cricket balls: could the Millers have claimed this expense from the club?

5. What if the Millers continued to sit in their garden during cricket matches and Mrs Miller was hit, and seriously injured, by a cricket ball: would the club be liable? Could the club raise the defence of contributory negligence?

6. Conversion requires an act denying the plaintiff's title in his moveable property: is merely playing with another's cricket ball conversion? Is it a trespass? If the owner of the land refused to return the cricket ball would he be liable today for conversion?[9]

7. The court awarded modest damages: was this in lieu of an injunction?[10]

8. What if the Millers had bought the house in the middle of winter?

9. How many separate reasons does Lord Denning give to support his decision?

10. Is this, in effect, an estoppel case?

11. Consider the notion of the *ratio decidendi* of a case (see p 91). What is the *ratio decidendi* of *Miller v Jackson*?

12. Was it unreasonable of the female plaintiff to develop 'a somewhat obsessive attitude'? Is this case a good example of a court deciding a case through the interpretation of the facts rather than the law?

6 THE ROLE OF LEGAL CATEGORIES

(a) Introduction

In Roman law the institutional system acted not just as a means of linking the social and the legal worlds; it also acted as the basis for legal classification. Law was to be divided into three areas each representing the institutional emphasis: the law of persons, the law of things and the law of actions. Within these generic categories there were further subdivisions expressly, or implicitly, recognised by the Romans themselves. Thus the law of persons could be sub-divided into

---

9   Cf Torts (Interference with Goods) Act 1977.
10   Cf Supreme Court Act 1981 s 50.

personality and status (a development that owes more to the modern civilian jurists) and the law of things into property and obligations; remedies, of course, could be subdivided into real (*in rem*) and personal (*in personam*) claims. However, there remains another important division recognised by the Romans which is still of the utmost importance today: at the beginning of the Digest the Roman jurist Ulpian tells us that the law falls into two branches – the *ius publicum* and the *ius privatum*. The former is concerned with the interests of the state, while the latter is concerned with the private interests of individuals. In English law the division into public and private law is by no means as pronounced as it is in France – indeed the division has traditionally been unrecognised at the formal level. Nevertheless, at the level of remedies there is an important distinction between judicial review and a claim for damages and this remedial distinction implies that the common law adheres to a dichotomy between public and private interests.[11] Perhaps where the common law differs from the civil law is in its failure to develop, at the institutional level, a notion of the state: common lawyers, as Lord Diplock once recognised,[12] continue to rely upon the notion of the 'crown' to represent government and the (so-called) public interest. And this reliance on a feudal institution has tended to engender a legal structure that sees all institutions as 'private' in the sense of having their own personality and particular interests. The Crown or a local authority, in this scheme, is like any other (commercial) organisation; and when it comes to litigation it has its own interest to advance and to protect with the result that there is little room for civil law ideas like *le bien public* or equality before public burdens principle.

In re State of Norway's Application [1990] 1 AC 723 House of Lords

Lord Goff: ... In France, as in other civil law countries, civil matters are categorised as a matter of substance and are regarded as limited to private law matters, excluding public law matters and in particular fiscal matters.

There appears to be little doubt that, in most if not all civil law countries, an important distinction is drawn between private law and public law, and that public law matters are generally excluded from civil or commercial matters.

In theory ... an English court would not treat a matter as civil or commercial which would, by English law, fall to be classified as criminal ...

[P]roceedings in any civil matter should include all proceedings other than criminal proceedings, and proceedings in any commercial matter should be treated as falling within proceedings in civil matters. On this simple approach,

---

11   See eg, *R v Secretary of State for Education and Science, Ex p Avon CC* [1991] 1 QB 558, 561.

12   *Town Investments Ltd v Dept of Environment* [1978] AC 359, 380-381.

I do not see why the expression should be read as excluding proceedings in a fiscal matter ...

In his case note ... Dr F A Mann stated that: "it can be asserted with confidence that very few states (if any) will ever regard a tax claim as a civil or commercial matter". I myself have little doubt that this is broadly true in the case of most civil law countries, with their classification of law into public law (including fiscal matters) and private law matters (with which alone civil and commercial matters are concerned) ... But, so far as common law countries are concerned, the matter is, on the material before your Lordships' House, completely unresolved ...

Notes and questions

1. 'The Divisions of English law are much less clear-cut than those of most other legal systems, and there has been much less discussion of what the divisions should be. The absence of clear divisions is principally attributable to two factors. First, the jurisdiction of the higher courts is unified, for they can deal with all justiciable matters, whether public, private, commercial, civil or criminal; divided jurisdictions tend to create, unified jurisdictions to conceal or prevent divisions of law. Secondly, English law has grown in bits according to need and was not laid down in slices by an act of will, and "any system of law in which legal rules are always created ad hoc must at its best lack form and symmetry" (Stone). Codes, by the application they require and the commentaries they induce, make lawyers think that the law is divided in a certain way; England has no codes in this sense. Since, then, it is unimportant to the English lawyer to which type of court or book he should turn in order to solve his problem, the law tends to seem seamless' (T Weir, The Common Law System, *International Encyclopedia of Comparative Law*, Vol II, Chapter 2, Part III, para 82). Would a division into public and private law help with the solving of case law problems? Take a case like *Dorset Yacht* (p 362): would this have been decided the same way in France?

2. The distinction between civil and commercial law does not have its formal roots in Roman law in the sense that the distinction is to be found in the *Corpus Iuris Civilis*. It is more a creature of the later civil law. Why and how do you think it developed? Is modern commercial law purely a matter of private law? What about economic law? What about the rise of the consumer?

(b) Civil and criminal law

Fisher v Bell [1961] 1 QB 394 Queen's Bench Division

(See p 12)

Questions

1. This case is often regarded as a contract problem. Why? Is it really an obligations case?
2. Is criminal law part of public or private law?

Archer v Brown [1985] QB 401 Queen's Bench Division

Peter Pain J: This case arises out of a swindle practised upon the plaintiff by the defendant ...

In cases of fraudulent misrepresentation the plaintiff has always been entitled to damages as well as rescission. (...) In cases of innocent misrepresentation a plaintiff was entitled to rescission only until recently. This was considered to work injustice and the Misrepresentation Act 1967 was passed to put this matter right. Even if the defendant's misrepresentation had been innocent the plaintiff would in my opinion have been entitled to claim damages as well as rescission by virtue of section 2 of that Act ...

While it is true that the measure of damages is different in tort and in contract, it makes no difference which measure one applies in this case: the damages are the same. The damages which flow from the defendant's deceit are no different from what must have been in the reasonable contemplation of the parties at the time of the contract ...

I do not think that the argument that the defendant could not make a profit here defeats the plaintiff's claim. It seems to follow from what Lord Diplock said in *Broome v Cassell & Co Ltd* that the wrongdoer may be caught if he weighs the risk of loss against the chance of getting away with it. In this case, as one sees from the course of proceedings, the defendant could well have got away with it against a less determined plaintiff. But what seems to put the claim under this head out of court is the fact that exemplary damages are meant to punish and the defendant has been punished. Even if he wins his appeal he will have spent a considerable time in gaol. It is not surprising that there is no authority as to whether this provides a defence, since there is no direct authority as to whether exemplary damages can be given in deceit. I rest my decision on the basic principle that a man should not be punished twice for the same offence. Since he has undoubtedly been punished, I should not enrich the plaintiff by punishing the defendant again ...

In recent years, damages for injured feelings have been awarded in a number of cases sounding in contract ...

I now have to ask myself: is there any reason why these damages should sound in breach of contract and not in deceit? ...

I find nothing in the passages ... from the speeches of Lord Hailsham of St Marylebone LC and Lord Diplock in *Broome v Cassell & Co Ltd* which should extend their doubts whether exemplary damages should be awarded for deceit to aggravated damages for deceit. I cannot help wondering whether the close relationship between contract and deceit mentioned by Lord Hailsham of St Marylebone LC is the reason why exemplary damages have not been awarded in deceit. Sachs LJ's reference to the *Theft Act 1968* in his judgment in *Mafo v Adams* leads me to ask whether the true reason why there is no reported case where exemplary damages have been given for deceit is that most deceits are punishable by the criminal law and that it would therefore be inappropriate to award exemplary damages. If this be so, then it is no reason for refusing to award damages which are compensatory for injured feelings. I can see no reason in logic or justice why such damages should not be awarded in deceit on the same basis as in contract. The authorities make it plain that the sum awarded should be moderate. In the light of the findings of fact which I have already made I think a sum of £500 would be appropriate under this head ...

Notes and questions

1. 'The distinction between civil and criminal law, though probably that best understood today by laymen, is not primitive. It is indeed a commonplace to point out how in an early state of society wrongs such as assault and murder, which we regard now as typical subjects for criminal law, are treated as giving rise merely to a sort of action for damages at the suit of the party injured or his relatives, and that these damages are the substitute for the yet more primitive right to vengeance ... Even in its most advanced period Roman law still kept traces of the old confusion between crime and tort in the penal damages it allowed, for example, in *furtum*, and "punitive" damages which combine punishment with reparation are familiar in English law' (HF Jolowicz, *Lectures on Jurisprudence* (1963), pp 344, 345). Does the English law of tort still have a punitive element? Is the development of criminal law dependent on a notion of the 'state'?

2. To what extent should one person be liable in private law for crimes committed by another person under his, her or its control?

3. Should victims of crimes be able to use the criminal trial process to obtain full compensatory damages? What are the arguments against such a procedure?

4. Could the whole of criminal law and the criminal process be privatised?

5. If the defendant had been able to prove that he was not at fault when he made the misrepresentation, would the plaintiff have been able to claim damages as well as rescission by virtue of s 2 of the Misrepresentation Act 1967?

(c) Contract

Moschi v Lep Air Services Ltd [1973] AC 331 House of Lords

Lord Diplock: The law of contract is part of the law of obligations. The English law of obligations is about their sources and the remedies which the court can grant to the obligee for a failure by the obligor to perform his obligation voluntarily. Obligations which are performed voluntarily require no intervention by a court of law. They do not give rise to any cause of action.

English law is thus concerned with contracts as a source of obligations. The basic principle which the law of contract seeks to enforce is that a person who makes a promise to another ought to keep his promise. This basic principle is subject to an historical exception that English law does not give the promisee a remedy for the failure by a promisor to perform his promise unless either the promise was made in a particular form, eg, under seal, or the promisee in return promises to do something for the promisor which he would not otherwise be obliged to do, ie, gives consideration for the promise ...

Each promise that a promisor makes to a promisee by entering into a contract with him creates an obligation to perform it owed by the promisor as obligor to the promisee as obligee. If he does not do so voluntarily there are two kinds of remedies which the court can grant to the promisee. It can compel the obligor to pay to the obligee a sum of money to compensate him for the loss that he has sustained as a result of the obligee's failure to perform his obligation. This is the remedy at common law in damages for breach of contract. But there are some kinds of obligation which the court is able to compel the obligor actually to perform. In some cases ... a remedy to compel performance by a decree of specific performance or by injunction is also available. It was formerly obtainable only in a court of equity ... But, since a court of common law could make and enforce orders for payment of a sum of money, where the obligation was itself an obligation to pay a sum of money, even a court of common law could compel the obligor to perform it ...

Questions

1. How does one recognise a set of facts as being contractual?

2. In *Fisher v Bell* (above p 12), if the owner of the shop had sold the knife on credit to the buyer, and the buyer had failed to pay the debt, could the owner have sued the buyer for a contractual debt?

3. If an employee of a supermarket steals goods from his employer and sells them to an acquaintance in his local pub, could the employee sue the acquaintance if the latter failed to pay for the goods? Could the supermarket sue the acquaintance?

4. Besides contract, what are the other parts of the law of obligations?

(d) Tort

Donoghue v Stevenson [1932] AC 562 House of Lords

Lord Atkin: My Lords, the sole question for determination in this case is legal: Do the averments made by the pursuer in her pleading, if true, disclose a cause of action? I need not restate the particular facts. The question is whether the manufacturer of an article of drink sold by him to a distributor, in circumstances which prevent the distributor or the ultimate purchaser or consumer from discovering by inspection any defect, is under any legal duty to the ultimate purchaser or consumer to take reasonable care that the article is free from defect likely to cause injury to health. I do not think a more important problem has occupied your Lordships in your judicial capacity: important both because of its bearing on public health and because of the practical test which it applies to the system under which it arises. The case has to be determined in accordance with Scots law ... but my own research, such as it is, satisfies me that the principles of the law of Scotland on such a question as the present are identical with those of English law; and I discuss the issue on that footing. The law of both countries appears to be that in order to support an action for damages for negligence the complainant has to show that he has been injured by the breach of a duty owed to him in the circumstances by the defendant to take reasonable care to avoid such injury. In the present case we are not concerned with the breach of the duty; if a duty exists, that would be a question of fact which is sufficiently averred and for present purposes must be assumed. We are solely concerned with the question whether, as a matter of law in the circumstances alleged, the defender owed any duty to the pursuer to take care ...

At present I content myself with pointing out that in English law there must be, and is, some general conception of relations giving rise to a duty of care, of which the particular cases found in the books are but instances. The liability for negligence, whether you style it such or treat it as in other systems as a species of 'culpa', is no doubt based upon a general public sentiment of moral wrongdoing for which the offender must pay. But acts or omissions which any moral code would censure cannot in a practical world be treated so as to give a right to every person injured by them to demand relief. In this way rules of law arise which limit the range of complainants and the extent of their remedy. The rule that you are to love your neighbour becomes in law, you must not injure your neighbour; and the lawyer's question, who is my neighbour? receives a restricted reply. You must take reasonable care to avoid acts or omissions which you can reasonably foresee would be likely to injure your neighbour. Who, then, in law is my neighbour? The answer seems to be – persons who are so closely and directly affected by my act that I ought reasonably to have them in contemplation as being so affected when I am directing my mind to the acts or omissions which are called in question. This appears to me to be the doctrine of *Heaven v Pender* ... There will no doubt arise cases where it will be difficult to determine whether the contemplated relationship is so close that the duty arises. But in the class of case now before the court I cannot conceive any difficulty to arise. A manufacturer puts up an article of food in a container which he knows will be opened by the actual consumer. There can be no inspection by any purchaser and no reasonable preliminary inspection by the consumer. Negligently, in the course of preparation, he allows the contents to be mixed with poison. It is said that the law of England and Scotland is that the poisoned consumer has no remedy against negligent manufacturer. If this were the result of the authorities, I should consider the result a grave defect in the law, and so contrary to principle that I should hesitate long before following any decision to that effect which had not the authority of this House. I would point out that, in the assumed state of the authorities, not only would the consumer have no remedy against manufacturer, he would have none against any one else, for in the circumstances alleged there would be no evidence of negligence against any one other than the manufacturer; and, except the case of a consumer who was also a purchaser, no contract and no warranty of fitness, and in the case of the purchase of a specific article under its patent or trade name, which might well the case in the purchase of some articles of food or drink, no warranty protecting even the purchaser-consumer ... I do not think so ill of our jurisprudence as to suppose that its principles are so remote from the ordinary needs of civilised society and the ordinary claims it makes upon its members as to deny a legal remedy where there is so obviously a social wrong ...

In my opinion several decided cases support the view that in such a case as the present the manufacturer owes a duty to the consumer to be careful ...

Lord Buckmaster (dissenting): ... The principle contended for must be this: that the manufacturer, or indeed the repairer, of any article, apart entirely from contract, owes a duty to any person by whom the article is lawfully used to see that it has been carefully constructed. All rights in contract must be excluded from consideration of this principle; such contractual rights as may exist in successive steps from the original manufacturer down to the ultimate purchaser are *ex hypothesi* immaterial. Nor can the doctrine be confined to cases where inspection is difficult or impossible to introduce. This conception is simply to misapply to tort doctrine applicable to sale and purchase.

The principle of tort lies completely outside the region where such considerations apply, and the duty, if it exists, must extend to every person who, in lawful circumstances, uses the article made. There can be no special duty attaching to the manufacture of food apart from that implied by contract or imposed by statute. If such a duty exists, it seems to me it must cover the construction of every article, and I cannot see any reason why it should not apply to the construction of a house. If one step, why not fifty? Yet if a house be, as it sometimes is, negligently built, and in consequence of that negligence the ceiling falls and injures the occupier or any one else, no action against the builder exists according to the English law, although I believe such a right did exist according to the laws of Babylon ...

Notes and questions

1. 'We have had several compendious theories as to the law of tort. Lynx-eyed predecessors who noticed that a tort suit often resulted in a transfer of funds from the defendant to the plaintiff inferred that it was the purpose of tort law to effect such transfers: the more transfers the better, or tort was being false to its purpose. This was especially true if the defendant could spread the loss, very thinly like jam so that no one could taste it ... An appropriate basis for discriminating between plaintiffs would be according to whether they were the victims of misfortune or of mismanagement, of bad

luck or of bad behaviour, that is, whether they have just a pain or a grievance as well, whether we can say of them that, the world being what it is, they should not have been hurt ... The purpose of fault would be to determine not who must pay but who may claim, to distinguish between plaintiffs rather than between defendants. And we would also distinguish according to the nature of the harm in issue, and make the law reflect society's proper value-judgments by letting people recover more easily in respect of personal injury than financial harm, and for property damage only if it also represented financial loss to them ...' (Tony Weir, *Governmental Liability* [1989] PL 40, 62-63). Is fault a realistic criterion for determining who should receive compensation in road accident cases? Was Mrs Donoghue the victim of misfortune or of mismanagement – of bad luck or of bad behaviour? What if the manufacturer had been able to prove that, on average, only one bottle in a million was defective?

2. 'It is submitted that a suitable criterion is to be found in the concept of risk and that a satisfactory body of legal rules could quite rapidly be developed by the courts if in every case they were to pose the question, 'Whose risk was it that this damage might occur?' in place of the present 'Whose fault was it that this damage did occur?' It is essential, however, that the traditional refusal of the courts to consider the factor of insurance be reversed. It is perhaps this refusal of the courts to face up to the facts of contemporary life which has led them to overlook loss distribution as it already exists and to insist on fault as the criterion of liability as if every defendant had to find the damages from his own pocket' (JA Jolowicz, *Liability for Accidents* [1968] CLJ 50, 60). If this thesis had been applied to *Dorset Yacht* (below p 360), what would have been the result? What about *Best v Samuel Fox* (p 358)?

3. 'The real weakness of the insurance argument is that insurance is essentially a group or social phenomenon, whereas the common law of obligations is concerned with individuals. Disputes between individuals do not provide a good medium through which to decide what is the best pattern of insurance in a particular area ... As Weinrib says, the invocation of insurance in tort disputes undermines the conception of tort law as concerned with the immediate personal interaction of the doer and the sufferer of harm.' (Peter Cane, *Tort Law and Economic Interests*, Oxford University Press, 1991, 460). Is the problem here an institutional one? If one were to move towards insurance-based liability, would the law of persons need rethinking? Is the law of tort founded upon the interests of individuals or the interest of groups (or classes) of individuals?

4. 'It cannot lightly be taken for granted, even as a matter of theory, that the purpose of the law of tort is compensation, still less that it ought

to be, an issue of large social import, or that there is something inappropriate or illogical or anomalous (a question-begging word) in including a punitive element in civil damages, or conversely that the criminal law, rather than the civil law is in these cases the better instrument for conveying social disapproval, or for redressing a wrong to the social fabric ... As a matter of practice English law has not committed itself to any of these theories, it may have been wiser than it knew ...' (Lord Wilberforce, *Cassell & Co Ltd v Broome* [1972] AC 1027). Ought punitive damages ever to be awarded in traffic accident cases? If the law of tort is not about compensation, what is, or are, its aim(s)? Could one run a whole tort course simply devoted to theories of tort? If one could run such a course, what would this tell us about legal knowledge?

(e) Restitution (unjust enrichment)

Lipkin Gorman v Karpnale Ltd [1991] 2 AC 548 House of Lords

(See p 145)

Woolwich Equitable Building Society v Inland Revenue Commissioners [1993] AC 70 House of Lords

(See p 54)

Notes and questions

1. 'It is clear that any civilised system of law is bound to provide remedies for cases of what has been called unjust enrichment or unjust benefit, that is to prevent a man from retaining the money of or some benefit derived from another which it is against conscience that he should keep. Such remedies in English law are generically different from remedies in contract or in tort, and are now recognised to fall within a third category of the common law which has been called quasi-contract or restitution' (Lord Wright in *Fibrosa Spolka Akcyjna v Fairbairn Lawson Combe Barbour Ltd* [1943] AC 32).

2. If the law of tort is concerned with non-contractual damages actions, could it be said that the law of unjust enrichment is concerned with non-contractual debt claims?

3. Does the English law of restitution belong more to the law of property than to the law of obligations?

(f) Property (1): Real and personal property

Beswick v Beswick [1966] Ch 538 Court of Appeal; [1968] AC 58 House of Lords

(See p 154)

Lord Denning MR (Court of Appeal): ... Section 56(1) of the Law of Property Act 1925 says that:

> "A person may take an immediate or other interest in land or other property, or the benefit of any condition, right of entry, covenant or agreement over or respecting land or other property, although he may not be named as a party to the conveyance or other instrument and by section 205(1) (xx) 'Property' includes any thing in action, and any interest in real or personal property".

Apply that section to this case. The promise of the nephew to pay the widow £5 a week was a "thing in action": for the simple reason that it could be enforced by action, namely, an action by the contracting party. This section says, as clearly as can be, that the widow can take the benefit of the agreement, although she is not named as a party to it. Seeing that she is to take the benefit of it, she must be able to sue for it, if not by herself alone, at least jointly with the contracting party. Otherwise the section is made of no effect. *Ubi jus, ibi remedium.* If there was, therefore, any doubt as to her ability to sue at common law or equity, that doubt is removed by this section. I adhere, therefore, to the view which I expressed on this section in *Smith and Snipes Hall Farm v River Douglas Catchment Board* and *Drive Yourself Hire Co (London) Ltd v Strutt*: and I am fortified by the judgment which Danckwerts LJ is about to deliver ...

Danckwerts LJ (Court of Appeal): ... The definition of "property" in s 205(1)(xx) "includes any thing in action, and any interest in real or personal property". The section replaces s 5 of the Real Property Act 1845 and applies to personal as well as real property. The Act of 1845 only applied to real property, and presumably there was some intelligible object in the extension. The new section obviously cannot be confined to covenants running with the land. Why should the section not be taken to mean what it says? There really is no ambiguity. The section says that "A person may take ... the benefit of ... any agreement over or respecting land or other property, although he may not be named as a party to the conveyance or other instrument". The section seems to have come as a shock to conventional lawyers who could not believe their eyes, but the section does say that a person not a party can take the benefit of a contract. Faced with the unexpected and unfamiliar there has been a tendency to take a timorous view of the provisions of this section ...

Lord Guest (House of Lords): ... It may be that the draftsman in incorporating the wide definition of "property" into s 56 had overlooked the result which it would have on the effect of this section by extending it beyond its predecessor. I am constrained to hold that if s 56 is to replace the previous law in s 5 of the Act of 1845, this can only be done by limiting the word "property" in s 56 to real property and thereby excluding the wide definition of "property" contained in s 205(1)(xx). The result is that the respondent has, in my view, no right to sue on the agreement of 14th March 1962 in her individual capacity ...

Notes and questions

1. Is the House of Lords' decision in this case an example of the courts ignoring the actual words of a statute?

2. Are obligations property? If so, can one own a debt?

3. Are all rights forms of property?

4. From a law of actions viewpoint, did the plaintiff succeed in her debt claim?

5. '[T]he Common Law systems differ radically from the Civil Law. Thus, although the distinction between real and personal rights is perfectly well understood by Common Law lawyers, its various applications are thought of as belonging not to property law but to the law of remedies, including the law of insolvency; and the much discussed question whether the beneficiary of a trust has a real or only a personal right is of little more than academic significance. Moreover, such personal claims arising out of contracts as debts are, along with industrial property such as patents, treated as property under the generic term of choses in action. Again, the relativity of most titles to things, and the frequent co-existence of interests in them, make it unprofitable to pay much attention to ownership ...' (FH Lawson, Structural Variations in Property Law: Comparative Conclusion, *International Encyclopedia of Comparative Law*, Vol VI, Chapter 2, Part VIII, para 274). Do Western legal systems need a definition of ownership? When one talks of 'interest' in the context of the law of property, does it have a special meaning?

6. 'Initially ... it will seem a little strange that property language should be chosen to express claims which have hitherto belonged largely within the public law domain ... But this merely goes to underline the fact that, in some important sense, all property rights enjoy an inherent public law character' (K Gray, Equitable Property, in M. Freeman or R Halson (eds), *Current Legal Problems 1994* (Oxford University Press, 1994), pp 210-211). In English law, has ownership not always been a public law as much as a private law device? Is this a result of feudalism?

(g) Property (2): bailment

Building and Civil Engineering Holidays Scheme Management Ltd v Post Office [1966] 1 QB 247 Court of Appeal

Lord Denning MR: ... At common law, bailment is often associated with a contract, but this is not always the case, see *R v McDonald, Meux v Great Eastern Railway*. An action against a bailee can often be put, not as an action in contract, nor in tort, but as an action on its own, *sui generis*, arising out of the possession had by the bailee of the goods, see Winfield on the *Province of the Law of Tort*, p 100, Fifoot's *History of the Common Law*, p 24, *Midland Silicones v Scrutton*. The incidents of this cause of action are not to be found by looking at the old books on detinue and trover. We have outlived those forms of action, together with trespass and case, see *Letang v Cooper*. Suffice it to say at the present day that if goods, which have been delivered to a bailee, are lost or damaged whilst in his custody he is liable to the person damnified (who may be the owner or the bailor) unless the bailee proves that the loss or damage is not due to any fault on his part, see *Coldman v Hill*, per Scrutton LJ ...

At common law in a case of bailment, the general principle is *restitutio in integrum*, which means that the party damnified is entitled to such a sum of money as will put him in as good a position as if the goods had not been lost or damaged. This is subject, however, to the qualification that the damages must not be too remote, that is, they must be such damages as flow directly and in the usual course of things from the loss or damage, see *The Argentino*. If the party damnified suffers damage of a special kind, he is entitled to recover it, subject to the qualification that the damages must not exceed such damages as would be produced in the ordinary course of things by the act complained of, see *Cory v Thames Ironworks*. When goods are lost or damaged in transit, the damage ordinarily produced is, in the case of loss, the cost of replacement; or in the case of damage, the cost of repair. That is the amount which, in the absence of contract, the bailor can recover. He cannot recover indirect or consequential damages (such as loss of profits on a business) because those can only be recovered in cases on contracts proper, where notice of special circumstances is brought home, see *British Columbia Saw-Mill Co v Nettleship* ...

Morris v CW Martin & Sons Ltd [1966] 1 QB 716 Court of Appeal

This was an action by the owner of a mink stole for its value brought against a firm of cleaners. The owner had sent her mink stole to one Beder, a furrier, for cleaning and Beder, with the owner's consent, gave it to the defendants to clean. The defendants' employee who was supposed to clean it stole it instead. The trial judge held the defendants not liable; an appeal to the Court of Appeal was allowed.

Lord Denning MR: ... [W]hen a principal has in his charge the goods or belongings of another in such circumstances that he is under a duty to take all reasonable precautions to protect them from theft or depredation, then if he entrusts that duty to a servant or agent, he is answerable for the manner in which that servant or agent carries out his duty. If the servant or agent is careless so that they are stolen by a stranger, the master is liable. So also if the servant or agent himself steals them or makes away with them. It follows that I do not think that *Cheshire v Bailey* can be supported. The job-master was clearly under a duty to take all reasonable precautions to protect the goods from being stolen, either as a bailee for reward or under the contract. He entrusted that duty to the coachman and must be answerable for the way in which the coachman carried out that duty; and it is all the same whether he did it negligently or fraudulently and whether he did it for his master's benefit or his own benefit. The decision cannot survive *Lloyd v Grace, Smith & Co* and should be overruled ...

Diplock LJ: ... Duties at common law are owed by one person to another only if there exists a relationship between them which the common law recognises as giving rise to such duty. One of such recognised relationships is created by the voluntary taking into custody of goods which are the property of another. By voluntarily accepting from Beder the custody of a fur which they knew to be the property of a customer of his, they brought into existence between the plaintiff and themselves the relationship of bailor and bailee by sub-bailment. The legal relationship of bailor and bailee of a chattel can exist independently of any contract, for the legal concept of bailment as creating a relationship which gives rise to duties owed by a bailee to a bailor is derived from Roman law and is older in our common law than the legal concept of parol contract as giving rise to legal duties owed by one party to the other party thereto. The nature of those legal duties, in particular as to the degree of care which the bailee is bound to exercise in the custody of the goods and as to his duty to redeliver them, varies according to the circumstances in which and purposes for which the goods are delivered to the bailee. But we are concerned here with conversion. This is a breach of a particular duty common to all classes of bailment. While most cases of bailment today are accompanied by a contractual relationship between bailee and bailor which may modify or extend the common law duties of the parties that would otherwise arise from the mere fact of bailment, this is not necessarily so – as witness gratuitous bailment or bailment by finding ...

One of the common law duties owed by a bailee of goods to his bailor is not to convert them, ie not to do intentionally in relation to the goods an act inconsistent with the bailor's right of property therein. (See *Caxton Publishing Co Ltd v Sutherland Publishing Co*, per Lord Porter.) This duty, which is common to all bailments as well as to other relationships which do not amount to bailment, is independent of and additional to the other common law duty of a bailee for reward to take reasonable care of his bailor's goods. Stealing goods is the simplest example of conversion; but, perhaps because in his classic judgment in *Coggs v Bernard* Sir John Holt CJ discusses the circumstances in which bailees are liable to their bailors for the loss of goods stolen not by the servant of the bailee but by a stranger, some confusion has, I think, arisen in later cases through failure to recognise the co-existence of the two duties of a bailee for reward; to take reasonable care of his bailor's goods and not to convert them – even by stealing.

If the bailee in the present case had been a natural person and had converted the plaintiff's fur by stealing it himself, no one would have argued that he was not liable to her for its loss. But the defendant bailees are a corporate person. They could not perform their duties to the plaintiffs to take reasonable care of the fur and not to convert it otherwise than vicariously by natural persons acting as their servants or agents. It was one of their servants to whom they had entrusted the care and custody of the fur for the purpose of doing work upon it who converted it by stealing it. Why should they not be vicariously liable for this breach of their duty by the vicar whom they had chosen to perform it? Sir John Holt, I think, would have answered that they were liable "for seeing that someone must be the loser by this deceit it is more reason that he who employs and puts a trust and confidence in the deceiver should be the loser than a stranger": *Hern v Nichols* ...

Salmon LJ: ... A bailee for reward is not answerable for a theft by any of his servants but only for a theft by such of them as are deputed by him to discharge some part of his duty of taking reasonable care. A theft by any servant who is not employed to do anything in relation to the goods bailed is entirely outside the scope of his employment and cannot make the master liable. So in this case, if someone employed by the defendants in another depot had broken in and stolen the fur, the defendants would not have been liable. Similarly in my view if a clerk employed in the same depot had seized the opportunity of entering the room where the fur was kept and had stolen it, the defendants would not have been liable. The mere fact that the master, by employing a rogue, gives him the opportunity to steal or defraud does not make the master liable for his depredations: *Ruben v Great Fingall Consolidated*. It might be otherwise if the master knew or ought to have known that his servant was dishonest, because then the master could be liable in negligence for employing him ...

Questions

1. Does bailment as a notion in itself give rise to duties and rights, or do the duties and rights associated with bailment arise from the law of contract and tort (conversion, trespass and negligence)?

2. Is bailment part of the law of obligations?

3. D delivers goods to P by mistake. An employee of P, thinking the goods belong to his employer, uses them while going about his work and is badly injured because the goods are defective. Can the employee claim compensation from D or P? Can P obtain compensation from D?

4. A bailee incurs expenditure looking after a bailor's goods. Is the bailor under a duty to reimburse the bailee? If so, what is the legal source of this duty?

5. In *Morris v Martin* what one difference of fact would have allowed the defendants to have escaped liability?

6. *Morris v Martin* should also be read in the law reports, for in addition to the bailment question there was a problem concerning an exclusion clause in the contract between bailee and sub-bailee. Why was the plaintiff's right not affected by the clause? Was her status as a consumer relevant?

7. Are Diplock LJ's last two sentences in the extract above of great relevance from a legal reasoning point of view? Is he basing his decision on a different legal notion than Salmon LJ?

(h) Equity

English v Dedham Vale Properties [1978] 1 All ER 382 Chancery

This was an action for damages and (or) an account of profits in equity brought by the vendors of a bungalow and land against the purchasers, a property company. Before conveyance of the property the purchasers had, without the knowledge of the vendors, successfully applied for planning permission using the name of the vendors, and the plaintiffs only became aware of what had happened after conveyance. The judge held that, although the purchasers were not guilty of fraud, they were liable in equity to account to the plaintiffs for the profit they had made as a result of the increase in the value of the land on the granting of planning permission.

Slade J: ... In my judgment, in the end the question of the liability, if any, of the defendants to account must depend on the view which the court takes as to the nature of the relationship subsisting between them and the plaintiffs at the date when the planning application was made. The liability to account would, in my judgment, arise if, though only if, the relationship was in the eyes of equity a fiduciary one in the sense that it imposed relevant fiduciary duties on the defendants towards the plaintiffs ...

Counsel for the defendants in effect submitted that the mere making of a planning application could not by itself have given rise to any such relationship when none would have otherwise existed. I see the force of this submission but am not in the end convinced by it. My reasons may be put in the form of two general propositions. (1) Where during the course of negotiations for a contract for the sale and purchase of property, the proposed purchaser, in the name of and purportedly as agent on behalf of the vendor, but without the consent or authority of the vendor, takes some action in regard to the property ... which, if disclosed to the vendor, might reasonably be supposed to be likely to influence him in deciding whether or not to conclude the contract, a fiduciary relationship in my judgment arises between the two parties. (2) Such fiduciary relationship gives rise to the consequences that there is a duty on the proposed purchaser to disclose to the vendor before the conclusion of the contract what he has done as the vendor's purported agent, and correspondingly, in the event of non-disclosure, there is a duty on him to account to him for any profit made in the course of the purported agency, unless the vendor consents to his retaining it ...

On my analysis of the facts of the present case, the plaintiffs never consented to the defendants ... purporting to make the planning application as their agent before contract; the fact that this had been done was never disclosed to them before the exchange of contracts; and they never consented to the defendants retaining the profit ultimately received by them as a result of the making of the planning application. In these circumstances, they are in my judgment accountable for such profit ...

Notes and questions

1. 'Although the principle of distinction between important parts of a legal system should be easy to identify and state, this is not possible for the division of English law into law and equity, since one cannot identify equity either by its sphere of application or by the intrinsic nature of its rules. The doctrines of equity are not confined to any particular area of substantive law; they have had differing effects in most areas at different times ... Nor is there any unifying principle within the system of equity. Whereas common law is conceivable as an independent and coherent though defective system, equity is not autonomous at all, but rather presupposes the law or is built round and upon it ...' (T Weir, The Common Law System, *International Encyclopedia of Comparative Law*, Vol II, Chapter 2, Part III, para 89).

Does this mean that equity cannot be defined as an independent system of law? Are the remedies of equity independent?

2. 'There is no precisely defined law setting limits to the equitable jurisdiction of a court to relieve against undue influence. This is the world of doctrine, not of neat and tidy rules. The courts of equity have developed a body of learning enabling relief to be granted where the law has to treat the transaction as unimpeachable unless it can be held to have been procured by undue influence. It is the unimpeachability at law of a disadvantageous transaction which is the starting-point from which the court advances to consider whether the transaction is the product merely of one's own folly or of the undue influence exercised by another. A court in the exercise of this equitable jurisdiction is a court of conscience. Definition is a poor instrument when used to determine whether a transaction is or is not unconscionable: this is a question which depends upon the particular facts of the case' (Lord Scarman in *National Westminster Bank v Morgan* [1985] AC 686). Are the equitable rules governing contractual transactions part of the law of contract or should they be seen as independent or as part of the law of actions (remedies)? Is Lord Scarman saying that equity cannot be reduced to rules?

3. 'When a servant, or agent, by a breach of duty damnifies his master or principal, the latter can, of course, recover in an ordinary action for breach of contract for any loss he has actually suffered. But there is a well established class of cases in which he can so recover, whether or not he has suffered any detriment in fact. These are cases in which the servant or agent has realised a secret profit, commission or bribe in the course of his employment; and the amount recoverable is a sum equal to such profit ... This amount the plaintiff can recover, either as money had and received to his use, or as an equitable debt ...' (Asquith LJ in *Reading v R* [1949] 2 KB 232). Are the equitable principles governing account part of the law of obligations? Could it be said that secret profits and the like belong to the principal?

7 THE ROLE OF THE CATEGORIES OF PUBLIC AND PRIVATE LAW

(a) Introduction

In re State of Norway's Application [1987] QB 433 Court of Appeal

Kerr LJ: ... [T]he common law does not – or at any rate not yet – recognise any clear distinction between public and private law. But the division is beginning to be recognised ...

Notes and questions

1. 'The distinction is vague and tenuous, and perhaps arises not so much from the different matter of public and private law as from the different remedies which may be sought; the Divisional Court dealing with an application for [judicial review] seems to think differently from a puisne judge hearing a claim for damages' (T Weir, The Common Law System, *International Encyclopedia of Comparative Law*, Vol II, Chapter 2, Part III, para 129). Is this difference in thinking engendered by a difference of remedies or a difference of substance? How is the thinking different?

2. Does the distinction between public and private law have any relevance in late 20th century economies?

3. Once utilities like gas, water, electricity and railways are privatised, should they immediately be the subject of a different legal regime? What about a commercial corporation whose shares are purchased by the state?

(b) Administrative contracts

Roy v Kensington & Chelsea Family Practitioner Committee [1992] 1 AC 624
House of Lords

A doctor brought, *inter alia*, an action in debt against his Family Practitioner Committee for breach of contract. The FPC sought to have the claim struck out as an abuse of process on the basis that the relationship between a doctor and the FPC was a matter only of public law and that the sole remedy available to the doctor was an action for judicial review. The House of Lords refused to strike out the claim.

Lord Bridge: ... I do not think the issue in the appeal turns on whether the doctor provides services pursuant to a contract with the family practitioner committee. I doubt if he does and am content to assume that there is no contract. Nevertheless, the terms which govern the obligations of the doctor on the one hand, as to the services he is to provide, and of the family practitioner committee on the other hand, as to the payments which it is required to make to the doctor, are all prescribed in the relevant legislation and it seems to me that the statutory terms are just as effective as they would be if they were contractual to confer upon the doctor an enforceable right in private law to receive the remuneration to which the terms entitle him. It must follow, in my view, that in any case of dispute the doctor is entitled to claim and recover in an action commenced by writ the amount of remuneration which he is able to prove as being due to him. Whatever remuneration he is entitled to under the statement is remuneration he has duly earned by the services he has rendered. The circumstance that the quantum of that remuneration, in the case of a particular dispute, is affected by a discretionary decision made by the committee cannot deny the doctor his private law right of recovery or subject him to the constraints which the necessity to seek judicial review would impose upon that right ...

Lord Lowry: ... An important point is that the court clearly has jurisdiction to entertain the doctor's action ... It is concerned with a private law right, it involves a question which could in some circumstances give rise to a dispute of fact and one object of the plaintiff is to obtain an order for the payment (not by way of damages) of an ascertained or ascertainable sum of money. If it is wrong to allow such a claim to be litigated by action, what is to be said of other disputed claims for remuneration? I think it is right to consider the whole spectrum of claims which a doctor might make against the committee. The existence of any dispute as to entitlement means that he will be alleging a breach of his private law rights through a failure by the committee to perform their public duty. If the committee's argument prevails, the doctor must in all these cases go by judicial review, even when the facts are not clear. I scarcely think that this can be the right answer ...

Although he seeks to enforce performance of a public law duty ... his private law rights dominate the proceedings ...

Davis Contractors Ltd v Fareham Urban District Council [1956] AC 696 House of Lords

(See p 343)

Staffordshire Area Health Authority v South Staffordshire Waterworks [1978] 1 WLR 1387 Court of Appeal

(See p 345)

Notes and questions

1. 'English law has conspicuously failed to develop any general theory of public contracts ... Even with individual departmental engagements the following may not be clear: whether the arrangement is contractual at all; whether certain obligations expressed in it bind the State; or whether (as in the case of transactions between private citizens) interpretation of the arrangement leads to the conclusion that it could have been, but in the event was not, a contract ... The result of this ... is that one of the commonest of everyday events [posting a letter], on which many people rely constantly, is entirely within the realm of non-law' (B Rudden, The Domain of Contract, in D Harris & D Tallon (eds), *Contract Law Today: Anglo-French Comparisons*, Oxford University Press, 1989, pp 95, 96, 97). A postman carelessly loses letters: can he be sued for the loss? Will his employer be liable? What if he deliberately destroys letters?

2. 'Contracts between private persons are not concluded in a preserve of unrestricted self-interest, and therefore even the ordinary civil law of contract of any country necessarily includes rules which reflect a public interest in the objects and terms of private contracts. The

element of the public interest is, however, significantly more prominent in the sphere of public contracting' (C Turpin, Public Contracts, *International Encyclopedia of Comparative Law*, Vol VII, Chapter 4, para 52). Is a local authority entitled to refuse to contract with anyone it does not like? (Cf Local Government Act 1988 s 17; *Blackpool & Fylde Aero Club Ltd v Blackpool BC*, below p 243.)

3. 'The *Cour de cassation*, in consistent case law since 1876, has always forbidden judges to annul or revise contracts for *imprévision*, whatever the consequences might be ... Contradicting the thesis upheld by the *Cour de cassation*, the *Conseil d'État* has elaborated since 1916 a theory of *imprévision* in administrative contracts ... The interests of the public service require that this extra-contractual situation should not release the contracting party from his obligation. By way of compensation, the government has come to his help and take its share of the additional costs due to the *imprévision* ... The basis for revision is precisely that the interests of a contracting party will be seriously prejudiced. It is a question of protecting an individual interest ... This can thus be called protective public policy' (Isabelle de Lamberterie, The Effect of Changes in Circumstances, in D Harris & D Tallon (eds), *Contract Law Today: Anglo-French Comparisons*, Oxford University Press, 1989, pp 228, 231, 233-234). Is the *Staffordshire* case authority for the proposition that inflation can frustrate an English contract?

4. Is an action for debt based on services rendered founded on contract (law) or the actual rendering of the services (fact)? Are all debts private law rights?

5. If contracts have force of legislation (see Article 1134 of Code civil), is it not logical to refuse to see any difference between contractual and statutory rights?

(c) Administrative liability in tort

Hill v Chief Constable of West Yorkshire [1989] AC 53 House of Lords

Lord Keith: ... There is no question that a police officer, like anyone else, may be liable in tort to a person who is injured as a direct result of his acts or omissions. So he may be liable in damages for assault, unlawful arrest, wrongful imprisonment and malicious prosecution, and also for negligence ... Further, a police officer may be guilty of a criminal offence if he wilfully fails to perform a duty which he is bound to perform by common law or by statute ... By common law police officers owe to the general public a duty to enforce the criminal law ... So the common law, while laying upon chief officers of police an obligation to enforce the law, makes no specific requirements as to the manner in which the obligation is to be discharged. That is not a situation where there can readily be inferred an intention of the common law to create a duty towards individual members of the public.

... [I]n my opinion there is another reason why an action for damages in negligence should not lie against the police in circumstances such as those of the present case, and that is public policy ...

Notes and questions

1. French law distinguishes between civil liability (private law) and adminstrative liability (public law): each is governed by a different set of courts with its own case law. In English law all legal and natural persons, public and private, are governed by the same tort regime with the result that tort, in addition to its compensatory role, has an important constitutional function. It is the tort of trespass that provides the remedy for wrongful arrest. However, the police or other government official can, in turn, use the law of tort against citizens who make a nuisance of themselves; the tort of defamation has proved a useful weapon to wield against those who complain or comment upon the activities of government officials. Is this healthy? Ought a local authority to be able to sue in defamation a ratepayer who accuses local officials of incompetence? Ought politicians to be able to sue those who criticise their abilities or their outside interests?

2. Read *Ministry of Housing v Sharp* [1970] 2 QB 223 in the law report. Is it really sensible that central government is here encouraged to sue local government because of an error made by an employee who is in effect a civil servant? Is the public interest being served?

3. In what circumstances should the state compensate citizens for damage arising through non-negligent government action? (Cf next case.)

4. Read *Elguzouli-Daf v Comr of Police of the Metropolis* [1995] 1 A11 ER 833 in the law report. Is 'public policy' not the central concept in actions for damages in negligence against public bodies? Is it really in the public interest that public bodies should be granted such immunities? Does French law take a similar view?

Rigby v Chief Constable of Northamptonshire [1985] 1 WLR 1242 Queen's Bench Division

Taylor J: On 17 December 1977, the Sportsman's Lodge, a gunsmiths shop in Northampton owned by the first plaintiff, Michael Rigby, was burned out. The cause of the fire was most unusual. A young psychopath had broken into the premises and armed himself. The police laid siege to the shop. Eventually they fired in a canister of CS gas to smoke out the intruder. The canister set the shop ablaze. The first plaintiff now sues the Chief Constable of Northamptonshire for damages for loss and damage to the premises and contents. The second plaintiff makes a small claim for damage to his guns which were in the first plaintiff's custody in the shop.

The case is put in a variety of ways; in trespass, in nuisance, in *Rylands v Fletcher* (1868) LR 3 HL 330 and in negligence. The defendant denies liability and raises, by way of specific defences, implied consent, necessity and contributory negligence of the first plaintiff ...

I now turn to consider the several ... heads under which the plaintiffs' claim is advanced. First, trespass or nuisance. Mr O'Brien concedes that the allegation of nuisance adds nothing to his claim in trespass. Mr Machin puts it more strongly. He contends that since the firing of the canister causing the damage was a direct rather than an indirect act, trespass rather than nuisance would be the appropriate cause of action. Either way, I do not need to consider nuisance any further.

It is common ground that to project an article such as the canister on to another's land from outside would, without justification or lawful excuse, constitute trespass. Mr Machin, however, puts the defence on three separate footings: first, implied consent; secondly, the necessary and proper exercise of police powers; and thirdly, the general defence of necessity.

As to implied consent, Mr Machin contends that the first plaintiff's evidence supports this defence. He said in cross-examination that he was prepared to leave things to the police to use their judgment from their experience. He gave the shop keys to the police. He had no objection to their going into the premises if they thought it right. Had they asked him if he minded their firing a CS canister into the shop he would have agreed with it. He added, however, that had he known the firing of a canister involved a fire risk he would have asked the police to make sure that there was a fire appliance immediately available. I am somewhat doubtful whether this evidence given seven years after the event, as to what the first plaintiff would have said had he been asked, is a sound footing for a defence of implied consent. In any event, I accept Mr O'Brien's contention that any implied consent would be limited to permitting the police to do what was necessary and no more. I therefore think that this head of defence merges with or is co-extensive with the defence of necessity ...

There is a surprising dearth of authority as to the nature and limits of necessity as a defence in tort. Mr Machin referred me to three cases. *Cope v Sharpe (No 2)* [1912] 1 KB 496 was a case of alleged trespass where the defendant had sought to prevent a heather fire from spreading. *Creswell v Sirl* [1948] 1 KB 241 was a case of alleged trespass to a dog which the defendant had shot to prevent it worrying sheep. In each case the defence prevailed. *Esso Petroleum Co Ltd v Southport Corporation* [1956] AC 218 is the leading case on the topic and both counsel referred to it in detail. It concerned an oil tanker stranded in a river estuary. Her master jettisoned 400 tons of oil cargo to prevent the tanker breaking her back. The tide carried the oil slick on to a fore-shore causing damage. The fore-shore owners sued the ship owners in trespass, nuisance and negligence. However, the only negligence alleged on the pleadings was faulty navigation by the master for which it was said the owners were vicariously liable. The owners' case was that the stranding was due to faulty steering gear caused by a crack in the stern frame. The defence of necessity was raised, *inter alia*, and Devlin J upheld it [1953] 3 WLR 773. The Court of Appeal reversed Devlin J's judgment [1954] 2 QB 182 but it was restored by the House of Lords ... The case is therefore clear authority for the application of necessity as a defence to trespass especially where human life is at stake.

However, Mr O'Brien relies on dicta in their Lordships' speeches to support the proposition that the defence is not available if the necessity is brought about by the defendant's own negligence, and that the burden of negativing negligence lies upon the defendant once the issue has been raised. The Court of Appeal took the view that the defendants had failed to discharge the burden of showing that the cracked frame causing a defect in the steering gear was not due to their negligence. Mr O'Brien says the House of Lords restored Devlin J's judgment solely on pleading grounds. There had been no allegation of negligence against the ship owners except in relation to the master's handling of the vessel.

Mr O'Brien's two propositions are clearly right. Necessity is not a good defence if the need to act is brought about by negligence on the part of the defendant. Once that issue is raised the defendant must show on the whole of the evidence that the necessity arose without negligence on his part. The more difficult question is as to what is meant by "negligence" in this context ... From these passages, Mr O'Brien argues that in the present case, where the issue has been raised, unless the defendant can show that to have equipped himself with Ferret would not have been a reasonable precaution, he fails to discharge the onus of proof. Necessity would therefore not avail him. I have already indicated that in my judgment the defendant was not negligent in exercising his discretion not to purchase Ferret. However, Mr O'Brien argues that, notwithstanding that, if the purchase of Ferret would have been a reasonable or a not unreasonable precaution then the necessity to use the CS canister would have been brought about by fault on the part of the defendant.

I cannot accept this argument. The passages cited ... were both in the context of a defence of inevitable accident as raised in *The Merchant Prince* [1892] p 179, upon which, as Lord Radcliffe said, much of the argument in *Esso Petroleum Co Ltd v Southport Corporation* [1956] AC 218 turned. I do not think that the observations of Lord Normand and Lord Radcliffe, which were *obiter* in any event, were intended to lay down a higher duty than the duty in the tort of negligence as a condition precedent to the application of the defence of necessity. It would be most unfair to do so. Whether or not the defendant has been negligent prior to the occurrence of the alleged necessity must surely be viewed as at the time of the alleged negligence. If by the ordinary criteria of negligence the defendant can show that at that time he was not at fault, it cannot be just when the necessity arises to impose retrospectively a higher duty on the defendant. Nor do I think *Southport Corporation*'s case is authority for that proposition. I am reinforced in this view by statements in two of the leading text books on the law of tort ...

I therefore hold that a defence of necessity is available in the absence of negligence on the part of the defendant creating or contributing to the necessity. In this case there was a dangerous armed psychopath whom it was urgently necessary to arrest. I have already found that it was not negligent of the defendant to be without Ferret. It is conceded that the only alternative was to fire in a CS gas canister, which was done. I therefore find that the defence of necessity prevails and that the cause of action in trespass fails.

Next, *Rylands v Fletcher* (1868) LR 3 HL 330. Mr O'Brien contends that this was an escape, albeit intentional, of a dangerous thing under the defendant's control on to the first plaintiff's property and that strict liability must attach. In answer, Mr Machin makes three submissions. First, he says, the *Rylands v Fletcher* principle only applies where there is an escape of a dangerous thing from land owned or occupied by the defendant at least under a franchise. A defendant who projects a missile on to the plaintiff's land from the highway has no sufficient interest in the land whence the missile escapes. He cited *West v Bristol Tramways Co* [1908] 2 KB 14 (escape of creosote fumes from wood blocks which the defendant had built into the highway) and *Powell v Fall* (1880) 5 QBD 597 (sparks from the highway). In neither of those cases was the point taken as to the sufficiency of the defendant's occupancy of the land. In *Jones v Ffestiniog Railway Co* (1868) LR 3 QB 733 (escape of sparks from the railway), the defendants were at least occupiers and managers of the railway track. I am unconvinced by this argument ... I can see no difference in principle between allowing a man-eating tiger to escape from your land on to that of another and allowing it to escape from the back of your wagon parked on the highway.

Secondly, and more fundamentally, Mr Machin says that *Rylands v Fletcher* does not apply to an intentional or voluntary release of a dangerous thing. The essence of the principle, he says, is an escape which predicates that there is no intentional or voluntary release. If the defendant deliberately releases or discharges the dangerous thing, then the right cause of action is trespass. *Rylands v Fletcher*, he says, derives from an action on the case for indirect damage. Mr Machin relies on a dictum of Viscount Simon in *Read v J Lyons & Co Ltd* [1947] AC 156, 166: "The circumstances in *Fletcher v Rylands* (1865) LR 1 Ex. 265 did not constitute a case of trespass because the damage was consequential, not direct." Mr O'Brien concedes that he can find no reported case of the principle being applied to an intentional release or firing of a dangerous thing. But, in principle, he argues that if the strict liability attaches in respect of an escaping tiger, the duty can be no lower in the case of a deliberately released tiger. The defendant's duty, he says, is to keep the tiger in at his peril. That makes sense but begs the question as to whether the liability for deliberate release is in trespass or *Rylands v Fletcher*.

I am inclined to the view that Mr Machin is right on this point. In any event, however, the issue on this cause of action is clinched by Mr Machin's third point, which is again the defence of necessity. In the classic and it may be the only *Rylands v Fletcher* situation, where there is an involuntary escape, the defence of necessity would be inappropriate. Since the defendant *ex hypothesi* would not have made any decision or choice whether to release the dangerous thing, he could hardly rely on necessity at that stage. He could at most rely upon the necessity of bringing the dangerous thing to the point whence it escaped. However, if one is to embrace cases of voluntary release or firing (such as this one) within the *Rylands v Fletcher* principle, it seems irresistibly logical that the defence of necessity must be open on the same basis as in trespass.

Mr O'Brien, whilst accepting that necessity can apply to *Rylands v Fletcher* liability, sought to argue that it has a more limited scope there than in answer to alleged trespass. He based this on the decision in *West v Bristol Tramways Co* [1908] 2 KB 14, the creosote case. However, there the defence was statutory authority and I do not think Mr O'Brien made his submission good. In the result, I conclude that if, which I doubt, this case falls to be considered at all under *Rylands v Fletcher*, necessity would provide a good defence as it does in trespass.

This leads me to consider the remaining allegation of negligence. I have already ruled that there was no negligence in being without the Ferret and in relying upon the CS canister. However, the plaintiffs allege, and have done since their action was brought, a number of heads of negligence in connection with the defendant's use of the canister or cartridge. These narrowed down in the end to allegation (v): "Firing the said cartridge when the fire brigade was not in attendance."

It is conceded that the defendant must be fixed with knowledge of the Green Goddess' departure. From 8.35pm, therefore, the defendant had constructive knowledge that there was no fire-fighting equipment standing by should it be necessary to use CS gas. The canister was not fired until 9.20pm. Although I consider Mr Greenwood overstated the fire risk, I am satisfied that it was a very real and substantial one, acceptable only if there was equipment readily available to put out any fire at an early stage. This would be so, in my judgment, even excluding the possibility of any accelerant happening to be present. Chief Inspector McGhee's first reaction, as one trained in the use and risks of the CS canister, was to have the fire brigade called to stand by even before he set out for the scene from the police station. I bear in mind the pressures and burdens upon the officers in the fraught situation with which they were dealing. Mr Machin argues that they could not have prevented the Green Goddess going to an existing fire elsewhere, that there is no evidence that another fire appliance could have been got to the scene in time, and that at 9.20 it would have been necessary to fire the canister even if Chief Inspector McGhee had known of the Green Goddess' departure.

On the other hand, had the police acted immediately at 8.35, Mr O'Brien argues the probability is that a fire appliance (for example the Wellingborough Green Goddess which in fact came later) could have been brought to the scene and would have arrived before 9.20. Bearing all these matters in mind, I conclude that the defendant by his officers was negligent in failing to react to the departure of the Green Goddess by seeking other help, and in using the canister without any fire-fighting equipment.

Mr Machin then says the burden remains on the plaintiffs to show that the damage would have been appreciably less if there had been a fire appliance nearby. The Green Goddess had been 80 to 100 yards away, agreed to be a proper distance. By the time it could be brought up in safety and deployed, the fire, accelerated by the presence of the powder, would inevitably have done as much damage as was in fact done. This argument, it seems to me, might have been of more substance if the shop had been totally razed to the ground. It was not, as can be seen on the photographs. True, there was no evidence from the plaintiffs' side to establish by expert opinion that less damage would have resulted had the fire been fought quicker and how much less. But it seems to me inevitable that some reduction in the damage would have been effected by quicker deployment of pumps. Part of the shop, in fact, remained unconsumed; appreciably more of it would have done so. I therefore find that the negligence was causative of actionable damage.

There remains the allegation of contributory negligence. This is based upon the Eley smokeless powder which Porter-Harris emptied on the floor. The first plaintiff said that all the tins of powder were locked in a safe in the back shop or should have been. He conceded that as it had been a busy Saturday, by human error they could have been left out on a shelf (as indeed he had said they were in his original statement). If the tins had been locked away, Porter-Harris could not have had ready access to them; powder would therefore not have been spilt on the floor. It may be that no fire would have been started by the canister, or at any rate such fire as did start would have been less dramatic and damaging. I bear in mind that the first plaintiff had a number of security devices which were correctly put into operation. There was the alarm system to the police station; there was armoured window glass; the door was heavily locked; there were grills on the outside of some windows and bars on the windows at the rear. Most of the weapons were in racks with security chains. In these circumstances I do not consider that leaving tins of powder on shelving in the back shop constituted contributory negligence.

I am not asked to consider the issue of damages. Suffice it to say, therefore, that in the upshot I find the defendant liable in negligence to both plaintiffs. The damages issue must be tried by another tribunal unless agreed.

Notes and questions

1. Do you think the real plaintiff in this action was an insurance company subrogated in the shop owner's rights? If not, could it not be said that the plaintiff deserved to lose the case for having an uninsured building? Might he have been insured, but the company had refused to pay?

2. *Rigby* concerned the police. But consider the position of local authorities: 'From the point of view of the tort lawyer, local government is much more important than central government. Local government may decide less, but it does more, and tort liability attaches to people who do rather than to people who decide ... The liability of central government may admittedly be in impressive in amount ... But generally, apart from the prisons and to a smaller extent the military, central government does not seem to be very vulnerable to tort suits. They do not occupy schools, though they seek increasingly to control them; and they do not mend the sidewalks, they only deny the ha'porth of tar required to mend them. Quite different is local government. Everyone sues them, even the Minister for Local Government himself ...' (T Weir, *Governmental Liability* [1989] PL 40, 47-48). Can the owner of a yacht damaged by escaping prisoners sue the Home Office for damages? (Cf *Home Office v Dorset Yacht Co* below p 362.)

2. 'There are, however, features of a local authority which may be regarded as distinguishing it from other types of corporation, whether trading or non-trading. The most important of these features is that it is a governmental body' (Lord Keith, *Derbyshire CC v Times Newspapers* [1993] AC 534). How should this distinction affect the question of liability in tort?

3. 'The jurisprudential basis for liability without fault [in French administrative law] has often been said to be that of the 'risk theory'. The activities of the state, even when conducted without fault, may in certain circumstances constitute the creation of a risk; if the risk materialises and an individual is occasioned injury or loss, it is only

just that the state should indemnify him. An alternative and perhaps more profound rationale is to connect liability without fault to the fundamental principle of the equality of all citizens in bearing public burdens. This principle of *"égalité devant les charges publiques"*, which is founded in Article 13 of the Declaration of the Rights of Man, has been vividly expressed by Duguit: "the activity of the state is carried on in the interest of the entire community; the burden that it entails should not weigh more heavily on some than others ..." ' (L Neville Brown & J Bell, *French Administrative Law*, Oxford University Press, 4th ed, 1993, p 184). Does English law subscribe to the *égalité* principle?[13]

4. 'France introduced a comprehensive system of workmen's compensation in 1898 (a year after the English Workmen's Compensation Act). But three years before ... the *Conseil d'État* had anticipated this legislation ... taking the view that the state owed an obligation to indemnify against the risks of employment (*le risque professionnel*) to those engaged in a public service. Even without statute, this principle has been used to give no-fault compensation to servicemen and women and their families for injuries on active service or in training ... Subsequently the *Conseil d'État* extended this right to compensation to those assisting in the public service even in a voluntary capacity ...' (L Neville Brown & J Bell, *French Administrative Law*, Oxford University Press, 4th ed, 1993, p 185). A government inspector is injured in a munitions factory by an unexplained explosion: can she recover damages in English law without proving fault? A fireman is injured while rushing to a fire: can he recover compensation or does he take the risk of such an injury?[14]

5. 'It is of the highest public importance that a democratically elected governmental body, or indeed any governmental body, should be open to uninhibited public criticism. The threat of a civil action for defamation must inevitably have an inhibiting effect on freedom of speech' (Lord Keith in *Derbyshire CC v Times Newspapers* [1993] AC 534). What might be the effect of this judicial statement on the right of a policeman to sue a newspaper or complaining citizen in defamation?

---

13   Cf *Dunne v NW Gas Board* [1964] 2 QB 806.
14   Cf *Read v J Lyons & Co* [1947] AC 156; *Watt v Hertfordshire CC* [1954] 1 WLR 835.

(d) Restitution and public law

Woolwich Equitable Building Society v Inland Revenue Commissioners [1993] AC 70 House of Lords

A building society paid several instalments of tax under regulations that it believed were void. In subsequent judicial review proceedings the regulations were finally declared void in a judgment by the House of Lords and the revenue repaid the money with interest from the date of the judgment. The building society brought an action in debt (money had and received) for interest from the date of payment. The trial judge refused the claim, but this was reversed by a majority of the Court of Appeal. A bare majority of the House of Lords dismissed an appeal.

Lord Goff: ... Take any tax or duty paid by the citizen pursuant to an unlawful demand. Common justice seems to require that tax to be repaid, unless special circumstances or some principle of policy require otherwise; *prima facie*, the taxpayer should be entitled to repayment as of right ...

I would ... hold that money paid by a citizen to a public authority in the form of taxes or other levies paid pursuant to an *ultra vires* demand by the authority is *prima facie* recoverable by the citizen as of right ... I do not consider that the principle of recovery should be inapplicable simply because the citizen has paid the money under a mistake of law.

Lord Browne-Wilkinson: ... Although there is in English law no general rule giving the plaintiff a right of recovery from a defendant who has been unjustly enriched at the plaintiff's expense, the concept of unjust enrichment lies at the heart of all the individual instances in which the law does give a right of recovery ...

In the present case, the concept of unjust enrichment suggests that the plaintiffs should have a remedy ... If the revenue is right, it will be enriched by the interest on money to which it had no right during that period. In my judgment, this is the paradigm of a case of unjust enrichment ...

There is in my view a close analogy to the right to recover money paid under a contract the consideration for which has wholly failed ...

The money was demanded by the state from the citizen and the inequalities of the parties' respective positions is manifest even in the case of a major financial institution like Woolwich. There are ... sound reasons by way of analogy for establishing the law in the sense which Lord Goff proposes.

Lord Slynn: ... I do not consider that the fact that Parliament has legislated extensively in this area means that no principle of recovery at common law can or should at this stage of the development of the law be found to exist ...

Although as I see it the facts do not fit easily into the existing category of duress or of claims *colore officii*, they shade into them. There is a common element of pressure which by analogy can be said to justify a claim for repayment ...

I find it quite unacceptable in principle that the common law should have no remedy for a taxpayer who has paid large sums or any sum of money to the revenue when those sums have been demanded pursuant to an invalid regulation and retained free of interest pending a decision of the courts.

Lord Keith (dissenting): ... The principle to be derived from [the cases], in my opinion, is that payments not lawfully due cannot be recovered unless they were made as a result of some improper form of pressure ... In the present case no pressure to pay was put upon Woolwich by the revenue. Woolwich paid because it calculated that it was in its commercial interest to do so. It could have resisted payment, and the revenue had no means other than the taking of legal proceedings which it might have used to enforce payment. The threat of legal proceedings is not improper pressure. There was no improper pressure ... and ... there was no duress.

Lord Jauncey (dissenting): ... Running through the authorities is the distinction between payments voluntary and payments made under compulsion or duress – the former being irrecoverable, the latter recoverable. The difference in the various authorities lies in the determinations as to what constitutes compulsion or duress ...

Duress to be relevant must be found within the four walls of the transaction. In this case Woolwich would, in relation to the revenue, have been no worse off if they had refused payment of the tax claimed and raised the defence which subsequently proved successful ...

That is sufficient for the disposal of this appeal which I would allow albeit with no little regret. The revenue obtained a huge sum of money which they had no right to demand and they are now hanging on to a very large amount of interest which they have no moral right to retain ...

However ... I do not consider that it would be appropriate for this House to make new law in this instance ...

For example ... how long should any right to repayment last? Is it in the public interest that a public authority's finances should be disrupted by wholly unexpected claims for repayment years after the money in question has been received? These are all matters ... with which the legislature is best equipped to deal.

Questions

1. Upon what principle was recovery allowed in this case?
2. Is this case an example of the private (commercial) interest being given precedence over the public interest?
3. Does Lord Slynn's view conflict with those expressed in *Murphy v Brentwood DC* [1991] AC 398?

Westdeutsche Landesbank Girozentrale v Islington London Borough Council [1994] 1 WLR 938 Court of Appeal

Leggatt LJ: The parties believed that they were making an interest swaps contract. They were not, because such a contract was *ultra vires* the council. So they made no contract at all. The council say that they should receive a windfall, because the purpose of the doctrine of *ultra vires* is to protect council taxpayers whereas restitution would disrupt the council's finances. They also contend that it would countenance "unconsidered dealings with local authorities." If that is the best that can be said for refusing restitution, the sooner it is enforced the better. Protection of council taxpayers from loss is to be distinguished from securing a windfall for them. The disruption of the council's finances is the result of ill-considered financial dispositions by the council and its officers. It is not the policy of the law to require others to deal at their peril with local authorities, nor to require others to undertake their own inquiries about whether a local authority has power to make particular contracts or types of contract. Any system of law, and indeed any system of fair dealing, must be expected to ensure that the council do not profit by the fortuity that when it became known that the contract was ineffective the balance stood in their favour. In other words, in circumstances such as these they should not be unjustly enriched ...

Questions

1. Is this a causation case?
2. What if the contract had turned out to be illegal rather than void?

The Powstaniec Wielkopolski [1989] QB 279 Queen's Bench

Sheen J: ... When construing an Act of Parliament it is to be presumed that Parliament intended to legislate in the public interest. My view as to what is in the public interest is based upon two factors, namely, (1) that one of the reasons for awarding salvage is to encourage mariners to go voluntarily to the assistance of ships in distress, and it is in the public interest that they should be so encouraged ...

Questions

1. Is the law of salvage part of public law or commercial law?
2. Is commercial law part of public or private law?

8 THE ROLE OF TEXTBOOKS

White v Jones [1993] 3 WLR 730 Court of Appeal

Steyn LJ: ... The question decided in *Ross v Caunters* was a difficult one. It lies at the interface of what has traditionally been regarded as the separate domains of contract and tort. It is therefore not altogether surprising that the appeal in the present case lasted three days, and that we were referred to about 40 decisions of English and foreign courts. Pages and pages were read from some of the judgments. But we were not referred to a single piece of academic writing on *Ross v Caunters*. Counsel are not to blame: traditionally counsel make very little use of academic materials other than standard textbooks. In a difficult case it is helpful to consider academic comment on the point. Often such writings examine the history of the problem, the framework into which a decision must fit, and countervailing policy considerations in greater depth than is usually possible in judgments prepared by judges who are faced with a remorseless treadmill of cases that cannot wait. And it is arguments that influence decisions rather than the reading of pages upon pages from judgments. I am not suggesting that to the already extremely lengthy appellate process there should be added the reading of lengthy passages from textbooks and articles. But such material, properly used, can sometimes help to give one a better insight into the substantive arguments. I acknowledge that in preparing this short judgment the arguments for and against the ruling in *Ross v Caunters* were clarified for me by academic writings ...

Notes and questions

1. 'Modern text-books are important ... as guides to the case law with which they are concerned. But if they are good they are more than mere guides, for they seek not only to arrange the cases systematically but to extract from them the general principles of the law and to show how those principles may be developed. And the same is true, on a smaller scale, of articles in the Law Reviews ... To deny persuasive authority to text-books today may be to state the formal position in England quite correctly, but it is to conceal the substantial and increasing importance of la doctrine in the formation of English law' (HF Jolowicz, *Lectures on Jurisprudence* (Athlone 1963), pp 314-315) Why do you think it is that *la doctrine* is not a formal source of law in the English system?

2. Is law based on general principles?

3. Are there different kinds of law textbooks – for example are there 'academic' and 'practitioner' textbooks? If you had written what you considered to be an 'academic' work, would you regard it as an insult if a colleague called it a 'practitioner' work?

9 THE ROLE OF FACTS

Geoffrey Samuel, The Foundations of Legal Reasoning (Maklu, 1994), pp 193-195 (footnotes omitted)

The notion of "what-if" is ... something that binds Roman and English law. What if one person lights a fire on his property, leaving another person to look after it, and the fire gets out of control and spreads to a neighbour's property? Who should be liable? What if the lease prohibited the lighting of fires? What if the person who failed to control it had a history of falling asleep on the job? What about a farmer who lights a fire to burn off the stubble in his field and the fire spreads to a neighbour's farm? Does it make any difference if it is a windy day or not? What if a carpenter, while working in another's house, goes out for a while leaving the house unguarded and a thief enters? These kinds of question are to be found in the *Corpus Iuris* and in the *All England Law Reports* and while the jurists in both systems are prepared to induce out of these 'what if' factual situations some general propositions, these propositions, in Roman law at least, were usually just a technique for explaining some further factual point. They were not designed to be part of a process for the construction of a deductive model of legal propositions ...

Accordingly, despite the occasional flights into generalisation, it can perhaps be said that on the whole English law continues to share the same interpretative closeness to the facts as the Roman law of the classical and medieval eras and this means that the technique of 'what if' could be a useful device for understanding the operation of institutions in both systems. Legal development is not a matter of inducing rules, terms or institutions out of a number of factual situations and applying these rules, terms or institutions to new factual situations. Rather it is a matter of pushing outwards from within the facts themselves. It is a matter of moving from one res, say a public highway, to another res like private property and seeing the extent to which the relationships between the various institutions themselves create a new normative situation. Legal development, in other words, is a matter of expanding the facts.

Questions

1. Are all the cases following *Donoghue v Stevenson* (above p 33) examples of pushing outwards from a bottle of ginger-beer?

2. The Romans, like the modern English jurist, seem to have reasoned at the level of fact; yet it was the Roman lawyers who developed the institutional system which rigidly distinguished between public and private law and between property and obligations. Is there a contradiction here? Why do the English jurists seem much less interested in systematics?

10 THE ROLE OF LEGAL CONCEPTS

Spartan Steel & Alloys Ltd v Martin & Co (Contractors) Ltd [1973] 1 QB 27

(See p 101)

In re KD (a minor) [1988] 1 AC 806

(See p 71)

Miller v Jackson [1977] QB 966

(See p 22)

Notes and questions

1. In these three cases three different concepts are used to justify each decision. What are the concepts and how do they differ between each other?
2. Are concepts simply a means of expressing policy?
3. Before one can have meaningful legal concepts, does one have need of a legal science?
4. What is the relationship between concepts and facts?
5. Is it useful and helpful to distinguish between legal concepts and legal institutions?[15] Would you describe legal personality as a concept? What about ownership or contract?

---

15 Cf G Samuel & J Rinkes, *Contractual and non-contractual obligations in English Law* (Ars Aequi, 1992), pp 231-257.

CHAPTER 2

LEGAL METHOD AND THE COMMON LAW

1 INTRODUCTION

An understanding of the English law of obligations requires knowledge not just of the law applicable to factual situations falling within its province, but also of the application process itself. This may seem a statement of the obvious. Yet it is only in more recent years that the importance of legal method as an object of study in itself has become fully recognised and this recognition is, in turn, having an impact both on substantive legal subjects and on legal theory. There are several reasons for the traditional lack of emphasis in legal education on methodology. First, it was assumed until quite recently that knowledge of law consisted of having knowledge of legal propositions, that is to say rules and principles[1]; and that these rules and principles applied themselves to factual situations in a rather mechanical fashion. Once the facts were established, the rule applied itself to these facts through the syllogism (deductive logic): the rule acted as the major premise, the facts as the minor and the court decision as the conclusion.[2] This logical approach to legal method has been particularly strong in the civil law tradition where the codes represented axiomatised – that is to say logically complete – systems of major premises ready to apply themselves to any factual situation that arose.[3]

Secondly, legal historians, despite having a profound knowledge of law (particularly Roman law) in terms of rules and institutions, have been less interested in the methods and habits of thought of the Roman jurists and their successors.[4] This is not to say that there are no profound studies. But the strength of the rule thesis of legal knowledge has been such that it has militated against the search for alternative methodological models. And so, as Susskind has observed, there is 'unequivocal help available neither from legal theory nor from the

---

1   See eg, R Susskind, *Expert Systems in Law* (Oxford, 1987), pp 78–79.
2   See G Samuel, *The Foundations of Legal Reasoning* (Maklu/Blackstone, 1994), pp 119–122, 137–140.
3   G Timsit, *Thèmes et systèmes de droit* (Presses Universitaires de France, 1986), pp 106–107.
4   S Strömholm, *A Short History of Legal Thinking in the West* (Norstedts, 1985), pp 46, 67.

primary or secondary sources of law' when it comes to alternatives to the rule thesis.[5] One must add that this lack of interest in alternatives has also been encouraged by the ideological factor that underpins the rule thesis; the idea that law is a set of ascertainable rules which are to be applied in a neutral fashion is part of a positivist philosophy that has been particularly strong for well over a century now.

It is only with the search for an escape from positivism that methodology has has come back into focus. Yet even a philosopher like Ronald Dworkin, who has done more than anyone in the common law world to re-emphasise the role of adjudication in the formulation of philosophical theory, continues to subscribe to the thesis that legal knowledge is based on rules and principles.[6] All the same, Dworkin has moved thinking away from the mechanics of the syllogism towards the interpretative role of the judge and while this shift has not undermined as such the rule thesis – indeed Dworkin specifically bases his theory on the existence of legal principles[7] – he has opened up the methodological debate in, for example, distinguishing between easy and hard cases.[8] In easy cases it may be that a legal rule applies itself in a mechanical fashion, but in hard cases – that is cases where there is no easy correspondence between the rule and the facts – the interpretative role of the judge becomes the central object of study. The judge, according to Dworkin, becomes involved in a process that is analogous to writing a chain novel. 'In this enterprise', writes Dworkin, 'a group of novelists writes a novel seriatim; each novelist in the chain interprets the chapters he has been given in order to write a new chapter, which is then added to what the next novelist receives, and so on'.[9] The problem with this otherwise valuable methodological analysis is that it assumes that legal reasoning is a matter of interpreting language – a matter of texts (*ars hermeneutica*). Can this ever be the basis of a scientific analysis of method? Does not a science function at one and the same time at the level of a discourse (language and texts) and at the level of the facts themselves? Does not a science organise the facts? Law of course may not be a science; yet it does seem to construct its own facts, as the materials in this chapter will hopefully show (see eg, *Re Rowland*, p 87), and, in addition, it seems to construct these facts using a discourse that has been formulated by a long historical process (see *Bryant v Herbert*, below). This history is not a history of events as such; it is 'above all a

---

5   Susskind, *supra*, p 154.

6   Susskind, *supra*, pp 78-79.

7   R Dworkin, *Taking Rights Seriously* (Duckworth, 1977), pp 24ff.

8   *Ibid*, pp 105-130.

9   R Dworkin, *Law's Empire* (Fontana, 1986), p 229.

genealogy of "categories" which have successively made up the objects of a science'[10] and it is these categories that will be one major focus of attention in this present chapter.

2 CAUSES OF ACTION

(a) Historical considerations: the forms of action

Bryant v Herbert (1877) 3 CPD 389 Court of Appeal

Bramwell LJ: It seems to me that the question in this case is, what is the meaning of the words "in any action founded on contract", and "on any action founded on tort"... The words are not words of art even as much as *ex contractu* or *ex delicto* would be. They are plain English words, and are to have the meaning ordinary Englishmen would give them. What is the foundation of an action? Those facts which it is necessary to state and prove to maintain it, and no others. This really seems a truism: unless those necessary facts exist, the action is unfounded. All other facts are no part of the foundation. There is a further observation. This statute passed after the Common Law Procedure Acts. They did not abolish forms of action in words. The Common Law Commissioners recommended that: but it was supposed that, if adopted, the law would be shaken to its foundations; so that all that could be done was to provide as far as possible that, though forms of actions remained, there never should be a question what was the form. This was accomplished save as to this very question of costs in actions within the county court jurisdiction. Until the passing of the statute [County Courts Act] we are discussing, it was necessary to see if an action was assumpsit, case &c. But the Common Law Procedure Act having passed, and the forms of actions being practically abolished, the legislature pass this Act dropping the words "*assumpsit, case*", &c., and using the words "founded on contract", "founded on tort". This shows to me that the substance of the matter was to be looked at. One may observe there is no middle term; the statute supposes all actions are founded either on contract or on tort. So that it is tort, if not contract, contract if not tort. Then is this action on the face of the statements of claim and defence founded on contract or on tort. All that is alleged is that the plaintiffs are owners of the picture, and that the defendant detains it. This means wrongfully detains it, not merely has in his possession, and negatively does not give it up. Then the action is manifestly founded on a tort on the pleadings. But so it is if the facts are looked at. I doubt if there was any contract between the parties ... These are the considerations on which I think this case ought to be decided, and not by inquiries whether detinue is an action *ex contractu* or *ex delicto*. I think that the legislature intended that the substance of the action and not its form should be looked at. It leaves out what was in the former Act, "*assumpsit*, case", &c., and uses general words "founded on contract", "founded on tort". But if the old learning as it was called is to be brought to help us, I should come to the same conclusion. No doubt dicta and

---

10   G-G Granger, *La ceience es les sciences* (Pressess Universitaire de France, 1993), p 115.

decisions are to be found that detinue is an action *ex contractu* or *ex quasi contractu*, &c., but there are dicta and decisions the other way. It is not easy to make sense of them: perhaps the nature of the thing does not admit of it. It cannot be settled by saying that debt and detinue could be joined, and that actions of tort could not be joined with actions on contract. Actions on contract could not be joined, eg, debt and *assumpsit*. The reason being unconnected with the question whether the action was *ex contractu* or *ex delicto* ... But I believe that it was intended that all this useless, and worse than useless, learning should be disregarded, and the matter decided on its substance.

Brett LJ: I concur in the judgment of my learned Brother, but I cannot agree with the reasons given ... With the greatest deference to my Brother Bramwell I cannot conceive that those words are what he calls plain English, because they seem to me to be technical terms. The conclusion to which I have come is this, that the action of detinue is technically an action founded on contract. The action was invented to avoid the technicalities of the old law: the invention was to state a contract which could not be traversed. Therefore I think the action of detinue, or the form of the action of detinue, so far as the remedy is concerned in its legal signification was founded on contract.

But, then, did the statute which we have to construe mean to use these terms in that sense? I have great doubts whether it did not, and whether using the terms "founded on contract", or "founded on tort", it was not having regard to the form of action. But I am not prepared to disagree with the conclusion that the statute meant to deal not with the form of action, but with the facts with reference to which the form of action is to be applied. Now, if that be so, the question then is, whether the cause of action in fact here is a cause of action founded on contract in the sense of its being a breach of contract, or whether it is founded on tort in the sense of its being founded on a wrongful act ... The real substantial cause of action is a wrongful act ...

My Brother Baggallay agrees in the result at which we have arrived.

Notes and questions

1. 'The principles of the common law were not laid down in the abstract, but grew around the forms through which justice was centralised and administered by the king's courts. There was a law of writs before there was a law of property, or of contract, or of tort ... A plaintiff did not ... concoct his own writ ... He had either to find a known formula to fit his case, or apply for a new one to be invented ... After [the 13th century], although occasional innovations were sanctioned by Parliament, the categories became more or less closed. The effect was momentous. Finding the right formula was no longer simply a matter of consistency and routine ... Formulae ... were seen as defining the rights and remedies recognised by the common law, and thus as fixing the common law within an immutable conceptual framework ... Later lawyers referred to the compartments of law and practice associated with different writs as the "forms of action". These forms of action were the first object of legal study' (JH Baker,

An Introduction to English Legal History (3rd ed, 1990), pp 63, 65, 66–67). How did the English law of actions differ from the Roman law of actions? How did the reforms of the 19th century change legal analysis? What must a plaintiff plead after the procedural reforms: just the facts or the facts plus the law?

2. Where do the categories 'contract' and 'tort' come from given that they do not appear to be part of the early history of English legal thought? What is the relationship between these two categories and the facts which go to make up a common law 'action'?

3. How does one know if a set of facts gives rise to an action founded on 'contract' or 'tort'? Must all actions for damages which cannot be classified under 'contract' be classified under 'tort'?

4. Is there a difference between an action founded on 'contract' and an action *ex contractu*?

5. What is Bramwell LJ advocating in respect of legal education? In what way does Brett LJ differ from Bramwell LJ?

6. 'The plaintiff has chosen to bring an action of trover, and he now says, I ought to be allowed to amend by turning this action into an action of account ... But the whole case is entirely different. The whole question before the jury would be different, and the whole account would have to be taken upon totally different principles from anything that was done before the jury ... That verdict has been founded on a notion of tort' (Lord Hatherley LC, *Jacobs v Seward* (1872) LR 5 App Cas 464). Is this an example of the forms of action ruling from the grave? Do judges still have to deal with these 'forms of action' problems? (Cf *Roy v Kensington & Chelsea FPC* p 44.)

(b) Modern law: remedies and rights

Letang v Cooper [1965] 1 QB 232 Court of Appeal

Diplock LJ: ... A cause of action is simply a factual situation the existence of which entitles one person to obtain from the court a remedy against another person. Historically, the means by which the remedy was obtained varied with the nature of the factual situation and causes of action were divided into categories according to the "form of action" by which the remedy was obtained in the particular kind of factual situation which constituted the cause of action. But that is legal history, not current law ... The Judicature Act, 1873 abolished forms of action. It did not affect causes of action; so it was convenient for lawyers and legislators to continue to use, to describe the various categories of factual situations which entitle one person to obtain from the court a remedy against another, the names of the various "forms of action" by which formerly the remedy appropriate to the particular category of factual situation was obtained. But it is essential to realise that when, since 1873, the name of a form of action is used to identify a cause of action, it is used as a convenient and succinct description of a particular category of factual situation which entitles one person to obtain from the court a remedy against another person. To forget this will indeed encourage the old forms of action to rule us from their graves ...

Notes and questions

1. 'The words "cause of action" comprise every fact, though not every piece of evidence, which it would be necessary for the plaintiff to prove, if traversed, to support his right to judgment of the court ... It seems to me clear that the facts which give rise to a remedy in England gave rise to a comparable civil remedy in Spain, albeit such remedy falls to be pursued in essentially criminal proceedings by intervention of the aggrieved party ...' (Potter J, *Black v Yates* [1991] 3 WLR 90). What is the process by which one goes from facts to remedy?

2. 'In the pragmatic way in which English law has developed, a man's legal rights are in fact those which are protected by a cause of action. It is not in accordance, as I understand it, with the principles of English law to analyse rights as being something separate from the remedy given to the individual ... [I]n my judgment, in the ordinary case to establish a legal or equitable right you have to show that all the necessary elements of the cause of action are either present or threatened' (Sir Nicolas Browne-Wilkinson, *Kingdom of Spain v Christie, Manson & Woods Ltd* [1986] 1 WLR 1120). Is the notion of a right (*le droit subjectif*) unknown in English law?

3. '[T]he question whether the right exists cannot be determined by inquiring whether the action for money had and received is the appropriate form of plea. If the right exists, the form of the plea is appropriate enough. If the right does not exist it cannot be enforced no matter how attractively it might be disguised by the pleader. The question is not now one of the appropriate form in which to clothe the right, but whether or not the right exists, although the absence of any clothing that fits may be an indication of the non-existence of the right' (Stable J, *Dies v British & International Mining & Finance Corporation* [1939] 1 KB 724). Compare and contrast the view of Stable J with that of Sir Nicolas Browne-Wilkinson.

3 PLEADINGS

Sterman v E W & W J Moore Ltd [1970] 1 QB 596 Court of Appeal

Lord Denning MR: ... Here was a plaintiff who issued his writ and served it on the defendants well within the period of limitation. They knew perfectly well that the plaintiff was claiming damages for his fall from the trestle because it was their fault. Yet they seek to bar him on the most technical consideration – just because he omitted the words 'for negligence and breach of statutory duty'. I do not think that we should allow this technical objection to prevail ... [W]e should allow the plaintiff to amend the writ so as to state in terms that his claim is for damages 'for negligence and breach of statutory duty'. I see no harm in adding the further claim for damages for 'breach of agreement' ...

Salmon LJ: I agree. I would emphasise that it is highly desirable that the indorsement to the writ should plainly set out the cause of action on which the plaintiff relies. It may be that it is sufficient ... if the writ merely gives a concise statement of the nature of the relief or remedy required by the plaintiff; but the disadvantage of confining the indorsement of the writ to a concise statement of the relief or remedy required (as the plaintiff has done in the present case) is that the plaintiff may find himself in considerable difficulty when he comes to deliver his statement of claim. It seems to me, although I am expressing no concluded view on the point, that the provisions of [the Rules of Supreme Court] preclude the plaintiff from including any cause of action in his statement of claim which is not mentioned in the writ ...

Notes and questions

1. What role do the pleadings play in the determination of the law applicable? Can a judge raise points of law not mentioned by the parties in their pleadings?

2. 'My Lords, I think this case ought to be decided in accordance with the pleadings. If it is, I am of opinion, as was the trial judge, that the respondents failed to establish any claim to relief that was valid in law. If it is not, we might do better justice to the respondents ... but I am certain that we should do worse justice to the appellants, since in my view they were entitled to conduct the case and confine their evidence in reliance upon ... the statement of claim ... It seems to me that it is the purpose of such particulars that they should help to define the issues ...' (Lord Radcliffe, *Esso Petroleum Ltd v Southport Corporation* [1956] AC 218). Does this view conflict with Lord Denning's view in *Sterman*?[11]

3. Is it not a principle of Western law that parties are under a duty only to plead the facts and that it is the court that applies the law? Are there any systems of law where the parties plead no law at all, only the facts?

---

11   Cf *Drane v Evangelou* [1978] 2 All ER 437.

4 THE LEGAL RULE

Spring v Guardian Assurance Plc [1994] 3 WLR 354 House of Lords

Lord Goff: ... The central issue in this appeal is whether a person who provides a reference in respect of another who was formerly engaged by him as a member of his staff (...) may be liable in damages to that other in respect of economic loss suffered by him by reason of negligence in the preparation of the reference ...

Lord Lowry: ... It is in the tradition of the English case law method to decide this appeal on its facts and not be deterred by reflecting on all possible situations in which a reference might be called for. Even if it is debatable where the line should be drawn, I am confident that from the plaintiff's point of view this case falls on the right side of it ...

Lord Woolf: ... It only remains for me to underline what I anticipate is already clear, that is, that the views which I have expressed are confined to the class of case with which I am now dealing. Some of the statements I have made I appreciate could be applied to analogous situations. However, I do not intend to express any view either way as to what will be the position in those analogous situations. I believe that they are better decided when, and if, a particular case comes before the court. This approach can lead to uncertainty which is undesirable. However, that undesirable consequence is in my view preferable to trying to anticipate the position in relation to other situations which are not the subject matter of this appeal ...

Notes and questions

1. '[L]*orsqu'un juge affirme, pour en faire application, une règle de droit, il ne peut le faire qu'au vu des circonstances de l'espèce dont il est saisi, et en relation avec ces circonstances*' ('When a judge asserts a legal rule to be applied, he does so only in view of, and in relation to, the facts of the case before him') (R David, *Le droit anglais*, Presses Universitaires de France, 5e.éd, 1987), p 20). What the late Professor David was alluding to here is the habit of common lawyers to formulate and apply rules only within specific factual situations; not for them the broad principle capable of covering a range of factual situations. Is his observation supported by the comments of the judges above?

2. Are rules formulated within very narrow and specific factual situations capable of being applied via the syllogism? What method of application does Lord Woolf envisage?

3. What do the Lords of Appeal envisage their role to be in the legal system?

5 GENERAL PRINCIPLES OF LAW

Woolwich Equitable Building Society v Inland Revenue Commissioners [1993] AC 70 House of Lords

(See p 54)

Notes and questions

1. 'I call a "principle" a standard that is to be observed, not because it will advance or secure an economic, political, or social situation deemed desirable, but because it is a requirement of justice or fairness or some other dimension of morality ... Rules are applicable in an all-or-nothing fashion ... But this is not the way ... principles ... operate ... A principle ... states a reason that argues in one direction, but does not necessitate a particular decision' (R Dworkin, *Taking Rights Seriously* (1977), pp 22, 24, 25, 26). Does the law of contract consist of rules or principles? (Cf Chapters 4-6.) What about the French or German civil code: are these codes of rules or principles?

2. '[I]f there is one thing which more than another public policy requires it is that men of full age and competent understanding shall have the utmost liberty of contracting, and that their contracts when entered into freely and voluntarily shall be held sacred and shall be enforced by Courts of Justice' (Sir George Jessel MR, *Printing and Numerical Registering Co v Sampson* (1875) LR 19 Eq 462). (Cf *Code civil* art 1134.) Is this a principle?

3. 'You must take reasonable care to avoid acts or omissions which you can reasonably foresee would be likely to injure your neighbour' (Lord Atkin, *Donoghue v Stevenson* [1932] AC 562). (Cf. *Code civil* art 1382; *Hedley Byrne & Co v Heller & Partners* [1964] AC 465). Is this a rule or a principle?

4. 'We think that the true rule of law is, that the person who for his own purposes brings on his lands and collects and keeps there anything likely to do mischief if it escapes, must keep it in at his peril, and, if he does not do so, is *prima facie* answerable for all the damage which is the natural consequence of its escape' (Blackburn J in *Rylands v Fletcher* (1866) LR 1 Ex 265). (Cf *Code civil* art 1384.) If this is a principle, would you expect it it function in much the same way as art 1384?[12]

---

12   Cf *Read v J Lyons & Co* [1947] AC 156.

5. 'By natural law it is equitable that no one should be enriched by the loss or injury of another' (Digest 50.17.206). Was this principle actually applied in *Lipkin Gorman v Karpnale Ltd* p 145 and in *Woolwich Building Society v IRC* [1993] AC 70?

6 LEGAL CONCEPTS

(a) Normative concepts

(i) Rights

Ex parte Island Records [1978] Ch 122 Court of Appeal

Lord Denning MR: ... The question ... becomes this: has the plaintiff a particular right which he is entitled to have protected? To this the answer which runs through all the cases is: a man who is carrying on a lawful trade or calling has a right to be protected from any unlawful interference with it ... It is a right which is in the nature of a right of property ... [The Attorney-General] has, we are told, refused his consent to a relator action – presumably because no public rights are involved. So perforce if the law is to be obeyed – and justice to be done – the courts must allow a private individual himself to bring an action against the offender – in those cases where his private rights and interests are specially affected by the breach [of the criminal law]. This principle is capable of extension so as to apply not only to rights of property or rights in the nature of it, but to other rights or interests ...

Questions

1. What is a relator action?[13]
2. Does a trader really have a right not to have his, her or its trade unlawfully interfered with? If D unlawfully causes a road accident with the result that a street is closed to the public for several hours, can traders in that street sue D for their loss of takings? What if D unlawfully sets up his market stall near a place where others are lawfully trading: can these traders sue D for any drop in their takings? Can they deprive D of any profit he might make? Can the local authority, which issues trading licences, sue D for damages?[14] Could the local authority obtain an injunction against D? Could they sue D in debt or account for the (illegal?) profit?
3. Is the purpose of the criminal law to protect individual rights?

---

13 Cf *Gouriet v UPOW* [1978] AC 435.
14 Cf *Stoke-on-Trent CC v W & J Wass Ltd* [1988] 1 WLR 1406.

4. Where does the notion of a right come from? Is it a product of legal history?

G Samuel & J Rinkes, Contractual and non-contractual obligations in English law (Ars Aequi, 1992), pp 238-239

A legal right ... is a construct of legal science: it takes its form from the relationship between *persona* and *res* and this is the reason why one always talks of a right to something. In other words a right is a legal concept that uses the conceptual structure of the property relationship between person and thing and applies it to other legal (and indeed political and social) relationships. Thus performance under a contract can be seen as a *res* to which the other contracting party (*persona*) is entitled and this leads to a situation where one can talk in terms of a right arising from a contract.

In re KD (a minor) [1988] 1 AC 806 House of Lords

Lord Oliver: ... The word 'right' is used in a variety of different senses, both popular and jurisprudential. It may be used as importing a positive duty in some other individual for the non-performance of which the law will provide an appropriate remedy, as in the case of a right to the performance of a contract. It may signify merely a privilege conferring no corresponding duty on any one save that of non-interference, such as the right to walk on the public highway. It may signify no more than the hope of or aspiration to a social order which will permit the exercise of that which is perceived as an essential liberty, such as, for instance, the so-called 'right to work' or a 'right' of personal privacy.

Questions

1. When one talks of rights in contract, is this to import into contract language from the law of property? Is a contractual right a property right? (Cf *Beswick v Beswick*, p 37.)

2. Are there such things as natural and/or human rights? Are such rights recognised by the English courts?

3. If there are certain rights that are inalienable, does this undermine the theory that legislation is the supreme source of law? Does it undermine the idea that law consists of positive rules?

4. Does one have a right to liberty?

R v Central Television Plc [1994] 3 WLR 20 Court of Appeal

Hoffman LJ: There are in the law reports many impressive and emphatic statements about the importance of the freedom of speech and the press. But they are often followed by a paragraph which begins with the word "nevertheless". The judge then goes on to explain that there are other interests which have to be balanced against press freedom. And in deciding upon the importance of press freedom in the particular case, he is likely to distinguish between what he thinks deserves publication in the public interest and things in which the public are merely interested. He may even advert to the commercial motives of the newspaper or television compared with the damage to the public or individual interest which would be caused by publication.

The motives which impel judges to assume a power to balance freedom of speech against other interests are almost always understandable and humane on the facts of the particular case before them. Newspapers are sometimes irresponsible and their motives in a market economy cannot be expected to be unalloyed by considerations of commercial advantage. Publication may cause needless pain, distress and damage to individuals or harm to other aspects of the public interest. But a freedom which is restricted to what judges think to be responsible or in the public interest is no freedom. Freedom means the right to publish things which government and judges, however well motivated, think should not be published. It means the right to say things which "right-thinking people" regard as dangerous or irresponsible. This freedom is subject only to clearly defined exceptions laid down by common law or statute.

Furthermore, in order to enable us to meet our international obligations under the *Convention for the Protection of Human Rights and Fundamental Freedoms* (1953) (Cmnd 8969), it is necessary that any exceptions should satisfy the tests laid down in article 10(2) ... It cannot be too strongly emphasised that outside the established exceptions, or any new ones which Parliament may enact in accordance with its obligations under the Convention, there is no question of balancing freedom of speech against other interests. It is a trump card which always wins ...

In any area of human rights like freedom of speech, I respectfully doubt the wisdom of creating judge-made exceptions, particularly when they require a judicial balancing of interests. The danger about such exceptions is that judges are tempted to use them. The facts of the individual case often seem to demand exceptional treatment because the newspaper's interest in publication seems trivial and the hurt likely to be inflicted very great. The interests of the individual litigant and the public interest in the freedom of the press are not easily commensurable. It is not surprising that in this case the misery of a five year old girl weighed more heavily with Kirkwood J than the television company's freedom to publish material which would heighten the dramatic effect of its documentary. This is what one would expect of a sensitive and humane judge exercising the wardship jurisdiction. But no freedom is without cost and in my view the judiciary should not whittle away freedom of speech with ad hoc exceptions. The principle that the press is free from both government and judicial control is more important than the particular case ...

I would not for a moment dispute ... the fact that a right of privacy may be a legitimate exception to freedom of speech. After all, other countries also a party to the Convention have a right of privacy for grown-ups as well. But we do not and there may be room for constitutional argument as to whether in a matter so fundamentally trenching upon the freedom of the press as the creation of a right of privacy, it would not be more appropriate for the remedy to be provided by the legislature rather than the judiciary ...

Questions

1. Does this judicial observation represent a new direction in English judicial thinking?

2. Can you detect the influence of any particular legal philosopher in Hoffman LJ's comments?

3. 'Politically conservative members of a former generation would doubtless find it unfamiliar that claims of civic or social right should nowadays be formulated in terms of the private law institution of property. But this merely goes to underline the fact that, in some important sense, all property rights enjoy an inherent public law character' (K Gray, Equitable Property, in M Freeman & R Halson (eds) *Current Legal Problems* 1994 (Oxford, 1994), p 211). Is the right to privacy a matter of public or private law? Do future generations have any present property rights in our planet?

(ii) Duty

Hyman v Nye (1881) 6 QBD 685 Queen's Bench Division

(See p 322)

Notes and questions

1. Is the correlative of a right a duty? In other words, if D is under a duty to pay P £50 does this mean that P has a right to £50?

2. If owners of vehicles for hire are under a duty to see that they are reasonably fit for their purpose, does this mean that consumers, as a class, have rights?

3. A road user owes a duty of care to other road users. What rights do road users have?

4. Rights and duties are described as normative concepts because their existence implies obligation: if P has a right, or if D is under a duty, no more is required in the sentence to make it a normative statement. Thus to say that P has a right to X means that he is entitled to X without further question. Equally to say that D is under a duty to do X implies that D must do X without further question. These normative concepts thus become central to legal reasoning since the moment one can construct a legal statement around one or other of them one has gone far in establishing both the reason for a decision and the justification for it. The classic right is of course that of ownership – an owner is entitled to vindicate what is his, her or its property without further question. And the Roman law word for ownership was *dominium* which implied power over a thing owned (*res*). Does this mean that all rights are power-conferring concepts? Does an owner have the right to issue orders to all those on his property? What are the constitutional implications of all this? If public law intervenes, for example to prohibit an owner of a listed building from knocking it down, does this mean that the owner no longer has a 'right' over the thing? Is a legislator entitled to revoke any individual right it sees fit to revoke?

(b) Quasi-normative concepts

(i) Interests

Miller v Jackson [1977] QB 966 Court of Appeal

(See p 22)

Notes and questions

1. 'Where a local authority consider it expedient for the promotion or protection of the interests of the inhabitants of their area ... they may prosecute ... any legal proceedings ...' (Local Government Act 1972 s 222(1)). Does this statute recognise that the inhabitants are a kind of *persona*?

2. Is an interest playing the role of a right in *Miller v Jackson*?

3. 'Now it is certainly true that consumer, worker and environmental interests are not to be found directly in traditional legal science. Yet the object of Roman legal science was – as is quite specifically stated in the Digest itself – public and private interests (*utilitas*) and when this notion is associated with the Roman institution of the legal subject (*persona*) it can be seen that the recognition of new social realities in modern law does not require any new epistemological discourse as such. The recognition by the law of new interests is simply the application of a traditional scientific structure (*persona* and *utilitas*) to new social circumstances' (G Samuel & J Rinkes, *Contractual and non-contractual obligations in English law* (1992), p 236). To what extent can this empirical interest relationship be used as a means of creating class rights?[15]

(ii) Damage

Khorasandijian v Bush [1993] 3 WLR 476 Court of Appeal

This was an action by a daughter, living in her parents' home, for an interlocutory injunction to prevent threatening phone calls from an ex boyfriend.

Dillon LJ: ... The substantive point of the appeal is, however, that it is said for the defendant that the judge had no jurisdiction to restrain the defendant from "harassing, pestering or communicating with" the plaintiff because those words did not reflect any tort known to the law and an interlocutory injunction could only be granted to protect a legal right of the plaintiff. On this point we have been referred to a substantial number of recent decisions, several of them as yet unreported, in a developing field of law. Many of the decisions are not easy to reconcile with each other. It is accepted, however, by Miss Harry Thomas, for the

---

15   Cf *Jolowicz* [1983] CLJ 222.

defendant, that an injunction to restrain the defendant from assaulting or attempting to assault the plaintiff, or, if preferred, from using violence to her, would be justifiable in law because trespass to the person is a recognised tort ...

The defendant was born on 13 August 1969 and thus is now a young man of 23. The plaintiff was born on 28 March 1974 and is thus now a girl of 18. They are not, and have never been, married to each other and they have never cohabited with each other. Thus there is no jurisdiction in this case to grant an injunction against "molestation" under section 1 of the Domestic Violence and Matrimonial Proceedings Act 1976, nor has the plaintiff sought to invoke that Act.

The power of the county court to grant injunctions, whether interlocutory or final, in cases where the county court has jurisdiction, is the same as the power of the High Court. The statutory authority is now section 37(1) of the Supreme Court Act 1981, which provides that the High Court may by order (whether interlocutory or final) grant an injunction "in all cases in which it appears to the court to be just and convenient to do so". It is well understood, however, despite the apparent width of those words, that, as Lord Diplock put it in relation to the predecessor of section 37(1) in *Siskina (Owners of cargo lately laden on board) v Distos Compania Naviera SA* [1979] A 210, 254:

> "That subsection, speaking as it does of interlocutory orders, presupposes the existence of an action, actual or potential, claiming substantive relief which the High Court has jurisdiction to grant and to which the interlocutory orders referred to are but ancillary."

Therefore it is necessary to consider what claims for substantive relief, or causes of action, the plaintiff has against the defendant. I say "has" against the defendant rather than "is asserting against the defendant by her pleadings" because it is conceded on behalf of the defendant that at this stage in this particular case the plaintiff should not be limited to her actual particulars of claim, which are in informal language and were issued in a hurry when the first application to the county court for an injunction was made. The pleadings can be amended, or, if technically necessary, a further action can be started and the two can be consolidated. It is therefore appropriate to consider the whole of the plaintiff's evidence, to determine what cause of action she appears to have on that evidence, and to consider what interlocutory injunctions the court has power to grant on that evidence. It is fair to the defendant to say that he has sworn affidavits disputing the plaintiff's account of events, but the immediate question is what causes of action the plaintiff has if she is right as to what has happened.

It is, of course, not in dispute that an interlocutory injunction can, in an appropriate case, be granted *quia timet* before an actual tort has been committed against a plaintiff. It is also clear that the form of an interlocutory injunction does not have to follow slavishly the form of the substantive relief which would be likely to be granted at the trial if the plaintiff succeeds ...

Miss Harry Thomas, for the defendant, concedes, as I have already indicated, that an injunction could be granted to restrain the defendant from assaulting or threatening to assault the plaintiff. She concedes also that an injunction could be granted to restrain the defendant from interfering with the plaintiff's property, eg there could be an injunction to restrain wrongful interference with goods such as the taking of the plaintiff's handbag, or to restrain malicious damage to property, such as, if sufficiently proved, the making of the scratches on the paintwork of the plaintiff's car. In relation to the telephone calls, she concedes that if the plaintiff's mother has a freehold or leasehold interest in the parental home, the plaintiff's mother could complain of persistent unwanted telephone calls made by the defendant to the plaintiff's mother in the parental home, as that would fall within the tort of private nuisance. But she submits, in reliance on the decision of this court in *Malone v Laskey* [1907] 2 KB 141, that the basis of the tort of private nuisance is interference with the enjoyment of a person's property, and therefore the plaintiff, as in law a mere licensee in her mother's property with no proprietary interest, cannot invoke the tort of private nuisance or complain of unwanted and harassing telephone calls made to her in her mother's home.

To my mind, it is ridiculous if in this present age the law is that the making of deliberately harassing and pestering telephone calls to a person is only actionable in the civil courts if the recipient of the calls happens to have the freehold or a leasehold proprietary interest in the premises in which he or she has received the calls. Miss Harry Thomas submits, however, that English law does not recognise any tort of harassment or invasion of privacy or, save in the different context of such a case as *Rookes v Barnard* [1964] AC 1129, intimidation. Therefore, she says that, save as expressly conceded as set out above, the defendant's conduct to the plaintiff is, even on the plaintiff's version of it, under the English civil law, legitimate conduct of which the plaintiff has no power or right to complain. I apprehend that it is correct, historically, that the tort of private nuisance, which originated as an action on the case, was developed in the beginning to protect private property or rights of property, in relation to the use or enjoyment of land. It is stated in Clerk & Lindsell on *Torts*, 16th ed (1989), p 1354, para 24-01 that "the essence of nuisance is a condition or activity which unduly interferes with the use or enjoyment of land".

That a legal owner of property can obtain an injunction, on the ground of private nuisance, to restrain persistent harassment by unwanted telephone calls to his home was decided by the Appellate Division of the Alberta Supreme Court in *Motherwell v Motherwell* (1976) 73 DLR (3d) 62. The court there rejected, by reference to English authority, a submission, at p 67:

"that the common law does not have within itself the resources to recognise invasion of privacy as either included in an existing category or as a new category of nuisance, and that it has lost its original power, by which indeed it created itself, to note new ills arising in a growing and changing society and pragmatically to establish a principle to meet the need for control and remedy; and then by categories to develop the principle as the interests of justice make themselves sufficiently apparent."

Consequently, notwithstanding *Malone v Laskey*, the court held that the wife of the owner had also the right to restrain harassing telephone calls to the matrimonial home. Clement JA who delivered the judgment of the court said, at p 78:

"Here we have a wife harassed in the matrimonial home. She has a status, a right to live there with her husband and children. I find it absurd to say that her occupancy of the matrimonial home is insufficient to found an action in nuisance. In my opinion she is entitled to the same relief as is her husband, the brother."

I respectfully agree, and in my judgment this court is entitled to adopt the same approach. The court has at times to reconsider earlier decisions in the light of changed social conditions; in this court we saw an example of that only the day before the hearing of this appeal began, when we were referred to *Dyson Holdings Ltd v Fox* [1976] QB 503. If the wife of the owner is entitled to sue in respect of harassing telephone calls, then I do not see why that should not also apply to a child living at home with her parents.

Damage is, in the relevant category, a necessary ingredient in the tort of private nuisance, and I shall have to refer further to that later. So far as the harassing telephone calls are concerned, however, the inconvenience and annoyance to the occupier caused by such calls, and the interference thereby with the ordinary and reasonable use of the property are sufficient damage. The harassment is the persistent making of the unwanted telephone calls, even apart from their content; if the content is itself as here threatening and objectionable, the harassment is the greater ...

In the present case, the plaintiff in her evidence referred to the defendant's conduct as putting her under an enormous weight of stress. This is amply borne out by much else that she says. On the facts in evidence that is the predictable and, so far as the defendant is concerned, intended effect of the defendant's conduct. There is no medical evidence, and it could not as yet be said, that the plaintiff is suffering from any physical or psychiatric illness. But there is, in my judgment, an obvious risk that the cumulative effect of continued and unrestrained further harassment such as she has undergone would cause such an illness. The law expects the ordinary person to bear the mishaps of life with fortitude and, as was put in a case cited by Lord Bridge in *McLoughlin v O'Brian*, customary phlegm; but it does not expect ordinary young women to bear indefinitely such a campaign of persecution as that to which the defendant has subjected the plaintiff. Therefore, in my judgment, on the facts of this case and in line with the law as laid down in *Janvier v Sweeney*, the court is entitled to look at the defendant's conduct as a whole and restrain those aspects on a *quia timet* basis also of his campaign of harassment which cannot strictly be classified as threats ...

I have had the advantage of reading in draft the judgment of Peter Gibson J. I note that he would qualify the injunction by adding words such as "by doing acts calculated to cause the [plaintiff] harm". I regard such a qualification as undesirable, because it would complicate enforcement of the injunction pending trial of the action; the defendant would assert that any act of pestering or harassment of which complaint was made was not by itself calculated to cause the plaintiff harm. I also regard the qualification as unnecessary because (i) the campaign of harassment has to be regarded as a whole without consideration of each ingredient in isolation, and viewed as a whole it is plainly calculated to cause the plaintiff harm, and can be restrained *quia timet* because of the danger to her health from a continuation of the stress to which she has been subjected; (ii) threats of violence can be restrained *per se*, whether or not the threat, without the subsequent violence, is calculated to cause the plaintiff harm; and (iii) telephone harassment is, in my judgment, as indicated above, an actionable interference with her ordinary and reasonable use and enjoyment of property where she is lawfully present, and thus, on the past history, can be restrained *quia timet* without further proof of damage.

Rose LJ: I agree with the judgment of Dillon LJ.

Peter Gibson J (dissenting): ... This is not a case to which the Domestic Violence and Matrimonial Proceedings Act 1976 applies, the parties being neither married to, nor cohabiting with, each other, nor are there children to protect. Although there have been calls for the extension of the domestic violence legislation so that the wide remedies under it (including the grant of injunctions to restrain any form of molestation, the exclusion of a party from a home or from a specified area including the home and the attachment of a power of arrest to certain injunctions) would become available in proceedings between parties whose relationships are not limited by reference to marriage and cohabitation (see, in particular, the Law Commission's *Report on Family Law: Domestic Violence and Occupation of the Family Home* (1992) (Law Com. No. 207)), no such extension has yet been enacted; and even if the Law Commission's recommendations were implemented, a person in the plaintiff's position would probably still be unable to invoke such remedies. Such a person must therefore look to the common law in order to obtain protection ...

The jurisdiction of the county court to grant an injunction is contained in section 38 of the County Courts Act 1984, which allows that court (subject to immaterial exceptions) to make any order, including an interlocutory order, which could be made by the High Court if the proceedings were in the High Court. By section 37 of the Supreme Court Act 1981 the High Court has power to grant an interlocutory or final injunction in all cases in which it appears to the court to be just and convenient to do so. But as Lord Diplock pointed out in *Siskina (Owners of cargo lately laden on board) v Distos Compania Naviera SA* [1979] AC 210, 254, the interlocutory order must be made in an action claiming substantive relief which the court has jurisdiction to grant and to which the interlocutory order is but ancillary. Normally, the interlocutory injunction will restrain conduct about which complaint is made in the pleadings and in respect of which relief is sought in the action, but as the usual purpose of the interlocutory order is to preserve the position until the rights of the parties have been determined in the action, the court can make whatever order best achieves that purpose even if that order would not be appropriate at the trial: *Fresh Fruit Wales Ltd. v Halbert, The Times*, 29 January 1991. While Mr Turl, for the plaintiff, relied on that authority in submitting that the judge had jurisdiction to make the order in the terms which he did, for my part I see no scope in the circumstances of this case for looking beyond the causes of action pleaded in the particulars of claim, amplified as they are by the affidavit evidence ...

Miss Harry Thomas, for the defendant, criticised the inclusion in the order of a restraint against harassment or pestering because that afforded the plaintiff far more protection than she was entitled to. She submitted that there was no tort of harassment or pestering, though she accepted that some acts of harassment may constitute an assault or threatened assault; but she submitted that threatening would not alone constitute an assault. Mr Turl contended that the law of tort had developed and that there now was a tort of unreasonable harassment. For this he relied on *Thomas v National Union of Mineworkers (South Wales Area)* [1986] Ch 20 ...

For my part, to the extent that Scott J was holding that there is now a tort of unreasonable harassment, with all respect to him, I cannot agree with him. There is no tort of harassment (*Patel v Patel* [1988] 2 FLR 179, 182, *per* Waterhouse J) and

I do not think that the addition of the adjective "unreasonable" would convert harassing conduct into tortious conduct ...

I know of no authority which would allow a person with no interest in land or right to occupy land to sue in private nuisance. Given that the purpose of an action in nuisance is to protect the right to use and enjoyment of land (see Salmond and Heuston on *The Law of Torts*, 20th ed (1992), p 67), it seems to me to be wrong in principle if a mere licensee or someone without such right could sue in private nuisance ...

Notes and questions

1. Can abusive telephone calls ever amount to a form of assault? Why can such calls, however mild, not be seen as a form of trespass if they cause damage?

2. An animal rights group advises sympathisers to telephone, late at night, various individuals said to be involved in experiments on animals. Can any of the individuals obtain an injunction against the group to stop them advising sympathisers to telephone? What if the group advised its sympathisers to telephone only during office hours?

3. The tendency of the English law of obligations is to classify damage into various kinds: (i) personal injury; (ii) physical damage to property; (iii) economic loss; (iv) nervous shock; (v) mental distress; and (vi) interference with the use and enjoyment of property. Under what heading would you classify the damage in *Khorasandijian*? Does the mere invasion of one of these interests entitle the person whose interest has been invaded to a remedy? If not, what more must be shown? Could the plaintiff in this case have obtained damages to compensate her for the harm suffered?

4. Is there now a tort of harassment?

5. The Nuclear Installations Act 1965 s 12 stipulates a right to compensation for 'any injury or damage ... caused in breach of a duty imposed by [the Act]'. A plaintiff suffers pure economic loss as a result of a breach of such a duty: is the plaintiff entitled to statutory compensation?[16]

(iii) Interests and damage

Linden Gardens Ltd v Lenesta Sludge Disposals Ltd [1994] AC 85 House of Lords

Lord Bridge: ... I cannot accept that in a contract of this nature, namely for work, labour and the supply of materials, the recovery of more than nominal damages

---

16   Cf *Merlin v BNF* [1990] 2 QB 557.

for breach of contract is dependent upon the plaintiff having a proprietary interest in the subject matter of the contract at the date of the breach. In everyday life contracts for work and labour are constantly being placed by those who have no proprietary interest in the subject matter of the contract. To take a common example, the matrimonial home is owned by the wife and the couple's remaining assets are owned by the husband and he is the sole earner. The house requires a new roof and the husband places a contract with a builder to carry out the work. The husband is not acting as agent for his wife, he makes the contract as principal because only he can pay for it. The builder fails to replace the roof properly and the husband has to call in and pay another builder to complete the work. Is it to be said that the husband has suffered no damage because he does not own the property? Such a result would in my view be absurd and the answer is that the husband has suffered loss because he did not receive the bargain for which he had contracted with the first builder and the measure of damages is the cost of securing the performance of that bargain by completing the roof repairs properly by the second builder.

Questions

1. Is the law in effect treating the family as a legal person?
2. In the example given by Lord Bridge, could the wife sue the builder who fails to replace the roof properly? (Cf *Beswick v Beswick*, p 154.) What kind of damage does the wife suffer – physical or economic?
3. What if the builder, while replacing the roof, managed to set fire to the house: could the husband and the wife sue the builder for the mental distress they suffer at seeing the family house burn down?
4. 'In the Lenesta Sludge case ... the House made available a remedy as a matter of law to solve the problem of transferred loss in the case before them' (Lord Goff in *White v Jones* [1995] 1 All ER 691). Discuss.

(c) Descriptive concepts

Caparo Industries Plc v Dickman [1990] 2 AC 605 House of Lords

Lord Oliver: ... 'Proximity' is, no doubt, a convenient expression so long as it is realised that it is no more than a label which embraces not a definable concept but merely a description of circumstances from which, pragmatically, the courts conclude that a duty of care exists.

Attia v British Gas Plc [1988] QB 304 Court of Appeal

(See p 299)

Questions

1. What is the relationship, if any, between the concepts of proximity and duty? Can they be compared?

2. Is proximity a notion that is ever of relevance to the law of contract?

3. P suffers an invasion of an interest by the act of a proximate person: is this ever, in itself, enough to give rise to a right to damages? If not, what more must be shown? (Cf Chapter 7 below.)

7 LAW AND FACT

(a) Questions of law and questions of fact

Qualcast (Wolverhampton) Ltd v Haynes [1959] AC 743 House of Lords

(See p 9)

Notes and questions

1. 'It is not the less a fact because that fact involves some knowledge or relation of law. There is hardly any fact which does not involve it. If you state that a man is in possession of an estate of £10,000 a year, the notion of possession is a legal notion, and involves knowledge of law; nor can any other fact in connection with property be stated which does not involve such knowledge of law' (Jessel MR, *Eaglesfield v Marquis of Londonderry* (1876) 4 Ch D 693). Is proximity a question of fact? Is damage a question of fact?

2. 'It is said, "*Ignorantia juris haud excusat*" [ignorance of the law never excuses]; but in that maxim the word "*jus*" is used in the sense of denoting general law, the ordinary law of the country. But when the word "*jus*" is used in the sense of denoting a private right, that maxim has no application. Private right of ownership is a matter of fact; it may be the result also of matter of law; but if parties contract under a mutual mistake and misapprehension as to their relative and respective rights, the result is, that that agreement is liable to be set aside as having proceeded upon a common mistake' (Lord Westbury, *Cooper v Phibbs* (1867) LR 2 HL 149). What is meant by 'private right'? Is this not a question of law?

3. '[C]ausation in the law of obligations is both a factual and a legal question each question in turn being governed by a different test. But what if the factual causal question is equally balanced: ought the court to find in favour of the defendant on the ground that the plaintiff has not actually proved his or her case? In deciding such a factual question an appeal court will in truth be secreting a normative (legal) principle with the result that factual and legal questions become inextricably intermixed revealing in turn just how

substantive law can both develop in the interstices of procedure and arise out of fact (*ex facto ius oritur*)' (G Samuel & J Rinkes, *Contractual and non-contractual obligations in English law* (1992), pp 48-49). P is able to prove that but for D's negligent failure to diagnose the correct medical condition he would have had a 25% chance of recovery: in losing this 25% has P lost something that can be classified as damage? Is this a question of fact or law?[17]

4. Read the case of *Bolton v Stone* [1951] AC 850 in the law report. Is the central question in this case one of fact or law?

(b) Establishing the facts

Ward v Tesco Stores Ltd [1976] 1 WLR 810 Court of Appeal

Lawton LJ: This is an appeal by the defendants from a judgment of his Honour Judge Nance given in the Liverpool County Court ... whereby he adjudged that the plaintiff should recover against the defendants £178.50 damages and her costs ... for personal injuries said to have been caused by the negligence of the defendants in the maintenance of the floor in their supermarket at Smithdown Road, Liverpool ...

The plaintiff went round the store, carrying a wire basket, as shoppers are expected to do in supermarkets. She was doing her shopping at the back of the store when she felt herself slipping. She appreciated that she was slipping on something which was sticky. She fell to the ground, and sustained minor injuries. She had not seen what had caused her to slip. It was not suggested ... that she had in any way been negligent in failing to notice what was on the floor as she walked along doing her shopping. When she was picking herself up she appreciated that she had slipped on some pink substance which looked to her like yoghourt. It was yoghourt. Later, somebody on the defendants' staff found a carton of yoghourt in the vicinity which was two-thirds empty ...

That is all the plaintiff was able to prove, save for one additional fact. About three weeks later when she was shopping in the same store she noticed that some orange squash had been spilt on the floor. She kept an eye on the spillage for about a quarter of an hour. During that time nobody came to clear it up.

The trial judge was of the opinion that the facts which I have related constituted a *prima facie* case against the defendants. I infer that this case, which involves only a small amount of damages, has been brought to this court because the defendants are disturbed that any judge should find that a *prima facie* case is established merely by a shopper proving that she had slipped on a supermarket floor.

At the trial the defendants called some evidence ... The defendants did not call any evidence as to when the store floor had last been brushed before the plaintiff's accident. It follows that there was no evidence before the court as to

---

17 Cf *McGhee v NCB* [1973] 1 WLR 1; *Wilsher v Essex Area Health Authority* [1988] AC 1074.

whether the floor had been brushed a few moments before the accident, or an hour, or possibly an hour and a half. The court was left without any information on what may have been an important matter ...

In this case the floor of this supermarket was under the management of the defendants and their servants. The accident was such as in the ordinary course of things does not happen if floors are kept clean and spillages are dealt with as soon as they occur. If an accident does happen because the floors are covered with spillage, then in my judgment some explanation should be forthcoming from the defendants to show that the accident did not arise from any want of care on their part; and in the absence of any explanation the judge may give judgment for the plaintiff. Such burden of proof as there is on the defendants in such circumstances is evidential, not probative. The trial judge thought that *prima facie* this accident would not have happened had the defendants taken reasonable care. In my judgment he was justified in taking that view because the probabilities were that the spillage had been on the floor long enough for it to have been cleaned up by a member of the staff ...

Megaw LJ: ... It is for the plaintiff to show that there has occurred an event which is unusual and which, in the absence of explanation is more consistent with fault on the part of the defendants than the absence of fault; and to my mind the learned judge was wholly right in taking that view of the presence of this slippery liquid on the floor of the supermarket in the circumstances of this case: ... that if it should happen ... it created a serious risk that customers would fall and injure themselves. When the plaintiff has established that, the defendants can still escape from liability ... if they could show that the accident must have happened, irrespective of the existence of a proper and adequate system ... to provide for the safety of customers ... That, in this case, they wholly failed to do ...

Ormrod LJ (dissenting): ... I do not think that it was established that this accident was caused by any want of care on the part of the defendants. The accident described by the plaintiff – and she did no more than describe the accident, namely that she slipped in some yoghourt which was on the floor of the supermarket – could clearly have happened no matter what degree of care these defendants had taken. The crucial question is how long before the accident the yoghourt had been on the floor ...

Notes and questions

1. Does this case actually lay down a rule? If so, what is the rule?

2. Why do the judges differ: is it because the majority focus on the operational system and the dissenting judge on the actual yoghourt?

3. Where the balance of probabilities is equally weighted, ought the court to find for the plaintiff or the defendant?

4. If Mrs Ward had been injured by an exploding bottle of lemonade in the supermarket, could she have sued them in contract? If not, why not?

5. 'The relevant events took place in the course of a few seconds; all or some of them were seen by 12 different witnesses ... and, as is

inevitable when honest witnesses give their recollections of what occurred in a very brief space of time there were wide divergences in their respective accounts. In such a case an appellate court will not lightly disturb the findings of the trial judge as to what in fact occurred' (Diplock LJ, *Wooldridge v Sumner* [1963] 2 QB 43). Is the court under a duty to attempt to establish the truth? If not, what is its duty with respect to the facts?

(c) The legal catergorisation of the facts

Lockett v A & M Charles Ltd [1938] 4 All ER 170 King's Bench

This was an action for damages by Mr and Mrs Lockett against a restaurant in respect of food poisoning caught from the whitebait hors d'oeuvre. Mr Lockett had paid the bill.

Tucker J: ... With regard to the female plaintiff's position in respect of breach of warranty, every proprietor of a restaurant is under a duty to take reasonable care to see that the food which he supplies to his guests is fit for human consumption. If he does not take such reasonable steps, and if he is negligent, a person who buys the food which he supplies can recover damages from him based on his negligence. As, however, there is no allegation of such negligence in this case, it must be assumed that the proprietor of the hotel and his servants could not be at fault in any way, and either plaintiff can recover only if he or she establishes that there was a contract between him or her and the proprietor of the hotel ...

Counsel for the plaintiffs is, in my opinion, right when he submits that, when persons go into a restaurant and order food, they are making a contract of sale in exactly the same way as they are making a contract of sale when they go into a shop and order any other goods. I think that the inference is that the person who orders the food in a hotel or restaurant *prima facie* makes himself or herself liable to pay for it, and when two people – whether or not they happen to be husband and wife – go into a hotel and each orders and is supplied with food, then, as between those persons and the proprietor of the hotel, each of them is making himself liable for the food which he orders, whatever may be the arrangement between the two persons who are eating at the hotel. On the facts in this case, it is, in my opinion, right to hold that there was a contract implied by the conduct of the parties between the plaintiff, Mrs Lockett, and the defendants when she ordered and was supplied with the whitebait at the Hotel de Paris ...

If that is so, it follows beyond all doubt that there is an implied warranty that the food supplied is reasonably fit for human consumption. I hold that the whitebait delivered in this case were not reasonably fit for human consumption, and that there was a breach of warranty. Accordingly I give judgment for the male plaintiff for the agreed sum of £98 8s, and for Mrs Lockett for £100.

Notes and questions

1. How does this case differ from *Donoghue v Stevenson* [1932] AC 562 (below p 33)? Why was Donoghue not a contract case?

2. 'To attribute a qualification is, from the formal point of view, to practice an act of classification. The class under consideration can be defined by objective describers and the qualification is then of a factual order ... The legal domain offers good examples of where the qualification is executed from explicit norms which nevertheless leave much room for argument. The qualification of a prohibited act by the law defines the court before which its author is going to be brought as well as the margin of punishment that he incurs ... The qualification is an argument since it operates in order to determine the decision of the judge or the jury. But it is also the consequence of an argument: it is the analysis of facts and the putting of them into contact with the legal texts which are going to determine the qualification' (P Oléron, *L'argumentation* (Presses Universitaires de France, 2nd ed, 1987), pp 87-88). What is the relationship between the qualification (categorisation) of facts and the operation of the syllogism? Is logic merely a means of argumentation? (Cf *Harbour Assurance Ltd v Kansa*, p 93.)

3. 'The goal of the sciences is a description as accurate as possible of facts ... But facts are never evident. They never directly thrust themselves upon one, and it can be said that they exist neither a priori nor separately. Facts have sense only in relation to a system of thought, through a pre-existing theory ...' (J-P Astolfi & M Develay, *La didactique des sciences* (Presses Universitaires de France, 1989), pp 25, 27). Does one have to know the law applicable before one can categorise the facts?

4. How would you classify the facts in *Lockett*: as contractual, tortious, sale of goods or consumer protection? Do you think the facts disclose a criminal offence?

(d) The response of the law to the facts

Financings Ltd v Stimson [1962] 1 WLR 1184 Court of Appeal

(See p 279)

Notes and questions

1. Would you classify the facts of this case as falling within the chapter on the formation of a contract or within a chapter dealing with rescission for mistake?

2. 'Either there is a situation of isomorphy (*lex clara est*), that is, correspondence between the norm and the case, or else there is a situation of doubt which calls for interpretation in the strict sense; in

this case directives of interpretation are needed, and the choice among them implies further evaluations' (J Bengoetxea, *The Legal Reasoning of the European Court of Justice* (Oxford, 1993), p 130). Was there any doubt as to the rule applicable in Stimson? What about *Fisher v Bell* (above p 12).

(e) The reception of facts by the law

Beswick v Beswick [1966] Ch 538 Court of Appeal

Lord Denning MR: ...The general rule undoubtedly is that "no third person can sue, or be sued, on a contract to which he is not a party"; but at bottom that is only a rule of procedure. It goes to the form of remedy, not to the underlying right. Where a contract is made for the benefit of a third person who has a legitimate interest to enforce it, it can be enforced by the third party in the name of the contracting party or jointly with him or, if he refuses to join, by adding him as a defendant. In that sense, and it is a very real sense, the third person has a right arising by way of contract. He has an interest which will be protected by law ... It is different when a third person has no legitimate interest, as when ... he is seeking to rely, not on any right given to him by the contract, but on an exemption clause ...

Notes and questions

1. Cf the decision of the House of Lords in *Beswick v Beswick* (See p 154) Did they find fault with this technique used by Lord Denning?

2. Can you isolate the various legal concepts employed by Lord Denning? How does he get from the world of fact to the world of law?

3. '... The reflections of jurists on the relationship between fact and law can also be brought to bear on the way in which the law ought to take in fact. Several difficulties are to be faced here ... In the first place, the jurist can hardly study the facts without seeing them through a pre-qualification. In the second place, the incessant coming-and-going from fact to law which permits him progressively to arrive at the best qualification available is evidently not independent of the opinion that he has on the just solution in the case. In the third place, the function of the qualification is not to describe reality, but to subject it to the most appropriate legal regime ... Consequently, the difficulty of the work of qualification consists in finding the balance between the consideration of fact and the objective to be promoted in law' (C Atias, *Épistémologie juridique* (Presses Universitaires de France, 1985), p 129). Does the approach of Lord Denning support this view of legal method?

(f) The reception of law by the facts

Blackpool & Fylde Aero Club Ltd v Blackpool Borough Council [1990] 1 WLR 1195 Court of Appeal

(See also p 243)

Bingham LJ: ... During the hearing the questions were raised: what if, in a situation such as the present, the council had opened and thereupon accepted the first tender received, even though the deadline had not expired and other invitees had not yet responded? Or if the council had considered and accepted a tender admittedly received well after the deadline? [Counsel for the defendant] answered that although by so acting the council might breach its own standing orders, and might fairly be accused of discreditable conduct, it would not be in breach of any legal obligation because at that stage there would be none to breach. This is a conclusion I cannot accept. And if it were accepted there would in my view be an unacceptable discrepancy between the law of contract and the confident assumptions of commercial parties ...

Questions

1. Is Bingham LJ using facts to change the law?
2. Are the facts being discussed by Bingham LJ actual facts? If not, are they being invented by the court? And, if so, is such invention an important aspect of legal reasoning?

(g) The utilisation of facts to determine the law

Re Rowland [1963] Ch 1 Court of Appeal

Lord Denning MR (dissenting): ... I decline ... to ask myself: what do the words mean to a grammarian? I prefer to ask: What did Dr Rowland and his wife mean by the word "coincide" in their wills? When they came to make their wills it is not difficult to piece together the thoughts that ran through their minds. The doctor might well say: "We are going off for three years to these far off places and in case anything happens to either of us we ought to make our wills. If I die before you, I would like everything to go to you, but if you die before me, I should like it to go to my brother and his boy". She might reply: "Yes, but what if we both die together. After all, one of those little ships might run on the rocks or something and we might both be drowned; or we might both be killed in an aeroplane crash". "To meet that," he would say, "I will put in that if your death coincides with mine, it is to go to my brother and his boy just the same". He would use the words 'coinciding with', not in the narrow meaning of 'simultaneous', but in the wider meaning of which they are equally capable, especially in this context, as denoting death on the same occasion by the same cause. It would not cross Dr Rowland's mind that anyone would think of such niceties as counsel for the first defendant has presented to us.

Russell LJ: ... If the evidence was that the testator and his wife were below decks in their cabin and the vessel plunged abruptly to the bottom of the sea, the view might be taken that their deaths were, metaphysics apart, coincident in point of time. But we simply do not know what happened to them. Counsel for the appellants could not suggest, in the case of either spouse, whether the correct inference was death by drowning, trapped in the ship, or death by drowning, sucked down by the sinking ship after going overboard, or death by shark or similar fish, or by thirst, or by drowning after swimming about or floating for a greater or less period with or without a lifebelt. This makes it plain that there is no evidence at all that the deaths were coincident in point of time (in the natural sense of simultaneous) in the mind of the ordinary man.

Questions

1. Is this case about the interpretation of a text (the will) or the interpretation of an event (the loss of the ship and the deaths)?

2. What was the cause of the testator's death according to (a) Lord Denning and (b) Russell LJ?

3. Why, exactly, did Lord Denning arrive at a different result from Russell LJ?

4. Did the judges invent their own facts? What role did the facts play in the interpretation of the will?

5. What reasoning technique(s) did the judges employ? Could it be described as methodological individualism – that is to say that, in a collection of events, each event is an event in itself? Or is only one judge employing this technique?

8 LEGAL REASONING

(a) Introduction

Home Office v Dorset Yacht Co Ltd [1970] AC 1004 House of Lords

(See p 362)

Questions

1. Lord Diplock suggests that in form legal method is a matter of induction and deduction, but that in substance there is much room for choice. Is this space for choice something inherent in induction and deduction itself or is it something special to legal reasoning? Does Sherlock Holmes reason by induction or deduction?

2. If choice is to be determined by the making of a policy decision, does this in effect mean that all legal reasoning is, in the final analysis, a matter of policy? What do you think is meant by policy in this context?

3. Viscount Dilhorne says that the absence of authority shows that no such duty exists in the facts of *Dorset*. How, then, do new duties ever come to be recognised? Should the House of Lords be bound in this way by authority? What actually is meant by 'authority' in this context?

4. Do you think the State should be made to pay for a new yacht if the yacht had been insured against damage?

Grant v Australian Knitting Mills Ltd [1936] AC 85 Privy Council

This was a successful action for damages, against a manufacturer of underpants, for injury caused to a purchaser by a pair of underpants which had not been properly decontaminated of chemicals before leaving the factory.

Lord Wright: ... But when the position of the manufacturers is considered different questions arise: there is no privity of contract between the appellant and the manufacturers: between them the liability if any, must be in tort, and the gist of the cause of action is negligence. The facts set out in the foregoing show, in their Lordships' judgment, negligence in manufacture ...

The appellant is not required to lay his finger on the exact person in all the chain who was responsible, or to specify what he did wrong. Negligence is found as a matter of inference from the existence of the defects taken in connection with all the known circumstances: even if the manufacturers could by apt evidence have rebutted that inference they have not done so ...

It is clear that [*Donoghue v Stevenson*] treats negligence, where there is a duty to take care, as a specific tort in itself, and not simply as an element in some more complex relationship or in some specialised breach of duty, and still less as having any dependence on contract. All that is necessary as a step to establish the tort of actionable negligence is to define the precise relationship from which the duty to take care is to be deduced. It is however, essential in English law that the duty should be established: the mere fact that a man is injured by another's act gives in itself no cause of action: if the act is deliberate, the party injured will have no claim in law even though the injury is intentional, so long as the other party is merely exercising a legal right: if the act involves lack of due care, again no case of actionable negligence will arise unless the duty to be careful exists. In *Donoghue's* case the duty was deduced simply from the facts relied on – namely, that the injured party was one of a class for whose use, in the contemplation and intention of the makers, the article was issued to the world, and the article was used by that party in the state in which it was prepared and issued without it being changed in any way and without there being any warning of, or means of detecting, the hidden danger: there was, it is true, no personal intercourse between the maker and the user; but though the duty is personal, because it is *inter partes*, it needs no interchange of words, spoken or written, or signs of offer or assent; it is thus different in character from any contractual relationship; no question of consideration between the parties is relevant: for these reasons the use of the word "privity" in this connection is apt to mislead, because of the suggestion of some overt relationship like that in contract, and the word "proximity" is open to the same objection ...

The principle of *Donoghue's* case can only be applied where the defect is hidden and unknown to the consumer, otherwise the directness of cause and effect is absent: the man who consumes or uses a thing which he knows to be noxious cannot complain in respect of whatever mischief follows, because it follows from his own conscious volition in choosing to incur the risk or certainty of mischance.

If the foregoing are the essential features of *Donoghue's* case they are also to be found, in their Lordships' judgment, in the present case. The presence of the deleterious chemical in the pants, due to negligence in manufacture, was a hidden and latent defect, just as much as were the remains of the snail in the opaque bottle: it could not be detected by any examination that could reasonably be made. Nothing happened between the making of the garments and their being worn to change their condition. The garments were made by the manufacturers for the purpose of being worn exactly as they were worn in fact by the appellant: it was not contemplated that they should be first washed. It is immaterial that the appellant has a claim in contract against the retailers, because that it a quite independent cause of action, based on different considerations, even though the damage may be the same. Equally irrelevant is any question of liability between the retailers and the manufacturers on the contract of sale between them. The tort liability is independent of any question of contract.

It was argued, but not perhaps very strongly, that *Donoghue's* case was a case of food or drink to be consumed internally, whereas the pants here were to be worn externally. No distinction, however, can be logically drawn for this purpose between a noxious thing taken internally and a noxious thing applied externally: the garments were made to be worn next to the skin: indeed Lord Atkin specifically puts as examples of what is covered by the principle he is enunciating things operating externally, such as "an ointment, a soap, a cleaning fluid or cleaning powder" ...

The decision in *Donoghue's* case did not depend on the bottle being stoppered and sealed: the essential point in this regard was that the article should reach the consumer or user subject to the same defect as it had when it left the manufacturer. That this was true of the garment is in their Lordships' opinion beyond question. At most there might in other cases be a greater difficulty of proof of the fact ...

No doubt many difficult problems will arise before the precise limits of the principle are defined: many qualifying conditions and many complications of fact may in the future come before the Courts for decision. It is enough now to say that their Lordships hold the present case to come within the principle of *Donoghue's* case ...

Notes and questions

1. Why can no logical distinction be drawn between a bottle of ginger-beer and a pair of underpants? Is a pair of underpants subject to the Food Safety Act 1990?

2. Was the plaintiff injured by a dangerous pair of underpants or by a dangerous product? Do 'products' exist or are they an invention of the legal mind?

3. What reasoning method was employed in this case: a method similar to that outlined by Lord Diplock in *Dorset Yacht* (above) or a method that one might describe as reasoning by analogy? What is the difference between induction, deduction and analogy?

4. Did *Grant* in any way alter the material facts of *Donoghue*?

5. 'The term "clear case" refers to a situation of isomorphy in which the applicability of a legal rule or a set of legal rules to certain facts is clear and unproblematic ... In these cases of isomorphy, where the facts of the case clearly fit into the operative facts of the legal rule, which attaches a legal consequence to those facts, judicial action can be accounted for by pointing to the fact that a rule is being almost unreflectively applied ...' (J Bengoetxea, *The Legal Reasoning of the European Court of Justice* (1993), pp 184, 186). Is *Grant* an easy case?

6. 'But problems arise when hard cases have to be decided and those decisions justified. What if no valid norm seems to govern the case? Which norm has to be chosen? What if a norm which tendentially governs the case leads to undesirable consequences? How must a norm be interpreted in order to obtain the best possible result? It is clear that all these questions take us to the domain of axiology, morality, or politics and yet legal justification is not expected to question the very system of law nor the ideology of adjudication embodied therein, ie the postulate that legal decisions have to be grounded on legally relevant sources, a postulate that embodies the rule of law ideal ...' (J Bengoetxea, *supra*, p 146). How do policy decisions fit into this scheme of easy and hard cases?

(b) The syllogism

FA & AB Ltd v Lupton [1972] AC 634 House of Lords

Lord Simon: ... A judicial decision will often be reached by a process of reasoning which can be reduced into a sort of complex syllogism, with the major premise consisting of a pre-existing rule of law (either statutory or judge-made) and with the minor premise consisting of the material facts of the case under immediate consideration. The conclusion is the decision of the case, which may or may not establish new law – in the vast majority of cases it will be merely the application of existing law to the facts judicially ascertained. Where the decision does constitute new law, this may or may not be expressly stated as a proposition of law: frequently the new law will appear only from subsequent comparison of, on the one hand, the material facts inherent in the major premise with, on the other, the material facts which constitute the minor premise. As a result of this comparison it will often be apparent that a rule has been extended by an analogy expressed or implied. I take as an example ... *National Telephone Co v Baker* (1893) 2 Ch 186. Major premise: the rule in *Rylands v Fletcher* (1866) LR 1 Exch 265, (1868) LR 3 HL 330. Minor premise: the defendant brought and stored electricity on his land for his own purpose; it escaped from the land; in so doing it injured the plaintiff's property. Conclusion: the defendant is liable in damages to the plaintiff (or would have been but for statutory protection). Analysis shows that the conclusion establishes a rule of law, which may be stated as 'for the purpose of the rule in *Rylands v Fletcher* electricity is analogous to water' or 'electricity is within the rule in *Rylands v Fletcher*'. That conclusion is now available as the major premise in the next case, in which some substance may be in question which in this context is not perhaps clearly analogous to water but is clearly analogous to electricity. In this way, legal luminaries are constituted which guide the wayfarer across uncharted ways.

Questions

1. Why is electricity analogous to water?

2. Does Lord Simon imply that knowledge of law consists of having knowledge of legal rules? If so, where does policy fit into the system?

3. What is meant by 'material facts'? What are the material facts of (a) *Donoghue v Stevenson* (see p 33) and (b) *Rylands v Fletcher* (see p 373)? Have the material facts of *Rylands* been altered by the *Cambridge Water* case (see p 375)?

4. Is this methodology an example of Lord Simon's 'one step at a time' approach (see pp 7-8)?

5. What is the hardest part of Lord Simon's complex syllogism: the decision that electricity is analogous to water or the decision that the defendant is or is not liable?

6. Is Lord Simon really telling us how law is applied to facts?

(c) Logic and categorisation

Whittaker v Campbell [1984] QB 318 Queen's Bench Division

Robert Goff LJ: ... We are concerned in the present case with the construction of certain words, viz., "without having the consent of the owner", in their context in a particular subsection of a criminal statute. However, the concept of consent is relevant in many branches of the law, including not only certain crimes but also the law of contract and the law of property. There is, we believe, danger in assuming that the law adopts a uniform definition of the word "consent" in all its branches ...

Questions

1. If the law adopts a uniform definition of 'offer', why should things be different with a word like 'consent'? (Cf *Fisher v Bell*, p 12.)

2. Are the categories of crime, contract and property distinct 'blocks' of rules? If so, to what extent do rules from different blocks interrelate?

Harbour Assurance Ltd v Kansa Ltd [1993] 3 WLR 42 Court of Appeal

This was a claim for a declaration that an arbitration clause contained in an insurance contract void for illegality was also void. The Court of Appeal held that the arbitration clause was not affected in this case by the illegality of the contract.

Hoffmann LJ: ... Mr Longmore's argument is extremely simple. He says that the question raised on the pleadings is whether the retrocession agreement was void *ab initio*. The arbitration clause formed part of the retrocession agreement. Therefore the issue must involve the validity of the arbitration clause itself.

Mr Longmore calls this logic. I call it over-simplification. The flaw in the logic, as it seems to me, lies in the ambiguity of the proposition that the arbitration clause "formed part" of the retrocession agreement. In one sense of course it did. It was clause 12 of a longer document which also dealt with the substantive rights and duties of the parties. But parties can include more than one agreement in a single document. They may say in express words that two separate agreements are intended. Or the question of whether the document amounts to one agreement or two may have to be answered by reference to the kind of provisions it contains ... There is no single concept of "forming part" which will provide the answer in every case ...

Notes and questions

1. Does this case indicate that logic is simply a form of argumentation? Or does it indicate that legal reasoning should never be seen as a matter of logic as such, but a matter of what premise is to be adopted?

2. 'It is clear for instance that if a man brings and keeps a wild beast on his land ... he may be liable for any damage occurring within or without his premises without proof of negligence. Such an exception will serve to illustrate the proposition that the law of torts has grown up historically in separate compartments and that beasts have travelled in a compartment of their own' (Lord Simonds, *Read v J Lyons & Co* [1947] AC 156). Is liability for a dangerous animal in France based on a general principle? If so, why should this principle not be relevant to English law?

3. '[T]he law should if possible be founded on comprehensive principles: compartmentalisation, particularly if producing anomaly, leads to the injustice of different results in fundamentally analogous circumstances' (Lord Simon, *National Carriers Ltd v Panalpina (Northern) Ltd* [1981] AC 675). Does this statement undermine Hoffman LJ's approach? Does it conflict with the view of Lord Simonds in *Read v Lyons* (above)? Does compartmentalisation always lead to injustice? What determines if something is 'fundamentally analogous'? Is electricity fundamentally analogous to water? Is a pair of underpants fundamentally analogous to a bottle of ginger-beer?

(d) Reasoning by elimination

Bryant v Herbert (1877) 3 CPD 389 Court of Appeal

(See p 63)

Notes and questions

1. Reasoning by elimination consists of examining and applying a complete range of categories, premises or hypotheses and eliminating all those that do not fit, so to speak. Thus the police might be said to reason in this way when they eliminate all potentional suspects but one: equally, the doctor who eliminates all the possible diseases save one. Is this a form of logical reasoning? Just how reliable is it?

2. If it is not contract then it must be tort. But what about unjust enrichment?

3. Read *Kingdom of Spain v Christie* (below p 112). Does reasoning by elimination play a role in the judgment?

(e) Mental imagery

Hall v Lorimer [1992] 1 WLR 939 Queen's Bench

Mummery J: ... In order to decide whether a person carries on business on his own account it is necessary to consider many different aspects of that person's work activity. This is not a mechanical exercise of running through items on a check list to see whether they are present in, or absent from, a given situation. The object of the exercise is to paint a picture from the accumulation of detail. The overall effect can only be appreciated by standing back from the detailed picture which has been painted, by viewing it from a distance and by making an informed, considered, qualitative appreciation of the whole. It is a matter of evaluation of the overall effect of the detail, which is not necessarily the same as the sum total of the individual details. Not all details are of equal weight or importance in any given situation. The details may also vary in importance from one situation to another.

Questions

1. Is Mummery J rejecting logic as the reasoning method in this particular case?

2. Were the judges in *Re Rowland* (above p 87) painting pictures?

3. Is the method being proposed by Mummery J very different from that proposed by Lord Simon in the *Lupton* case (above p 91)? Do

you think they are two different methods appealing to different aspects of the mind? Do humans think in terms of pictures?

4. What is the relationship, if any, between visual imagery, symmetry and logic? To what extent does the syllogism use visual imagery as its means of operation?[18]

(f) Analogy

Stocks v Magna Merchants Ltd [1973] 2 All ER 329 Queen's Bench Division

Arnold J: ... There is no authority on the point and the parties agree that it is a matter of principle, that is that it falls to be determined by reference to the proper method of assessing damages in such a case as the present ...

The present question, in my judgment, falls to be answered in favour of the plaintiff if the redundancy payment in quality and, in particular, as regards its remoteness or proximity in relation to the dismissal of the plaintiff is analogous to a retirement pension, or predominantly analogous to that, but in favour of the defendants if it is analogous, or predominantly analogous, in those respects to unemployment benefit ...

My view is that there is a closer analogy, as regards remoteness or proximity to the dismissal of the plaintiff, between the payment of unemployment benefit and the payment of a sum for redundancy under the 1965 Act than there is between the payment of a retirement pension and a redundancy payment. Consequently, in my judgment ... the right conclusion here is that the amount of the redundancy payment does fall to be deducted in calculating the damages payable by the defendants to the plaintiff ...

Questions

1. Why is there 'a closer analogy' between these two kinds of payments?

2. Is this a 'painting a picture' case?

The Mediana [1900] AC 113 House of Lords

Earl of Halsbury LC: ... Now, in the particular case before us ... the broad proposition seems to me to be that by a wrongful act of the defendants the plaintiffs were deprived of their vessel. When I say deprived of their vessel, I will not use the phrase 'the use of the vessel'. What right has a wrongdoer to consider what use you are going to make of your vessel? More than one case has been put to illustrate this: for example, the owner of a horse, or of a chair. Supposing a person took away a chair out of my room and kept it for 12 months, could anybody say you had a right to diminish the damages by showing that I

---

18 Cf G Samuel, *The Foundations of Legal Reasoning*, Maklu/Blackstone, 1994, p 121.

did not usually sit in that chair, or that there were plenty of other chairs in the room? The proposition so nakedly stated appears to me to be absurd ...

Questions

1. Why should a rule applicable to a chair also be applicable to a lightship? Are they not entirely different kinds of property?
2. Why would it be absurd for a defendant who mistakenly deprived an owner of one of his chairs to argue that the owner had suffered no damage?

Butler Machine Tool Co Ltd v Ex-Cell-O Corporation [1979] 1 WLR 401 Court of Appeal

Lord Denning MR: ... Applying this guide, it will be found that in most cases when there is a 'battle of forms' there is a contract as soon as the last of the forms is sent and received without objection being taken to it ... The difficulty is to decide which form, or which part of which form, is a term or condition of the contract. In some cases the battle is won by the man who fires the last shot. He is the man who puts forward the latest term and conditions: and, if they are not objected to by the other party, he may be taken to have agreed to them ... In some cases, however, the battle is won by the man who gets the blow in first ... There are yet other cases where the battle depends on the shots fired on both sides ...

Lawton LJ: ... In my judgment, the battle has to be conducted in accordance with set rules. It is a battle more on classical 18th century lines when convention decided who had the right to open fire first rather than in accordance with the modern concept of attrition ...

Notes and questions

1. Is war a useful analogy through which to understand contractual relationships?
2. 'Perhaps ... the most that can be attempted is a broad categorisation of the decided cases according to the type of situation in which liability has been established in the past in order to found an argument by analogy' (Lord Oliver, *Caparo Industries Plc v Dickman* [1990] 1 AC 605). Does this mean that English case law is not actually about the induction of general principles of liability?
3. 'The owner or keeper of ... an animal has an absolute duty to confine and control it so that it shall not do injury to others ... But such an exceptional case as this affords no justification for its extension by analogy' (Lord MacMillan, *Read v J Lyons & Co* [1947] AC 156). Why?
4. Is reasoning by analogy a form of painting a picture along the lines suggested in *Hall v Lorimer* (above p 94)?
5. Are metaphors forms of analogy?

(g) Metaphor

**Spartan Steel & Alloys Ltd v Martin & Co (Contractors) Ltd [1973] 1 QB 27
Court of Appeal**

Lord Denning MR: ... I do not like this doctrine of 'parasitic damages'. I do not like the very word 'parasite'. A 'parasite' is one who is a useless hanger-on sucking the substance out of others. 'Parasitic' is the adjective derived from it. It is a term of abuse. It is an opprobrious epithet. The phrase 'parasitic damages' conveys to my mind the idea of damages which ought not in justice to be awarded, but which somehow or other have been allowed to get through by hanging on to others. If such be the concept underlying the doctrine, then the sooner it is got rid of the better.

Questions

1. If Lord Denning finds parasitic damages so offensive, why does he allow the plaintiff in *Jackson v Horizon Holidays* (below p 121) to recover them?

2. Is this reasoning through painting a picture?

3. Is Lord Denning proposing a reason or putting forward an argument?

4. Read M G Duncan, 'In Slime and Darkness' (1994) 68 *Tulane Law Review* 725. Are metaphors central to our understanding of criminal law?

(h) The appeal to the facts

Re Rowland [1963] 1 Ch 1 Court of Appeal

(See p 87)

Notes and questions

1. "[Imagination] contributes to the fulfilment of theorising through the hypothetical variation of specific factual situations so as to bring out the essential core and borderlines of legal ideas. What is crucial here is imagination's capacity for conjuring up and holding-fast to an infinity of hypothetical situations which present exemplifications of legal problems and doctrines both as if they were actual and under the governance of the operationalism principle of legal ideas .... Imagination allows both judges and theorists to both make available and explore the nature and limits of legal ideas *qua* ideas. For example, in legal education we frequently take the facts of a decided

case and ask students to reflectively consider, on a 'what-if' basis, a series of imaginative variations ...' (M Salter, Towards a Phenomenology of Legal Thinking (1992) 23 *Journal of the British Society for Phenomenology* 167, 172). Does *Re Rowland* provide a good illustration of this thesis?

2. 'Much of the strength of Roman law is due to the fact that it is both rooted in actuality and linked to procedure. It contrived to avoid the patchiness of a purely casuistic system because, rather like professors of law in the United States when teaching with the method that Socrates used in conversation with slaves, the jurists hypothetically varied the actual facts of the situations presented to them, and considered what the legal effect of such hypothetical variations would be' (T Weir, Contracts in Rome and England (1992) 66 *Tulane Law Review* 1615, 1616-1617). Do common lawyers reason in the same way as the classical Roman lawyers?[19]

3. Does the 'what-if' approach nevertheless involve the use of logic?

Blackpool & Fylde Aero Club Ltd v Blackpool Borough Council [1990] 1 WLR 1195 Court of Appeal

(See also p 243)

Bingham LJ: ... [I]f he submits a conforming tender before the deadline he is entitled, not as a matter of mere expectation but of contractual right, to be sure that his tender will after the deadline be opened and considered ... Had the club, before tendering, inquired of the council whether it could rely on any timely and conforming tender being considered along with others, I feel quite sure that the answer would have been "of course". The law would, I think, be defective if it did not give effect to that.

Questions

1. Is Bingham LJ adopting a similar reasoning approach to that adopted by Lord Denning in *Re Rowland*?

2. What justifies the move from 'expectation' to 'right'? What facilitates the move?

(i) Values

R v Central Television Plc [1994] 3 WLR 20 Court of Appeal

(See p 71)

---

19 For some good examples of Roman legal reasoning see C Kolbert, *Justinian: The Digest of Roman Law*, Penguin 1979.

Notes and questions

1. 'In practical terms the effectiveness of a legal argument is tied to its conformity with the values held by the person to whom it is addressed. It presupposes a tacit, but vital, accord on the values held by society in whose name the judge renders justice. This accord has to be carried even as far as the hierarchy established between these values. There are the "universal hierarchies: the values relative to persons are superior to the values relative to things; a man is not to be run over in order to avoid a dog; a human life is worth more than private property". And the "hierarchies that are often said to be social: the testimony of a retired general is worth more, in support of a proposition, than that of an active tramp" [*BREDIN*]' (J Ghestin & G Goubeaux, *Traité de droit civil: introduction générale* (3rd ed, 1990), pp 46-47). Has the criminal law always accepted that human life is worth more than private property? To what extent does the law of tort put human life before economic interests?

2. 'There are several good things in life, such as liberty, bodily integrity, land, possessions, reputation, wealth, privacy, dignity, perhaps even life itself. Lawyers call these goods "interests". These interests are all good, but they are not all equally good. This is evident when they come into conflict (one may jettison cargo to save passengers, but not *vice versa*, and one may detain a thing, but not a person, as security for a debt). Because these interests are not equally good, the protection afforded to them by the law is not equal: the law protects the better interests better. Accordingly, the better the interest invaded, the more readily does the law give compensation for that harm. In other words, whether you get the money you claim depends on what you are claiming it for. It would be surprising if it were otherwise' (T Weir, *A Casebook on Tort* (7th ed, 1992), pp 4-5). Does English law protect bodily integrity better than it protects reputation? Is it easier for an employer to obtain compensation for financial loss caused by a uncaring workers going on strike than it is for a worker to obtain compensation for personal injury caused by an uncaring employer?

3. Did the law of defamation better protect the interests of the late Robert Maxwell than the interests of the pensioners who once worked for one of his companies?

4. Does the Unfair Contract Terms Act 1977 s 2(1) and the Consumer Protection Act 1987 s 5(1) reflect values?

(j) Policy

Barclays Bank v O'Brien [1992] 3 WLR 593 Court of Appeal [1993] 3 WLR 786 House of Lords

(See also p 157)

Scott LJ: ... These authorities seem to me to leave the developing law, if not at the crossroads, at least at the junction of two diverging roads ... The choice between the two roads cannot, in my opinion, be made simply by reference to binding authority. Binding authority can be found to justify either. The choice should, I think, be a matter of policy. Ought the law to treat married women who provide security for their husband's debts, and others in an analogous position, as requiring special protection? The position of married women today, both generally and *vis-à-vis* their husbands is very different from what it was ... But.... in the culturally and ethnically mixed community in which we live, the degree of emancipation of women is uneven.

Lord Browne-Wilkinson: ... On the other hand, it is important to keep a sense of balance in approaching these cases. It is easy to allow sympathy for the wife who is threatened with the loss of her home at the suit of a rich bank to obscure an important public interest *viz*, the need to ensure that the wealth currently tied up in the matrimonial home does not become economically sterile. If the rights secured to wives by the law renders vulnerable loans granted on the security of matrimonial homes, institutions will be unwilling to accept such security, thereby reducing the flow of loan capital to business enterprises. It is therefore essential that a law designed to protect the vulnerable does not render the matrimonial home unacceptable as security to financial institutions.

Notes and question

1. 'In previous times, when faced with a new problem, the judges have not openly asked themselves the question: what is the best policy for the law to adopt? But the question has always been there in the background. It has been concealed behind such questions as: Was the defendant under a duty to the plaintiff? Was the relationship between them sufficiently proximate? Was the injury direct or indirect? Was it foreseeable, or not? Was it too remote? And so forth' (Lord Denning MR, *Dutton v Bognor Regis UDC* [1972] 1 QB 373). Does an appeal to 'policy' really help decide cases? Are not judges usurping the role of politicians?

2. 'Of course, every rule of law is a legal manifestation of public policy. But your Lordships are ... instantly concerned with "public policy" in a narrower sense – namely, consideration of social interests beyond the purely legal which call for the modification of a normal legal rule ...' (Lord Simon, *D v NSPCC* [1978] AC 171). Is policy simply the link between the notion of a legal rule and the notion of an interest?

3. What is the relationship between legal rights and policy?

(k) Interpretation of rights

**Spartan Steel & Alloys Ltd v Martin & Co (Contractors) Ltd [1973] 1 QB 27
Court of Appeal**

This was an action for damages by the owners of a factory against a firm of contractors for damage and loss suffered when the supply of electricity was cut off as a result of the contractors, while excavating with a mechanical shovel on the highway, carelessly cutting through an electric cable. The factory owners claimed damages under three heads: (i) damage to metal in a furnace when the power failed; (ii) loss of profit on the ruined metal in the furnace; (iii) loss of profit on four other metal melting operations that could have been carried out if the electricity had not been off. A majority of the Court of Appeal held that the plaintiffs could recover under heads (i) and (ii), but not under head (iii).

Lord Denning MR: ... At bottom I think the question of recovering economic loss is one of policy. Whenever the courts draw a line to mark out the bounds of duty, they do it as matter of policy so as to limit the responsibility of the defendant. Whenever the courts set bounds to the damages recoverable – saying that they are, or are not, too remote – they do it as matter of policy so as to limit the liability of the defendant

In many of the cases where economic loss has been held not to be recoverable, it has been put on the ground that the defendant was under no duty to the plaintiff. Thus where a person is injured in a road accident by the negligence of another, the negligent driver owes a duty to the injured man himself, but he owes no duty to the servant of the injured man – see *Best v Samuel Fox & Co Ltd*: nor to the master of the injured man – *Inland Revenue Commissioners v Hambrook*: nor to anyone else who suffers loss because he had a contract with the injured man – see *Simpson & C v Thomson*: nor indeed to anyone who only suffers economic loss on account of the accident: see *Kirkham v Boughey*. Likewise, when property is damaged by the negligence of another, the negligent tortfeasor owes a duty to the owner or possessor of the chattel, but not to one who suffers loss only because he had a contract entitling him to use the chattel or giving him a right to receive it at some later date: see *Elliott Steam Tug Co Ltd v Shipping Controller* and *Margarine Union GmbH v Cambay Prince Steamship*.

In other cases, however, the defendant seems clearly to have been under a duty to the plaintiff, but the economic loss has not been recovered because it is too remote. Take the illustration given by Blackburn J in *Cattle v Stockton Waterworks Co*, when water escapes from a reservoir and floods a coal mine where many men are working. Those who had their tools or clothes destroyed could recover: but those who only lost their wages could not. Similarly, when the defendants' ship negligently sank a ship which was being towed by a tug, the owner of the tug lost his remuneration, but he could not recover it from the negligent ship: though the same duty (of navigation with reasonable care) was owed to both tug and tow: see *Société Anonyme de Remorquage à Hélice v Bennetts*. In such cases if the plaintiff or his property had been physically injured, he would have recovered: but, as he only suffered economic loss, he is held not entitled to recover. This is, I should think, because the loss is regarded by the law as too remote: see *King v Phillips*.

On the other hand, in the cases where economic loss by itself has been held to be recoverable, it is plain that there was a duty to the plaintiff and the loss was not too remote. Such as when one ship negligently runs down another ship, and damages it, with the result that the cargo has to be discharged and reloaded. The negligent ship was already under a duty to the cargo owners: and they can recover the cost of discharging and reloading it, as it is not too remote: see *Morrison Steamship Co Ltd v Greystoke Castle (Cargo Owners)*. Likewise, when a banker negligently gives a reference to one who acts on it, the duty is plain and the damage is not too remote: see *Hedley Byrne & Co Ltd v Heller & Partners Ltd*.

The more I think about these cases, the more difficult I find it to put each into its proper pigeon-hole. Sometimes I say: "There was no duty". In others I say: "The damage was too remote". So much so that I think the time has come to discard those tests which have proved so elusive. It seems to me better to consider the particular relationship in hand, and see whether or not, as a matter of policy, economic loss should be recoverable, or not. Thus in *Weller & Co v Foot and Mouth Disease Research Institute* it was plain that the loss suffered by the auctioneers was not recoverable, no matter whether it is put on the ground that there was no duty or that the damage was too remote. Again in *Electrochrome Ltd. v Welsh Plastics Ltd*, it is plain that the economic loss suffered by the plaintiffs' factory (due to the damage to the fire hydrant) was not recoverable, whether because there was no duty or that it was too remote ...

The second consideration is the nature of the hazard, namely, the cutting of the supply of electricity. This is a hazard which we all run. It may be due to a short circuit, to a flash of lightning, to a tree falling on the wires, to an accidental cutting of the cable, or even to the negligence of someone or other. And when it does happen, it affects a multitude of persons; not as a rule by way of physical damage to them or their property, but by putting them to inconvenience, and sometimes to economic loss. The supply is usually restored in a few hours, so the economic loss is not very large. Such a hazard is regarded by most people as a thing they must put up with – without seeking compensation from anyone. Some there are who install a stand-by system. Others seek refuge by taking out an insurance policy against breakdown in the supply. But most people are content to take the risk on themselves. When the supply is cut off, they do not go running round to their solicitor. They do not try to find out whether it was anyone's fault. They just put up with it. They try to make up the economic loss by doing more work next day. This is a healthy attitude which the law should encourage ...

Edmund Davies LJ (dissenting): ... For my part, I cannot see why the £400 loss of profit here sustained should be recoverable and not the £1,767. It is common ground that both types of loss were equally foreseeable and equally direct consequences of the defendants' admitted negligence, and the only distinction drawn is that the former figure represents the profit lost as a result of the physical damage done to the material in the furnace at the time when power was cut off. But what has that purely fortuitous fact to do with legal principle? In my judgment, nothing ...

Notes and questions

1. 'But suppose ... that a judge successfully justifies a decision in a hard case, like *Spartan Steel*, on grounds not of policy but of principle.

Suppose, that is, that he is able to show that the plaintiff has a right to recover its damages ... [A]n argument of principle fixes on some interest presented by the proponent of the right it describes, an interest alleged to be of such a character as to make irrelevant the fine discriminations of any argument of policy that might oppose it. A judge who is insulated from the demands of the political majority whose interests the right would trump is, therefore, in a better position to evaluate the argument ... The rights thesis ... provides a more satisfactory explanation of how judges use precedent in hard cases than the explanation provided by any theory that gives a more prominent place to policy ... The rights thesis provides that judges decide hard cases by confirming or denying concrete rights ...' (R Dworkin, *Taking Rights Seriously* (1977), pp 85, 87, 101, 116-117). Dworkin talks of rights but then switches to the notion of an interest: is he not undermining his own argument? Is there not a major difference between rights and interests? If the law endows some interest with the status of a right, is this not a matter of policy? Do English lawyers, as far as tort cases are concerned at any rate, think in terms of rights?

2. 'We can find an even more fruitful comparison between literature and law ... by constructing an artificial genre of literature that we might call the chain novel. In this enterprise a group of novelists writes a novel seriatim; each novelist in the chain interprets the chapters he has been given in order to write a new chapter, which is then added to what the next novelist receives, and so on. Each has the job of writing his chapter so as to make the novel being constructed the best it can be, and the complexity of this task models the complexity of deciding a hard case under law ...' (R Dworkin, *Law's Empire* (1986), p 229). Can you reconcile this chain novel method with his rights approach outlined above? Is Dworkin proposing a theory of legal method or is he simply providing an interpretative analogy? Does this Dworkin analogy tell us anything about law and legal reasoning as objects of a science?

3. Can *Spartan* be said to involve 'concrete rights'? Are rights dependent upon texts?

(I) Practical reasoning

The Eurymedon [1975] AC 154 Privy Council

Lord Wilberforce: ... If the choice, and the antithesis, is between a gratuitous promise and a promise for consideration, as it must be, in the absence of a *tertium quid*, there can be little doubt which, in commercial reality, this is ... English law, having committed itself to a rather technical and schematic doctrine of contract, in application takes a practical approach, often at the cost of forcing the facts to fit uneasily into the marked slots of offer, acceptance and consideration ...

Ex parte King [1984] 3 All ER 897 Court of Appeal

Griffiths LJ: ... [T]he common law of England has not always developed on strictly logical lines, and where logic leads down a path that is beset with practical difficulties the courts have not been frightened to turn aside and seek the pragmatic solution that will best serve the needs of society.

Smith v Eric Bush [1990] 1 AC 831 House of Lords

Lord Templeman: ... The public are exhorted to purchase their homes and cannot find houses to rent ... In these circumstances it is not fair and reasonable for building societies and valuers to agree together to impose on purchasers the risk of loss arising as a result of incompetence or carelessness on the part of valuers.

Bridge v Campbell Discount Co Ltd [1962] AC 600 House of Lords

Lord Denning: ... Let no one mistake the injustice of this. It means that equity commits itself to this absurd paradox: it will grant relief to a man who breaks his contract but will penalise the man who keeps it. If this be the state of equity today, then it is in sore need of an overhaul so as to restore its first principles.

Re Grosvenor [1944] Ch 138 Court of Appeal

Lord Greene MR: ... The statement that time is infinitely divisible was said to be a scientific fact. I should prefer to call it a metaphysical conception. No doubt, when a bevy of angels is performing saltatory exercises on the point of a needle it is always possible to find room for one more, but propositions of this character appear to me to be ill suited for adoption by the law of this country which proceeds on principles of practical common sense.

Notes and questions

1. 'If patriotism is the last refuge of the scoundrel, then common sense must be the last refuge of the incompetent ... Common sense is a quintessentially English obsession. It suits the English self-image to suppose that in any area of life and experience there is a corpus of plain, simple, unadorned, instinctive ways of doing things ... Nothing fancy is how we like it. Nothing intellectual. Nothing Continental. British common sense is, of course, particularly sensible' (Martin Kettle, *The Guardian*, 19 February 1994, p 25). Is this a fair comment in respect of some forms of reasoning in English courts?

2. What do you think Lord Wilberforce means by 'commercial reality'? Does such a notion imply 'commercial unreality'? Industry lobbied against strict liability in the area of products: were they advocating a

position based on 'commercial reality'? Is, then, the *Consumer Protection Act 1987* founded on commercial unreality?

R v Self [1992] 1 WLR 657 Court of Appeal

Garland J: ... The view of this court is that little profit can be had from taking examples and trying to reduce them to absurdity. The words of the statute are clear and applying those words to this case there was no arrestable offence committed. It necessarily follows that the two offences ... [of assault] could not be committed because there was no power to apprehend or detain the appellant.

Re Dick [1953] Ch 343 Court of Appeal

Evershed MR: ... I confess that I have found the case one of most vexing difficulty, and I have been conscious of some vacillation and many doubts during the course of the careful arguments to which we have listened. I have, however, come to the conclusion that I cannot hold that the judge wrongly determined the issue presented to him, and my doubts have been, perhaps, assuaged by the circumstance that my two brethren have felt, perhaps with less nervousness than I, that the conclusion reached is right.

X Ltd v Morgan-Grampian Plc [1990] 2 WLR 421 Court of Appeal.

Lord Donaldson MR: ... Lord Hailsham once said that "the rule of law is a confidence trick". What he meant was that the rule of law depends upon public confidence and public acceptance of the system whereby Parliament makes the laws, the courts enforce them and the vast majority of citizens accept them until they can get them changed. The stance of the journalists' profession in relation to this particular law, of which it happens to disapprove, threatens this confidence and acceptance. This, surely, is contrary to the highest possible public interest.

Questions

1. If it turns out that as a matter of human rights the journalist was justified, does this mean that it is judges like Lord Donaldson who are undermining confidence?[20] (Compare Lord Donaldson's views with those of Hoffmann LJ in *R v Central Television Plc* (above p 71.))

2. If law is a confidence trick, what does this say about legal reasoning? Is Lord Donaldson's observation of much help to the law student?

3. Is freedom of the press not the highest possible public interest?

Fothergill v Monarch Airlines Ltd [1981] AC 251 House of Lords

Lord Diplock: ... Elementary justice or ... the need for legal certainty demands that the rules by which a citizen is to be bound should be ascertainable by him (or, more realistically, by a competent lawyer advising him) ...

---

20 See also *McIlkenny v Chief Constable of W Midlands* [1980] 2 All ER 227.

Parry v Cleaver [1970] AC 1 House of Lords

Lord Reid: ... It would be revolting to the ordinary man's sense of justice, and therefore contrary to public policy, that the sufferer should have his damages reduced so that he would gain nothing from the benevolence of his friends or relations or of the public at large, and that the only gainer would be the wrongdoer.

Questions

1. What is meant by 'justice' in Lord Diplock's and Lord Reid's comment? (Cf Lord Denning in *Willis*, below.)

2. Because something is revolting to an ordinary person's sense of justice, does it actually follow that it is therefore against public policy? Are not justice and policy expressing quite different ideas?

Dunne v North Western Gas Board [1964] 2 QB 806 Court of Appeal

Sellers LJ: ... Gas, water and also electricity services are well-nigh a necessity of modern life, or at least are generally demanded as a requirement for the common good ... It would seem odd that facilities so much sought after by the community and approved by their legislators should be actionable at common law because they have been brought to places where they are required and have escaped without negligence by an unforeseen sequence of mishaps.

Questions

1. Would the *Conseil d'État* find it so odd? (Cf Chapter 1.)

2. Does Denning LJ in *Watt v Hertfordshire CC* [1954] 1 WLR 835 take a similar approach to Sellers LJ?

3. Does the conclusion follow from the premise? Could it not be argued that the 'common good' is a ground for imposing strict liability? Why should an individual be made to suffer for the common good? Is the ordinary man's sense of justice of any relevance here?

RH Willis & Son v British Car Auctions [1978] 2 All ER 392 Court of Appeal

Lord Denning MR: ... This system is the commercial way of doing justice between the parties. It means that all concerned are protected. The true owner is protected by the strict law of conversion. He can recover against the innocent acquirer and the innocent handler. But those innocents are covered by insurance so that the loss is not borne by any single individual but spread through the community at large.

Kingdom of Spain v Christie, Manson & Woods Ltd [1986] 1 WLR 1120 Chancery Division

(See also p 112)

Sir Nicolas Browne-Wilkinson VC: ... In the pragmatic way in which English law has developed, a man's legal rights are in fact those which are protected by a cause of action. It is not in accordance, as I understand it, with the principles of English law to analyse rights as being something separate from the remedy given to the individual ... [I]n my judgment, in the ordinary case to establish a legal or equitable right you have to show that all the necessary elements of the cause of action are either present or threatened ...

Hill v C A Parsons & Co Ltd [1972] Ch 305 Court of Appeal

Lord Denning MR: ... The judge said that he felt constrained by the law to refuse an injunction. But that is too narrow a view of the principles of law. He has overlooked the fundamental principle that, whenever a man has a right, the law should give a remedy. The Latin maxim is *ubi jus ibi remedium*. This principle enables us to step over the trip-wires of previous cases and to bring the law into accord with the needs of today ...

Questions

1. Can you reconcile the approach of Brown-Wilkinson VC with that of Lord Denning in *Parsons*?
2. Is the approach of Brown-Wilkinson VC *ubi remedium ibi jus*?

News of the World Ltd v Friend [1973] 1 All ER 422 House of Lords

Lord Simon of Glaisdale: My Lords, the philosopher FH Bradley described metaphysics as the finding of bad reasons for what we believe on instinct. An opinion on a short point of construction is apt to be the rationalisation of a first impression; and I am all the more conscious of Bradley's jibe when I find myself differing from my noble and learned friends whose judgment I deeply respect ...

Notes and questions

1. Can you list the various different types of arguments and reasons set out in this sub-section on practical reasoning? How do they relate to each other and to the other methodologies set out in this chapter?
2. Is there a difference between reasoning, argumentation and justification? How would you classify the various statements in this sub-section?
3. Is the role of the judge simply to apply the rules?
4. 'Traditional rule systems are brittle, and can be made to capture ... detailed phenomena only awkwardly (eg, by having a separate rule for each 'exception') ... Rules and symbols have their most obvious use in building higher-level models that abstract away from many of the detailed phenomena exhibited in behavioural data. When the details are not needed these are the models of choice (at least for description); but to model the actual mechanisms of cognition, more

detailed, less brittle models are needed ... [T]he behaviour of the cognitive system is not rule-governed, but rather is only (approximately) rule-described' (W Bechtel & A Abrahamsen, *Connectionism and the Mind* (1991), p 227). When one argues about causes of actions and rights is one arguing about rules? Is knowledge of law knowledge of rules?

5. Just how important is logic to legal method?

6. '[A] theory dealing with human facts is constantly menaced, if one is not careful, with becoming an ideology, substituting myths for concepts and prescriptions for descriptions' (G-G Granger, *La science et les sciences* (Presses Universitaires de France, 1993), p 99). Discuss in relation to the judicial statements set out in this chapter. Is Dworkin's chain novel thesis in danger of reducing legal method to a 'mythical', rather than 'scientific', process?

(m) Symmetry

Read v J Lyons & Co [1947] AC 156 House of Lords

Lord Simonds: ... My Lords, it was urged by counsel for the appellant that a decision against her when the plaintiff in the *Rainham* case succeeded would show a strange lack of symmetry in the observation. But your Lordships will not fail to observe that such a decision is in harmony with the development of a strictly analogous branch of the law, the law of nuisance, in which also negligence is not a necessary ingredient in the case ... To confine the rule in *Rylands v Fletcher* ... appears to me consistent and logical.

Questions

1. What is meant by 'symmetry in the law'?

2. What is the relationship between symmetry and (a) reasoning by syllogism and (b) reasoning by analogy?

3. '*L'article 1384 [du Code civil] ... retrouve sa symétrie'* (J Ghestin, Note, sub Ass plén., 29 mars 1991, JCP 1991.II.21673 no 1). Discuss.

4. Does symmetry play a role in legal theory?

5. Is the symmetry of the German Civil Code (BGB) similar to that of the French Civil Code? What about the new Dutch Civil Code – does this have a quite different symmetry?

6. Is symmetry in law (and/or legal theory) capable of acting as an object in itself of legal knowledge?

7. Is symmetry important in the understanding of analogies and metaphores?

8. Is there a symmetry between art 1382 and art 1384 of the Code Civil? If so, what is the effect of an absence of such symmetry in other legal systems?

CHAPTER 3

REMEDIES

1 INTRODUCTION

One of the themes to have emerged from the previous chapters is the tension between rights and remedies. According to one judge it is the entitlement to a remedy that defines the existence of rights (see p 107 and below p 112), whereas, according to another judge, the idea of a legal right has now liberated itself from the law of actions.[1] *Ubi ius ibi remedium* (p 117). Yet whatever the actual situation with respect to the relationship between rights and remedies, there is no doubt that English law continues to see the remedy as an active institution in the sense that it is a focal point for legal rules capable of operating at the level both of law and of fact. Indeed it is the remedy which takes the initiative when it comes to expanding liability (see eg, *Jackson v Horizon Holidays*, below p 121). Thus the tendency of the common lawyer is to ask 'Has my client a remedy?' rather than 'Has my client a right to ... ?' And while this thinking is the result of English legal history, as various writers have pointed out,[2] it is not merely a piece of antiquarian thinking and practice; the remedy, being a legal institution (that is a factual and legal focal point to which rules attach), can act as a vehicle for organising the facts in such a way as they appear to reveal legal rights. This is why a celebrated medieval jurist said of Roman law (which also used the law of actions in an active sense), *ex facto ius oritur* (law arises out of fact). If P is entitled to an injunction (*actio*) to stop D interfering with P's live musical performances by illegally recording them, this in itself will both turn the live performances into a form of property and create a legal relationship (*dominium*) between P and his performances.[3] One does not need, as the next case illustrates, a theory of ownership or possession.

---

1   For the historical and theoretical background see H F Jolowicz, *Roman Foundations of Modern Law* (Oxford, 1957), pp 61-81.
2   See eg, J A Jolowicz, *The Judicial Protection of Fundamental Rights under English Law* (Cambridge/Tilburg Lectures, 1980), pp 5-6.
3   See *Ex p Island Records* [1978] 1 Ch 122.

Kingdom of Spain v Christie, Mason & Woods Ltd [1986] 1 WLR 1120
Chancery Division

Sir Nicholas Browne-Wilkinson VC: These proceedings relate to an oil painting by Goya called "La Marquesa de Santa Cruz". By an originating summons dated 5 March 1986 the Kingdom of Spain claims certain declarations relating to three documents; two of them are dated 30 March 1983 and the third is dated 5 April 1983. Those three documents purport to be official documents of the Government of Spain authorising the export of the picture from Spain. The declarations are sought against the first defendant, Christie Manson & Woods Ltd ("Christie's"), who is offering the picture for sale at auction in London on 11 April this year on the instructions of the owner of the picture, the second defendant, Overseas Art Investments Ltd ("OAI") ...

At first sight I thought that ... if it were established that the picture had been exported from Spain with the use of forged documents, Christie's, giving effect to that clause, would not have been prepared to auction it. That certainly was the view of the plaintiffs when they started these proceedings. However, in the course of argument counsel for Christie's made it clear that even if it were to be declared by the court that the documents were forgeries, Christie's would feel free to continue with the sale. They take the view that [the Dealers Code of Practice] does not apply where the vendor has acquired the picture innocently (ie, is not implicated in the illegal export) and that such a case falls to be dealt with under clause 4. Christie's also apparently take the view that the Spanish Government have refused to agree "satisfactory reimbursement" to OAI.

Whether Christie's are right on either of those views is not for this court to say. The fact is that Christie's are prepared to and will go ahead with the sale, even if the documents are found by the court to be forgeries. In any event the Code is not a document on which the Spanish Government can directly rely; it is not a party to the Code ...

Against that background I turn to the law.

This is an application to strike out the proceedings before trial. That is an extreme step for a court to take and is only done when it is obvious and clear beyond doubt that the plaintiff has no claim fit to go to trial. To shut out somebody from the judgment seat has been said many times to be an extreme step. Only in exceptional circumstances, therefore, is it right on such an application finally to determine any difficult point of law. Normally, if a case involves sustained argument, it is not a case for striking out but for a preliminary point of law to be set down.

In the present case, as will emerge, as the argument went on, the basis of possible resistance to striking out changed, and what at one time might have been thought to have been a plain and obvious case may no longer be so.

For the purpose of considering whether a case should be struck out as disclosing no cause of action, it is necessary for the court to assume the truth of the facts alleged by the plaintiffs; but I must emphasise that that is an assumption.

The fundamental difficulty in this case is that the plaintiffs have chosen only to claim declarations. They have made no claim against the defendants by way of injunction or for damages. It is clearly established by the authorities that in proceedings for a declaration, other than for judicial review, the court will only make such a declaration in defence of a legal or equitable right of the plaintiff: see *Gouriet v Union of Post Office Workers* [1978] AC 435, 501 ... Obviously in that statement "legal rights" include equitable rights ...

The defendants in this case contend that the Spanish Government have no rights as against them at all relating to the use of the allegedly forged documents. The central question therefore is what legal or equitable rights do the Spanish Government have in relation to these documents and as against these defendants.

During the course of the argument my view has changed more than once. At the outset it seemed to me extraordinary if the law of England provided no civil remedy to a man, whose signature or stamp has been forged on a document, to prevent the continued circulation of that document as a genuine document. If the law provides no such remedy for a citizen of this country to prevent the continued circulation of a false representation in the form of a document, in my judgment the law is defective.

However, as the argument developed it seemed to me more and more likely that I was going to be forced to the conclusion that no such right did exist. Mr Littman, for the plaintiffs, put his case in this way. He said he did not need to show an accrued cause of action to restrain the use of the documents; all he had to do was to isolate a right which, when other factors were added to it, would constitute a cause of action. He relied on three well known forms of action: the right to restrain passing off, malicious falsehood and defamation. As I understand it, he did not claim that he had an accrued cause of action for any of those wrongs; and, indeed, in my judgment he plainly has not.

The requisite constituent elements of a claim in passing off are, first, that there has to be misrepresentation; second, that it is made by a trader in the course of trade; third, to a prospective customer of his, or to consumers of goods or services supplied by him; fourth, which is calculated to injure the business or goodwill of another trader; and fifth, which causes actual damage to the business or goodwill of the trader by whom the action is brought. It would be stretching concepts of trade and business in this case well beyond anything that has previously occurred to suggest either that the Spanish Government are traders or that OAI is a trader in business.

As to malicious falsehood, there has to be not only an untrue statement but that untrue statement must be made maliciously and said without any belief in its truth. The evidence here certainly does not suggest that that is the current position.

Finally, in relation to defamation, in addition to any untrue statement there has to be at least damage to the reputation of the plaintiff. At the moment I can see no way in which it can be said that the continued circulation of forged documents would be defamatory to the Spanish Government.

However, Mr Littman submits that that is not the question. He says that the underlying right in each of those forms of action is the basic right of a citizen not to have untruths told about himself. Having identified that as the right, he says that the other elements necessary to bring an action successfully are mere appendages or conditions attached to the possession of a cause of action rather than being a basic legal right protected. Therefore, says Mr Littman, he is entitled in this case to a declaration of the falsity of the documents, there being a general right to restrain the circulation of untrue statements. He has shown a basic right and therefore is entitled to a declaration to the effect that the documents are untrue. I was unpersuaded by that analysis. In the pragmatic way in which English law has developed, a man's legal rights are in fact those which are protected by a cause of action. It is not in accordance, as I understand it, with the principles of English law to analyse rights as being something separate from the remedy given to the individual. Of course, in *quia timet* proceedings you do not have, for example, to show that damage has occurred even if damage is a necessary constituent of the cause of action. It is enough to show that the defendant has an intention to do an act which, if done, will cause damage. But in my judgment, in the ordinary case to establish a legal or equitable right you have to show that all the necessary elements of the cause of action are either present or threatened. I am fortified in that view by submissions made by Mr Scott for OAI that if there were any such general right as Mr Littman contends for, it is impossible to see why the specific constituent elements of passing off or malicious falsehood have ever developed. If every man can protect the false use of his name or reputation by having a basic right so to do, why is it that the courts have developed the very limited class of cases in which an action for passing off or malicious falsehood can be brought?

Therefore, I was very far from satisfied that Mr Littman had shown that the plaintiffs had any legal or equitable right as against the defendants that they were entitled to enforce by way of declaration. The case is just not one in which the defendants have done or are threatening to do acts which constitute defamation, malicious falsehood or passing off.

However, the case took a new turn when a number of cases were cited, one of which at least was directly in point. *Emperor of Austria v Day* (1861) 3 De GF & J 217 is a decision of the Court of Appeal in Chancery ...

I find it very difficult to discover what was the cause of action of the Emperor of Austria in that case. The judgments make it clear that the court was not enforcing the prerogative rights of the Emperor as sovereign of Hungary. The essential ingredient concentrated on by the court was that the acts of the defendant in printing the notes were a threat to do some act which would injure the property or cause pecuniary damage to the Emperor and to his subjects. So far as I can see, the court proceeded on the basis that if the acts of the defendant did threaten such damage, it was self-evident that there was a threat of an equitable wrong which should be restrained by injunction: see *per* Lord Campbell LC, at pp 233, 240, and Knight Bruce LJ, at p 245. The proposition being put forward by the Court of Appeal in that case appears to be that a deliberate act of the defendant which will cause injury to the plaintiff's property or pecuniary damage to him will be restrained by injunction in the Courts of Equity ...

Is such damage possible in this case? It is certainly not currently alleged in the originating summons as such. However, in my judgment it is certainly arguable in the present case that the continued use of forged documents of the Spanish state, purporting to show the lawful export of works of art from Spain, is directly comparable to the false currency which was under consideration in the Emperor of Austria case. The issue of false currency could debase the lawful currency of Hungary; the use of forged documents of the Government of Spain could debase the credibility of genuine export documents issued by that government. The question in this case will be whether such debasement would cause damage to the property of the Kingdom of Spain or the property of its subjects.

It is plain that in the Emperor of Austria case "property" in relation to a claim by a foreign sovereign was used in rather a loose sense: see *RCA Corporation v Pollard* [1983] Ch 135, 153 *per* Oliver LJ. Mr Littman suggested that such damage flowing from the continued use of forged documents is in this case to be found in the diminution in the value of pictures still in Spain for which genuine export licences could be obtained in the future and the fact that, if illicitly exported pictures can continue to be sold with forged documents, the expense to the Kingdom of Spain of buying them back for the benefit of Spain will be *pro tanto* increased. To that I would add that possibly the ability to continue to use forged documents after illicit export is a factor calculated to increase the attractions of illicit export to wrongdoers, thereby depriving the inhabitants of Spain of public works of art owned by the Kingdom of Spain and injury to the property in Spain.

Whether those arguments are well founded or not is not for me to determine finally on this application. *The Emperor of Austria* case, 3 de GF & J 217 has satisfied me that there may be – and I say no more than that – a legal right in this case which the plaintiffs are entitled to have declared by way of declaration in the way sought. It is not plain and obvious that the action cannot succeed.

I turn then to consider the second ground on which the defendants seek to strike out this claim, namely, that the claim is an abuse of the process of the court.

It is submitted on behalf of the defendants that the purpose of these proceedings is to denigrate the value of the picture at the forthcoming sale by a collateral attack so as to secure the eventual return of the picture to Spain at a cheaper price. They point to what they say is delay in the bringing of proceedings; that although the Government of Spain had known of the illegal export since 1983, and indeed have known that OAI were the owners since then, they have not thought fit to bring proceedings until just before the forthcoming sale. The defendants say that there is no way in which this action can be determined before the sale on 11 April, and the intention is to have it as a blight cast on the sale. They point to the statements made in the Spanish press to the effect that the government are going to do everything they can to stop the sale. They point also to the fact that the Spanish Government have not sought to proceed by way of an application for an injunction which would require them to give a cross-undertaking in damages, but have satisfied themselves with this unusual procedure of a simple declaration as to truth and falsity.

In the light of all those circumstances, it is said that the court is being used by the Spanish Government for a collateral purpose and not *bona fide* for the purpose for which the right of action, if any, exists.

I agree with the defendants that if they could make out that case it would be a case for striking out. But I am not myself satisfied that the Spanish Government are motivated either exclusively or primarily by the collateral motive suggested. First, as to delay, I can see no grounds for criticising the Spanish Government in not having taken proceedings. For purposes which are no doubt good ones, the defendants OAI are a cosmopolitan body of people spread over many jurisdictions, Liberia, British Virgin Islands, Channel Islands and Paris. There is no obvious jurisdiction in which those people could be sued. What is more, the whereabouts of the picture have been unknown since it was with the Getty Museum. There was no cause for proceedings when the picture was with the Getty museum because that museum declined to go on in any event. I ask rhetorically: where could these proceedings have been brought, unless and until the Spanish Government knew that the picture was to be in this country and that there was to be a sale of it? I can see no ground for criticism of the Spanish Government on that head.

Secondly, as to the chances of the matter being tried before 11 April, although I have not yet decided or indeed heard full argument I am bound to say that my present impression coincides with that of the defendants, namely, that there is really no hope of this matter being tried before 11 April on the merits. The Spanish Government are advised by very reputable and skilled solicitors and counsel, and I am told that the legal advisers took the view that the case could be determined before 11 April, and it was for that purpose that the claim for relief was limited to a declaration. I am satisfied that that was a view genuinely, if possibly mistakenly, held.

In my judgment the Spanish Government have here, if I am right on there being a possible cause of action, a legitimate interest which they are seeking to defend in this action, namely, in preventing the continued use of forged documents of the Spanish state.

As to the failure to apply for an interim injunction, it is not a necessity that a party threatened with an injury is forced to apply for interlocutory relief. If they choose not to do so, that is for them to decide. The Spanish Government say that they will continue with this action, even if the sale does take place on 11 April and is not postponed. It is suggested that that is in some way indicative also of an abuse. I cannot see it that way. Proceedings now having started in a jurisdiction in which OAI has consented to be joined, it seems to me no hardship for the action to continue (if it is to go on) until judgment, even if the defendants choose not to postpone the sale.

It may well be that the Spanish Government will receive a collateral advantage by pursuing this action in the form of a diminution in the price of the picture. They have said that they are not intending to bid at the sale, but there is no suggestion that they are no longer interested in buying under any circumstances. But I am not satisfied that their sole or predominant objective in this case is to force down the price. It appears to be a much wider concern, namely, the concern not to permit false documents to continue to circulate in support of a picture which they say has been illicitly exported. Often in litigation parties hope to use the litigation as a weapon to achieve wider results. In my judgment, in such cases the action cannot be struck out as an abuse of the process until it is shown that that is their predominant objective as opposed to a collateral benefit. I therefore refuse also to strike out the whole summons as an abuse of the process of the court.

Finally, in fairness to the defendants I should emphasise two points, because it is important that the existence of these proceedings should not be either misconstrued or misunderstood. The action does not in any way impugn the title of OAI to sell the picture. The title to the picture of any buyer will not be affected by anything which eventually happens in this action. The action only relates to the question whether the picture was or was not lawfully exported from Spain.

Secondly, I must emphasise that for the purposes of this judgment I have had to assume that the allegations as to forgery as made by the Government of Spain are correct. This judgment in no way constitutes a finding or any indication that those allegations have been proved.

Notes and questions

1. '*Ubi jus ibi remedium*: where there's a right there's a remedy. To this the realist replies – *ubi remedium ibi jus*: where there's a remedy there's a right' (FH Lawson, *Remedies of English Law* (2nd ed, 1980), p 1). Does *Spain v Christie* support this realist view?

2. 'The effectiveness of the system of English civil justice may be attributed to the vast number, variety, diversity and flexibility of its judicial remedies. The remedies depend on the nature of the legal rights, claims and interests established, and as these may themselves vary considerably, so the corresponding remedies will vary also, which is why civil remedies are by their nature so multifarious and multi-varied ... [T]he categories of civil remedies are not closed, and the judicial machinery ... may devise and operate new remedies, or variations of old remedies ...' (Sir Jack I H Jacob, *The Fabric of English Civil Justice* (Stevens, 1987), pp 171-172). To what extent can the courts themselves devise new remedies as opposed to thinking up new variations of old remedies? Do they have the power actually to devise new remedies?

3. What substantive rights are in issue in the *Spain* case?

4. Are rights and causes of action synonymous? Can one ever have a right without a cause of action? Can one ever have a cause of action without a right? (Cf *Jackson v Horizon Holidays*, below p 121.)

2 REMEDIES AND RIGHTS

Bryant v Herbert (1877) 3 CPD 389 Court of Appeal

(See p 63)

Notes and questions

1. What comes first, the right or the remedy?

2. 'I think that many rules which are recognised as rules of substantive law could be classified merely as rules of practice. It may be that, in some jurisprudential theory, it is possible to classify as a legal right some claim which will not be enforced by the court, but on a

practical level the existence of a right depends upon the existence of a remedy for its infringement ...' (Oliver LJ, *Techno-Impex v Geb Van Weelde* [1981] QB 648). Is this true of EU law? Is it true of public law? Is it true of contract?

3. What about the remedy of a declaration? Is not the sole purpose of this remedy to declare pre-existing rights?

4. Is there such a thing as the English law of obligations or should the topic be called the law of causes of action? What if one pleads the wrong cause of action?

Esso Petroleum Co Ltd v Southport Corporation [1953] 3 WLR 773 Queen's Bench Division; [1954] 2 QB 182 Court of Appeal; [1956] AC 218 House of Lords

This was an action for damages brought by Southport Corporation against an oil company whose tanker had run aground and whose cargo of oil, when deliberately released from the stricken ship by the captain in order to avoid loss of life, had polluted the Corporation's beaches. The Corporation pleaded as causes of action trespass, nuisance (private and public) and negligence of the captain; they subsequently, at the appeal stage, attempted to plead a further cause of action, namely that the company itself was negligent in putting to sea an unseaworthy ship. The trial judge held that the captain had not been negligent and dismissed the damages action; the Court of Appeal allowed an appeal on the ground that it was for the defendants to disprove any negligence; the House of Lords restored the trial judge's decision.

Devlin J (Queen's Bench Division): ... If there is an unlawful interference with the plaintiff's property, the question whether it is a trespass or a nuisance depends upon whether or not it is a direct physical interference. I incline to the view that in this case it is; but having regard to the views which I have expressed about nuisance I think it is unnecessary to enter into this matter, which is not covered exactly by precedent. It may well be that it is one of those cases which are described in the books as a nuisance of a particular kind analogous to trespass ...

In my judgment the plaintiffs have a good cause of action in trespass or nuisance subject to the special defences raised by the defendants which I shall next consider.

On the first of these, if one seeks an analogy from traffic on land, it is well established that persons whose property adjoins the highway cannot complain of damage done by persons using the highway unless it is done negligently: ... These cases amplify the principle in *Holmes v Mather* which dealt with collisions on the highway itself and which is the foundation of the modern practice whereby a plaintiff in a running-down action sues for negligence and not for trespass ...

Denning LJ (Court of Appeal): ...

(1) *Trespass to land* ... I am clearly of opinion that the Southport Corporation cannot here sue in trespass. This discharge of oil was not done directly on to

their foreshore, but outside in the estuary. It was carried by the tide on to their land, but that was only consequential, not direct. Trespass, therefore, does not lie.

(2) *Private nuisance.* In order to support an action on the case for a private nuisance the defendant must have used his own land or some other land in such a way as injuriously to affect the enjoyment of the plaintiffs' land. "The ground of responsibility", said Lord Wright in *Sedleigh-Denfield v O'Callaghan*, "is the possession and control of the land from which the nuisance proceeds". Applying this principle, it is clear that the discharge of oil was not a private nuisance, because it did not involve the use by the defendants of any land, but only of a ship at sea.

(3) *Public nuisance.* The term "public nuisance" covers a multitude of sins, great and small ... Suffice it to say that the discharge of a noxious substance in such a way as to be likely to affect the comfort and safety of Her Majesty's subjects generally is a public nuisance ...

Applying the old cases to modern instances, it is, in my opinion, a public nuisance to discharge oil into the sea in such circumstances that it is likely to be carried on to the shores and beaches of our land to the prejudice and discomfort of Her Majesty's subjects. It is an offence punishable by the common law. Furthermore, if any person should suffer greater damage or inconvenience from the oil than the generality of the public, he can have an action to recover damages on that account, provided, of course, that he can discover the offender who discharged the oil. This action would have been described in the old days as an action on the case, but it is now simply an action for a nuisance ...

(4) *Burden of proof.* One of the principal differences between an action for a public nuisance and an action for negligence is the burden of proof. In an action for a public nuisance, once the nuisance is proved and the defendant is shown to have caused it, then the legal burden is shifted on to the defendant to justify or excuse himself. If he fails to do so, he is held liable, whereas in an action for negligence the legal burden in most cases remains throughout on the plaintiff. In negligence, the plaintiff may gain much help from provisional presumptions like the doctrine of *res ipsa loquitur*, but, nevertheless, at the end of the case the judge must ask himself whether the legal burden is discharged. If the matter is left evenly in the balance, the plaintiff fails. But in public nuisance, as in trespass, the legal burden shifts to the defendant, and it is not sufficient for him to leave the matter in doubt. He must plead and prove a sufficient justification or excuse.

(5) *Justification or excuse.* The defendants seek to justify themselves by saying that it was necessary for them to discharge the oil because their ship was in danger. She had been driven by rough seas on to the revetment wall, and it was necessary to discharge the oil in order to get her off. If she had not done so, lives might have been lost. This is, no doubt, true at that stage in the story, but the question is, how came she to get upon the wall? If it was her own fault, then her justification fails, because no one can avail himself of a necessity produced by his own default. Where does the legal burden rest in this respect? Must the Southport Corporation prove that the ship was at fault in getting on to the wall, or must the ship prove that she herself was not at fault? In my opinion the burden is on the ship. She does not justify herself in law by necessity alone, but only by unavoidable necessity, and the burden is on her to show it was unavoidable.

Public nuisance is, in this respect, like unto a trespass, as to which it was said by the Court of King's Bench as long ago as 1616 in *Weaver v Ward*, that no man shall be excused "except it may be judged utterly without his fault" ...

Those were, it is true, cases in trespass; but the same principle applies to cases of public nuisance. That is shown by *Tarry v Ashton*, where a lamp which projected over the Strand fell on to a passer-by. This was described by Lord Wright as private action for a public nuisance: see *Sedleigh-Denfield v O'Callaghan*. Another example is *Wringe v Cohen*, where the gable of a house next the highway was blown down in a storm (which was treated by this court as a public nuisance). In both cases the defendant was held liable because his premises were in a defective state. He did not know of the defect, and he was not negligent in not knowing, but, nevertheless, he was liable because he did not prove any sufficient justification or excuse. He did not prove inevitable accident ...

Lord Radcliffe (House of Lords): My Lords, I think that this case ought to be decided in accordance with the pleadings. If it is, I am of opinion, as was the trial judge, that the respondents failed to establish any claim to relief that was valid in law. If it is not, we might do better justice to the respondents – I cannot tell, since the evidence is incomplete – but I am certain that we should do worse justice to the appellants, since in my view they were entitled to conduct the case and confine their evidence in reliance upon the further and better particulars of the statement of claim which had been delivered by the respondents. It seems to me that it is the purpose of such particulars that they should help to define the issues and to indicate to the party who asks for them how much of the range of his possible evidence will be relevant and how much irrelevant to those issues. Proper use of them shortens the hearing and reduces costs. But if an appellate court is to treat reliance upon them as pedantry or mere formalism, I do not see what part they have to play in our trial system ...

Notes and questions

1. 'The expressions "private law" and "public law" have recently been imported into the law of England from countries which, unlike our own, have separate systems concerning public law and private law. No doubt they are convenient expressions for descriptive purposes. In this country they must be used with caution, for, typically, English law fastens not on principles but on remedies. The principle remains intact that public authorities and public servants are, unless clearly exempted, answerable in the ordinary courts for wrongs done to individuals' (Lord Wilberforce, *Davy v Spelthorne BC* [1984] AC 262). Is *Esso* a public or a private law case?

2. Did the plaintiffs lose in the House of Lords because they did not plead the right cause (form?) of action?

3. What kind of damage did Southport Corporation suffer: physical damage or economic loss?

4. Read *Benjamin v Storr* (1874) LR 9 CP 400 in the law report. Why did Devlin J not draw an analogy with this case rather than with the traffic accident cases?

5. Did Esso have control of the tanker? Under what circumstances should control, of itself, give rise to liability on the part of the person in control when the thing controlled does damage? Should something more than control itself be required before one can attribute liability? (Cf Chapter 7.)

6. Maitland said that the forms of action continue to rule from the grave. Do you agree?

7. Does *Esso* and *Cambridge Water* (see p 375), when taken together, reject the principle that it is the polluter who should pay?

3 REMEDIES AND INTERESTS

Jackson v Horizon Holidays Ltd [1975] 1 WLR 1468 Court of Appeal

This was an action for damages brought by a father against a tour operator in respect of a holiday booked by the father for himself and his family. The father had booked the holiday in reliance upon statements made over the telephone and in the tour operator's brochure. Many of the promised facilities were not available and the hotel and food were of poor quality. The father sought compensation for mental distress in respect of himself, his wife and his children and the trial judge, who thought that they had had half a holiday, awarded half the total price of the holiday, plus another £500 for mental distress. An appeal by the defendants as to the amount awarded was dismissed by the Court of Appeal.

Lord Denning MR: ... The judge said that he could only consider the mental distress to Mr Jackson himself, and that he could not consider the distress to his wife and children. He said:

> "The damages are the plaintiff's ... I can consider the effect upon his mind of the wife's discomfort, vexation, and the like, although I cannot award a sum which represents her own vexation."

Mr Davies, for Mr Jackson, disputes that proposition. He submits that damages can be given not only for the leader of the party – in this case, Mr Jackson's own distress, discomfort and vexation – but also for that of the rest of the party.

We have had an interesting discussion as to the legal position when one person makes a contract for the benefit of a party. In this case it was a husband making a contract for the benefit of himself, his wife and children. Other cases readily come to mind. A host makes a contract with a restaurant for a dinner for himself and his friends. The vicar makes a contract for a coach trip for the choir. In all these cases there is only one person who makes the contract. It is the husband, the host or the vicar, as the case may be. Sometimes he pays the whole price himself. Occasionally he may get a contribution from the others. But in any case it is he who makes the contract. It would be a fiction to say that the contract was made by all the family, or all the guests, or all the choir and that he was only an agent for them. Take this very case. it would be absurd to say that the twins of three years old were parties to the contract or that the father was making the contract on their behalf as if they were principals. It would equally be a mistake to say that in any of these instances there was a trust. The transaction bears no resemblance to a trust. There was no trust fund and no trust property. No, the real truth is that in each instance, the father, the host or the vicar, was making a contract himself for the benefit of the whole party. In short, a contract by one for the benefit of third persons.

What is the position when such a contract is broken? At present the law says that the only one who can sue is the one who made the contract. None of the rest of the party can sue, even though the contract was made for their benefit. But when that one does sue, what damages can he recover? Is he limited to his own loss? Or can he recover for the others? Suppose the holiday firm puts the family into a hotel which is only half built and the visitors have to sleep on the floor? Or suppose the restaurant is fully booked and the guests have to go away, hungry and angry, having spent so much on fares to get there? Or suppose the coach leaves the choir stranded halfway and they have to hire cars to get home? None of them individually can sue. Only the father, the host or the vicar can sue. He can, of course, recover his own damages. But can he not recover for the others? I think he can. The case comes within the principle stated by Lush LJ in *Lloyd's v Harper*:

"I consider it to be an established rule of law that where a contract is made with A. for the benefit of B., A. can sue on the contract for the benefit of B., and recover all that B. could have recovered if the contract had been made with B. himself."

It has been suggested that Lush LJ was thinking of a contract in which A was trustee for B. But I do not think so. He was a common lawyer speaking of common law. His words were quoted with considerable approval by Lord Pearce in *Beswick v Beswick*. I have myself often quoted them. I think they should be accepted as correct, at any rate so long as the law forbids the third persons themselves from suing for damages. It is the only way in which a just result can be achieved. Take the instance I have put. The guests ought to recover from the restaurant their wasted fares. The choir ought to recover the cost of hiring the taxis home. Then is no one to recover from them except the one who made the contract for their benefit? He should be able to recover the expense to which he has been put, and pay it over to them. Once recovered, it will be money had and received to their use. (They might even, if desired, be joined as plaintiffs.) If he can recover for the expense, he should also be able to recover for the discomfort, vexation and upset which the whole party have suffered by reason of the breach of contract, recompensing them accordingly out of what he recovers.

Applying the principles to this case, I think that the figure of £1,100 was about right. It would, I think, have been excessive if it had been awarded only for the damage suffered by Mr Jackson himself. But when extended to his wife and children, I do not think it is excessive. People look forward to a holiday. They expect the promises to be fulfilled. When it fails, they are greatly disappointed and upset. It is difficult to assess in terms of money; but it is the task of the judges to do the best they can. I see no reason to interfere with the total award of £1,100. I would therefore dismiss the appeal.

Notes and questions

1. 'The legal action is open to anyone who has a legitimate interest in the success or failure of the claim' (*Nouveau code de procédure civile art. 31*).[4] Is this true of English law? (Cf *Miller v Jackson*, above p 22.)[5]

2. 'Take ... a landowner who collects pestilential rubbish near a village ... The householders nearest to it suffer the most, but everyone in the neighbourhood suffers too. In such cases the Attorney-General can take proceedings for an injunction to restrain the nuisance: and when he does so he acts in defence of the public right, not for any sectional interest ... But when the nuisance is so concentrated that only two or three property owners are affected by it ... then they ought to take proceedings on their own account to stop it and not expect the community to do it for them ...' (Denning LJ, *Att-Gen v PYA Quarries* [1957] 2 QB 169). How does one distinguish between 'sectional interest' and 'public right'?

3. The notion of an interest can apply either to the institutional relationship between a party and a remedy (see eg, *Beswick v Beswick*, p 86) or between a party and the kind of harm they suffer (see eg, *Surrey CC v Bredero Homes*, p 178). How easy is it for an English lawyer to move from an 'interest' to a 'right'? Are there any intermediate terms that help facilitate the movement?

4. If the father refused to hand over to his wife the damages he had obtained on her behalf, could the wife bring an action in debt against him to recover them (cf Chapter 7)?

5. Could the wife and children have sued in their own right Horizon Holidays for damages?

6. Would it make sense to allow a family to contract, to own property and to sue as a legal subject in itself? Does the family exist as a social reality? Does it have its own interests which the law should recognise?

---

4   '*L'action est ouvert à tous ceux qui ont un intérêt légitime au succès ou au rejet d'une prétention, ...*'.

5   See also Local Government Act 1972 s 222(1); Supreme Court Act 1981 s 31(3); *Lall v Lall* [1965] 3 All ER 330.

4 SELF-HELP

(a) Personal justice

Bradford Corporation v Pickles [1895] AC 587 House of Lords

This was an action for an injunction brought by a local authority against a landowner who, so it was alleged, was deliberately interfering with the natural supply of water to the corporation's waterworks by digging holes on his land. The landowner, it seemed, was trying to bring pressure on the corporation to purchase his land. The House of Lords gave judgment for the landowner.

Lord Halsbury LC: ... The acts done, or sought to be done, by the defendant were all done upon his own land, and the interference whatever it is, with the flow of water is an interference with water, which is underground and not shown to be water flowing in any defined stream, but is percolating water, which, but for such interference, would undoubtedly reach the plaintiff's works, and in that sense does deprive them of the water which they would otherwise get. But although it does deprive them of water which they would otherwise get, it is necessary for the plaintiffs to establish that they have a right to the flow of water, and that the defendant has no right to do what he is doing ...

The very question was ... determined by this House, [in *Chasemore v Richards*], and it was held that the landowner had a right to do what he had done whatever his object or purpose might be, and although the purpose might be wholly unconnected with the enjoyment of his own estate ...

The only remaining point is the question of fact alleged by the plaintiffs, that the acts done by the defendant are done, not with any view which deals with the use of his own land or the percolating water through it, but is done, in the language of the pleader, "maliciously" ...

This is not a case in which the state of mind of the person doing the act can affect the right to do it. If it was a lawful act, however ill the motive might be, he had a right to do it. If it was an unlawful act, however good his motive might be, he would have no right to do it ...

Lord Macnaghten: ... But the real answer to the claim of the corporation is that in such a case motives are immaterial. It is the act, not the motive for the act, that must be regarded. If the act, apart from motive, gives rise merely to damage without legal injury, the motive, however reprehensible it may be, will not supply that element ...

Notes and questions

1. 'Self-redress is a summary remedy, which is justified only in clear and simple cases, or in an emergency' (Lloyd LJ, *Burton v Winters* [1993] 1 WLR 1077). Was the defendant in *Bradford* actually exercising a self-help remedy?

2   Does *Bradford* mean that English law has no doctrine of abuse of rights? (Cf Chapter 7.)?[6]

3.   If the parties had been reversed – that is to say, if it had been the Corporation that was digging the holes – would Mr Pickles have had a remedy?

4.   The defendant builds a wall that intrudes by a couple of inches into the plaintiff's land. The plaintiff is refused an injunction against the defendant. Is the plaintiff entitled to knock the wall down himself? (Cf *Burton v Winters*, above.)

5.   If the Corporation had made a contract to purchase Mr Pickles' land as a result of his digging the holes, could the contract have been set aside in equity on the basis of duress?

(b) Self-protection

R v Self [1992] 1 WLR 657 Court of Appeal

Garland J: ... This matter comes before the court by leave of the single judge on a point of law. There is one point central to the appeal. It is this. Since the appellant was acquitted of theft neither Mr Frost nor Mr Mole were entitled by virtue of section 24 of the Police and Criminal Evidence Act 1984 to effect a citizen's arrest. If they were not entitled to do that then this appellant could not be convicted of an assault with intent to resist or prevent the lawful apprehension or detainer of himself, that is to say his arrest ...

The view of this court is that little profit can be had from taking examples and trying to reduce them to absurdity. The words of the statute are clear and applying those words to this case there was no arrestable offence committed. It necessarily follows that the two offences under section 38 of the Offences against the Person Act 1861 could not be committed because there was no power to apprehend or detain the appellant.

It follows also, that that being the law, as this court sees it, the convictions on counts 2 and 3 must be quashed and this appeal allowed.

Notes and questions

1.   A person is entitled to use reasonable force to resist a trespass: thus self-help can be used in cases of assault, false imprisonment and trespass to land and goods. But what are the limits? What if a trespasser gains actual possession of the land or goods of another: can the owner use force to recover the land or goods? If not, why not?

---

6   Cf *Hollywood Silver Fox Farm v Emmett* [1936] 2 KB 468; *Wheeler v Leicester* CC [1985] AC 1054.

2. D, without any justification whatsoever, attacks C on a public highway and C, in order to protect himself, throws a large brick at D. The brick misses D and hits P, an innocent passer-by. Can P sue C or D for trespass?

3. A bolt of lightning starts a fire on D's land. P, worried by the fire and the fact that D is making no effort to put it out, enters D's and puts the fire out himself. If D assaults P while on the land, could P sue D for trespass?

(c) Refusal to pay

Vigers v Cook [1919] 2 KB 475 Court of Appeal

(See p 296)

Bolton v Mahadeva [1972] 1 WLR 1009 Court of Appeal

This was a debt action for £560 brought by a firm of heating engineers against a householder who had contracted with the engineers to have a central heating system installed in his house for £560. The householder claimed that the work of installation was so defective that it amounted to a non-performance of the contract and that, accordingly, he was not liable to pay anything. The trial judge held that the system was defective and would cost £174.50 to remedy; he gave judgment for £385.50 plus another £46 for extras. The Court of Appeal allowed an appeal by the householder.

Cairns LJ: ... The main question in the case is whether the defects in workmanship found by the judge to be such as to cost £174 to repair – that is, between one-third and one-quarter of the contract price – were of such a character and amount that the plaintiff could not be said to have substantially performed his contract. That is, in my view, clearly the legal principle which has to be applied to cases of this kind.

The rule which was laid down many years ago in *Cutter v Powell* in relation to lump sum contracts was that unless the contracting party had performed the whole of his contract, he was not entitled to recover anything. That strong rule must now be read in the light of certain more recent cases ...

Perhaps the most helpful case is the most recent one of *Hoenig v Isaacs*. That was a case where the plaintiff was an interior decorator and designer of furniture who had entered into a contract to decorate and furnish the defendant's flat for a sum of £750; and, as appears from the statement of facts, the official referee who tried the case at first instance found that the door of a wardrobe required replacing, that a bookshelf which was too short would have to be re-made, which would require alterations being made to a bookcase, and that the cost of remedying the defects was £55 18s. 2s. That is on a £750 contract. The ground on which the Court of Appeal in that case held that the plaintiff was entitled to succeed, notwithstanding that there was not complete performance of the contract, was that there was substantial performance of the contract and that the defects in the work which there existed were not sufficient to amount to a substantial degree of non-performance.

In considering whether there was substantial performance I am of opinion that it is relevant to take into account both the nature of the defects and the proportion between the cost of rectifying them and the contract price. It would be wrong to say that the contractor is only entitled to payment if the defects are so trifling as to be covered by the *de minimis* rule ...

Now, certainly it appears to me that the nature and amount of the defects in this case were far different from those which the court had to consider in *H Dakin & Co Ltd v Lee* and *Hoenig v Isaacs*. For my part, I find it impossible to say that the judge was right in reaching the conclusion that in those circumstances the contract had been substantially performed. The contract was a contract to install a central heating system. If a central heating system when installed is such that it does not heat the house adequately and is such, further, that fumes are given out, so as to make living rooms uncomfortable, and if the putting right of those defects is not something which can be done by some slight amendment of the system, then I think that the contract is not substantially performed.

The actual amount of expenditure which the judge assessed as being necessary to cure those particular defects were £40 in each case. Taking those matters into account and the other matters making up the total of £174, I have reached the conclusion that the judge was wrong in saying that this contract had been substantially completed; and, on my view of the law, it follows that the plaintiff was not entitled to recover under that contract ...

Notes and questions

1. One of the most effective remedies that a consumer has against a supplier who provides shoddy goods or services is the option not to pay the bill. In effect the consumer is either (a) simply repudiating the contract for serious breach by the other party (see Chapter 6) or (b) refusing to perform because the other party has not performed. What is the difference between breach of contract and non-performance of a contract? Were the consumers in *Vigers* and *Mahadeva* refusing to pay because the other party was in breach?

2. If, of course, the consumer is not justified in repudiating because (a) the breach by the supplier does not go to the root of the contract or (b) the other party has substantially performed, then the consumer will be in breach of contract. What remedies will the supplier then have against the consumer? If the refusal to pay the bill caused the undertaker or the firm of heating engineers to borrow money at a high rate of interests to stop them going bankrupt, could they claim this interest in an action for damages against the consumer?

3. In both *Vigers* and *Mahadeva* it could be said that the consumer received something from the supplier. Ought they to pay for this something? If the houseowner in *Mahadeva* had brought another firm

in to get the heating working for a price of £100 (1972 prices), would it be just and equitable that the owner could obtain a heating system so cheaply? Had he unjustly enriched himself at the expense of the first heating firm? What if the firm had been a cowboy firm of builders: can one unjustly enrich himself or herself at the expense of a cowboy firm of builders?

4. In *Mahadeva* the refusal to pay was a particularly effective remedy. But what if the heating engineers had not only installed a bad system, but also had caused extensive damage to the owner's house? In this situation the owner would have had to sue for damages for breach of contract and such a remedy covers only the actual loss suffered by the plaintiff. Would the court, then, have set-off the cost of the pipes, radiators etc, against the loss suffered by the owner?

5. What if this case had come before the courts in the days when there were still juries in civil cases and the jury had decided that the heating engineers had substantially performed the contract: could the Court of Appeal have reversed their finding?

Eller v Grovecrest Investments Ltd [1994] 4 All ER 845 Court of Appeal

Hoffmann LJ: The question in this appeal is whether set-off against a claim for rent can be invoked against a landlord exercising the ancient common law remedy of distress ...

[The] authorities can be understood only against the background of the principles which governed set-off at common law and equity before the Judicature Acts. At common law, a defendant could resist a money claim on the ground that he had already paid money to the plaintiff's use ... But no cross-claim could be set off in any proceedings until the Insolvent Debtors Relief Act 1729 ...

Nevertheless, set-off under the statute was restricted to mutual debts and did not, for example, allow the set-off of a claim for unliquidated damages such as the tenant makes in this case ...

So much for the position at common law. The Court of Chancery approached set-off on a wider basis and would relieve a debtor against a common law liability when he had a cross-claim "so directly connected with [the claim] that it would be manifestly unjust to the claimant to recover without taking into account the cross-claim" (see *Cia Sud Americana de Vapores v Shipmair BV, The Teno* [1977] 2 Lloyd's Rep 289 at 297 *per* Parker J). The procedural remedy given by the Court of Chancery was to injunct the plaintiff from bringing or proceeding with his common law action until the cross-claim had been taken into account ...

What fair dealing requires seems clear enough. It is contrary to principle that a landlord should be able to recover more by distress than he can by action ...

In my judgment, therefore, this court is free to hold that set-off is available against a claim to levy distress. Mr Philip Wood, in his comprehensive book on *English and International Set-Off* (1989) para 4.86 says that this is the better view. I agree ...

Neill LJ: ... It is necessary to remember that before the passing of the statutes of set-off in the time of George II there was no right of set-off in an action at law ...

The introduction of the statutory right of set-off represented an important development, but the set-off was only available in the circumstances prescribed in the statute, that is, in respect of debts or liquidated demands due between the same parties in the same right. It followed, therefore, that a claim for damages for tort or in pursuit of a remedy in respect of some tortious liability could not be used by way of a set-off under the statutes ...

It would appear that another effect of the strict rules governing a statutory set-off at law was that in the eighteenth and nineteenth centuries, before the Judicature Acts 1873 and 1875, courts of equity were very reluctant to intervene where the position of the parties *inter se* was regulated by their rights at law ...

The position was different, however, where the set-off relied on was a true equitable set-off and one which was not even arguably within the statutes ...

Notes and questions

1. Two important self-help remedies in commercial law are set-off and liens: the first operates within the remedy of debt (see below), while the second is, like the landlord's remedy of distress, a self-help remedy *in rem* exercised against the goods of another. Thus a bailee may in certain circumstances have a lien on the thing bailed. What are the circumstances?

2. Could banking function without set-off? What is the relationship, if any, between set-off and subrogation?

3. P buys an expensive washing machine using his credit card. The washing machine explodes after the third use and damages clothes and surrounding property. Can P set-off the cost of all this against his credit card bill?[7] What if the Conditions of Use in the credit card contract contains a clause denying the right of any credit card holder to use the remedy of set-off?

---

7   Consumer Credit Act 1974 s 75.

5 DEBT

(a) Introduction

United Australia Ltd v Barclays Bank Ltd [1941] AC 1 House of Lords

Lord Atkin: ... The story starts with the action of debt which was not necessarily based upon the existence of a contract, for it covered claims to recover sums due to customary dues, penalties for breaches of by-laws, and the like. The action of debt had its drawbacks, the chief being that the defendant could wage his law. There followed the application of the action on the case of assumpsit to debt. "The defendant being indebted then promised." At first there must be an express promise; then the Courts implied a promise from an executory contract: Slade's case. Slade's case was not a claim *in indebitatus assumpsit*, but the principle was applied, and it became unnecessary to prove an express promise in those cases. Then the action was allowed in respect of cases where there was no contract, executory or otherwise, as in the cases where debt would have lain for customary fees and the like; and by a final and somewhat forced application to cases where the defendant had received money of the plaintiff to which he was not entitled. These included cases where the plaintiff had intentionally paid money to the defendant, eg claims for money paid on a consideration that wholly failed and money paid under a mistake: cases where the plaintiff had been deceived into paying money, cases where money had been extorted from the plaintiff by threats or duress of goods. They also included cases where money had not been paid by the plaintiff at all but had been received from third persons, as where the defendant had received fees under colour of holding an office which in fact was held by the plaintiff: and finally cases like the present where the defendant had been wrongfully in possession of the plaintiff's goods, had sold them and was in possession of the proceeds. Now to find a basis for the actions in any actual contract whether express or to be implied from the conduct of the parties was in many of the instances given obviously impossible. The cheat or the blackmailer does not promise to repay to the person he has wronged the money which he has unlawfully taken: nor does the thief promise to repay the owner of the goods stolen the money which he has gained from selling the goods. Nevertheless, if a man so wronged was to recover the money in the hands of the wrongdoer, and it was obviously just that he should be able to do so, it was necessary to create a fictitious contract: for there was no action possible other than debt or assumpsit on the one side and action for damages for tort on the other. The action of indebitatus assumpsit for money had and received to the use of the plaintiff in the cases I have enumerated was therefore supported by the imputation by the Court to the defendant of a promise to repay ...

Fibrosa Spolka Akcyjna v Fairbairn Lawson Combe Barbour Ltd [1943] AC 32 House of Lords

Lord Wright: My Lords, the claim in the action was to recover a prepayment of £1,000 made on account of the price under a contract which had been frustrated. The claim was for money paid for a consideration which had failed. It is clear that any civilised system of law is bound to provide remedies for cases of what has been called unjust enrichment or unjust benefit, that is to prevent a man from retaining the money of or some benefit derived from another which it is against conscience that he should keep. Such remedies in English law are generically different from remedies in contract or in tort, and are now recognised to fall within a third category of the common law which has been called quasi-contract or restitution. The root idea was stated by three Lords of Appeal, Lord Shaw, Lord Sumner and Lord Carson, in *RE Jones Ltd v Waring & Gillow Ltd*, which dealt with a particular species of the category, namely, money paid under a mistake of fact. Lord Sumner referring to *Kelly v Solari*, where money had been paid by an insurance company under the mistaken impression that it was due to an executrix under a policy which had in fact been cancelled, said: "There was no real intention on the company's part to enrich her". Payment under a mistake of fact is only one head of this category of the law. Another class is where, as in this case, there is prepayment on account of money to be paid as consideration for the performance of a contract which in the event becomes abortive and is not performed, so that the money never becomes due. There was in such circumstances no intention to enrich the payee. This is the class of claims for the recovery of money paid for a consideration which has failed. Such causes of action have long been familiar and were assumed to be common-place by Holt CJ in *Holmes v Hall* in 1704. Holt CJ was there concerned only about the proper form of action and took the cause of the action as beyond question. He said: "If A gives money to B to pay to C upon C's giving writings etc. and C will not do it, indebit will lie for A against B for so much money received to his use. And many such actions have been maintained for earnests in bargains, when the bargainer would not perform, and for premiums for insurance, when the ship etc. did not go the voyage". The Chief Justice is there using earnest as meaning a prepayment on account of the price, not in the modern sense of an irrevocable payment to bind the bargain, and he is recognising that the *indebitatus assumpsit* had by that time been accepted as the appropriate form of action in place of the procedure which had been used in earlier times to enforce these claims such as debt, account or case.

By 1760 actions for money had and received had increased in number and variety. Lord Mansfield CJ, in a familiar passage in *Moses v Macferlan*, sought to rationalise the action for money had and received, and illustrated it by some typical instances. "It lies", he said, "for money paid by mistake; or upon a consideration which happens to fail – or for money got through imposition (express, or implied); or extortion; or oppression; or an undue advantage taken of the plaintiff's situation, contrary to laws made for the protection of persons under those circumstances. In one word, the gist of this kind of action is, that the defendant, upon the circumstances of the case, is obliged by the ties of natural justice and equity to refund the money". Lord Mansfield prefaced this pronouncement by observations which are to be noted. "If the defendant be under an obligation from the ties of natural justice, to refund; the law implies a debt and gives this action [*sc. indebitatus assumpsit*] founded in the equity of the plaintiff's case, as it were, upon a contract (*quasi ex contractu* as the Roman law expresses it)". Lord Mansfield does not say that the law implies a promise. The law implies a debt or obligation which is a different thing. In fact, he denies that there is a contract; the obligation is as efficacious as if it were upon a contract. The obligation is a creation of the law, just as much as an obligation in tort. The obligation belongs to a third class, distinct from either contract or tort, though it resembles contract rather than tort. This statement of Lord Mansfield has been the basis of the modern law of quasi-contract, notwithstanding the criticisms which have been launched against it. Like all large generalisations, it has needed and received qualifications in practice. There is, for instance, the qualification that an action for money had and received does not lie for money paid under an erroneous judgment or for moneys paid under an illegal or excessive distress. The law has provided other remedies as being more convenient. The standard of what is against conscience in this context has become more or less canalised or defined, but in substance the juristic concept remains as Lord Mansfield left it.

The gist of the action is a debt or obligation implied, or, more accurately imposed, by law in much the same way as the law enforces as a debt the obligation to pay a statutory or customary impost. This is important because some confusion seems to have arisen though perhaps only in recent times when the true nature of the forms of action have become obscured by want of user. If I may borrow from another context the elegant phrase of Viscount Simon LC in *United Australia Ltd v Barclays Bank Ltd*, there has sometimes been, as it seems to me, "a misreading of technical rules, now happily swept away". The writ of *indebitatus assumpsit* involved at least two averments, the debt or obligation and the *assumpsit*. The former was the basis of the claim and was the real cause of action. The latter was merely fictitious and could not be traversed, but was necessary to enable the convenient and liberal form of action to be used in such cases. This fictitious *assumpsit* or promise was wiped out by the Common Law Procedure Act 1852 ... Yet the ghosts of the forms of action have been allowed at times to intrude in the ways of the living and impede vital functions of the law. Thus in *Sinclair v Brougham*, Lord Sumner stated that "all these causes of action [sc. for money had and received] are common species of the *genus assumpsit*. All now rest, and long have rested, upon a notional or imputed promise to repay". This observation, which was not necessary for the decision of the case, obviously does not mean that there is an actual promise of the party. The phrase "notional or implied promise" is only a way of describing a debt or obligation arising by construction of law. The claim for money had and received always rested on a debt or obligation which the law implied or more accurately imposed, whether the procedure actually in vogue at any time was debt or account or case or *indebitatus assumpsit*. Even the fictitious *assumpsit* disappeared after the Act of 1852. I prefer Lord Sumner's explanation of the cause of action in *Jones's* case. This agrees with the words of Lord Atkin which I have just quoted, yet serious legal writers have seemed to say that these words of the great judge in *Sinclair v Brougham* closed the door to any theory of unjust enrichment in English law. I do not understand why or how. It would indeed be a *reductio ad absurdum* of the doctrine of precedents. In fact, the common law still employs the action for money had and received as a practical and useful, if not complete or ideally perfect, instrument to prevent unjust enrichment, aided by the various methods of technical equity which are also available, as they were found to be in *Sinclair v Brougham* ...

Notes and questions

1. The distinction between an action for debt and an action for damages is a modern reflection of the old forms of action distinction between the writ of debt and the writ of trespass. These categories preceded those of contract and tort which, as we have seen (*Bryant v Herbert*, p 63), were imported from civil law into the common law in the 19th century. Debt got largely subsumed by contract not just because many debt claims were the result of contractual transactions, but also

because even in those situations where a debt might be claimed in the absence of a contractual relationship the theory adopted by the majority of the judges, until recently (Lord Wright was an exception), was that all debt claims were deemed contractual. Quasi-contractual debt claims were based on the obligations theory of an implied contract.[8] This theory is now giving way to an unjust enrichment theory as envisaged by Lord Wright (see *Lipkin Gorman v Karpnale*, p 145? and *Woolwich Building Society v IRC*, p 54). However, in *Lipkin Gorman* Lord Goff seemed to advance the idea that non-contractual debt claims were based on a property right in the debt. Is this property idea any less of a fiction than an implied contract?

2.   If the law of obligations has found categories for both contractual and non-contractual (tort) damages claims, why have they had such difficulty in finding a category for non-contractual debt claims?

3.   Is a claim for salvage or expenses a claim in debt or damages? (Cf *The Aldora*, below p 140.)

(b) Contractual debt

White & Carter (Councils) Ltd v McGregor [1962] AC 413 House of Lords (Scotland)

Lord Reid: My Lords, the pursuers supply to local authorities litter bins which are placed in the streets. They are allowed to attach to these receptacles plates carrying advertisements, and they make their profit from payments made to them by the advertisers. The defender carried on a garage in Clydebank and in 1954 he made an agreement with the pursuers under which they displayed advertisements of his business on a number of these bins. In June 1957 his sales manager made a further contract with the pursuers for the display of these advertisements for a further period of three years. The sales manager had been given no specific authority to make this contract and when the defender heard of it later on the same day he at once wrote to the pursuers to cancel the contract. The pursuers refused to accept this cancellation. They prepared the necessary plates for attachment to the bins and exhibited them on the bins from 2nd November 1957 onwards.

The defender refused to pay any sums due under the contract and the pursuers raised the present action in the Sheriff Court craving payment of £196 4s. the full sum due under the contract for the period of three years. After sundry procedure the Sheriff-Substitute on 15th March 1960 dismissed the action ...

The case for the defender (now the respondent) is that, as he repudiated the contract before anything had been done under it, the appellants were not entitled to go on and carry out the contract and sue for the contract price: he

---

8   See eg, *Sinclair v Brougham* [1914] AC 398.

maintains that in the circumstances the appellants' only remedy was damages, and that, as they do not sue for damages, this action was rightly dismissed ...

The general rule cannot be in doubt. It was settled in Scotland at least as early as 1848 and it has been authoritatively stated time and again in both Scotland and England. If one party to a contract repudiates it in the sense of making it clear to the other party that he refuses or will refuse to carry out his part of the contract; the other party, the innocent party, has an option. He may accept that repudiation and sue for damages for breach of contract, whether or not the time for performance has come; or he may if he chooses disregard or refuse to accept it and then the contract remains in full effect ...

I need not refer to the numerous authorities. They are not disputed by the respondent but he points out that in all of them the party who refused to accept the repudiation had no active duties under the contract. The innocent party's option is generally said to be to wait until the date of performance and then to claim damages estimated as at that date. There is no case in which it is said that he may, in face of the repudiation, go on and incur useless expense in performing the contract and then claim the contract price. The option, it is argued, is merely as to the date as at which damages are to be assessed ...

Of course, if it had been necessary for the defender to do or accept anything before the contract could be completed by the pursuers, the pursuers could not and the court would not have compelled the defender to act, the contract would not have been completed and the pursuers' only remedy would have been damages ...

It might be said that, because in most cases the circumstances are such that an innocent party is unable to complete the contract and earn the contract price without the assent or co-operation of the other party, therefore in cases where he can do so he should not be allowed to do so. I can see no justification for that.

[Another] ground would be that there is some general equitable principle or element of public policy which requires this limitation of the contractual rights of the innocent party. It may well be that, if it can be shown that a person has no legitimate interest, financial or otherwise, in performing the contract rather than claiming damages, he ought not to be allowed to saddle the other party with an additional burden with no benefit to himself. If a party has no interest to enforce a stipulation, he cannot in general enforce it: so it might be said that, if a party has no interest to insist on a particular remedy, he ought not to be allowed to insist on it. And, just as a party is not allowed to enforce a penalty, so he ought not to be allowed to penalise the other party by taking one course when another is equally advantageous to him. If I may revert to the example which I gave of a company engaging an expert to prepare an elaborate report and then repudiating before anything was done, it might be that the company could show that the expert had no substantial or legitimate interest in carrying out the work rather than accepting damages: I would think that the *de minimis* principle would apply in determining whether his interest was substantial, and that he might have a legitimate interest other than an immediate financial interest. But if the expert had no such interest then that might be regarded as a proper case for the exercise of the general equitable jurisdiction of the court. But that is not this case. Here the respondent did not set out to prove that the appellants had no legitimate interest in completing the contract and claiming the contract price rather than claiming damages; there is nothing in the findings of fact to support such a case, and it seems improbable that any such case could have been proved. It is, in my judgment, impossible to say that the appellants should be deprived of their right to claim the contract price merely because the benefit to them, as against claiming damages and re-letting their advertising space, might be small in comparison with the loss to the respondent: that is the most that could be said in favour of the respondent. Parliament has on many occasions relieved parties from certain kinds of improvident or oppressive contracts, but the common law can only do that in very limited circumstances. Accordingly, I am unable to avoid the conclusion that this appeal must be allowed and the case remitted so that decree can be pronounced as craved in the initial writ.

Lord Keith of Avonholm (dissenting): ... If I understand aright, counsel for the appellants would read time of performance as time of performance by the defender after the appellants had discharged their part of performance under the contract. Their claim then becomes a claim, not for damages for breach of contract, but for a debt due by the defender under the contract. In other words, there would be an anticipatory repudiation by the defender which the appellants were not bound to accept as a breach of contract and which did not cease to be anticipatory until the moment when the defender was due to make payment under the contract. This, I think, goes beyond anything that has been decided in the cases where anticipatory repudiation has been considered. It makes an arbitrary distinction and one differing in its consequences according as performance is first called for under the contract from the repudiating party, or from the other party. In the former case there is a plain breach of contract making the repudiating party liable in damages, unless where a claim for specific implement is available. In the latter case, according to the submission made, he is liable contractually for a debt at least where the consideration for performance by the other party is expressed in money. The law of Scotland has always stressed the mutuality of contracts and it should follow, in my opinion, that the consequences of breach of contract by either party should correspond. I would state the position in the case of an anticipatory repudiation not accepted by the other party as a breach of contract thus: If the contract is to take operative effect in the first place by performance of the repudiating party and he maintains his repudiation by refusing, or failing to give performance, the other party has a cause of action for either damages or specific implement. If performance is first to be given by the other party and the time for his performance has arrived he must tender performance, in the sense of showing that he is now ready and able to give performance, and if this tender is still rejected by the repudiating party his only cause of action again arises to him as at that date.

I would refer first to contracts for the sale of goods which were touched on in the course of the debate, for the reason that one of the remedies provided to the seller by the Sale of Goods Act 1893, is an action for the price. This, however, applies only in two cases. One is where the property in the goods has passed to the buyer. But property cannot pass without the intention of the buyer as well as that of the seller and, except in some such cases as fraud or lack of consensus in idem or breach of contract by the seller, no question of repudiation can arise. The contract is completed and finished apart from delivery and nothing remains but payment of the price. The only other case is where parties have contracted for payment on a day certain, irrespective of delivery or the passing of property. This is a clear case of a contractual debt unconditioned by any question of performance by the other party. A much closer parallel with the present case is a contract to sell future, or unascertained goods. In this case there can be no appropriation of, and therefore passing of, property in the goods without the assent of both buyer and seller. If therefore the buyer repudiates the contract before appropriation, or refuses his assent to appropriation, there can be no passing of property. The seller is then confined to an action of damages for breach of contract. This, of course, is a rule of statute. But the Act is largely declaratory of English law, though not of Scots law. So the rule can only be treated as an analogy, but it is an analogy which seems to me to make a hole in the principle contended for by the appellants ...

I find the argument advanced for the appellants a somewhat startling one. If it is right it would seem that a man who has contracted to go to Hong Kong at his own expense and make a report, in return for remuneration of £10,000, and who, before the date fixed for the start of the journey and perhaps before he has incurred any expense, is informed by the other contracting party that he has cancelled or repudiates the contract, is entitled to set off for Hong Kong and produce his report in order to claim in debt the stipulated sum. Such a result is not, in my opinion, in accordance with principle or authority, and cuts across the rule that where one party is in breach of contract the other must take steps to minimise the loss sustained by the breach ...

Notes and questions

1. 'The two causes of action, namely, that for debt or money due under the contract and that for damages for breach of contract, are quite different ...' (Davies LJ, *Overstone Ltd v Shipway* [1962] 1 WLR 117). Does this mean that if the plaintiff in *White & Carter* had lost his debt claim he could, at a later date, have brought a quite separate damages action?

2. Might it be an abuse of a right to sue in debt rather than damages? Does equity have a doctrine of abuse of rights? Does the common law? What about EU law?

3. What is meant by 'legitimate interest' in this context?

Attica Sea Carriers Corp v Ferrostaal Poseidon [1976] 1 Ll Rep 250 Court of Appeal

Lord Denning MR: ... [*White & Carter (Councils) Ltd v McGregor*] has no application whatever in a case where the plaintiff ought, in all reason, to accept the repudiation and sue for damages – provided that damages would provide an adequate remedy for any loss suffered by him. The reason is because, by suing for the money, the plaintiff is seeking to enforce specific performance of the contract — and he should not be allowed to do so when damages would be an adequate remedy ... [The owners] cannot sue for specific performance – either of the promise to pay the charter hire, or of the promise to do the repairs – because damages are an adequate remedy for the breach. What is the alternative which the shipowners present to the charterers? Either the charterers must pay the charter hire for years to come, whilst the vessel lies idle and useless for want of repair. Or the charterers must do the repairs which would cost twice as much as the ship would be worth when repaired – after which the shipowners might sell it as scrap, making the repairs a useless waste of money. In short, on either alternative, the shipowners seek to compel specific performance of one or other of the provisions of the charter – with most unjust and unreasonable consequences – when damages would be an adequate remedy. I do not think the law allows them to do this.

Questions

1. Is it true to say that English law is reluctant specifically to enforce contracts?

2. Were the defendants abusing their right? Did equity prevent them suing in debt?

Rowland v Divall [1923] 2 KB 500 Court of Appeal

This was an action for money had and received by a purchaser of a car, which subsequently turned out to be stolen and had to be surrendered to its true owner, for the return of the price paid. The Court of Appeal allowed the purchaser to recover the full price.

Atkin LJ: ... It seems to me that in this case there has been a total failure of consideration, that is to say that the buyer has not got any part of that for which he paid the purchase money. He paid the money in order that he might get the property, and he has not got it. It is true that the seller delivered to him the *de facto* possession, but the seller had not got the right to possession and consequently could not give it to the buyer. Therefore the buyer, during the time that he had the car in his actual possession had no right to it, and was at all times liable to the true owner for its conversion. Now there is no doubt that what the buyer had a right to get was the property in the car, for the Sale of Goods Act expressly provides that in every contract of sale there is an implied condition that the seller has a right to sell; and the only difficulty that I have felt in this case arises out of the wording of s 11, sub-s l(c), which says that: "Where a contract of sale is not severable, and the buyer has accepted the goods ... the breach of any condition to be fulfilled by the seller can only be treated as a breach of warranty, and not as a ground for rejecting the goods and treating the contract as repudiated, unless there be a term of the contract, express or implied, to that effect." It is said that this case falls within that provision, for the contract of sale was not severable and the buyer had accepted the car. But I think that the answer is that there can be no sale at all of goods which the seller has no right to sell. The whole object of a sale is to transfer property from one person to another. And I think that in every contract of sale of goods there is an implied term to the effect that a breach of the condition that the seller has a right to sell the goods may be treated as a ground for rejecting the goods and repudiating the contract notwithstanding the acceptance, within the meaning of the concluding words of sub-s (c); or in other words that the subsection has no application to a breach of that particular condition. It seems to me that in this case there must be a right to reject, and also a right to sue for the price paid as money had and received on failure of the consideration, and further that there is no obligation on the part of the buyer to return the car, for *ex hypothesi* the seller had no right to receive it. Under those circumstances can it make any difference that the buyer has used the car before he found out that there was a breach of the condition? To my mind it makes no difference at all. The buyer accepted the car on the representation of the seller that he had a right to sell it, and inasmuch as the seller had no such right he is not entitled to say that the buyer has enjoyed a benefit under the contract. In fact the buyer has not received any part of that which he contracted to receive – namely, the property and right to possession – and, that being so, there has been a total failure of consideration. The plaintiff is entitled to recover the £334 which he paid.

Questions

1. Is this case the reverse side of the coin, so to speak, of *Bolton v Mahadeva* (above p 126)? Did the plaintiff, by succeeding in debt, get a benefit that he did not have to pay for?

2. What is meant by total failure of consideration? Was the consideration for the promise to pay the price that title actually be transferred?

(c) Debt and damages

Wadsworth v Lydall [1981] 1 WLR 598 Court of Appeal

Brightman LJ: ... The second question on the appeal is a little more difficult. It is whether the plaintiff is entitled to recover as special damages the loss which he has suffered as a result of the defendant's failure to pay his debt under the contract on the due date ... The defendant contends that ... although interest can be awarded nowadays under [statute], damages cannot be awarded in respect of unpaid indebtness. The plaintiff is confined, the defendant says, to such interest as he is able to claim under the [statute], but is not entitled to damages ... In my view the court is not so constrained by the decision of the House of Lords. In *London, Chatham and Dover Railway Co v South Eastern Railway Co* [1893] AC 429 the House of Lords was not concerned with a claim for special damages. The action was an action for an account. The House was concerned only with a claim for interest by way of general damages. If a plaintiff pleads and can prove that he has suffered special damages as a result of the defendant's failure to perform his obligation under a contract, and such damage is not too remote on the principle of *Hadley v Baxendale* (1854) 9 Exch 341, I can see no logical reason why such special damage should be irrecoverable merely because the obligation on which the defendant defaulted was an obligation to pay money and not some other type of obligation ...

Ormrod LJ: ... The court has to look not at what this particular defendant knew or contemplated but what a reasonable person in his position would have contemplated ... This case is not on all fours with – and can be distinguished from – the *London, Chatham and Dover* case and clearly ought to be so distinguished.

Questions

1. Is it an abuse of a right when a debtor fails to pay a debt on time and this causes damage to the creditor? Or is it a simple breach of contract causing damage?

2. Why has the common law been so reluctant to award interest on debts not paid on time?

Damon Compania Naviera SA v Hapag-Lloyd [1985] 1 WLR 435 Court of Appeal

This was an action for damages brought by a seller of three ships against prospective buyers who, in breach of a contract concluded via telexes, failed to sign a formal contract of purchase. The telex contract contained a clause that a deposit of 10% would be payable on the signing of the formal contract. The disappointed sellers claimed this 10% by way of damages, and a majority of the Court of Appeal upheld their claim.

Fox LJ: ... Damages for breach of contract are a compensation for the loss which the plaintiff has suffered through the breach. Accordingly, the plaintiff is entitled to be placed in the same position as if the contractual obligation had been performed. In the present case, if the obligation had been performed, Hapag-Lloyd could have sued Damon in debt for the amount of the deposit and it seems to me that that should be reflected in the damages recoverable for breach of the obligation.

Robert Goff LJ (dissenting): ... If the repudiation occurred after Damon had paid the deposit, Hapag-Lloyd would be safe: they would have the deposit and could keep it. If the repudiation occurred after the obligation to pay the deposit had accrued due, but before Damon had paid it, Hapag-Lloyd could sue Damon for the deposit as a debt ... But if the repudiation occurred before Damon's obligation to pay the deposit had fallen due, then Hapag-Lloyd could only recover damages for repudiation, which would fall to be assessed on the usual basis of compensating Hapag-Lloyd for the loss of their bargain ... The normal measure, in a contract of sale of goods, is of course the difference between the contract and market prices for the goods. I can see no reason for departing from that ordinary measure of damages in the present case. To award Hapag-Lloyd damages assessed on the basis of the amount of the deposit would be to compare their present position with what their position would have been if the contract had only been partially performed (ie, the deposit paid), and not with their position if the contract had been performed in full; if damages were assessed in that way, they would be over-compensated for the loss of their bargain. In truth, the inability of Hapag-Lloyd to obtain the protection of the deposit, in the circumstances of the present case, flows from their contracting on such terms that the deposit was not payable forthwith upon the making of the contract.

Stephenson LJ: ... On the last point I am attracted by the logic of Robert Goff LJ's contrary opinion. But the measure of damages resulting from Damon's repudiatory breach is, in my opinion, the loss directly and naturally resulting from the breach in the ordinary course of events, and I agree with Fox LJ that that loss is the amount of the deposit ...

Questions

1. What interest does an action in debt protect? Is this an interest that is always protected by an action in damages? What must the plaintiff show in order to succeed in protecting this interest via damages?

2. What was the cause of the plaintiffs' loss?

(d) Non-contractual debt

The Aldora [1975] QB 748 Queen's Bench

Brandon J: ... I do not think that a claim for salvage is a proceeding for the recovery of damages, and the question is accordingly reduced to this: whether it is a proceeding for the recovery of a debt. As to this it is to be observed that the words used are 'any debt', indicating that the net is being spread as widely as possible. Those words are, as it seems to me, apt to cover sums, whether liquidated or unliquidated, which a person is obliged to pay either under a contract, express or implied, or under a statute. They would, therefore, cover a common law claim on a '*quantum meruit*', or a statutory claim for a sum recoverable as a debt, for instance a claim for damages done to harbour works under s 74 of the Harbour, Docks, and Piers Clauses Act 1847.

United Australia Ltd v Barclays Bank Ltd [1941] AC 1 House of Lords

(See p 130)

Fibrosa Spolka Akcyjna v Fairbairn Lawson Combe Barbour Ltd [1943] AC 32 House of Lords

(See p 130)

Notes and questions

1. If the focal point of an action for damages is loss, what is the focal point for an action in debt?
2. The common law recognises three categories of non-contractual debt claims: (i) the action for money had and received; (ii) the action for money paid; and (iii) an action on a *quantum-meruit* (see Chapter 7). What is the obligation basis of these claims? Is this an area where civil law learning can be helpful? What is the relationship, if any, between these common law claims and equitable remedies?

6 TRACING

Agip (Africa) Ltd v Jackson [1990] Ch 265 Chancery Division [1991] Ch 547 Court of Appeal

Millet J (Chancery Division): ... The plaintiffs claim to recover money paid under a mistake ... Unlike a tracing claim in equity, the common law claim for money had and received is a personal and not a proprietary claim and the cause of action is complete when the money is received. With only limited exceptions, it is no defence that the defendant has parted with the money. The claim does not depend on any impropriety or want of probity on the part of the defendants ...

Tracing at common law

... Tracing at common law, unlike its counterpart in equity, is neither a cause of action nor a remedy but serves an evidential purpose. The cause of action is for money had and received. Tracing at common law enables the defendant to be identified as the recipient of the plaintiff's money and the measure of his liability to be determined by the amount of the plaintiff's money he is shown to have received.

The common law has always been able to follow a physical asset from one recipient to another. Its ability to follow an asset in the same hands into a changed form was established in *Taylor v Plumer*, 3 M & S 562. In following the plaintiff's money into an asset purchased exclusively with it, no distinction is drawn between a chose in action such as the debt of a bank to its customer and any other asset: *In re Diplock* [1948] Ch 465, 519. But it can only follow a physical asset, such as a cheque or its proceeds, from one person to another. It can follow money but not a chose in action. Money can be followed at common law into and out of a bank account and into the hands of a subsequent transferee, provided that it does not cease to be identifiable by being mixed with other money in the bank account derived from some other source: *Banque Belge pour l'Etranger v Hambrouck* [1921] 1 KB 321 ...

The cause of action for money had and received is complete when the plaintiff's money is received by the defendant. It does not depend on the continued retention of the money by the defendant. Save in strictly limited circumstances it is no defence that he has parted with it. *A fortiori* it can be no defence for him to show that he has so mixed it with his own money that he cannot tell whether he still has it or not. Mixing by the defendant himself must, therefore, be distinguished from mixing by a prior recipient. The former is irrelevant, but the latter will destroy the claim, for it will prevent proof that the money received by the defendant was the money paid by the plaintiff ...

That case [*Banque Belge*] apart, there is none so far as I am aware in which a claim for money had and received has been successfully brought against anyone other than the immediate recipient of the money or his principal. In that case H obtained by fraud from his employer a number of cheques purporting to be drawn by the employer on the plaintiff bank. He paid the cheques into a bank account in his own name. His bank collected the proceeds from the plaintiff bank and credited them to H's account. H then drew cheques on his account in favour of S, his mistress, who paid them into her own account at her own bank. She spent most of the money but a balance of £315 remained. This sum was paid into court by her bank and was claimed by the plaintiff bank. The plaintiff bank was held entitled to it.

It is not easy to know what that case decided. The plaintiff bank sought a declaration that the £315 was its property. The relief it claimed was not a money judgment but an order for payment of the £315. In other words, it was making a proprietary claim. The trial judge, however, treated it as a common law action for money had and received and entered an ordinary money judgment against S for the sum claimed. Her appeal was dismissed.

The plaintiff had limited its claim to the £315 in court. That was also consistent with a proprietary claim, though the decision to limit the claim may have been due to other considerations. But there is no hint in any of the judgments in Court of Appeal that the claim need not have been so limited; although if S was in truth personally accountable for money had and received, the fact that she had dissipated the money was irrelevant. On the contrary, Banks LJ was concerned to show that the money had not been mixed in her account, which indicates that he considered the claim to be a proprietary one in which it was necessary to establish not what S had received but what she still retained.

Scrutton LJ held that the money could be traced in equity. It is not clear whether he relied on this to support the common law claim or to found relief in equity, but since the plaintiff had limited its claim to the £315, this made no difference to the result. Atkin LJ alone drew attention to the difference between the two types of claim. He, too, held that the money could be followed in equity, and that this entitled the plaintiff to a specific order for the return of the money in question. He then dealt expressly with the common law action for money had and received and held that the plaintiff's ability to follow the money at common law entitled it to bring such an action.

I think that at first instance I am bound to regard that case as authority for the proposition that an action for money had and received is not limited to the immediate recipient or his principal but may be brought against a subsequent transferee into whose hands the money can be followed and who still retains it. But it is no authority for the proposition that it lies against a subsequent transferee who has parted with the money, and I doubt that it does. At this remove the action begins to take on the aspect of a proprietary claim rather than the enforcement of a personal liability to account. Should it be sought to impose personal liability on a person who has parted with the money, recourse can be made to equity which has developed appropriate principles by which such liability can be determined. The alternative is to expose an innocent transferee who has dissipated the money to a claim at law where none would exist in equity and to make that liability depend on the fortuitous circumstance that the money had not been mixed with other money prior to its receipt by him. Such a difference in outcome cannot be justified as reflecting the fact that in one case the defendant is being required to account to the former legal owner while in the other he is accounting merely to an owner in equity, for the equitable remedies are available to the former legal owner who has been deprived of his property as the result of a breach of fiduciary obligation ...

There is no difficulty in tracing the plaintiffs' money in equity, which has well developed principles by which the proceeds of fraud can be followed and recovered from those through whose hands they pass. Whether equity can make its tracing rules available in aid of common law remedies, or whether, as I think, it would be preferable to develop a unified restitutionary remedy for the recovery of property transferred without consideration to a recipient with no legitimate justification for receiving it, are questions which must be left for others to decide. There is certainly no need for recourse to the common law action for money had and received, which is not well equipped for the task. In my judgment, the plaintiffs' attempted reliance on the common law was unnecessary and misplaced.

The claim in equity

There is no difficulty in tracing the plaintiffs' property in equity, which can follow the money as it passed through the accounts of the correspondent banks in New York or, more realistically, follow the chose in action through its transmutation as a direct result of forged instructions from a debt owed by the Banque du Sud to the plaintiffs in Tunis into a debt owed by Lloyds Bank to Baker Oil in London.

The only restriction on the ability of equity to follow assets is the requirement that there must be some fiduciary relationship which permits the assistance of equity to be invoked. The requirement has been widely condemned and depends on authority rather than principle, but the law was settled by *In re Diplock* [1948] Ch 465. It may need to be reconsidered but not, I venture to think, at first instance. The requirement may be circumvented since it is not necessary that the fund to be traced should have been the subject of fiduciary obligations before it got into the wrong hands; it is sufficient that the payment to the defendant itself gives rise to a fiduciary relationship: *Chase Manhattan Bank NA v Israel-British Bank (London) Ltd* [1981] Ch 105. In that case, however, equity's assistance was not needed in order to trace the plaintiff's money into the hands of the defendant; it was needed in order to ascertain whether it had any of the plaintiff's money left. The case cannot, therefore, be used to circumvent the requirement that there should be an initial fiduciary relationship in order to start the tracing process in equity.

The requirement is, however, readily satisfied in most cases of commercial fraud, since the embezzlement of a company's funds almost inevitably involves a breach of fiduciary duty on the part of one of the company's employees or agents ...

The tracing remedy

The tracing claim in equity gives rise to a proprietary remedy which depends on the continued existence of the trust property in the hands of the defendant. Unless he is a *bona fide* purchaser for value without notice, he must restore the trust property to its rightful owner if he still has it. But even a volunteer who has received trust property cannot be made subject to a personal liability to account for it as a constructive trustee if he has parted with it without having previously acquired some knowledge of the existence of the trust: *In re Montagu's Settlement Trusts* [1987] Ch 264.

The plaintiffs are entitled to the money in court which rightfully belongs to them. To recover the money which the defendants have paid away the plaintiffs must subject them to a personal liability to account as constructive trustees and prove the requisite degree of knowledge to establish the liability ...

Knowing assistance

A stranger to the trust will also be liable to account as a constructive trustee if he knowingly assists in the furtherance of a fraudulent and dishonest breach of trust. It is not necessary that the party sought to be made liable as a constructive trustee should have received any part of the trust property, but the breach of trust must have been fraudulent. The basis of the stranger's liability is not receipt of trust property but participation in a fraud ...

In my judgment it necessarily follows that constructive notice of the fraud is not enough to make him liable. There is no sense in requiring dishonesty on the part of the principal while accepting negligence as sufficient for his assistant. Dishonest furtherance of the dishonest scheme of another is an understandable basis for liability; negligent but honest failure to appreciate that someone else's scheme is dishonest is not ...

Fox LJ (Court of appeal): ... Agip's claim was for money paid under a mistake of fact. The defendants' contention was that Agip had disclosed no title to sue. The basis of that contention was that the relationship between banker and customer was one of debtor and creditor. When the customer paid money into the bank, the ownership of the money passed to the bank. The bank could do what it liked with it. What the bank undertook to do was to credit the amount of the money to the customer's account, and to honour his drafts or other proper directions in relation to it ... The banker's instruction is to pay from the customer's account. He does so by a payment from his own funds and a corresponding debit. The reality is a payment by the customer, at any rate in a case where the customer has no right to require a re-crediting of his account. Nothing passes *in specie*. The whole matter is dealt with by accounting transactions partly in the paying bank and partly in the clearing process ...

The order, after all, was an order to pay with Agip's money. I agree, therefore, with the view of Millett J [1990] Ch 265, 283H that "the fact remains that the Banque du Sud paid out the plaintiffs' money and not its own". If Banque du Sud paid away Agip's money, Agip itself must be entitled to pursue such remedies as there may be for its recovery. The money was certainly paid under a mistake of fact ...

Tracing at common law

The judge held that Agip was not entitled to trace at law. Tracing at law does not depend upon the establishment of an initial fiduciary relationship. Liability depends upon receipt by the defendant of the plaintiff's money and the extent of the liability depends on the amount received. Since liability depends upon receipt the fact that a recipient has not retained the asset is irrelevant. For the same reason dishonesty or lack of inquiry on the part of the recipient are irrelevant. Identification in the defendant's hands of the plaintiff's asset is, however, necessary. It must be shown that the money received by the defendant was the money of the plaintiff. Further, the very limited common law remedies make it difficult to follow at law into mixed funds ...

Tracing in equity

Both common law and equity accepted the right of the true owner to trace his property into the hands of others while it was in an identifiable form. The common law treated property as identified if it had not been mixed with other property. Equity, on the other hand, will follow money into a mixed fund and charge the fund. There is, in the present case, no difficulty about the mechanics of tracing in equity. The money can be traced through the various bank accounts to Baker Oil and onwards. It is, however, a prerequisite to the operation of the remedy in equity that there must be a fiduciary relationship which calls the equitable jurisdiction into being ...

Questions

1. Is tracing at common law based on a right of property in the money?
2. What is the relationship between tracing at common law and an action for money had and received?
3. Will tracing at common law ever be available in circumstances where tracing in equity is not available?
4. E steals £500 from P, his employer, and gives the cash to his mother, D, who invests it on the stock exchange and ends up with £50,000. Can P claim the £50,000 from D? What if D had invested the money in an old painting that turned out to be worth £50,000: could P claim the painting?

Lipkin Gorman v Karpnale Ltd [1991] 2 AC 548 House of Lords

A partner in a firm of solicitors embezzled cash from the firm's bank account and lost the money gambling at the defendants' casino. When the solicitors brought an action in debt (money had and received) to recover the lost cash, the gambling club claimed that they were *bona fide* purchasers for value having exchanged the money for gambling chips. The House of Lords allowed the solicitors to succeed in debt on the basis that they could trace their money into the defendants' bank account.

Lord Goff: ... The solicitors' claim is, in substance, as follows. They say, first, that the cash handed over by the bank to Chapman in exchange for the cheques drawn on the solicitors' client account by Cass was in law the property of the solicitors. That is disputed by the respondents who say that, since the cheques were drawn on the bank by Cass without the authority of his partners, the legal property in the money immediately vested in Cass; that argument was however rejected by the Court of Appeal. If that argument is rejected, the respondents concede for present purposes that the cash so obtained by Cass from the client account was paid by him to the club, but they nevertheless resist the solicitors' claim on two grounds: first, that they gave valuable consideration for the money in good faith, as held by a majority of the Court of Appeal; and second that, in any event, having received the money in good faith and having given Cass the opportunity of winning bets and, in some cases, recovering substantial sums by way of winnings, it would be inequitable to allow the solicitors' claim ...

Title to the money

... [I]n the present case, the solicitors seek to show that the money in question was their property at common law. But their claim in the present case for money had and received is nevertheless a personal claim; it is not a proprietary claim, advanced on the basis that money remaining in the hands of the respondents is their property. Of course there is no doubt that, even if legal title to the money did vest in Cass immediately on receipt, nevertheless he would have held it on trust for his partners, who would accordingly have been entitled to trace it in equity into the hands of the respondents. However, your Lordships are not concerned with an equitable tracing claim in the present case, since no such case is advanced by the solicitors, who have been content to proceed at common law by a personal action, *viz* an action for money had and received. I should add that, in the present case, we are not concerned with the fact that money drawn by Cass from the solicitors' client account at the bank may have become mixed by Cass with his own money before he gambled it away at the club. For the respondents have conceded that, if the solicitors can establish legal title to the money in the hands of Cass, that title was not defeated by mixing of the money with other money of Cass while in his hands. On this aspect of the case, therefore, the only question is whether the solicitors can establish legal title to the money when received by Cass from the bank by drawing cheques on the client account without authority.

It is well established that a legal owner is entitled to trace his property into its product, provided that the latter is indeed identifiable as the product of his property. Thus, in *Taylor v Plumer* (1815) 3 M & S 562, where Sir Thomas Plumer gave a draft to a stockbroker for the purpose of buying exchequer bills, and the stockbroker instead used the draft for buying American securities and doubloons for his own purposes, Sir Thomas was able to trace his property into the securities and doubloons in the hands of the stockbroker, and so defeat a claim made to them by the stockbroker's assignees in bankruptcy. Of course, "tracing" or "following" property into its product involves a decision by the owner of the original property to assert his title to the product in place of his original property ...

I return to the present case. Before Cass drew upon the solicitors' client account at the bank, there was of course no question of the solicitors having any legal property in any cash lying at the bank. The relationship of the bank with the solicitors was essentially that of debtor and creditor; and since the client account was at all material times in credit, the bank was the debtor and the solicitors were its creditors. Such a debt constitutes a chose in action, which is a species of property; and since the debt was enforceable at common law, the chose in action was legal property belonging to the solicitors at common law.

There is in my opinion no reason why the solicitors should not be able to trace their property at common law in that chose in action, or in any part of it, into its product, ie cash drawn by Cass from their client account at the bank. Such a claim is consistent with their assertion that the money so obtained by Cass was their property at common law. Further, in claiming the money as money had and received, the solicitors have not sought to make the respondents liable on the basis of any wrong, a point which will be of relevance at a later stage, when I come to consider the defence of change of position ...

Whether the respondents gave consideration for the money

There is no doubt that the respondents received the money in good faith; but, as I have already recorded, there was an acute difference of opinion among the members of the Court of Appeal whether the respondents gave consideration for it. Parker LJ was of opinion that they did so, for two reasons. (1) The club supplied chips in exchange for the money. The contract under which the chips were supplied was a separate contract, independent of the contracts under which bets were placed at the club; and the contract for the chips was not avoided as a contract by way of gaming and wagering under s 18 of the Gaming Act 1845. (2) Although the actual gaming contracts were void under the Act, nevertheless Cass in fact obtained in exchange for the money the chance of winning and of then being paid and so received valuable consideration from the club.

May LJ agreed with the first of these two reasons. Nicholls LJ disagreed with both.

I have to say at once that I am unable to accept the alternative basis upon which Parker LJ held that consideration was given for the money, *viz* that each time Cass placed a bet at the casino, he obtained in exchange the chance of winning and thus of being paid. In my opinion, when Cass placed a bet, he received nothing in return which constituted valuable consideration. The contract of gaming was void; in other words, it was binding in honour only. Cass knew, of course, that, if he won his bet, the club would pay him his winnings. But he had no legal right to claim them. He simply had a confident expectation that, in fact, the club would pay; indeed, if the club did not fulfil its obligations binding in honour upon it, it would very soon go out of business. But it does not follow that, when Cass placed the bet, he received anything that the law recognises as valuable consideration. In my opinion he did not do so. Indeed, to hold that consideration had been given for the money on this basis would, in my opinion, be inconsistent with *Clarke v Shee and Johnson*, 1 Cowp 197. Even when a winning bet has been paid, the gambler does not receive valuable consideration for his money. All that he receives is, in law, a gift from the club ...

But this broad approach does not solve the problem, which is essentially one of analysis. I think it best to approach the problem by taking a situation unaffected by the impact of the Gaming Acts.

Suppose that a large department store decides, for reasons of security, that all transactions in the store are to be effected by the customers using chips instead of money. On entering the store, or later, the customer goes to cash desk and obtains chips to the amount he needs in exchange for cash or a cheque. When he buys goods, he presents chips for his purchase. Before he leaves the store, he presents his remaining chips, and receives cash in return. The example may be unrealistic, but in legal terms it is reasonably straightforward. A contract is made when the customer obtains his chips under which the store agrees that, if goods are purchased by the customer, the store will accept chips to the equivalent value of the price, and further that it will redeem for cash any chips returned to it before the customer leaves the store. If a customer offers to buy a certain item of goods at the store, and the girl behind the counter accepts his offer but then refuses to accept the customer's chips, the store will be in breach of the contract for chips. Likewise if, before he leaves the store, the customer hands in some or all of his chips at the cash desk, and the girl at the cash desk refuses to redeem them, the store will be in breach of the contract for chips.

Each time that a customer buys goods, he enters into a contract of sale, under which the customer purchases goods at the store. This is a contract for the sale of goods; it is not a contract of exchange, under which goods are exchanged for chips, but a contract of sale, under which goods are bought for a price, ie for a money consideration. This is because, when the customer surrenders chips of the appropriate denomination, the store appropriates part of the money deposited with it towards the purchase. This does not however alter the fact that an independent contract is made for the chips when the customer originally obtains them at the cash desk. Indeed that contract is not dependent upon any contract of sale being entered into; the customer could walk around the store and buy nothing, and then be entitled to redeem his chips in full under the terms of his contract with the store.

But the question remains: when the customer hands over his cash at the cash desk, and receives his chips, does the store give valuable consideration for the money so received by it? In common sense terms, the answer is no. For, in substance and in reality, there is simply a gratuitous deposit of the money with the store, with liberty to the customer to draw upon that deposit to pay for any goods he buys at the store. The chips are no more than the mechanism by which that result is achieved without any cash being handed over at the sales counter, and by which the customer can claim repayment of any balance remaining of his deposit. If a technical approach is adopted, it might be said that, since the property in the money passes to the store as depositee, it then gives consideration for the money in the form of a chose in action created by its promise to repay a like sum, subject to draw-down in respect of goods purchased at the store. I however prefer the common sense approach. Nobody would say that the store has purchased the money by promising to repay it: the promise to repay is simply the means of giving effect to the gratuitous deposit of the money with the store. It follows that, by receiving the money in these circumstances, the store does not for present purposes give valuable consideration for it. Otherwise a bank with which money was deposited by an innocent donee from a thief could claim to be a bona fide purchaser of the money simply by virtue of the fact of the deposit.

Let me next take the case of gambling at a casino. Of course, if gaming contracts were not void under English law by virtue of section 18 of the Gaming Act 1845, the result would be exactly the same. There would be a contract in respect of the chips, under which the money was deposited with the casino; and then separate contracts would be made when each bet was placed, at which point of time part or all of the money so deposited would be appropriated to the bets.

However, contracts by way of gaming or wagering are void in English law. What is the effect of this? It is obvious that each time a bet is placed by the gambler, the agreement under which the bet is placed is an agreement by way of gaming or wagering, and so is rendered null and void. It follows, as I have said, that the casino, by accepting the bet, does not thereby give valuable consideration for the money which has been wagered by the gambler, because the casino is under no legal obligation to honour the bet. Of course, the gambler cannot recover the money from the casino on the ground of failure of consideration; for he has relied upon the casino to honour the wager – he has in law given the money to the casino, trusting that the casino will fulfil the obligation binding in honour upon it and pay him if he wins his bet – though if the casino does so its payment to the gambler will likewise be in law a gift. But suppose it is not the gambler but the true owner of the money (from whom the gambler has perhaps, as in the present case, stolen the money) who is claiming it from the casino. What then? In those circumstances the casino cannot, in my opinion, say that it has given valuable consideration for the money, whether or not the gambler's bet is successful. It has given no consideration if the bet is unsuccessful, because its promise to pay on a successful bet is void; nor has it done so if the gambler's bet is successful and the casino has paid him his winnings, because that payment is in law a gift to the gambler by the casino.

For these reasons I conclude, in agreement with Nicholls LJ, that the respondents did not give valuable consideration for the money. But the matter does not stop there; because there remains the question whether the respondents can rely upon the defence of change of position.

Change of position

I turn then to the last point on which the respondents relied to defeat the solicitors' claim for the money. This was that the claim advanced by the solicitors was in the form of an action for money had and received, and that such a claim should only succeed where the defendant was unjustly enriched at the expense of the plaintiff. If it would be unjust or unfair to order restitution, the claim should fail. It was for the court to consider the question of injustice or unfairness, on broad grounds. If the court thought that it would be unjust or unfair to hold the respondents liable to the solicitors, it should deny the solicitors recovery. Mr Lightman, for the club, listed a number of reasons why, in his submission, it would be unfair to hold the respondents liable. These were (1) the club acted throughout in good faith, ignorant of the fact that the money had been stolen by Cass; (2) although the gaming contracts entered into by the club with Cass were all void, nevertheless the club honoured all those contracts; (3) Cass was allowed to keep his winnings (to the extent that he did not gamble them away); (4) the gaming contracts were merely void not illegal; and (5) the solicitors' claim was no different in principle from a claim to recover against an innocent third party to whom the money was given and who no longer retained it.

I accept that the solicitors' claim in the present case is founded upon the unjust enrichment of the club, and can only succeed if, in accordance with the principles of the law of restitution, the club was indeed unjustly enriched at the expense of the solicitors. The claim for money had and received is not, as I have previously mentioned, founded upon any wrong committed by the club against the solicitors. But it does not, in my opinion, follow that the court has carte blanche to reject the solicitors' claim simply because it thinks it unfair or unjust in the circumstances to grant recovery. The recovery of money in restitution is not, as a general rule, a matter of discretion for the court. A claim to recovery of money at common law is made as a matter of right; and even though the underlying principle of recovery is the principle of unjust enrichment, nevertheless, where recovery is denied, it is denied on the basis of legal principle.

It is therefore necessary to consider whether Mr Lightman's submission can be upheld on the basis of legal principle. In my opinion it is plain, from the nature of his submission, that he is in fact seeking to invoke a principle of change of position, asserting that recovery should be denied because of the change in position of the respondents, who acted in good faith throughout.

Whether change of position is, or should be, recognised as a defence to claims in restitution is a subject which has been much debated in the books. It is, however, a matter on which there is a remarkable unanimity of view, the consensus being to the effect that such a defence should be recognised in English law. I myself am under no doubt that this is right ...

In these circumstances, it is right that we should ask ourselves: why do we feel that it would be unjust to allow restitution in cases such as these? The answer must be that, where an innocent defendant's position is so changed that he will suffer an injustice if called upon to repay or to repay in full, the injustice of requiring him so to repay outweighs the injustice of denying the plaintiff restitution. If the plaintiff pays money to the defendant under a mistake of fact, and the defendant then, acting in good faith, pays the money or part of it to charity, it is unjust to require the defendant to make restitution to the extent that he has so changed his position. Likewise, on facts such as those in the present case, if a thief steals money and pays it to a third party who gives it away to charity, that third party should have a good defence to an action for money had and received. In other words, bona fide change of position should of itself be a good defence in such cases as these. The principle is widely recognised throughout the common law world ... The time for its recognition in this country is, in my opinion, long overdue.

I am most anxious that, in recognising this defence to actions of restitution, nothing should be said at this stage to inhibit the development of the defence on a case by case basis, in the usual way. It is, of course, plain that the defence is not open to one who has changed his position in bad faith, as where the defendant has paid away the money with knowledge of the facts entitling the plaintiff to restitution; and it is commonly accepted that the defence should not be open to a wrongdoer. These are matters which can, in due course, be considered in depth in cases where they arise for consideration. They do not arise in the present case. Here there is no doubt that the respondents have acted in good faith throughout, and the action is not founded upon any wrongdoing of the respondents. It is not however appropriate in the present case to attempt to identify all those actions in restitution to which change of position may be a defence. A prominent example will, no doubt, be found in those cases where the plaintiff is seeking repayment of money paid under a mistake of fact; but I can see no reason why the defence should not also be available in principle in a case such as the present, where the plaintiff's money has been paid by a thief to an innocent donee, and the plaintiff then seeks repayment from the donee in an action for money had and received. At present I do not wish to state the principle any less broadly than this: that the defence is available to a person whose position has so changed that it would be inequitable in all the circumstances to require him to make restitution, or alternatively to make restitution in full. I wish to stress however that the mere fact that the defendant has spent the money, in whole or in part, does not of itself render it inequitable that he should be called upon to repay, because the expenditure might in any event have been incurred by him in the ordinary course of things. I fear that the mistaken assumption that mere expenditure of money may be regarded as amounting to a change of position for present purposes has led in the past to opposition by some to recognition of a defence which in fact is likely to be available only on comparatively rare occasions. In this connection I have particularly in mind the speech of Lord Simonds in *Ministry of Health v Simpson* [1951] AC 251, 276.

I wish to add two further footnotes. The defence of change of position is akin to the defence of *bona fide* purchase; but we cannot simply say that *bona fide* purchase is a species of change of position. This is because change of position will only avail a defendant to the extent that his position has been changed; whereas, where *bona fide* purchase is invoked, no inquiry is made (in most cases) into the adequacy of the consideration. Even so, the recognition of change of position as a defence should be doubly beneficial. It will enable a more generous approach to be taken to the recognition of the right to restitution, in the knowledge that the defence is, in appropriate cases, available; and while recognising the different functions of property at law and in equity, there may also in due course develop a more consistent approach to tracing claims, in which common defences are recognised as available to such claims, whether advanced at law or in equity ...

Notes and questions

1. 'For my part, I think that the true distinction lies between a proprietary claim on the one hand, and a claim which seeks only a money judgment on the other. A proprietary claim is one by which the plaintiff seeks the return of chattels or land which are his property, or claims that a specified debt is owed by a third party to him and not to the defendant ...' (Staughton LJ, *Republic of Haiti v Duvalier* [1990] 1 QB 202). Are all proprietary claims tracing actions?[9]

2. Is a tracing claim at common law an *actio in rem* or *in personam*?

3. What is the relationship, if any, between change of position and estoppel?

4. How can one own a debt? Why was it that the widow in *Beswick v Beswick* (below p 37) could not claim that she was owner of the debts owed to her by the nephew?

5. Does one need a defence of change of position? Could it not be said that tracing, *vis-à-vis* any particular defendant, ends where that defendant in good faith has paid money forming the object of a tracing claim to a third party?

6. Should tracing attach to the money (or other tangible thing) or to the value? What difference would it make? Is the distinction between *res* and value important in respect of the defence of change of position?

7. Did the plaintiff in *Rowland v Divall* (above p 137) have any property right in the purchase price while it remained in the defendant's possession?

In re Goldcorp Exchange Ltd [1994] 3 WLR 199 Privy Council

Lord Mustill: On 11 July 1988 the Bank of New Zealand Ltd (...) caused receivers to be appointed under the terms of a debenture issued by Goldcorp Exchange Ltd (...), dealer in gold and other precious metals. The company was then and still remains hopelessly insolvent ... The discovery that not only was there a shortfall in available bullion but also that the stock of bullion had been dealt with internally in a manner quite different from what had been promised by the vendors in their promotional literature has aroused great indignation amongst the members of the public (more than 1,000) whose faith in the promises made by the vendors has proved to be misplaced. These feelings were exacerbated when it was realised that the debt secured by the debenture and the floating charge which it created were in excess of the entire assets of the company, including the stocks of bullion, so that if the secured interest of the bank is satisfied in preference to the claims of the purchasers, the latter will receive nothing at all. This has impelled the private investors (...) to assert in the liquidation of the company, not their unanswerable personal claims against the

---

9   Cf *Ingram v Little* [1961] 1 QB 31; *Bowmakers Ltd v Barnett Instruments Ltd* [1945] KB 45.

company for damages or for the repayment of sums paid in advance, but claims of a proprietary nature ...

In the High Court all the claims were founded on the proposition that the customers had, or must be deemed to have, proprietary interests in the bullion which could be traced into the stock remaining on liquidation ...

Their Lordships begin with the question whether the customer obtained any form of proprietary interest, legal or equitable, simply by virtue of the contract of sale, independently of the collateral promises. In the opinion of their Lordships the answer is so clearly that he did not that it would be possible simply to quote ... section 16 of the Sale of Goods Act 1893 ... and one reported case, and turn to more difficult issues. It is common ground that the contracts in question were for the sale of unascertained goods ...

Approaching these situations *a priori* common sense dictates that the buyer cannot acquire title until it is known to what goods the title relates. Whether the property then passes will depend upon the intention of the parties and in particular on whether there has been a consensual appropriation of particular goods to the contract ...

A more plausible ... argument posits that the company, having represented to its customers that they had title to bullion held in the vaults, cannot now be heard to say that they did not. At first sight this argument gains support from a small group of cases, of which *Knights v Wiffen* (1870) LR 5 QB 660 is the most prominent ...

Assuming that the decision was nevertheless correct the question is whether it applies to the present case. Their Lordships consider that, notwithstanding the apparent similarities, it does not ... The present case is quite different, for there was no existing bulk and therefore nothing from which a title could be carved out by a deemed appropriation. The reasoning of *Knights v Wiffen* does not enable a bulk to be conjured into existence for this purpose simply through the chance that the vendor happens to have some goods answering the description of the *res vendita* in its trading stock at the time of the sale – quite apart, of course, from the fact that if all the purchasers obtained a deemed title by estoppel there would not be enough bullion to go around ...

Let it be assumed, however, that the company could properly be described as a fiduciary and let it also be assumed that notwithstanding the doubts expressed above the non-allocated claimants would have achieved some kind of proprietary interest if the company had done what it said. This still leaves the problem, to which their Lordships can see no answer, that the company did not do what it said. There never was a separate and sufficient stock of bullion in which a proprietary interest could be created. What the non-allocated claimants are really trying to achieve is to attach the proprietary interest, which they maintain should have been created on the non-existent stock, to wholly different assets. It is understandable that the claimants, having been badly let down in a transaction concerning bullion should believe that they must have rights over whatever bullion the company still happens to possess. Whilst sympathising with this notion their Lordships must reject it, for the remaining stock, having never been separated, is just another asset of the company, like its vehicles and office furniture. If the argument applies to the bullion it must apply to the latter as well, an obviously unsustainable idea ...

Finally, it is argued that the court should declare in favour of the claimants a remedial constructive trust, or to use another name a restitutionary proprietary interest, over the bullion in the company's vaults ... Their Lordships ... are unable to understand how the doctrine in any of its suggested formulations could apply to the facts of the present case. By leaving its stock of bullion in a non-differentiated state the company did not unjustly enrich itself by mixing its own bullion with that of the purchasers: for all the gold belonged to the company. It did not act wrongfully in acquiring, maintaining and using its own stock of bullion, since there was no term of the sale contracts or of the collateral promises, and none could possibly be implied, requiring that all bullion purchased by the company should be set aside to fulfil the unallocated sales. The conduct of the company was wrongful in the sense of being a breach of contract, but it did not involve any injurious dealing with the subject matter of the alleged trust ... The company's stock of bullion had no connection with the claimants' purchases, and to enable the claimants to reach out and not only abstract it from the assets available to the body of creditors as a whole, but also to afford a priority over a secured creditor, would give them an adventitious benefit devoid of the foundation in logic and justice which underlies this important new branch of the law ...

Whilst it is convenient to speak of the customers "getting their money back" this expression is misleading. Upon payment by the customers the purchase moneys became, and rescission or no rescission remained, the unencumbered property of the company. What the customers would recover on rescission would not be "their" money, but an equivalent sum. Leaving aside for the moment the creation by the court of a new remedial proprietary right, to which totally different considerations would apply, the claimants would have to contend that in every case where a purchaser is misled into buying goods he is automatically entitled upon rescinding the contract to a proprietary right superior to those of all the vendor's other creditors, exercisable against the whole of the vendor's assets. It is not surprising that no authority could be cited for such an extreme proposition ...

It may be ... that where one party mistakenly makes the same payment twice it retains a proprietary interest in the second payment which (if tracing is practicable) can be enforced against the payees' assets in a liquidation ahead of unsecured creditors. But in the present case, the customers intended to make payment, and they did so because they rightly conceived that that was what the contracts required ... As in the case of the misrepresentation, the alleged mistake might well have been a ground for setting aside the contract if the claimants had ever sought to do so; and in such a case they would have had a personal right to recover the sum equivalent to the amount paid. But even if they had chosen to exercise this right, it would not by operation of law have carried with it a proprietary interest ...

There remains the question whether the court should create after the event a remedial restitutionary right superior to the security created by the charge. The nature and foundation of this remedy were not clearly explained in argument. This is understandable, given that the doctrine is still in an early stage and no single juristic account of it has yet been generally agreed ... The bank relied on the floating charge to protect its assets; the customers relied on the company to deliver the bullion and to put in place the separate stock. The fact that the claimants are private citizens whereas their opponent is a commercial bank could not justify the court in simply disapplying the bank's valid security. No case cited has gone anywhere near to this, and the Board would do no service to the nascent doctrine by stretching it past breaking point

So far as concerns an equitable interest deemed to have come into existence from the moment when the transaction was entered into, it is hard to see how this could coexist with a contract which, so far as anyone knew, might be performed by actual delivery of the goods. And if there was no initial interest, at what time before the attachment of the security, and by virtue of what event, could the court deem a proprietary right to have arisen? None that their Lordships are able to see ...

For these reasons the Board must reject all the ways in which the non-allocated claimants assert a proprietary interest over the purchase price and its fruits ...

Questions

1. Did the company not enrich itself as a result of its breaches of contract?
2. Does not a person who mistakenly makes the same payment twice nevertheless intend to make the second payment?
3. If the bullion company was a fiduciary, why should equity be prevented from intervening with its remedy of an equitable lien over the purchase price?
4. If the bullion company asserted that the customers had property rights, why should the company not be estopped from denying this assertion? Is not the existence of the *res* itself irrelevant? Or, alternatively, could it not be said that the company is estopped from denying the existence of the *res*?

7 SPECIFIC PERFORMANCE

Beswick v Beswick [1968] AC 58 House of Lords

Lord Guest: My Lords, by agreement, dated March 14, 1962, the late Peter Beswick assigned to Joseph Beswick his business as coal merchant in consideration of Joseph employing Peter as a consultant for the remainder of his life at a weekly salary of £6.10s.0d. For the like consideration Joseph, in the event of Peter's death, agreed to pay his widow an annuity charged on the business at the rate of £5 per week. Peter Beswick died on November 3, 1963, and the respondent is the administratrix of his estate. She claims in these proceedings personally and as administratrix of her late husband against Joseph Beswick the appellant for specific performance of the agreement and for payment of the annuity ...

The first question is whether the respondent as administratrix of the estate of the late Peter Beswick is entitled to specific performance of the agreement of March 14, 1962. On this matter I have had the opportunity of reading the speech of my noble and learned friend, Lord Reid. I agree with him in thinking that the respondent is entitled to succeed on this branch of the case ...

Lord Reid: ... [T]he respondent in her personal capacity has no right to sue, but she has a right as administratrix of her husband's estate to require the appellant to perform his obligation under the agreement. He has refused to do so and he maintains that the respondent's only right is to sue him for damages for breach of his contract. If that were so, I shall assume that he is right in maintaining that the administratrix could then recover only nominal damages, because his breach of contract has caused no loss to the estate of her deceased husband. If that were the only remedy available the result would be grossly unjust. It would mean that the appellant keeps the business which he bought and for which he has only paid a small part of the price which he agreed to pay ...

I am of opinion that specific performance ought to be ordered ...

Lord Hodson: ... It is no part of the law that in order to sue on a contract one must establish that it is in one's interest to do so ...

In such a case as this, there having been an unconscionable breach of faith, the equitable remedy sought is apt. The appellant has had the full benefit of the contract and the court will be ready to see that he performs his part ...

Lord Pearce: My Lords, if the annuity had been payable to a third party in the lifetime of Beswick, senior, and there had been default, he could have sued in respect of the breach. His administratrix is now entitled to stand in his shoes and to sue in respect of the breach which has occurred since his death. It is argued that the estate can recover only nominal damages and that no other remedy is open, either to the estate or to the personal plaintiff. Such a result would be wholly repugnant to justice and commonsense. And if the argument were right it would show a very serious defect in the law ...

The administratrix is entitled, if she so prefers, to enforce the agreement rather than accept its repudiation, and specific performance is more convenient than an action for arrears of payment followed by separate actions as each sum falls due. Moreover, damages for breach would be a less appropriate remedy since the parties to the agreement were intending an annuity for a widow; and a lump sum of damages does not accord with this; and if (contrary to my view) the argument that a derisory sum of damages is all that can be obtained be right, the remedy of damages in this case is manifestly useless. The present case presents all the features which led the equity courts to apply their remedy of specific performance. The contract was for the sale of a business. The appellant could on his part clearly have obtained specific performance of it if Beswick senior or his administratrix had defaulted. Mutuality is a ground in favour of specific performance. Moreover, the appellant on his side has received the whole benefit of the contract and it is a matter of conscience for the court to see that he now performs his part of it ...

Lord Upjohn: ... In this case the court ought to grant a specific performance order all the more because damages are nominal. [The defendant] has received all the property; justice demands that he pay the price and this can only be done in the circumstances by equitable relief ...

Questions

1. Does it not seem a little bizarre that equity should order specific performance of a common law duty of specific performance (see debt above)?

2. Is it really the law that a person who has no interest in the performance of a contract can sue for a remedy for breach of the contract? Did Mrs Beswick have an interest in the performance of the contract?

3. Read the case of *White v Jones* [1995] 1 All ER 691 in the Appendix. Was this not a case where equity could have intervened on behalf of the third party (plaintiff)? What equitable remedy might have been appropriate?

4. The contractor (nephew) in *Beswick* intentionally refused to peform his contractuel duty and this caused a loss of expection to a third party (Mrs Beswick). If he had carelessly forgotten to pay her, could she have sued him for damages in the tort of negligence (cf *White v Jones*, Appendix)?

Price v Strange [1978] Ch 337 Court of Appeal

Buckley LJ: ... Considering the position *a priori* and apart from authority, it would seem that the questions which should be asked by any court which is invited to enforce specific performance of a contractual obligation should be: (1) is the plaintiff entitled to a remedy of some kind in respect of the alleged breach of contract? (2) if so, would damages be an adequate remedy? (3) if not, would specific performance be a more adequate remedy for the plaintiff? (4) if so, would it be fair to the defendant to order him to perform his part of the contract specifically? The first question goes to the validity and enforceability of the contract. Only if it is answered affirmatively do the subsequent questions arise. If the second question is answered affirmatively there is no occasion for equity to interfere, so that again the subsequent questions do not arise. If the second question is answered in the negative it will not necessarily follow that the third question must be answered affirmatively. For instance, the circumstances may not be such as to admit of specific performance, as where the subject-matter of the contract no longer exists. Only in the event of the third question arising and being answered in the affirmative can the fourth question arise. It is here, as it seems to me, that the alleged principle of mutuality comes in.

If one party were compelled to perform his obligations in accordance with the terms of the contract while the obligations of the other party under the contract, or some of them, remained unperformed, it might be unfair that the former party should be left to his remedy in damages if the latter party failed to perform any of his unperformed obligations. This is a consideration which bears on the appropriateness of specific performance as a remedy in the particular case; it has no bearing on the validity or enforceability of the contract, that is to say, on whether the plaintiff has a cause of action. A contract of which mutual specific performance cannot be enforced may yet afford a good cause of action for a remedy in damages at law ...

Questions

1. Is mutuality a general principle of the law of contract itself?
2. Could Mrs Beswick have been in breach of contract *vis-à-vis* the nephew? What effect would any breach have had on the nephew's obligation to pay the annuity? Was there mutuality between Mrs Beswick and the nephew?

8 RESCISSION IN EQUITY

Barclays Bank Plc v O'Brien [1993] 3 WLR 786 House of Lords

This was an action by a bank for possession of a matrimonial home which had been used as security for an overdraft extended to a company in which the husband, but not the wife, had an interest. The wife resisted the possession action on the ground that she signed the charge documents in reliance on her husband's false representation that it was limited to £60,000. The Court of Appeal held that the wife was entitled to special protection in equity and that the charge was enforceable against her only to the extent of £60,000. The House of Lords, although not agreeing with the special protection in equity, dismissed an appeal.

Lord Browne-Wilkinson: My Lords, in this appeal your Lordships for the first time have to consider a problem which has given rise to reported decisions of the Court of Appeal on no less than 11 occasions in the last eight years and which has led to a difference of judicial view. Shortly stated the question is whether a bank is entitled to enforce against a wife an obligation to secure a debt owed by her husband to the bank where the wife has been induced to stand as surety for her husband's debt by the undue influence or misrepresentation of the husband ...

The decision of the Court of Appeal

The Court of Appeal (Purchas, Butler-Sloss and Scott LJJ) reversed [the trial judge's order for possession]. The leading judgment in the Court of Appeal was given by Scott LJ who found that there were two lines of authority. One line would afford no special protection to married women: the rights of the creditor bank could only be adversely affected by the wrongful acts of the principal debtor, the husband, in procuring the surety's liability if the principal debtor was acting as the agent of the creditor in procuring the surety to join or the creditor had knowledge of the relevant facts. I will call this theory "the agency theory". The other line of authority detected by Scott LJ (which I will call "the special equity theory") considers that equity affords special protection to a protected class of surety viz. those where the relationship between the debtor and the surety is such that influence by the debtor over the surety and reliance by the surety on the debtor are natural features of the relationship. In cases where a surety is one of this protected class, the surety obligation is unenforceable by the creditor bank if (1) the relationship between the debtor and the surety was known to the creditor (2) the surety's consent was obtained by undue influence or by misrepresentation or without "an adequate understanding of the nature and effect of the transaction" and (3) the creditor had failed to take reasonable steps to ensure that the surety had given a true and informed consent to the transaction. The Court of Appeal preferred the special equity principle. They held that the legal charge on the O'Brien's matrimonial home was not enforceable by the bank against Mrs O'Brien save to the extent of the £60,000 which she had thought she was agreeing to secure.

Policy considerations

The large number of cases of this type coming before the courts in recent years reflects the rapid changes in social attitudes and the distribution of wealth which have recently occurred. Wealth is now more widely spread. Moreover a high proportion of privately owned wealth is invested in the matrimonial home. Because of the recognition by society of the equality of the sexes, the majority of matrimonial homes are now in the joint names of both spouses. Therefore in order to raise finance for the business enterprises of one or other of the spouses, the jointly owned home has become a main source of security. The provision of such security requires the consent of both spouses.

In parallel with these financial developments, society's recognition of the equality of the sexes has led to a rejection of the concept that the wife is subservient to the husband in the management of the family's finances. A number of the authorities reflect an unwillingness in the court to perpetuate law based on this outmoded concept. Yet, as Scott LJ in the Court of Appeal rightly points out [1993] QB 109, 139, although the concept of the ignorant wife leaving all financial decisions to the husband is outmoded, the practice does not yet coincide with the ideal. In a substantial proportion of marriages it is still the husband who has the business experience and the wife is willing to follow his advice without bringing a truly independent mind and will to bear on financial decisions. The number of recent cases in this field shows that in practice many wives are still subjected to, and yield to, undue influence by their husbands. Such wives can reasonably look to the law for some protection when their husbands have abused the trust and confidence reposed in them.

On the other hand, it is important to keep a sense of balance in approaching these cases. It is easy to allow sympathy for the wife who is threatened with the loss of her home at the suit of a rich bank to obscure an important public interest viz, the need to ensure that the wealth currently tied up in the matrimonial home does not become economically sterile. If the rights secured to wives by the law renders vulnerable loans granted on the security of matrimonial homes, institutions will be unwilling to accept such security, thereby reducing the flow of loan capital to business enterprises. It is therefore essential that a law designed to protect the vulnerable does not render the matrimonial home unacceptable as security to financial institutions.

With these policy considerations in mind I turn to consider the existing state of the law. The whole of modern law is derived from the decision of the Privy Council in *Turnbull & Co v Duval* [1902] AC 429 which, as I will seek to demonstrate, provides an uncertain foundation. Before considering that case however, I must consider the law of undue influence which (though not directly applicable in the present case) underlies both *Duval's* case and most of the later authorities.

Undue influence

A person who has been induced to enter into a transaction by the undue influence of another ("the wrongdoer") is entitled to set that transaction aside as against the wrongdoer. Such undue influence is either actual or presumed. In *Bank of Credit and Commerce International SA v Aboody* [1990] 1 QB 923, 953, the Court of Appeal helpfully adopted the following classification.

Class 1: Actual undue influence

In these cases it is necessary for the claimant to prove affirmatively that the wrongdoer exerted undue influence on the complainant to enter into the particular transaction which is impugned.

Class 2: Presumed undue influence

In these cases the complainant only has to show, in the first instance, that there was a relationship of trust and confidence between the complainant and the wrongdoer of such a nature that it is fair to presume that the wrongdoer abused that relationship in procuring the complainant to enter into the impugned transaction. In Class 2 cases therefore there is no need to produce evidence that actual undue influence was exerted in relation to the particular transaction impugned: once a confidential relationship has been proved, the burden then shifts to the wrongdoer to prove that the complainant entered into the impugned transaction freely, for example by showing that the complainant had independent advice. Such a confidential relationship can be established in two ways, *viz.*

Class 2(A)

Certain relationships (for example solicitor and client, medical advisor and patient) as a matter of law raise the presumption that undue influence has been exercised.

Class 2(B)

Even if there is no relationship falling within Class 2(A), if the complainant proves the *de facto* existence of a relationship under which the complainant generally reposed trust and confidence in the wrongdoer, the existence of such relationship raises the presumption of undue influence. In a Class 2(B) case therefore, in the absence of evidence disproving undue influence, the complainant will succeed in setting aside the impugned transaction merely by proof that the complainant reposed trust and confidence in the wrongdoer without having to prove that the wrongdoer exerted actual undue influence or otherwise abused such trust and confidence in relation to the particular transaction impugned.

As to dispositions by a wife in favour of her husband, the law for long remained in an unsettled state. In the 19th century some judges took the view that the relationship was such that it fell into Class 2(A) ie as a matter of law undue influence by the husband over the wife was presumed. It was not until the decisions in *Howes v Bishop* [1909] 2 KB 390 and *Bank of Montreal v Stuart* [1911] AC 120 that it was finally determined that the relationship of husband and wife did not as a matter of law raise a presumption of undue influence within Class 2(A). It is to be noted therefore that when the *Duval* case was decided in 1902 the question whether there was a Class 2(A) presumption of undue influence as between husband and wife was still unresolved.

An invalidating tendency?

Although there is no Class 2(A) presumption of undue influence as between husband and wife, it should be emphasised that in any particular case a wife may well be able to demonstrate that *de facto* she did leave decisions on financial affairs to her husband thereby bringing herself within Class 2(B) ie that the relationship between husband and wife in the particular case was such that the wife reposed confidence and trust in her husband in relation to their financial affairs and therefore undue influence is to be presumed. Thus, in those cases which still occur where the wife relies in all financial matters on her husband and simply does what he suggests, a presumption of undue influence within Class 2(B) can be established solely from the proof of such trust and confidence without proof of actual undue influence ...

In my judgment [the] special tenderness of treatment afforded to wives by the courts is properly attributable to two factors. First, many cases may well fall into the Class 2(B) category of undue influence because the wife demonstrates that she placed trust and confidence in her husband in relation to her financial affairs and therefore raises a presumption of undue influence. Second, the sexual and emotional ties between the parties provide a ready weapon for undue influence: a wife's true wishes can easily be overborne because of her fear of destroying or damaging the wider relationship between her and her husband if she opposes his wishes.

For myself, I accept that the risk of undue influence affecting a voluntary disposition by a wife in favour of a husband is greater than in the ordinary run of cases where no sexual or emotional ties affect the free exercise of the individual's will.

Undue influence, misrepresentation and third parties

Up to this point I have been considering the right of a claimant wife to set aside a transaction as against the wrongdoing husband when the transaction has been procured by his undue influence. But in surety cases the decisive question is whether the claimant wife can set aside the transaction, not against the wrongdoing husband, but against the creditor bank. Of course, if the wrongdoing husband is acting as agent for the creditor bank in obtaining the surety from the wife, the creditor will be fixed with the wrongdoing of its own agent and the surety contract can be set aside as against the creditor. Apart from this, if the creditor bank has notice, actual or constructive, of the undue influence exercised by the husband (and consequentially of the wife's equity to set aside the transaction) the creditor will take subject to that equity and the wife can set aside the transaction against the creditor (albeit a purchaser for value) as well as against the husband: see *Bainbrigge v Browne* (1881) 18 ChD 188 and *Bank of Credit and Commerce International SA v Aboody* [1990] 1 QB 923, 973. Similarly, in cases such as the present where the wife has been induced to enter into the transaction by the husband's misrepresentation, her equity to set aside the transaction will be enforceable against the creditor if either the husband was acting as the creditor's agent or the creditor had actual or constructive notice.

Turnbull & Co v Duval [1902] AC 429

This case provides the foundation of the modern law: the basis on which it was decided is, to say the least, obscure ... [His Lordship considered *Duval* and subsequent authorities and concluded ...]

Accordingly, the present law is built on the unsure foundations of the *Duval* case. Like most law founded on obscure and possibly mistaken foundations it has developed in an artificial way, giving rise to artificial distinctions and conflicting decisions. In my judgment your Lordships should seek to restate the law in a form which is principled, reflects the current requirements of society and provides as much certainty as possible.

Conclusions

(a) Wives

My starting point is to clarify the basis of the law. Should wives (and perhaps others) be accorded special rights in relation to surety transactions by the recognition of a special equity applicable only to such persons engaged in such transactions? Or should they enjoy only the same protection as they would enjoy in relation to their other dealings? In my judgment, the special equity theory should be rejected. First, I can find no basis in principle for affording special protection to a limited class in relation to one type of transaction only. Second, to require the creditor to prove knowledge and understanding by the wife in all cases is to reintroduce by the back door either a presumption of undue influence of Class 2(A) (which has been decisively rejected) or the *Romilly* heresy (which has long been treated as bad law). Third, although Scott LJ found that there were two lines of cases one of which supported the special equity theory, on analysis although many decisions are not inconsistent with that theory the only two cases which support it are *Yerkey v Jones*, 63 CLR 649, and the decision of the Court of Appeal in the present case. Finally, it is not necessary to have recourse to a special equity theory for the proper protection of the legitimate interests of wives as I will seek to show.

In my judgment, if the doctrine of notice is properly applied, there is no need for the introduction of a special equity in these types of cases. A wife who has been induced to stand as a surety for her husband's debts by his undue influence, misrepresentation or some other legal wrong has an equity as against him to set aside that transaction. Under the ordinary principles of equity, her right to set aside that transaction will be enforceable against third parties (eg against a creditor) if either the husband was acting as the third party's agent or the third party had actual or constructive notice of the facts giving rise to her equity. Although there may be cases where, without artificiality, it can properly be held that the husband was acting as the agent of the creditor in procuring the wife to stand as surety, such cases will be of very rare occurrence. The key to the problem is to identify the circumstances in which the creditor will be taken to have had notice of the wife's equity to set aside the transaction.

The doctrine of notice lies at the heart of equity. Given that there are two innocent parties, each enjoying rights, the earlier right prevails against the later right if the acquirer of the later right knows of the earlier right (actual notice) or would have discovered it had he taken proper steps (constructive notice). In particular, if the party asserting that he takes free of the earlier rights of another knows of certain facts which put him on inquiry as to the possible existence of the rights of that other and he fails to make such inquiry or take such other steps as are reasonable to verify whether such earlier right does or does not exist, he will have constructive notice of the earlier right and take subject to it. Therefore where a wife has agreed to stand surety for her husband's debts as a result of undue influence or misrepresentation, the creditor will take subject to the wife's equity to set aside the transaction if the circumstances are such as to put the creditor on inquiry as to the circumstances in which she agreed to stand surety ...

What, then are the reasonable steps which the creditor should take to ensure that it does not have constructive notice of the wife's rights, if any? Normally the reasonable steps necessary to avoid being fixed with constructive notice consist of making inquiry of the person who may have the earlier right (ie the wife) to see whether such right is asserted. It is plainly impossible to require of banks and other financial institutions that they should inquire of one spouse whether he or she has been unduly influenced or misled by the other. But in my judgment the creditor, in order to avoid being fixed with constructive notice, can reasonably be expected to take steps to bring home to the wife the risk she is running by standing as surety and to advise her to take independent advice. As to past transactions, it will depend on the facts of each case whether the steps taken by the creditor satisfy this test. However for the future in my judgment a creditor will have satisfied these requirements if it insists that the wife attend a private meeting (in the absence of the husband) with a representative of the creditor at which she is told of the extent of her liability as surety, warned of the risk she is running and urged to take independent legal advice. If these steps are taken in my judgment the creditor will have taken such reasonable steps as are necessary to preclude a subsequent claim that it had constructive notice of the wife's rights. I should make it clear that I have been considering the ordinary case where the creditor knows only that the wife is to stand surety for her husband's debts. I would not exclude exceptional cases where a creditor has knowledge of further facts which render the presence of undue influence not only possible but probable. In such cases, the creditor to be safe will have to insist that the wife is separately advised ...

If the law is established as I have suggested, it will hold the balance fairly between on the one hand the vulnerability of the wife who relies implicitly on her husband and, on the other hand, the practical problems of financial institutions asked to accept a secured or unsecured surety obligation from the wife for her husband's debts. In the context of suretyship, the wife will not have any right to disown her obligations just because subsequently she proves that she did not fully understand the transaction: she will, as in all other areas of her affairs, be bound by her obligations unless her husband has, by misrepresentation, undue influence or other wrong, committed an actionable wrong against her. In the normal case, a financial institution will be able to lend with confidence in reliance on the wife's surety obligation provided that it warns her (in the absence of the husband) of the amount of her potential liability and of the risk of standing surety and advises her to take independent advice.

Mr Jarvis, for the bank, urged that this is to impose too heavy a burden on financial institutions. I am not impressed by this submission. The Report by Professor Jack's *Review Committee on Banking Services: Law and Practice* (1989) (Cmnd. 622), recommended that prospective guarantors should be adequately warned of the legal effects and possible consequences of their guarantee and of the importance of receiving independent advice. Pursuant to this recommendation, the Code of Banking Practice (adopted by banks and building societies in March 1992) provides in paragraph 12.1 as follows:

"Banks and building societies will advise private individuals proposing to give them a guarantee or other security for another person's liabilities that: (i) by giving the guarantee or third party security he or she might become liable instead of or as well as that other person; (ii) he or she should seek independent legal advice before entering into the guarantee or third party security. Guarantees and other third party security forms will contain a clear and prominent notice to the above effect."

Thus good banking practice (which applies to all guarantees, not only those given by a wife) largely accords with what I consider the law should require when a wife is offered as surety. The only further substantial step required by law beyond that good practice is that the position should be explained by the bank to the wife in a personal interview. I regard this as being essential because a number of the decided cases show that written warnings are often not read and are sometimes intercepted by the husband. It does not seem to me that the requirement of a personal interview imposes such an additional administrative burden as to render the bank's position unworkable.

(b) Other persons

I have hitherto dealt only with the position where a wife stands surety for her husband's debts. But in my judgment the same principles are applicable to all other cases where there is an emotional relationship between cohabitees. The "tenderness" shown by the law to married women is not based on the marriage ceremony but reflects the underlying risk of one cohabitee exploiting the emotional involvement and trust of the other. Now that unmarried cohabitation, whether heterosexual or homosexual, is widespread in our society, the law should recognise this. Legal wives are not the only group which are now exposed to the emotional pressure of cohabitation. Therefore if, but only if, the creditor is aware that the surety is cohabiting with the principal debtor, in my judgment the same principles should apply to them as apply to husband and wife.

In addition to the cases of cohabitees, the decision of the Court of Appeal in *Avon Finance Co Ltd v Bridger* [1985] 2 All ER 281 shows (rightly in my view) that other relationships can give rise to a similar result. In that case a son, by means of misrepresentation, persuaded his elderly parents to stand surety for his debts. The surety obligation was held to be unenforceable by the creditor *inter alia* because to the bank's knowledge the parents trusted the son in their financial dealings. In my judgment that case was rightly decided: in a case where the creditor is aware that the surety reposes trust and confidence in the principal debtor in relation to his financial affairs, the creditor is put on inquiry in just the same way as it is in relation to husband and wife.

Summary

I can therefore summarise my views as follows. Where one cohabitee has entered into an obligation to stand as surety for the debts of the other cohabitee and the creditor is aware that they are cohabitees: (1) the surety obligation will be valid and enforceable by the creditor unless the suretyship was procured by the undue influence, misrepresentation or other legal wrong of the principal debtor; (2) if there has been undue influence, misrepresentation or other legal wrong by the principal debtor, unless the creditor has taken reasonable steps to satisfy himself that the surety entered into the obligation freely and in knowledge of the true facts, the creditor will be unable to enforce the surety obligation because he will be fixed with constructive notice of the surety's right to set aside the transaction; (3) unless there are special exceptional circumstances, a creditor will have taken such reasonable steps to avoid being fixed with constructive notice if the creditor warns the surety (at a meeting not attended by the principal debtor) of the amount of her potential liability and of the risks involved and advises the surety to take independent legal advice.

I should make it clear that in referring to the husband's debts I include the debts of a company in which the husband (but not the wife) has a direct financial interest.

The decision of this case

Applying those principles to this case, to the knowledge of the bank Mr and Mrs O'Brien were man and wife. The bank took a surety obligation from Mrs O'Brien, secured on the matrimonial home, to secure the debts of a company in which Mr O'Brien was interested but in which Mrs O'Brien had no direct pecuniary interest. The bank should therefore have been put on inquiry as to the circumstances in which Mrs O'Brien had agreed to stand as surety for the debt of her husband. If the Burnham branch had properly carried out the instructions from Mr Tucker of the Woolwich branch, Mrs O'Brien would have been informed that she and the matrimonial home were potentially liable for the debts of a company which had an existing liability of £107,000 and which was to be afforded an overdraft facility of £135,000. If she had been told this, it would have counteracted Mr O'Brien's misrepresentation that the liability was limited to £60,000 and would last for only three weeks. In addition according to the side letter she would have been recommended to take independent legal advice.

Unfortunately, Mr Tucker's instructions were not followed and to the knowledge of the bank (through the clerk at the Burnham branch) Mrs O'Brien signed the documents without any warning of the risks or any recommendation to take legal advice. In the circumstances the bank (having failed to take reasonable steps) is fixed with constructive notice of the wrongful misrepresentation made by Mr O'Brien to Mrs O'Brien. Mrs O'Brien is therefore entitled as against the bank to set aside the legal charge on the matrimonial home securing her husband's liability to the bank.

For these reasons I would dismiss the appeal with costs.

Notes and questions

1. 'According to the decisions of courts of equity it was not necessary, in order to set aside a contract obtained by material false representation, to prove that the party who obtained it knew at the time when the representation was made that it was false' (Jessel MR, *Redgrave v Hurd* (1881) 20 Ch D 1). Is *Redgrave* authority for the proposition that contributory negligence is never a defence against

fraudulent misrepresentation? Is it a defence against negligent misrepresentation?

2. 'In my judgment ... a voluntary transaction ... will be set aside for mistake whether the mistake is a mistake of law or fact, so long as the mistake is as to the effect of the transaction itself and not merely as to its consequences or the advantages to be gained by entering into it. The proposition that equity will never relieve against mistakes of law is clearly too widely stated ...' (Millet J, *Gibbon v Mitchell* [1990] 1 WLR 1304). Why have legal systems traditionally distinguished between mistakes of law and mistakes of fact?

3. 'A person who has been induced to enter into a transaction by the undue influence of another ("the wrongdoer") is entitled to set that transaction aside as against the wrongdoer. Such undue influence is either actual or presumed' (Lord Browne-Wilkinson, *Barclays Bank Plc v O'Brien*). Can one commercial corporation be guilty of undue influence over another commercial corporation?

4. 'Equity in this jurisdiction acts upon the conscience of the creditor. In coming to the conclusion whether it would be unconscionable for the creditor to enforce the charge against the surety, all the circumstances involving the relationships between the creditor, the debtor and the surety will be taken into account' (Purchas LJ, *Barclays Bank v O'Brien* [1992] 3 WLR 593). Does this mean that the equitable remedy of rescission is not governed by specific rules as such?

5. Under what circumstances can a contract be rescinded in equity for mistake? What about unconscionable transactions?

6. Is *Barclays Bank v O'Brien* a policy decision? If so, what is the policy?

9 RECTIFICATION IN EQUITY

Thomas Bates & Son Ltd v Wyndham's (Lingerie) Ltd [1981] 1 WLR 505 Court of Appeal

This was an action by a landlord for rectification of a lease which, to the knowledge of the tenant, did not actually reflect what had been agreed between them during negotiations. The Court of Appeal held that the lease should be rectified.

Buckley LJ: ... The landlords claim rectification in the present case on the basis of a principle enunciated by Pennycuick J in *A Roberts & Co Ltd v Leicestershire Council* [1961] Ch 555, 570 where he said:

"The second ground rests upon the principle that a party is entitled to rectification of a contract upon proof that he believed a particular term to be included in the contract, and that the other party concluded the contract with the omission or a variation of that term in the knowledge that the first party believed the term to be included ...

The principle is stated in Snell on *Equity*, 25th ed (1960), p 569 as follows: 'By what appears to be a species of equitable estoppel, if one party to a transaction knows that the instrument contains a mistake in his favour but does nothing to correct it, he (and those claiming under him) will be precluded from resisting rectification on the ground that the mistake is unilateral and not common.' "

Of course if a document is executed in circumstances in which one party realises that in some respect it does not accurately reflect what down to that moment had been the common intention of the parties, it cannot be said that the document is executed under a common mistake, because the party who has realised the mistake is no longer labouring under the mistake. There may be cases in which the principle enunciated by Pennycuick J applies although there is no prior common intention, but we are not, I think, concerned with such a case here, for it seems to me, upon the facts that I have travelled through, that it is established that the parties had a common intention down to the time when Mr Avon realised the mistake in the terms of the lease, a common intention that the rent in respect of any period after the first five years should be agreed or, in default of agreement, fixed by an arbitrator.

The principle so enunciated by Pennycuick J was referred to, with approval, in this court in *Riverlate Properties Ltd v Paul* [1975] Ch 133, where Russell LJ, reading the judgment of the court, said, at p 140:

"It may be that the original conception of reformation of an instrument by rectification was based solely upon common mistake: but certainly in these days rectification may be based upon such knowledge on the part of the lessee: see, for example, *A Roberts & Co Ltd v Leicestershire County Council* [1961] Ch 555. Whether there was in any particular case knowledge of the intention and mistake of the other party must be a question of fact to be decided upon the evidence. Basically it appears to us that it must be such as to involve the lessee in a degree of sharp practice."

In that case the lessee against whom the lessor sought to rectify a lease was held to have had no such knowledge as would have brought the doctrine into play. The reference to "sharp practice" may thus be said to have been an *obiter dictum*. Undoubtedly I think in any such case the conduct of the defendant must be such as to make it inequitable that he should be allowed to object to the rectification of the document. If this necessarily implies some measure of "sharp practice", so be it; but for my part I think that the doctrine is one which depends more upon the equity of the position. The graver the character of the conduct involved, no doubt the heavier the burden of proof may be; but, in my view, the conduct must be such as to affect the conscience of the party who has suppressed the fact that he has recognised the presence of a mistake.

For this doctrine – that is to say the doctrine of *A Roberts & Co Ltd v Leicestershire County Council* – to apply I think it must be shown: first, that one party A erroneously believed that the document sought to be rectified contained a particular term or provision, or possibly did not contain a particular term or provision which, mistakenly, it did contain; secondly, that the other party B was aware of the omission or the inclusion and that it was due to a mistake on the part of A; thirdly, that B has omitted to draw the mistake to the notice of A. And I think there must be a fourth element involved, namely, that the mistake must be one calculated to benefit B. If these requirements are satisfied, the court may regard it as inequitable to allow B to resist rectification to give effect to A's intention on the ground that the mistake was not, at the time of execution of the document, a mutual mistake ...

For these reasons I think that the judge ... reached the right conclusion on the matter relating to rectification. I would accordingly uphold that part of his order which directed rectification ...

Questions

1. Is rectification a form of estoppel?

2. Is *Wyndam* an unjust enrichment case?

3. What is actually meant by "the equity of the position"? Is this something that is entirely bound up with the conduct of the parties? Or might the nature of the transaction be a consideration?

4. Is the remedy of rectification governed by rules?

10 ACCOUNT

London, Chatham & Dover Railway Co v South Eastern Railway Co [1892] 1 Ch 120 Court of Appeal

Lindley LJ: ... Before the Judicature Acts a suit for an account could be maintained in equity in the following cases: – (1) Where the plaintiff had a legal right to have money payable to him ascertained and paid, but which right, owing to defective legal machinery, he could not practically enforce at law. Suits for an account between principal and agent, and between partners, are familiar instances of this class of case. (2) Where the plaintiff would have had a legal right to have money ascertained and paid to him by the defendant, if the defendant had not wrongfully prevented such right from accruing to the plaintiff. In such a case a court of law could only give unliquidated damages for the defendant's wrongful act; and there was often no machinery for satisfactorily ascertaining what would have been due and payable if the defendant had acted properly. In such a case, however, a Court of Equity decreed an account, ascertained what would have been payable if the defendant had acted as he ought to have done and ordered him to pay the amount: *M'Intosh v Great Western Railway Company* ((1865) 4 Giff 683), is the leading authority in this class of case. (3) Where the plaintiff had no legal but only equitable rights against the defendant, and where an account was necessary to give effect to those equitable rights. Ordinary suits by *cestuis que trust* against their trustees and suits for equitable waste fell within this class. (4) Combination of the above cases.

Att-Gen v Guardian Newspapers (No 2) [1990] AC 109 House of Lords

Lord Goff: ... The statement that a man shall not be allowed to profit from his own wrong is in very general terms, and does not of itself provide any sure guidance to the solution of a problem in any particular case. That there are groups of cases in which a man is not allowed to profit from his own wrong, is certainly true ... The plaintiff's claim to restitution is usually enforced by an account of profits made by the defendant through his wrong at the plaintiff's expense. This remedy of an account is alternative to the remedy of damages ...

English v Dedham Vale Properties [1978] 1 All ER 382 Chancery Division

(See p 41)

Questions

1. What is the relationship between an action in debt and an action in account? Could the plaintiff in *English* have sued in common law debt (money had and received) for the profit? If not, why not?
2. Read the case of *Cuckmere Brick Co v Mutual Finance Ltd* [1971] Ch 949 in the law report. Was this an action in account?
3. Must there always be a fiduciary relationship before account will lie?
4. Is account a remedy or a procedural process? What is the relationship, if any, between account and tracing in equity?

11 SUBROGATION

Orakpo v Manson Investments Ltd [1978] AC 95 House of Lords

Lord Diplock: ... My Lords, there is no general doctrine of unjust enrichment recognised in English law. What it does is to provide specific remedies in particular cases of what might be classified as unjust enrichment in a legal system that is based on the civil law. There are some circumstances in which the remedy takes the form of 'subrogation', but this expression embraces more than a single concept in English law. It is a convenient way of describing a transfer of rights from one person to another, without assignment or assent of the person from whom the rights are transferred and which takes place by operation of law in a whole variety of widely different circumstances. Some rights by subrogation are contractual in their origin, as in the case of contracts of insurance. Others, such as the right of an innocent lender to recover from a company moneys borrowed *ultra vires* to the extent that these have been expended on discharging the company's lawful debts, are in no way based on contract and appear to defeat classification except as an empirical remedy to prevent a particular kind of unjust enrichment.

This makes particularly perilous any attempt to rely on analogy to justify applying to one set of circumstances which would otherwise result in unjust enrichment a remedy of subrogation which has been held to be available for that purpose in another and different set of circumstances.

One of the sets of circumstances in which a right of subrogation arises is when a liability of a borrower B to an existing creditor C secured on the property of B is discharged out of moneys provided by the lender L and paid to C either by L himself at B's request and on B's behalf or directly by B pursuant to his agreement with L. In these circumstances L is *prima facie* entitled to be treated as if he were the transfee of the benefit of C's security on the property to the extent that the moneys lent by L to B were applied to the discharge of B's liability to C. This subrogation of L to the security on the property of B is based on the presumed mutual intentions of L and B; in other words where a contract of loan provides that moneys lent by L to B are to be applied in discharging a liability of B to C secured on property, it is an implied term of that contract that L is to be subrogated to C's security ...

Lord Salmon: ... The test whether the courts will apply the doctrine of subrogation to the facts of any particular case is entirely empirical. It is, I think, impossible to formulate any narrower principle than that the doctrine will be applied only when the courts are satisfied that reason and justice demand that it should be. Typical cases in which the doctrine has been held to apply are, eg, (1) A is insured against damage done to his car; his car is damaged in a collision with another car driven by Y; the insurers pay for the repair to A's car and are subrogated to any rights which A may have against Y for causing the damage by negligence. The right to subrogation may be stipulated for in the insurance policy; but if it is not, it will be implied by the law. (2) When A, acting as B's agent, pays out of his own pocket at B's request, the price of the land which B has contracted to buy from V, and V thereupon conveys the land to B. The law will subrogate to A the rights which V had over the land after the contract of sale and before completion ...

Notes and questions

1. Subrogation is best understood as an institutional structure rather than as a remedy defined and governed by rules. It concerns the relationship between *persona* (legal subject) and *res* (legal object) and is a means by which one legal object (*res*) is substituted for another legal object (real subrogation) or one legal subject (*persona*) is substituted for another legal subject (personal subrogation). It was probably imported into the common law from the civil law. Subrogation plays a central role in the English law of obligations since it is the means by which an insurance company is able to gain access to the courts: thus in *Dorset Yacht* (p 362) and *Lister* (p 307) the real plaintiff was an insurance company subrogated to the rights of the plaintiff. Can such a remedy defeat the loss spreading policy of the law of obligations?

2. Is it still true to say that there is no doctrine of unjust enrichment in English law? Does the remedy of subrogation ever defeat the doctrine of unjust enrichment? (Cf *Lister v Romford Ice Co* p 307.)

3. To what extent is the idea of retention of title in supply of goods contracts dependent upon a form of subrogation?[10]

4. Should subrogation in insurance be governed by principles from the common law (contract) or by principles from equity?[11]

5. Was *Photo Production v Securicor* (p 312) a subrogation case? If so, did the existence of subrogation radically affect the outcome of the litigation?

12 INJUNCTION

(a) The nature of an injunction

Wookey v Wookey [1991] 3 WLR 135 Court of Appeal

Butler-Sloss LJ: ... The grant of an injunction is a discretionary remedy derived from the equitable jurisdiction which acts *in personam* and only against those who are amenable to its jurisdiction; nor will it act in vain by granting an injunction which is idle and ineffectual. An injunction should not, therefore, be granted to impose an obligation to do something which is impossible or cannot be enforced. The injunction must serve a useful purpose for the person seeking the relief and there must be a real possibility that the order, if made, will be enforceable by the process *in personam*. However, the courts expect and assume that their orders will be obeyed and will not normally refuse an injunction because of the respondent's likely disobedience to the order.

Notes and questions

1. 'It is obvious ... that there may be orders of the court which are not injunctions. The direction as to the removal of the children is such an order. It is neither an injunction nor in the nature of an injunction' (Lloyd LJ, *In re P (Minors)* [1990] 1 WLR 613). What is so special about an injunction and why is it different from other orders?

2. 'The High Court may by order (whether interlocutory or final) grant an injunction or appoint a receiver in all cases in which it appears to the court to be just and convenient to do so' (Supreme Court Act 1981 s 37(1)). Does this statutory rule allow a court to issue an injunction in every case where they think it 'just and convenient' to do so?

---

10 Cf *Aluminium Industrie Vaassen BV v Romalpa Aluminium Ltd* [1976] 2 All ER 552.

11 Cf *Morris v Ford Motor Co* [1973] 1 QB 792.

3. Can injunctions ever bind those who are not parties to the litigation? If so, does this mean that they do act *in rem*?

4. In what circumstances will a court issue an injunction to prevent breaches of the criminal law?

5. In what ways can an injunction be used to develop the law? Can they be used in ways that are not available to other remedies such as debt, damages and rescission?

(b) Interlocutory injunction

American Cyanamid Co v Ethicon Ltd [1975] AC 396 House of Lords

Lord Diplock: ... The object of the interlocutory injunction is to protect the plaintiff against injury by violation of his right for which he could not be adequately compensated in damages recoverable in the action if the uncertainty were resolved in his favour at the trial; but the plaintiff's need for such protection must be weighed against the corresponding need of the defendant to be protected against injury resulting from his having been prevented from exercising his own legal rights for which he could not be adequately compensated under the plaintiff's undertaking in damages ... The court must weigh one need against another and determine where 'the balance of convenience' lies ...

The court no doubt must be satisfied that the claim is not frivolous or vexatious; in other words, that there is a serious question to be tried ...

It is no part of the court's function at this stage of the litigation to try to resolve conflicts of evidence on affidavit as to facts on which the claims of either party may ultimately depend nor to decide difficult questions of law which call for detailed argument and mature considerations. These are matters to be dealt with at the trial ... So unless the material available to the court at the hearing of the application for an interlocutory injunction fails to disclose that the plaintiff has any real prospect of succeeding in his claim for a permanent injunction at the trial, the court should go on to consider whether the balance of convenience lies in favour of granting or refusing the interlocutory relief that is sought.

As to that, the governing principle is that the court should first consider whether if the plaintiff were to succeed at the trial in establishing his right to a permanent injunction he would be adequately compensated by an award of damages for the loss he would have sustained as a result of the defendant's continuing to do what was sought to be enjoined between the time of the application and the time of the trial. If the damages ... would be adequate ... no interlocutory injunction should normally be granted ...

It is where there is doubt as to the adequacy of the respective remedies in damages available to either party or to both, that the question of balance of convenience arises. It would be unwise to attempt even to list all the various matters which may need to be taken into consideration in deciding where the balance lies, let alone to suggest the relative weight to be attached to them. These will vary from case to case ...

The court is not justified in embarking on anything resembling a trial of the action ...

Khorasandijian v Bush [1993] 3 WLR 476 Court of Appeal (see p 74)

Questions

1. Is an interlocutory injunction a discretionary remedy that bears little relationship to the substantive rights of the parties?

2. An employer seeks an interlocutory injunction against a trade union or group of employees in respect of a threatened strike: is the 'balance of convenience' question a matter of political judgment? Whose 'convenience' is to be considered?

3. Was the interlocutory injunction responsible for protecting the reputation of the late Robert Maxwell?

Allen v Jambo Holdings Ltd [1980] 2 All ER 502 Court of Appeal

Lord Denning MR: ... It is a new case altogether. In the past *Mareva* injunctions have been confined to the commercial court. The judges of that court have granted injunctions to restrain foreign companies from removing moneys so as to defeat their creditors ... But this is new. Not because it concerns an aircraft. There was one case where an aircraft ran up a bill for fuel. Its bill was not paid. The aircraft was restrained from moving until it was paid. But this is the first case we have had of a personal injury (this is a fatal accident case) where a *Mareva* injunction has been sought. The nearest parallel is a ship in an English port where there is an accident causing personal injuries or death. It has been settled for centuries that the claimant can bring an action *in rem* and arrest the ship. She is not allowed to leave the port until security is provided so as to ensure that any proper claim will be duly met. The question in this case is whether a similar jurisdiction can be exercised in regard to an aircraft. In principle I see no reason why it should not, except that it is to be done by a *Mareva* injunction instead of an action *in rem* ...

Notes and questions

1. 'If it appears that the debt is due and owing, and there is a danger that the debtor may dispose of his assets so as to defeat it before judgment, the court has jurisdiction in a proper case to grant an interlocutory judgment so as to prevent him disposing of those assets' (Lord Denning MR, *Mareva Compania Naviera v International Bulkcarriers* [1980] 1 All ER 213). Does this mean that the interlocutory injunction is now a remedy *in rem*? How does the law enforce such an injunction?

2. There are two particular kinds of interlocutory injunction of the utmost importance to English commercial law: (i) the *Mareva* injunction (above) and (ii) the *Anton Piller* order (below). Are these

examples of the creativity of the common law? Could the civil law judges ever have developed such remedies? Would civil law judges want to develop such remedies? Does the power to issue interlocutory remedies in civil law systems attach to the remedy or to the judge?

Anton Piller KG v Manufacturing Processes Ltd [1976] 1 All ER 779 Court of Appeal

Lord Denning MR: ... Let me say at once that no court in this land has any power to issue a search warrant to enter a man's house so as to see if there are papers or documents there which are of an incriminating nature ... But the order sought in this case is not a search warrant. It does not authorise the plaintiffs' solicitors or anyone else to enter the defendants' premises against their will. It does not authorise the breaking down of any doors, nor the slipping in by the back door, nor getting in by an open door or window. It only authorises entry and inspection by the permission of the defendants. The plaintiffs must get the defendants' permission. But it does do this: it brings pressure on the defendants to give permission. It does more. It actually orders them to give permission - with, I suppose, the result that if they do not give permission, they are guilty of contempt of court.

Ormrod LJ: ... The proposed order is at the extremity of this court's powers. Such orders, therefore, will rarely be made ... There are three essential pre-conditions for the making of such an order, in my judgment. First, there must be an extremely strong *prima facie* case. Secondly, the damage, potential or actual, must be very serious for the plaintiff. Thirdly, there must be clear evidence that the defendants have in their possession incriminating documents or things, and that there is a real possibility that they may destroy such material before any application *inter partes* can be made. The form of the order makes it plain that the court is not ordering or granting anything equivalent to a search warrant. The order is an order on the defendant *in personam* to permit inspection. It is therefore open to him to refuse to comply with such an order, but at his peril either of further proceedings for contempt of court ... but more important, of course, the refusal to comply may be the most damning evidence against the defendant at the subsequent trial ...

Questions

1. Were the judges being realistic when they said that such orders would only rarely be made?

2. Do you think *Anton Piller* orders belong in the category of private or public law?

Columbia Picture Industries Inc v Robinson [1987] Ch 38 Chancery Division

Scott J: ... It is implicit in the nature of *Anton Piller* orders that they should be applied for *ex parte* and dealt with by the courts in secrecy. In the Queen's Bench Division applications ... are heard in chambers. Secrecy is ensured. In this division applications are heard in court but it is customary for the court to sit *in camera*. ... [T]he most significant feature of *Anton Piller* orders is that they are mandatory in form and are designed for immediate execution ... It is a fundamental principle of civil jurisprudence in this country that citizens are not to be deprived of their property by judicial or quasi-judicial order without a fair hearing. *Audi alterem partem* is one of the principles of natural justice and contemplates a hearing at which the defendant can, if so advised, be represented and heard ... What is to be said of the *Anton Piller* procedure which, on a regular and institutionalised basis, is depriving citizens of their property and closing down their businesses by orders made *ex parte*, on applications of which they know nothing and at which they cannot be heard, by orders which are forced, on pain of committal, to obey, even if wrongly made? ... It is the experience of [the solicitors acting for plaintiffs] that, when they apply for *Anton Piller* orders, they almost invariably succeed in getting them ...

Questions

1. Would it be unreasonable to say that legal remedies tend to be available for the convenience of commerce rather than the convenience of the citizen?

2. If the UK had had a written constitution, together with a constitutional court, would *Anton Piller* orders have ever been allowed?

Lock Plc v Beswick [1989] 1 WLR 1268 Chancery Division

Hoffmann J: ... Even in cases in which the plaintiff has strong evidence that an employee has taken what is undoubtedly specific confidential information, such as a list of customers, the court must employ a graduated response. To borrow a useful concept from the jurisprudence of the European Community, there must be *proportionality* between the perceived threat to the plaintiff's rights and the remedy granted. The fact that there is overwhelming evidence that the defendant has behaved wrongfully in his commercial relationships does not necessarily justify an *Anton Piller* order ... The making of an intrusive order *ex parte* even against a guilty defendant is contrary to normal principles of justice and can only be done when there is a paramount need to prevent a denial of justice to the plaintiff. The absolute extremity of the court's powers is to permit a search of a defendant's dwelling house, with the humiliation and family distress which that frequently involves.

Questions

1. Ought the principle of proportionality to be applicable to all types of interlocutory injunctions? Do you think, in substance, it is a principle that the English courts have always tried to apply? Does it apply to remedies other than injunctions?

2. Is the interlocutory injunction a remedy that is sometimes difficult to reconcile with the idea of human rights? Or is it a remedy that supports human rights?

3. Should interlocutory injunctions ever be available to inhibit publication of a true story that is in the public interest?

(c) The role of injunctions

Warner Brothers Pictures Inc v Nelson [1937] 1 KB 209 King's Bench

Branson J: The facts of this case are few and simple. The plaintiffs are a firm of film producers in the United States of America. In 1931 the defendant [Bette Davis] then not well known as a film actress, entered into a contract with the plaintiffs. Before the expiration of that contract the present contract was entered into between the parties. Under it the defendant received a considerably enhanced salary, the other conditions being substantially the same. This contract was for fifty-two weeks and contains options to the plaintiffs to extend it for further periods of fifty-two weeks at ever-increasing amounts of salary to the defendant ... It is a stringent contract, under which the defendant agrees "to render her exclusive services as a motion picture and/or legitimate stage actress" to the plaintiffs, and agrees to perform solely and exclusively for them. She also agrees, by way of negative stipulation, that "she will not, during such time" – that is to say, during the term of the contract – "render any services for or in any other phonographic, stage or motion picture production ... or engage in any other occupation without the written consent of the producer ..."

In June of this year the defendant, for no discoverable reason except that she wanted more money, declined to be further bound by the agreement, left the United States and, in September, entered into an agreement in this country with a third person. This was a breach of contract on her part, and the plaintiffs ... commenced this action claiming a declaration that the contract was valid and binding, an injunction to restrain the defendant from acting in breach of it, and damages ...

I turn then to the consideration of the law applicable to this case on the basis that the contract is a valid and enforceable one. It is conceded that our courts will not enforce a positive covenant of personal service; and specific performance of the positive covenants by the defendant to serve the plaintiffs is not asked in the present case ...

The defendant, having broken her positive undertakings in the contract without any cause or excuse which she was prepared to support in the witnessbox, contends that she cannot be enjoined from breaking the negative covenants also ...

The conclusion to be drawn from the authorities is that, where a contract of personal service contains negative covenants the enforcement of which will not amount either to a decree of specific performance of the positive covenants of the contract or to the giving of a decree under which the defendant must either remain idle or perform those positive covenants, the court will enforce those negative covenants; but this is subject to a further consideration. An injunction is a discretionary remedy, and the court in granting it may limit it to what the court considers reasonable in all the circumstances of the case ...

The case before me is, therefore, one in which it would be proper to grant an injunction unless to do so would in the circumstances be tantamount to ordering the defendant to perform her contract or remain idle or unless damages would be the more appropriate remedy.

With regard to the first of these considerations, it would, of course, be impossible to grant an injunction covering all the negative covenants in the contract. That would, indeed, force the defendant to perform her contract or remain idle; but this objection is removed by the restricted form in which the injunction is sought. It is confined to forbidding the defendant, without the consent of the plaintiffs, to render any services for or in any motion picture or stage production for any one other than the plaintiffs.

It was also urged that the difference between what the defendant can earn as a film artiste and what she might expect to earn by any other form of activity is so great that she will in effect be driven to perform her contract. That is not the criterion adopted in any of the decided cases. The defendant is stated to be a person of intelligence, capacity and means, and no evidence was adduced to show that, if enjoined from doing the specified acts otherwise than for the plaintiffs, she will not be able to employ herself both usefully and remuneratively in other spheres of activity, though not as remuneratively as in her special line. She will not be driven, although she may be tempted, to perform the contract, and the fact that she may be so tempted is no objection to the grant of an injunction ...

I think ... that an injunction should be granted ...

Miller v Jackson [1977] QB 966 Court of Appeal

(See p 22)

Notes and questions

1. 'I have before me an application by three plaintiffs for injunctions to restrain tower cranes erected and operated by the defendants from oversailing their respective properties ... [Counsel for the plaintiff] has submitted that if I am satisfied, as I am, that the oversailing booms ... are committing a trespass ... the plaintiffs are entitled to an injunction as of course. An injunction is a discretionary remedy, but it is well settled that the discretion must be exercised in accordance with judicial precedent and principle and there is authority ... that a trespass threatened to be continued will be restrained by injunction as of course. There is a sense in which the grant of an injunction against trespass enables a landowner to behave like a dog in a manger ... But ... [t]he authorities establish, in my view, that the plaintiffs are entitled as of course to injunctions ...' (Scott J, *Anchor Brewhouse Developments v Berkley House* [1987] EG 173). If the injunction is not available as of course, would this not make nonsense of any notion of ownership in English law? In *Miller v*

Jackson was the discretion exercised in accordance with judicial precedent?

2. Can a court issue an injunction simply to protect the public interest?[12]

3. Do injunctions protect rights or interests?

13 DAMAGES

(a) The role of damages

Cassell & Co v Broome [1972] AC 1027 House of Lords

Lord Hailsham: ... Of all the various remedies available at common law, damages are the remedy of most general application at the present day, and they remain the prime remedy in actions for breach of contract and tort. They have been defined as "the pecuniary compensation, obtainable by success in an action, for a wrong which is either a tort or a breach of contract". They must normally be expressed in a single sum to take account of all the factors applicable to each cause of action ...

In almost all actions for breach of contract, and in many actions for tort, the principle of *restitutio in integrum* is an adequate and fairly easy guide to the estimation of damage, because the damage suffered can be estimated by relation to some material loss. It is true that where loss includes a pre-estimate of future losses, or an estimate of past losses which cannot in the nature of things be exactly computed, some subjective element must enter in. But the estimate is in things commensurable with one another ...

In many torts, however, the subjective element is more difficult. The pain and suffering endured, and the future loss of amenity, in a personal injuries case are not in the nature of things convertible into legal tender ... The principle of *restitutio in integrum*, which compels the use of money as its sole instrument for restoring the *status quo*, necessarily involves a factor larger than any pecuniary loss.

In actions of defamation and in any other actions where damages for loss of reputation are involved, the principle of *restitutio in integrum* has necessarily an even more highly subjective element. Such actions involve a money award which may put the plaintiff in a purely financial sense in a much stronger than he was before the wrong ...

The next point to notice is that it has always been a principle in English law that the award of damages when awarded must be a single lump sum in respect of each separate cause of action ...

---

12   Cf *Thomas v NUM* [1986] Ch 20; *Associated British Ports v TGWU* [1989] 1 WLR 939.

Lord Diplock: ... The award of damages as the remedy for all civil wrongs was in England the creature of the common law. It is a field of law in which there has been but little intervention by Parliament. It is judge-made law par excellence. Its original purpose in cases of trespass was to discourage private revenge in a primitive society inadequately policed, at least as much as it was to compensate the victim for the material harm occasioned to him ...

Notes and questions

1. Are most county court contractual claims actions for damages?

2. 'The general rule in English law today as to the measure of damages recoverable for the invasion of a legal right, whether by breach of a contract or by commission of a tort, is that damages are compensatory. Their function is to put the person whose right has been invaded in the same position as if it had been respected so far as the award of a sum of money can do so ...' (Lord Diplock, *The Albazero* [1977] AC 774). Is the role of damages only to compensate?

3. '[W]here any injury is to be compensated by damages, in settling the sum of money to be given for reparation of damages you should as nearly as possible get at that sum of money which will put the party who has been injured, or who has suffered, in the same position as he would have been in if he had not sustained the wrong for which he is now getting his compensation or reparation' (Lord Blackburn, *Livingstone v Rawyards Coal Co* (1880) 5 App Cas 25). Was there *restitutio in integrum* in *Spartan Steel v Martin* (p 101)?

(b) Contractual liability and damages

Surrey County Council v Bredero Homes Ltd [1993] 1 WLR 1361 Court of Appeal

Dillon LJ: This is an appeal by the plaintiffs, the Surrey County Council ... against a decision of Ferris J given on 21 November 1991 ... By his decision the judge awarded the plaintiffs nominal damages only against the defendant, Bredero Homes Ltd, for breaches of virtually identical positive covenants contained in transfers by the plaintiffs to the defendant of certain land in Surrey in 1981 ...

The plaintiffs object to the development of the final 3.64 acres ... As a legal basis it is said by the plaintiffs, and conceded by the defendant, that in building 77 houses in all under the later planning permission, rather than 72 under the first planning permission, the defendant acted in breach of the covenants in the transfers.

The plaintiffs therefore seek damages. They have never sought an interim injunction to restrain the defendant from developing the land otherwise than in accordance with the first planning permission. They never sought an injunction at the trial requiring the defendant to pull down the completed houses. They recognised that there was never any practical possibility of such an injunction being granted ... The plaintiffs accept that they have not suffered any damage at all of the nature of damage to adjoining property owned or occupied by them. What they claim as damages is essentially the profit made by the defendant by breaking the covenants and building 77 houses and not just 72 ...

The starting point, however, in my judgment is that the remedy at common law for a breach of contract is an award of damages, and damages at common law are intended to compensate the victim for his loss, not to transfer to the victim if he has suffered no loss the benefit which the wrongdoer has gained by his breach of contract ...

Every student is taught that the basis of assessing damages for breach of contract is the rule in *Hadley v Baxendale* (1854) 9 Ex 341, which is wholly concerned with the losses which can be compensated by damages. Such damages may, in an appropriate case, cover profit which the injured plaintiff has lost, but they do not cover an award, to a plaintiff who has himself suffered no loss, of the profit which the defendant has gained for himself by his breach of contract.

In the field of tort there are areas where the law is different and the plaintiff can recover in respect of the defendant's gain. Thus in the field of trespass it is well established that if one person has, without leave of another, been using that other's land for his own purposes he ought to pay for such user. Thus even if he had done no actual harm to the land he was charged for the user of the land .... The same principle was applied to patent infringement ... The infringer was ordered to pay by way of damages a royalty for every infringing article because the infringement damaged the plaintiff's property right, that is to say, his patent monopoly. So in a case of detinue the defendant was ordered to apply a hire for chattels he had detained: *Strand Electric and Engineering Co Ltd v Brisford Entertainments Ltd* [1952] 2 QB 246 ...

As I see it, therefore, there never was in the present case, even before the writ was issued, any possibility of the court granting an injunction ... The plaintiffs' only possible claim from the outset was for damages only, damages at common law. The plaintiffs have suffered no damage. Therefore on basic principles, as damages are awarded to compensate loss, the damages must be merely nominal. For these reasons, which substantially accord with those of Ferris J I would dismiss this appeal.

Steyn LJ: ... An award of compensation for breach of contract serves to protect three separate interests. The starting principle is that the aggrieved party ought to be compensated for loss of his positive or expectation interests. In other words, the object is to put the aggrieved party in the same financial position as if the contract had been fully performed. But the law also protects the negative interest of the aggrieved party. If the aggrieved party is unable to establish the value of a loss of bargain he may seek compensation in respect of his reliance losses. The object of such an award is to compensate the aggrieved party for expenses incurred and losses suffered in reliance on the contract. These two complementary principles share one feature. Both are pure compensatory principles ...

There is, however, a third principle which protects the aggrieved party's restitutionary interest. The object of such an award is not to compensate the plaintiff for a loss, but to deprive the defendant of the benefit he gained by the breach of contract. The classic illustration is a claim for the return of goods sold and delivered where the buyer has repudiated his obligation to pay the price. It is not traditional to describe a claim for restitution following a breach of contract as damages. What matters is that a coherent law of obligations must inevitably extend its protection to cover certain restitutionary interests ...

The object of the award in the *Wrotham Park* case [[1974] 1 WLR 798] was not to compensate the plaintiffs for financial injury, but to deprive the defendants of an unjustly acquired gain. Whilst it must be acknowledged that the *Wrotham Park* case represented a new development, it seems to me that it was based on a principled legal theory, justice and sound policy ... The *Wrotham Park* case is analogous to cases where a defendant has made use of the aggrieved party's property and thereby saved expense ... I readily accept that "property" in this context must be interpreted in a wide sense. I would also not suggest that there is no scope for further development in this branch of the law.

But, in the present case, we are asked to extend considerably the availability of restitutionary remedies for breach of contract. I question the desirability of any such development ...

The present case involves no breach of fiduciary obligations. It is a case of breach of contract. The principles governing expectation or reliance losses cannot be invoked. Given the fact of the breach of contract the only question is whether restitution is an appropriate remedy for this wrong. The case does not involve any invasion of the plaintiffs' property interests even in the broadest sense of that word, nor is it closely analogous to the *Wrotham Park* position. I would therefore rule that no restitutionary remedy is available and there is certainly no other remedy available. I would dismiss the appeal.

Rose LJ: I agree ...

Questions

1. Could the plaintiff have obtained the defendant's profit via an action of account?

2. Is expectation interest equivalent to *lucrum cessans* in the civil law?

3. Did the defendant unjustly enrich himself (or itself)? Was it at the expense of the plaintiff?

4. What if the builder had made a huge profit as a result of his breach of the planning permission: who should be entitled to this profit? Might the Local Government Act 1972 s 222 provide any clues?

5. Is *Bredero* a hard case?

6. If *Spartan Steel v Martin* (p 101) had been a contract case, would the plaintiff have recovered a higher figure?

Jarvis v Swans Tours Ltd [1973] 1 QB 233 Court of Appeal

This was an action for damages brought by a customer against a tour operator in respect of a holiday which fell far short of the promises made in the brochure.

The winter holiday in Switzerland cost £63.45 and the brochure promised a series of exciting events which included afternoon teas, parties, yodlers and an English-speaking mein-host; also promised were nearby ski-runs with adequate ski-hire facilities. Few of the promised events and facilities were forthcoming. In an action by the plaintiff against the operator the county court judge awarded damages of £31.72, based on the idea that the plaintiff got only half a holiday. On appeal the Court of Appeal raised the damages to £125.

Lord Denning MR: ... What is the legal position? I think that the statements in the brochure were representations or warranties. The breaches of them give Mr Jarvis a right to damages. It is not necessary to decide whether they were representations or warranties because since the Misrepresentation Act 1967, there is a remedy in damages for misrepresentation as well as for breach of warranty.

The one question in the case is: What is the amount of damages? The judge seems to have taken the difference in value between what he paid for and what he got. He said that he intended to give "the difference between the two values and no other damages" under any other head. He thought that Mr Jarvis had got half of what he paid for. So the judge gave him half the amount which he bad paid, namely, £31.72. Mr Jarvis appeals to this court. He says that the damages ought to have been much more ...

What is the right way of assessing damages? It has often been said that on a breach of contract damages cannot be given for mental distress. Thus in *Hamlin v Great Northern Railway Co*, Pollock CB said that damages cannot be given "for the disappointment of mind occasioned by the breach of contract". And in *Hobbs v London & South Western Railway Co*, Mellor J said that:

> "for the mere inconvenience, such as annoyance and loss of temper, or vexation, or for being disappointed in a particular thing which you have set your mind upon, without real physical inconvenience resulting, you cannot recover damages."

The courts in those days only allowed the plaintiff to recover damages if he suffered physical inconvenience, such as having to walk five miles home, as in *Hobbs'* case; or to live in an over crowded house, *Bailey v Bullock*.

I think that those limitations are out of date. In a proper case damages for mental distress can be recovered in contract, just as damages for shock can be recovered in tort. One such case is a contract for a holiday, or any other contract to provide entertainment and enjoyment. If the contracting party breaks his contract, damages can be given for the disappointment, the distress, the upset and frustration caused by the breach. I know that it is difficult to assess in terms of money, but it is no more difficult than the assessment which the courts have to make every day in personal injury cases for loss of amenities. Take the present case. Mr Jarvis has only a fortnight's holiday in the year. He books it far ahead, and looks forward to it all that time. He ought to be compensated for the loss of it.

A good illustration was given by Edmund Davies LJ in the course of the argument. He put the case of a man who has taken a ticket for Glyndbourne. It is the only night on which he can get there. He hires a car to take him. The car does not turn up. His damages are not limited to the mere cost of the ticket. He is entitled to general damages for the disappointment he has suffered and the loss of the entertainment which he should have had. Here, Mr Jarvis's fortnight's winter holiday has been a grave disappointment. It is true that he was conveyed to Switzerland and back and had meals and bed in the hotel. But that is not what he went for. He went to enjoy himself with all the facilities which the defendants said he would have. He is entitled to damages for the lack of those facilities, and for his loss of enjoyment.

A similar case occurred in 1951. It was *Stedman v Swan's Tours*. A holiday-maker was awarded damages because he did not get the bedroom and the accommodation which he was promised. The county court judge awarded him £13.15. This court increased it to £50.

I think the judge was in error in taking the sum paid for the holiday £63.45 and halving it. The right measure of damages is to compensate him for the loss of entertainment and enjoyment which he was promised, and which he did not get.

Looking at the matter quite broadly, I think the damages in this case should be the sum of £125. I would allow the appeal, accordingly.

Watts v Morrow [1991] 1 WLR 1421 Court of Appeal

Bingham LJ: ... A contract-breaker is not in general liable for any distress, frustration, anxiety, displeasure, vexation, tension or aggravation which his breach of contract may cause to the innocent party ... But the rule is not absolute. Where the very object of a contract is to provide pleasure, relaxation, peace of mind or freedom from molestation, damages will be awarded if the fruit of the contract is not provided or if the contrary result is procured instead ... A contract to survey the condition of a house for a prospective purchaser does not, however, fall within this exceptional category. In cases not falling within this exceptional category, damages are in my view recoverable for physical inconvenience and discomfort caused by the breach and mental suffering directly related to that inconvenience and discomfort ... But I also agree that awards should be restrained ...

Questions

1. Is mental distress a form of damage now recognised by the common law? Will it be protected by the law of tort? Should the the plaintiff in *Best v Samuel Fox* (p 358) have been given damages for mental distress? Is her case not more deserving than that of the disappointed holiday-maker?

2. D runs over Tibbins, P's much loved cat, causing P to suffer much mental distress. If the cat had a value of 50p, how much can P claim from D in an action for damages? Does it make any difference whether the case is pleaded in contract or tort?

3. Can a parent claim damages for mental distress for a child killed by the wrongful act of another?[13]

4. Are damages for misrepresentation governed by the same rules as damages for breach of warranty (ie breach of contract)

Vacwell Engineering Co Ltd v BDH Chemicals Ltd [1971] 1 QB 88 Queen's Bench Division

This was an action for damages in respect of death and damage arising out of an explosion in the plaintiffs' laboratory. The explosion occurred when a chemical, marketed and sold by the defendants, came into contact with water while one of the plaintiffs' employees was washing labels off the chemical's glass containers. The only warning on the label referred to "Harmful Vapour" and both the defendants, who had done inadequate research, and the plaintiffs were unaware of its explosive habits.

Rees J: ... The term and its breach having been established, the next question is whether Vacwell have shown that the accident was caused by BDH's breach of contract. It was strenuously and helpfully argued by Mr Tapp that the conduct for which Vacwell is responsible, which gave immediate rise to the explosion, was not foreseeable and amounted to a *novus actus interveniens* which broke the chain of causation. Upon the hypothesis that BDH foresaw, or should have foreseen, that an ampoule might be washed with water and might be dropped or that in some other way the contents of one or two ampoules might come into contact with water, the damage to be expected would be a small, violent reaction with consequent burning, minor cuts from glass, or, at worst, injury to one or more eyes. But, so his argument runs, no one could foresee, or should have foreseen, that the contents of 40 to 100 ampoules of boron tribromide would suddenly come into contact with such an amount of water as would produce the violent and lethal explosion which occurred in this case. The explosion itself and its consequences are, he says, of a different order from those foreseeable. Thus he takes the point as going to causation and also to remoteness of damage ...

As a result of the breach of contract in the instant case, an explosion, albeit of a small or minor kind, was reasonably foreseeable. An explosion of the magnitude which did occur was not reasonably foreseeable but I find that it was the direct result of the supply of boron tribromide without an adequate warning label, for use in Vacwell's manufacturing process. Looking at the whole of the circumstances as disclosed by the evidence, I hold that the explosion was caused by the breach of contract ...

... Taking all these circumstances into account, including that an explosion involving some damage to property caused by the explosion was reasonably foreseeable, I am unable to find that because the damage to property was much greater than could have been reasonably foreseen, it was too remote to be recoverable in law. When one bears in mind that the delicate glassware which constituted the equipment in connection with which boron tribromide was to be used was of the value of over £800,000, it may be unduly favourable to BDH to hold, as I do, that damage to property of the order of £74,000 was not reasonably

---

13   Cf Fatal Accidents Act 1976 s 1A.

foreseeable. Accordingly I find that Vacwell has established a breach of contract and that the explosion and its consequences were caused thereby ...

[On appeal the parties came to an agreement on the basis that Rees J's judgment dealing with remoteness should not be challenged: [1971] 1 QB 111.]

Questions

1. In damages actions for breach of contract is it true to say that defendants are liable for all direct damage arising out of the breach? Does foreseeability have a role?

2. Did the defendants contemplate the actual explosion and damage at the time they made the contract?

Ruxley Electronics Ltd v Forsyth [1994] 1 WLR 650 Court of Appeal

Dillon LJ (dissenting): Mr Forsyth stipulated in his agreement with Mr Hall that the pool to be constructed for him should have a maximum water depth of 7 feet 6 inches. But the pool as actually constructed has a maximum depth at its deepest point of only 6 feet 9 inches. Therefore Mr Forsyth claims damages, and claims in particular the cost of making good the defect, ie, providing a pool of the maximum depth of 7 feet 6 inches. But, on the judge's findings of fact which are not challenged, the only satisfactory way the defect can be made good would be to strip out the whole of the existing pool, excavate further to the required depth and then construct a completely new pool. The judge held that the cost of doing that would be £21,560, and Mr Forsyth accordingly claims that sum as damages instead of the mere £2,500 for loss of amenity which the judge awarded him ...

It is submitted on the present appeal that the requirement that reinstatement should be reasonable if the cost of reinstatement is sought as damages only arises in the context of mitigation of damages. Therefore it is submitted that the requirement is irrelevant in the present case where there is no alternative course by way of mitigation and the choice is between full reinstatement at the cost of £21,560 and leaving Mr Forsyth (subject to the judge's award of damages for loss of amenity) with the inferior pool which Mr Hall, in breach of contract, constructed for him. It is, of course, true that reasonableness lies at the heart of the doctrine of mitigation of damages. But that is not, in my judgment, the only impact of the concept of reasonableness on the law of damages.

If the evidence had been that the value of the pool as constructed was less than the value of a pool with a depth of 7 feet 6 inches as contracted for, but that the loss of value was substantially less than the £21,560 cost of reinstatement, then, given the finding that the pool as constructed is still deep enough to be perfectly safe to dive into, the obvious course would have been to award Mr Forsyth the loss of value. The basis of that would have been reasonableness. He has no absolute right to be awarded the cost of reinstatement. I see no reason, therefore, why if there has been no loss in value, he should automatically become entitled to the cost of reinstatement, however high. That would be a wholly unreasonable conclusion in law. Accordingly I agree with the judge's approach and would dismiss this appeal ...

Staughton LJ: ... In the present case Mr Forsyth has without question suffered a loss; he has a swimming pool which is less well suited to diving than the one he contracted for. What money will place him "in the same situation ... as if the contract had been performed?" The answer, on the facts of this case, is the cost of replacing the pool. Otherwise a builder of swimming pools need never perform his contract. He can always argue that 5 feet in depth is enough for diving, even if the purchaser has stipulated for 6, 7 or 8 feet, and pay no damages. In my judgment the key lies in the proposition of Oliver J that reasonableness is a matter of mitigation. It is unreasonable of a plaintiff to claim an expensive remedy if there is some cheaper alternative which would make good his loss. Thus he cannot claim the cost of reinstatement if the difference in value would make good his loss by enabling him to purchase the building or chattel that he requires elsewhere. But if there is no alternative course which will provide what he requires, or none which will cost less, he is entitled to the cost of repair or reinstatement even if that is very expensive. Suppose that I booked a hotel room in York during race week and the hotelier later told me that he was full and I could not come. It transpires that only one other hotel has room which is the local equivalent of the Ritz and very expensive. Otherwise I must go and stay in Manchester and will miss the first race. It is nothing to the point that a man spending his own money would rather miss one race than pay the cost of staying at the Ritz Hotel. Since there is no other alternative which will provide that which he has contracted for, he is entitled to incur that expense and charge it to the defendant ...

I would therefore award £21,560 as damages to Mr Forsyth against Ruxley to be deducted from the balance of the price. But I would set aside the existing award of £2,500 general damages which was the judge's compensation for loss of pleasure and amenity by reason of the lack of depth. That has now been dealt with ...

Mann LJ: ... Upon the facts two matters are to be observed. First, Mr Forsyth did not secure that for which he had contracted, and second, the pool was safe for diving. It is also to be observed that there was no finding to the effect that the shortage of depth had any effect upon the value of the estate.

The question is whether Mr Forsyth has to be content with a sum for the loss of this amenity of diving into a 6 feet 9 inches pool rather than an entitlement to the cost of that for which he contracted, a 7 feet 6 inches pool. This simple question attracted interesting arguments which went to the foundation of the measure of damages for breach of contract. The foundation is found in the judgment of Parke B in *Robinson v Harman*, I Ex. 850, 855, where he said:

> "The rule of the common law is, that where a party sustains a loss by reason of a breach of contract, he is, so far as money can do it, to be placed in the same situation, with respect to damages, as if the contract had been performed."

This very general principle is shadowed by another, which is that the damages should reflect a reasonable culmination of the relationship which has occurred between the parties. Thus damages will not reflect an unreasonable failure to mitigate loss. However, here we are not concerned with any failure to mitigate but rather with disappointment at the unfulfilled bargain. Before the judge there was no intent to reconstruct the pool. Now an undertaking to rebuild has been given. I regard the gift as unimportant and unnecessary: see *Dean v Ainley* [1987]

I WLR 1729, 1737H, by Kerr LJ. What a plaintiff intends to do, or does, with his damages is not material.

I think that this appeal is answered by Oliver J in *Radford v De Froberville* [1977] I WLR 1262, 1270, when he said:

> "*Pacta sunt servanda*. If he contracts for the supply of that which he thinks serves his interests – be they commercial, aesthetic or merely eccentric – then if that which is contracted for is not supplied by the other contracting party I do not see why, in principle, he should not be compensated by being provided with the cost of supplying it through someone else or in a different way, subject to the proviso, of course, that he is seeking compensation for a genuine loss and not merely using a technical breach to secure an uncovenanted profit."

Mr Forsyth did not secure what served his interests and for which he had bargained. The only way in which his interest can be served is by the construction of a new pool which I do not think is an unreasonable adventure. There can be instances where the cost of rectifying a failed project is not reasonable, as, for example, where no personal preference is served or where there is no preference and the value of the estate is undiminished. In my judgment this is not such a case. The bargain was for a personal preference. I would accordingly allow this appeal and award the sum of £21,560 against Ruxley. The award of general damages should consequently be set aside.

Questions

1. Does every contractor who does not get what he stipulated for suffer damage? What about the mental distress?
2. Could the plaintiff have refused to pay anything for the swimming pool as constructed?
3. Imagine that the House of Lords reinstates the decision of the trial judge and that Mr Forsyth has to be content with £2500. If Mr Forsyth subsequently suffers severe personal injury as a result of the depth being only 6ft 9ins, will he be able to claim compensation from Ruxley?

(c) Tortious liability and damages

Spartan Steel & Alloys Ltd v Martin & Co [1973] 1 QB 27 Court of Appeal

(See p 101)

Dominion Mosaics & Tile Ltd v Trafalgar Trucking Co Ltd [1990] 2 All ER 246 Court of Appeal

Taylor LJ: ... The basic principle governing the measure of damages where the defendant's tort has caused damage to the plaintiff's land or building is *restitutio integrum*. The damages should be such as will, so far as money can, put the plaintiff in the same position as he would have held had the tort not occurred. In applying that principle to particular cases, the problem has been whether *restitutio* is to be achieved by assessing the diminution in value of the damaged premises or the cost of reinstatement or possibly on some other basis ...

It is important to remember, however ... that insurance moneys are not to be taken into account. In fact [the new property] was purchased with insurance moneys. The insurance company has therefore stood out of its £390,000 and is entitled, by way of subrogation, to the return of its money, plus interest, from the proceeds of this action. Thus the respondents are not enriched in cash to the tune of £390,000, plus interest. True ... they got a more valuable building than they had before, but on the authority of the *Harbutt's Plasticine Ltd* case [1970] 1 QB 447 that does not necessarily render the award excessive or require any discount for betterment ...

Had it been argued that in fairness to the appellants some discount from £65,000 should have been allowed to reflect the depreciation of the machines in their few months of service, the point would have merited consideration. But no such submission was made, nor was there any evidence on which to base an assessment of an appropriate discount ...

Notes and questions

1. Is it right that the law of damages should confer benefits upon plaintiffs in addition to compensating them for their losses?

2. Was counsel for the appellants negligent in any way? To what extent is the measure of damages dependent upon the parties themselves?

3. Why does the law of damages not take account of insurance money? Does not such money diminish the loss? Is it because the tortfeasor should not receive a benefit at the plaintiff's expense?

4. 'It is not, I think, possible to say we must adopt, or seek to adopt, any rigid standard of comparison between a nuisance case and personal injury litigation. Nevertheless, overall the law ought to remain consistent when it is dealing with analogous situations ... One must bear in mind also a further general principle, that, when one is removed from the world of pecuniary loss and is attempting to measure damages for non-pecuniary loss, an element in reasonableness is the fairness of the compensation to be awarded. There must be moderation; some attention must be paid to the rights of the offending defendant as well as to the rights of the injured plaintiff ...' (Scarman LJ, *Bone v Seale* [1975] 1 All ER 787). What amount should be awarded to a person who has to put up with unpleasant smells from a neighbour's pig farm?

(d) Exemplary damages

Rookes v Barnard [1964] AC 1129 House of Lords

Lord Devlin: ... The first category [for an award of exemplary damages] is oppressive, arbitrary or unconstitutional action by servants of the government. I should not extend this category ... Where one man is more powerful than another ... he is not to be punished simply because he is the more powerful. In the case of the government it is different, for the servants of the government are also servants of the people and the use of their power must always be subordinate to their duty of service ... Cases in the second category are those in which the defendant's conduct has been calculated by him to make a profit for himself which may well exceed the compensation payable to the plaintiff ... Exemplary damages can properly be awarded whenever it is necessary to teach a wrongdoer that tort does not pay.

Notes and questions

1. 'It cannot lightly be taken for granted, even as a matter of theory, that the purpose of the law of tort is compensation ...' (Lord Wilberforce, *Cassell & Co Ltd v Broome* [1972] AC 1027). What are the other purposes of a damages action founded in the law of tort?

2. 'I thought and still think that that is highly anomalous. It is confusing the function of the civil law which is to compensate with the function of the criminal law which is to inflict deterrent and punitive penalties ... [But the] right to give punitive damages in certain cases is so firmly embedded in our law that only Parliament can remove it ... Local government is as much government as national government, and the police and many other persons are exercising governmental functions ...' (Lord Reid, *Cassell & Co Ltd v Broome* [1972] AC 1027). Do exemplary damages compensate the defendant or do they simply give the plaintiff a windfall?

3. 'Exemplary damages are anomalous. Indeed it is difficult to find any satisfactory basis for allowing such damages against a small local authority and refusing them against a powerful international company. But the anomaly exists and governmental bodies, including local authorities, are treated as being in a special category. I do not find it possible to accept the suggestion that when the applicant was being interviewed the committee were carrying out some private function of the council ... Cases where exemplary damages are justified will be rare, probably very rare. Before awarding such damages the court or tribunal will need to consider whether the conduct which is criticised falls within one of the special categories ... It will also have to consider whether the award of compensatory damages, including aggravated damages, is not by

itself sufficient to punish the defendant ...' (Neill LJ, *Bradford City Council v Arora* [1991] 2 QB 507). Are not public bodies in a different position from the private body? Do not organs of the state have a special duty to conform to the law?

4. Exemplary damages cannot be awarded in contract: *Addis v Gramophone Co Ltd* [1909] AC 488. Why not?

5. Can punitive (exemplary) damages be awarded in negligence and/or trepass cases?

(e) Personal injury

Wright v British Railways Board [1983] 2 AC 773 House of Lords

Lord Diplock: ... My Lords, claims for damages in respect of personal injuries constitute a high proportion of civil actions that are started in the courts in this country. If all of them proceeded to trial the administration of civil justice would break down; what prevents this is that a high proportion of them are settled before they reach the expensive and time-consuming stage of trial, and an even higher proportion of claims, particularly the less serious ones, are settled before the stage is reached of issuing and serving a writ. This is only possible if there is some reasonable degree of predictability about the sum of money that would be likely to be recovered if the action proceeded to trial.

The principal characteristics of actions for personal injuries that militate against predictability as to the sum recoverable are, first, that the English legal system requires that any judgment for tort damages, not being a continuing tort, shall be for one lump sum to compensate for all loss sustained by the plaintiff in consequence of the defendant's tortious act whether such loss be economic or non-economic, and whether it has been sustained during the period prior to the judgment or is expected to be sustained thereafter. The second characteristic is that non-economic loss constitutes a major item in the damages. Such loss is not susceptible of measurement in money. Any figure at which the assessor of damages arrives cannot be other than artificial and, if the aim is that justice metered out to all litigants should be even-handed instead of depending on idiosyncrasies of the assessor, whether jury or judge, the figure must be "basically a conventional figure derived from experience and from awards in comparable cases".

So Lord Denning MR put it, speaking for a unanimous five-member Court of Appeal in *Ward v James* ...

The Court of Appeal, with its considerable case-load of appeals in personal injury actions and the relatively recent experience of many of its members in trying such cases themselves, is, generally speaking, the tribunal best qualified to set the guidelines for judges currently trying such actions, particularly as respects non-economic loss ...

As regards assessment of damages for non-economic loss in personal injury cases, the Court of Appeal creates the guidelines as to the appropriate conventional figure by increasing or reducing awards of damages made by judges in individual cases for various common kinds of injuries. Thus so-called "brackets" are established broad enough to make allowance for circumstances which make the deprivation suffered by an individual plaintiff in consequence of the particular kind of injury greater or less than in the general run of cases, yet clear enough to reduce the unpredictability of what is likely to be the most important factor in arriving at settlement of claims ...

Notes and questions

1. 'In an action for personal injuries the damages are always divided into two main parts. First, there is what is referred to as special damage, which has to be specially pleaded and proved. This consists of out-of-pocket expenses and loss of earnings incurred down to the date of trial, and is generally capable of substantially exact calculation. Secondly, there is general damage which the law implies and is not especially pleaded. This includes compensation for pain and suffering and the like, and, if the injuries suffered are such as to lead to continuing or permanent disability, compensation for loss of earning power in the future ...' (Lord Goddard, *British Transport Commission v Gourley* [1956] AC 185). To what extent is general damage compensation for mental injury?

2. '[R]ecent cases show the desirability of three things: First, assessability: In cases of grave injury ... the award must basically be a conventional figure, derived from experience or from awards in comparable cases. Secondly, uniformity ... Thirdly, predictability ...' (Lord Denning MR, *Ward v James* [1966] 1 QB 273). Why have these three principles been ignored for so long in defamation cases?

3. Would it not be cheaper and more efficient if liability for serious personal injury was placed on a no-fault basis? What about accidents in the home?

4. What is the scientific object of the legal science of personal injury damages: the injuries or the Court of Appeal? If the latter, does this not mean that law is the object of its own science? Could the object be the amounts attributed by the Court of Appeal to various types of injury? If so, does mathematics then become the object?

(f) Fraud

Doyle v Olby (Ironmongers) Ltd [1969] 2 QB 158 Court of Appeal

Lord Denning MR: ... Damages for fraud and conspiracy are assessed differently from damages for breach of contract ... On principle, the distinction seems to be this: in contract, the defendant has made a promise and broken it. The object of damages is to put the plaintiff in as good a position as far as money can do it, as if the promise had been performed. In fraud, the defendant has been guilty of a deliberate wrong by inducing the plaintiff to act to his detriment. The object of damages is to compensate the plaintiff for all the loss he has suffered, so far again, as money can do it ...

Archer v Brown [1985] QB 401 Queen's Bench Division

(See p 30)

Questions

1. If the law of damages is about compensation (*restitutio in integrum*) ought not the behaviour of the defendant to be irrelevant?
2. Is an action for damages founded upon s 2(1) of the Misrepresentation Act 1967 technically an action in the tort of deceit? If so, will damages be awarded on the basis of fraud?
3. In the *Ruxley* case (p 184), if the breach of contract had been deliberate, would the court have had little difficulty in awarding the £21,560 damages?

(g) Damages for wrongful interference

IBL Ltd v Coussens [1991] 2 All ER 133 Court of Appeal

Neill LJ: ... At common law an action in conversion was purely a personal action and it resulted in a judgment for pecuniary damages only. An action in detinue however, (...), was akin to an action *in rem* and was appropriate where the plaintiff sought specific restitution of his chattel. Before the Common Law Procedure Act 1854 a plaintiff who wished to insist on the return of his chattel had to have recourse to Chancery ...

It is to be observed that the 1977 Act does not give any guidance as to the date at which the value of the goods is to be assessed ...

In considering any award of damages in an action in tort it is necessary to bear in mind the general principle which was restated by Brandon LJ in *Brandeis* ...

At the same time it is necessary to bear in mind that where the goods are irreversibly converted and are not recovered the general rule is that the measure of damages is the value of the goods at the time of conversion ...

I have come to the conclusion that if one takes account of all these considerations and the fact that several different remedies are available under s 3 of the 1977 Act it is not possible, or indeed appropriate, to attempt to lay down any rule which is intended to be of universal application as to the date by reference to which the value of goods is to be assessed. The method of valuation and the date of valuation will depend on the circumstances.

Notes and questions

1. Why should damages in the tort of conversion be measured by the value of the goods converted? Is not the role of an action for damages to compensate for loss?

2. 'If a wrongdoer has made use of goods for his own purpose, then he must pay a reasonable hire for them, even though the owner has in fact suffered no loss ... The claim for a hiring charge is ... not based on the loss to the plaintiff, but on the fact that the defendant has used the goods for his own purposes. It is an action against him because he has had the benefit of the goods. It resembles, therefore, an action for restitution, rather than an action of tort' (Denning LJ, *Strand Electric & Engineering Ltd v Brisford Entertainments Ltd* [1952] 2 QB 246 Court of Appeal). Is it not debt that should be fulfilling this role?

3. '[W]hat was in effect held in [the *Strand Electric*] case was that, in the case of conversion of a profit earning chattel which a defendant has used for his own benefit, the owner can recover by way of damages a hire charge plus either the return of the chattel or, if there has been a subsequent conversion by disposal, the value of the chattel at the date of such conversion ... Thirdly, although damages for conversion normally consist in the value of the goods at the date of conversion, consequential damages are always recoverable if not too remote ... What the plaintiffs have lost is the use of the car over the whole period from the original conversion until ultimate return' (Parker J, *Hillesden Securities v Ryjack* [1983] 1 WLR 959). Why should owners of profit earning chattels be treated more favourably by the law of damages than owners of non-profit earning chattels? Is it the role of the law of tort to protect expectation interests?

4. 'In the field of tort there are areas where the law is different and the plaintiff can recover in respect of the defendant's gain. Thus in the field of trespass it is well established that if one person has, without leave of another, been using that other's land for his own purposes he ought to pay for such user ... So in a case of detinue the defendant was ordered to pay a hire for chattels he had detained: *Strand Electric and Engineering Co Ltd v Brisford Entertainments Ltd* ....' (Dillon LJ, *Surrey CC v Bredero Homes Ltd* [1993] 1 WLR 1361). Should tort continue to play this unjust enrichment role now that there appears to be an independent category of restitution?

(h) The limitation of liability

Hadley v Baxendale (1854) 156 ER 145 Court of Exchequer

Alderson B: ... We think the proper rule in such a case as the present is this. Where two parties have made a contract which one of them has broken the damages which the other party ought to receive in respect of such breach of contract should be such as may fairly and reasonably be considered as either arising naturally, ie, according to the usual course of things, from such breach of contract itself, or such as may reasonably be supposed to have been in the contemplation of both parties at the time they made the contract as the probable result of the breach of it. If special circumstances under which the contract was actually made were communicated by the plaintiffs to the defendants, and thus known to both parties, the damages resulting from the breach of such a contract which they would reasonably contemplate would be the amount of injury which would ordinarily follow from a breach of contract under the special circumstances so known and communicated. But, on the other hand, if these special circumstances were wholly unknown to the party breaking the contract, he, at the most, could only be supposed to have had in his contemplation the amount of injury which would arise generally, and in the great multitude of cases not affected by any special circumstances, from such a breach of contract. For, had the special circumstances been known, the parties might have specially provided for the breach of contract by special terms as to the damages in that case; and of this advantage it would be very unjust to deprive them. In the present case, if we are to apply the principles above laid down, we find that the only circumstances here communicated by the plaintiffs to the defendants at the time the contract was made were that the article to be carried was the broken shaft of a mill and that the plaintiffs were the millers of that mill. But how do these circumstances show reasonably that the profits of the mill must be stopped by an unreasonable delay in the delivery of the broken shaft by the carrier to the third person? Suppose the plaintiffs had another shaft in their possession and that they only wished to send back the broken shaft to the engineer who made it; it is clear that this would be quite consistent with the above circumstances, and yet the unreasonable delay in the delivery would have no effect upon the intermediate profits of the mill.

It follows, therefore, that the loss of profits here cannot reasonably be considered such a consequence of the breach of contract as could have been fairly and reasonably contemplated by both the parties when they made this contract. For such loss would neither have flowed naturally from the breach of this contract in the great multitude of such cases occurring under ordinary circumstances, nor were the special circumstances, which, perhaps, would have made it a reasonable and natural consequence of such breach of contract, communicated to or known by the defendants. The judge ought, therefore, to have told the jury that, upon the facts there before them, they ought not to take the loss of profits into consideration at all in estimating the damages. There must, therefore, be a new trial in this case.

Notes and questions

1. This famous case remains the starting point for the measure of damages in actions for breach of contract. It has a European flavour in that it is generally considered to have been influenced by Pothier and by the rule in the French Code civil which stipulates: '*Le débiteur n'est tenu que des dommages et intérêts qui ont été prévus ou qu'on a pu prévoir lors du contrat, lorsque ce n'est point par son dol que l'obligation n'est point exécutée.*' (Article 1150). However, the use of the word 'contemplation' has attracted much attention since it appears to mean, in the context of a contractual relationship, something different from the word 'forseeability' used, subsequently, in the context of a tort situation. Can one contemplate something that the reasonable man would not forsee? Can one forsee something that the reasonable contractor, at the time of the contract, would not contemplate?

2. How many rules are being formulated by Alderson B? Can one be liable for damage which, although not in the contemplation of the parties at the time of the contract, arises naturally from the breach?

3. What was the plaintiff's expectation interest in *Hadley*? Did the court protect this interest? What interest did the court protect?

4. P hired a horse from D and used it in battle. The horse proved most unsuitable for war and as a result P was captured and spent five years in captivity. Ought D to be liable for the five years in captivity?

5. Does Article 1150CC (above) function as a statutory limitation of liability clause? If so, does this mean that the rule in *Hadley v Baxendale* is an implied limitation clause?

Diamond v Campbell-Jones [1960] 1 All ER 583 Chancery Division

Buckley J: In this case I have to determine the amount of damages payable by the defendants to the plaintiff under a judgment of Harman J ... By that judgment it was declared that the defendants had wrongfully repudiated an agreement ... for the sale by the defendants to the plaintiff of No 44, Green Street, Mayfair, for £6,000, and an inquiry was directed as to what damages (if any) the plaintiff had suffered as a result of such repudiation ...

The plaintiff carries on business as a dealer in real estate, and in the course of that business he has bought and converted a number of houses in the centre of London. In his affidavit he says as follows: ...

"The purpose of my acquiring No 44, Green Street, as the defendants at all material times well knew, was to obtain vacant possession so that I could develop the same by sub-division thereof ..."

The plaintiff contends that the proper measure of damages is the profit which it is reasonable to suppose he would have made had he converted the four upper floors into two maisonettes, the ground floor into offices, and the basement into a self-contained flat ... The defendants, on the other hand, contend that the proper measure is the difference between the sale price and the market value of the property at the date of their breach of contract.

The general rule of common law is that where a party has sustained a loss by reason of a breach of contract he is, so far as money can do it, to be placed by way of damages in the same position as if the contract had been performed ...

It will be convenient for me to read a very well-known passage from ... *Hadley v Baxendale* ...

[C]ounsel for the plaintiff says that the damage to the plaintiff consequent on the defendants' repudiation of their contract which the defendants could reasonably have foreseen at the date of the contract depends on the circumstances of which knowledge at the date of the contract ought to be imputed to the defendants. This imputed knowledge, he says, includes the general conditions of everyday life and the general circumstances of the business of the parties. He says that the subject-matter of the contract was a house which everyone considered to be fit only for conversion and no longer to be suited to single occupation. He says that it was at least "on the cards" that a purchaser would convert the house before disposing of it. It follows, he says, that if the purchaser in fact intended to do this, and can show that by doing so it was reasonable to suppose that his profit would have been greater than if he had sold the property for its market value at the date of the breach of contract, he is entitled to damages measured by that probable profit.

I have had no evidence at all of any such knowledge or of any actual knowledge by the defendants that the plaintiff either intended or was likely to carry out the conversion of the property himself ...

In some cases the nature or the subject-matter of a contract may be such as to make it clear that one of the parties is entering into the contract for the purpose of a particular business, and the circumstances may be such that the court will infer that the other party must have appreciated that this was so. It seems to me, however, that this can rarely be the case where the contract is for the sale of land. The vendor of a shop equipped for use as a butcher's shop would not, in my judgment, be justified by that circumstance alone in assuming, and ought not to be treated as knowing, that the purchaser would intend to use it for the business of a butcher rather than that of a baker or candlestick-maker. Special circumstances are necessary to justify imputing to a vendor of land a knowledge that the purchaser intends to use it in any particular manner. In my judgment neither the fact that No 44, Green Street was ripe for conversion, nor indeed the fact that everybody recognised this, was sufficient ground for imputing to the vendors knowledge that the purchaser was a person whose business it was to carry out such conversions, or that he intended, or was even likely, to convert the house himself for profit.

For these reasons, in my judgment, the plaintiff is not entitled to damages measured by reference to the profit obtainable by converting the property. The damages should be assessed in accordance with the principle normally applicable to cases of breach of contract for the sale of land, that is to say, by reference to the difference between the purchase price and the market value at the date of the breach of contract. [His Lordship then proceeded to consider the evidence as to the market value in February, 1956, of No 44, Green Street and

continued:] I hold that the market value of the property at the relevant date was
£14,500. The difference between this figure and the purchase price is accordingly
£8,500 ...

Notes and questions

1. 'The law cannot take account of everything that follows a wrongful
   act; it regards some subsequent matters as outside the scope of its
   selection ... In the varied web of affairs, the law must abstract some
   consequences as relevant, not perhaps on grounds of pure logic but
   simply for practical reasons' (Lord Wright, *The Liesbosch* [1933] AC
   449). When a court regards certain matters as being outside the scope
   of its selection, is it saying that there is no causal link between the
   matters and the wrongful act? What caused the lost profits in *Hadley
   v Baxendale* (above p 193)?

2. 'In cases like *Hadley v Baxendale* or the present case it is not enough
   that in fact the plaintiff's loss was directly caused by the defendant's
   breach of contract. It clearly was so caused in both. The crucial
   question is whether ... the loss ... should have been within his
   contemplation. The modern rule in tort is quite different and it
   imposes a much wider liability. The defendant will be liable for any
   type of damage which is reasonably foreseeable as liable to happen
   even in the most unusual case ...' (Lord Reid, *The Heron II* [1969] 1 AC
   350). Is Lord Reid accurate: do not most contractors suffering direct
   damage get compensated? (See eg, *Parsons v Uttley Ingham*, below;
   Vacwell Engineering v BDH Chemicals, p 183.)

3. 'The test of remoteness is similar to that in tort. The contractor is
   liable for all such loss or expense as could reasonably have been
   foreseen, at the time of the breach, as a possible consequence of it.
   Applied to this case, it means that the makers of the hopper are liable
   for the death of the pigs. They ought reasonably to have foreseen
   that, if the mouldy pig nuts were fed to the pigs, there was a
   possibility that they might become ill. Not a serious possibility. Not a
   real danger. But still a slight possibility' (Lord Denning MR, *Parsons
   (Livestock) Ltd v Uttley Ingham & Co* [1978] QB 791). In this case a
   vendor of a hopper failed to remove, when erecting the hopper on
   the buyer's farm, some sticky tape holding the ventilator closed; the
   closed ventilator could not be seen from the ground and the nuts
   stored in the hopper went mouldy. The farmer nevertheless
   continued to feed the nuts to his pigs and as a result the herd was
   decimated by a very rare disease. Who caused the pigs to die?

6. 'While, on his finding, nobody at the time of contract could have
   expected E coli to ensue from eating mouldy nuts [the judge] is
   clearly, and, as a matter of common sense, rightly, saying that people

would contemplate ... the serious possibility of injury and even death among the pigs' (Scarman LJ, *Parsons (Livestock) Ltd v Uttley Ingham & Co* [1978] QB 791). Why, then, did the farmer continue to feed mouldy nuts to his pigs? If the farmer had sued in tort, would he have got the same damages?[14]

7. How much should the farmer in *Parsons* get for his dead pigs? Should he get (i) the cost of replacing the pigs; (ii) the cost of replacing the pigs plus compensation for the trouble and mental distress at seeing, and clearing up, the dead animals; (iii) the sale value of the pigs; (iv) the sale value plus compensation for mental distress etc? Does the distinction between *damnum emergens* and *lucrum cessans* have any meaning in English law?

8. What if a neighbouring farmer had borrowed (mouldy) nuts from the hopper: should he be able to sue the vendor of the hopper? Or the buyer of the hopper? How much should the neighbouring farmer get if successful?

The Borag [1981] 1 WLR 274 Court of Appeal

Lord Denning MR: In this case a vessel was wrongfully arrested. It was afterwards released on the owner providing security. The question is: what is the proper measure of compensation for the owner? ... It seems to me, as a matter of common sense and common law, that expenditure made to obtain the release of a vessel from arrest should be regarded as an item of damages, and not as mitigation ... Next there was the question of causation or remoteness. I would agree that the overdraft interest was in a sense a consequence of the unlawful arrest. It flowed from it in the sense that, if there had been no unlawful arrest, the overdraft would not have been incurred. But, as we all know, it is not every consequence of a wrongful act which is the subject of compensation. The law has to draw a line somewhere ... Although the overdraft interest may be a consequence of the initial unlawful arrest, is it such a consequence that ought to be visited in damages? Upon this point – I do not care whether you call it "causation" or whether you call it "remoteness" – causation and remoteness are two different ways of stating the same question. Is the consequence sufficiently closely connected with the cause as to be the subject of compensation or not? To my mind causation and remoteness here are the same ...

Shaw LJ: ... [The umpire] looked at the whole matter as should a man of business who was sufficiently informed in regard to the broad legal principles involved in breach of contract and the right and reasonable basis for compensation for the damage occasioned by a particular breach ...

Templeman LJ: ...The managers, in breach of contract, arrested the owners' vessel to secure payment of the owners' debts. The managers became liable for the reasonably foreseeable damages suffered by the owners as a result of that breach of contract.... Whatever principle is invoked – whether it be the principle of causation or mitigation – the acid test in the present circumstances must have

---

14 Cf Law Reform (Contributory Negligence) Act 1945.

been reasonableness; and, if the interest charges were unreasonable, they were not damages for which the managers are liable ... [I]f the interest charges were unreasonable – they were too remote; they were not caused by the breach; they were not part of a reasonable form of mitigation – all these matters hang together.

Notes and questions

1. The principle of mitigation is discussed after *Gainsford v Carroll* (below p 199). Is there really no difference between the rules of causation, remoteness and mitigation?

2. English law tackles the difficult problem of causation by splitting it up into a number of quite separate rules and principles.[15] These different rules function, as it were, at different levels. The first level of operation is actionability: some causes of action are not complete unless the damage has been caused directly (eg false imprisonment).[16] The second level is that of fact (and thus was once in the province of the jury): there must be factual cause and connection between the wrongful act and the damage. Thus the negligent doctor who fails to save the life of a patient mortally injured by another will not be liable for the patient's death; only if he caused the death will he be liable.[17] The third level is that of law (and thus in the province of the judge): even although there might be cause and connection between the wrongful act and the damage, the law might exclude all or part of the damage on the ground that it is too remote.[18] Here, as we have seen, there appear to be two different tests depending upon whether the claim is in contract[19] or in tort.[20] In fact the position can become more complex when one moves into the area of the property torts and bailment (see above pp 191-192) since remoteness, causation and actionability often become one and the same question: is the defendant liable for the full value of the plaintiff's property stolen in unforeseeable circumstances from the bailee?[21] The fourth level is that of the law of damages: here, it might be said, the rules attach themselves more to the institution of the *actio* (remedy) rather than to the substantive legal relationship between

---

15 See generally G Samuel & J Rinkes, *Contractual and non-contractual obligations in English law* (Ars Aequi, 1992), pp 213-217.
16 *Harnett v Bond* [1925] AC 669.
17 *Barnett v Chelsea & Kensington Hospital Management Committee* [1969] 1 QB 428.
18 *The Wagon Mound (No 1)* [1961] AC 388.
19 *Hadley v Baxendale* (1854) 156 ER 145.
20 *The Wagon Mound (No 1)* [1961] AC 388.
21 *Mitchell v Ealing LBC* [1979] QB 1.

the parties and thus the cases do not as such raise questions about the liability itself. It is at this level that contributory negligence and mitigation function.

3. An important defence in the English law of tort is *volenti non fit injuria* – a plaintiff who consents to damage has no claim. Thus if someone willingly decides to go on an aeroplane flight with a drunken pilot then the claim might be barred (although statute prevents this rule applying in respect of motor vehicles). A moment's thought will reveal just how important consent is to the law of tort and, of course, it is an idea that is reflected in contractual exclusion and limitation clauses (see eg, *Photo Productions v Securicor*, p 312). At what level does consent function in contract and tort: at the level of actionability, causation or damages? Can a dead person ever be deemed to consent?

Gainsford v Carroll (1824) 107 ER 516 Court of King's Bench

Action for the non-performance of three contracts entered into by the defendants with the plaintiff for the sale of fifty bales of bacon, to be shipped by them from Waterford, in the months of January, February, and March 1823 respectively. The defendant suffered judgment by default, and, upon the execution of the writ of enquiry in London, the secondary told the jury that they were at liberty to calculate the damages according to the price of bacon on the day when the enquiry was executed, and that the difference between that and the contract price ought to be the measure of damages. Parke had obtained a rule nisi for setting aside the enquiry on the ground that the plaintiff was only entitled to recover the difference between the contract price and the price which the article bore at or about the time when, by the terms of the contract, it ought to have been delivered. In the case of a purchase of goods, the vendee is in possession of his money, and he has it in his power, as soon as the vendor has failed in the performance of the contract, to purchase other goods of the like quality and description, and it is his own fault it he does not do so.

Per curiam. Here the plaintiff had his money in his possession and he might have purchased other bacon of the like quality the very day after the contract was broken, and if he has sustained any loss, by neglecting to do so, it is his own fault. We think that the under sheriff ought to have told the jury that the damages should be calculated according to the price of the bacon at or about the day when the goods ought to have been delivered.

Notes and questions

1. 'A plaintiff is under no duty to mitigate his loss, despite the habitual use by the lawyers of the phrase "duty to mitigate". He is completely free to act as he judges to be in his best interests. On the other hand, a defendant is not liable for all loss suffered by the plaintiff in consequence of his so acting. A defendant is only liable for such part of the plaintiff's loss as is properly to be regarded as caused by the

defendant's breach of duty ... Whether a loss is avoidable by reasonable action on the part of the plaintiff is a question of fact not law' (Sir John Donaldson MR, *The Solholt* [1983] 1 Ll Rep 605). Is the distinction between duty and interests helpful in this context? What are the rights of a plaintiff *vis-à-vis* a defendant in breach of an obligation? What are the rights of a defendant in these circumstances? If the defendant has certain rights, is not the plaintiff under certain duties?

2. 'In short, [a plaintiff] is fully entitled to be as extravagant as he pleases but not at the expense of the defendant ... [The plaintiff] was fully entitled to have his damaged vehicle repaired at whatever cost because he preferred it. But he was not justified in charging against the defendant the cost of repairing the damaged vehicle when that cost was more than twice the replacement market value and he had made no attempt to find a replacement vehicle ... It is vital, for the purpose of assessing damages fairly between the plaintiff and the defendant, to consider whether the plaintiff's course of action was economic or uneconomic, and if it was uneconomic it cannot ... form a proper basis for assessment of damages. The question has to be considered from the point of view of a businessman' (Pearson LJ, *Darbishire v Warran* [1963] 1 WLR 1067). If the plaintiff is not entitled to rebuild a much loved chattel at the full expense of the wrongdoer, is the plaintiff entitled to damages for mental distress instead? If the tort of conversion distinguishes between profit earning and non-profit earning chattels, why cannot other torts distinguish between economic and non-economic chattels?

Thomas v Countryside Council for Wales [1994] 4 All ER 853 Queen's Bench Division

Rougier J: ... [I]n order to assess the net profits foregone, the arbitrator first estimated the profit which the appellants would have earned had they been allowed to continue as before, and as the second half of the equation he assessed what was the maximum income the farm could produce, the sole criterion being that of finance; no other considerations entered the picture.

In my judgment that approach is wrong in law. It would have appealed to Mr Gradgrind but it does not appeal to me ... Take the case of a farmer who farms sheep and nothing else because that is what he wishes to do. Restrictions are placed upon him which will entail a very considerable diminution of the number of sheep he is able to farm; bowing to the inevitable he takes advice and is told that rather than continue with a limited herd he will make more money if he converts his entire farm to turnips and mangoldwurzels. Is he not to be allowed to say: "I don't like turnips and mangoldwurzels; I don't like their smell, I don't like the mud they produce, and I fail to see why this intrusive body, 'drest in a little brief authority', should come and radically alter the amenities and tenor of the life that I have led for many years." Are not such arguments to be heard? If the answer is No then the world will have grown grey indeed. For these reasons the matter must be remitted to the arbitrator for him to apply the correct test.

This naturally leads to the question what is the correct test? ...

I think that the wording of the guidelines, although far short of ideal, was intended to equate the manner of assessing compensation with the normal law applicable to cases of contractual or tortious liability ...

Under the normal law of contract and tort the fundamental basis for the measure of damages is compensation for pecuniary loss which directly and naturally flows from the breach ... There is, however, a qualification that a plaintiff suing for breach of contract or, for that matter, for tort cannot call upon a defendant to pay the full direct consequences unless he himself has acted reasonably to mitigate the loss. It is sometimes loosely described as a plaintiff's duty to mitigate ...

If he wishes to claim the full measure of his loss, a plaintiff must act reasonably, but, as was recently pointed out in ... The Solholt ... a plaintiff is under no duty to mitigate his loss. He is completely free to act as he judges to be in his best interests. The significance of his failure to act in a reasonable manner is merely that he cannot then call upon the defendant to pay for losses which he might have avoided had he taken reasonable steps to do so. For the purposes of the present remission to the arbitrator I would stress that fundamentally the matter is one of causation – that is to say the assessment of the loss which has naturally flowed as a result of the restrictions.

Put another way, was the appellants' decision to adopt the farming system which they did a reasonable one? That question is not to be answered solely in terms of the commercial optimum ...

Questions

1. Can one apply Sir John Donaldson's reasoning in *The Solholt* to the law of obligations in general: for example could one say that one is under no 'duty' in the law of contract to execute one's promises but that if one does not then one must pay damages?

2. If you had to put Rougier LJ's reasoning method in the chapter on legal reasoning (see Chapter 2), what heading would you put it under?

Law Reform (Contributory Negligence) Act 1945 (8 & 9 Geo VI, c 28)

1. Apportionment of liability in case of contributory negligence

(1) Where any person suffers damage as the result partly of his own fault and partly of the fault of any other person or persons, a claim in respect of that damage shall not be defeated by reason of the fault of the person suffering the damage, but the damages recoverable in respect thereof shall be reduced to such extent as the court thinks just and equitable having regard to the claimant's share in the responsibility of the damage ...

4 Interpretation

...

"damage" includes loss of life and personal injury ...

"fault" means negligence, breach of statutory duty or other act or omission which gives rise to liability in tort or would, apart from this Act, give rise to the defence of contributory negligence.

Notes and questions

1. Before this Act contributory negligence was treated as a matter of factual causation: that is to say it operated in an all-or-nothing fashion. Either the defendant caused the plaintiff's damage or, because of the contributory negligence, he did not. Many plaintiffs whose own carelessness had contributed to their damage were thus debarred from obtaining compensation. The effect of the 1945 statute was to change the level at which contributory negligence functioned; instead of functioning at the level of causation itself, it now functions at the level of the assessment of damages. In other words carelessness by the plaintiff need not affect liability itself. However, can a court still hold that a plaintiff was the cause of his or her own damage?

2. Would the Act be applicable to the facts of *Redgrave v Hurd* (below, p 272)?

3. Why was the Act not applied to the facts of *Parsons v Uttley Ingham* (above, p 196)?

4. Should the Act be applicable to a plaintiff who is suing in debt?

5. To what extent should (i) smoking (ii) drinking (iii) eating too much butter be treated as contributory negligence?

6. What about a plaintiff who is injured while indulging in unlawful behaviour?

CHAPTER 4

INTRODUCTION TO CONTRACTUAL OBLIGATIONS

1 INTRODUCTION

The law of contract has acted as the paradigm obligation in the civil law systems since the development of the law of obligations itself. Even in the modern codes *delict* (tort) and restitution can still seem an afterthought and it is only the case law that reveals the impact of the industrial revolution. In English law the historical position is much more complex since contract is a relatively new import; yet once it had taken hold during the 19th century nearly all obligations problems assumed a contractual flavour.[1] The modern tort of negligence retains a 'contractual' element in its insistence upon a duty of care based on the empirical requirement of proximity.

Given this central role that contract has now assumed in the common law, it is tempting to think in terms of harmonisation in Europe. Indeed one recent French introduction to English law, while fully appreciating *le fossé* which separates the English from the French legal mentality, suggests that it might only a matter of time before the common law and civil law become assimilated.[2] Yet such thinking, as positive as it is, can mask important differences of structure, approach and mentality; the common law of contract and the civil law of contract do start out from different positions and while there might be *rapprochement* these differing positions can lead to misunderstanding if not approached with care. That said, the differences can also act as positive vehicles for transmitting knowledge of English contract law.

Moschi v Lep Air Services Ltd [1973] AC 331 House of Lords

(See p 32)

Notes and questions

1. The basis upon which English law has built its law of contract is the notion of promise. This, as we shall see, is in contrast to the

---

1   P Atiyah, *The Rise and Fall of Freedom of Contract* (Oxford, 1979).
2   R David & X Blanc-Jouvan, *Le droit anglais* (Presses Universitaires de France, 1994), p 125-126.

Romanist systems which have used the idea of agreement. Of course one can say that English contract law is about agreements and many writers do say this, but the judges are, on the whole, more circumspect. Agreement suggests a meeting of subjective minds and this in turn implies that mistake will undermine the contract; promise, in contrast, is much more objective. Once one has launched a promise others may come to rely upon it. Is this why the common law (in contrast to equity) has never developed a doctrine of mistake?

2. Lord Diplock also recognises the important role of the remedy in English contract law. An action for damages is, for example, quite different from a claim in debt – the latter is more akin to a claim for specific performance. Compare his analysis in *Moschi* with his analysis in *Photo Production* (p 312). Does he not overlook something in the latter analysis which he does not overlook in the former?

3. Lord Diplock says that contract is part of the English law of obligations. What are the other parts of the English law of obligations?

2 TYPES OF CONTRACT

(a) Bilateral contracts

United Dominions Trust Ltd v Eagle Aircraft Services Ltd [1968] 1 WLR 74
Court of Appeal

Diplock LJ: ... [T]he present appeal does turn on the difference in legal character between contracts which are synallagmatic (a term which I prefer to bilateral, for there may be more than two parties), and contracts which are not syllagmatic but only unilateral, an expression which, like synallagmatic, I have borrowed from French law (Code Civil, art 1102 and art 1103). Under contracts of the former kind, each party undertakes to the other party to do or to refrain from doing something, and, in the event of his failure to perform his undertaking, the law provides the other party with a remedy. The remedy of the other party may be limited to recovering monetary compensation for any loss which he has sustained as a result of the failure, without relieving him from his own obligation to do that which he himself has undertaken to do and has not yet done, or to continue to refrain from doing that which he himself has undertaken to refrain from doing. It may, in addition, entitle him, if he so elects, to be released from any further obligation to do or to refrain from doing anything ... The mutual obligations of parties to a synallagmatic contract may be subject to conditions precedent, that is to say, they may not arise until a described event has occurred; but the event must not be one which one party can prevent from occurring, for if it is, it leaves that party free to decide whether or not he will enter into any obligations to the other party at all. The obligations under the contract lack that mutuality which is an essential characteristic of a synallagmatic contract ...

Notes and questions

1. Are there not important differences between the French notion of a bilateral contract and the English notion? Is not the English notion bound up with the requirement of consideration (which the French do not have)?

2. What if a contract between A and B contains an exclusion clause that exonerates A from any contractual liability towards B in any circumstances: will the contract be void for lack of mutuality?

3. A contracts to work for B. A is then found guilty of a serious crime and sent to prison for a long period. Is A in breach of his contract with B?

4. How does a condition precedent actually operate in English law? Are they individual promises or are they events upon which other promises are based?

(b) Unilateral contracts

United Dominions Trust Ltd v Eagle Aircraft Services Ltd [1968] 1 WLR 74
Court of Appeal

Diplock LJ:.... Under contracts which are only unilateral – which I have elsewhere described as "if" contracts – one party, whom I will call "the promisor", undertakes to do or to refrain from doing something on his part if another party, "the promisee", does or refrains from doing something, but the promisee does not himself undertake to do or to refrain from doing that thing. The commonest contracts of this kind in English law are options for good consideration to buy or to sell or to grant or take a lease, competitions for prizes, and such contracts as that discussed in *Carlill v Carbolic Smoke Ball Co* [1893] 1 QB 256. A unilateral contract does not give rise to any immediate obligation on the part of either party to do or to refrain from doing anything except possibly an obligation on the part of the promisor to refrain from putting it out of his power to perform his undertaking in the future. This apart, a unilateral contract may never give rise to any obligation on the part of the promisor; it will only do so on the occurence of the event specified in the contract, *viz*, the doing (or refraining from doing) by the promisee of a particular thing. It never gives rise, however, to any obligation on the promisee to bring about the event by doing or refraining from doing that particular thing. Indeed, a unilateral contract of itself never gives rise to any obligation on the promisee to do or to refrain from doing anything. In its simplist form (eg, "If you pay the entrance fee and win the race, I will pay you £100"), no obligations on the part of the promisee result from it at all. But in its more complex and more usual form, as in an option, the promisor's undertaking may be to enter into a synallagmatic contract with the promisee on the occurance of the event specified in the unilateral contract, and in that case the event so specified must be, or at least include, the communication by the promisee to the promisor of the promisee's acceptance of his obligations under the synallagmatic contract. By entering into the subsequent synallagmatic contract on the occurrence of the specified event, the promisor discharges his obligation under the unilateral contract and accepts new obligations under the synallagmatic contract. Any obligations of the promisee arise, not out of the unilateral contract, but out of the subsequent synallagmatic contract into which he was not obliged to enter but has chosen to do so.

Two consequences follow from this. The first is that there is no room for any inquiry whether any act done by the promisee in purported performance of a unilateral contract amounts to a breach of warranty or a breach of condition on his part, for he is under no obligation to do or to refrain from doing any act at all. The second is that, as respects the promisor, the initial inquiry is whether the event, which under the unilateral contract gives rise to obligations on the part of the promisor, has occurred. To that inquiry the answer can only be a simple "Yes" or "No"...

Questions

1. A yacht club stipulates, 'If any yachtsmen pays the entrance fee and wins the yacht race to be held on Saturday at 2 pm, we will pay the yachtsman £1000'. D pays the fee and enters the race; however during the race he collides with P's yacht and sinks it. Can P sue D for breach of contract? What if D won the race by cheating: can the yacht club sue D to recover the £1000 and (or) can C, who would be the winner if D is disqualified, sue D for £1000. Could C sue D in damages for all his expenditure in entering the race?

2. At what point in a unilateral contract is the contractual offer accepted?

3. D advertises in his local newspaper that he will pay £10 to anyone who returns his lost wallet. P finds the wallet, which contains D's address, and returns it to D who says nothing about the reward. The next day P sees the advert in the paper: can he claim the £10? What if P, after seeing the advert and then finding the wallet, carelessly loses it while taking it to D's house: can D sue P for the value of the wallet and its contents?

4. In *Carlill v Carbolic Smoke Ball Co* (p 237) the plaintiff sued in debt on the basis of a unilateral contract. Did the plaintiff gain any kind of property right in the debt the moment the condition precedent matured?

(c) Contract or contracts

Ashington Piggeries Ltd v Christopher Hill Ltd [1972] AC 441 House of Lords

Lord Diplock: ... My Lords, the claim in each of these appeals is for damages for breach of a contract for the sale of goods. It will, therefore, be necessary to relate them to the relevant statutory provisions of the Sale of Goods Act 1893. In the form in which the Bill was originally drafted by Sir MacKenzie Chalmers that

Act was intended to state the common law rules relating to the sale of goods as they had been developed by judicial decision up to 1889. Although a number of amendments were made in committee during the passage of the Bill through Parliament, they did not alter the essential character of the Act as expository of the common law of England at the date at which it was passed. But the exposition contained in the Act is only partial. It does not seek to codify the general law of contract of England or of Scotland. It assumes the existence as a basic principle of the English law of contract that, subject to any limitations imposed by statute or by common law rules of public policy, parties to contracts have freedom of choice not only as to what each will mutually promise to do but also as to what each is willing to accept as the consequences of the performance or non-performance of those promises so far as those consequences affect any other party to the contract ... The provisions of the Act are in the main confined to statements of what promises are to be implied on the part of the buyer and the seller in respect of matters upon which the contract is silent, and statements of the consequences of performance or non-performance of promises, whether expressed or implied, where the contract does not state what those consequences are to be. Even a code whose content is so limited must proceed by classifying promises, both those which are expressed and those to be implied; the circumstances which give rise to implied promises, and how they are to be performed and the consequences of performing each class of promise or of failing to perform it. Because of the source of the rules stated in the Sale of Goods Act 1893 the classification adopted is by reference to the promises made in relatively simple types of contracts for the sale of goods which were commonly made in the nineteenth century and had been the subject of judicial decision before 1893. But although the language in which the rules are expressed is appropriate to these simple types of contracts, it has to be applied today to promises made in much more complicated contracts which cannot be readily allotted to any single class of contract which appears to be primarily envisaged by a particular section or subsection of the code. Unless the Sale of Goods Act 1893 is to be allowed to fossilise the law and to restrict the freedom of choice of parties to contracts for the sale of goods to make agreements which take account of advances in technology and changes in the way in which business is carried on today, the provisions set out in the various sections and subsections of the code ought not to be construed so narrowly as to force upon parties to contracts for the sale of goods promises and consequences different from what they must reasonably have intended. They should be treated rather as illustrations of the application to simple types of contract of general principles for ascertaining the common intention of the parties as to their mutual promises and their consequences which ought to be applied by analogy in cases arising out of contracts which do not appear to have been within the immediate contemplation of the draftsman of the Act in 1893.

In each of the instant appeals the dispute is as to what the seller promised to the buyer by the words which he used in the contract itself and by his conduct in the course of the negotiations which led up to the contract. What he promised is determined by ascertaining what his words and conduct would have led the buyer reasonably to believe that he was promising. That is what is meant in the English law of contract by the common intention of the parties. The test is impersonal. It does not depend upon what the seller himself thought he was promising, if the words and conduct by which he communicated his intention to the seller would have led a reasonable man in the position of the buyer to a different belief as to the promise; nor does it depend upon the actual belief of the buyer himself as to what the seller's promise was, unless that belief would have been shared by a reasonable man in the position of the buyer. The result of the application of this test to the words themselves used in the contract is "the construction of the contract". So far as the reasonable belief of the buyer as to what the seller's promise was, would have been influenced by any conduct of the seller before the contract was made, any implication as to the nature of his promise falls to be determined by applying to his conduct the general principles for ascertaining the common intention of parties to a contract for the sale of goods which underlie the relevant provisions of the Sale of Goods Act 1893 ...

A contract for the sale of goods is one whereby the property in goods which have been physically identified is transferred from the seller to the buyer (see: ss 1(1) and 16). But a contract may be made for the sale of unascertained goods before the actual goods in which the property is to be transferred are physically identified and agreed upon. At the time of making such a contract the kind of goods which are its subject-matter can only be identified verbally and/or by reference to a sample ...

Notes and questions

1. English law, unlike classical Roman law, is committed in theory to the idea of a law of contract rather than contracts. Accordingly, the hire of a supertanker is in principle governed by the same general rules as the sale of an orange. In practice of course things are different; and even in law different types of contract can be governed by different statutes. Thus the sale of an orange will be governed by the Sale of Goods Act 1979 while the hire of a supertanker will not. What statutes will govern the hire of a supertanker? Will any statutes govern all types of contract?

2. Lord Diplock talks about the classification of promises into those that are express and those that are implied. If it is statute that implies some promises, is it true to say that such promises (terms) have been agreed by the parties? Are they not simply rules imposed upon those entering certain kinds of transactions? To what extent can parties, today, exclude implied terms?

3. Is Lord Diplock reinforcing the thesis that English contract law is based upon promise rather than agreement?

4. Is the Sale of Goods Act a code? If so, how does it differ from those statutes that are not codes? Would you call the Consumer Credit Act 1974 a code?

3 LEVEL OF DUTY

Greaves & Co (Contractors) Ltd v Baynham Meikle & Partners [1975] 1 WLR 1095 Court of Appeal

Lord Denning MR: ... [I]t has often been stated that the law will only imply a term when it is reasonable and necessary to do so in order to give business efficacy to the transaction; and, indeed, so obvious that both parties must have intended it. But those statements must be taken with considerable qualification. In the great majority of cases it is no use looking for the intention of both parties. If you asked the parties what they intended, they would say that they never gave it a thought; or, if they did, the one would say that he intended something different from the other. So that courts imply – or, as I would say, impose – a term such as is just and reasonable in the circumstances. Take some of the most familiar of implied terms in the authorities cited to us. Such as the implied condition of fitness on a sale of goods at first implied by the common law and afterwards embodied in the Sale of Goods Act 1893. Or the implied warranty of fitness on a contract for work and materials: *Young & Marten Ltd v McManus Childs Ltd*. Or the implied warranty that a house should be reasonably fit for human habitation: see *Hancock v B W Brazier*. And dozens of other implied terms. If you should read the discussions in the cases, you will find that the judges are not looking for the intention of both parties; nor are they considering what the parties would answer to an officious bystander. They are only seeking to do what is "in all the circumstances reasonable". That is how Lord Reid put it in *Young & Marten Ltd v McManus Childs Ltd*; and Lord Upjohn said quite clearly that the implied warranty is "imposed by law".

Apply this to the employment of a professional man. The law does not usually imply a warranty that he will achieve the desired result, but only a term that he will use reasonable care and skill. The surgeon does not warrant that he will cure the patient. Nor does the solicitor warrant that he will win the case. But, when a dentist agrees to make a set of false teeth for a patient, there is an implied warranty that they will fit his gums: see *Samuels v Davis*.

What then is the position when an architect or an engineer is employed to design a house or a bridge? Is he under an implied warranty that, if the work is carried out to his design, it will be reasonably fit for the purpose? Or is he only under a duty to use reasonable care and skill? This question may require to be answered some day as matter of law ...

Supply of Goods and Services Act 1982 (c. 29)

9. Implied terms about quality or fitness

(2) Where ... the bailor bails goods in the course of a business, there is (...) an implied condition that the goods supplied under the contract are of satisfactory quality.

13. Implied term about care and skill

In a contract for the supply of a service where the supplier is acting in the course of a business, there is an implied term that the supplier will carry out the service with reasonable care and skill.

Hyman v Nye (1881) 6 QBD 685 Queen's Bench Division

(See p 322)

Frost v Aylsbury Dairy Co Ltd [1905] 1 KB 608

(See p 19)

Lockett v A & M Charles Ltd [1938] 4 All ER 170 King's Bench Division

(See p 84)

Notes and questions

1. One of the central questions in the law of obligations is, for want of a better word, the intensity of the obligation itself. This can express itself in a number of ways – for example, in French law it is the difference between obligations attaching to the means and obligations attaching to the ends – but it usually comes down to the role of fault. In what circumstances will a person incur liability in the absence of fault? The dichotomy is particularly evident in the 1982 Act extracted above: if goods are not of satisfactory quality then the bailor will be liable even if he himself was in no way to blame. The seller of goods incurs a similar liability. This strict liability is justified on economic and social grounds in *Hyman v Nye*, but it still leaves open the question as to why, particularly in a consumer society, services are treated differently. Ought one to start off from the assumption that an action for breach of contract is based upon fault? Should contributory negligence be a defence? Does the Sale of Goods Act (see p 228) (and the Supply of Goods and Services Act) recognise contributory negligence as a defence?

2. One reason for the difference between goods and services is to be found in the wording and institutional structure of the statutory provisions. Section 9 of the Supply of Goods and Services Act 1982, like s 14 of the Sale of Goods Act 1979, is framed around the *res* (goods) rather than the *persona* (seller). Thus liability becomes dependent upon the state and condition of the goods. In s 13 of the 1982 Act, however, the rule is framed around the *persona* (supplier) and this automatically brings into play the behaviour of the supplier. The obligation, in other words, attaches to the person rather than to

the thing. Imagine that Parliament had wanted to introduce strict liability for services: can you redraft s 13 so as to reflect Parliament's wishes?

3. English contract law is often said to be an obligation of strict liability rather than one that is fault-based; the civilian systems, in contrast, are said to be fault-based.[3] There is truth in this at the level of contractual theory, but in practice it often comes down to interpretation. What did the parties actually promise (common law) or agree (civil law)? And policy has its role as well. Who ought to bear the risk of this damage or loss: the plaintiff or the defendant? Does, or should, insurance have a role here?

Consumer Protection Act 1987 (c.43)

2. Liability for defective products

(1) Subject to the following provisions of this Part, where any damage is caused wholly or partly by a defect in a product, every person to whom subsection (2) below applies shall be liable for the damage.

(2) This subsection applies to –

(a) the producer of the product;

(b) any person who, by putting his name on the product, has held himself out to be the producer of the product;

(c) any person who has imported the product into a member State from a place outside the member States in order, in the course of any business of his, to supply it to another ...

3. Meaning of 'defect'

(1) Subject to ... there is a defect in a product for the purpose of this Part if the safety of the product is not such as persons generally are entitled to expect ...

4. Defences

(1) In any civil proceedings by virtue of this Part against any person (...) in respect of a defect in a product it shall be a defence for him to show ...

(e) that the state of scientific and technical knowledge at the relevant time was not such that a producer of products of the same description as the product in question might be expected to have discovered the defect if it had existed in his products while they were under his control ...

---

3   For an excellent analysis see G Treitel, *Remedies for Breach of Contract: A Comparative Account* (Oxford, 1988).

5 Damage giving rise to liability

(1) Subject to ... 'damage' means death or personal injury or any loss of or damage to any property (including land)

(2) A person shall not be liable under section 2 above in respect of any defect in a product for the loss of or any damage to the product itself or for the loss of or any damage to the whole or any part of any product which has been supplied with the product in question comprised in it.

(3) A person shall not be liable under section 2 above for any loss of or damage to any property which, at the time it is lost or damaged, is not –

(a) of a description of property ordinarily intended for private use, occupation or consumption; and

(b) intended by the person suffering the loss or damage mainly for his own private use, occupation or consumption.

(4) No damages shall be awarded ... if the amount which would fall to be so awarded ... does not exceed £275.

6 Application of certain enactments etc

(7) It is hereby declared that liability by virtue of this Part is to be treated as liability in tort ...

Questions

1. Despite s 6, is it really realistic to continue to distinguish between contract and tort in the area of products liability?

2. Is the 1987 Act one that actually introduces strict liability into English products law? Does the Act conform to the Directive of 25 July 1985?

3. Imagine that the facts of the following cases arose after the 1987 Act had come into force and re-assess the cases: (i) *Lockett v Charles* (p 84); (ii) *Roe v MOH* (below); (iii) *Parsons v Uttley Ingham* (p 196).

Roe v Minister of Health [1954] 2 Q.B. 66 Court of Appeal

Denning LJ: No one can be unmoved by the disaster which has befallen these two unfortunate men. They were both working men before they went into the Chesterfield Hospital in October 1947. Both were insured contributors to the hospital, paying a small sum each week, in return for which they were entitled to be admitted for treatment when they were ill. Each of them was operated on in the hospital for a minor trouble, one for something wrong with a cartilage in his knee, the other for a hydrocele. The operations were both on the same day, 13th October 1947. Each of them was given a spinal anaesthetic by a visiting anaesthetist, Dr Graham. Each of them has in consequence been paralysed from the waist down.

The judge has said that those facts do not speak for themselves, but I think that they do. They certainly call for an explanation. Each of these men is entitled to say to the hospital: "While I was in your hands something has been done to me which has wrecked my life. Please explain how it has come to pass". The reason why the judge took a different view was because he thought that the hospital authorities could disclaim responsibility for the anaesthetist, Dr Graham: and, as it might be his fault and not theirs, the hospital authorities were not called upon to give an explanation. I think that that reasoning is wrong. In the first place, I think that the hospital authorities are responsible for the whole of their staff, not only for the nurses and doctors, but also for the anaesthetists and the surgeons. It does not matter whether they are permanent or temporary, resident or visiting, whole-time or part-time. The hospital authorities are responsible for all of them. The reason is because, even if they are not servants, they are the agents of the hospital to give the treatment. The only exception is the case of consultants or anaesthetists selected and employed by the patient himself. I went into the matter with some care in *Cassidy v Ministry of Health* and I adhere to all I there said. In the second place, I do not think that the hospital authorities and Dr Graham can both avoid giving an explanation by the simple expedient of each throwing responsibility on to the other. If an injured person shows that one or other or both of two persons injured him, but cannot say which of them it was, then he is not defeated altogether. He can call on each of them for an explanation: see *Baker v Market Harborough Industrial Co-operative Society*.

I approach this case, therefore, on the footing that the hospital authorities and Dr Graham were called on to give an explanation of what has happened. But I think that they have done so. They have spared no trouble or expense to seek out the cause of the disaster. The greatest specialists in the land were called to give evidence. In the result, the judge has found that what happened was this. [His lordship discussed how the accident had occurred: disinfectant had seeped into the anaesthetic by means of invisible cracks in the ampoules; the anaesthetic was thus contaminated when used.] ... That is the explanation of the disaster, and the question is: were any of the staff negligent? I pause to say that once the accident is explained, no question of *res ipsa loquitur* arises. The only question is whether on the facts as now ascertained anyone was negligent ... If the anaesthetists had foreseen that the ampoules might get cracked with cracks that could not be detected on inspection they would no doubt have dyed the phenol a deep blue; and this would have exposed the contamination. But I do not think that their failure to foresee this was negligence. It is so easy to be wise after the event and to condemn as negligence that which was only a misadventure. We ought always to be on our guard against it, especially in cases against hospitals and doctors. Medical science has conferred great benefits on mankind, but these benefits are attended by considerable risks. Every surgical operation is attended by risks. We cannot take the benefits without taking the risks. Every advance in technique is also attended by risks. Doctors, like the rest of us, have to learn by experience; and experience often teaches in a hard way. Something goes wrong and shows up a weakness, and then it is put right. That is just what happened here. Dr Graham sought to escape the danger of infection by disinfecting the ampoule. In escaping that known danger he unfortunately ran into another danger. He did not know that there could be undetectable cracks, but it was not negligent for him not to know it at that time. We must not look at the 1947 accident with 1954 spectacles. The judge acquitted Dr Graham of negligence and we should uphold his decision ...

One final word. These two men have suffered such terrible consequences that there is a natural feeling that they should be compensated. But we should be doing a disservice to the community at large if we were to impose liability on hospitals and doctors for everything that happens to go wrong. Doctors would be led to think more of their own safety than of the good of their patients. Initiative would be stifled and confidence shaken. A proper sense of proportion requires us to have regard to the conditions in which hospitals and doctors have to work. We must insist on due care for the patient at every point, but we must not condemn as negligence that which is only a misadventure. I agree with my Lord that these appeals should be dismissed.

Thake v Maurice [1986] QB 644 Court of Appeal

(See p 324)

Questions

1. What implications, if any, does *Roe* have for the law of contract?
2. If the plaintiff in *Roe* had been injured in a private hospital in business for profit would the result have been different?
3. Should the hospital have informed the plaintiffs of the risks of having an operation before carrying it out? What if the plaintiffs had claimed that they would never have consented to surgery if they had known of the risks?
4. The benefits of modern medicine may well be attended by considerable risks. But does it follow that individual citizens should be the people who have to carry the risk? If doctors have to learn the hard way, why is it that they (or their employers) do not have to bear the risks? Why should the community not bear the risks since the community benefits from good health?

4 LAW OF PERSONS AND LAW OF PROPERTY

Stevenson v Beverley Bentinck Ltd [1976] 1 WLR 483 Court of Appeal

This was an action in conversion and detinue by the purchaser of a motor car, which unknown to the purchaser was still on hire-purchase from a finance company, against the finance company who had seized the vehicle. The action failed in the Court of Appeal.

Roskill LJ: ... Ever since hire-purchase was invented, round about the turn of the century, there have been hire-purchase frauds, and the books are full of examples of such frauds, which have caused loss to innocent parties. Again and again – and the present case is yet another example – courts have to decide where as between two wholly innocent parties, that loss should fall. This is particularly so in the case of motor-cars, because persons who hire motor-cars under hire-purchase agreements persist in selling them or purporting to sell them, to innocent purchasers when as persons in possession they have no right whatever to sell.

The common law had a plain answer in those cases. It said that the true owner was never divested of his title, but as things have progressed through this century (if "progress" is the right word) Parliament thought it necessary to alter the common law position and to give limited protection to those who bought vehicles or other goods in such circumstances.

There was nothing new in that concept. The Factors Acts go back to the early part of the last century, and came to rest, after a number of amendments, in 1889. The 1889 Act is still on the statute book. Section 25(2) of the Sale of Goods Act 1893 is another example of the statutory protection of an innocent purchaser of goods. Now under ss 27 and 29 of the Hire-Purchase Act 1964 we have yet further though limited protection given to an innocent purchaser of a car on hire-purchase whose hirer has purported to convey a title to that car which at common law he cannot give. The sole question, to my mind, is whether the plaintiff can bring himself within that protection. The argument advanced by counsel for the plaintiff (I think it was in substance the argument which junior counsel for the plaintiff advanced in the court below, and which failed) was this. The plaintiff did not acquire this Jaguar in his capacity as a part-time motor trader. He acquired it in his private capacity. Therefore, it is said, he is within the protection given to a "private purchase" under ss 27 and 29.

If it were relevant to look at the capacity in which he bought the car, that would be a very attractive argument, and if this were a case under the Factors Act 1889 that might well be the position, but this is not a case under the Factors Act. As I ventured to point out to counsel for the plaintiff, the Factors Act is entirely different, both in concept and in expression, from the language of ss 27 and 29 of the 1964 Act. The Factors Act in the type of case to which counsel for the plaintiff referred unquestionably requires the court to look both at the status of the person said to be a mercantile agent, and also at the capacity in which he has dealt with the particular goods in question.

Counsel for the defendants, if I may say so, put the point in a succinct sentence when he said that under the present Act the court is concerned not with capacity, but only with status. I think that is right. I think Parliament created a clear dichotomy. It may work hardly in some cases. In the present case it seems to work hardly on the plaintiff as an innocent purchaser, but we cannot stretch the construction of s 27 and the definitions in s 29 merely to meet a hard case. When one looks at the sections, here is, as Bridge J put it, a clear dichotomy between a "trade or inance purchaser" on the one hand and a "private purchaser" on the other. A "private purchaser" does not mean a person who buys a car otherwise than in his capacity as a "trade or finance purchaser". It means someone who does not at the material time carry on any such business as is defined as being the business of a "trade or finance purchaser".

So one has to resolve the question by asking oneself, as did the learned judge: at the time when the disposition in question was effected, was the purchaser carrying on wholly or partly the business of a "trade or finance purchaser"? The learned judge, by a slip of the tongue, used the word "date" instead of "time". That question in this case seems to me to be susceptible of only one answer. The purchaser (the plaintiff) was at the time of the disposition carrying on in part the business of a motor dealer – a trade or finance purchaser – and that disentitles him to the statutory protection given to a "private purchaser" under s 27. I would, therefore, dismiss this appeal. It follows that I am afraid that I am unable to agree with the passage in *Goode on Hire-Purchase* on which counsel for the plaintiff relies.

Notes and questions

1. This case, if it does nothing else, proves that one needs a knowledge of Roman law in order to be able to understand legal thought and legal reasoning in any of the Western systems of law. English law may not adhere to the rigid systematics of Gaius and Justinian, but it still distinguishes between the law of persons and the law of things. In general one is in the realm of the law of persons when dealing with status and personality; the former is usually encountered when one is handling problems about nationality and the latter forms the basis of company law. However, a knowledge of the law of persons is vital even when in the area of the law of things since the law of obligations raises problems about corporate liability. Where *Stevenson* is interesting is in its use of the law of persons to decide a problem from the law of property: ownership of a car is directly dependent upon the status of the plaintiff. Ought ownership to be dependent upon status? Is this not to confuse concepts?

2. Are the following matters of status: (i) a visitor and an occupier in the Occupiers' Liability Act 1957; (ii) a consumer in the Unfair Contract Terms Act 1977; (iii) a bailor and a bailee; (iv) a seller of goods in the course of a business in the Sale of Goods Act 1979? Are there other law of obligations statutes that might raise questions of status?

5 PROMISE AND AGREEMENT

Hopkins v Tanqueray (1854) 139 ER 369 Court of Common Pleas

This was an action for damages by the purchaser, at an auction at Tattersall's, of a horse subsequently found to be unsound and resold at a loss by the plaintiff. The purchaser claimed that the horse was warranted as sound because of statements by the seller to the plaintiff on the day previous to the auction; but it was established that horses sold at Tattersall's were not warranted unless so stated in the catalogue and that the horse in question was not warranted. The jury found in favour of the plaintiff, but the Court of Common Pleas held that there was no evidence to support their finding.

Jervis CJ: ... I am of opinion that the rule to enter a nonsuit in this case must be made absolute. No doubt, there is no necessity that the word "warrant" or "promise" should occur in the bargain ... Nor is it necessary that the statement or representation should be simultaneous with the close of the bargain: if it be part of the contract, it matters not at what period of the negotiation it is made ... Whether, assuming what was said in this case prior to the sale, to have amounted to a warranty, such warranty would under the circumstances have been binding between the parties, I give no opinion, because I think it is quite clear that what passed amounted to a representation only, and not to a warranty. The facts were simply these: The defendant seeing the plaintiff in the stable on the Sunday prior to the sale, examining the horse's legs, said to him, "You need not examine his legs: you have nothing to look for: I assure you he is perfectly sound in every respect" to which the plaintiff replied, "If you say so, I am satisfied." The plaintiff made no further examination; and he did not employ a veterinary surgeon, relying upon a representation made by an honourable man. The defendant, doubtless, believed the horse to be as he represented it: no fraud is imputed to him: on the contrary, indeed, the plaintiff expressly disclaims it. There is, consequently, no basis on which to rest this action. On the day following, Mr Tattersall announces that he is about to sell California without a warranty: and the defendant becomes the purchaser. It seems to me to be perfectly clear, that, in what took place between them on the Sunday, the defendant did not mean to warrant the horse, but was merely making a representation of that which he bona fide believed to be the fact; and that the plaintiff so understood it. What passed afterwards cannot in any degree affect the case: it only amounts to this, that the parties thought at one time that there had been a warranty. I think the rule must be made absolute.

Maule J: I also am of opinion that the rule to enter a nonsuit in this case must be made absolute, the event in which the leave for that purpose was reserved having arisen, viz. that there was no evidence to go to the jury that the horse was sold with a warranty. That there was no warranty at the time of the actual sale, is perfectly clear; for, it was shown to be the course of dealing at Tattersall's, that no horse is sold with a warranty unless it is expressly mentioned; and this has been dealt with as a case in which no mention of warranty was made at the time of the sale. The question, then, is, whether we can import a warranty of soundness, as between the plaintiff and the defendant, from that which took place at Tattersall's on the day preceding the auction – a conversation pointing towards a sale of the horse ... The evidence, properly understood, and appreciated, amounts to no more than this, that the defendant was believed to be a gentleman of veracity, as well as of skill in horses, and the plaintiff was about to examine the horse in question, as persons who are, or affect to be, very knowing usually perform that operation, when the defendant says to him, "You need not take the trouble to examine my horse to ascertain if there is any defect that may be seen or felt: he is perfectly sound." That is a clear representation: and, if it were made with intent to deceive, the defendant would undoubtedly be liable. That, however, is not only not insinuated, but actually disclaimed on the part of the plaintiff, and I think very properly. There appears to have been no more than an honest representation that the horse in the defendant's opinion, and so far as his knowledge went, was a perfectly sound horse. There is nothing whatever to show that the representation was one that was to subject the defendant to a liability to pay damages in the event of the horse proving to be unsound – nothing to show that the defendant meant more than what he actually did say on the occasion. The fact of that conversation passing between the plaintiff and the defendant at the time when it was known to both that the sale was to take place by public competition on the following day, affords to my mind a very strong reason for thinking that the defendant could not have intended what he then said to be imported as a warranty into the transaction. If there be any ambiguity, that affords an additional presumption that that conversation was not intended for a warranty. I therefore think there was no evidence to go to the jury, and consequently that a nonsuit must be entered pursuant to the leave reserved. It is unnecessary to say anything as to the other point which was thrown out in the course of the argument.

Cresswell J (concurred).

Crowder J: I am of the same opinion. The conversation which took place between the parties on the Sunday was a mere representation, and was evidently not made with an intention to warrant the horse. A representation, to constitute a warranty, must be shown to have been intended to form part of the contract. I think it abundantly clear upon the evidence that the matter here relied on was not understood or intended as forming part of the contract which might be made at the auction on the following day, which it was well known to both parties would be without a warranty. It was a mere representation, quite distinct from any intention to warrant the animal. It is unnecessary to consider whether a party may lawfully warrant as between himself and a particular individual under circumstances like these. It is a very grave question whether such a contract could be upheld in a court of justice, in the case of a sale by auction, where all have a right to suppose they are bidding upon equal terms ...

Notes and questions

1. 'If a man covenant, for a valid consideration, that it shall rain tomorrow, he cannot afterwards say, "I could not make it rain; I did all I could to make it rain; but it would not." He chooses to covenant that such a thing shall happen, and if it does not, he has broken his covenant. If a man enter into a covenant that a thing shall be of a particular quality, it would be no answer to say, "it is impossible the thing can be of that quality' (Maule J in *Canham v Barry* (1855) 24 LJCP 100). Would a promise that it shall rain tomorrow be capable of forming the basis of a contract in French law?

2. 'When a person has been induced to enter into a contract by a representation which, whether wilfully or not, was a mistake, equity will give relief ...' (Byles J in *Stears v South Essex Gaslight & Coke Co* (1861) 30 LJCP 49). Could the plaintiff in *Hopkins v Tanqueray* have claimed relief in equity?

3. 'If there is one principle more clear than another, it is, that if a man has made a deliberate statement, and another has acted upon it, he cannot be at liberty to deny the truth of the statement he has made.'

(Bramwell B in *McCance v L & NW Ry* (1861) 31 LJ Exch 65). Is this a principle that is reflected both in common law (contract and deceit) and in equity (estoppel)?

4. In the civil law systems contract has, since classical Roman law, been based on the agreement (*conventio*). In Roman law itself this did not have a great deal of meaning since the classical jurists did not think in terms of a general theory of contract; what mattered was the type of transaction in issue.[4] *Conventio* was a common denominator that linked all the various types of contract. It was the medieval Roman and canon lawyers who turned this common denominator into a principle and the 19th century jurists who made it an axiom. The history of contract in the common law is founded on a rather different institutional basis: the role of covenant, deceit and *assumpsit* saw liability more in terms of broken promises rather than unperformed obligations and while, at first sight, it may seem of little relevance whether the notion of contract is based on promise or on agreement the difference can have practical effects. For example, agreement founded upon consent implies a doctrine of error. How can there be true consent when one party is labouring under a mistake? A doctrine of promise, on the other hand, does not necessarily imply that mistake should undermine a contract. It is perfectly possible to say that a promisor takes the risk of error. Does this difference between promise and agreement act as an obstacle to harmonisation?

5. What is the value in distinguishing between representations and warranties? Was the court in *Hopkins* in effect treating the representation as a mere 'puff' which would not attract legal liability?

Gibson v Manchester City Council [1978] 1 WLR 520 Court of Appeal; [1979] 1 WLR 294 House of Lords

Lord Denning MR (Court of Appeal): ... We have had much discussion as to whether Mr Gibson's letter of 18th March 1971 was a new offer or whether it was an acceptance of the previous offer which had been made. I do not like detailed analysis on such a point. To my mind it is a mistake to think that all contracts can be analysed into the form of offer and acceptance. I know in some of the textbooks it has been the custom to do so; but, as I understand the law, there is no need to look for a strict offer and acceptance. You should look at the correspondence as a whole and at the conduct of the parties and see therefrom whether the parties have come to an agreement on everything that was material. If by their correspondence and their conduct you can see an agreement on all

---

4   See generally T Weir, Contracts in Rome and England (1992) 66 *Tulane Law Review* 1615.

material terms, which was intended thencefoward to be binding, then there is a binding contract in law even though all the formalities have not been gone through ...

Lord Diplock (House of Lords): ... My Lords, there may be certain types of contract, although I think they are exceptional, which do not fit easily into the normal analysis of a contract as being constituted by offer and acceptance; but a contract alleged to have been made by an exchange of correspondence between the parties in which the successive communications other than the first are in reply to one another is not one of these. I can see no reason in the instant case for departing from the conventional approach of looking at the handful of documents relied on as constituting the contract sued on and seeing whether on their true construction there is to be found in them a contractual offer by the council to sell the house to Mr Gibson and an acceptance of that offer by Mr Gibson. I venture to think that it was by departing from this conventional approach that the majority of the Court of Appeal was led into error ...

Questions

1. Was Lord Denning attempting to replace the promise thesis with the theory that contract was a matter of agreement? Was this attempt rejected in the House of Lords? (Cf Swiss Code of Obligations Article 2.)

2. Is contractual liability to be found within the actual facts of a dispute or is it to be found within the intention of the parties? In a case like *Gibson*, does a court have to look only at the documents or must it look beyond the documents?

3. Read *Clarke v Dunraven* [1897] AC 59 in the law reports. Is this one of Lord Diplock's exceptional cases?

6 FREEDOM OF CONTRACT

Printing and Numerical Registering Co v Sampson (1875) LR 19 Eq 462 Chancery

Sir George Jessel: ... If there is one thing more than another which public policy requires, it is that men of full age and competent understanding shall have the utmost liberty of contracting and that their contracts, when entered into freely and voluntarily, shall be held sacred and shall be enforced by courts of justice ...

Notes and questions

1. 'I think, if we held this action to be maintainable, we should violate a most important principle of law, that parties to contracts are to be allowed to regulate their contracts and liabilities themselves; and that the Court will only give effect to the intention of the parties as it is expressed by the contract' (Erle J in *Gott v Gandy* (1853) 23 LJQB 1). Is contract a form of private legislation? (cf French Code civil art 1134.)

2. '[T]he defendants are at liberty to make any contract they please, and where the question is, what were the terms of the bailment so made? the reasonableness of the terms is an irrelevant inquiry, the parties being at liberty to choose their own terms ...' (Erle CJ in *Van Toll v SE Ry* (1862) LJCP 241). Will courts enforce unreasonable contracts?

3. Is (or was) the doctrine of freedom of contract a device to suit the City of London? If the influence of commerce was of importance, why did English law not distinguish between commercial and non-commercial transactions? Does it do so today?

4. If parties have the right to make contracts on their own terms, is this a right that can be abused? (Cf Chapter 7.)

Photo Production Ltd v Securicor Transport Ltd [1980] AC 827 House of Lords

(See p 312)

Unfair Contract Terms Act 1977 (c 50)

1 Scope of Part I

(1) For the purposes of this Part of this Act, "negligence" means the breach –

(a) of any obligation, arising from the express or implied terms of a contract, to take reasonable care or exercise reasonable skill in the performance of the contract;

(b) of any common law duty to take reasonable care or exercise reasonable skill (but not any stricter duty); ...

(3) In the case of both contract and tort, sections 2 to 7 apply ... only to business liability ...

2 Negligence liability

(1) A person cannot by reference to any contract term or to a notice given to persons generally or to particular persons exclude or restrict his liability for death or personal injury resulting from negligence.

(2) In the case of other loss or damage, a person cannot so exclude or restrict his liability for negligence except in so far as the term or notice satisfies the requirement of reasonableness ...

(See also p 315)

Questions

1. Does this statute undermine in a significant way the doctrine of freedom of contract? Do contractual promises in business liability situations now have to be reasonable? (Cf below p 315.)

2. Why does the Act distinguish between business liability and non-business liability?

3. Do the courts now distinguish between commercial and consumer transactions?

Interfoto Picture Library Ltd v Stiletto Visual Programmes Ltd [1989] QB 433
Court of Appeal

Dillon LJ: ...The plaintiffs run a library of photographic transparencies. The defendants are engaged in advertising. On 5 March 1984 Mr Beeching, a director of the defendants, wanting photographs for a presentation for a client, telephoned the plaintiffs, whom the defendants had never dealt with before. He spoke to a Miss Fraser of the plaintiffs and asked her whether the plaintiffs had any photographs of the 1950s which might be suitable for the defendants' presentation. Miss Fraser said that she would research his request, and a little later on the same day she sent round by hand to the defendants 47 transparencies packed in a jiffy bag. Also packed in the bag, among the transparencies, was a delivery note which she had typed out ...

Having received the transparencies, Mr Beeching telephoned the plaintiffs at about 3.10 on the afternoon of 5 March, and told Miss Fraser ... that he was very impressed with the plaintiffs' fast service, that one or two of the transparencies could be of interest, and that he would get back to the plaintiffs.

Unfortunately, he did not get back on to the plaintiffs and the transparencies seem to have been put on one side and overlooked by the defendants. The plaintiffs tried to telephone Mr Beeching on 20 and again on 23 March, but only spoke to his secretary. In the upshot the transparencies, which the defendants did not use for their presentation, were not returned to the plaintiffs until 2 April.

The plaintiffs thereupon sent an invoice to the defendants for £3,783.50 as a holding charge for the transparencies. The invoice was rejected by the defendants, and accordingly in May 1984 the plaintiffs started this action claiming £3,783.50, the amount of the invoice. That is the sum for which the judge awarded the plaintiffs judgment by his order now under appeal. The plaintiffs' claim is based on conditions printed on their delivery note ...

The sum of £3,783.50 is calculated by the plaintiffs in strict accordance with condition 2 as the fee for the retention of 47 transparencies from 19 March to 2 April 1984. It is of course important to the plaintiffs to get their transparencies back reasonably quickly, if they are not wanted, since if a transparency is out with one customer it cannot be offered to another customer, should occasion arise. It has to be said, however, that the holding fee charged by the plaintiffs by condition 2 is extremely high, and in my view exorbitant. The judge held that on a *quantum meruit* a reasonable charge would have been £3.50 per transparency per week, and not £5 per day ...

The question is therefore whether condition 2 was sufficiently brought to the defendants' attention to make it a term of the contract which was only concluded after the defendants had received, and must have known that they had received the transparencies and the delivery note.

This sort of question was posed, in relation to printed conditions, in the ticket cases, such as *Parker v South Eastern Railway Co* (1877) 2 CPD 416, in the last century. At that stage the printed conditions were looked at as a whole and the question considered by the courts was whether the printed conditions as a whole had been sufficiently drawn to a customer's attention to make the whole set of conditions part of the contract; if so the customer was bound by the printed conditions even though he never read them.

More recently the question has been discussed whether it is enough to look at a set of printed conditions as a whole. When for instance one condition in a set is particularly onerous does something special need to be done to draw customers' attention to that particular condition? ...

[I]n *Thornton v Shoe Lane Parking Ltd* [1971] 2 QB 163 both Lord Denning MR and Megaw LJ held as one of their grounds of decision, as I read their judgments, that where a condition is particularly onerous or unusual the party seeking to enforce it must show that that condition, or an unusual condition of that particular nature, was fairly brought to the notice of the other party ...

Counsel for the plaintiffs submits that *Thornton v Shoe Lane Parking Ltd* [1971] 2 QB 613 was a case of an exemption clause and that what their Lordships said must be read as limited to exemption clauses and in particular exemption clauses which would deprive the party on whom they are imposed of statutory rights. But what their Lordships said was said by way of interpretation and application of the general statement of the law by Mellish LJ in *Parker v South Eastern Railway Co*, 2 CPD 416, 423–424 and the logic of it is applicable to any particularly onerous clause in a printed set of conditions of the one contracting party which would not be generally known to the other party.

Condition 2 of these plaintiffs' conditions is in my judgment a very onerous clause. The defendants could not conceivably have known, if their attention was not drawn to the clause, that the plaintiffs were proposing to charge a "holding fee" for the retention of the transparencies at such a very high and exorbitant rate.

At the time of the ticket cases in the last century it was notorious that people hardly ever troubled to read printed conditions on a ticket or delivery note or similar document. That remains the case now. In the intervening years the printed conditions have tended to become more and more complicated and more and more one-sided in favour of the party who is imposing them, but the other parties, if they notice that there are printed conditions at all, generally still tend to assume that such conditions are only concerned with ancillary matters of form and are not of importance. In the ticket cases the courts held that the common law required that reasonable steps be taken to draw the other parties' attention to the printed conditions or they would not be part of the contract. It is, in my judgment, a logical development of the common law into modern conditions that it should be held, as it was in *Thornton v Shoe Lane Parking Ltd* [1971] 2 QB 163, that, if one condition in a set of printed conditions is particularly onerous or unusual, the party seeking to enforce it must show that that particular condition was fairly brought to the attention of the other party.

In the present case, nothing whatever was done by the plaintiffs to draw the defendants' attention particularly to condition 2; it was merely one of four columns' width of conditions printed across the foot of the delivery note. Consequently condition 2 never, in my judgment, became part of the contract between the parties.

I would therefore allow this appeal and reduce the amount of the judgment which the judge awarded against the defendants to the amount which he would have awarded on a quantum meruit on his alternative findings, ie the reasonable charge of £3.50 per transparency per week for the retention of the transparencies beyond a reasonable period, which he fixed at 14 days from the date of their receipt by the defendants.

Bingham LJ: In many civil law systems, and perhaps in most legal systems outside the common law world, the law of obligations recognises and enforces an overriding principle that in making and carrying out contracts parties should act in good faith. This does not simply mean that they should not deceive each other, a principle which any legal system must recognise; its effect is perhaps most aptly conveyed by such metaphorical colloquialisms as "playing fair", "coming clean" or "putting one's cards face upwards on the table". It is in essence a principle of fair and open dealing. In such a forum it might, I think, be held on the facts of this case that the plaintiffs were under a duty in all fairness to draw the defendants' attention specifically to the high price payable if the transparencies were not returned in time and, when the 14 days had expired, to point out to the defendants the high cost of continued failure to return them.

English law has, characteristically, committed itself to no such overriding principle but has developed piecemeal solutions in response to demonstrated problems of unfairness. Many examples could be given. Thus equity has intervened to strike down unconscionable bargains. Parliament has stepped in to regulate the imposition of exemption clauses and the form of certain hire-purchase agreements. The common law also has made its contribution, by holding that certain classes of contract require the utmost good faith, by treating as irrecoverable what purport to be agreed estimates of damage but are in truth a disguised penalty for breach, and in many other ways.

The well known cases on sufficiency of notice are in my view properly to be read in this context. At one level they are concerned with a question of pure contractual analysis, whether one party has done enough to give the other notice of the incorporation of a term in the contract. At another level they are concerned with a somewhat different question, whether it would in all the circumstances be fair (or reasonable) to hold a party bound by any conditions or by a particular condition of an unusual and stringent nature ...

The tendency of the English authorities has, I think, been to look at the nature of the transaction in question and the character of the parties to it; to consider what notice the party alleged to be bound was given of the particular condition said to bind him; and to resolve whether in all the circumstances it is fair to hold him bound by the condition in question. This may yield a result not very different from the civil law principle of good faith, at any rate so far as the formation of the contract is concerned.

Turning to the present case, I am satisfied for reasons which Dillon LJ has given that no contract was made on the telephone when the defendants made their initial request. I am equally satisfied that no contract was made on delivery of the transparencies to the defendants before the opening of the jiffy bag in which they were contained. Once the jiffy bag was opened and the transparencies taken out with the delivery note, it is in my judgment an inescapable inference that the defendants would have recognised the delivery note as a document of a kind likely to contain contractual terms and would have seen that there were conditions printed in small but visible lettering on the face of the document. To the extent that the conditions so displayed were common form or usual terms regularly encountered in this business, I do not think the defendants could successfully contend that they were not incorporated into the contract.

The crucial question in the case is whether the plaintiffs can be said fairly and reasonably to have brought condition 2 to the notice of the defendants. The judge made no finding on the point, but I think that it is open to this court to draw an inference from the primary findings which he did make. In my opinion the plaintiffs did not do so. They delivered 47 transparencies, which was a number the defendants had not specifically asked for. Condition 2 contained a daily rate per transparency after the initial period of 14 days many times greater than was usual or (so far as the evidence shows) heard of. For these 47 transparencies there was to be a charge for each day of delay of £235 plus value added tax. The result would be that a venial period of delay, as here, would lead to an inordinate liability. The defendants are not to be relieved of that liability because they did not read the condition, although doubtless they did not; but in my judgment they are to be relieved because the plaintiffs did not do what was necessary to draw this unreasonable and extortionate clause fairly to their attention. I would accordingly allow the defendants' appeal and substitute for the judge's award the sum which he assessed upon the alternative basis of *quantum meruit*.

In reaching the conclusion I have expressed I would not wish to be taken as deciding that condition 2 was not challengeable as a disguised penalty clause. This point was not argued before the judge nor raised in the notice of appeal. It was accordingly not argued before us. I have accordingly felt bound to assume, somewhat reluctantly, that condition 2 would be enforceable if fully and fairly brought to the defendants' attention.

Council Directive of 5 April 1993 93/13EEC: L 95/29 (Unfair terms in consumer contracts)

Article 3. 1. A contractual term which has not been individually negotiated shall be regarded as unfair if, contrary to the requirement of good faith, it causes a significant imbalance in the parties' rights and obligations arising under the contract, to the detriment of the consumer.

Questions

1. On what legal ground was the debt clause in *Interfoto* set aside?
2. Will Bingham LJ (now Sir Thomas Bingham MR) have to change his views on good faith in English law? Or was he simply preparing English law for change from outside?

3. Will Parliament have to legislate as a result of the Directive?

4. Are consumer contracts now subject to their own regime? Is there still freedom of contract when one of the parties deals as a consumer?

5. Are consumers, as a group, now a legal subject with their own rights and interests? Or, put another way, are they, as a class, a quasi-subject in a law of persons sense? If so, does this not undermine the individualism upon which the traditional law of contract is based? To what extent is the law of obligations now a matter of quasi-subjects rather than individuals?

6. If parties are under a duty only to plead the facts, why is it that a court cannot raise any question of law (for example whether the clause is a penalty) to be found in the facts (cf *Esso*, p 118).

7. Bingham LJ suggests that the cases on sufficiency of notice function on two levels. Is this true of all cases? What implications might this have for legal analysis?

7 THE INTERPRETATION OF CONTRACTS

The Moorcock (1889) 14 PD 64 Court of Appeal

This was an action for damages by the owner of a ship against the owners of a wharf in respect of damage sustained by the ship when she rested on hard ground at low tide. The Court of Appeal held the wharf owners liable.

Bowen LJ: ... The question which arises here is whether, when a contract is made to let the use of this jetty to a ship which can only use it, as is known to both parties, by taking the ground, there is any implied warranty on the part of the owners of the jetty, and if so, what is the extent of that warranty. Now, an implied warranty, or as it is called, a covenant in law, as distinguished from an express contract or express warranty, really is in all cases founded on the presumed intention of the parties, and upon reason. The implication which the law draws from what must obviously have been the intention of the parties, the law draws with the object of giving efficacy to the transaction and preventing such a failure of consideration as cannot have been within the contemplation of either side; and I believe if one were to take all the cases, and they are many, of implied warranties and covenants in law, it will be found that in all them the law is raising an implication from the presumed intention of the parties with the object of giving to the transaction such efficacy as both parties must have intended that in all events it should have. In business transactions such as this, what the law desires to effect by the implication is to give such business efficacy to the transaction as must have been intended at all events by both parties who are business men; not to impose on one side all the perils of the transaction, or to emancipate one side from all the chances of failure, but to make each party promise in law as much, at all events, as it must have been in the contemplation of both parties that he should be responsible for in respect of those perils or chances.

Now what did each party in a case like this know? For if we are examining into their presumed intention, we must examine into their minds as to what the transaction was. Both parties knew that this jetty was let for hire, and knew that it could only be used under the contract by the ship taking the ground. They must have known that it was by grounding that she used the jetty; in fact ... they must have known, both of them, that unless the ground was safe the ship would be simply buying an opportunity of danger, and that all consideration would fail unless some care had been taken to see that the ground was safe. In fact the business of the jetty could not be carried on except upon such a basis. The parties also knew that with regard to the safety of the ground outside the jetty the shipowner could know nothing at all, and the jetty owner might with reasonable care know everything. The owners of the jetty, or their servants, were there at high and low tide, and with little trouble they could satisfy themselves, in case of doubt, as to whether the berth was reasonably safe. The ship's owner, on the other hand, had not the means of verifying the state of the jetty, because the berth itself opposite the jetty might be occupied by another ship at any moment.

[I]t may well be said that the law will not imply that the persons who have not control of the place have taken reasonable care to make it good, but it does not follow that they are relieved from all responsibility. They are on the spot. They must know the jetty cannot be used unless reasonable care is taken, if not to make it safe, at all events to see whether it is safe. No one can tell whether reasonable safety has been secured except themselves, and I think if they let out their jetty for use they at all events imply that they have taken reasonable care to see that the berth, which is the essential part of the use of the jetty, is safe, and if it is not safe, and if they have not taken such reasonable care, it is their duty to warn persons with whom they have dealings that they have not done so ...

Notes and questions

1. The notion of an implied term is central to English contract law since it is the means by which a court can interpret contractual facts in order to insert into the facts a normative element which can then be used to establish liability. Thus the wharf owner was liable, not because he was at fault (one possible normative concept), but because he had 'promised' (another normative concept) that the berth was safe. The berth was not safe, so the wharf owner was liable to compensate in damages because he was in breach of his promise. Fault and the implied term do, however, often come together: if in *Bolton v Mahadeva* (above p 126) a fire had accidentally started the question of the level of duty (fault or strict liability) would have centred on the implied term. Did the heating engineers promise to use care and skill or did they warrant that the materials they used were safe?

2. Is the implied term a means by which courts can remake contracts?

3. Do employees impliedly promise their employers in their contracts of employment that they will not be negligent? Does an employer

impliedly promise to warn employees about any lack of insurance cover when the employer asks the employee to work abroad?[5]

4   What if the owner of the ship had been compensated for the damage by his insurance company: would the court still have implied the term so as to allow the insurance company to recover via the doctrine of subrogation?

Sale of Goods Act 1979 (c 54)

14. Implied terms about quality or fitness

(1) Except as provided by this section and section 15 below and subject to any other enactment, there is no implied term about the quality or fitness for any particular purpose of goods supplied under a contract of sale.

(2) Where the seller sells goods in the course of a business, there is an implied term that the goods supplied under the contract are of satisfactory quality;

(2A) For the purposes of this Act, goods are of satisfactory quality if they meet the standard that a reasonable person would regard as satisfactory, taking account of any description of the goods, the price (if relevant) and all the other relevant circumstances.

(2B) For the purposes of this Act, the quality of goods includes their state and condition and the following (among others) are in appropriate cases aspects of the quality of goods –

(a) fitness for all the purposes for which goods of the kind in question are commonly supplied,

(b) appearance and finish,

(c) freedom from minor defects,

(d) safety, and

(e) durability.

(2C) The term implied by subsection (2) above does not extend to any matter making the quality of goods unsatisfactory –

(a) which is specifically drawn to the buyer's attention before the contract is made,

(b) where the buyer examines the goods before the contract is made, which that examination ought to reveal, or

(c) in the case of a contract for sale by sample, which would have been apparent on a reasonable examination of the sample.

---

5   Cf *Reid v Rush & Tompkins plc* [1990] 1 WLR 212.

(3) Where the seller sells goods in the course of a business and the buyer, expressly or by implication, makes known –

(a) to the seller ...

(b) ... any particular purpose for which the goods are being bought, there is an implied term that the goods supplied under the contract are reasonably fit for that purpose, whether or not that is a purpose for which such goods are commonly supplied, except where the circumstances show that the buyer does not rely, or that it is unreasonable for him to rely, on the skill or judgment of the seller ...

(6) As regards England and Wales and Northern Ireland, the terms implied by subsections (2) and (3) above are conditions ...

Notes and questions

1. Terms can be implied in fact and in law. Or, put another way, there are some contracts where implied promises will automatically apply either because of precedent or because of legislation. The notion of an implied term can thus become a means of importing objective rules into contractual situations. To what extent can these objective rules be expressly excluded by the parties to a contract?

2. Does s 14 embody the idea that contributory negligence is a complete defence to an action for damages in contract?

3. Is a new car with a deep scratch on one of its doors reasonably fit for its purpose and (or) of satisfactory quality?

Greaves & Co v Baynham Meikle & Partners [1975] 1 WLR 1095

(See p 209)

Questions

1. Will the court imply a term when it is reasonable to do so? Or must something more be shown?

2. Would it be reasonable to imply into all contracts a term that the contract be performed in good faith? Are there any contracts were good faith is an implied term?

3. Can an implied term ever be dependent upon the status of one or both parties to a contract?

4. Can an implied term ever exist independently of the main contract?

L Schuler AG v Wickman Machine Tool Sales Ltd [1974] AC 235 House of Lords

This was a dispute as to whether Schuler, a German company, was entitled to repudiate a contract for breach of a term of the written contract, described as a "condition", whereby a certain number of visits would be made by employees of Wickman, an English company, to clients in respect of promoting Schuler's products. Most of the visits were made by Wickman, but on a few occasions they failed to make the required number of visits stipulated for in the contract. The arbitrator held that Schuler was not entitled to repudiate or terminate the contract and a majority of the House of Lords confirmed this decision.

Lord Reid: ... In the ordinary use of the English language "condition" has many meanings, some of which have nothing to do with agreements. In connection with an agreement it may mean a pre-condition: something which must happen or be done before the agreement can take effect. Or it may mean some state of affairs which must continue to exist if the agreement is to remain in force ...

No doubt some words used by lawyers do have a rigid inflexible meaning. But we must remember that we are seeking to discover intention as disclosed by the contract as a whole. Use of the word "condition" is an indication – even a strong indication – of such an intention but it is by no means conclusive. The fact that a particular construction leads to a very unreasonable result must be a relevant consideration. The more unreasonable the result the more unlikely it is that the parties can have intended it, and if they do intend it the more necessary it is that they shall make that intention abundantly clear ...

Lord Morris: ... Subject to any legal requirements businessmen are free to make what contracts they choose but unless the terms of their agreement are clear a court will not be disposed to accept that they have agreed something utterly fantastic. If it is clear what they have agreed a court will not be influenced by any suggestion that they would have been wiser to have made a different agreement. If a word employed by the parties in a contract can have only one possible meaning, unless any question of rectification arises, there will be no problem. If a word either by reason of general acceptance or by reason of judicial construction has come to have a particular meaning then, if used in a business or technical document, it will often be reasonable to suppose that the parties intended to use the word in its accepted sense. But if a word in a contract may have more than one meaning then, in interpreting the contract, a court will have to decide what was the intention of the parties as revealed by or deduced from the terms and subject-matter of their contract.

Words are but the instruments by which meanings or intentions are expressed. Often the same word has in differing contexts to do service to convey differing meanings ...

Lord Wilberforce (dissenting): ... The general rule is that extrinsic evidence is not admissible for the construction of a written contract; the parties' intentions must be ascertained, on legal principles of construction, from the words they have used ...

There are of course exceptions. I attempt no exhaustive list of them ... [E]vidence may be admitted of surrounding circumstances or in order to explain technical expressions or to identify the subject-matter of an agreement; or (an overlapping exception) to resolve a latent ambiguity. But ambiguity in this context is not to be equated with difficulty of construction, even difficulty to a point where judicial opinion as to meaning has differed. This is, I venture to think, elementary law ...

I would only add that, for my part, to call the clause arbitrary, capricious or fantastic, or to introduce as a test of its validity the ubiquitous reasonable man (I do not know whether he is English or German) is to assume, contrary to the evidence, that both parties to this contract adopted a standard of easygoing tolerance rather than one of aggressive, insistent punctuality and efficiency ...

Lord Simon: ... Most words in English are capable of a number of meanings, either in popular usage or as legal terms of art or both. In either category, *prima facie* they will be read in their most usual and natural (or primary) sense. But this again is a rebuttable presumption; so that a word will be construed in a less usual or natural (or secondary) sense if the instrument shows that it is intended in such sense ...

Questions

1. Does this case suggest that a contractor will not be permitted to exercise his right to repudiate a contract if it is unreasonable for him to do so?

2. Could Schuler have sued Wickman for damages? If not (because they could not prove loss), ought this to effect their self-help remedy of repudiation?

3. Is this case an example of the courts remaking a contract for two commercial parties?

4. P contracts to paint D's building for a fixed price. The written contract stipulates that it is a 'condition' that only a particular named type of paint is used. P paints the building but does not use the paint stipulated for in the contract. Can D refuse to pay P? What if the paint, although not the one stipulated for in the contract, is a better quality and more expensive paint?

5. Read *The Chikuma* [1981] 1 WLR 314 and *The General Capinpin* [1991] 1 L1 Rep 1 in the law reports. Is the approach adopted by the majority in *Schuler* still good law?

6. Is *Schuler* a proportionality (cf Lock, pp 174) case?

CHAPTER 5

THE FORMATION OF A CONTRACT

1 INTRODUCTION

Whittaker v Campbell [1984] QB 318 Queen's Bench Division

Robert Goff LJ: ... [T]here is, in our opinion, no general principle of law that fraud vitiates consent. Let us consider this proposition first with reference to the law of contract. In English law every valid contract presupposes an offer by one party which has been accepted by the offeree. Plainly there can be no such acceptance unless offer and acceptance correspond, so the offer can only be accepted by the offeree, the acceptance must relate to the same subject matter as the offer and must also be, in all material respects, in the same terms as the offer. But the test whether there has been correspondence between offer and acceptance is not subjective but objective. If there is objective agreement, there may be a binding contract, even if in his mind one party or another has not consented to it, a principle recently affirmed by the Court of Appeal in *Centrovincial Estates plc v Merchant Investors Assurance Co Ltd* (1983) *The Times*, 8 March. Furthermore putting on one side such matters as the ancient doctrine of *non est factum* and relief from mistake in equity, there is no principle of English law that any contract may be 'avoided', ie, not come into existence, by reason simply of a mistake, whether a mistake of one or both parties. The question is simply whether objective agreement has been reached and, if so, on what terms. If objective has been reached, in the sense we have described, then the parties will be bound, unless on a true construction the agreement was subject to a condition precedent, express or implied, failure of which has in the event prevented a contract from coming into existence.

What is the effect of fraud? Fraud is, in relation to a contract, a fraudulent misrepresentation by one party which induces the other to enter into a contract or apparent contract with the representor. Apart from the innocent party's right to recover damages for the tort of deceit, the effect of the fraud is simply to give the innocent party the right, subject to certain limits, to rescind the contract. These rights are similar to (though not identical with) the rights of a party who has been induced to enter into a contract by an innocent, as opposed to a fraudulent, misrepresentation, though there the right to recover damages derives from statute, and the limits to rescission are somewhat more severe. It is plain, however, that in this context fraud does not 'vitiate consent', any more than an innocent misrepresentation 'vitiates consent'. Looked at realistically, a misrepresentation, whether fraudulent or innocent, induces a party to enter into a contract in circumstances where it may be unjust that the representor should be permitted to retain the benefit (the chose in action) so acquired by him. The remedy of rescission, by which the unjust enrichment of the representor is prevented, though for historical and practical reasons treated in books on the law of contract, is a straightforward remedy in restitution subject to limits which are characteristic of that branch of the law.

The effect of rescission of a contract induced by a misrepresentation is that property in goods transferred under it may be revested in the transferor (the misrepresentee). But this may not be possible if the goods have been transferred to a third party, for the intervention of third party rights may preclude rescission. In such a case, especially if the misrepresentor has disappeared from the scene or is a man of straw so that damages are an ineffective remedy, the misrepresentee's only practical course may be to seek to establish that there never was any contract (ie, that the supposed contract was 'void'), so that he never parted with the property in the goods and can claim the goods or their value from the third party. To succeed in such a claim, he has generally to show that there was no objective agreement between him and the representor. For that purpose, however, the misrepresentation (fraudulent or innocent) is simply the origin of a set of circumstances in which it may be shown that there was no objective agreement, eg, that the offer was, objectively speaking, made to one person and (perhaps as a result of fraud), objectively speaking, accepted by another. Again, it cannot be said that fraud 'vitiates consent'; fraud was merely the occasion for an apparent contract which was, in law, no contract at all ...

Notes and questions

1. It has already been noted in the previous chapter that English contract law is founded upon the notion of promise rather than agreement. Does this extract from Goff LJ confirm this thesis?

2. In French law fraud can undermine the agreement since it undermines the consent upon which contract is based. In English law, however, fraud does not of itself undermine agreement; it simply gives rise to the equitable remedy of rescission (cf Chapter 3) which, when viewed from the position of the common law, means that the contract is 'voidable'. In addition damages may be available in tort. Of course, as Goff LJ points out, fraud may result in a court holding that there never was a contract because the fraud prevented effective offer and acceptance, an essential requirement for most contracts. In this situation one talks of a 'void' contract, even although this is actually a contradiction in terms. However, the courts are usually reluctant to hold that a contract for the sale of goods is void rather than voidable. Why?

3. In addition to offer and acceptance, there must also be consideration and intention to create legal relations in order that a valid contract be constituted. The sub-sections that follow examine these main requirements (except intention to create legal relations) and additional sections look at the main factors that can vitiate a contract. One question that should be borne in mind while reading the materials in this chapter (indeed in all the chapters on contractual and non-contractual obligations) is the extent to which the cases can be reduced to actual rules. We have already seen from Lord Simon in *Lupton* (p 91) that no case is an authority outside of its 'material

facts'. To what extent, then, is a subject like contract determined by the kind of transactional disputes that find themselves before the courts? And what factors, in addition to the strict 'principles' of the law of contract, might be relevant in determining the actual decision?

2 OFFER AND ACCEPTANCE

(a) Fact and law

Gibson v Manchester City Council [1979] 1 WLR 294 House of Lords

This was an action for specific performance by a potential purchaser of a council house against a local authority which, after a number of preliminary letters indicating a willingness to sell, and setting out the steps to be followed, suddenly, and as a result of a change of political control, refused to carry on with the sale. The Court of Appeal granted the specific performance, but an appeal to the House of Lords was allowed.

Lord Diplock: ... My Lords, the words ... make it quite impossible to construe this letter as a contractual offer capable of being converted into a legally enforceable open contract for the sale of land by Mr Gibson's written acceptance of it. The words 'may be prepared to sell' are fatal to this ...

My Lords, the application form and letter of March 18, 1971 were relied on by Mr Gibson as an unconditional acceptance of the council's offer to sell the house; but this cannot be so unless there was a contractual offer by the council available for acceptance, and, for the reason already given I am of opinion that there was none ...

(See also p 219)

Notes and questions

1. If English contract law was based on agreement and consent, as in French law, would there have been a contract in this case?
2. What if the letter had read 'will be prepared to sell'?
3. What if the incoming political party had promised, during the local election, not to deprive council house tenants of their 'right' to buy?
4. What if the a letter formally offering to sell the house to the plaintiff had not been sent before the change of political control owing to the negligence of a council official? What if it had not been sent owing to deliberate action on behalf of some council officials opposed on political grounds to the sale of council houses?
5. Did the plaintiff fail because of the facts or because of the existence of a clear legal rule?

(b) Offers and the consumer

Pharmaceutical Society of Great Britain v Boots [1953] 1 QB 401 Court of Appeal

Somervell LJ: ... The point taken by the plaintiffs is this: it is said that the purchase is complete if and when a customer going round the shelves takes an article and puts it in the receptacle which he or she is carrying, and that therefore, if that is right, when the customer comes to the pay desk, having completed the tour of the premises, the registered pharmacist, if so minded, has no power to say: "This drug ought not to be sold to this customer." Whether and in what circumstances he would have that power we need not inquire, but one can, of course, see that there is a difference if supervision can only be exercised at a time when the contract is completed.

Whether the view contended for by the plaintiffs is a right view depends on what are the legal implications of this layout – the invitation to the customer. Is a contract to be regarded as being completed when the article is put into the receptacle, or is this to be regarded as a more organised way of doing what is done already in many types of shops – and a bookseller is perhaps the best example – namely, enabling customers to have free access to what is in the shop, to look at the different articles, and then, ultimately, having got the ones which they wish to buy, to come up to the assistant saying: "I want this"? The assistant in 999 times out of 1,000 says: "That is all right," and the money passes and the transaction is completed. I agree with what the Lord Chief Justice has said, and with the reasons which he has given for his conclusion, that in the case of an ordinary shop, although goods are displayed and it is intended that customers should go and choose what they want, the contract is not completed until, the customer having indicated the articles which he needs, the shopkeeper, or someone on his behalf, accepts that offer. Then the contract is completed. I can see no reason at all, that being clearly the normal position, for drawing any different implication as a result of this layout.

The Lord Chief Justice, I think, expressed one of the most formidable difficulties in the way of the plaintiffs' contention when he pointed out that, if the plaintiffs are right, once an article has been placed in the receptacle the customer himself is bound and would have no right, without paying for the first article to substitute an article which he saw later of a similar kind and which he perhaps preferred. I can see no reason for implying from this self-service arrangement any implication other than that which the Lord Chief Justice found in it, namely, that it is a convenient method of enabling customers to see what there is and choose, and possibly put back and substitute, articles which they wish to have, and then to go up to the cashier and offer to buy what they have so far chosen. On that conclusion the case fails ...

Notes and questions

1. In a French case involving a bottle of lemonade which exploded just as the customer was handling it to the cashier the French courts decided that a contract for the sale of goods in a supermarket is

complete as soon as the customer takes the goods from the shelf and puts it in the trolley or basket provided.[1] The customer was thus able to recover damages in contract for her injury. Why do you think the French courts took this approach? What problems does the French rule give rise to? How would English law have dealt with the facts of the French case?

2. Are goods displayed in a shop window contractual offers if they have a ticket attached saying 'special offer'?

3. What legal problems might Virtual Reality shopping present future contract lawyers?

4. A shopkeeper rings up on his till the price of a packet of cigarettes before realising that the customer buying the cigarettes is under age: must the shopkeeper hand over the cigarettes to the customer?

Carlill v Carbolic Smoke Ball Co [1893] 1 QB 256 Court of Appeal

This was an action in debt against a manufacturer who had inserted in newspapers an advertisement offering "£100 reward" to anyone who caught influenza after using their smoke ball inhalant as per directions for two weeks. The advert also stated that £1,000 had been deposited with the Alliance Bank "showing our sincerity in the matter". On the faith of the advertisement the plaintiff bought one of the inhalants and used it as directed for two weeks; the product proved ineffective and the defendants insincere. The plaintiff sued for the £100 and the Court of Appeal allowed her to recover.

Bowen LJ: ... It is ... contended that the advertisement is rather in the nature of a puff or a proclamation than a promise or offer intended to mature into a contract when accepted. But the main point seems to be that the vagueness of the document shows that no contract whatever was intended. It seems to me that in order to arrive at a right conclusion we must read this advertisement in its plain meaning, as the public would understand it. It was intended to be issued to the public and to be read by the public. How would an ordinary person reading this document construe it? It was intended unquestionably to have some effect, and I think the effect which it was intended to have, was to make people use the smoke ball, because the suggestions and allegations which it contains are directed immediately to the use of the smoke ball as distinct from the purchase of it. It did not follow that the smoke ball was to be purchased from the defendants directly, or even from agents of theirs directly. The intention was that the circulation of the smoke ball should be promoted, and that the use of it should be increased ... And it seems to me that the way in which the public would read it would be this, that if anybody, after the advertisement was published, used three times daily for two weeks the carbolic smoke ball, and then caught cold, he would be entitled to the reward ...

Was it intended that the £100 should, if the conditions were filled, be paid? The advertisement says that £1,000 is lodged at the bank for the purpose. Therefore, it cannot be said that the statement that £100 would be paid was intended to be a

---

1   See Cass.civ 20 October 1964, Dalloz-Sirey 1965.62; cf Tunc [1962] Rev trim dr civ 305.

mere puff. I think it was intended to be understood by the public as an offer which was to be acted upon.

But it was said there was no check on the part of the persons who issued the advertisement, and that it would be an insensate thing to promise £100 to a person who used the smoke ball unless you could check or superintend his manner of using it. The answer to that argument seems to me to be that if a person chooses to make extravagant promises of this kind he probably does so because it pays him to make them, and, if he has made them, the extravagance of the promises is no reason in law why he should not be bound by them ...

A L Smith LJ: ... In my judgment, the advertisement was an offer intended to be acted upon, and when accepted and the conditions performed constituted a binding promise on which an action would lie, assuming there was consideration for that promise. The defendants have contended that it was a promise in honour or an agreement or a contract in honour – whatever that may mean. I understand that if there is no consideration for a promise, it may be a promise in honour, or, as we should call it, a promise without consideration and *nudum pactum*; but if anything else is meant, I do not understand it. I do not understand what a bargain or a promise or an agreement in honour is unless it is one on which an action cannot be brought because it is *nudum pactum*, and about *nudum pactums* I will say a word in a moment ....

[I]t was said that there was no consideration, and that it was *nudum pactum*. There are two considerations here. One is the consideration of the inconvenience of having to use this carbolic smoke ball for two weeks three times a day; and the other more important consideration is the money gain likely to accrue to the defendants by the enhanced sale of the smoke balls, by reason of the plaintiff's user of them. There is ample consideration to support this promise. I have only to add that as regards the policy and the wagering points, in my judgment, there is nothing in either of them ...

Notes and questions

1. This most famous of contract cases remains of central importance to English contract law for several reasons. First, because it indicates, once again, how objective promise rather than subjective agreement acts as the foundation of liability; the defendant was liable because it launched on to the consumer market (so to speak) a promise and this promise was taken up by a consumer who, as an individual, was never known to the promisor. Secondly, because it shows that an offer made to the world at large, or at least to a class, does not have to be specifically accepted by verbal communication by the person taking up the offer. All that the promisee has to do, if he or she wants what is promised, is to perform the required act which will constitute the consideration moving from the promisee. Thirdly, because it established an important role for the collateral contract in the world of commerce and consumer affairs. Mrs Carlill did not buy the product from the manufacturers; she probably purchased it from her local chemist and thus if it had been defective causing her injury she

would probably have sued the shop under the contract of sale for breach of an implied term. Collateral contracts continue to have an important role in the area of formation of contracts. Fourthly, because it illustrates the importance of conditions in contracts; if Mrs Carlill had not caught flu she could not have sued for the money. Before she caught flu, was there, however, a contractual relationship between her and the Carbolic Smoke Ball Co?

2. The case is also of importance in terms of the remedy. Was Mrs Carlill seeking compensation for breach of contract or specific enforcement of a contractual obligation based on the idea of non-performance? Could Mrs Carlill have sued the company in damages? If not, why not?

3. Under what circumstances might a manufactuer of a product be liable, on the basis of an advertising campaign, to compensate a consumer in damages?

4. Would these facts have given rise to a contractual obligation in a system where contract is founded on agreement rather than promise?

5. The defendants attempted to argue that there was no intention to create legal relations. Is such as argument ever likely to be successful (in the absence of a specific clause) in commercial and/or consumer transactions?

(c) Offers and commerce

Butler Machine Tool Co Ltd v Ex-Cell-O Corporation [1979] 1 WLR 401 Court of Appeal

This was an action in debt by sellers of a machine in respect of an amount over and above the original sale price of the machine. The sellers claimed they were entitled to this extra sum as a result of a price variation clause contained in their original written offer of sale; but the buyers claimed that the contract was governed by their written acceptance form which did not contain a price variation clause and which contained a tear-off acknowledgement slip which the plaintiffs had returned. The Court of Appeal, allowing an appeal, held that the plaintiffs were not entitled to recover.

Lord Denning MR: ... In the present case the judge thought that the sellers in their original quotation got their blow in first; especially by the provision that "These terms and conditions shall prevail over any terms and conditions in the Buyer's order." It was so emphatic that the price variation clause continued through all the subsequent dealings and that the buyer must be taken to have agreed to it. I can understand that point of view. But I think that the documents have to be considered as a whole. And, as a matter of construction, I think the acknowledgement of June 5, 1969 is the decisive document. It makes clear that the contract was on the buyers' terms and not on the sellers' terms: and the buyers' terms did not include a price variation clause ...

Lawton LJ: ... It cannot be said that the buyers accepted the counter-offer by reason of the fact that ultimately they took physical delivery of the machine. By the time they took physical delivery of the machine, they made it clear by correspondence that they were not accepting that there was any price escalation clause in any contract which they had made with the plaintiffs.

(See also p 96)

Questions

1. Is the rule that a counter-offer amounts to the rejection (and destruction) of the original offer a realistic one in the world of standard form commercial documents?

2. If English contract law was based on agreement rather than promise would the plaintiffs have recovered their debt?

3. What if the plaintiffs had not returned the acknowledgement slip but had simply delivered the machine which the buyers had accepted?

4. Would such a price variation clause now be covered by the Unfair Contract Terms Act 1977?

Interfoto Picture Library Ltd v Stiletto Visual Programmes Ltd [1989] QB 433 Court of Appeal

(See p 222)

Questions

1. Was there *consensus ad idem* (meeting of the minds)? If not, why was there a contract? Do the parties not have to be agreed on the price?

2. Was the plaintiff in breach of contract? Was it this breach that prevented him for suing for the contractual debt?

3. Civil lawyers recognise three fundamental principles: abuse of rights, good faith and unjust enrichment. Which of these principles, if any, found expression in *Interfoto*?

4.. Why was the clause not covered by the Unfair Contract Terms Act 1977?

5. Why was a non-contractual debt claim (*quantum meruit*) allowed in a situation that was plainly covered by contract?

6. What if the plaintiffs' photographs had been deliberately destroyed by one of the defendant's employees? (Cf *Photo Production v Securicor*, p 312).

(d) The end of an offer

Financings Ltd v Stimson [1962] 1 WLR 1184 Court of Appeal

(See p 279)

Notes and questions

1. An offer can only be accepted if it remains in existence. The most obvious way in which an offer can come to an end is by revocation; clearly, however, this must be done before acceptance. Could the Carbolic Smoke Ball Co have revoked its offer after Mrs Carlill had purchased the smoke ball but before the two weeks usage time had elapsed?

2. In *Financings* was there any kind of contractual relationship between the hire-purchase company and the defendant during the period the car was in the defendant's possession?

3. Was the plaintiff in *Financings* under a duty to repay to the defendant the deposit?

4. Besides revocation, in what other ways may an offer lapse or come to an end?

(e) Pre-contractual liability

Entores Ltd v Miles Far East Corporation [1955] 2 QB 327 Court of Appeal

Denning LJ: ... When a contract is made by post it is clear law throughout the common law countries that the acceptance is complete as soon as the letter is put into the post box, and that is the place where the contract is made. But there is no clear rule about contracts made by telephone or by Telex. Communications by these means are virtually instantaneous and stand on a different footing.

The problem can only be solved by going in stages. Let me first consider a case where two people make a contract by word of mouth in the presence of one another. Suppose, for instance, that I shout an offer to a man across a river or a courtyard but I do not hear his reply because it is drowned by an aircraft flying overhead. There is no contract at that moment. If he wishes to make a contract, he must wait till the aircraft is gone and then shout back his acceptance so that I can hear what he says. Not until I have his answer am I bound ...

Now take a case where two people make a contract by telephone. Suppose, for instance, that I make an offer to a man by telephone and, in the middle of his reply, the line goes "dead" so that I do not hear his words of acceptance. There is no contract at that moment. The other man may not know the precise moment when the line failed. But he will know that the telephone conversation was abruptly broken off: because people usually say something to signify the end of the conversation. If he wishes to make a contract, he must therefore get through again so as to make sure that I heard. Suppose next, that the line does not go dead, but it is nevertheless so indistinct that I do not catch what he says and I ask him to repeat it. He then repeats it and I hear his acceptance. The contract is made, not on the first time when I do not hear, but only the second time when I do hear. If he does not repeat it, there is no contract. The contract is only complete when I have his answer accepting the offer.

Lastly, take the Telex. Suppose a clerk in a London office taps out on the teleprinter an offer which is immediately recorded on a teleprinter in a Manchester office, and a clerk at that end taps out an acceptance. If the line goes dead in the middle of the sentence of acceptance, the teleprinter motor will stop. There is then obviously no contract. The clerk at Manchester must get through again and send his complete sentence. But it may happen that the line does not go dead, yet the message does not get through to London. Thus the clerk at Manchester may tap out his message of acceptance and it will not be recorded in London because the ink at the London end fails, or something of that kind. In that case, the Manchester clerk will not know of the failure but the London clerk will know of it and will immediately send back a message "not receiving". Then, when the fault is rectified, the Manchester clerk will repeat his message. Only then is there a contract. If he does not repeat it, there is no contract. It is not until his message is received that the contract is complete.

In all the instances I have taken so far, the man who sends the message of acceptance knows that it has not been received or he has reason to know it. So he must repeat it. But, suppose that he does not know that his message did not get home. He thinks it has. This may happen if the listener on the telephone does not catch the words of acceptance, but nevertheless does not trouble to ask for them to be repeated: or the ink on the teleprinter fails at the receiving end, but the clerk does not ask for the message to be repeated: so that the man who sends an acceptance reasonably believes that his message has been received. The offeror in such circumstances is clearly bound, because he will be estopped from saying that he did not receive the message of acceptance. It is his own fault that he did not get it. But if there should be a case where the offeror without any fault on his part does not receive the message of acceptance – yet the sender of it reasonably believes it has got home when it has not – then I think there is no contract.

My conclusion is, that the rule about instantaneous communications between the parties is different from the rule about the post. The contract is only complete when the acceptance is received by the offeror: and the contract is made at the place where the acceptance is received.

In a matter of this kind, however, it is very important that the countries of the world should have the same rule. I find that most of the European countries have substantially the same rule as that I have stated. Indeed, they apply it to contracts by post as well as instantaneous communications. But in the United States of America it appears as if instantaneous communications are treated in the same way as postal communications. In view of this divergence, I think that we must consider the matter on principle: and so considered, I have come to the view I have stated, and I am glad to see that Professor Winfield in this country (55 *Law Quarterly Review*, 514), and Professor Williston in the United States of America (*Contracts*, § 82, p 239), take the same view ...

Notes and questions

1. There can be no formal contract between two parties until there has been offer and acceptance. Yet what is the position if one of the parties thinks that there is a contract and incurs expenditure, or acts in some other way, in carrying out what he thinks is his contractual duty? Obviously, the person incurring the expenditure or doing the act cannot found any claim upon the non-existent contract; but he might be able to found a claim in some other area of the law of obligations. Much will depend upon the behaviour of the other party as Denning LJ indicates in his famous *obiter dictum* in *Entores*. Thus, if the other party is somehow at fault and this fault can be seen as a cause of the plaintiff's expenditure loss, then an action might lie in the tort of negligence, although the economic loss rule will present a serious obstacle. Alternatively, as we shall see, the plaintiff may be able to claim any benefit conferred on the other party via a quasi-contractual debt claim. Another possibility, of course, is estoppel. Yet how can one be estopped from denying the existence of a contract? Does the existence of such an equitable principle confirm, yet again, that English law is based on promise rather than agreement?

2. Is this case relevant for contractual negotiations carried out by fax?

3. Why was the nephew in *Beswick* (p 154) not estopped from denying the existence of an obligation to pay Mrs Beswick?

Blackpool & Fylde Aero Club Ltd v Blackpool Borough Council [1990] 1 WLR 1195 Court of Appeal

Bingham LJ: In this action the plaintiffs ("the club") sued the defendants ("the council") for damages for breach of contract and common law negligence. It was in issue between the parties whether there was any contract between them and whether the council owed the club any duty of care in tort. These issues of liability came before Judge Jolly sitting as a judge of the Queen's Bench Division and he decided them both in favour of the club, all questions of *quantum* being deferred. The council appeal, contending that the judge was wrong on each point.

The council own and manage Blackpool Airport. For purposes of raising revenue they have made it a practice to grant a concession to an air operator to operate pleasure flights from the airport, no doubt largely for the entertainment of holiday-makers. The club, one of whose directors was and is a Mr Bateson, tendered for and were granted this concession in 1975 and again in 1978 and again in 1980. In 1983 the most recently granted concession was due to expire. The council accordingly prepared an invitation to tender. This was sent to the club and to six other parties, all of them in one way or another connected with the airport. This document was headed and began as follows:

"... The council do not bind themselves to accept all or any part of any tender. No tender which is received after the last date and time specified shall be admitted for consideration ..."

Only three of the selected tenderers responded to the council's invitation. One put in a low bid for the lighter size of aircraft only. The second, Red Rose Helicopters Ltd, submitted a larger bid, also for the lighter size of aircraft. Mr Bateson for the club filled in the form of tender, submitting a bid substantially larger, on its face, than the others' for the lighter size of aircraft, and also submitting a bid for the heavier size. He put it in the envelope provided by the council, took it to the town hall and posted it in the town hall letter box at about 11 am on Thursday 17 March. This was about an hour before the advertised deadline expired. The town clerk's staff were supposed to empty the letter box each day at 12 o'clock. They failed to do so. The club's tender accordingly remained in the letter box until the next morning, 18 March, when the letter box was next opened. The envelope was then taken out and date-stamped 18 March 1983 by the town clerk's department. At some time thereafter the word "late" was written on the envelope, because that is what the club's tender was mistakenly thought to be.

On 29 March 1983 the chairman of the council's relevant committee considered which tender to accept. The club's tender had been recorded as being late, and was in accordance with the council's standing orders excluded from consideration when the chairman made his decision. He accordingly made his choice between the two tenders believed to be in time, recommending acceptance of Red Rose Helicopters' tender, no doubt because it was bigger. An indication that its tender was accepted was given to Red Rose Helicopters. The town clerk wrote to the club to say that their tender was not received until 18 March and was therefore received too late for consideration. Mr Bateson replied that the club's tender had been delivered to the town hall before the deadline. "You will appreciate," he wrote, "that this matter is of some considerable importance to our company." The council evidently made inquiries and established that the club's tender had been received in time ...

The judge resolved the contractual issue in favour of the club, holding that an express request for a tender might in appropriate circumstances give rise to an implied obligation to perform the service of considering that tender. Here, the council's stipulation that tenders received after the deadline would not be admitted for consideration gave rise to a contractual obligation, on acceptance by submission of a timely tender, that such tenders would be admitted for consideration ...

Mr Toulson [counsel for the council] submitted that the warranty contended for by the club was simply a proposition "tailor-made to produce the desired result" (*per* Lord Templeman in *CBS Songs Ltd v Amstrad Consumer Electronics Plc* [1988] AC 1013, 1059F) on the facts of this particular case. There was a vital distinction between expectations, however reasonable, and contractual obligations: see *per* Diplock LJ in *Lavarack v Woods of Colchester Ltd* [1967] 1 QB 278, 294. The club here expected its tender to be considered. The council fully intended that it should be. It was in both parties' interests that the club's tender should be considered. There was thus no need for them to contract. The court should not subvert well-understood contractual principles by adopting a woolly pragmatic solution designed to remedy a perceived injustice on the unique facts of this particular case ...

I found great force in the submissions made by Mr Toulson and agree with much of what he said. Indeed, for much of the hearing I was of opinion that the judge's decision, although fully in accord with the merits as I see them, could not be sustained in principle. But I am in the end persuaded that Mr Toulson's argument proves too much. During the hearing the questions were raised: what if, in a situation such as the present, the council had opened and thereupon accepted the first tender received, even though the deadline had not expired and other invitees had not yet responded? Or if the council had considered and accepted a tender admittedly received well after the deadline? Mr Toulson answered that although by so acting the council might breach its own standing orders, and might fairly be accused of discreditable conduct, it would not be in breach of any legal obligation because at that stage there would be none to breach. This is a conclusion I cannot accept. And if it were accepted there would in my view be an unacceptable discrepancy between the law of contract and the confident assumptions of commercial parties, both tenderers (as reflected in the evidence of Mr Bateson) and invitors (as reflected in the immediate reaction of the council when the mishap came to light).

A tendering procedure of this kind is, in many respects, heavily weighted in favour of the invitor. He can invite tenders from as many or as few parties as he chooses. He need not tell any of them who else, or how many others, he has invited. The invitee may often, although not here, be put to considerable labour and expense in preparing a tender, ordinarily without recompense if he is unsuccessful. The invitation to tender may itself, in a complex case, although again not here, involve time and expense to prepare, but the invitor does not commit himself to proceed with the project, whatever it is; he need not accept the highest tender; he need not accept any tender; he need not give reasons to justify his acceptance or rejection of any tender received. The risk to which the tenderer is exposed does not end with the risk that his tender may not be the highest or, as the case may be, lowest. But where, as here, tenders are solicited from selected parties all of them known to the invitor, and where a local authority's invitation prescribes a clear, orderly and familiar procedure – draft contract conditions available for inspection and plainly not open to negotiation, a prescribed common form of tender, the supply of envelopes designed to preserve the absolute anonymity of tenderers and clearly to identify the tender in question, and an absolute deadline – the invitee is in my judgment protected at least to this extent: if he submits a conforming tender before the deadline he is entitled, not as a matter of mere expectation but of contractual right, to be sure that his tender will after the deadline be opened and considered in conjunction with all other conforming tenders or at least that his tender will be considered if others are. Had the club, before tendering, inquired of the council whether it could rely on any timely and conforming tender being considered along with others, I feel quite sure that the answer would have been "of course". The law would, I think, be defective if it did not give effect to that.

It is of course true that the invitation to tender does not explicitly state that the council will consider timely and conforming tenders. That is why one is concerned with implication. But the council do not either say that they do not bind themselves to do so, and in the context a reasonable invitee would understand the invitation to be saying, quite clearly, that if he submitted a timely and conforming tender it would be considered, at least if any other such tender were considered.

I readily accept that contracts are not to be lightly implied ... In all the circumstances of this case, and I say nothing about any other, I have no doubt that the parties did intend to create contractual relations to the limited extent contended for. Since it has never been the law that a person is only entitled to enforce his contractual rights in a reasonable way (*White and Carter (Councils) Ltd v McGregor* [1962] AC 413, 430A, *per* Lord Reid), Mr Shorrock was in my view right to contend for no more than a contractual duty to consider. I think it plain that the council's invitation to tender was, to this limited extent, an offer, and the club's submission of a timely and conforming tender an acceptance ...

I accordingly agree with the judge's conclusion on the contractual issue, essentially for the reasons which he more briefly gave.

This conclusion makes it unnecessary to consider at length the club's alternative argument, which the judge also accepted, that if there was no contract at all between the parties the council nonetheless owed the club a duty to take reasonable care to see to it that if the club submitted a tender by the deadline it would be considered along with other tenders duly returned when the decision to grant the concession was made ...

I am reluctant to venture into this somewhat unvirginal territory when it is unnecessary to do so for the purpose of deciding this case. Having heard the argument, I am tentatively of opinion that Mr Toulson's objections are correct and that the club cannot succeed on this point if they fail on the other. But I do not think it necessary or desirable to express a final conclusion.

I would accordingly dismiss the appeal. The practical consequences of deciding the contractual issue on liability in the club's favour must, if necessary, be decided hereafter.

Stocker LJ: ... I ... agree that in all the circumstances of this case there was an intention to create binding legal obligations if and when a tender was submitted in accordance with the terms of the invitation to tender, and that a binding contractual obligation arose that the club's tender would be before the officer or committee by whom the decision was to be taken for consideration before a decision was made or any tender accepted. This would not preclude or inhibit the council from deciding not to accept any tender or to award the concession, provided the decision was *bona fide* and honest, to any tenderer. The obligation was that the club's tender would be before the deciding body for consideration before any award was made. Accordingly, in my view, the conclusion of the judge and his reasons were correct ...

Farquharson LJ: I agree.

Notes and questions

1. This rather extraordinary case is important for a whole range of reasons. First and foremost because it shows that knowledge of law is not simply a matter of knowing rules. Indeed this case seems to defy most of the settled contract rules, yet its process of reasoning is typical of the common law jurist. Bingham LJ starts from within the facts and works outward towards the notion of an expectation which in turn, rather by sleight of hand, becomes a 'right' (see Chapter 2). This methodology does not consist of knowing rules and applying them to a set of facts; and if *Blackpool* does nothing else, it certainly

will prove a challenge to those who think that law is amenable to some existing Artificial Intelligence system. Can a *ratio decidendi* be drawn out of this decision?

2   Secondly the case is important because it indicates the important role of the collateral contract in pre-contractual liability problems. Thus in addition to the possibilities outlined above (in the note after *Entores v Miles Far East Corporation*), there is the possibility that the court can turn the pre-contractual behaviour into an independent contract in itself. Is the case in effect an example of a contract to negotiate? What damage did the plaintiff suffer? Was it caused by the defendants?

3.   Thirdly, the case is interesting because of the status of the defendant. No doubt the decision deserves its place in law of obligations books, but one may ask whether its real place is in works on administrative law. The duty attached to the procedures rather than to the transaction and while Bingham LJ recognised that a contracting party is under no duty to exercise his rights in a reasonable way, he nevertheless seems to be intervening to prevent an abuse of position. Note, also, how Stocker LJ refers to *bona fides*. Public law, both in the caselaw[2] and in statute,[3] has recognised for some time now that a public body does not have the same contractual rights and liberties as a private person, particularly at the pre-contract stage. If the defendant had been a private commercial body seeking tenders for a private commercial venture would the result have been the same?

Walford v Miles [1992] 2 AC 128 House of Lords

This was an action for damages for misrepresentation and breach of contract brought by disappointed prospective purchasers of a business against the owners of the business who had eventually sold it, not to the plaintiffs, but to a third party. The plaintiffs claimed that the defendants had orally agreed to negotiate only with the plaintiffs and were thus in breach of this 'lock-out' agreement when they sold the business to the third party. The trial judge awarded damages for breach of contract and misrepresentation, but a majority of the Court of Appeal allowed an appeal on the breach of contract decision. An appeal to the House of Lords was dismissed.

Lord Ackner: ... The [plaintiffs] relied upon an oral agreement, collateral to the negotiations which were proceeding to purchase the company and land it occupied "subject to contract". The consideration for this oral agreement was twofold – firstly the [plaintiffs] agreeing to continue the negotiations and not withdraw and secondly, their providing the comfort letter from their bankers in the terms requested ...

---

2   See *R v Lewisham LBC ex p Shell UK* [1988] 1 All ER 938.
3   See Local Government Act 1988 s 17.

As thus pleaded, the agreement purported to be what is known as a "lock-out" agreement, providing the plaintiffs with an exclusive opportunity to try and come to terms with the defendants, but without expressly providing any duration for such an opportunity ...

[Counsel for the plaintiffs] accepted that as the law now stands and has stood for approaching 20 years, an agreement to negotiate is not recognised as an enforceable contract. This was first decided in terms in *Courtney and Fairbairn Ltd v Tolaini Brothers (Hotels) Ltd* [1975] 1 WLR 297 ...

Before your Lordships it was sought to argue that the decision in Courtney's case ... was wrong. Although the cases in the United States did not speak with one voice your Lordships' attention was drawn to the decision of the United States' Court of Appeal, Third Circuit, in *Channel Home Centers, Division of Grace Retail Corporation v Grossman* (1986) 795 F. 2d 291 as being "the clearest example" of the American cases in the appellants' favour. That case raised the issue whether an agreement to negotiate in good faith, if supported by consideration, is an enforceable contract. I do not find the decision of any assistance. While accepting that an agreement to agree is not an enforceable contract, the Court of Appeal appears to have proceeded on the basis that an agreement to negotiate in good faith is synonymous with an agreement to use best endeavours and as the latter is enforceable, so is the former. This appears to me, with respect, to be an unsustainable proposition. The reason why an agreement to negotiate, like an agreement to agree, is unenforceable, is simply because it lacks the necessary certainty. The same does not apply to an agreement to use best endeavours. This uncertainty is demonstrated in the instant case by the provision which it is said has to be implied in the agreement for the determination of the negotiations. How can a court be expected to decide whether, subjectively, a proper reason existed for the termination of negotiations? The answer suggested depends upon whether the negotiations have been determined "in good faith". However the concept of a duty to carry on negotiations in good faith is inherently repugnant to the adverserial position of the parties when involved in negotiations. Each party to the negotiations is entitled to pursue his (or her) own interest, so long as he avoids making misrepresentations. To advance that interest he must be entitled, if he thinks it appropriate, to threaten to withdraw from further negotiations or to withdraw in fact, in the hope that the opposite party may seek to reopen the negotiations by offering him improved terms. [Counsel for the plaintiffs], of course, accepts that the agreement upon which he relies does not contain a duty to complete the negotiations. But that still leaves the vital question – how is a vendor ever to know that he is entitled to withdraw from further negotiations? How is the court to police such an "agreement?" A duty to negotiate in good faith is as unworkable in practice as it is inherently inconsistent with the position of a negotiating party. It is here that the uncertainty lies. In my judgment, while negotiations are in existence either party is entitled to withdraw from those negotiations, at any time and for any reason. There can be thus no obligation to continue to negotiate until there is a "proper reason" to withdraw. Accordingly, a bare agreement to negotiate has no legal content ...

... I believe it helpful to make ... observations about a so-called "lock-out" agreement. There is clearly no reason in the English contract law why A, for good consideration, should not achieve an enforceable agreement whereby B, agrees for a specified period of time, not to negotiate with anyone except A in relation to the sale of his property. There are often good commercial reasons why

A should desire to obtain such an agreement from B ... But I stress that this is a negative agreement – B by agreeing not to negotiate for this fixed period with a third party, locks himself out of such negotiations. He has in no legal sense locked himself into negotiations with A. What A has achieved is an exclusive opportunity, for a fixed period, to try and come to terms with B, an opportunity for which he has, unless he makes his agreement under seal, to give good consideration ...

Notes and questions

1. If the *Blackpool* case had gone to the House of Lords do you think the decision of the Court of Appeal would have been upheld? Who do you think was the dissenting judge in the Court of Appeal decision in *Walford*?

2. *Walford* is a very good case to compare with cases from civilian jurisdictions where, for example, the doctrine of good faith has been used to impose duties upon parties at a pre-contractual stage. Why is it that English law insists upon a different approach: is it really because the doctrine is 'unworkable'? What if A has expended much money on the basis that some kind of contract will be negotiated with B: ought B to be allowed to have the right to disregard completely the interests of A? Ought B to be free to pull out of negotiations without giving reasons? What if B is a public body?

3. Does *Walford* stipulate that there is no principle of pre-contractual liability in English law? Could *Walford* be an obstacle to the harmonisation of the law of obligations in the EU?

4. Is Lord Ackner's analysis of a lock-out agreement convincing? Is B's duty, in Lord Ackner's example, simply one not to negotiate with anyone else?

5. Can the courts imply a 'lock-out' agreement? If so, might such an implication be based on reasonableness and fairness?

Pitt v PHH Asset Management Ltd [1994] 1 WLR 327 Court of Appeal

Sir Thomas Bingham MR: ... For very many people their first and closest contact with the law is when they come to buy or sell a house. They frequently find it a profoundly depressing and frustrating experience. The vendor puts his house on the market. He receives an offer which is probably less than his asking price. He agonises over whether to accept or hold out for more. He decides to accept, perhaps after negotiating some increase. A deal is struck. Hands are shaken. The vendor celebrates relaxes, makes plans for his own move and takes his house off the market. Then he hears that the purchaser who was formerly pleading with him to accept his offer has decided not to proceed. No explanation is given, no apology made. The vendor has to embark on the whole dreary process of putting his house on the market all over again.

For the purchaser the process is, if anything, worse. After a series of futile visits to unsuitable houses he eventually finds the house of his dreams. He makes an offer, perhaps at the asking price, perhaps at what the agent tells him the vendor is likely to accept. The offer is accepted. A deal is done. The purchaser instructs solicitors to act. He perhaps commissions an architect to plan alterations. He makes arrangements to borrow money. He puts his own house on the market. He makes arrangements to move. He then learns that the vendor has decided to sell to someone else, perhaps for the price already offered and accepted, perhaps for an increased price achieved by a covert, unofficial auction. Again, no explanation, no apology. The vendor is able to indulge his self-interest, even his whims, without exposing himself to any legal penalty.

The reasons why purchaser and vendor can act in this apparently unprincipled manner are to be found in two legal rules of long standing: first, the rule that contracts for the sale and purchase of land must be evidenced (or now made) in writing; secondly, the rule that terms agreed subject to contract do not give rise to a binding contract. These rules are deeply imbedded in statute and authority. They make possible the behaviour I have described, but the validity and merits of those rules are not, and could not be, the subject of challenge in this appeal.

For the purchaser there is, however, one means of protection: to make an independent agreement by which the vendor agrees for a clear specified period not to deal with anyone other than that purchaser. The effect is to give that purchaser a clear run for the period in question. The vendor does not agree to sell to that purchaser, such an agreement would be covered by section 2 of the [Law of Property (Miscellaneous Provisions) Act 1989], but he does give a negative undertaking that he will not for the given period deal with anyone else. That, I am quite satisfied, is what happened here, as the judge rightly held. The vendor and the prospective purchaser made what has come to be called a "lock out agreement". That was a contract binding on them both. The vendor broke it. He is liable to the prospective purchaser for damages which remain to be assessed. I would dismiss the appeal.

Questions

1. How does a lock-out agreement differ from a contract to contract?
2. Could a lock-out agreement ever be the basis of an injunction or specific performance?
3. If *PHH* were to go to the House of Lords do you think the views of Sir Thomas Bingham would be upheld?

British Steel Corporation v Cleveland Bridge & Engineering Co Ltd [1984] 1 All ER 504 Queen's Bench Division

This was a successful action in debt (*quantum meruit*) for work done, at the request of the defendants, in anticipation of a formal contract that never materialised. The defendants conterclaimed for damages for breach of contract.

Robert Goff LJ: ... Now the question whether in a case such as the present any contract has come into existence must depend on a true construction of the relevant communications which have passed between the parties and the effect (if any) of their actions pursuant to those communications. There can be no hard and fast answer to the question whether a letter of intent will give rise to a binding agreement: everything must depend on the circumstances of the particular case. In most cases, where work is done pursuant to a request contained in a letter of intent, it will not matter whether a contract did or did not come into existence, because, if the party who has acted on the request is simply claiming payment, his claim will usually be based on a *quantum meruit*, and it will make no difference whether that claim is contractual or quasi-contractual. Of course, a *quantum meruit* claim (like the old actions for money had and received and for money paid) straddles the boundaries of what we now call contract and restitution, so the mere framing of a claim as a *quantum meruit* claim, or a claim for a reasonable sum, does not assist in classifying the claim as contractual or quasi contractual. But where, as here, one party is seeking to claim damages for breach of contract, the question whether any contract came into existence is of crucial importance.

As a matter of analysis the contract (if any) which may come into existence following a letter of intent may take one of two forms: either there may be an ordinary executory contract, under which each party assumes reciprocal obligations to the other; or there may be what is sometimes called an 'if' contract, ie a contract under which A requests B to carry out a certain performance and promises B that, if he does so, he will receive a certain performance in return, usually remuneration for her performance. The latter transaction is really no more than a standing offer which, if acted on before it lapses or is lawfully withdrawn, will result in a binding contract ...

In my judgment, the true analysis of the situation is simply this. Both parties confidently expected a formal contract to eventuate. In these circumstances, to expedite performance under that anticipated contract, one requested the other to commence the contract work, and the other complied with that request. If thereafter, as anticipated, a contract was entered into, the work done as requested will be treated as having been performed under that contract; if, contrary to their expectation, no contract was entered into, then the performance of the work is not referable to any contract the terms of which can be ascertained, and the law simply imposes an obligation on the party who made the request to pay a reasonable sum for such work as has been done pursuant to that request, such an obligation sounding in quasi contract or, as we now say, in restitution. Consistently with that solution, the party making the request may find himself liable to pay for work which he would not have had to pay for as such if the anticipated contract had come into existence, eg preparatory work which will, if the contract is made, be allowed for in the price of the finished work ... I only wish to add to this part of my judgment the footnote that, even if I had concluded that in the circumstances of the present case there was a contract between the parties and that that contract was of the kind I have described as an 'if' contract, then I would still have concluded that there was no obligation under that contract on the part of BSC to continue with or complete the contract work, and therefore no obligation on their part to complete the work within a reasonable time. However, my conclusion in the present case is that the parties never entered into any contract at all.

Questions

1. Is a *quantum meruit* founded upon a contractual relationship?
2. Is this case an example of pre-contractual liability?
3. Was the defendant held liable in debt or damages?
4. Compare and contrast *Cleveland* with *Blackpool & Fylde*. Could the plaintiff in *Blackpool* have sued on a *quantum meruit* for all the expenses incurred in preparing and submitting the tender?

3 CONSIDERATION

(a) Validity of consideration

Williams v Roffey Brothers & Nicholls (Contractors) Ltd [1991] 1 QB 1 Court of Appeal

This was an action in debt for building work done pursuant to a promise made by the defendants whereby they undertook to pay more for this work than they had stipulated in the original contract. The defendant claimed that the promise to pay the extra money was unsupported by consideration, but the Court of Appeal disagreed; the defendants had received a real benefit in return for their promise to pay more.

Glidewell LJ: ... Mr Evans [counsel for the defendants] submits that, though his clients may have derived, or hoped to derive, practical benefits from their agreement to pay the "bonus", they derived no benefit in law, since the plaintiff was promising to do no more than he was already bound to do by his subcontract, ie, continue with the carpentry work and complete it on time. Thus there was no consideration for the agreement. Mr Evans relies on the principle of law which, traditionally, is based on the decision in *Stilk v Myrick* (1809) 2 Camp. 317. That was a decision at first instance of Lord Ellenborough CJ. On a voyage to the Baltic, two seamen deserted. The captain agreed with the rest of the crew that if they worked the ship back to London without the two seamen being replaced, he would divide between them the pay which would have been due to the two deserters. On arrival at London this extra pay was refused, and the plaintiff's action to recover his extra pay was dismissed. Counsel for the defendant argued that such an agreement was contrary to public policy, but Lord Ellenborough CJ's judgment was based on lack of consideration ...

In *North Ocean Shipping Co Ltd v Hyundai Construction Co Ltd* [1979] QB 705, Mocatta J regarded the general principle of the decision in *Stilk v Myrick*, 2 Camp. 317 as still being good law. He referred to two earlier decisions of this court, dealing with wholly different subjects, in which Denning LJ sought to escape from the confines of the rule, but was not accompanied in his attempt by the other members of the court ...

It was suggested to us in argument that, since the development of the doctrine of promissory estoppel, it may well be possible for a person to whom a promise has been made, on which he has relied, to make an additional payment for services which he is in any event bound to render under an existing contract or by operation of law, to show that the promisor is estopped from claiming that there was no consideration for his promise. However, the application of the doctrine of promissory estoppel to facts such as those of the present case has not yet been fully developed ...

There is, however, another legal concept of relatively recent development which is relevant, namely, that of economic duress. Clearly if a subcontractor has agreed to undertake work at a fixed price, and before he has completed the work declines to continue with it unless the contractor agrees to pay an increased price, the subcontractor may be held guilty of securing the contractor's promise by taking unfair advantage of the difficulties he will cause if he does not complete the work. In such a case an agreement to pay an increased price may well be voidable because it was entered into under duress. Thus this concept may provide another answer in law to the question of policy which has troubled the courts since before *Stilk v Myrick*, 2 Camp. 317, and no doubt led at the date of that decision to a rigid adherence to the doctrine of consideration.

This possible application of the concept of economic duress was referred to by Lord Scarman, delivering the judgment of the Judicial Committee of the Privy Council in *Pao On v Lau Yiu Long* [1980] AC 614 ...

Accordingly, following the view of the majority in *Ward v Byham* [1956] 1 WLR 496 and of the whole court in *Williams v Williams* [1957] 1 WLR 148 and that of the Privy Council in *Pao On* [1980] AC 614 the present state of the law on this subject can be expressed in the following proposition: (i) if A has entered into a contract with B to do work for, or to supply goods or services to, B in return for payment by B; and (ii) at some stage before A has completely performed his obligations under the contract B has reason to doubt whether A will, or will be able to, complete his side of the bargain; and (iii) B thereupon promises A an additional payment in return for A's promise to perform his contractual obligations on time; and (iv) as a result of giving his promise, B obtains in practice a benefit, or obviates a disbenefit; and (v) B's promise is not given as a result of economic duress or fraud on the part of A; then (vi) the benefit to B is capable of being consideration for B's promise, so that the promise will be legally binding ...

Russell LJ: ... [W]hilst consideration remains a fundamental requirement before a contract not under seal can be enforced, the policy of the law in its search to do justice between the parties has developed considerably since the early 19th century when *Stilk v Myrick*, 2 Camp. 317 was decided by Lord Ellenborough CJ. In the late 20th century I do not believe that the rigid approach to the concept of consideration to be found in *Stilk v Myrick* is either necessary or desirable. Consideration there must still be but, in my judgment, the courts nowadays should be more ready to find its existence so as to reflect the intention of the parties to the contract where the bargaining powers are not unequal and where the finding of consideration reflect the true intention of the parties ...

Purchase LJ: ... In my judgment ... the rule in *Stilk v Myrick*, 2 Camp. 317 remains valid as a matter of principle, namely that a contract not under seal must be supported by consideration. Thus, where the agreement upon which reliance is placed provides that an extra payment is to be made for work to be done by the payee which he is already obliged to perform then unless some other consideration is detected to support the agreement to pay the extra sum that agreement will not be enforceable. The two cases, *Harris v Watson*, Peake 102 and *Stilk v Myrick*, 2 Camp. 317 involved circumstances of a very special nature, namely the extraordinary conditions existing at the turn of the 18th century under which seamen had to serve their contracts of employment on the high seas. There were strong public policy grounds at that time to protect the master and owners of a ship from being held to ransom by disaffected crews. Thus, the decision that the promise to pay extra wages even in the circumstances established in those cases, was not supported by consideration is readily understandable. Of course, conditions today on the high seas have changed dramatically and it is at least questionable, as Mr Makey submitted, whether these cases might not well have been decided differently if they were tried today. The modern cases tend to depend more upon the defence of duress in a commercial context rather than lack of consideration for the second agreement. In the present case the question of duress does not arise ... Nevertheless, the court is more ready in the presence of this defence being available in the commercial context to look for mutual advantages which would amount to sufficient consideration to support the second agreement under which the extra money is paid ...

The question must be posed: what consideration has moved from the plaintiff to support the promise to pay the extra £10,300 added to the lump sum provision? In the particular circumstances which I have outlined above, there was clearly a commercial advantage to both sides from a pragmatic point of view in reaching the agreement of 9 April. The defendants were on risk that as a result of the bargain they had struck the plaintiff would not or indeed possibly could not comply with his existing obligations without further finance. As a result of the agreement the defendants secured their position commercially. There was, however, no obligation added to the contractual duties imposed upon the plaintiff under the original contract. *Prima facie* this would appear to be a classic *Stilk v Myrick* case. It was, however, open to the plaintiff to be in deliberate breach of the contract in order to "cut his losses" commercially. In normal circumstances the suggestion that a contracting party can rely upon his own breach to establish consideration is distinctly unattractive. In many cases it obviously would be and if there was any element of duress brought upon the other contracting party under the modern development of this branch of the law the proposed breaker of the contract would not benefit. With some hesitation ... I consider that the modern approach to the question of consideration would be that where there were benefits derived by each party to a contract of variation even though one party did not suffer a detriment this would not be fatal to the establishing of sufficient consideration to support the agreement. If both parties benefit from an agreement it is not necessary that each also suffers a detriment. In my judgment, on the facts as found by the judge, he was entitled to reach the conclusion that consideration existed and in those circumstances I would not disturb that finding. This is sufficient to determine the appeal ...

Notes and questions

1. The second formal requirement for a valid contract in English law is consideration. The standard definition is: 'A valuable consideration,

in the sense of the law, may consist either in some right, interest, profit, or benefit accruing to one party, or some forbearance, detriment, loss, or responsibility, given, suffered, or undertaken by the other' (Lush J in *Currie v Misa* (1875) LR 10 Ex 153, 162). What do you think is the role of consideration in contract law? Does the definition need amending in the light of *Roffey*?

2. A and B exchange Christmas presents every year. Is the exchange a contract? If not, is this only because the parties do not intend legal relations?

3. In *Roffey* is it a material fact that the transaction was one for building work?

4. What is meant by economic duress? (Cf *CTN Cash & Carry v Gallaher Ltd*, below p 290.)

5. How does *Roffey* differ from *D & C Builders v Ress* (below)?

(b) Consideration and abuse of rights

D & C Builders Ltd v Rees [1966] 2 QB 617 Court of Appeal

This was an action in debt by a firm of builders in respect of money owed for work done. The debtor argued that the plaintiffs had accepted a lesser figure in full and final settlement of the debt. The creditor argued that this lesser sum had been accepted only after the debtor had threatened to pay them nothing at a time when the firm was on the verge of bankruptcy. The Court of Appeal gave judgment in favour of the builders.

Lord Denning MR: ... This case is of some consequence: for it is a daily occurrence that a merchant or tradesman, who is owed a sum of money, is asked to take less. The debtor says he is in difficulties. He offers a lesser sum in settlement, cash down. He says he cannot pay more. The creditor is considerate. He accepts the proffered sum and forgives him the rest of the debt. The question arises: Is the settlement binding on the creditor? The answer is that, in point of law, the creditor is not bound by the settlement. He can the next day sue the debtor for the balance: and get judgment. The law was so stated in 1602 by Lord Coke in *Pinnel's* Case (1602) 5 Co Rep 117a – and accepted in 1889 by the House of Lords in *Foakes v Beer* (1884) 9 App Cas 605.

Now, suppose that the debtor, instead of paying the lesser sum in cash, pays it by cheque. He makes out a cheque for the amount. The creditor accepts the cheque and cashes it. Is the position any different? I think not. No sensible distinction can be taken between payment of a lesser sum by cash and payment of it by cheque. The cheque, when given, is conditional payment. When honoured, it is actual payment. It is then just the same as cash. If a creditor is not bound when he receives payment by cash, he should not be bound when he receives payment by cheque ...

In point of law payment of a lesser sum, whether by cash or by cheque, is not discharge of a greater sum.

This doctrine of the common law has come under heavy fire. It was ridiculed by Sir George Jessel in *Couldery v Bartram* (1881) 19 Ch D 394 at p 399. It was said to be mistaken by Lord Blackburn in *Foakes v Beer*. It was condemned by the Law Revision Committee (Cmd 5449, 1945) paras 20 and 21. But a remedy has been found. The harshness of the common law has been relieved. Equity has stretched out a merciful hand to help the debtor. The courts have invoked the broad principle stated by Lord Cairns in *Hughes v Metropolitan Railway Co*.

> "It is the first principle upon which all courts of equity proceed that if parties, who have entered into definite and distinct terms involving certain legal results, afterwards by their own act or with their own consent enter upon a course of negotiation which has the effect of leading one of the parties to suppose that the strict rights arising under the contract will not be enforced or will be kept in suspense, or held in abeyance, the person who otherwise might have enforced those rights will not be allowed to enforce them when it would be inequitable having regard to the dealings which have taken place between the parties."

It is worth noticing that the principle may be applied, not only so as to suspend strict legal rights, but also so as to preclude the enforcement of them.

This principle has been applied to cases where a creditor agrees to accept a lesser sum in discharge of a greater. So much so that we can now say that, when a creditor and a debtor enter upon a course of negotiation, which leads the debtor to suppose that, on payment of the lesser sum, the creditor will not enforce payment of the balance, and on the faith thereof the debtor pays the lesser sum and the creditor accepts it as satisfaction: then the creditor will not be allowed to enforce payment of the balance when it would be inequitable to do so. This was well illustrated during the last war. Tenants went away to escape the bombs and left their houses unoccupied. The landlords accepted a reduced rent for the time they were empty. It was held that the landlords could not afterwards turn round and sue for the balance, see *Central London Property Trust Ltd v High Trees House Ltd*. This caused at the time some eyebrows to be raised in high places. But they have been lowered since. The solution was so obviously just that no one could well gainsay it.

In applying this principle, however, we must note the qualification: The creditor is only barred from his legal rights when it would be inequitable for him to insist upon them. Where there has been a true accord, under which the creditor voluntarily agrees to accept a lesser sum in satisfaction, and the debtor acts upon that accord by paying the lesser sum and the creditor accepts it, then it is inequitable for the creditor afterwards to insist on the balance. But he is not bound unless there has been truly an accord between them.

In the present case, on the facts as found by the judge, it seems to me that there was no true accord. The debtor's wife held the creditor to ransom. The creditor was in need of money to meet his own commitments, and she knew it. When the creditor asked for payment of the £480 due to him, she said to him in effect "We cannot pay you the £480. But we will pay you £300 if you will accept it in settlement. If you do not accept it on those terms you will get nothing. £300 is better than nothing." She had no right to say any such thing. She could properly have said: "We cannot pay you more than £300. Please accept it on account." But she had no right to insist on his taking it in settlement. When she said: "We will pay you nothing unless you accept £300 in settlement", she was putting undue pressure on the creditor. She was making a threat to break the contract (by paying nothing) and she was doing it so as to compel the creditor to do what he was unwilling to do (to accept £300 in settlement): and she succeeded. He complied with her demand. That was on recent authority a case of intimidation: see *Rookes v Barnard* and *Stratford (JT) & Son Ltd v Lindley*. In these circumstances there was no true accord so as to found a defence of accord and satisfaction: see *Day v McLea*. There is also no equity in the defendant to warrant any departure from the due course of law. No person can insist on a settlement procured by intimidation.

In my opinion there is no reason in law or equity why the creditor should not enforce the full amount of the debt due to him. I would, therefore, dismiss this appeal.

Notes and questions

1. *Rees* is obviously a useful case to compare with *Williams v Roffey*. Why was the Court of Appeal prepared to find consideration in one but not in the other? Did the parties in *Rees* not receive a benefit?

2. Would the result of *Roffey* have been different if the plaintiff had simply threatened not to continue with the building work unless the plaintiff promised to pay more?

3. If the creditor's debt claim had failed in *Rees*, would the defendant have been unjustly enriched? In which chapter in a book on the law of restitution would you expect to find this case?

4. If the plaintiff in *Rees* had suffered considerable financial loss as a result of the defendant's refusal to pay the full bill, could the plaintiff have sued for damages for breach of contract or for a tort?

5. The workers at P's factory threaten to go on strike unless P agrees to pay them higher wages. P agrees to the demands because he wishes to fulfill an urgent order. After the order is fulfilled, P wishes to know if he is bound by the promise to pay higher wages.

Central London Property Trust Ltd v High Trees House Ltd [1957] 1 KB 130 King's Bench Division

This was an action in debt by a landlord company against a tenant company claiming arrears of rent, for the year of 1945 only, in respect of a block of flats let during the war years. The arrears were based on the amount of rent payable as stipulated in the formal lease, but the tenant claimed that the landlord had agreed to take a reduced rent from 1941 because of the difficulty of letting the flats during the war.

Denning J: ... If I were to consider this matter without regard to recent developments in the law, there is no doubt that, had the plaintiffs claimed it, they would have been entitled to recover ground rent at the rate of £2,500 a year from the beginning of the term, since the lease under which it was payable was a lease under seal which, according to the old common law, could not be varied by an agreement by parol (whether in writing or not), but only by deed. Equity, however, stepped in, and said that if there had been a variation of a deed by a simple contract (which in the case of a lease required to be in writing would have to be evidenced by writing), the courts may give effect to it as is shown in *Berry v Berry*. That equitable doctrine, however, could hardly apply in the present case because the variation here might be said to have been made without consideration. With regard to estoppel, the representation made in relation to reducing the rent was not a representation of an existing fact. It was a representation, in effect, as to the future, namely, that payment of the rent would not be enforced at the full rate but only at the reduced rate. Such a representation would not give rise to an estoppel because, as was said in *Jorden v Money*, a representation as to the future must be embodied as a contract or be nothing.

But what is the position in view of developments in the law in recent years? The law has not been standing still since *Jorden v Money*. There has been a series of decisions over the past 50 years which, although they are said to be cases of estoppel are not really such. They are cases in which a promise was made which was intended to create legal relations and which, to the knowledge of the person making the promise, was going to be acted on by the person to whom it was made, and which was in fact so acted on. In such cases the courts have said that the promise must be honoured ... The logical consequence, no doubt, is that a promise to accept a smaller sum in discharge of a larger sum, if acted upon, is binding notwithstanding the absence of consideration: and if the fusion of law and equity leads to this result, so much the better ...

I am satisfied that a promise such as that to which I have referred is binding and the only question remaining for my consideration is the scope of the promise in the present case. I am satisfied on all the evidence that the promise here was that the ground rent should be reduced to £1,250 a year as a temporary expedient while the block of flats was not fully, or substantially fully let, owing to the conditions prevailing. That means that the reduction in the rent applied throughout the years down to the end of 1944, but early in 1945 it is plain that the flats were fully let, and, indeed, the rents received from them (many of them not being affected by the Rent Restrictions Acts), were increased beyond the figure at which it was originally contemplated that they would be let. At all events the rent from them must have been very considerable. I find that the conditions prevailing at the time when the reduction in rent was made, had completely passed away by the early months of 1945. I am satisfied that the promise was understood by all parties only to apply under the conditions prevailing at the time when it was made, namely, when the flats were only partially let, and that it did not extend any further than that. When the flats became fully let, early in 1945, the reduction ceased to apply.

In those circumstances, under the law as I hold it, it seems to me that rent is payable at the full rate for the quarters ending September 29 and December 25, 1945.

If the case had been one of estoppel it might be said that in any event the estoppel would cease when the conditions to which the representation applied came to an end, or it also might be said that it would only come to an end on notice. In either case it is only a way of ascertaining what is the scope of the representation. I prefer to apply the principle that a promise intended to be binding, intended to be acted on and in fact acted on, is binding so far as its terms properly apply. Here it was binding as covering the period down to the early part of 1945, and as from that time full rent is payable.

I therefore give judgment for the plaintiff company for the amount claimed.

Questions

1. Is this an example of equity modifying a contract? Did not the landlord have the contractual right to the full rent? Was the landlord in effect estopped in equity from abusing his common law right?

2. If the facts of *High Trees* arose again today, would recourse to equity still be necessary?

Crabb v Arun District Council [1976] Ch 179 Court of Appeal

This was an action for a declaration that the plaintiff had a right of access over the defendants' land in order to reach one of his plots which no longer had an access owing to the sale of part of his land. The plaintiff claimed that he would not have gone ahead with the sale of part of his property if the council representative had not given the clear impression in discussions that the plaintiff would be granted access at point B. The council at first left a gap at point B, but later fenced it off, denying the plaintiff access unless he paid £3,000 for such a right. The Court of Appeal granted the declaration.

Lord Denning MR: ... When counsel for Mr Crabb said that he put his case on an estoppel, it shook me a little, because it is commonly supposed that estoppel is not itself a cause of action. But that is because there are estoppels and estoppels. Some do give rise to a cause of action. Some do not. In the species of estoppel called proprietary estoppel, it does give rise to a cause of action. We had occasion to consider it a month ago in *Moorgate Mercantile Co Ltd v Twitchings* where I said that the effect of estoppel on the true owner may be that:

> "his own title to the property, be it land or goods, has been held to be limited or extinguished, and new rights and interests have been created therein. And this operates by reason of his conduct – what he has led the other to believe – even though he never intended it."

The new rights and interests, so created by estoppel in or over land, will be protected by the courts and in this way give rise to a cause of action ...

The basis of this proprietary estoppel – as indeed of promissory estoppel – is the interposition of equity. Equity comes in, true to form, to mitigate the rigours of strict law. The early cases did not speak of it as 'estoppel'. They spoke of it as 'raising an equity' ...

What then are the dealings which will preclude him from insisting on his strict legal rights? If he makes a binding contract that he will not insist on the strict legal position, a court of equity will hold him to his contract. Short of a binding contract, if he makes a promise that he will not insist upon his strict legal rights – even though that promise may be unenforceable in point of law for want of consideration or want of writing – and if he makes the promise knowing or intending that the other will act upon it, and he does act upon it, then again a court of equity will not allow him to go back on that promise: see *Central London Property Trust Ltd v High Trees House Ltd* and *Charles Rickards Ltd v Oppenheim*. Short of an actual promise, if he, by his words or conduct, so behaves as to lead another to believe that he will not insist on his strict legal rights – knowing or intending that the other will act on that belief – and he does so act, that again will raise an equity in favour of the other, and it is for a court of equity to say in what way the equity may be satisfied. The cases show that this equity does not depend on agreement but on words or conduct. In *Ramsden v Dyson* Lord Kingsdown spoke of a verbal agreement 'or what amounts to the same thing, an expectation, created or encouraged'. In *Birmingham and District Land Co v London and North Western Railway Co*, Cotton LJ said that '... what passed did not make a new agreement, but what took place ... raised an equity against him' ...

The question then is: were the circumstances here such as to raise an equity in favour of Mr Crabb? True the council on the deeds had the title to their land, free of any access at point B. But they led Mr Crabb to believe that he had or would be granted a right of access at point B ...

The council actually put up the gates at point B at considerable expense. That certainly led Mr Crabb to believe that they agreed that he should have the right of access through point B without more ado ...

The council knew that Mr Crabb intended to sell the two portions separately and that he would need an access at point B as well as point A. Seeing that they knew of his intention – and they did nothing to disabuse him, but rather confirmed it by erecting gates at point B – it was their conduct which led him to act as he did; and this raises an equity in favour against them ...

Questions

1. Did the plaintiff gain a *ius in rem* as a result of the injunction? Would a continental lawyer classify this case in the law of obligations?

2. How, and in what court, would this case have been decided in France? Do you think the status of the defendant influenced the Court of Appeal in *Crabb*?

3. Was there not promise and consideration in this case?

(c) Third parties

Jackson v Horizon Holidays Ltd [1975] 1 WLR 1468 Court of Appeal

(See p 121)

Beswick v Beswick [1968] AC 58 House of Lords

(See p 154)

Notes and questions

1. Three-party situations have presented problems in the law of contract since Roman times. Both in civil law and in the common law the idea that one person could use contract to the benefit or the burden of a third party has been only reluctantly overcome and then, usually, by recourse either to fiction or to tort. The reason in the civil law for this reluctance is to be found in the idea of an *in personam* obligation itself: an obligation is a *vinculum juris* (legal chain) which binds only two named parties. If contract could confer rights or duties on third parties, then it would become a matter of *iura in rem*. In the common law, which did not inherit the legacy of Roman legal science, the problem of the third party is founded in the notion of consideration which must move from the promisee. *Beswick* indicates that the doctrine remains alive, although it is likely that legislation will intervene sooner or later. Why do you think it is that the judges, who have often criticised the doctrine of privity, have not actually reformed the law themselves?

2. *Jackson* shows how the courts can outflank the doctrine if they wish. Sometimes this is done through the use of the tort of negligence (although the economic loss rule can present a problem)[4]; at other times the courts find a collateral contract between one of the main contractors and the third party.[5] What is interesting about *Jackson* is that it uses the law of remedies (damages) to allow the third parties to obtain compensation. The reasoning in the case has been criticised, subsequently, by the House of Lords in *Woodar Investment Development Ltd v Wimpey Construction UK Ltd*,[6] but the actual decision was upheld. Does *Jackson* confirm that the law of actions in English law continues to play an important independent and creative role in the development of the law of obligations?

4 MISTAKE

(a) Introduction

William Sindall Plc v Cambridgeshire County Council [1994] 1 WLR 1016 Court of Appeal

Evans LJ: This could be a textbook case on the law of mistake in contract. Cambridgeshire sold 6.71 acres of land, which had been used for nearly 20 years

---

4   See eg, *Smith v Eric Bush* [1990] 1 AC 831; *White v Jones* [1995] 1 A11 ER 691 (HL).
5   See eg, *The Eurymedon* [1975] AC 154.
6   [1980] 1 WLR 277.

as a school playing field, to a firm of builders, Sindall, who intended to develop an estate of about 70 houses and 30 flats. The sale was duly completed in March 1989 but then Sindall's troubles began. Obtaining detailed planning permission took longer than had been expected and by October 1990 that process was far from complete. Meanwhile, the value of the land, even with planning permission, had fallen dramatically due to the general decline in market prices. The contract price in 1988 was £5,082,500. The value in 1990 was less than half that figure. Sindall had borrowed the whole of the amount which they had paid, and interest rates were high.

Then came the chance discovery in October 1990 of a sewage pipe crossing the land diagonally about two metres below the surface. Because the land had been used as a playing field, the manhole which would have revealed its existence had been covered and grassed over. The pipe carried foul sewage, as opposed to surface water drainage, from a neighbouring block of flats owned by the Cambridge City Council. It discharged into a public sewer outside the boundary on the far corner of the site. It also served a building, the youth centre, which had been constructed on that part of the site but which would inevitably be demolished in order to make room for the housing development planned.

Neither Sindall nor the officers of Cambridgeshire at the time of the sale knew of the existence of the sewer. Sindall seek to set aside the contract and thus to recover the sum of £5,082,500 which they paid in 1989, on grounds of misrepresentation and mistake. The judge held that they are entitled to do so, and Cambridgeshire now appeals, contending that Sindall are not entitled to any remedy, or alternatively, that Sindall should be restricted to a claim for damages under section 2(1) of the Misrepresentation Act 1967.

First, mistake. There are certain circumstances in which the courts will hold that an agreement made between two parties, each labouring under fundamental mistake, is invalid as a contract, that is to say, it has no legal effect. The judge applied the test established by the majority judgments of the House of Lords in *Bell v Lever Brothers* [1932] AC 161 as defined by Steyn J in *Associated Japanese Bank (International) Ltd v Crédit du Nord SA* [1989] I WLR 255, and he reached the following conclusion: "there are undoubtedly important differences between what was contracted for and what was purchased. They do not, as it seems to me, meet the essential test of being essentially and radically different." There is no appeal against that finding or against the judge's conclusion that the builders failed to establish any common law remedy on the basis of mistake. I would add merely this, that the concept of a factual situation "essentially and radically different" from that by reference to which the parties made their agreement is the same concept, in my view, as that which may lead to frustration of the contract where there has been a change in circumstances due to a supervening event. Before 1956, there was much debate as to the legal basis for the discharge of contracts by frustration, but this was authoritatively settled by the House of Lords in *Davis Contractors Ltd v Fareham Urban District Council* [1956] AC 696 and in particular by the speech of Viscount Radcliffe, at p 729:

> "frustration occurs whenever the law recognises that without default of either party a contractual obligation has become incapable of being performed because the circumstances in which performance is called for

would render it a thing radically different from that which was undertaken by the contract. *Non haec in foedera veni.* It was not this that I promised to do."

The judge proceeded to consider Sindall's claim for rescission on the ground of mutual mistake, that is to say, for the equitable remedy which is available in circumstances like those described by Denning LJ in *Solle v Butcher* [1950] I KB 671, 692. He found in this context that there was "such a mistake as would entitle equity to order rescission". This implies that the mistake was "fundamental" *(per* Denning LJ, at p 693) and the question arises whether simultaneously the mistake can be fundamental yet the land not "essentially and radically different" from what it was supposed to be. But it is unnecessary and inappropriate, in my judgment, to consider this issue at this stage, because on any view of the matter, as Mr Sher I think accepts, the first question is whether the contract on its true construction covers the new situation which has arisen by reason of a change of circumstances (frustration) or the emergence of a factual situation different from that which was assumed (mutual mistake). If the scope of the contract is wide enough to cover the new, or newly discovered, situation, then there is no room either for discharge by frustration or for rescission in equity on the grounds of mistake. Put another way, if the agreed terms provide for this situation, then the parties have "allocated the risk" as between themselves, as Mr Etherton submits that they did in the present case ...

Equitable mistake

Logically, there remains the question whether the contract, notwithstanding that on its true construction it covers the situation which has arisen, and that it cannot be set aside for misrepresentation, nevertheless may be rescinded on the ground of equitable mistake, as defined by Denning LJ in *Solle v Butcher* [1950] 1 KB 671. It must be assumed, I think, that there is a category of mistake which is "fundamental", so as to permit the equitable remedy of rescission, which is wider than the kind of "serious and radical" mistake which means that the agreement is void and of no effect in law: see Chitty on *Contracts*, 26th ed (1989), vol 1, para 401; Treitel, *The Law of Contract*, 8th ed (1991), p 276; and Cheshire, Fifoot and Furmston's *Law of Contract*, 11th ed (1991), p 245. The difference may be that the common law rule is limited to mistakes with regard to the subject matter of the contract, whilst equity can have regard to a wider and perhaps unlimited category of "fundamental" mistake. However, that may be, I am satisfied that the judge's finding in the present case was vitiated by his assumption that the presence of the sewer and of the city's easement had serious consequences for the proposed development, even if the sewer was incorporated into the public sewer that was envisaged for the development itself (option 2A). This would not involve the loss of seven houses and three flats, as the judge appears to have thought, but, at most, of one three-bedroomed house. The additional cost of the alterations to the sewer would not have exceeded about £20,000. Given the breadth of the contract terms, in particular condition No 14 which on its face was intended to cover precisely such a situation as this, and the relatively minor consequences of the discovery of the sewer, even if some period of delay as well as additional cost was involved, it is impossible to hold, in my judgment, that there is scope for rescission here ...

Notes and questions

1. Mistake is one area of the law of contract where the distinction between promise and agreement has a practical effect. In French law, where contract is based on consent and agreement, it logically follows that mistake ought in principle to be a vitiating factor: for if the parties have agreed on the basis of an error then there cannot be true agreement. In a system where promise is the basis of a contract it does not logically have to follow that mistake will nullify the contract since a promise is a promise even if based on a mistake. In other words one does not need to look into the minds of one or both of the parties; one need only look at the objective promise. Here is the reason why the common law (as opposed to equity) has no doctrine of mistake (see *Bell v Lever Bros*, below). However, as Evans LJ points out, there some situations where the court will seemingly set aside a contract based on mistake; these cases are not, it must be stressed, in theory based on some substantive doctrine of error. They are either offer and acceptance problems, where the court holds that the mistake vitiates the formation of a contract, or implied condition precedent problems, where the court holds that there is an implied condition that, for example, the object of the contract is in existence or is of a certain quality (see *Financings Ltd v Stimson*, below). Is this approach now outdated? Ought the courts to start thinking in terms of a substantive doctrine of error?

2. Before answering the questions posed above, consider the following problem. B sees an old painting in a junk shop and asks P, the owner, how much he wants to sell it for. P says he thinks the painting is by a minor artist and is worth around £500 and he offers it to B for £480 which B readily accepts. Having purchased the picture B takes it to an antiques expert for a valuation and the expert says that the picture is a missing masterpiece by a major artist and is worth at least half a million pounds. The find is widely reported in the press and P is much put out. Can P ask for the contract to be set aside? Would your answer be different if B had verbally agreed with P that the painting was by a minor artist knowing full well that it was not?

3. When viewed from the position of a substantive law of contract mistake may seem to lack any fundamental principles. If one shifts to the law of remedies the position changes quite dramatically in that there are a number of remedies which become available depending on the kind of error in issue. If the source of the error is a statement by one of the contracting parties ("this painting is by Constable" or "this car has done only 20,000 miles") then there may be remedies for misrepresentation or, sometimes, for breach of contract (see *Dick Bentley*, below). If the source of the error cannot be attributed to a

pre-contractual statement, then one of the parties will usually be seeking either to have the contract declared void (an action for a declaration) or to enforce a contract that the other party is refusing to perform (specific performance or damages). If the error concerns a document a special defence of *non est factum* (this is not my deed) comes into play; and if the mistake concerns the identity of a person the tort of conversion is usually the remedy in play since mistake of identity often involves property problems. In fact many cases involving *non est factum* and mistake of identity deserve to be classed more in the law of property than the law of obligations. Why do you think it is that the common law distinguishes between misrepresentation and mistake?

4. One fundamental remedy distinction that must always be borne in mind when dealing with mistake and misrepresentation problems is the difference between the remedy of damages at common law and the remedy of rescission in equity (see Chapter 3). A party who has entered a contract under a misrepresentation made by the other party can in principle ask the court to rescind the contract in equity; and such rescission will be available irrespective of fault. Thus, even if the misrepresentation was made on reasonable grounds, the representee can, in principle, still ask the court for rescission. However, the court now has power to grant damages in lieu of the equitable remedy of rescission in non-fraudulent misrepresentation cases (see Misrepresentation Act 1967 s 2(2)). If a contracting party suffers loss as a result of the misrepresentation the common law remedy of damages might be available if the representee suffering the loss can establish (i) the tort of deceit (as modified by the Misrepresentation Act 1967 s 2(1)); (ii) the tort of negligence (see *Hedley Byrne*, below); or (iii) breach of contract (or a collateral contract). Before *Hedley Byrne* it was extremely difficult to found a damages action in tort since deceit required proof of fraud (see *Bradford v Borders*, below); and even after 1964 establishing all the requirements for an action in negligence was not easy. The effect of the 1967 Act is to remove the requirement of proving fraud or negligence in a damages claim for misrepresentation, although if a defendant can establish that he was not negligent he will have a defence. What if a representee can establish all the requirements for the equitable remedy of rescission: ought this to be enough to found a damages action as well?[7]

5. The equitable remedy of rescission may also be available for mistake as well as misrepresentation. Thus there are now, seemingly, two

---

7   Cf *Banque Keyser Ullmann v Skandia Insurance* [1990] 1 QB 665 CA; [1992] 2 AC 249 HL.

doctrines of mistake in contract: there is the position at common law (offer and acceptance and implied condition precedent) and the position in equity (remedy of rescission). When viewed from the position in equity it may be that the courts take a broad view: rescission depends upon the circumstances of each case and is in principle available to prevent unjustified enrichment or to stop abuses of power or rights. When analysing factual problems involving error it is, then, worth keeping these two broad principles in mind. Is this distinction between common law and equity helpful or should the courts move towards developing a single doctrine?

(b) Liability in contract

Hopkins v Tanqueray (1854) 139 ER 369 Court of Common Pleas

(See p 216)

Dick Bently Productions Ltd v Harold Smith (Motors) Ltd [1965] 1 WLR 623 Court of Appeal

Lord Denning MR: The plaintiff, Charles Walter Bentley, sometimes known as Dick Bentley, brings an action against Harold Smith (Motors) Ltd for damages for breach of warranty on the sale of a car ... The county court judge found that there was a warranty, that it was broken, and that the damages were more than £400; but as the claim was limited to £400, he gave judgment for the plaintiff for that amount.

The first point is whether this representation, namely, that it had done 20,000 miles only since it had been fitted with a replacement engine and gearbox, was an innocent misrepresentation (which does not give rise to damages), or whether it was a warranty. It was said by Holt CJ, and repeated in *Heilbut, Symons & Co v Buckleton*, that: "An affirmation at the time of the sale is a warranty, provided it appear on evidence to be so intended". But that word "intended" has given rise to difficulties. I endeavoured to explain in *Oscar Chess Ltd v Williams* that the question whether a warranty was intended depends on the conduct of the parties, on their words and behaviour, rather than on their thoughts. If an intelligent bystander would reasonably infer that a warranty was intended, that will suffice. What conduct, then? What words and behaviour lead to the inference of a warranty?

Looking at the cases once more as we have done so often, it seems to me that if a representation is made in the course of dealings for a contract for the very purpose of inducing the other party to act upon it, and actually inducing him to act upon it, by entering into the contract, that is *prima facie* ground for inferring that it was intended as a warranty. It is not necessary to speak of it as being collateral. Suffice it that it was intended to be acted upon and was in fact acted on. But the maker of the representation can rebut this inference if he can show that it really was an innocent misrepresentation, in that he was in fact innocent of fault in making it, and that it would not be reasonable in the circumstances for him to be bound by it. In the *Oscar Chess* case the inference was rebutted. There a man had bought a second-hand car and received with it a log-book which stated the year of the car, 1948. He afterwards resold the car. When he resold it he simply repeated what was in the log-book and passed it on to the buyer. He honestly believed on reasonable grounds that it was true. He was completely innocent of any fault. There was no warranty by him, but only an innocent misrepresentation. Whereas in the present case it is very different. The inference is not rebutted. Here we have a dealer, Smith, who was in a position to know, or at least to find out, the history of the car. He could get it by writing to the makers. He did not do so. Indeed, it was done later. When the history of this car was examined, his statement turned out to be quite wrong. He ought to have known better. There was no reasonable foundation for it ...

The judge found that the representations were not dishonest. Smith was not guilty of fraud. But he made the statement as to 20,000 miles without any foundation. And the judge was well justified in finding that there was a warranty ...

It seems to me that on this point there is nothing wrong in the way the judge has dealt with the case, and therefore ... I would hold the appeal fails and should be dismissed.

Danckwerts LJ: I agree with the judgment of Lord Denning MR.

Salmon LJ: I agree. I have no doubt at all that the judge reached a correct conclusion when he decided that Smith gave a warranty to the plaintiff and that that warranty was broken. Was what Smith said intended and understood as a legally binding promise? If so, it was a warranty and as such may be part of the contract of sale or collateral to it. In effect, Smith said: "If you will enter into a contract to buy this motor car from me for £1,850, I undertake that you will be getting a motor car which has done no more than 20,000 miles since it was fitted with a new engine and a new gearbox". I have no doubt at all that what was said by Smith was so understood and was intended to be so understood by Bentley. I accordingly agree that the appeal should be dismissed.

Questions

1. 'Where there is a contract for the sale of goods by description, there is an implied condition (now 'term') that the goods will correspond with the description' (Sale of Goods Act 1979 s 13(1)). Why did the plaintiff not seek damages under this section?
2. Is this a collateral contract case?
3. If these facts occurred again today, would the plaintiff have to rely upon the law of contract in order to get damages?
4. Did the plaintiff get what he contracted for in (i) *Hopkins v Tanqueray* and (ii) *Dick Bentley*?
5. To what extent was the status of the defendant of importance in *Dick Bentley*?
6. If *Hopkins v Tanqueray* had arisen after the Sales of Goods Act 1893, would the result have been different?

(c) Liability in tort

(i) Deceit

Bradford Building Society v Borders [1941] 2 All ER 205 House of Lords

Viscount Maugham: ... My Lords, we are dealing here with a common law action of deceit, which requires four things to be established. First, there must be a representation of fact made by words, or, it may be, by conduct. The phrase will include a case where the defendant has manifestly approved and adopted a representation made by some third person. On the other hand, mere silence, however morally wrong, will not support an action of deceit: *Peek v Gurney per* Lord Chelmsford, and *per* Lord Cairns, and *Arkwright v Newbold*. Secondly, the representation must be made with a knowledge that it is false. It must be wilfully false, or at least made in the absence of any genuine belief that it is true: *Derry v Peek* and *Nocton v Ashburton (Lord)*. Thirdly, it must be made with the intention that it should be acted upon by the plaintiff, or by a class of persons which will include the plaintiff, in the manner which resulted in damage to him: *Peek v Gurney* and *Smith v Chadwick*. If, however, fraud be established, it is immaterial that there was no intention to cheat or injure the person to whom the false statement was made: *Derry v Peek*, and *Peek v Gurney*. Fourthly, it must be proved that the plaintiff has acted upon the false statement and has sustained damage by so doing: *Clarke v Dickson*. I am not, of course, attempting to make a complete statement of the law of deceit, but only to state the main facts which a plaintiff must establish ...

(ii) Negligence

Hedley Byrne & Co v Heller & Partners Ltd [1964] AC 465 House of Lords

This was an action for damages brought by a firm of advertising agents against a bank in respect of financial loss incurred by the agents when one of their clients, to whom they had extended credit, went into liquidation. The advertising agents had extended the credit on the basis of a credit reference supplied by the defendant bank. The bank denied liability on the ground either that they owed no duty of care to the agency or that they were protected by an exclusion clause. The House of Lords, while giving judgment for the bank on the basis of the clause, nevertheless decided that such facts could give rise to a duty of care.

Lord Reid: ... The appellants' first argument was based on *Donoghue v Stevenson*. That is a very important decision, but I do not think that it has any direct bearing on this case. That decision may encourage us to develop existing lines of authority, but it cannot entitle us to disregard them. Apart altogether from authority, I would think that the law must treat negligent words differently from negligent acts. The law ought so far as possible to reflect the standards of the reasonable man, and that is what *Donoghue v Stevenson* sets out to do. The most obvious difference between negligent words and negligent acts is this. Quite careful people often express definite opinions on social or informal occasions even when they see that others are likely to be influenced by them; and they often do that without taking that care which they would take if asked for their opinion professionally or in a business connection. The appellant agrees that there can be no duty of care on such occasions, and we were referred to American and South African authorities where that is recognised, although their law appears to have gone much further than ours has yet done. But it is at least unusual casually to put into circulation negligently made articles which are dangerous. A man might give a friend a negligently-prepared bottle of home-made wine and his friend's guests might drink it with dire results. But it is by no means clear that those guests would have no action against the negligent manufacturer.

Another obvious difference is that a negligently made article will only cause one accident, and so it is not very difficult to find the necessary degree of proximity or neighbourhood between the negligent manufacturer and the person injured. But words can be broadcast with or without the consent or the foresight of the speaker or writer. It would be one thing to say that the speaker owes a duty to a limited class, but it would be going very far to say that he owes a duty to every ultimate "consumer" who acts on those words to his detriment. It would be no use to say that a speaker or writer owes a duty but can disclaim responsibility if he wants to. He, like the manufacturer, could make it part of a contract that he is not to be liable for his negligence: but that contract would not protect him in a question with a third party, at least if the third party was unaware of it.

So it seems to me that there is good sense behind our present law that in general an innocent but negligent misrepresentation gives no cause of action. There must be something more than the mere misstatement. I therefore turn to the authorities to see what more is required. The most natural requirement would be that expressly or by implication from the circumstances the speaker or writer has undertaken some responsibility, and that appears to me not to conflict with any authority which is binding on this House ...

A reasonable man, knowing that he was being trusted or that his skill and judgment were being relied on, would, I think have three courses open to him. He could keep silent or decline to give the information or advice sought: or he could give an answer with a clear qualification that he accepted no responsibility for it or that it was given without that reflection or inquiry which a careful answer would require: or he could simply answer without any such qualification. If he chooses to adopt the last course he must, I think, be held to have accepted some responsibility for his answer being given carefully, or to have accepted a relationship with the inquirer which requires him to exercise such care as the circumstances require ...

The appellants founded on a number of cases in contract where very clear words were required to exclude the duty of care which would otherwise have flowed from the contract. To that argument there are, I think, two answers. In the case of a contract it is necessary to exclude liability for negligence, but in this case the question is whether an undertaking to assume duty to take care can be inferred: and that is a very different matter. And, secondly, even in cases of contract general words may be sufficient if there was no other kind of liability to be excluded except liability for negligence: the general rule is that a party is not exempted from liability for negligence "unless adequate words are used" – *per* Scrutton LJ in *Rutter v Palmer*. It being admitted that there was here a duty to give an honest reply, I do not see what further liability there could be to exclude except liability for negligence: there being no contract there was no question of warranty.

I am therefore of opinion that it is clear that the respondents never undertook any duty to exercise care in giving their replies. The appellants cannot succeed unless there was such a duty and therefore in my judgment this appeal must be dismissed.

Lord Morris: ... My Lords, I consider that it follows and that it should now be regarded as settled that if someone possessed of a special skill undertakes, quite irrespective of contract, to apply that skill for the assistance of another person who relies upon such skill, a duty of care will arise. The fact that the service is to be given by means of or by the instrumentality of words can make no difference. Furthermore, if in a sphere in which a person is so placed that others could reasonably rely upon his judgment or his skill or upon his ability to make careful inquiry, a person takes it upon himself to give information or advice to, or allows his information or advice to be passed on to, another person who, as he knows or should know, will place reliance upon it, then a duty of care will arise ...

Lord Devlin: ... [T]he distinction is now said to depend on whether financial loss is caused through physical injury or whether it is caused directly. The interposition of the physical injury is said to make a difference of principle. I can find neither logic nor common sense in this. If irrespective of contract, a doctor negligently advises a patient that he can safely pursue his occupation and he cannot and the patient's health suffers and he loses his livelihood, the patient has a remedy. But if the doctor negligently advises him that he cannot safely pursue his occupation when in fact he can and he loses his livelihood, there is said to be no remedy. Unless, of course, the patient was a private patient and the doctor accepted half a guinea for his trouble: then the patient can recover all. I am bound to say my Lords, that I think this to be nonsense. It is not the sort of nonsense that can arise even in the best system of law out of the need to draw nice distinctions between borderline cases. It arises, if it is the law, simply out of a refusal to make sense. The line is not drawn on any intelligible principle. It just happens to be the line which those who have been driven from the extreme assertion that negligent statements in the absence of contractual or fiduciary duty give no cause of action have in the course of their retreat so far reached ...

I think ... that there is ample authority to justify your Lordships in saying now that the categories of special relationships which may give rise to a duty to take care in word as well as in deed are not limited to contractual relationships or to relationships of fiduciary duty, but include also relationships which in the words of Lord Shaw in *Nocton v Lord Ashburton* are "equivalent to contract", that is, where there is an assumption of responsibility in circumstances in which, but for the absence of consideration, there would be a contract. Where there is an express undertaking, an express warranty as distinct from mere representation, there can be little difficulty. The difficulty arises in discerning those cases in which the undertaking is to be implied. In this respect the absence of consideration is not irrelevant. Payment for information or advice is very good evidence that it is being relied upon and that the informer or adviser knows that it is. Where there is no consideration, it will be necessary to exercise greater care in distinguishing between social and professional relationships and between those which are of a contractual character and those which are not. It may often be material to consider whether the adviser is acting purely out of good nature or whether he is getting his reward in some indirect form. The service that a bank performs in giving a reference is not done simply out of a desire to assist commerce. It would discourage the customers of the bank if their deals fell through because the bank had refused to testify to their credit when it was good ...

Lord Pearce: ... To import such a duty the representation must normally, I think, concern a business or professional transaction whose nature makes clear the gravity of the inquiry and the importance and influence attached to the answer ...

Questions

1. Is *Hedley Byrne*, in effect, an extension of the tort of deceit?
2. Is it an extension of the law of contract?
3. Is it an extension of the equitable notion of fiduciary relationship?
4. Is *Hedley Byrne* an extension of the *Donoghue v Stevenson* principle or is it a new principle within the law of tort?

(iii) Statute

Misrepresentation Act 1967 (c 7)

1. Removal of certain bars to rescission for innocent misrepresentation

Where a person has entered into a contract after a misrepresentation has been made to him, and

(a) the misrepresentation has become a term of the contract; or

(b) the contract has been performed; or both, then, if otherwise he would be entitled to rescind the contract without alleging fraud, he shall be so entitled, subject to the provisions of this Act, notwithstanding the matters mentioned in paragraphs (a) and (b) of this section.

2. Damages for misrepresentation

(1) Where a person has entered into a contract after a misrepresentation has been made to him by another party thereto and as a result thereof he has suffered loss, then, if the person making the misrepresentation would be liable to damages in respect thereof had the misrepresentation been made fraudulently, that person shall be so liable notwithstanding that the misrepresentation was not made fraudulently, unless he proves that he had reasonable ground to believe and did believe up to the time the contract was made that the facts represented were true.

(2) Where a person has entered into a contract after a misrepresentation has been made to him otherwise than fraudulently and he would be entitled, by reason of the misrepresentation, to rescind the contract, then, if it is claimed, in any proceedings arising out of the contract, that the contract ought to be or has been rescinded, the court or arbitrator may declare the contract subsisting and award damages in lieu of rescission, if of opinion that it would be equitable to do so,

having regard to the nature of the misrepresentation and the loss that would be caused by it if the contract were upheld, as well as to the loss that rescission would cause to the other party.

(3) Damages may be awarded against a person under subsection (2) of this section whether or not he is liable to damages under subsection (1) thereof, but where he is so liable any award under the said subsection (2) shall be taken into account in assessing his liability under the said subsection (1).

Questions

1. Is misrepresentation part of the law of contract or of tort?
2. Are all breaches of contract torts?
3. Is an action for damages under s 2(1) of the 1967 Act an action in the tort of deceit?
4. Can one now get damages for innocent misrepresentation?

(d) Rescission in equity

Redgrave v Hurd (1881) 20 ChD 1 Court of Appeal

This was an action, brought by the seller, for specific performance of a contract to buy a house and solicitor's practice. The defendant counterclaimed for rescission of the contract on the basis that the plaintiff had seriously misrepresented the amount of income from the business. It appeared that the defendant had not examined the books of the business to see if the plaintiff's representations were accurate; and the trial judge gave judgment for the plaintiff on the basis that the defendant ought to have examined the books and papers. An appeal to the Court of Appeal was allowed.

Jessel MR: ... As regards the rescission of a contract, there was no doubt a difference between the rules of courts of equity and the rules of courts of common law – a difference which, of course, has now disappeared by the operation of the Judicature Act, which makes the rules of equity prevail. According to the decisions of court of equity it was not necessary, in order to set aside a contract obtained by material false representation, to prove that the party who obtained it knew at the time when the representation was made that it was false. It was put in two ways, either of which was sufficient. One way of putting the case was, "A man is not to be allowed to get a benefit from a statement which he now admits to be false. He is not to be allowed to say, for the purpose of civil jurisdiction, that when he made it he did not know it to be false; he ought to have found that out before he made it." The other way of putting it was this: "Even assuming that moral fraud must be shown in order to set aside a contract, you have it where a man, having obtained a beneficial contract by a statement which he now knows to be false, insists upon keeping that contract. To do so is a moral delinquency: no man ought to seek to take advantage of his own false statements." The rule in equity was settled, and it does not matter on which of the two grounds it was rested ...

There is another proposition of law of very great importance which I think it is necessary for me to state, because, with great deference to the very learned judge from whom this appeal comes, I think it is not quite accurately stated in his judgment. If a man is induced to enter into a contract by a false representation it is not a sufficient answer to him to say, "If you had used due diligence you would have found out that the statement was untrue. You had the means afforded you of discovering its falsity, and did not choose to avail yourself of them." I take it to be a settled doctrine of equity, not only as regards specific performance but also as regards rescission, that this is not an answer ... One of the most familiar instances in modern times is where men issue a prospectus in which they make false statements of the contracts made before the formation of a company, and then say that the contracts themselves may be inspected at the offices of the solicitors. It has always been held that those who accepted those false statements as true were not deprived of their remedy merely because they neglected to go and look at the contracts. Another instance with which we are familiar is where a vendor makes a false statement as to the contents of a lease, as, for instance, that it contains no covenant preventing the carrying on of the trade which the purchaser is known by the vendor to be desirous of carrying on upon the property. Although the lease itself might be produced at the sale, or might have been open to the inspection of the purchaser long previously to the sale, it has been repeatedly held that the vendor cannot be allowed to say, "You were not entitled to give credit to my statement." It is not sufficient, therefore, to say that the purchaser had the opportunity of investigating the real state of the case, but did not avail himself of that opportunity ...

[W]hen a person makes a material representation to another to induce him to enter into a contract, and the other enters into that contract, it is not sufficient to say that the party to whom the representation is made does not prove that he entered into the contract relying upon the representation. If it is a material representation calculated to induce him to enter into the contract, it is an inference of law that he was induced by the representation to enter into it, and in order to take away his title to be relieved from the contract on the ground that the representation was untrue, it must be shown either that he had knowledge of the facts contrary to the representation, or that he stated in terms, or showed clearly by his conduct, that he did not rely on the representation. If you tell a man, "You may enter into partnership with me, my business is bringing in between £300 and £400 a year", the man who makes that representation must know that it is a material inducement to the other to enter into the partnership, and you cannot investigate as to whether it was more or less probable that the inducement would operate on the mind of the party to whom the representation was made. Where you have neither evidence that he knew facts to show that the statement was untrue, or that he said or did anything to show that he did not actually rely upon the statement, the inference remains that he did so rely, and the statement being a material statement, its being untrue is a sufficient ground for rescinding the contract ...

Questions

1. Who caused the defendant's damage?
2. Has the difference between the rules of the court of equity and the rules of the courts of common law disappeared?

Leaf v International Galleries [1950] 2 KB 86 Court of Appeal

This was a rescission action brought by the purchaser of a painting. In 1944 the plaintiff purchased a picture called "Salisbury Cathedral" from the defendant for £85. At the time of the purchase the defendant said that the picture was a Constable; but when the plaintiff came to sell the painting five years later he was informed that it had not been painted by Constable. The Court of Appeal dismissed the plaintiff's claim.

Denning LJ: The question is whether the plaintiff is entitled to rescind the contract on the ground that the picture in question was not painted by Constable. I emphasise that it is a claim to rescind only: there is no claim in this action for damages for breach of condition or breach of warranty. The claim is simply one for rescission ... No claim for damages is before us at all. The only question is whether the plaintiff is entitled to rescind.

The way in which the case is put by Mr Weitzman, on behalf of the plaintiff, is this: he says that this was an innocent misrepresentation and that in equity he is, or should be, entitled to claim rescission even of an executed contract of sale on that account. He points out that the judge has found that it is quite possible to restore the parties to their original position. It can be done by simply handing back the picture to the defendants.

In my opinion, this case is to be decided according to the well known principles applicable to the sale of goods. This was a contract for the sale of goods. There was a mistake about the quality of the subject-matter, because both parties believed the picture to be a Constable; and that mistake was in one sense essential or fundamental. But such a mistake does not avoid the contract: there was no mistake at all about the subject-matter of the sale. It was a specific picture, "Salisbury Cathedral". The parties were agreed in the same terms on the same subject-matter, and that is sufficient to make a contract: see *Solle v Butcher*.

There was a term in the contract as to the quality of the subject-matter: namely, as to the person by whom the picture was painted – that it was by Constable. That term of the contract was, according to our terminology, either a condition or a warranty. If it was a condition, the buyer could reject the picture for breach of the condition at any time before he accepted it, or is deemed to have accepted it; whereas, if it was only a warranty, he could not reject it at all but was confined to a claim for damages.

I think it right to assume in the buyer's favour that this term was a condition, and that, if he had come in proper time he could have rejected the picture, but the right to reject for breach of condition has always been limited by the rule that, once the buyer has accepted, or is deemed to have accepted, the goods in performance of the contract, then he cannot thereafter reject, but is relegated to his claim for damages: see s 11, sub-s 1 (c) of the Sale of Goods Act 1893, and *Wallis, Son & Wells v Pratt & Haynes*.

The circumstances in which a buyer is deemed to have accepted goods in performance of the contract are set out in s 35 of the Act, which says that the buyer is deemed to have accepted the goods, amongst other things, "when, after the lapse of a reasonable time, he retains the goods without intimating to the seller that he has rejected them". In this case the buyer took the picture into his house and, apparently, hung it there, and five years passed before he intimated any rejection at all. That, I need hardly say, is much more than a reasonable time. It is far too late for him at the end of five years to reject this picture for breach of any condition. His remedy after that length of time is for damages only, a claim which he has not brought before the court.

Is it to be said that the buyer is in any better position by relying on the representation, not as a condition, but as an innocent misrepresentation ? ...

Although rescission may in some cases be a proper remedy, it is to be remembered that an innocent misrepresentation is much less potent than a breach of condition; and a claim to rescission for innocent misrepresentation must at any rate be barred when a right to reject for breach of condition is barred. A condition is a term of the contract of a most material character, and if a claim to reject on that account is barred, it seems to me *a fortiori* that a claim to rescission on the ground of innocent misrepresentation is also barred.

So, assuming that a contract for the sale of goods may be rescinded in a proper case for innocent misrepresentation, the claim is barred in this case for the self-same reason as a right to reject is barred. The buyer has accepted the picture. He had ample opportunity for examination in the first few days after he bad bought it. Then was the time to see if the condition or representation was fulfilled. Yet he has kept it all this time. Five years have elapsed without any notice of rejection. In my judgment he cannot now claim to rescind. His only claim, if any, as the county court judge said, was one for damages, which he has not made in this action. In my judgment, therefore, the appeal should be dismissed.

Questions

1. Could the plaintiff in *Leaf* have sued the defendants for damages?
2. If the facts of *Leaf* occurred again today, could the plaintiff get damages under s 2(2) of the Misrepresentation Act 1967?
3. Section 35 of the Sale of Goods Act 1979 has now been amended by section 2 of the Sale and Supply of Goods Act 1994. How might the new s 35 effect the facts of *Leaf*?

Associated Japanese Bank (International) Ltd v Crédit du Nord [1989] 1 WLR 255 Queen's Bench Division

(See p 280)

(e) Error *in corpore*

Smith v Hughes (1871) LR 6 QB 597 Court of Queen's Bench

This was an action in debt brought by a farmer for the price of new oats sold to the defendant, a trainer of racehorses. The defendant did not want "new" oats - as the farmer knew – and thus he argued that he was not bound by the contract; but the plaintiff claimed that the defendant had offered to buy "good oats", making no mention of the word "old". The jury returned a verdict for the defendant and the plaintiff appealed. The Court of Queen's Bench ordered a new trial.

Cockburn CJ: ... [W]e must assume that nothing was said on the subject of the defendant's manager desiring to buy old oats, nor of the oats having been said to be old; while, on the other hand, we must assume that the defendant's manager believed the oats to be old oats, and that the plaintiff was conscious of the existence of such belief, but did nothing, directly or indirectly, to bring it about, simply offering his oats and exhibiting his sample, remaining perfectly passive as to what was passing in the mind of the other party. The question is whether, under such circumstances, the passive acquiescence of the seller in the self-deception of the buyer will entitle the latter to avoid the contract. I am of opinion that it will not.

The oats offered to the defendant's manager were a specific parcel, of which the sample submitted to him formed a part. He kept the sample for twenty-four hours, and had, therefore, full opportunity of inspecting it and forming his judgment upon it. Acting on his own judgment, he wrote to the plaintiff, offering him a price. Having this opportunity of inspecting and judging of the sample, he is practically in the same position as if he had inspected the oats in bulk. It cannot be said that, if he had gone and personally inspected the oats in bulk, and then, believing – but without anything being said or done by the seller to bring about such a belief – that the oats were old, had offered a price for them, he would have been justified in repudiating the contract, because the seller, from the known habits of the buyer, or other circumstances, had reason to infer that the buyer was ascribing to the oats a quality they did not possess, and did not undeceive him .

I take the true rule to be, that where a specific article is offered for sale, without express warranty, or without circumstances from which the law will imply a warranty – as where, for instance, an article is ordered for a specific purpose – and the buyer has full opportunity of inspecting and forming his own judgment, if he chooses to act on his own judgment, the rule *caveat emptor* applies ... The question is not what a man of scrupulous morality or nice honour would do under such circumstances ...

Blackburn J: ... The jury were directed that, if they believed the word "old" was used, they should find for the defendant – and this was right; for if that was the case, it is obvious that neither did the defendant intend to enter into a contract on the plaintiff's terms, that is, to buy this parcel of oats without any stipulation as to their quality; nor could the plaintiff have been led to believe he was intending to do so.

But the second direction raises the difficulty. I think that, if from that direction the jury would understand that they were first to consider whether they were satisfied that the defendant intended to buy this parcel of oats on the terms that it was part of his contract with the plaintiff that they were old oats, so as to have the warranty of the plaintiff to that effect, they were properly told that, if that was so, the defendant could not be bound to a contract without any such warranty unless the plaintiff was misled. But I doubt whether the direction would bring to the minds of the jury the distinction between agreeing to take the oats under the belief that they were old, and agreeing to take the oats under the belief that the plaintiff contracted that they were old.

The difference is the same as that between buying a horse believed to be sound, and buying one believed to be warranted sound; but I doubt if it was made obvious to the jury, and I doubt this the more because I do not see much evidence to justify a finding for the defendant on this latter ground if the word "old" was not used ... I agree, therefore, in the result that there should be a new trial.

Questions

1. Is this case authority for the proposition that English contract law has no doctrine of *bona fides*?

2. Who caused the buyer's loss?

3. Is this case authority for the proposition that silence is no misrepresentation?

4. Would this case be decided the same way today?

5. Is this case further evidence in support of the idea that English contract law is based on promise rather than agreement?

Bell v Lever Brothers Ltd [1932] AC 161 House of Lords

This was an action for rescission of two contracts, together with a claim for the repayment of monies paid thereunder, made between a company and two of its directors whereby the directors terminated their employment contracts in return for large compensation payments. After the compensation payments had been made, the company discovered that they could legally, and without compensation, have dismissed the two directors for breaches of their employments contracts. The jury found that the two directors had not fraudulently concealed their breaches. The trial judge, Court of Appeal and two Law Lords thought that the compensation contracts were void for mistake; a majority of the House of Lords thought that they were not.

Lord Atkin: ... Two points present themselves for decision. Was the agreement of March 19, 1929, void by reason of a mutual mistake ...?

Could the agreement of March 19, 1929, be avoided by reason of the failure of Mr Bell to disclose his misconduct ...?

My Lords, the rules of law dealing with the effect of mistake on contract appear to be established with reasonable clearness. If mistake operates at all it operates so as to negative or in some cases to nullify consent. The parties may be mistaken in the identity of the contracting parties, or in the existence of the subject-matter of the contract at the date of the contract, or in the quality of the subject-matter of the contract. These mistakes may be by one party, or by both, and the legal effect may depend upon the class of mistake above mentioned. Thus a mistaken belief by A that he is contracting with B whereas in fact he is contracting with C, will negative consent where it is clear that the intention of A was to contract only with B ...

Mistake as to quality of the thing contracted for raises more difficult questions. In such a case a mistake will not affect assent unless it is the mistake of both parties, and is as to the existence of some quality which makes the thing without the quality essentially different from the thing as it was believed to be ...

It is essential on this part of the discussion to keep in mind the finding of the jury acquitting the defendants of fraudulent misrepresentation or concealment in procuring the agreements in question. Grave injustice may be done to the defendants and confusion introduced into the legal conclusion, unless it is quite clear that in considering mistake in this case no suggestion of fraud is admissible and cannot strictly be regarded by the judge who has to determine the legal issues raised. The agreement which is said to be void is the agreement contained in the letter of March 19, 1929, that Bell would retire from the Board of the Niger Company ... and that in consideration of his doing so Levers would pay him as compensation the sum of £30,000 in full satisfaction ... I have come to the conclusion that it would be wrong to decide that an agreement to terminate a definite specified contract is void if it turns out that the agreement had already been broken and could have been terminated otherwise. The contract released is the identical contract in both cases, and the party paying for release gets exactly what he bargains for. It seems immaterial that he could have got the same result in another way, or that if he had known the true facts he would not have entered into the bargain. A buys B's horse; he thinks the horse is sound and he pays the price of a sound horse; he would certainly not have bought the horse if he had known, as the fact is, that the horse is unsound. If B has made no representation as to soundness and has not contracted that the horse is sound, A is bound and cannot recover back the price. A buys a picture from B; both A and B believe it to be the work of an old master, and a high price is paid. It turns out to be a modern copy. A has no remedy in the absence of representation or warranty ... A buys a roadside garage business from B abutting on a public thoroughfare: unknown to A, but known to B it has already been decided to construct a by-pass road which will divert substantially the whole of the traffic from passing A's garage. Again A has no remedy. All these cases involve hardship on A and benefit B, as most people would say, unjustly. They can be supported on the ground that it is of paramount importance that contracts should be observed, and that if parties honestly comply with the essentials of the formation of contracts ie, agree in the same terms on the same subject-matter they are bound, and must rely on the stipulations of the contract for protection from the effect of facts unknown to them.

[His Lordship then went on to hold that the defendants owed no duty to the Lever Company to disclose the impugned transactions.]

Lord Thankerton: ... [I]n the present case, there being no obligation to disclose [misconduct], Bell and Snelling, if they had had their misconduct in mind, would have been entitled to say nothing and Lever would have been bound by the contract. I have difficulty in seeing how the fact that Bell and Snelling did not remember at the time is to put Lever in a better position ...

Questions

1. Is the decision in this case inevitable given that English law does not in general treat silence as a misrepresentation?
2. Did the plaintiffs consent to the payments to the directors?

3. Did the directors unjustly enrich themselves at the expense of the plaintiffs?

4. If these facts arose again today would the contracts be voidable in equity?[8]

Sale of Goods Act 1979 (.54)

6. Goods which have perished

Where there is a contract for the sale of specific goods, and the goods without the knowledge of the seller have perished at the time when a contract is made, the contract is void.

Questions

1. Why is the contract 'void'?

2. S agrees to sell a wrecked ship to B and supplies B with details of its position on some reef in the ocean. B spends much time and money looking for the wreck but is never able to locate it. Can B sue S for breach of contract?

Financings Ltd v Stimson [1962] 1 WLR 1184 Court of Appeal

This was an action for damages for breach of contract brought by a finance company against a defendant who had signed a hire-purchase form at the premises of a motor dealer, paid a deposit, and then took possession of a car. The hire-purchase form stated that the hire-purchase contract would become binding only upon acceptance by the finance company. The defendant later returned the car to the dealer saying that he was dissatisfied with it and that he did not want to go on with the agreement; he also offered to forgo his deposit. Before the finance company had signed the agreement, but after the car had been returned to the dealer, the vehicle was stolen from the dealer's premises and severely damaged. The finance company then signed the agreement and claimed there was a contract. A majority of the Court of Appeal dismissed the finance company's claim for damages.

Donovan LJ: The dealer in this case was clearly the plaintiff finance company's agent to do a variety of things: to receive an offer of hire-purchase; to tell the proposed hire purchaser, the defendant, that the plaintiffs would accept the business; to ensure that comprehensive insurance was effected by the defendant; and thereafter to deliver the car to him. In the written hire-purchase form of agreement there was no clause negativing agency between the plaintiffs and the dealer. In these circumstances, authority to receive a notice of revocation of the hire-purchase offer was, in my opinion, within the dealer's authority as ostensible agent for the plaintiffs ...

---

8 Cf *Solle v Butcher* [1950] 1 KB 671.

Then was a notice of revocation given before the offer was accepted? That acceptance must be taken to have taken place not earlier than 25th March 1961. Before then, namely, on 20th March, the defendant had taken the car back to the dealer, told him he did not want to go on with the transaction and offered to forfeit his deposit. The dealer said words to the effect that he would get in touch with the plaintiffs to see what could be arranged, and told the defendant that he himself should also communicate with the plaintiffs, which the defendant did not do. Clearly both parties were under the impression that what was in view was the rescission of an existing concluded contract, whereas at this moment there was no contract at all. But it is conceded, and I think rightly so, that, if an offeror makes it clear that he does not want to go on with the transaction, it is properly treated as a revocation of his offer, notwithstanding that the words used would be more appropriate to a case of rescission. Thus one reaches the stage that an offer here has been revoked before acceptance and the revocation communicated to the ostensible agent of the offered. There is thus an end of the matter in favour of the defendant.

But if this view be wrong, I would agree that the offer here was on the basis that the car remained substantially in the same condition until acceptance, and that this did not happen ...

Questions

1. Should this case be classified under offer and acceptance or mistake?
2. What if the car had been defective and the defendant had been injured while driving it back to the dealer? Could the defendant have sued the plaintiff for his injuries?
3. What if the car had been defective and it had gone out of control while in the hands of the thief injuring both the thief and another road user? Could the thief and/or the other road user sue (i) the dealer; (ii) the hire-purchase company; (iii) the manufacturer of the vehicle; (iv) the thief?

Associated Japanese Bank (International) Ltd v Crédit du Nord [1989] 1 WLR 255 Queen's Bench Division

Steyn J: Throughout the law of contract two themes regularly recur – respect for the sanctity of contract and the need to give effect to the reasonable expectations of honest men. Usually, these themes work in the same direction. Occasionally, they point to opposite solutions. The law regarding common mistake going to the root of a contract is a case where tension arises between the two themes. That is illustrated by the circumstances of this extraordinary case.

In broad but necessarily imprecise terms the shape of this case is as follows. In February 1984 Mr Jack Bennett concluded a sale and leaseback transaction with the plaintiffs in respect of four machines, which were described by serial numbers. In other words, Mr Bennett sold the machines to the plaintiffs, and the plaintiffs then leased the machines to Mr Bennett. The plaintiffs had been unwilling to enter into the transaction unless the lessee's obligations were guaranteed by an acceptable guarantor. The defendants proved to be acceptable guarantors, and for a guarantee fee the defendants guaranteed the obligations of the lessee under the lease agreement. The plaintiffs paid a sum in excess of £1m. to Mr Bennett. Out of the proceeds of the sale Mr Bennett paid the first quarterly rental. But in May 1984 he was arrested. The second quarterly rental was never paid. And it was discovered that the machines, which were the subject matter of the sale and lease, did not exist. Mr Bennett had committed a fraud upon both the plaintiffs and the defendants. Pursuant to the terms of the lease, the plaintiffs claimed the total outstanding balance from Mr Bennett. In July 1984 Mr Bennett was adjudged bankrupt. The plaintiffs sued the defendants on the guarantee ...

The central ... question to be resolved is whether the plaintiffs are entitled under the guarantee to judgment in the sum of £1,021,000 together with interest. The principal issues to which most of counsel's submissions were directed related to the questions (a) whether the guarantors were excused from liability by the non-fulfilment of an express or implied condition precedent of the guarantee, viz the existence of the machines, or (b) whether the guarantee was void *ab initio* by reason of a common mistake affecting the guarantee, *viz* the existence of the machines ...

The construction point

The first question to be considered is whether the guarantee was expressly made subject to a condition precedent that the four machines existed ...

Clause 6 of the guarantee ... contemplated the existence of the machines, and made provision for a right of substitution only if the guarantors granted consent. Against that background the question is whether it was expressly agreed that the guarantee would only become effective if there was a lease of four existing machines. The point is not capable of elaborate analysis. It is a matter of first impression. On balance, my conclusion is that, sensibly construed against its objective setting, the guarantee was subject to an express condition precedent that there was a lease in respect of four existing machines. If this conclusion is right, the plaintiffs' claim against the defendants as guarantors or as sole or principal debtors under clause 11 fails.

If my conclusion about the construction of the guarantee is wrong, it remains to be considered whether there was an implied condition precedent that the lease related to four existing machines. In the present contract such a condition may only be held to be implied if one of two applicable tests is satisfied. The first is that such an implication is necessary to give business efficacy to the relevant contract, ie the guarantee. In other words, the criterion is whether the implication is necessary to render the contract (the guarantee) workable. That is usually described as the *Moorcock* test, being a reference to *The Moorcock* (1889) 14 PD 64. It may well be that this stringent test is not satisfied because the guarantee is workable in the sense that all that is required is that the guarantors who assumed accessory obligations must pay what is due under the lease. But there is another type of implication, which seems more appropriate in the present context. It is possible to imply a term if the court is satisfied that reasonable men, faced with the suggested term which was *ex hypothesi* not expressed in the contract, would without hesitation say: yes, of course, that is "so obvious that it goes without saying": see *Shirlaw v Southern Foundries* (1926) Ltd [1939] 2 KB 206, 227, *per* MacKinnon LJ. Although broader in scope than the *Moorcock* test, it is nevertheless a stringent test, and it will only be permissible to hold that an implication has been established on this basis in comparatively rare cases, notably when one is dealing with a commercial instrument such as a guarantee for reward. Nevertheless, against the contextual background of the fact that both parties were informed that the machines existed, and the express terms of the guarantee, I have come to the firm conclusion that the guarantee contained an implied condition precedent that the lease related to existing machines. Again, if this conclusion is right, the plaintiffs' claim against the defendants as guarantors or as sole or principal debtors under clause 11 fails ...

Notwithstanding these conclusions, which are determinative of the case, I will now consider the arguments as to common or mutual mistake which played such a large part at the hearing of this case.

Mistake

The common law regarding mutual or common mistake

There was a lively debate about the common law rules governing a mutual or common mistake of the parties as to some essential quality of the subject matter of the contract. Counsel for the defendants submitted that *Bell v Lever Brothers Ltd* [1932] AC 161 authoritatively established that a mistake by both parties as to the existence of some quality of the subject matter of the contract, which makes the subject matter of the contract without the quality essentially different from the subject matter as it was believed to be, renders the contract void *ab initio*. Counsel for the plaintiffs contested this proposition. He submitted that at common law a mistake even as to an essential quality of the subject matter of the contract would not affect the contract unless it resulted in a total failure of consideration. It was not clear to me that this formulation left any meaningful and independent scope for the application of common law rules in this area of the law. In any event, it is necessary to examine the legal position in some detail.

The landmark decision is undoubtedly *Bell v Lever Brothers Ltd*. Normally a judge of first instance would simply content himself with applying the law stated by the House of Lords. There has, however, been substantial controversy about the rule established in that case. It seems right therefore to examine the effect of that decision against a somewhat wider framework. In the early history of contract law the common law's preoccupation with consideration made the development of a doctrine of mistake impossible. Following the emergence in the 19th century of the theory of *consensus ad idem* it became possible to treat misrepresentation, undue influence and mistake as factors vitiating consent. Given that the will theory in English contract law was cast in objective form, judging matters by the external standard of the reasonable man, both as to contract formation and contractual interpretation, it nevertheless became possible to examine in what circumstances mistake might nullify or negative consent. But even in late Victorian times there was another powerful policy consideration militating against upsetting bargains on the ground of unexpected circumstances, which occurred before or after the contract. That was the policy of *caveat emptor* which held sway outside the field of contract law subsequently codified by the Sale of Goods Act 1893. Nevertheless, principles affecting the circumstances in which consent may be vitiated gradually emerged. The most troublesome areas proved to be two related areas, *viz* common mistake as to an essential quality of the subject matter of the contract and post-contractual frustration. Blackburn J, an acknowledged master of the common law, who yielded to no one in his belief in the sanctity of contract, led the way in both areas. In *Taylor v Caldwell* (1863) 3 B & S 826 Blackburn J first stated the doctrine of frustration in terms which eventually led to the adoption of the "radical change in obligation" test of commercial frustration in modern law: see *Davis Contractors Ltd v Fareham Urban District Council* [1956] AC 696 ... In *Kennedy v Panama, New Zealand, and Australian Royal Mail Co Ltd* (1867) LR 2 QB 580 ... Blackburn J, delivering the judgment of the court, held, LR 2 QB 580, 588:

"the principle of our law is the same as that of the civil law; and the difficulty in every case is to determine whether the mistake or misapprehension is as to the substance of the whole consideration, going, as it were, to the root of the matter, or only to some point, even though a material point, an error as to which does not affect the substance of the whole consideration."

None of the cases between the decisions in *Kennedy v Panama, New Zealand, and Australian Royal Mail Co Ltd* and *Bell v Lever Brothers Ltd* [1932] AC 161 significantly contributed to the development of this area of the law. But *Bell v Lever Brothers Ltd* was a vitally important case. The facts of that case are so well known as to require no detailed exposition ...

It seems to me that the better view is that the majority in *Bell v Lever Brothers Ltd* [1932] AC 161 had in mind only mistake at common law. That appears to be indicated by the shape of the argument, the proposed amendment (see p 191) placed before the House of Lords, and the speeches of Lord Atkin and Lord Thankerton. But, if I am wrong on this point, it is nevertheless clear that mistake at common law was in the forefront of the analysis in the speeches of the majority. The law has not stood still in relation to mistake in equity. Today, it is clear that mistake in equity is not circumscribed by common law definitions. A contract affected by mistake in equity is not void but may be set aside on terms: *Solle v Butcher* [1950] 1 KB 671; *Magee v Pennine Insurance Co Ltd* [1969] 2 QB 507 and *Grist v Bailey* [1967] Ch 532. It does not follow, however, that *Bell v Lever Brothers Ltd* is no longer an authoritative statement of mistake at common law. On the contrary, in my view the principles enunciated in that case clearly still govern mistake at common law ...

No one could fairly suggest that in this difficult area of the law there is only one correct approach or solution. But a narrow doctrine of common law mistake (as enunciated in *Bell v Lever Brothers Ltd* [1932] AC 161), supplemented by the more flexible doctrine of mistake in equity (as developed in *Solle v Butcher* [1950] 1 KB 671 and later cases), seems to me to be an entirely sensible and satisfactory state of the law: see *Sheikh Bros Ltd v Ochsner* [1957] AC 136. And there ought to be no reason to struggle to avoid its application by artificial interpretations of *Bell v Lever Brothers Ltd*.

It might be useful if I now summarised what appears to me to be a satisfactory way of approaching this subject. Logically, before one can turn to the rules as to mistake, whether at common law or in equity, one must first determine whether the contract itself, by express or implied condition precedent or otherwise, provides who bears the risk of the relevant mistake. It is at this hurdle that many pleas of mistake will either fail or prove to have been unnecessary. Only if the contract is silent on the point, is there scope for invoking mistake. That brings me to the relationship between common law mistake and mistake in equity. Where common law mistake has been pleaded, the court must first consider this plea. If the contract is held to be void, no question of mistake in equity arises. But, if the contract is held to be valid, a plea of mistake in equity may still have to be considered: see *Grist v Bailey* [1967] Ch 532 and the analysis in Anson's *Law of Contract*, 26th ed (1984), p 290. Turning now to the approach to common law mistake, it seems to me that the following propositions are valid although not necessarily all entitled to be dignified as propositions of law.

The first imperative must be that the law ought to uphold rather than destroy apparent contracts. Secondly, the common law rules as to a mistake regarding the quality of the subject matter, like the common law rules regarding commercial frustration, are designed to cope with the impact of unexpected and wholly exceptional circumstances on apparent contracts. Thirdly, such a mistake in order to attract legal consequences must substantially be shared by both parties, and must relate to facts as they existed at the time the contract was made. Fourthly, and this is the point established by *Bell v Lever Brothers Ltd* [1932] AC 161, the mistake must render the subject matter of the contract essentially and radically different from the subject matter which the parties believed to exist. While the civilian distinction between the substance and attributes of the subject matter of a contract has played a role in the development of our law (and was cited in speeches in *Bell v Lever Brothers Ltd*), the principle enunciated in *Bell v Lever Brothers Ltd* is markedly narrower in scope than the civilian doctrine. It is therefore no longer useful to invoke the civilian distinction. The principles enunciated by Lord Atkin and Lord Thankerton represent the *ratio decidendi* of *Bell v Lever Brothers Ltd*. Fifthly, there is a requirement which was not specifically discussed in *Bell v Lever Brothers Ltd*. What happens if the party, who is seeking to rely on the mistake, had no reasonable grounds for his belief? An extreme example is that of the man who makes a contract with minimal knowledge of the facts to which the mistake relates but is content that it is a good speculative risk. In my judgment a party cannot be allowed to rely on a common mistake where the mistake consists of a belief which is entertained by him without any reasonable grounds for such belief: cf *McRae v Commonwealth Disposals Commission* (1951) 84 CLR 377, 408. That is not because principles such as estoppel or negligence require it, but simply because policy and good sense dictate that the positive rules regarding common mistake should be so qualified. Curiously enough this qualification is similar to the civilian concept where the doctrine of error *in substantia* is tempered by the principles governing *culpa in contrahendo*. More importantly, a recognition of this qualification is consistent with the approach in equity where fault on the part of the party adversely affected by the mistake will generally preclude the granting of equitable relief: *Solle v Butcher* [1950] 1 KB 671, 693.

Applying the law to the facts

It is clear, of course, that in this case both parties – the creditors and the guarantors – acted on the assumption that the lease related to existing machines. If they had been informed that the machines might not exist, neither the plaintiffs nor the defendants would for one moment have contemplated entering into the transaction. That by itself, I accept, is not enough to sustain the plea of common law mistake. I am also satisfied that the defendants had reasonable grounds for believing that the machines existed ... No doubt the guarantors relied to some extent on the creditworthiness of Mr Bennett. But I find that the prime security to which the guarantors looked was the existence of the four machines as described to both parties ... The non-existence of the subject matter of the principal contract is therefore of fundamental importance. Indeed the analogy of the classic *res extincta* cases, so much discussed in the authorities, is fairly close. In my judgment the stringent test of common law mistake is satisfied: the guarantee is void *ab initio* ...

Equitable mistake

Having concluded that the guarantee is void *ab initio* at common law, it is strictly unnecessary to examine the question of equitable mistake. Equity will give relief against common mistake in cases where the common law will not, and it provides more flexible remedies including the power to set aside the contract on terms. It is not necessary to repeat my findings of fact save to record again the fundamental nature of the common mistake, and that the defendants were not at fault in any way. If I had not decided in favour of the defendants on construction and common law mistake, I would have held that the guarantee must be set aside on equitable principles. Unfortunately, and counsel are not to blame for that, the question of the terms (if any) to be imposed (having regard particularly to sums deposited by Mr Bennett with the defendants) were not adequately explored in argument. If it becomes necessary to rule on this aspect, I will require further argument ...

Conclusion

Subject to any observations by counsel as to the form of the order, my conclusion is that the plaintiffs' claim must be dismissed ...

Questions

1. Does the common law of contract actually have independent rules governing mistake?
2. Would the contracts in *Bell v Lever Brothers* now be subject to rescission in equity?
3. What role does fault play in mistake problems?
4. What are the reasonable expectations of honest men?
5. 'It is a matter of first impression'. Discuss, from a legal reasoning point of view.

William Sindall Plc v Cambridgeshire County Council [1994] 1 WLR 1016 Court of Appeal

(See p 261)

Questions

1. Is mistake now governed by rules similar to those used in frustration problems? (Cf Chapter 6.)
2. Could the equitable remedy of rescission now have a role to play in frustration problems?

(f) Error *in negotio*

Avon Finance Co Ltd v Bridger [1985] 2 All ER 281 Court of Appeal

The plaintiffs brought an action for possession of the defendants' house which had been charged to the plaintiffs as security for a loan. The charge had been signed by the defendants, but only because they had been misled as to the nature of the document by their son. The judge dismissed the plaintiffs' claim on the basis of *non est factum* and an appeal to the Court of Appeal was unsuccessful.

Lord Denning MR: A few years ago we had a case about old Herbert Bundy, a father who was let down by his son. Now we have the case of George Bridger, a postman, who has also been let down by his son ...

It is plain that the son was a very bad lot. He went missing. He owed debts all round. Newspapers reported him as saying that his life had crumbled; that he had been sleeping in his car; and so forth. It seems to me that the legal position was not fully canvassed before the county court judge. One could not expect Mr Bridger to understand the law. He set out the facts. In his pleadings he was only bound to set out the material facts. The case was argued as though it depended on the legal doctrine of *non est factum* ... The judge thought that the issue depended on whether or not Mr and Mrs Bridger were careless in not checking the documents and unreasonable in trusting their son ...

The judge ... held that it was a case of *non est factum* and that the parents were not liable.

Now I am afraid I cannot agree with the judge about *non est factum*. The doctrine is of very limited application as was explained in the Court of Appeal in *Saunders v Anglia Building Society, sub nom Gallie v Lee* ... as modified by Lord Pearson in the House of Lords ... In that case Mrs Gallie's signature was obtained by fraud just as Mr and Mrs Bridger's was here. Yet the plea of *non est factum* did not prevail.

But I think the case should be considered on a different footing altogether, namely on the principle of 'inequality of bargaining' as set out in *Lloyds Bank Ltd v Bundy* ...

Here this son brought undue pressures on his parents for the benefit of the plaintiffs, and for himself of course, because he wanted the loan. They left it all to him. They said that he was to procure the execution of the deed. He brought undue pressure to bear on his parents by giving them an entirely misleading account of the documents. It seems to me that the parents' bargaining power was impaired by their own ignorance, and that this court should not uphold the transaction. On this ground I would uphold the judge's decision.

I would just like to comment on a point which was not canvassed in the court below. We were referred to the Consumer Credit Act 1974, which now replaces many of the provisions of the old Moneylenders Acts 1900 to 1927 which were in force. Without going into the details of the sections ... it seems to me that under the statute now, in regard to an agreement such as the one in this case, if it grossly contravenes the ordinary principles of fair dealing, and if regard is had to factors such as the age, experience and business capacity of Mr and Mrs

Bridger, this is a case which may well come within the provisions of the 1974 Act. The agreement should be regarded as extortionate and the court can set aside the whole of the obligation. It is unnecessary to consider those matters in detail because they were not gone into. But, as far as I can see, if that statute were considered in detail, it is very likely that the same result would be reached as I would reach in this case, which is that the plaintiffs in these circumstances cannot enforce this legal charge against the parents.

Brandon LJ: The deputy county court judge found in favour of the defendants on the basis of the defence *non est factum*. I would not agree with the decision of the deputy county court judge on that aspect of the case. A defendant can only rely on that plea when he has exercised reasonable care in the circumstances in connection with the transaction. The deputy county court judge found as a fact that the defendants had exercised reasonable care; but his decision on that matter, although one of fact, was a decision based on an inference from primary facts which are not in dispute, and this court is as well placed to draw the appropriate inference as was the deputy county court judge. In my judgment, it is impossible on the facts of this case to find that the defendants exercised such reasonable care as was appropriate in the circumstances in entering into the transaction. I would therefore find it impossible to support the judgment on the ground on which it was given.

In this court, however, a different defence has been discussed, which I think it is right the court should consider because the defendants were in person and were not in a position to put all the relevant legal arguments before the court below. That defence is that the transaction relating to the second mortgage is voidable in equity ...

The matters which seem to me to give rise to an equity in favour of the defendants are three. The first matter is that the plaintiffs chose to appoint the son, who was the debtor, to procure from his parents the security which he and they needed to further the transaction on which they were engaged. It was for the plaintiffs' benefit to have this security because they are in business for money lending, and they wanted a good secure money-lending contract. They chose to appoint the son, a young accountant in the prime of life, to procure this contract from his parents, both of whom were old-age pensioners, much less well educated than he was. The person whom they chose to appoint, being a son, could be expected to have some influence over his elderly parents, and that is something of which the plaintiffs could or should have been aware. In fact, the son was fraudulent. He deceived his parents, and by his deception induced them to enter into this transaction. We have those two matters, the procurement of the security by the son and the relationship between the son and his elderly parents of different educational attainment. Finally we have the third factor of the absence of any independent advice.

The fact is that there was no independent advice, and, in so far as the plaintiffs thought there was independent advice, they were in error ...

Questions

1. Where is the line to be drawn between error and undue influence? Does it matter?

2. Was the son acting as agent of the plaintiffs?

3. Could the plaintiffs sue the son for their legal expenses incurred in the action against the parents?

4. Is this a mistake case? If so, which party was labouring under a mistake?

5. Does this case conflict with the House of Lords' decision in *Esso Petroleum v Southport Corporation* (above p 118)?

(g) Error *in persona*

Lewis v Averay [1972] 1 QB 198 Court of Appeal

This was an action in the tort of conversion by the seller of a motor car for its return after it had been resold by the original purchaser, who had misrepresented his identity to the plaintiff, to a *bona fide* purchaser. The plaintiff claimed that the original sale contract was void for mistake of identity and thus no title could pass. The Court of Appeal dismissed the plaintiff's claim.

Lord Denning MR: ... Who is entitled to the goods? The original seller? Or the ultimate buyer? The courts have given different answers ...

[T]here was, to all outward appearance, a contract: but there was a mistake by the seller as to the identity of the buyer. This mistake was fundamental. In each case it led to the handing over of the goods. Without it the seller would not have parted with them.

This case therefore raises the question: What is the effect of a mistake by one party as to the identity of the other? It has sometimes been said that if a party makes a mistake as to the identity of the person with whom he is contracting there is no contract, or, if there is a contract, it is a nullity and void, so that no property can pass under it. This has been supported by a reference to the French jurist Pothier; but I have said before, and I repeat now, his statement is no part of English law ... Pothier's statement has given rise to such refinements that it is time it was dead and buried altogether ...

Again it has been suggested that a mistake as to the identity of a person is one thing: and a mistake as to his attributes is another. A mistake as to identity, it is said, avoids a contract: whereas a mistake as to attributes does not. But this is a distinction without a difference. A man's very name is one of his attributes. It is also a key to his identity. If then, he gives a false name, is it a mistake as to his identity? Or a mistake as to his attributes? These fine distinctions do no good to the law.

As I listened to the argument in this case, I felt it wrong that an innocent purchaser (who knew nothing of what had passed between the seller and the rogue) should have his title depend on such refinements. After all, he has acted with complete circumspection and in entire good faith: whereas it was the seller who let the rogue have the goods and thus enabled him to commit the fraud. I do not, therefore, accept the theory that a mistake as to identity renders a contract void ... When two parties have come to a contract – or rather what appears, on the face of it, to be a contract the fact that one party is mistaken as to the identity of the other does not mean that there is no contract, or that the contract is a nullity and void from the beginning. It only means that the contract is voidable, that is, liable to be set aside at the instance of the mistake person, so long as he does so before third parties have in good faith acquired rights under it ...

In this case Mr Lewis made a contract of sale with the very man, the rogue, who came to the flat. I say that he "made a contract" because in this regard we do not look into his intentions, or into his mind to know what he was thinking or into the mind of the rogue. We look to the outward appearances. On the face of the dealing, Mr Lewis made a contract under which he sold the car to the rogue, delivered the car and the log book to him, and took a cheque in return. The contract is evidenced by the receipts which were signed. It was, of course, induced by fraud. The rogue made false representations as to his identity. But it was still a contract, though voidable for fraud. It was a contract under which this property passed to the rogue, and in due course passed from the rogue to [the bona fide purchaser], before the contract was avoided.

Though I very much regret that either of these good and reliable gentlemen should suffer, in my judgment it is [the plaintiff] who should do so. I think the appeal should be allowed and judgment entered for the defendant.

Questions

1. These cases assume that the conveyance of title stood or fell with the contract. But why could the handing over of the car not pass title? Did not the seller in both cases intend to pass ownership and the rogue intend to acquire ownership?

2. Is the reference to Pothier misleading given Article 2279 of the Code civil which states that possession is equivalent to ownership in the case of the sale of moveable property? If English law had the same rule as the one to be found in Article 2279, what relevance would such a rule have to the facts of *Lewis*?

3. Does this case belong more to the law of property than to the law of obligations?

5 FRAUD

Whittaker v Campbell [1984] QB 318 Queen's Bench Division

(See p 233)

Questions

1. Is fraud part of the law of restitution rather than the law of contract?

2. Why does English law distinguish between promise as a legal act and fraud as a legal fact? Surely the latter could be said to undermine the former?

3. Does fraud vitiate consent as far as the tort of trespass is concerned? A fraudulently conceals from B that he has the AIDS virus: could it be said that B consents to having sexual intercourse with A?

Bradford Building Society v Borders [1941] 2 All ER 205 House of Lords

(See p 268)

Questions

1. A newspaper accuses a politician of fraud and the politician successfully sues the newspaper for damages in defamation on the basis that the newspaper cannot actually prove the allegation. It is subsequently proved in criminal proceedings that the politician is guilty of fraud. Could the newspaper recover the defamation damages it has paid to the politician in an action either for damages or for debt? Would it make any difference if, during the defamation proceedings, the politician had specifically denied the fraud, but later admitted it after the criminal proceedings?

2. Will all fraudulent behaviour which causes loss now give rise to an action for damages in the tort of negligence?

3. If it is ever proved that a cigarette manufacturer has suppressed evidence that smoking causes cancer will this be enough to found an action for deceit on behalf of anyone who can show that they have developed cancer from smoking that manufacturer's cigarettes?

6 DURESS

CTN Cash and Carry Ltd v Gallaher Ltd [1994] 4 All ER 714 Court of Appeal

Steyn LJ: A buyer paid a sum of money to his supplier. The sum of money was in truth not owed by the buyer to the supplier. The buyer paid the sum as a result of the supplier's threat to stop the buyer's credit facilities in their future dealings if the sum was not paid. The supplier acted in the bona fide belief that the sum was owing. Does the doctrine of economic duress enable the buyer to recover the payment? In a judgment given on 8 August 1991 Judge Michael Kershaw QC gave a negative answer to this question. This appeal challenges the correctness of the deputy judge's conclusion ...

Miss Heilbron QC, who appeared for the plaintiffs, submitted that the deputy judge erred in rejecting the plea of duress. She submitted that the payment was made under illegitimate pressure. She emphasised that there was objectively no legal basis for demanding the price of the goods, and the threat of withdrawing the credit facilities was made solely in order to obtain the payment. The threat was powerful because the removal of credit would have seriously jeopardised the plaintiffs' business. The clear purpose, she said, was to extort money to which the plaintiffs were in truth not entitled. In the circumstances, the threat was illegitimate and the case of duress was made out.

Miss Heilbron cited a number of authorities which illustrate developments in this branch of the law. While I found the exercise of interest, I was reminded of the famous aphorism of Oliver Wendell Holmes that general propositions do not solve concrete cases. It may only be a half-truth, but in my view the true part applies to this case. It is necessary to focus on the distinctive features of this case, and then to ask whether it amounts to a case of duress.

The present dispute does not concern a protected relationship. It also does not arise in the context of dealings between a supplier and a consumer. The dispute arises out of arm's length commercial dealings between two trading companies. It is true that the defendants were the sole distributors of the popular brands of cigarettes. In a sense the defendants were in a monopoly position. The control of monopolies is, however, a matter for Parliament. Moreover, the common law does not recognise the doctrine of inequality of bargaining power in commercial dealings (see *National Westminster Bank plc v Morgan* [1985] AC 686). The fact that the defendants were in a monopoly position cannot therefore by itself convert what is not otherwise duress into duress.

A second characteristic of the case is that the defendants were in law entitled to refuse to enter into any future contracts with the plaintiffs for any reason whatsoever or for no reason at all. Such a decision not to deal with the plaintiffs would have been financially damaging to the defendants, but it would have been lawful. *A fortiori*, it was lawful for the defendants, for any reason or for no reason, to insist that they would no longer grant credit to the plaintiffs. The defendants' demand for payment of the invoice, coupled with the threat to withdraw credit, was neither a breach of contract nor a tort.

A third, and critically important, characteristic of the case is the fact that the defendants *bona fide* thought that the goods were at the risk of the plaintiffs and that the plaintiffs owed the defendants the sum in question. The defendants exerted commercial pressure on the plaintiffs in order to obtain payment of a sum which they bona fide considered due to them. The defendants' motive in threatening withdrawal of credit facilities was commercial self-interest in obtaining a sum that they considered due to them.

Given the combination of these three features, I take the view that none of the cases cited to us assist the plaintiffs' case. Miss Heilbron accepted that there is no decision which is in material respects on all fours with the present case. It is therefore unnecessary to disinter all those cases and to identify the material distinctions between each of those decisions and the present case. But Miss Heilbron rightly emphasised to us that the law must have a capacity for growth in this field. I entirely agree.

I also readily accept that the fact that the defendants have used lawful means does not by itself remove the case from the scope of the doctrine of economic duress ...

We are being asked to extend the categories of duress of which the law will take cognisance. That is not necessarily objectionable, but it seems to me that an extension capable of covering the present case, involving 'lawful act duress' in a commercial context in pursuit of a *bona fide* claim, would be a radical one with far-reaching implications. It would introduce a substantial and undesirable element of uncertainty in the commercial bargaining process. Moreover, it will often enable *bona fide* settled accounts to be reopened when parties to commercial dealings fall out. The aim of our commercial law ought to be to encourage fair dealing between parties. But it is a mistake for the law to set its sights too highly when the critical inquiry is not whether the conduct is lawful but whether it is morally or socially unacceptable. That is the inquiry in which we are engaged. In my view there are policy considerations which militate against ruling that the defendants obtained payment of the disputed invoice by duress.

Outside the field of protected relationships, and in a purely commercial context, it might be a relatively rare case in which 'lawful act duress' can be established. And it might be particularly difficult to establish duress if the defendant *bona fide* considered that his demand was valid. In this complex and changing branch of the law I deliberately refrain from saying 'never'. But as the law stands, I am satisfied that the defendants' conduct in this case did not amount to duress.

It is an unattractive result, inasmuch as the defendants are allowed to retain a sum which at the trial they became aware was not in truth due to them. But in my view the law compels the result.

For these reasons, I would dismiss the appeal.

Farquharson LJ: I agree.

Sir Donald Nicholls V-C: I also agree. It is important to have in mind that the sole issue raised by this appeal and argued before us was duress. The plaintiff claims payment was made by it under duress and is recoverable accordingly. I agree, for the reasons given by Steyn LJ, that the claim must fail. When the defendant company insisted on payment, it did so in good faith. It believed the risk in the goods had passed to the plaintiff company, so it considered it was entitled to be paid for them. The defendant company took a tough line. It used its commercial muscle. But the feature underlying and dictating this attitude was a genuine belief on its part that it was owed the sum in question. It was entitled to be paid the price for the goods. So it took the line: the plaintiff company must pay in law what it owed, otherwise its credit would be suspended.

Further, there is no evidence that the defendant's belief was unreasonable. Indeed, we were told by the defendant's counsel that he had advised his client that on the risk point the defendant stood a good chance of success. I do not see how a payment demanded and made in those circumstances can be said to be vitiated by duress.

So that must be an end to this appeal ...

Questions

1. If the plaintiff paid the money to retain the credit facilities, was this a contract? Is it a contract that might be set aside in equity via the remedy of rescission?

2. How does this case differ from *D & C Builders v Rees* (p 255)?

3. If the defendants had decided to withdraw the credit facilities out of malice, would this have been a tort? What would be the position if the defendants did not genuinely believe they were owed the money by the plaintiffs?

4. The disputed invoice arose because the suppliers had delivered cigarettes to the plaintiffs – but to the wrong warehouse – and these cigarettes were stolen from the plaintiffs' warehouse. What was the insurance position with respect to the theft of the cigarettes and how, if at all, might the insurance position be of importance to the case?

5. Does *CTN* deny the thesis that abuse of power is a tort?

6. If English contract law had a doctrine of good faith would *CTN* have been decided differently?

7. If the plaintiff had brought an action for money had and received, based on payment made under a mistake, would they have been able to recover? (Cf Chapter 7.)

8. Under what circumstances, if any, might the plaintiff have been allowed to trace the money they paid to the defendant?

9. Read *Atlas Express Ltd v Kafko Ltd*[9] in the law report. If this case had been heard after *CTN* would the result be different? How do the two cases differ?

D & C Builders Ltd v Rees [1966] 2 QB 617 Court of Appeal

(See p 255)

Avon Finance Co Ltd v Bridger [1985] 2 All ER 281 Court of Appeal

(See p 286)

Barclays Bank plc v O'Brien [1992] 3 WLR 593 Court of Appeal; [1993] 3 WLR 786 House of Lords

(See p 157)

---

9   [1989] QB 833; [1989] 3 WLR 389; [1989] 1 All ER 641.

Notes and questions

1. Undue influence is an equitable form of duress which may give rise to the equitable remedy of rescission. What about actual duress to the person (ie, threats of violence): does this give rise only to an action in equity for rescission or are there some forms of duress that will make a contract void?

2. Was the husband in *O'Brien* acting as agent of the bank?

3. Could the bank sue the husband in *O'Brien* for all its losses arising out of the mortgage transaction?

4. Do the courts have a general equitable power to set aside unconscionable transactions?

5. Is it duress for a trade union to threaten industrial action? If so, can any person who suffers loss as a result of the duress obtain, at common law, damages? What about equity: will it always allow rescission of any contract entered into as a result of a threat of industrial action?[10]

6. Is the threat of unemployment a form of duress?

7. Is the threat of legal action duress when the person making the threat knows full well that he has no legal basis for his threat?

8. Can a threat to withdraw from pre-contractual negotiations ever amount to duress?

9. Are there situations where one has a right to make threats?[11]

---

10 Cf *Dimskal Shipping Co v ITWF* [1992] 2 AC 152.
11 Cf *Thorne v MTA* [1937] AC 797.

CHAPTER 6

NON-PERFORMANCE OF A CONTRACT

1 INTRODUCTION

Contracts that are fully performed by both parties rarely raise problems involving the courts. There seems little point therefore in describing the contents of a contractual obligation in the abstract. Indeed even when one party fails fully to perform his, her or its side of a contract the two parties may prefer to settle the matter outside of the law. It is when one person suffers injury, damage and (or) loss that the courts usually become involved and even then the chances are that the matter will be settled before getting to court. Most contracts are performed by both sides usually satisfactorily and if this were not the case commerce would cease to function.

When problems do arise between contracting parties it is, as far as the common law is concerned at any rate, helpful to start out from the nature of the complaint (something which is true in respect of non-contractual obligations as well: Chapter 7). Is the plaintiff claiming compensation for damage or loss caused by the act or omission of the other party? Or is the plaintiff complaining that the other party is failing to do what he had undertaken to do (for example pay a debt) or undertaken not to do (work for someone else for example)? Again, is the plaintiff trying to escape from an obligation which he had taken on when market conditions were different or which he had taken on as a result of what he had been lead to believe by the other party? Or is he trying to renegotiate the price because of a change of circumstances or whatever? These questions lead one towards the appropriate remedy which, in turn, helps the lawyer to conceptualise the obligational problem at a substantive level. Thus a rescission claim usually raises a question about the events surrounding the formation of a contract (see Chapter 5); a claim in damages, on the other hand, often leads to problems about the contents of a contract (implied terms, exclusion clauses and the like). In addition there may well be a dispute surrounding the nature of the damage itself and whether it is of a type which the defendant should compensate (see Chapter 3). However, when a debt case gets to court and into the law reports it is usually because such a claim has raised a problem about the very existence of a contract (see eg, *Carlill*, p 237) or about whether the creditor has performed his side of the bargain (see *Bolton v Mahadeva*, p 126); it is not in the nature of such claims to raise questions about causation and foreseeability as such, although sometimes behaviour and fault can prove indirectly relevant (see eg, *Vigers v Cook*, below). Equally, a debt claim can raise a question about just who has the right to claim performance of a contract as in *Beswick v Beswick* (see p 154). And this, in its turn, can give rise to the more abstract questions about the difference between rights and interests (see Chapter 2) and the relationship between rights and remedies (see Chapter 3).

The point to remember in all of this, is that the type of damage suffered by a contractor or other plaintiff is an excellent starting point for an analysis of a set of facts. One then works from the damage towards the actors (*personae*, ie, parties), the props (*res*, eg, goods sold or hired, factory guarded and so on) and the possible actions (remedies, eg, debt, damages, injunction, rescission or whatever) that could come into play. And the interplay of all of these should reveal the relevant relationships (contractual terms, unilateral promise, duty of care, bailment and the like) which will motivate and justify the granting or refusal of a remedy.

2 BREACH AND NON-PERFORMANCE

Vigers v Cook [1919] 2 KB 475 Court of Appeal

This was an action in debt by a funeral undertaker against the defendant in respect of a funeral of the defendant's son. The Court of Appeal held that the defendant was justified in refusing to pay the bill.

Bankes LJ: ... The first question is, what was the contract between the parties? ...

Undertaking an order for a funeral indicates not a single but a complex operation, that is to say, a series of single operations; and naturally there must have been a discussion in reference to these various single operations which went to make up the entire transaction in respect of which the contract was made. For instance, there must have been an intimation as to where the interment was to take place, and as to the kind of coffin desired ... But, having been concluded, in my opinion it is one entire contract ... Not a word has been said against the plaintiff in this case. He is an undertaker of repute ... He took the order, and the order included the supply of the elm shell, the lead coffin, and the oak case ... On August 1 the lead coffin was soldered down in the mortuary, and the pinhole was left ... On August 2 the complaint came from the mortuary authorities, and on that day the pinhole was closed. As the natural result of closing the pinhole, the gas accumulated in the lead coffin to such an extent that by the time the coffin arrived at the entrance to the church the lead coffin had burst, and there was a leakage from the coffin, sufficient, to render it extremely undesirable that the body should be taken into the church ... and as a result the body was not taken in.

In my opinion the contract which was made between the parties included ... as an essential term the conveying of the body into the church for a part of the service, subject to this condition, that the body was in such a state as to permit of that being done. The body in this coffin was not in that state, but the onus was on the plaintiff to establish that it was not in that state owing to no default on his part. In my opinion he he did not discharge that onus ... I think that, although the plaintiff down to the time of the closing of the aperture did nothing other than what a competent and careful undertaker would do, in the difficult circumstances which arose when he felt it necessary to close the aperture, he has not shown that it was owing to no fault on his part that one essential term of his contract was not fulfilled; and it being one entire contract, in my opinion he fails in proving that he is entitled to any portion of the one entire price which was payable for the entire contract ...

Notes and questions

1. It has been observed many times in the previous chapter that the difference between contract in French and English law is that one is based on agreement and the other is based on promise. This distinction becomes evident, once again, in the way failure to perform a contract is envisaged. In French law all failures to perform are labelled 'non-performance' (*inexécution*), but in English law the notion of promise gives rise to a different expression. A failure to do what one has promised to do is called a 'breach' of promise and this has given rise to the notion of breach of contract. However the idea of a non-performance cannot be disregarded in English law because in a unilateral contract the promisee cannot ever be in breach since such a person has never promised anything. Thus Mrs Carlill (see p 237) could never be in breach of contract; all she could ever be accused of by the Carbolic Smoke Ball Company is non-performance of the consideration stipulated in the advertisement. Was the Carbolic Smoke Ball Co in breach of the contract with Mrs Carlill or were they guilty only of a non-performance?

2. From the position of the law of remedies the difference between breach and non-performance can be important. If a contractor wishes to claim damages it must be established that the other party is in breach of contract and that this breach has caused the plaintiff's damage. But say if the damage suffered by the plaintiff as a result of the other party's failure to perform is less than the price that the plaintiff had agreed to pay for the performance? Is a claim in damages on the basis of breach the best way of conceptualising the problem? (Cf *Bolton v Mahadeva*, p 126.)

3. What if a contractor performs most, but not all, of his obligations under a contract: can the other party refuse to pay any of the agreed price?

Hoenig v Isaacs [1952] 2 All ER 176 Court of Appeal

This was an action in debt for the balance outstanding in respect of decoration and furnishing work carried out in the defendant's flat. The defendant claimed that the plaintiff had not performed the contract and it was found at first instance that, although the contract had been substantially performed, there were some defects in the workmanship which would cost just under £56 to put right. The Court of Appeal held that the plaintiff was entitled to the outstanding balance of £350 less the cost of the defects by way of set-off.

Denning LJ: ... In determining this issue the first question is whether, on the true construction of the contract, entire performance was a condition precedent to payment. It was a lump sum contract, but that does not mean that entire performance was a condition precedent to payment. When a contract provides for a specific sum to be paid on completion of specified work, the courts lean against a construction of the contract which would deprive the contractor of any payment at all simply because there are some defects or omissions. The promise to complete the work is, therefore, construed as a term of the contract, but not as a condition. It is not every breach of that term which absolves the employer from his promise to pay the price, but only a breach which goes to the root of the contract, such as an abandonment of the work when it is only half done. Unless the breach does go to the root of the matter, the employer cannot resist payment of the price. He must pay it and bring a cross-claim for the defects and omissions, or, alternatively, set them up in diminution of the price ... It is, of course, always open to the parties by express words to make entire performance a condition precedent ...

Even if entire performance was a condition precedent, nevertheless, the result would be the same, because I think the condition was waived ... [The defendant] did not refuse to accept the work. On the contrary, he entered into possession of the flat and used the furniture as his own, including the defective items. That was a clear waiver of the condition precedent. Just as in a sale of goods the buyer who accepts the goods can no longer treat a breach of condition as giving a right to reject but only a right to damages, so also in a contract for work and labour an employer who takes the benefit of the work can no longer treat entire performance as a condition precedent, but only as a term giving rise to damages ...

Questions

1. Are all non-performances breaches of contract?

2. D offers £10 to anyone who will cut his hedge. P cuts three-quarters of the hedge and then gives up and goes home. Is P entitled to any money from D? What if D finishes the last quarter himself?[1]

3. At what point does non-performance become substantial performance?

---

1 Cf *Sumpter v Hedges* [1898] 1 QB 673.

Bolton v Mahadeva [1972] 1 WLR 1009 Court of Appeal

(See p 126)

Questions

1. Is this an example of a self-help remedy?
2. Was the houseowner in *Bolton* enriched at the expense of the heating contractor? Does it matter? Is your answer to this second question influenced by the fact that the houseowner could be described as a consumer?

Attia v British Gas Plc [1988] QB 304 Court of Appeal

Bingham LJ: The plaintiff's claim pleaded in this action is a simple one. She alleges that the defendants were installing central heating in her house and that a fire occurred as a result of the defendants' negligent work. This the defendants admit. The plaintiff further pleads that she returned home to see smoke coming from the loft of the house and then witnessed the burning of the house for over four hours until the fire was brought under control. This experience, she alleges, caused her "nervous shock in the form of a serious psychological reaction evidenced by an anxiety state and depression".

Her claim is accordingly one for what have in the authorities and the literature been called damages for nervous shock. Judges have in recent years become increasingly restive at the use of this misleading and inaccurate expression, and I shall use the general expression "psychiatric damage", intending to comprehend within it all relevant forms of mental illness, neurosis and personality change. But the train of events (all of which must be causally related) with which this action, like its predecessors, is concerned remains unchanged: careless conduct on the part of the defendant causing actual or apprehended injury to the plaintiff or a person other than the defendant; the suffering of acute mental or emotional trauma by the plaintiff on witnessing or apprehending that injury or witnessing its aftermath; psychiatric damage suffered by the plaintiff.

There is, however, one respect in which this case differs from all the decided cases; or almost all: *Owens v Liverpool Corporation* [1939] 1 KB 394 would appear to be an exception. Although the plaintiff suffered injury in that her home and presumably her possessions were burned and damaged, it is not said that she was at any time in fear for her own personal safety or that of anyone else, nor is it said that physical injury (as opposed to the psychiatric damage of which she complains) was suffered by anyone. It was no doubt this singular feature of the case which led the parties to agree to the trial of a preliminary issue:

> "Can the plaintiff recover damages for nervous shock caused by witnessing her home and possessions damaged and/or destroyed by a fire caused by the defendants' negligence while installing central heating in the plaintiff's home?"

The parties are not to be criticised for adopting a procedure which they conscientiously believed would save costs and time. But it would, I think, have been better if the action had proceeded to trial, at any rate on liability, perhaps leaving the assessing of damages, if any, to a later date. For I think that there are, within the issue set down for trial, two distinct questions. One is a question of far-reaching legal principle: is a claim for damages for psychiatric damage suffered by one who has witnessed the destruction of her property, in the absence of any actual or apprehended physical injury, one that must necessarily fail as a matter of law? In the light of such illustrious precedents as *Donoghue v Stevenson* [1932] AC 562 and *Dorset Yacht Co Ltd v Home Office* [1970] AC 1004, questions such as this cannot be regarded as unsuitable for determination on, in effect, demurrer. But there is in this case a special feature to which I shall return, namely, a pre-existing relationship between the defendants as contractors and the plaintiff as occupant of a house in which they were working. I would be happier deciding even this legal question against a background of full and proven, rather than outline and assumed, facts. The second question is much more limited. It is whether on the facts pleaded it was reasonably foreseeable by the defendants that careless performance of their work might cause psychiatric damage to the plaintiff. This is a question of fact which, for reasons I shall give, cannot in my view be fairly decided at this stage ...

Since the defendants were working in the house where the plaintiff lived, it must have been obvious to them that she would be so closely and directly affected by their performance of their work that they ought reasonably to have her in contemplation as being so affected when they carried out the work. It is not, I think, contested that the defendants owed her a duty to take reasonable care to carry out the work so as to avoid damaging her home and property. But it is said that the defendants owed her no duty to take reasonable care to carry out the work so as to avoid causing her psychiatric damage. This analytical approach cannot, I think, be said to be wrong, but it seems to me to be preferable, where a duty of care undeniably exists, to treat the question as one of remoteness and ask whether the plaintiff's psychiatric damage is too remote to be recoverable because not reasonably foreseeable as a consequence of the defendant's careless conduct. The test of reasonable foreseeability is, as I understand, the same in both contexts, and the result should be the same on either approach. So the question in any case such as this, applying the ordinary test of remoteness in tort, is whether the defendant should reasonably have contemplated psychiatric damage to the plaintiff as a real, even if unlikely, result of careless conduct on his part ...

Whether the psychiatric damage suffered by this plaintiff as a result of the carelessness of the defendants was reasonably foreseeable is not something which can be decided as a question of law. In considering the present question of principle reasonable foreseeability must for the present be assumed in the plaintiff's favour. So the question is whether, assuming everything else in the plaintiff's favour, this court should hold this claim to be bad in law because the mental or emotional trauma which precipitated the plaintiff's psychiatric damage was caused by her witnessing the destruction of her home and property rather than apprehending or witnessing personal injury or the consequences of personal injury.

It is submitted, I think rightly, that this claim breaks new ground. No analogous claim has ever, to my knowledge, been upheld or even advanced. If, therefore, it were proper to erect a doctrinal boundary stone at the point which the onward march of recorded decisions has so far reached, we should answer the question of principle in the negative and dismiss the plaintiff's action, as the deputy judge did. But I should for my part erect the boundary stone with a strong presentiment that it would not be long before a case would arise so compelling on its facts as to cause the stone to be moved to a new and more distant resting place. The suggested boundary line is not, moreover, one that commends itself to me as either fair or convenient. Examples which arose in argument illustrate the point. Suppose, for example, that a scholar's life's work of research or composition were destroyed before his eyes as a result of a defendant's careless conduct, causing the scholar to suffer reasonably foreseeable psychiatric damage. Or suppose that a householder returned home to find that his most cherished possessions had been destroyed through the carelessness of an intruder in starting a fire or leaving a tap running, causing reasonably foreseeable psychiatric damage to the owner. I do not think a legal principle which forbade recovery in these circumstances could be supported. The only policy argument relied on as justifying or requiring such a restriction was the need to prevent a proliferation of claims, the familiar floodgates argument. This is not an argument to be automatically discounted. But nor is it, I think, an argument which can claim a very impressive record of success. All depends on one's judgment of the likely result of a particular extension of the law. I do not myself think that refusal by this court to lay down the legal principle for which the defendants contend, or (put positively) our acceptance that a claim such as the plaintiff's may in principle succeed, will lead to a flood of claims or actions, let alone a flood of successful claims or actions. Insistence that psychiatric damage must be reasonably foreseeable, coupled with clear recognition that a plaintiff must prove psychiatric damage as I have defined it, and not merely grief, sorrow or emotional distress, will in my view enable the good sense of the judge to ensure, adopting Lord Wright's language in *Bourhill v Young* [1943] AC 92, 110, that the thing stops at the appropriate point. His good sense provides a better, because more flexible, mechanism of control than a necessarily arbitrary rule of law.

I would therefore answer this broad question of principle in favour of the plaintiff ...

Dillon LJ: ... The law has developed step by step and is still developing. In those circumstances I would be particularly reluctant to lay down any general rule as to the conditions in which such damages can or cannot be recovered as a matter of public policy ...

[A] great deal of difficulty which has been felt over the development of the law as to damages for "nervous shock" has arisen in relation to what, in the terminology of the tort of negligence, is described as the question of proximity .... But that difficulty does not arise in the present case because in the present case there is no problem of proximity .... The defendants knew about the plaintiff .... I can see no good reason why, in such a context, the law should have refused to allow her damages for "nervous shock" if she could get over the hurdles of causation and foreseeability as an aspect of remoteness ...

Questions

1. Is *Attia* a contract case?
2. If the fire had been caused, not by British Gas, but by lightning: do you think that the householder would have had to pay for the work

done by British Gas even if the house had been completely destroyed?[2] What if the cause of the fire was unexplained? Upon whom is the burden of proof?

3. What if the householder, while at the office, had been informed by a neighbour that her house was on fire: would she still be entitled to damages for nervous shock?

4. Does the law of property (possession) play a fundamental role in this case?

3 THE ROLE OF FAULT

Vigers v Cook [1919] 2 KB 475 Court of Appeal

(See p 296)

Notes and questions

1. The distinction between agreement and promise is to be found at the root of the problem of the role of fault in contract. In systems based on agreement the normative dimension to non-performance is provided by fault[3]; accordingly, if the non-performance is due to factors that cannot be attributed to the fault of the non-performing party he has, *prima facie*, a defence. Only if such a party has agreed to guarantee a particular result will the plaintiff be entitled to damages irrespective of fault. In English law the normative dimension is provided by the notion of promise itself; thus all that a contractor has, *prima facie*, to show in order in order to obtain damages for breach is a breach of promise. Whether or not the defendant is guilty of fault is, *prima facie*, irrelevant.[4] However, as *Vigers* indicates, the English position is not quite so simple. Could it not be said that the undertaker was unable to claim in debt because he could not prove he was not at fault? Is debt based on fault?

2. The position regarding fault in English contract law is not so simple because although promise is a normative concept in itself much will depend on what was actually promised. This problem has already been encountered under the heading of level of duty (see Chapter 4). In contracts where the object is a physical thing the commercial

---

2   Cf *BP Exploration (Libya) Ltd v Hunt (No 2)* [1979] 1 WLR 783.

3   See generally G H Treitel, *Remedies for Breach of Contract: A Comparative Account* (Oxford, 1988), pp 7–42.

4   *Raineri v Miles* [1981] AC 1050, 1086.

supplier will usually be promising that the thing supplied will be reasonably fit and of satisfactory quality; if the goods are not fit then there will be a breach of promise irrespective of the fault of the supplier (see *Hyman v Nye* below p 322 and *Frost v Alysbury Dairy*, p 19). The supplier is liable because he is in breach of a promise now implied by statute (see the paradigm provision: Sale of Goods Act 1979 s 14, below p 228). Where the object of the contract is a service rather than the supply of goods a quite different promise is implied as s 13 of the Supply of Goods and Services Act 1982 now makes clear. A supplier of a service promises to carry out the service with reasonable care and skill. Accordingly, in order to show a breach of promise the contractor suffering damage must show fault (ie lack of reasonable care and skill). Is this the same requirement as for the tort of negligence?

3.   Where fault is relevant, upon whom is the burden of proving fault?

Reed v Dean [1949] 1 KB 188 King's Bench Division

This was an action for damages by the hirers of a motor launch who had suffered injury and loss when the boat caught fire.

Lewis J: ... In my view, the present case is governed by cases like *Hyman v Nye* and *Jones v Page*. Where a vessel or other thing is hired there is an implied term that the vessel or thing hired shall be as fit for the purpose as reasonable care and skill can make it. In my view the plaintiffs are right in saying that that term was implied in the present contract.

But it has been argued that the fact that the "Golden Age" caught fire does not of necessity show that it was not fit for the purpose for which it was hired. I think I am entitled to say that, when a motor launch catches fire, apparently for an entirely unexplained cause, there is a presumption that the launch was not reasonably fit for that purpose. The evidence was that the launch, including the engine, was in perfect condition at the commencement of the hire, except that there was evidence that when the engine was cold the device known as "tickling the carburettor" was necessary, and that that caused a certain amount of petrol to flow outside the engine into the bilge. It is quite clear that there was a leak of petrol somewhere or somehow. This engine caught fire and, in my view, it is necessary for the defendants to satisfy me that it was not through any fault of theirs. I do not think that the admission by the plaintiff husband to the fireman that he might have spilt some petrol was sufficient to rebut the presumption that there was something wrong with the engine, as is proved by the fact that it caught fire, and the defendant has not discharged the onus of showing that the fire was not caused through any deficiency in the engine.

One other matter has caused me considerable anxiety. There was no form of fire appliance on this vessel, except an extinguisher which was useless. It was argued for the plaintiffs that proper fire-fighting equipment was part of the necessary equipment of a motor launch, that failure to provide such equipment was a breach of the implied warranty of fitness and that the fact that the "Golden Age" had no proper fire-fighting appliances was therefore a breach of the implied warranty. I was not referred by counsel to any authority directly on the point as to whether the implied warranty of fitness, where there is one, requires that a vessel shall be provided with equipment that is unnecessary to make it go or with equipment such as any reasonable person would supply in order that the vessel should be safe. I do not know; I have tried to find whether there is any such authority and my researches have failed to find any case immediately in point. I venture to suggest that in the case of a ship or motor launch one knows that one of the essentials of the vessel is to have lights. The lights do not assist in making the vessel go, but I should be very much surprised to learn that a vessel which was hired out to be sent to sea without any port or starboard lights was as fit as reasonable care and skill could make it for the purpose for which it was hired. I hold therefore that the defendant was under an implied obligation to make the "Golden Age" as reasonably safe as care and skill could make it, that that obligation included an obligation to provide fire-fighting equipment and that one of the causes of the loss that the plaintiffs have suffered was the failure by him to provide efficient fire-fighting equipment. There will therefore be judgment for the plaintiffs.

Notes and questions

1. This modest case is possibly more important than it looks in that it goes some way in tackling a problem exposed in the decision of *Joseph Constantine SS Ltd v Imperial Smelting Corp.*[5] A ship on hire to the plaintiffs exploded for a reason never properly explained. The House of Lords, reversing the Court of Appeal, held that the plaintiffs were not entitled to damages since the owners of the ship, the defendants, could rely upon frustration. There was no onus on the defendants to prove that the ship exploded through no fault on their part. Why could the owners of the motor launch not plead frustration?

2. Would the owner of the motor launch be entitled to the hire fee up to the moment the boat sank?

3. Has this decision been modified by the Supply of Goods and Services Act 1982?

4. Could the defendants have raised the defence of contributory negligence?

5. Does reasoning by analogy play an important role in Lewis J's decision?

Heil v Hedges [1951] 1 TLR 512 King's Bench Division

The plaintiff consumed a pork chop for lunch that had only been partly cooked by her maid and she suffered trichinosis as a result. The plaintiff unsuccessfully

---

5   [1942] AC 154.

brought an action for damages against the butcher who had sold the pork, claiming that the chop was neither of merchantable quality nor reasonably fit for its purpose.

McNair J: ... The next question is whether the defendant was in breach of the implied condition of reasonable fitness and merchantability under s 14 ... of the Sale of Goods Act 1893. I have already stated that the evidence satisfies me that if pork infested with trichinella is subjected to a temperature of 131 deg F., or on a more conservative estimate 137 deg. F., the trichinella is killed and the pork is innocuous. I am also satisfied on the evidence called by the defendant that it is common knowledge among the general public, as distinct from experts in nutrition and dietectics, that pork should be cooked substantially longer than other meat, given the same temperature, and that the proper way to cook pork is to cook it until it is white. A well-qualified witness called by the defendant told me that she had consulted 40 or 50 cookery books on the subject and that they were all to the same effect. She had also, by way of reinforcing her view, asked a number of housewives of humble station as to their views, and they had unanimously formed the view which she had formed.

In these circumstances it seems to me that, so far as trichinella spiralis is concerned, the implied condition of fitness or merchantability is complied with if the pork, when supplied, is in such condition that if properly cooked according to accepted standards it is innocuous ...

It being the common contemplation of the parties that the pork will be cooked before consumption, it seems to me that the implied condition must be applied in relation to pork which is not only cooked but properly cooked according to accepted standards. In my opinion, on the facts, it is plain that the pork in question in this case was not properly cooked according to accepted and known standards, but was fit for human consumption and merchantable if so cooked. Accordingly, in my judgment, the plaintiff's allegation that the implied conditions of fitness and merchantability were broken fails.

If liability had been established, I should have assessed the damages recoverable at £209 6s. 10d. in respect of special damage and £750 as general damages, but as I have taken the view that no liability is established there will be judgment for the defendant.

Questions

1. If the meat had been lamb rather than pork would the result have been different? What about beef?
2. Is this decision confined (i) to meat, (ii) to food or (iii) to products?
3. Will this decision apply to eggs purchased in the UK?

Ingham v Emes [1955] 2 QB 366 Court of Appeal

This was an action for damages brought by a customer, Mrs Ingham, against "Maison Emes", a ladies' hairdressers in Godalming. Mrs Ingham had gone to the hairdressers to have her hair dyed by the use of a product called Inecto, a preparation known to be dangerous in some cases, but she had failed to disclose to the hairdressers that she had suffered acute dermatitis when Inecto had been used on her some seven years previously. This second use of the product again caused dermatitis, but the Court of Appeal rejected the damages claim.

Denning LJ: ... The difficulty that I have felt is that this looks like a plea of contributory negligence, or a plea that Mrs Ingham was the author of her own misfortune; and that has never been pleaded or found. But I think the same result is reached by saying that the implied term as to fitness is dependent on proper disclosure by the customer of any relevant peculiarities known to her, and in particular of the fact that she knew by experience that Inecto might have a bad effect on her. The way this result is reached in law is this: in a contract for work and materials (such as the present) there is an implied term that the materials are reasonably fit for the purpose for which they are required: see *Myers v Brent Cross Service Co*. This term is analogous to the corresponding term in the sale of goods: see *Stewart v Reavell's Garage*. In order for the implied term to arise, however, the customer must make known to the contractor expressly or by implication the "particular purpose" for which the materials are required so as to show that he relies on the contractor's skill or judgment. The particular purpose in this case was to dye the hair, not of a normal person, but of a person known to be allergic to Inecto. Mrs Ingham did not make that particular purpose known to the assistant. She cannot therefore recover on the implied term ...

Notes and questions

1. It can easily be forgotten that it is a fundamental principle of the law of obligations that the breach of the obligation must be the cause of the plaintiff's damage. Contributory negligence, as we have seen (Chapter 3), is simply one device for dealing with difficult causal problems. In *Ingham v Emes* did the plaintiff fail because the hairdresser was not the factual cause of the plaintiff's dermatitis?

2. What if the plaintiff had forgotten that she was allergic to Inecto?

3. What if the plaintiff had suffered the dermatitis for the first time at the defendants' salon but could not actually prove beyond doubt that Inecto causes dermatitis; she could only prove that there was a 50% chance that her illness was caused by the product?[6]

4. Is a person with a bad cold or flu under a duty to disclose to the hairdresser that they have such an illness? If not, why not?

5. What if a hairdresser accidently cuts the ear off a customer after having been startled by a car back-firing in the street outside?

Poole v Smith's Car Sales (Balham) Ltd [1962] 1 WLR 744 Court of Appeal

This was a successful action in debt by one car dealer against another for the price of a car. The vehicle had been transferred by the plaintiff to the defendants with a view to the latter selling it to one of their customers for £325. Subsequently, the plaintiffs, without success, asked for the return of the vehicle

---

6   Cf *McGhee v NCB* [1973] 1 WLR 1; *Wilsher v Essex Area Health Authority* [1988] AC 1074.

and it was only after a final demand that the car was returned in a very bad condition. It seemed that this damage had been caused by two of the defendants' employees who had used the car without permission.

Willmer LJ: ... Had the defendants returned the car within a reasonable time, and had the plaintiff then refused to accept it because of the damage it had sustained, I think a really interesting question could have arisen. Our attention has been called to *Elphick v Barnes* which shows that where goods delivered under a sale or return contract are lost or damaged without default on the part of the defendant, the plaintiff cannot maintain an action for the price so long as the stipulated time or a reasonable time has not elapsed. For the party to whom the goods are delivered is not an insurer. I accept that. Such party would doubtless be liable in the event of loss or damage occurring through his fault while the goods are in his possession, but not if the damage occurred without any fault on his part. Had the defendants returned this car within a reasonable time in its damaged condition, it would at least have been open to them to contend that the damage was caused by no fault on their part, and that, accordingly, the plaintiff, on the principle of *Elphick v Barnes*, would be bound to accept the return of the car. But that could only be on the basis that the property had never passed under rule 4(b). On the view to which we have come in this case, however, this very interesting question does not, in my judgment, arise. I think that the plaintiff is entitled to recover, quite regardless of the fact of the car having been damaged, on the basis that a reasonable time had elapsed, so that the property had passed to the defendants. Accordingly, the contract price of £325 was, in my judgment, payable.

I would allow the appeal.

Questions

1. This case once again illustrates the important difference between debt and damages. The defendant can be liable in contractual debt only if property in the goods (the car) had passed to him. Yet is not the prospective purchaser a bailee of the car on sale or return and would not the defendant be liable in damages? Might he be liable in trespass or conversion for the value of the car?[7]

2. Could the defendant garage have claimed that they were not responsible for the acts of the employees who used the car without authority? Could the plaintiffs have sued the employees for (a) debt and/or (b) damages? Could the defendant garage have recovered the cost of the car from one or both of the employees?

Lister v Romford Ice & Cold Storage Co Ltd [1957] AC 555 House of Lords

This was an action in damages and (or) debt by an insurance company, subrogated to the rights of an assured employer, against an employee who had negligently injured a fellow-employee. The fellow-employee had obtained

---

7   Cf Torts (Interference with Goods) Act 1977 s 2(2).

damages, paid by the insurance company, on the basis that the employer was vicariously liable for the fault of its employee. The insurance company based their claims on breach of an implied term of the employee's contract of employment (damages) and (or) on statutory rights of contribution and indemnity (debt). A majority of the House of Lords gave judgment for the insurance company.

Viscount Simonds: ... [referring to Denning LJ's dissenting judgment in the Court of Appeal] ... [H]e says: "This shows that there is an implied term in these cases whereby, if the employer is insured, he will not seek to recover contribution or indemnity from the servant."

It will be observed that the implied term which thus commended itself to the learned Lord Justice is limited in its scope. The driver is to be relieved from liability if his master is covered by insurance against the claim. If he is not covered, for instance, because the accident takes place not on a road but on private premises and the law does not require him to insure against such a risk, and he has not done so, then under this plea the driver must bear the consequences of his negligence if he is himself sued. This consideration led counsel to yet another variation of the plea. This was that the driver was entitled to be indemnified not only if the employer was in fact insured or was required by law to be insured, but also if he ought, as a reasonable and prudent man, to have been insured against the risk in question ...

My Lords, undoubtedly there are formidable obstacles in the path of the appellant ... First, it is urged that it must be irrelevant to the right of the master to sue his servant for breach of duty that the master is insured against its consequences. As a general proposition it has not, I think, been questioned for nearly 200 years that in determining the rights *inter se* of A and B the fact that one or other of them is insured is to be disregarded ... And this general proposition no doubt, applies if A is a master and B his man. But its application to a case or class of case must yield to an express or implied term to the contrary, and, as the question is whether that term should be implied, I am not constrained by an assertion of the general proposition to deny the possible exception. Yet I cannot wholly ignore a principle so widely applicable as that a man insures at his own expense for his own benefit and does not thereby suffer any derogation of his rights against another man ...

Here, it was said, was a duty alleged to arise out of the relation of master and servant in this special sphere of employment which was imposed by the common law. When, then, did it first arise? Not, surely, when the first country squire exchanged his carriage and horses for a motor car or the first haulage contractor bought a motor lorry. Was it when the practice of insurers against third-party risk became so common that it was to be expected of the reasonable man or was it only when the Act of 1930 made compulsory and therefore universal what had previously been reasonable and usual? ...

It was contended, too, that a term should not be implied by law of which the social consequences would be harmful. The common law demands that the servant should exercise his proper skill and care in the performance of his duty: the graver the consequences of any dereliction, the more important it is that the sanction which the law imposes should be maintained. That sanction is that he should be liable in damages to his master: Other sanctions there may be, dismissal perhaps and loss of character and difficulty of getting fresh employment, but an action for damages, whether for tort or for breach of contract, has, even if rarely used, for centuries been available to the master, and now to grant the servant immunity from such an action would tend to create a feeling of irresponsibility in a class of persons from whom, perhaps more than any other, constant vigilance is owed to the community ...

Lord Radcliffe (dissenting): ... Now, the insurance policy required [by the Road Traffic Act 1930] could not come into existence of its own motion. One of the two parties, employer and employed, had to assume responsibility for taking it out or keeping it running and for paying up the necessary premiums to buy the cover. To which of them ought we to attribute that responsibility, having regard to the relationship of the parties? In my view, to the employer. I cannot suppose that, short of special stipulation, any other answer would be given in such a case ...

Then it is sought to show that the term in question cannot exist in law because it has never been heard of before this case. When did it first enter into the relations of employer and employed? Could it really have existed since the Road Traffic Act, 1930, if it did not exist before it? My Lords, I do not know because I do not think that I need to know. After all we need not speak of the master's action against his servant for negligence as if it had been common fare at the law for centuries. Economic reasons alone would have made the action a rarity. If such actions are now to be the usual practice I think it neither too soon nor too late to examine afresh some of their implications in a society which has been almost revolutionised by the growth of all forms of insurance ...

Lord Somerville (dissenting): ... Romer LJ [in the Court of Appeal], at the end of his judgment said that it was not in the public interest that drivers should be immune from the financial consequences of their negligence. The public interest has for long tolerated owners being so immune, and it would, I think, be unreasonable if it was to discriminate against those who earned their living by driving. Both are subject to the sanction of the criminal law as to careless or dangerous driving. The driver has a further sanction in that accidents causing damage are likely to hinder his advancement ...

Questions

1. Is there an implied term in a contract of employment that, in the case of an employee working abroad in a country where there is no compulsory driving insurance, an employer will make sure the employee is covered by an insurance policy? If not, is there at least a duty to warn the employee of the insurance position?[8]

2. In French law a judge must search for the real intention of the parties and in case of ambiguity must find for the debtor rather than the creditor. If this principle had been applied in *Lister* would the result have had to be different?

---

8   Cf *Reid v Rush & Tompkins plc* [1990] 1 WLR 212.

3. Research appears to show that drivers make one mistake about every two minutes. Does this mean that commercial drivers are in constant breach of contract?

4. Ought any judge with shares in an insurance company be allowed to sit in judgment on cases involving, directly or indirectly, insurance companies?

5. This extraordinary, and rightly much criticised, decision illustrates what can happen when attention is not carefully given to each institution in play (person, thing and action) together with the role of each category (tort, contract and equity). Of course, the majority ought to have considered the reality of the insurance position and Viscount Simonds' reasoning seems a bit daft by today's standards. Nevertheless, if the majority had focused just on the equitable remedy of subrogation they, like Lord Denning MR in a later case,[9] could have arrived at a different result without having to admit as such insurance into the law of tort. Ought subrogation to have been available to the insurance company? Were they not paid to carry the risk of motor accidents? Perhaps the absence of a third category in the law of obligations is partly to blame: for categories allow jurists to think about the roles of each subject and the role of restitution is to prevent unjust enrichment. Allowing an insurance company to recover an indemnity from an employee via the equitable remedy of subrogation is to undermine the role of equity and the law of tort at one and the same time. Equally it undermines the law of contract because the implied term is contrary to anything that employees would have ever agreed to (as insurance companies recognised). It is often said that hard cases make bad law, but might it not be better to say that bad lawyers make bad law?

Keppel Bus Co Ltd v Sa'ad bin Ahmad [1974] 2 All ER 700 Privy Council

This was an action for damages brought against a bus company in respect of personal injuries suffered by a passenger when he was assaulted by an angry bus conductor. The Singapore Court of Appeal held the company liable, but this decision was reversed by the Privy Council.

Lord Kilbrandon: ... The question in the case is whether the conductor did what he did "in the course of his employment". The course of the employment is not limited to the obligations which lie on an employee in virtue of his contract of service. It extends to acts done on the implied authority of the master. In *Poland v John Parr & Sons* a carter, who had handed over his wagon and was going home to his dinner, struck a boy whom he suspected, wrongly but on reasonable grounds, of stealing his master's property. The master was held liable for the consequences, since a servant has implied authority, at least in an emergency, to protect his master's property ...

---

9   *Morris v Ford Motor Co Ltd* [1973] 1 QB 782.

There is no dispute about the law. The Court of Appeal relied on the well-known passage from *Salmond on Torts* which was approved in *Canadian Pacific Railway Co v Lockhart*; it is not necessary to repeat it.

The Court of Appeal rightly point out that the question in every case is whether on the facts the act done, albeit unauthorised and unlawful, is done in the course of the employment; that question is itself a question of fact ... It is necessary, accordingly, in the present appeal to examine the grounds on which the learned judge held that, on the facts, this assault was committed in the course of carrying out, by a wrong mode, work which the conductor was expressly or impliedly authorised and therefore employed to do, and to see whether there is any evidence to support them. If there be no evidence, it is a matter of law that his conclusions could not stand ...

On the facts as found by the learned judge, and after examining, with the assistance of learned counsel, the testimony of those witnesses whom the judge accepted as credible, their Lordships are unable to find any evidence which, if it had been under the consideration of a jury, could have supported a verdict for the respondent. It may be accepted that the keeping of order among the passengers is part of the duties of a conductor. But there was no evidence of disorder among the passengers at the time of the assault. The only sign of disorder was that the conductor had gratuitously insulted the respondent, and the respondent had asked him in an orderly manner not to do it again ... Their Lordships are of opinion that no facts have been proved from which it could be properly inferred that there was present in that bus an emergency situation, calling for forcible action, justifiable on any express or implied authority, with which the appellants could be said on the evidence to have clothed the conductor.

A similar criticism can be levelled at the second ground on which the learned judge found that the conductor was acting under authority. There is no evidence that the respondent was interfering with the conductor in his due performance of his duty. His interference, if so it could be described, was a protest against the conductor's insulting language. Insults to passengers are not part of the due performance of a conductor's duty, as the learned judge seems to recognise in the paragraph of his judgment which follows.

The function of a bus conductor, from which could be deduced the scope of the authority committed to him, was attractively put by counsel for the respondent as "managing the bus"; it was said that what he did arose out of that power and duty of management. But this concept, it seems, if pushed to its extremes could serve to bring anything which the conductor did during his employment within the class of things done in the course of it. There must be room for some distinction between the acts of a manager, however foreign to his authority, and acts of management, properly so called. Probably this way of putting the case is fundamentally no different from that which the learned trial judge adopted and their Lordships reject, because there is no evidence of circumstances which would suggest that what the manager actually did was, although wrongful, within the scope of his authority, express or implied, and thus an act of management ...

Questions

1. Is this a contract case?

2. Were the defendants guilty of a breach of contract?

3. Do bus companies make promises to passengers? If so, what are these promises?

4. Did the defendants escape liability because they were not themselves at fault? What if they had had evidence that the bus conductor could be violent on occasions?

5. Do you think that it is an affront to common sense, as a leading English law professor (with a great knowledge of French law) once argued, that because the bus conductor's behaviour was worse than merely careless the company should not be liable?

6. Is this yet another example of poor lawyers making bad law?

4 EXCLUSION AND LIMITATION CLAUSES

Photo Production Ltd v Securicor Transport Ltd [1980] AC 827 House of Lords

This was an action for damages brought by the owners of a factory (or more precisely their insurance company) against a security company in respect of a fire deliberately started by one of the security company's patrolmen. The fire completely destroyed the plaintiffs' factory, but the security company resisted liability on the basis of a clause in the contract which stipulated that "under no circumstances" were the defendants to be "responsible for any injurious act or default by any employee unless such act or default could have been foreseen and avoided by the exercise of due diligence on the part of the [defendants] as his employer; nor, in any event, [were the defendants to] be held responsible for any loss suffered by the [plaintiffs] through fire or any other cause, except in so far as such loss [was] solely attributable to the negligence of the [defendants'] employees acting within the course of their employment." The trial judge gave judgment for the security company; the Court of Appeal reversed this decision; an appeal to the House of Lords was allowed.

Lord Diplock: ... My Lords, the contract in the instant case was entered into before the passing of the Unfair Contract Terms Act 1977. So what we are concerned with is the common law of contract, of which the subject-matter is the legally enforceable obligations as between the parties to it of which the contract is the source ...

My Lords, it is characteristic of commercial contracts, nearly all of which today are entered into not by natural legal persons, but by fictitious ones, ie companies, that the parties promise to one another that something will be done, for instance, that property and possession of goods will be transferred, that goods will be carried by ship from one port to another, that a building will be constructed in accordance with agreed plans, that services of a particular kind will be provided. Such a contract is the source of primary legal obligations on each party to it to procure that whatever he has promised will be done is done (...).

Where what is promised will be done involves the doing a physical act, performance of the promise necessitates procuring a natural person to do it ... If that person fails to do it in the manner in which the promiser has promised to procure it to be done, as, for instance, with reasonable skill and care, the promisor has failed to fulfil his own primary obligation ...

A basic principle of the common law of contract, to which there are no exceptions that are relevant in the instant case, is that parties to a contract are free to determine for themselves what primary obligations they will accept. They may state these in express words in the contract itself and, where they do, the statement is determinative; but in practice a commercial contract never states all the primary obligations of the parties in full; many are left to be incorporated by implication of law from the legal nature of the contract into which the parties are entering. But if the parties wish to reject or modify primary obligations which would otherwise be so incorporated, they are fully at liberty to do so by express words.

Leaving aside those comparatively rare cases in which the court is able to enforce a primary obligation by decreeing specific performance of it, breaches of primary obligations give rise to substituted secondary obligations on the part of the party in default, and, in some cases, may entitle the other party to be relieved from further performance of his own primary obligations. These secondary obligations of the contract breaker and any concomitant relief of the other party from his own primary obligations also arise by implication of law, generally common law, but sometimes statute, as in the case of codifying statutes passed at the turn of the century, notably the Sale of Goods Act 1893. The contract, however, is just as much the source of secondary obligations as it is of primary obligations; and like primary obligations that are implied by law secondary obligations too can be modified by agreement between the parties, although, for reasons to be mentioned later, they cannot, in my view, be totally excluded. In the instant case, the only secondary obligations and concomitant reliefs that are applicable arise by implication of the common law as modified by the express words of the contract.

Every failure to perform a primary obligation is a breach of contract. The secondary obligation on the part of the contract breaker to which it gives rise by implication of the common law is to pay monetary compensation to the other party for the loss sustained by him in consequence of the breach ...

My Lords, an exclusion clause is one which excludes or modifies an obligation, whether primary, or secondary, that would otherwise arise under the contract by implication of law. Parties are free to agree to whatever exclusion or modification of obligations they please within the limits that the agreement must retain the legal characteristics of a contract and must not offend against the equitable rule against penalties, that is to say, it must not impose on the breaker of a primary obligation a general secondary obligation to pay to the other party a sum of money that is manifestly intended to be in excess of the amount which would fully compensate the other party for the loss sustained by him in consequence of the breach of the primary obligation. Since the presumption is that the parties by entering into the contract intended to accept the implied obligations, exclusion clauses are to be construed strictly and the degree of strictness appropriate to be applied to their construction may properly depend on the extent to which they involve departure from the implied obligations. Since the obligations implied by law in a commercial contract are those which, by judicial consensus over the years or by Parliament in passing a statute, have been regarded as obligations which a reasonable businessman would realise that he was accepting when he entered into a contract of a particular kind, the court's view of the reasonableness of any departure from the implied obligations which would be involved in construing the express words of an exclusion clause in one sense that they are capable of bearing rather than another is a relevant consideration in deciding what meaning the words were intended by the parties to bear. But this does not entitle the court to reject the exclusion clause, however unreasonable the court itself may think it is, if the words are clear and fairly susceptible of one meaning only.

My Lords, the reports are full of cases in which what would appear to be very strained constructions have been placed on exclusion clauses, mainly in what today would be called consumer contracts and contracts of adhesion. As Lord Wilberforce has pointed out, any need for this kind of judicial distortion of the English language has been banished by Parliament's having made these kinds of contracts subject to the Unfair Contract Terms Act 1977. In commercial contracts negotiated between businessmen capable of looking after their own interests and of deciding how risks inherent in the performance of various kinds of contract can be most economically borne (generally by insurance), it is, in my view, wrong to place a strained construction on words in an exclusion clause which are clear and fairly susceptible of one meaning only even after due allowance has been made for the presumption in favour of the implied primary and secondary obligations.

Applying these principles to the instant case, in the absence of the exclusion clause a primary obligation of Securicor under the contract, which would be implied by law, would be an absolute obligation to procure that the visits by the night patrol to the factory were conducted by natural persons who would exercise reasonable skill and care for the safety of the factory. That primary obligation is modified by the exclusion clause. Securicor's obligation to do this is not to be absolute, but is limited to exercising due diligence in their capacity as employers of the natural persons by whom the visits are conducted, to procure that those persons shall exercise reasonable skill and care for the safety of the factory.

For the reasons given by Lord Wilberforce it seems to me that this apportionment of the risk of the factory being damaged or destroyed by the injurious act of an employee of Securicor while carrying out a visit to the factory is one which reasonable businessmen in the position of Securicor and Photo Productions might well think was the most economical ... The risk that a servant of Securicor would damage or destroy the factory or steal goods from it, despite the exercise of all reasonable diligence by Securicor to prevent it, is what in the context of maritime law would be called a "misfortune risk", is something which reasonable diligence of neither party to the contract can prevent. Either party can insure against it. It is generally more economical for the person by whom the loss will be directly sustained to do so rather than that it should be covered by the other party by liability insurance ...

Lord Wilberforce: ... Securicor undertook to provide a service of periodical visits for a very modest charge ... It did not agree to provide equipment. It would have no knowledge of the value of Photo Productions' factory; that and the efficacy of their fire precautions, would be known to Photo Productions. In these circumstances nobody could consider it unreasonable that as between these two equal parties the risk assumed by Securicor should be a modest one, and that Photo Productions should carry the substantial risk of damage or destruction ...

Lord Salmon: ... I think that any businessman entering into this contract could have had no doubt as to the real meaning of this clause and would have made his insurance arrangements accordingly ...

Questions

1. Why is it that an employer is, in principle, liable for violence done by its employee to a building but not liable (see *Keppel* above) for violence done by its employee to a person? If you had to devise an artificial intelligence programme on the law of obligations how would you deal with *Keppel* and *Photo Production*?
2. Did the court focus on risk rather than fault? If so, why?
3. Would the plaintiffs have had to pay for the services rendered by Securicor?
4. Which legal subject caused the plaintiffs' damage?
5. In his analysis of contract into primary and secondary obligations does Lord Diplock overlook the action for debt? Does this action not enforce directly a primary obligation?

Unfair Contract Terms Act 1977 (c 50)

1. Scope of Part I

(1) For the purposes of this Part of this Act, "negligence" means the breach –

(a) of any obligation, arising from the express or implied terms of a contract, to take reasonable care or exercise reasonable skill in the performance of the contract;

(b) of any common law duty to take reasonable care or exercise reasonable skill (but not any stricter duty) ...

(3) In the case of both contract and tort, sections 2 to 7 apply ... only to business liability, that is liability for breach of obligations or duties arising

(a) from things done or to be done by a person in the course of a business (whether his own business or another's); or

(b) from the occupation of premises used for business purposes of the occupier; and references to liability are to be read accordingly ...

(4) In relation to any breach of duty or obligation, it is immaterial for any purpose of this Part of this Act whether the breach was inadvertent or intentional, or whether liability for it arises directly or vicariously.

2. Negligence liability

(1) A person cannot by reference to any contract term or to a notice given to persons generally or to particular persons exclude or restrict his liability for death or personal injury resulting from negligence.

(2) In the case of other loss or damage, a person cannot so exclude or restrict his liability for negligence except in so far as the term or notice satisfies the requirement of reasonableness.

(3) Where a contract term or notice purports to exclude or restrict liability for negligence a person's agreement to or awareness of it is not of itself to be taken as indicating his voluntary acceptance of any risk.

3. Liability arising in contract

(1) This section applies as between contracting parties where one of them deals as consumer or on the other's written standard terms of business.

(2) As against that party, the other cannot by reference to any contract term –

(a) when himself in breach of contract, exclude or restrict any liability of his in respect of the breach; or

(b) claim to be entitled –

(i) to render a contractual performance substantially different from that which was reasonably expected of him, or

(ii) in respect of the whole or any part of his contractual obligation, to render no performance at all.

Except in so far as (in any of the cases mentioned above in this subsection) the contract term satisfies the requirement of reasonableness.

4. Unreasonable indemnity clauses

(1) A person dealing as consumer cannot by reference to any contract term be made to indemnify another person (whether a party to the contract or not) in respect of liability that may be incurred by the other for negligence or breach of contract, except in so far as the contract term satisfies the requirement of reasonableness.

(2) This section applies whether the liability in question –

(a) is directly that of the person to be indemnified or is incurred by him vicariously;

(b) is to the person dealing as consumer or to someone else.

5. "Guarantee" of consumer goods

(1) In the case of goods of a type ordinarily supplied for private use or consumption, where loss or damage –

(a) arises from the goods proving defective while in consumer use; and

(b) results from the negligence of a person concerned in the manufacture or distribution of the goods

liability for the loss or damage cannot be excluded or restricted by reference to any contract term or notice contained in or operating by reference to a guarantee of the goods.

13. Varieties of exemption clause

(1) To the extent that this Part of this Act prevents the exclusion or restriction of any liability it also prevents –

(a) making the liability or its enforcement subject to restrictive or onerous conditions;

(b) excluding or restricting any right or remedy in respect of the liability, or subjecting a person to any prejudice in consequence of his pursuing any such right or remedy;

(c) excluding or restricting rules of evidence or procedure ...

Questions

1. Does this Act treat consumers as incapables? Does it treat the class of consumers as a legal person?
2. Is s 13 in effect wide enough to cover almost any contractual clause that puts duties on one of the parties? Does s 13 conform to Lord Diplock's thesis of primary and secondary obligations?
3. Will the Act need to be modified in the light of the EU Directive on unfair terms in consumer contracts?[10]

George Mitchell (Chesterhall) Ltd v Finney Lock Seeds Ltd [1983] QB 284 Court of Appeal; [1983] 2 AC 803 House of Lords

This was an action for damages by a farmer against the seller of Dutch Winter cabbage seed. The seed, which cost £201.60, turned out to be of inferior quality and useless to the farmer and he claimed compensation for all his losses when the crop of cabbages had to be destroyed; the sellers relied on a clause on the invoice purporting to limit their liability, should the seed prove defective, to replacing the seed or repaying the price. The trial judge awarded the farmer £61,513.78 damages plus £30,756 interest and appeals to the Court of Appeal and House of Lords were dismissed.

Lord Denning MR (Court of Appeal) [having reviewed the case law and the Unfair Contract Terms Act 1977]:

---

10   See Council Directive of 5 April 1993 (93/13/EEC:L 95/29).

The effect of the changes

What is the result of all this? To my mind it heralds a revolution in our approach to exemption clauses; not only where they exclude liability altogether and also where they limit liability; not only in the specific categories in the Unfair Contract Terms Act 1977, but in other contracts too. Just as in other fields of law we have done away with the multitude of cases on "common employment", "last opportunity," "invitees" and "licensees" and so forth, so also in this field we should do away with the multitude of cases on exemption clauses. We should no longer have to go through all kinds of gymnastic contortions to get round them. We should no longer have to harass our students with the study of them. We should set about meeting a new challenge. It is presented by the test of reasonableness ...

Fair and reasonable

There is only one case in the books so far on this point. It is *RW Green Ltd v Cade Bros Farm*. There Griffiths J held that it was fair and reasonable for seed potato merchants to rely on a limitation clause which limited their liability to the contract price of the potatoes. That case was very different from the present.The terms had been evolved over 20 years. The judge said: "They are therefore not conditions imposed by the strong upon the weak; but are rather a set of trading terms upon which both sides are apparently content to do business." The judge added: "No moral blame attaches to either party; neither of them knew, nor could be expected to know, that the potatoes were infected." In that case the judge held that the clause was fair and reasonable and that the seed merchants were entitled to rely on it.

Our present case is very much on the borderline. There is this to be said in favour of the seed merchants. The price of this cabbage seed was small: £192. The damages claimed are high: £61,000. But there is this to be said on the other side. The clause was not negotiated between persons of equal bargaining power. It was inserted by the seed merchants in their invoices without any negotiation with the farmers.

To this I would add that the seed merchants rarely, if ever, invoked the clause. Their very frank director said: "The trade does not stand on the strict letter of the clause ... Almost invariably when a customer justifiably complains, the trade pays something more than a refund." The papers contain many illustrations where the clause was not invoked and a settlement was reached.

Next, I would point out that the buyers had no opportunity at all of knowing or discovering that the seed was not cabbage seed, whereas the sellers could and should have known that it was the wrong seed altogether. The buyers were not covered by insurance against the risk. Nor could they insure. But, as to the seed merchants, the judge said:

> "I am entirely satisfied that it is possible for seedsmen to insure against this risk. I am entirely satisfied that the cost of so doing would not materially raise the price of seeds on the market. I am entirely satisfied that the protection of this clause for the purposes of protecting against the very rare case indeed, such as the present, is not reasonably required. If and in so far as it may be necessary to consider the matter, I am also satisfied that it is possible for seedsmen to test seeds before putting the-on to the market."

To that I would add this further point. Such a mistake as this could not have happened without serious negligence on the part of the seed merchants themselves or their Dutch suppliers. So serious that it would not be fair to enable them to escape responsibility for it.

In all the circumstances I am of opinion that it would not be fair or reasonable to allow the seed merchants to rely on the clause to limit their liability.

Kerr LJ (Court of Appeal): ... I would unhesitatingly also decide this case in favour of the plaintiffs on the ground that it would not be fair and reasonable to allow the defendants to rely on this clause ...

The plaintiffs have suffered a loss of some £61,000 in terms of money; and in terms of time and labour the productivity of over 60 acres has been wasted for over a year. There was nothing whatever the plaintiffs could have done to avoid this. As between them and the defendants all the fault lay admittedly on the side of the defendants. Further, farmers do not, and cannot be expected to, insure against this kind of disaster; but suppliers of seed can ...

Lord Bridge (House of Lords): ... My Lords, it seems to me, with all due deference, that the judgments of the learned trial judge and of Oliver LJ on the common law issue come dangerously near to re-introducing by the back door the doctrine of "fundamental breach" which this House in Securicor 1, had so forcibly evicted by the front. The learned judge discusses what I may call the "peas and beans" or "chalk and cheese" cases, sc. those in which it has been held that exemption clauses do not apply where there has been a contract to sell one thing, eg, a motor car, and the seller has supplied quite another things eg, a bicycle. I hasten to add that the judge can in no way be criticised for adopting this approach since counsel appearing for the appellants at the trial had conceded "that if what had been delivered had been beetroot seed or carrot seed, he would not be able to rely upon the clause". Different counsel appeared for the appellants in the Court of Appeal, where that concession was withdrawn ...

This is the first time your Lordships' House has had to consider a modern statutory provision giving the court power to override contractual terms excluding or restricting liability, which depends on the court's view of what is "fair and reasonable" ... It may ... be appropriate to consider how an original decision of what is "fair and reasonable" made in the application of any of these [statutory] provisions should be approached by an appellate court. It would not be accurate to describe such a decision as an exercise of discretion. But ... the court must entertain a whole range of considerations, put them in the scales on one side or the other and decide at the end of the day on which side the balance comes down ...

The question of relative bargaining strength under paragraph (a) and of the opportunity buy seeds without a limitation of the seedsman's liability under paragraph (b) were inter-related. The evidence was that a similar limitation of liability was universally embodied in the terms of trade between seedsmen and farmers and had been so for very many years. The limitation had never been negotiated between representative bodies but, on the other hand, had not been the subject of any protest by the National Farmers' Union. These factors, if considered in isolation, might have been equivocal. The decisive factor, however, appears from the evidence of four witnesses called for the appellants, two independent seedsmen, the chairman of the appellant company, and a director of a sister company (both being wholly-owned subsidiaries of the same parent). They said that it had always been their practice, unsuccessfully attempted in the instant case, to negotiate settlements of farmers' claims for damages in excess of the price of the seeds, if they thought that the claims were "genuine" and "justified". This evidence indicated a clear recognition by seedsmen in general, and the appellants in particular, that reliance on the limitation of liability imposed by the relevant condition would not be fair or reasonable.

Two further factors, if more were needed, weight the scales in favour of the respondents. The supply of autumn, instead of winter, cabbage seeds was due to the negligence of the appellants' sister company. Irrespective of its quality, the autumn variety supplied could not, according to the appellants' own evidence, be grown commercially in East Lothian. Finally, as the trial judge found, seedsmen could insure against the risk of crop failure caused by supplying ahe wrong variety of seeds without materially increasing the price of seeds.

My Lords, even if I felt doubts about the statutory issue, I should not, for the reasons explained earlier, think it right to interfere with the unanimous original decision of that issue by the Court of Appeal. As it is, I feel no such doubts. If I were making the original decision, I should conclude without hesitation that would not be fair or reasonable to allow the [defendants] to rely on the contractual limitation of their liability ...

Questions

1. Did fault play a central role in determining the outcome of this case? If so, how can this be reconciled with risk which is, surely, the notion which underpins insurance?

2. Did the House of Lords base their decision on an issue of fact?

5 BREACH AND LEVEL OF DUTY

Readhead v Midland Railway Co (1869) LR 4 QB 379 Court of Exchequer Chamber

Montague Smith J: In this case the plaintiff, a passenger for hire on the defendants' railway, suffered an injury in consequence of the carriage in which he travelled getting off the line and upsetting; the accident was caused by the breaking of the tyre of one of the wheels of the carriage owing to "a latent defect in the tyre which was not attributable to any fault on the part of the manufacturer, and could not be detected previously to the breaking".

Does an action lie against the company under these circumstances?

This question involves the consideration of the true nature of the contract made between a passenger and a general carrier of passengers for hire. It is obvious, that for the plaintiff on this state of facts to succeed in this action, he must establish either that there is a warranty, by way of insurance on the part of the carrier to convey the passenger safely to his journey's end, or, as the learned counsel mainly insisted, a warranty that the carriage in which he travels shall be in all respects perfect for its purpose, that is to say, free from all defects likely to cause peril, although those defects were such that no skill, care, or foresight could have detected their existence.

We are of opinion, after consideration of the authorities, that there is no such contract either of general or limited warranty and insurance entered into by the carrier of passengers, and that the contract of such a carrier and the obligation undertaken by him are to take due care (including in that term the use of skill and foresight) to carry a passenger safely. It of course follows that the absence of such care, in other words negligence, would alone be a breach of this contract, and as the facts of this case do not disclose such a breach, and on the contrary negative any want of skill, care or foresight, we think the plaintiff has failed to sustain his action and that the judgment of the Court below in favour of the defendant ought to be affirmed.

The law of England has, from the earliest times, established a broad distinction between the liabilities of common carriers of goods and of passengers. Indeed the responsibility (like the analogous one of innkeepers) of the carrier to redeliver the goods in a sound state can attach only in the case of goods. This responsibility has been so long fixed, and is so universally known, that carriers of goods undertake to carry on contracts well understood to comprehend this implied liability ...

The Court is now asked to declare the same law to be applicable to contracts to carry passengers ...

The reason suggested was, as we understood it, that a passenger when placed in a carriage was as helpless as a bale of goods, and therefore entitled to have for his personal safety a warranty that the carriage was sound ... The argument founded on this reason, however, would obviously carry the liability of the carrier far beyond the limited warranty of the roadworthiness of the carriage in which the passenger happened to travel. His safety is no doubt dependent on the soundness of the carriage in which he travels, but in the case of a passenger on a railway it is no less dependent on the roadworthiness of the other carriages in the same train and of the engine drawing them, on the soundness of the rails, of the points, of the signals, of the masonry, in fact of all the different parts of the system employed and used in his transport, and he is equally helpless as regards them all.

If then there is force in the above reason, why stop short at the carriage in which the passenger happens to travel? ...

An obligation to use all due and proper care is founded on reasons obvious to all, but to impose on the carrier the burden of a warranty that everything he necessarily uses is absolutely free from defects likely to cause peril, when from the nature of things defects must exist which no skill can detect, and the effects of which no care or foresight can avert, would be to compel a man, by implication of law and not by his own will, to promise the performance of an impossible thing, and would be directly opposed to the maxims of law, *lex non cogit ad impossibilia – Nemo tenetur ad impossibilia.*

If the principle of implying a warranty is to prevail in the present case, there seems to be no good reason why it should not be equally applied to a variety of other cases, as for instance to the managers of theatres and other places of public resort, who provide seats or other accommodation for the public. Why are they not to be equally held to insure by implied warranty the soundness of the structures to which they invite the public? But we apprehend it to be clear that such persons do no more than undertake to use due care that their buildings shall be in a fit state ...

"Due care", however, undoubtedly means, having reference to the nature of the contract to carry, a high degree of care, and casts on carriers the duty of exercising all vigilance to see that whatever is required for the safe conveyance of their passengers is in fit and proper order. But the duty to take due care, however widely construed or however rigorously enforced, will not, as the present action seeks to do, subject the defendants to the plain injustice of being compelled by the law to make reparation for a disaster arising from a latent defect in the machinery which they are obliged to use, which no human skill or care could either have prevented or detected.

In the result we come to the conclusion that the case of the plaintiff, so far as it relies on authority, fails in precedent; and so far as it rests on principle, fails in reason ...

Notes and questions

1. Why is there one rule for goods and another for passengers? What justification(s) for the difference does Montague Smith J offer? Are they convincing?

2. In order for a contractor to be in breach of contract he, she or it must be in breach of one of the actual promises (terms) which go to make up the contract. However, as the above case makes clear ("after a consideration of the authorities"), this exercise is one of interpretation, not of the parties' minds, but of the law; yet the parties' minds become one reason for not implying an absolute promise since that would, according to the court, lead to a situation where the parties have promised the impossible. Why, however, does Lindley J in the case below seem to take a different approach?

Hyman v Nye (1881) 6 QBD 685 Queen's Bench Division

Lindley J: The defendant in this case was a job-master at Brighton, letting out carriages and horses for hire. The plaintiff hired of him a landau, and a pair of horses, and a driver, for a drive from Brighton to Shoreham and back. After having driven some way, and whilst the carriage was going down hill and slowly over a newly mended part of the road, a bolt in the underpart of the carriage broke. The splinter-bar became displaced; the horses started off; the carriage was upset; the plaintiff was thrown out and injured, and he brought this action for compensation.

It was proved at the trial that no fault could be imputed to the horses nor to the driver; and although the plaintiff was charged with having caused the accident by pulling the reins, the jury found in the plaintiff's favour on this point, and nothing now turns upon it.

It further appeared that the carriage had been built by a good builder some eight or nine years before the accident; had been repaired by a competent person about 15 months before it; that the defendant had no reason to suppose that there was any defect in the carriage or in any of its bolts; and that the defect, if any, in the bolt which broke could not have been discovered by any ordinary inspection. The bolt itself was not produced at the trial, and the nature of the defect, if any, in it when the carriage started was not proved.

The learned judge at the trial told the jury in substance that the plaintiff was bound to prove that the injury which he had sustained was caused by the negligence of the defendant; and if in their opinion the defendant took all reasonable care to provide a fit and proper carriage their verdict ought to be for him. Being thus directed, the jury found a verdict for the defendant; and in particular they found that the carriage was reasonably fit for the purpose for which it was hired, and that the defect in the bolt could not have been discovered by the defendant by ordinary care and attention. The plaintiff complains of this direction, and of the verdict founded upon it, and we have to consider whether the direction was correct ...

A careful study of these authorities leads me to the conclusion that the learned judge at the trial put the duty of the defendant too low. A person who lets out carriages is not, in my opinion, responsible for all defects discoverable or not; he is not an insurer against all defects; nor is he bound to take more care than coach proprietors or railway companies who provide carriages for the public to travel in; but in my opinion, he is bound to take as much care as they; and although not an insurer against all defects, he is an insurer against all defects which care and skill can guard against. His duty appears to me to be to supply a carriage as fit for the purpose for which it is hired as care and skill can render it; and if whilst the carriage is being properly used for such purpose it breaks down, it becomes incumbent on the person who has let it out to show that the breakdown was in the proper sense of the word an accident not preventable by any care or skill. If he can prove this, as the defendant did in *Christie v Griggs*, and as the railway company did in *Readhead v Midland Ry Co*, he will not be liable; but no proof short of this will exonerate him. Nor does it appear to me to be at all unreasonable to exact such vigilance from a person who makes it his business to let out carriages for hire. As between him and the hirer the risk of defects in the carriage, so far as care and skill can avoid them, ought to be thrown on the owner of the carriage. The hirer trusts him to supply a fit and proper carriage; the lender has it in his power not only to see that it is in a proper state, and to keep it so, and thus protect himself from risk, but also to charge his customers enough to cover his expenses.

Such being, in my opinion, the law applicable to the case, it follows that the direction given to the jury did not go far enough, and that it was not sufficient, in order to exonerate the defendant from liability for him to prove that he did not know of any defect in the bolt; had no reason to suppose it was weak, and could not see that it was by an ordinary inspection of the carriage. It further follows that, in my opinion, the evidence was not such as to warrant the finding that the carriage was in a fit and proper state when it left the defendant's yard.

In many of the cases bearing on this subject, the expression "reasonably fit and proper" is used. This is a little ambiguous, and requires explanation. In a case like the present, a carriage to be reasonably fit and proper must be as fit and proper as care and skill can make it for use in a reasonable and proper manner, ie as fit and proper as care and skill can make it to carry a reasonable number of people, conducting themselves in a reasonable manner, and going at a reasonable pace on the journey for which the carriage was hired; or (if no journey was specified) along roads, or over ground reasonably fit for carriages. A carriage not fit and proper in this sense would not be reasonably fit and proper, and vice versa. The expression "reasonably fit" denotes something short of absolutely fit; but in a case of this description the difference between the two expressions is not great.

It was objected on the part of the defendant that the plaintiff had in his statement of claim based his case on negligence on the part of the defendant, and not on any breach of warranty express or implied, and consequently that the plaintiff could not recover in this action, at least, without amending. But the absence of such care as a person is by law bound to take is negligence; and whether the plaintiff sues the defendant in tort for negligence in not having supplied such a fit and proper carriage as he ought to have supplied, or whether the plaintiff sues him in contract for the breach of an implied warranty that the carriage was as fit and proper as it ought to have been, appears to me wholly immaterial. Upon this point I adopt the opinion of Baron Martin in *Francis v Cockrell*, which is based upon and warranted by *Brown v Boorman* ...

For the above reasons I am of opinion that there should be a new trial.

Mathew J [concurred].

Notes and questions

1. Is Lindley J applying to the facts before him exactly the same rule as the court in *Readhead* applied to the facts before it? If so, why the different result?

2. Is there any concept which is applied in *Hyman* but was not applied in *Readhead*?

3. Did the defendant in *Hyman* promise the impossible?

4. Why did the court in *Hyman* order a new trial rather than make its own decision?

5. Are railway carriages (and the like) 'products'?

6. Does the Supply of Goods and Services Act 1982 impose the same level of duty on an owner as *Hyman*?

7. Is the duty on the defendant in *Hyman* the same as the duty on the defendants in: (i) *Henderson v Jenkins* (p 399); (ii) *Ward v Tesco* (p 82); (iii) *Grant v Australian Knitting Mills* (p 89)?

Thake v Maurice [1986] QB 644 Court of Appeal

Kerr LJ (dissenting): This is an appeal by the defendant, a consultant surgeon in general practice, from a judgment delivered by Peter Pain J [1985] 2 WLR 215 on 26 March 1984 after a trial which occupied five days. The facts and the parties' contentions are set out with admirable clarity, and, save on one issue, the judge's findings of facts were unchallenged on this appeal. Since the facts are highly unusual, it is desirable to set them out in full, and I cannot do better than by quoting extensively from the judgment itself. The background and the issues are summarised, at pp 217-218:

"In 1975 the two plaintiffs, Mr and Mrs Thake, were at their wits' end. They had four children and a fifth on the way. Mr Thake was a railway guard and they were having the greatest difficulty in managing on his pay, so Mr Thake had a vasectomy which was performed by the defendant. The operation appeared to be a success and both plaintiffs were convinced that Mr Thake was now sterile. They resumed normal sexual intercourse without any further contraceptive precaution. In 1978 Mrs Thake began to miss her periods. She did not worry because she was convinced that it was impossible for her to conceive. She put it down to an early onset of the change of life. Eventually she went to her doctor and was shattered to find that she was four months pregnant. Her husband was tested and it was found that he had become fertile again. He was one of those rare cases in which nature had formed a bridge of scar tissue between the cut ends of the vas through which the sperm could pass. The two plaintiffs now claim damages against the defendant on three alternative grounds. First, they assert that the contract was not simply a contract to carry out a vasectomy, but was a contract to sterilise Mr Thake which was broken when he became fertile again. Secondly, they put their case on breach of collateral warranty or innocent misrepresentation. They submit that they were induced to enter into the contract by a false warranty or representation that the operation would render Mr Thake irreversibly sterile. Thirdly, they allege contractual negligence in that the defendant failed to warn them that there was a small risk that Mr Thake would become fertile again. An interesting point also arises as to the assessment of damages, should the plaintiffs succeed on liability. The defendant asserts that, as a matter of public policy, damages may not be awarded for the birth of a healthy child."

The claim in contract

The judge reached the conclusion that in the unusual circumstances of this case the plaintiffs had established that the revival of Mr Thake's fertility gave rise to a breach of the contract concluded between the defendant and the plaintiffs ...

On this issue I have reached the same conclusion as the judge. Having regard to everything that passed between the defendant and the plaintiffs at the meeting, coupled with the absence of any warning that Mr Thake might somehow again become fertile after two successful sperm tests, it seems to me that the plaintiffs could not reasonably have concluded anything other than that his agreement to perform the operation meant that, subject to two successful sperm tests, he had undertaken to render Mr Thake permanently sterile. In my view this follows from an objective analysis of the undisputed evidence of what passed between the parties, and it was also what the plaintiffs understood and intended to be the effect of the contract with the defendant.

The considerations which lead me to this conclusion can be summarised as follows. First, we are here dealing with something in the nature of an amputation, not treatment of an injury or disease with inevitably uncertain results. The nature of the operation was the removal of parts of the channels through which sperm had to pass to the outside in such a way that the channels could not reunite. This was vividly demonstrated to the plaintiffs by the defendant pulling apart his arms and fists and turning back his wrists, as well as by a sketch. The defendant repeatedly and carefully explained that the effect of the operation was final, as the plaintiffs said again and again in their evidence, subject only to a remote possibility of surgical reversal, and that was the only warning which the defendant impressed on them. Subject to this and the two sperm tests of which the plaintiffs were told, designed to make sure that the operation had in fact been successful, I cannot see that one can place any interpretation on what the defendant said and did other than that he undertook to render Mr Thake permanently sterile by means of the operation. Nor can I see anything in the transcripts of the evidence which leads to any other conclusion, and the defendant himself agreed that in the context of the discussion as a whole, the word "irreversible" would have been understood by the plaintiffs as meaning 'irreversible by God or man'. On the evidence in this case the position is quite different, in my view, from what was in the mind of Lord Denning MR in *Greaves & Co (Contractors) Ltd v Baynham Meikle & Partners* [1975] 1 WLR 1095, 1100, when he said: "The surgeon does not warrant that he will cure the patient." That was said in the context of treatment or an operation designed to cure, not in the context of anything in the nature of an amputation. The facts of the present case are obviously extremely unusual, but I do not see why the judge's and my conclusion on these unusual facts should be viewed by surgeons with alarm, as mentioned by the judge. If the defendant had given his usual warning, the objective analysis of what he conveyed would have been quite different ...

Accordingly, I would uphold the judge's conclusion that the plaintiffs succeed in their claim that the revival of Mr Thake's fertility gave rise to a breach of contract on the part of the defendant ...

Neill LJ: I have had the advantage of reading in draft the judgment of Kerr LJ and ... I regret to say, however, that I am unable to agree with his conclusion as to the claim in contract ...

I accept that there may be cases where, because of the claims made by a surgeon or physician for his method of treatment, the court is driven to the conclusion that the result of the treatment is guaranteed or warranted. But in the present case I do not regard the statements made by the defendant as to the effect of his treatment as passing beyond the realm of expectation and assumption. It seems to me that what he said was spoken partly by way of warning and partly by way of what is sometimes called "therapeutic reassurance". Both the plaintiffs and the defendant expected that sterility would be the result of the operation and the defendant appreciated that that was the plaintiffs' expectation. This does not mean, however, that a reasonable person would have understood the defendant to be giving a binding promise that the operation would achieve its purpose or that the defendant was going further than to give an assurance that he expected and believed that it would have the desired result. Furthermore, I do not consider that a reasonable person would have expected a responsible medical man to be intending to give a guarantee. Medicine, though a highly skilled profession, is not, and is not generally regarded as being, an exact science. The reasonable man would have expected the defendant to exercise all the proper skill and care of a surgeon in that speciality; he would not in my view have expected the defendant to give a guarantee of 100 per cent success.

Accordingly, though I am satisfied that a reasonable person would have left the consulting room thinking that Mr Thake would be sterilised by the vasectomy operation, such a person would not have left thinking that the defendant had given a guarantee that Mr Thake would be absolutely sterile. For these reasons I would allow the appeal in so far as the claim in contract is concerned ...

Nourse LJ: ... The question ... is whether the defendant contracted to carry out a vasectomy or to render Mr Thake permanently sterile. The latter alternative necessarily involved a guarantee; in other words, a warranty that there was not the remotest chance, not one in ten thousand, that the operation would not succeed. Peter Pain J held, in my view correctly, that the contract was contained partly in the words used between the parties and partly in the words of the consent form. The object of the operation, as stated in the form, was to render Mr Thake sterile and incapable of parenthood. The contract contained an implied warranty that, in carrying out the operation, the defendant would exercise the ordinary skill and care of a competent surgeon. It did not contain an implied warranty that, come what may, the objective would be achieved: see *Greaves & Co (Contractors) Ltd v Baynham Meikle & Partners* [1975] 1 WLR 1095, 1100, *per* Lord Denning MR ...

Lord Denning thought, and I respectfully agree with him, that a professional man is not usually regarded as warranting that he will achieve the desired result. Indeed, it seems that that would not fit well with the universal warranty of reasonable care and skill, which tends to affirm the inexactness of the science which is professed. I do not intend to go beyond the case of a doctor. Of all sciences medicine is one of the least exact. In my view a doctor cannot be objectively regarded as guaranteeing the success of any operation or treatment unless he says as much in clear and unequivocal terms. The defendant did not do that in the present case ...

Questions

1. Should the level of duty ever be dependent upon the price of the service?

2. If one supplies faulty goods the seller is strictly liable (see p 19): why is there a different rule for services? Is the distinction a sensible one when viewed from the position of the consumer? What about when viewed from the position of the supplier?

3. Is there a policy issue behind this decision?

6 REMEDIES AND BREACH

(a) Self-help

Hong Kong Fir Shipping Co Ltd v Kawasaki Kishen Kaisha Ltd [1962] 2 QB 26 Court of Appeal

This was an action for damages by the owners of a ship against the charterers of the vessel for wrongful repudiation of the charterparty. The charterers claimed they were entitled to repudiate the contract because the ship was unseaworthy and the crew inadequate. The trial judge held that the owners were in breach of contract, but that the charterers had not been entitled to repudiate. An appeal to the Court of Appeal was dismissed.

Diplock LJ: ... Every synallagmatic contract contains in it the seeds of the problem: in what event will a party be relieved of his undertaking to do that which he has agreed to do but has not yet done? The contract may itself expressly define some of these events, as in the cancellation clause in a charterparty; but, human prescience being limited, it seldom does so exhaustively and often fails to do so at all. In some classes of contracts such as sale of goods, marine insurance, contracts of affreightment evidenced by bills of lading and those between parties to bills of exchange, Parliament has defined by statute some of the events not provided for expressly in individual contracts of that class; but where an event occurs the occurrence of which neither the parties nor Parliament have expressly stated will discharge one of the parties from further performance of his undertakings, it is for the court to determine whether the event has this effect or not.

The test whether an event has this effect or not has been stated in a number of metaphors all of which I think amount to the same thing: does the occurrence of the event deprive the party who has further undertakings still to perform of substantially the whole benefit which it was the intention of the parties as expressed in the contract that he should obtain as the consideration for performing those undertakings?

This test is applicable whether or not the event occurs as a result of the default of one of the parties to the contract, but the consequences of the event are different in the two cases. Where the event occurs as a result of the default of one party, the party in default cannot rely upon it as relieving himself of the performance of any further undertakings on his part, and the innocent party, although entitled to, need not treat the event as relieving him of the further performance of his own undertakings. This is only a specific application of the fundamental legal and moral rule that a man should not be allowed to take advantage of his own wrong. Where the event occurs as a result of the default of neither party, each is relieved of the further performance of his own undertakings, and their rights in respect of undertakings previously performed are now regulated by the Law Reform (Frustrated Contracts) Act 1943.

This branch of the common law has reached its present stage by the normal process of historical growth, and the fallacy in Mr Ashton Roskill's [counsel for the charterer] contention that a different test is applicable when the event occurs as a result of the default of one party from that applicable in cases of frustration where the event occurs as a result of the default of neither party lies, in my view, from a failure to view the cases in their historical context. The problem: "in what event will a party to a contract be relieved of his undertaking to do that which he has agreed to do but has not yet done?" has exercised the English courts for centuries, probably ever since *assumpsit* emerged as a form of action distinct from covenant and debt and long before even the earliest cases which we have been invited to examine ...

Once it is appreciated that it is the event and not the fact that the event is a result of a breach of contract which relieves the party not in default of further performance of his obligations, two consequences follow. (1) The test whether the event relied upon has this consequence is the same whether the event is the result of the other party's breach of contract or not, as Devlin J pointed out in *Universal Cargo Carriers Corporation v Citati*. (2) The question whether an event which is the result of the other party's breach of contract has this consequence cannot be answered by treating all contractual undertakings as falling into one of two separate categories: "conditions" the breach of which gives rise to an event which relieves the party not in default of further performance of his obligations, and "warranties" the breach of which does not give rise to such an event.

Lawyers tend to speak of this classification as if it were comprehensive, partly for the historical reasons which I have already mentioned and partly because Parliament itself adopted it in the Sale of Goods Act, 1893, as respects a number of implied terms in contracts for the sale of goods and has in that Act used the expressions "condition" and "warranty" in that meaning. But it is by no means true of contractual undertakings in general at common law.

No doubt there are many simple contractual undertakings, sometimes express but more often because of their very simplicity ("It goes without saying") to be implied, of which it can be predicated that every breach of such an undertaking must give rise to an event which will deprive the party not in default of substantially the whole benefit which it was intended that he should obtain from the contract. And such a stipulation, unless the parties have agreed that breach of it shall not entitle the non-defaulting party to treat the contract as repudiated, is a "condition." So too there may be other simple contractual undertakings of which it can be predicated that no breach can give rise to an event which will deprive the party not in default of substantially the whole benefit which it was intended that he should obtain from the contract; and such a stipulation, unless the parties have agreed that breach of it shall entitle the non-defaulting party to treat the contract as repudiated, is a "warranty".

There are, however, many contractual undertakings of a more complex character which cannot be categorised as being "conditions" or "warranties", if the late nineteenth century meaning adopted in the Sale of Goods Act, 1893, and used by Bowen LJ in *Bentsen v Taylor, Sons & Co* be given to those terms. Of such undertakings all that can be predicated is that some breaches will and others will not give rise to an event which will deprive the party not in default of substantially the whole benefit which it was intended that he should obtain from the contract; and the legal consequences of a breach of such an undertaking, unless provided for expressly in the contract, depend upon the nature of the event to which the breach gives rise and do not follow automatically from a prior classification of the undertaking as a "condition" or a "warranty." For instance, to take Bramwell B's example in *Jackson v Union Marine Insurance Co Ltd* itself, breach of an undertaking by a shipowner to sail with all possible dispatch to a named port does not necessarily relieve the charterer of further performance of his obligation under the charterparty, but if the breach is so prolonged that the contemplated voyage is frustrated it does have this effect ...

As my brethren have already pointed out, the shipowners' undertaking to tender a seaworthy ship has, as a result of numerous decisions as to what can amount to "unseaworthiness", become one of the most complex of contractual undertakings. It embraces obligations with respect to every part of the hull and machinery, stores and equipment and the crew itself. It can be broken by the presence of trivial defects easily and rapidly remediable as well as by defects which must inevitably result in a total loss of the vessel.

Consequently the problem in this case is, in my view, neither solved nor soluble by debating whether the shipowner's express or implied undertaking to tender a seaworthy ship is a "condition" or a "'warranty". It is like so many other contractual terms an undertaking one breach of which may give rise to an event which relieves the charterer of further performance of his undertakings if he so elects and another breach of which may not give rise to such an event but entitle him only to monetary compensation in the form of damages ...

What the judge had to do in the present case, as in any other case where one party to a contract relies upon a breach by the other party as giving him a right to elect to rescind the contract, and the contract itself makes no express provision as to this, was to look at the events which had occurred as a result of the breach at the time at which the charterers purported to rescind the charterparty and to decide whether the occurrence of those events deprived the charterers of substantially the whole benefit which it was the intention of the parties as expressed in the charterparty that the charterers should obtain from the further performance of their own contractual undertakings ...

The question which the judge had to ask himself was, as he rightly decided, whether or not at the date when the charterers purported to rescind the contract, namely, June 6, 1957, or when the shipowners purported to accept such rescission, namely, August 8, 1957, the delay which had already occurred as a result of the incompetence of the engine-room staff, and the delay which was likely to occur in repairing the engines of the vessel and the conduct of the shipowners by that date in taking steps to remedy these two matters, were, when taken together, such as to deprive the charterers of substantially the whole benefit which it was the intention of the parties they should obtain from further use of the vessel under the charterparty ...

Upjohn LJ: ... Why is this apparently basic and underlying condition of seaworthiness not, in fact, treated as a condition? It is for the simple reason that the seaworthiness clause is breached by the slightest failure to be fitted "in every way" for service. Thus, to take examples from the judgments in some of the cases I have mentioned above, if a nail is missing from one of the timbers of a wooden vessel or if proper medical supplies or two anchors are not on board at the time of sailing, the owners are in breach of the seaworthiness stipulation. It is contrary to common sense to suppose that in such circumstances the parties contemplated that the charterer should at once be entitled to treat the contract as at an end for such trifling breaches ...

It is open to the parties to a contract to make it clear either expressly or by necessary implication that a particular stipulation is to be regarded as a condition which goes to the root of the contract, so that it is clear that the parties contemplate that any breach of it entitles the other party at once to treat the contract as at an end. That matter has to be determined as a question of the proper interpretation of the contract ... Where, however, upon the true construction of the contract, the parties have not made a particular stipulation a condition, it would in my judgment be unsound and misleading to conclude that, being a warranty, damages is necessarily a sufficient remedy.

In my judgment the remedies open to the innocent party for breach of a stipulation which is not a condition strictly so called, depend entirely upon the nature of the breach and its foreseeable consequences. Breaches of stipulation fall, naturally, into two classes. First there is the case where the owner by his conduct indicates that he considers himself no longer bound to perform his part of the contract; in that case, of course, the charterer may accept the repudiation and treat the contract as at an end. The second class of case is, of course, the more usual one and that is where, due to misfortune such as the perils of the sea, engine failures, incompetence of the crew and so on, the owner is unable to perform a particular stipulation precisely in accordance with the terms of the contract try he never so hard to remedy it. In that case the question to be answered is, does the breach of the stipulation go so much to the root of the contract that it makes further commercial performance of the contract impossible, or in other words is the whole contract frustrated? If yea, the innocent party may treat the contract as at an end. If nay, his claim sounds in damages only.

If I have correctly stated the principles, then as the stipulation as to the seaworthiness is not a condition in the strict sense the question to be answered is, did the initial unseaworthiness as found by the judge, and from which there has been no appeal, go so much to the root of the contract that the charterers were then and there entitled to treat the charterparty as at an end? The only unseaworthiness alleged, serious though it was, was the insufficiency and incompetence of the crew, but that surely cannot be treated as going to the root of the contract for the parties must have contemplated that in such an event the crew could be changed and augmented. In my judgment, on this part of his case counsel for the charterers necessarily fails ...

Notes and questions

1. A contractor faced with a serious breach of contract on the part of his co-contractor has the self-help remedy of repudiation of the contract, sometimes referred to as a right of rescission. However, rescission is confusing in this context since the common law remedy of repudiation has, conceptually speaking, nothing in common with the equitable remedy of rescission. The power to repudiate is a self-help remedy in that a party does not need permission of the court. All the same if a contractor repudiates when the breach does not justify it, then the person repudiating will themselves be in breach rendering them liable in damages. This, of course, is what happened in *Hong Kong*. Ought a party to be able to exercise a self-help remedy in this way?

2. The difficulty facing lawyers is one of determining when a breach is serious. Basically there are two approaches to the problem: either the breach can be measured in relation to the status of the actual promise (term) broken or it can be measured in relation to the actual consequences of the breach itself. The former approach, developed in respect of sale of goods contracts, was, until *Hong Kong*, considered

good for all contracts; however, it gave rise to logical problems in that the breach of a serious term, labelled a "condition" (on which see *Schuler v Wickman* p 229), might lead to little or no damage. Consequently, the courts started to take account of the consequences flowing from the breach. Did this new approach invent a new type of term that was neither a "condition" nor a "warranty"? Or did it simply require the courts to look at the consequences of the breach?[11]

3.. Can a breach of warranty ever give rise to a breach which goes to the root of the contract? Can a breach of condition ever give rise to a breach which does not go to the root of the contract?

4. Could the employers in *Lister v Romford Ice* (p 307) have dismissed the employee for his breach of contract in injuring his fellow employee?

5. Could the hirers of the motor launch in *Reed v Dean* have repudiated the contract of hire the moment they discovered there was no fire extinguisher?

6. Was the hairdresser in *Ingham v Emes* in breach of any contractual term? If so was it a breach of a condition or a warranty?

(b) Damages

Surrey CC v Bredero Homes Ltd [1993] 1 WLR 1361 Court of Appeal

(See p 178)

Notes and questions

1. The award of damages in contract will protect three different types of interest: the expectation interest; the reliance interest; and the restitution interest. How is a lawyer to know which interest the court will protect? Is it for the plaintiff to decide? Where a plaintiff suffers personal injury as a result of the defendant's breach of contract, will the assessment of damages fall under one of the above heads? If so, which one?

2. Is the object of the law of damages social interests? What defines these interests: social science or legal science or a mixtrue of both?

3. Do you think the status of the plaintiff is of relevance in this case?

4. Could the plaintiffs have brought an equitable account action for the profit made by the defendant?

---

11   See *Bunge Corporation v Tradax SA* [1981] 1 WLR 711.

Lazenby Garages Ltd v Wright [1976] 1 WLR 459 Court of Appeal

Lord Denning MR: Mr Wright works on the land. On 19th February 1974 he went to the showrooms of motor dealers called Lazenby Garages Ltd. He saw some second-hand cars there. He agreed to buy a BMW 2002. He signed a contract to pay £1,670 for it. It was to be delivered to him on 1st March 1974. He went back home to his wife and told her about it. she persuaded him not to buy it. So next day he went back to the garage and said he would not have it after all. They kept it there offering it for resale. Two months later on 23rd April 1974 they resold it for £1,770, that is for £100 more than Mr Wright was going to pay.

Notwithstanding this advantageous resale, the garage sued Mr Wright for damages. They produced evidence that they had themselves bought the car second-hand on 14th February 1974, that is five days before Mr Wright had come in and agreed to buy it. They said that they had bought it for £1,325. He had agreed to buy it from them for £1,670. So they had lost £345 and they claimed that sum as damages.

In answer Mr Wright said: "You haven't lost anything; you've sold it for a higher price". The garage people said that they were dealers in second-hand cars; that they had had a number of cars of this sort of age and type, BMW 2002s; and that they had lost the sale of another car. They said that, if Mr Wright had taken this car, they would have been able to sell one of those other cars to the purchaser. So they had sold one car less and were entitled to profit accordingly.

The judge thought that they had not proved that they had sold one car less but that there was a 50:50 chance that they would have sold an extra car. So he gave them damages for half the sum claimed. Instead of £345 he gave them £172.50.

Now there is an appeal to this court. The cases show that if there are a number of new cars, all exactly of the same kind, available for sale, and the dealers can prove that they sold one car less than they otherwise would have done, they would be entitled to damages amounting to their loss of profit on the one car: see the judgment of Upjohn J in *W L Thompson v Robinson (Gunmakers) Ltd*. The same has been held in the United States: *Torkomian v Russell* and *Stewart v Hawsen*; in Canada, *Mason & Risch Ltd v Christner*; and in Australia, *Cameron v Campbell & Worthington*.

But it is entirely different in the case of a second-hand car. Each second-hand car is different from the next, even though it is the same make. The sales manager of the garage admitted in evidence that some second-hand cars, of the same make, even of the same year, may sell better than others of the same year. Some may sell quickly, others sluggishly. You simply cannot tell why. But they are all different.

In the circumstances the cases about new cars do not apply. We have simply to apply to s 50 of the Sale of Goods Act 1893. There is no available market for second-hand cars. So its not sub-s (3) but sub-s (2). The measure of damages is the estimated loss directly and naturally resulting in the ordinary course of events from the buyer's breach of contract. That throws us back to the test of what could reasonably be expected to be in the contemplation of the parties as a natural consequence of the breach. The buyer in this case could not have contemplated that the dealer would sell one car less. At most he would contemplate that, if they resold this very car at a lower price, they would suffer by reason of that lower price and should recover the difference. But if they resold this very car at a higher price, they would suffer no loss. Seeing that these plaintiffs resold this car for £100 more than the sale to Mr Wright, they clearly suffered no damage at all.

In my opinion the appeal should be allowed and judgment entered for the defendant, Mr Wright.

[Lawton and Bridge LJJ agreed.]

Questions

1. Is this case an example of the court refusing to accept loss of a chance as a form of damage?
2. What if the plaintiffs had resold the car for £1670?
3. Is the object (*res*) in this case a car or a particular second-hand BMW 2002? If the latter, does this mean that English law is more interested in actual things as opposed to words?

Heywood v Wellers [1976] QB 446 Court of Appeal

This was an action in debt, for the return of money paid, and damages, for mental distress, brought by a client against a firm of negligent solicitors who had failed to take proper legal proceedings to stop the client from being molested by an off-duty policeman.

Lord Denning MR: ... [T]he solicitors were entitled to nothing for costs; and Mrs Heywood could recover the £175 as money paid on a consideration which had wholly failed. She was, therefore, entitled to recover it as of right. And she is entitled to recover as well damages for negligence. Take this instance. If you engage a driver to take you to the station to catch a train for a day trip to the sea, you pay him £2 – and then the car breaks down owing to his negligence. So that you miss your holiday. In that case you can recover, not only your £2, but also damages for the disappointment, upset and mental distress which you suffered – see *Jarvis v Swan's Tours Ltd; Jackson v Horizon Holidays Ltd.*

So here, Mrs Heywood employed the solicitors to take proceedings at law to protect her from molestation by Mr Marrion. They were under a duty by contract to use reasonable care. Owing to their want of care she was molested by this man on three or four occasions. This molestation caused her much mental distress and upset. It must have been in their contemplation that, if they failed in their duty, she might be further molested and suffer much upset and distress. This damage she suffered was within their contemplation within the rule in *Hadley v Baxendale*. That was the test applied by Lawson J in the recent case of *Cox v Phillips Industries Ltd*. Counsel for the solicitors urged that damages for mental distress were not recoverable. He relied on *Groom v Crocker* and *Cook v S*. But those cases may have to be reconsidered. In any case they were different from this. Here Wellers were employed to protect her from molestation causing mental distress – and should be responsible in damages for their failure.

It was suggested that, even if Wellers had done their duty and taken the man to court, he might still have molested her. But I do not think they can excuse themselves on that ground. After all, it was not put to the test; and it was their fault it was not put to the test. If they had taken him to court as she wished – and as they ought to have done – it might well have been effective to stop him from molesting her any more. We should assume that it would have been effective to protect her, unless they prove that it would not: see *Coldman v Hill* by Scrutton LJ; *Scottish Co-operative Wholesale Society Ltd v Meyer*.

So the remaining question is: what damages should be awarded to Mrs Heywood for the molestation she suffered on three or four occasions, and the mental distress and upset she suffered? The judge, unfortunately, did not quantify the damages. In her claim as amended she put them at £150. I would allow her that sum. Some reduction should be made for the fact that, if Wellers had done their duty (and saved her from the molestation), it would have cost her something. I should put that at the figure which Mr Price gave in the beginning, £25 ...

Questions

1. Is Lord Denning treating the plaintiff in this case quite differently from the plaintiff in *Miller v Jackson* (p 22)?
2. Is mental distress a form of damage – an 'interest' – protected by the law of obligations? Or is it an interest protected only by certain causes of action? If the latter, does this mean that the notion of an 'interest' as a social concept is rather meaningless? Is not an interest, in other words, just another legal concept?
3. Is law a science that creates its own object?
4. Why was the burden of proving causation put onto the shoulders of the defendant?

(c) Debt

White & Carter (Councils) Ltd v McGregor [1962] AC 413 House of Lords (Scotland)

(See p 133).

Bridge v Campbell Discount Co Ltd [1962] AC 600 House of Lords

This was an action in debt brought by a finance company against a hire-purchaser of a car who had written to the finance company terminating the hire-purchase contract. The company was claiming two-thirds of the hire-purchase price which the contract stipulated was to be payable if the purchaser decided to terminate the agreement. The purchaser claimed that this two-thirds clause was a penalty and thus unenforceable in equity (doctrine of relief against penalties). The Court of Appeal held that the equitable doctrine applied only to breaches of contract and thus had no application where the contract was lawfully terminated; the House of Lords, allowing an appeal, held that on the facts of this case the hire-purchaser had been in breach of contract.

Lord Denning: ... When hire-purchase transactions were first validated by this House in 1895 in *Helby v Matthews*, the contract of hire had most of the features of an ordinary hiring. In particular, the hirer was at liberty to terminate the hiring at any time without paying any penalty. He could return the goods and not be liable to make any further payments beyond the monthly sum then due. There was no clog on his right to terminate. And this was one of the reasons why the House saw nothing wrong with the transaction ...

Since that time, however, the finance houses have imposed a serious clog on the hirer's right to terminate the hiring. They have introduced into their printed forms a "minimum-payment" clause such as never appeared in *Helby v Matthews*. The Clause in this case is a good example. The minimum payment is two-thirds of the hire-purchase price ...

What possible justification have the finance houses for inserting this "minimum-payment" clause? They call it "agreed compensation for depreciation". But it is no such thing. It is not "agreed". Nor is it "compensation for depreciation". There is not the slightest evidence that Bridge ever agreed it, and I do not suppose for a moment that he did. He simply signed the printed form. And as for "depreciation", everyone knows that a car depreciates more and more as it gets older and older, but this sum gets less and less. It is obvious that the initial rental of £105 (which was one-quarter of the cash price) would compensate at once for a 25 per cent depreciation: and the monthly rentals covered any remaining depreciation over the next three years. The truth is that this minimum-payment is not so much compensation for depreciation but rather compensation for loss of the future instalments which the hire-purchase company expected to receive, but which they had no right to receive. It is a penal sum which they exact because the hiring is terminated before two-thirds has been paid. In cases when the hiring is terminated, as it was here, within a few weeks, it is beyond doubt oppressive and unjust.

Is not this, then, a classic case for equity to intervene? The contract is contained in a printed form. Not one hirer in a thousand reads it, let alone understands it. He takes it on trust and signs it. It is binding at law but when it comes to be examined it is found to contain a penalty which is oppressive and unjust. It seems to me that such a case comes within the very first principles on which equity intervenes to grant relief. "The whole system of equity jurisprudence proceeds upon the ground that a party, having a legal right, shall not be permitted to avail himself of it for the purpose of injustice, or fraud, or oppression, or harsh and vindictive injury". See Story's *Commentaries on Equity Jurisprudence* (1839), Vol II, p 508.

The Court of Appeal acknowledge that in some cases there is room for the intervention of equity. They accept that, where the hiring is terminated because the hirer is in breach, equity will relieve him from payment of the penalty, see *Cooden Engineering Co Ltd v Stanford*. But they say that when it is terminated for any other reason, as, for instance, if the hirer gives notice of termination himself, or if he dies, there is no equity to relieve him or his executors from the rigours of the law, see *Associated Distributors Ltd v Hall*. The jurisdiction of equity is confined, they say, to relief against penalties for breach of contract and does not extend further. Applied to this case it means this: if Bridge, after few weeks, finds himself unable to keep up the instalments and, being a conscientious man, gives notice of termination and returns the car, without falling into arrear, he is liable to pay the penal sum of £206 3s. 4d. without relief of any kind. But if he is an unconscientious man who falls into arrear without saying a word, so that the company retake the car for his default, he will be relieved from payment of the penalty.

Let no one mistake the injustice of this. It means that equity commits itself to this absurd paradox: it will grant relief to a man who breaks his contract but will penalise the man who keeps it. If this be the state of equity today, then it is in sore need of an overhaul so as to restore its first principles. But I am quite satisfied that such is not the state of equity today. This case can brought within long-established principles without recourse to any new equity. From the very earliest times equity has relieved not only against penalties for breach of contract, but also against penalties for non-performance of a condition. And the stipulation for a "minimum-payment" was, it seems to me, a penalty which was payable upon non-performance of a condition ...

In my judgment, therefore, the courts have power to grant relief against the penal sum contained in this "minimum-payment" clause, no matter for what reason the hiring is terminated. The "minimum-payment" clause is single and indivisible, and no just distinction can be drawn between the cases where the hirer is in breach and where he is not ...

If I am wrong about all this, however, and there is no jurisdiction to grant relief unless the hirer is in breach, then I would be prepared to hold in this case Bridge was in breach ...

Lord Radcliffe: ... Having regard to the view that your Lordships have taken as to the true facts of the case, our decision does not, I take it, conclude the question of an owner's rights under such agreements, when the hiring is determined under a hirer's option or by an event specified in the contract but not involving breach. Such questions are closely related to what we have to consider here, but it does not follow that the legal arguments that sustain the hirer, when he is sued on breach, would be capable of sustaining him in these other situations. Indeed, although I wish to decide nothing, I appreciate that the doctrine of penalties can only be applied to those situations by the construction of almost a new set of arguments that would not arise naturally out of the arguments and considerations that have prevailed with courts either of equity or of common law, when relieving against penalties in the past. "Unconscionable" must not be taken to be a panacea for adjusting any contract between competent persons when it shows a rough edge to one side or the other, and equity lawyers are, I notice, sometimes both surprised and discomfited by the plentitude of jurisdiction, and the imprecision of rules that are attributed to "equity" by their more enthusiastic colleagues. Since the courts of equity never undertook to serve as a general adjuster of men's bargains, it was inevitable that they should in course of time evolve definite rules as to the circumstances in which, and the conditions under which, relief would be given, and I do not think that it would be at all an easy task, and I am not certain that it would be a desirable achievement to try to reconcile all the rules under some simple general formula. Even such masters of equity as Lord Eldon and Sir George Jessel, it must be remembered, were highly sceptical of the court's duty to apply the epithet "unconscionable" or its consequences to contracts made between persons of full age in circumstances that did not fall within the familiar categories of fraud, surprise, accident, etc even though such contracts involved the payment of a larger sum of money on breach of an obligation to pay a smaller sum (see the latter's judgment in *Wallis v Smith*). But I do not speculate as to what principles they would have thought applicable to a hire-purchase contract, in which the hirer, I dare say willingly enough, transacts only with a dealer who is not the agent of the owner and if he signs up at all, signs up to an elaborate fixed menu of stipulations and conditions, which he probably does not bother himself to read and very likely does not or cannot understand.

I agree that the appeal should be allowed.

Questions

1. Is this case an example of the House of Lords deciding a question of fact?

2. Leaving aside the Consumer Credit Act 1974 s 100, would the facts of this case now be covered by the Unfair Contract Terms Act 1977? Do the facts fall within the EC Directive of 5 April 1993 on unfair terms in consumer contracts?

3. What role, if any, does causation play in debt claims?

4. Could the court have implied into the contract in *White & Carter* a *bona fides* term? If they had, could the debtor have sued the creditor for damages for breach of this term? Could the debtor have repudiated the whole contract?

5. Do Lords Radcliffe and Scarman (p 43) view the role of equity and contract in the same way?

Central London Property Trust Ltd v High Trees House Ltd [1947] KB 130 King's Bench Division

(See p 257).

Questions

1. Were the defendants in *High Trees* guilty of a breach of contract?

2. Can a refusal to pay a debt which causes damage to the creditor be the basis for an action for damages for breach of contract?

7 IMPOSSIBILITY OF PERFORMANCE

Taylor v Caldwell (1863) 122 ER 309 Court of Queen's Bench

Blackburn J: In this case the plaintiffs and defendants had, on May 27, 1861, entered into a contract by which the defendants agreed to let the plaintiffs have the use of The Surrey Gardens and Music Hall on four days then to come ... for the purpose of giving a series of four grand concerts ... and the plaintiffs agreed to take the Gardens and Hall on those days, and pay £100 for each day ...

After the making of the agreement, and before the first day on which a concert was to be given, the Hall was destroyed by fire. This destruction, we must take it on the evidence, was without the fault of either party, and was so complete that in consequence the concerts could not be given as intended. And the question we have to decide is whether, under these circumstances, the loss which the plaintiffs have sustained is to fall upon the defendants. The parties when framing their agreement evidently had not present to their minds the possibility of such a disaster, and have made no express stipulation with reference to it, so that the answer to the question must depend upon the general rules of law applicable to such a contract.

There seems no doubt that where there is a positive contract to do a thing, not in itself unlawful, the contractor must perform it or pay damages for not doing it, although in consequence of unforeseen accidents, the performance of his contract has become unexpectedly burthensome or even impossible ... But this rule is only applicable when the contract is positive and absolute, and not subject to any condition either express or implied: and ... where, from the nature of the contract, it appears that the parties must from the beginning have known that it could not be fulfilled unless when the time for the fulfilment of the contract arrived some particular specified thing continued to exist, so that, when entering into the contract, they must have contemplated such continuing existence as the foundation of what was to be done; there, in the absence of any express or implied warranty that the thing shall exist, the contract is not to be construed as a positive contract, but as subject to an implied condition that the parties shall be excused in case, before breach, performance becomes impossible from the perishing of the thing without default of the contractor.

There seems little doubt that this implication tends to further the great object of making the legal construction such as to fulfil the intention of those who entered into the contract. For in the course of affairs men in making such contracts in general would, if it were brought to their minds, say that there should be such a condition.

Accordingly, in the civil law, such an exception is implied in every obligation of the class which they call *obligatio de certo corpore*. The rule is laid down in the Digest, lib. XLV., tit. 1, de verborum obligationibus ... The general subject is treated of by Pothier, who in his *Traité des Obligations*, Partie 3, Chap. 6, art. 3, 668, states the result to be that the debtor *corporis certi* is freed from his obligation when the thing has perished, neither by his act, nor his neglect, and before he is in default, unless by some stipulation he has taken on himself the risk of the particular misfortune which has occurred.

Although the civil law is not, of itself, authority in an English court, it affords great assistance in investigating the principles on which the law is grounded. And it seems to us that the common law authorities establish that in such a contract the same condition of the continued existence of the thing is implied by English law.

There is a class of contracts in which a person binds himself to do something which requires to be performed by him in person; and such promises, e.g., promises to marry, or promises to serve for a certain time, are never in practice qualified by an express exception of the death of the party ...

These are instances where the implied condition is of the life of a human being, but there are others in which the same implication is made as to the continued existence of a thing ...

In none of these cases is the promise in words other than positive, nor is there any express stipulation that the destruction of the person or thing shall excuse the performance; but that excuse is by law implied, because from the nature of the contract it is apparent that the parties contracted on the basis of the continued existence of the particular person or chattel. In the present case, looking at the whole contract, we find that the parties contracted on the basis of the continued existence of the Music Hall at the time when the concerts were to be given; that being essential to their performance.

We think, therefore, that the Music Hall having ceased to exist, without fault of either party, both parties are excused, the plaintiffs from taking the gardens and paying the money, the defendants from performing their promise to give the use of the Hall and Gardens and other things.

Notes and questions

1. In French law non-performance (*inexécution*) of a contract will usually give rise to no liability if the defendant can show that the cause of the non-performance is some act or event outside of, and beyond, his control. In other words, if the defendant can show he is not at fault he may escape liability. Such a principle was imported into English law by Blackburn J via the notion of an implied term; fault, in other words, got translated into promise. Take the following example. A promises his friend B that he will attend B's birthday party 'come what may'; on the day of the party A does not turn up and B is most put out until he learns that his friend has been badly injured by a bus while crossing the road on the way to the party. Why is it that B does not 'blame' A for failing to turn up? Is it because there was an implied understanding that A's promise to turn up was subject to obvious exceptions? Or is it because A was not 'at fault'? What if A had been careless in crossing the road, would B have good grounds to be put out?

2. Much, of course, depends on the nature of the arrangement or transaction within which the promises are made. If A promises B that he will look after B's car while B is away, B will no doubt not hold it against A if the car is damaged in a freak thunderstorm. But what if it is damaged by a freak thunderstorm partly because A has failed to put the car in a safe parking place? In these circumstances carelessness on the part of the promisor becomes important because the 'institution' (*res*) damaged is B's property. Ownership and property change the nature of the problem – the nature of the interest – and thus the nature of the promises. Can this be translated into a

question of 'duty'? What is the duty of A in respect of B's car? Does such a notion depend upon fault or promise?

3. Why could the defendant in *Reed v Dean* (p 303) not claim that the contract of hire was frustrated by the fire? D contracts with P to perform in P's theatre on a certain night but when the night arrives D fails to turn up and later claims, and can prove, that he was ill. Will the contract be frustrated if P can show that D was ill only because he had carelessly neglected to take proper care of himself? What if, before the night he was supposed to perform, D had been arrested for possession of illegal drugs and was in custody the night he was supposed to perform?[12] What if part of D's attraction is his adherence to a 'drug culture'?

4. How often do the English courts resort to Roman law or to Pothier in order to help them analyse and solve a problem? Do they ever do this today? Did they do it often during the 19th century? Were many translations made of continental law books? If so, during what period? Why do the English courts not make many references today to the various civil codes? (But is this beginning to change?) Do you think it would be desirable that knowledge of one civil law system should be a core subject in all law degrees? If not, why not?

5. Could one ever teach English law to a French or German lawyer without one having a knowledge of the civil codes?

Krell v Henry [1903] 2 KB 740 Court of Appeal

This was an action in debt for rent owing for the use of rooms overlooking Pall Mall. The defendant had contracted to rent the rooms for £75 for two days during the coronation of the King and had paid the plaintiff £25 in advance. However when the coronation was cancelled, owing to the illness of the King, the defendant refused to pay the £50 and counterclaimed for the return of his £25. The trial judge gave judgment for the defendant on the claim and counterclaim. The plaintiff appealed.

Vaughan Williams LJ: The real question in this case is the extent of the application in English law of the principle of the Roman law which has been adopted and acted on in many English decisions, and notably in the case of *Taylor v Caldwell* ... I do not think that the principle of the civil law as introduced into the English law is limited to cases in which the event causing the impossibility of performance is the destruction or non-existence of some thing which is the subject-matter of the contract or of some condition or state of things expressly specified as a condition of it. I think that you first have to ascertain, not necessarily from the terms of the contract, but, if required, from necessary inferences, drawn from surrounding circumstances recognised by both contracting parties, what is the substance of the contract, and then to ask the question whether that substantial contract needs for its foundation the

---

12   Cf *Shepherd & Co v Jerrom* [1986] 3 All ER 589.

assumption of the existence of a particular state of things. If it does, this will limit the operation of the general words, and in such case, if the contract becomes impossible of performance by reason of the non-existence of the state of things assumed by both contracting parties as the foundation of the contract there will be no breach of the contract thus limited. Now what are the facts of the present case? The contract is contained in two letters of June 20 which passed between the defendant and the plaintiff's agent, Mr Cecil Bisgood. These letters do not mention the coronation, but speak merely of the taking of Mr Krell's chambers, or, rather, of the use of them, in the daytime of June 26 and 27, for the sum of £75, £25 then paid, balance £50 to be paid on the 24th. But the affidavits, which by agreement between the parties are to be taken as stating the facts of the case, show that the plaintiff exhibited on his premises, third floor, 56A, Pall Mall, an announcement to the effect that windows to view the Royal coronation procession were to be let, and that the defendant was induced by that announcement to apply to the housekeeper on the premises, who said that the owner was willing to let the suite of rooms for the purpose of seeing the Royal procession for both days, but not nights, of June 26 and 27. In my judgment the use of the rooms was let and taken for the purpose of seeing the Royal procession. It was not a demise of the rooms, or even an agreement to let and take the rooms. It is a licence to use rooms for a particular purpose and none other. And in my judgment the taking place of those processions on the days proclaimed along the proclaimed route, which passed 56A, Pall Mall, was regarded by both contracting parties as the foundation of the contract; and I think that it cannot reasonably be supposed to have been in the contemplation of the contracting parties, when the contract was made, that the coronation would not be held on the proclaimed days, or the processions not take place on those days along the proclaimed route ...

I think for the reasons which I have given that the principle of *Taylor v Caldwell* ought to be applied. This disposes of the plaintiff's claim for £50 unpaid balance of the price agreed to be paid for the use of the rooms. The defendant at one time set up a cross-claim for the return of the £25 he paid at the date of the contract. As that claim is now withdrawn it is unnecessary to say anything about it ...

[The other judges concurred]

Questions

1. What was the object of the contract in *Krell v Henry*: was it to hire a room or to hire a viewing place? Is the answer to this question determined by the owner's pre-contractual statement? What if the contract had contained a clause stipulating that it was a contract for the demise of rooms? Might it be said that it is the law of property which determined whether or not the contract was frustrated?

2. Why should the owner of the rooms and not the hirer be the one to shoulder the risk of the coronation being cancelled?

3. Ought the defendant to have been able to reclaim the £25 in debt?

Davis Contractors Ltd v Fareham Urban District Council [1956] AC 696 House of Lords

This was an action in debt (*quantum meruit*) by a firm of building contractors for expenditure incurred over and above the agreed contract price of £92,425 to build 78 houses. The extra expenditure had been incurred as a result of an unforeseen serious shortage of skilled labour and building materials; and the plaintiffs claimed that the contract itself had been frustrated by these unforeseen shortages. The House of Lords held that the contract had not been not frustrated.

Lord Radcliffe: ... The theory of frustration belongs to the law of contract and it is represented by a rule which the courts will apply in certain limited circumstances for the purpose of deciding that contractual obligations, *ex facie* binding, are no longer enforceable against the parties. The description of the circumstances that justify the application of the rule and, consequently, the decision whether in a particular case those circumstances exist are, I think necessarily questions of law.

It has often been pointed out that the descriptions vary from one case of high authority to another ...

Lord Loreburn ascribes the dissolution to an implied term of the contract that was actually made. This approach is in line with the tendency of English courts to refer all the consequences of a contract to the will of those who made it. But there is something of a logical difficulty in seeing how the parties could even impliedly have provided for something which *ex hypothesi* they neither expected nor foresaw; and the ascription or frustration to an implied term of the contract has been criticised as obscuring the true action of the court which consists in applying an objective rule of the law of contract to the contractual obligations that the parties have imposed upon themselves ...

By this time it might seem that the parties themselves have become so far disembodied spirits that their actual persons should be allowed to rest in peace. In their place there rises the figure of the fair and reasonable man. And the spokesman of the fair and reasonable man, who represents after all no more than the anthropomorphic conception of justice, is and must be the court itself. So perhaps it would be simpler to say at the outset that frustration occurs whenever the law recognises that without default of either party a contractual obligation has become incapable of being performed because the circumstances in which performance is called for would render it a thing radically different from that which was undertaken by the contract. *Non haec in foedera veni.* It was not this that I promised to do.

There is, however, no uncertainty as to the materials upon which the court must proceed. "The data for decision are, on the one hand, the terms and construction of the contract, read in the light of the then existing circumstances, and on the other hand the events which have occurred" ... But, even so, it is not hardship or inconvenience or material loss itself which calls the principle of frustration into play. There must be as well such a change in the significance of the obligation that the thing undertaken would, if performed, be a different thing from that contracted for.

I am bound to say that, if this is the law, the appellants' case seems to me a long way from a case of frustration. Here is a building contract entered into by a housing authority and a big firm of contractors in all the uncertainties of the post-war world. Work was begun shortly before the formal contract was executed and continued, with impediments and minor stoppages but without actual interruption, until the 78 houses contracted for had all been built. After the work had been in progress for a time the appellants raised the claim, which they repeated more than once, that they ought to be paid a larger sum for their work than the contract allowed; but the respondents refused to admit the claim and, so far as appears, no conclusive action was taken by either side which would make the conduct of one or the other a determining element in the case.

That is not in any obvious sense a frustrated contract ... The contract, it is said, was an eight month contract, as indeed it was. Through no fault of the parties it turned out that it took 22 months to do the work contracted for. The main reason for this was that, whereas both parties had expected that adequate supplies of labour and material would be available to allow for completion in eight months, the supplies that were in fact available were much less than adequate for the purpose. Hence, it is said, the basis or the footing of the contract was removed before the work was completed; or, slightly altering the metaphor, the footing of the contract was so changed by the circumstance that the expected supplies were not available and the contract built upon that footing became void ...

Two things seem to me to prevent the application of the principle of frustration to this case. One is that the cause of the delay was not any new state of things which the parties could not reasonably be thought to have foreseen. On the contrary, the possibility of enough labour and materials not being available was before their eyes and could have been the subject of special contractual stipulation. It was not made so. The other thing is that, though timely completion was no doubt important to both sides, it is not right to treat the possibility of delay as having the same significance for each. The owner draws up his conditions in detail, specifies the time within which he requires completion, protects himself both by a penalty clause for time exceeded and by calling for the deposit of a guarantee bond and offers a certain measure of security to a contractor by his escalator clause with regard to wages and prices. In the light of these conditions the contractor makes his tender, and the tender must necessarily take into account the margin of profit that he hopes to obtain upon his adventure and in that any appropriate allowance for the obvious risks of delay. To my mind, it is useless to pretend that the contractor is not at risk if the delay does occur, even serious delay. And I think it a misuse of legal terms to call in frustration to get him out of his unfortunate predicament ...

Questions

1. Why should the contractor and not the local authority be the one to shoulder the risk of the unforeseen shortages? Would it be in the public interest to bankrupt the private contractor?

2. Were the shortages to be foreseen or not? Ought they to have been foreseen?

3. What if the houses had been only partially completed and the builders were facing bankruptcy unless the local authority agreed to pay more?

4. Do you find the reasons for abandoning the implied term theory of frustration convincing? If contract is based upon the act of the

parties, is not frustration a matter of implied condition precedent with reference to the status of the parties? Or might it not be a question of level of duty and is duty not a question of terms?

5. Does *Davies* introduce a new remedy of rescission at common law?

6. Is it a material fact that the builders were a "big firm of contractors"?

Staffordshire Area Health Authority v South Staffordshire Waterworks [1978] 1 WLR 1387 Court of Appeal

This was an action for a declaration that an agreement made in 1929 between a water company and a local area health authority could be determined by the water company on reasonable notice and without the consent of the area health authority.

Lord Denning MR: ... [T]here were negotiations between the hospital authorities and the water company. It resulted in an agreement dated 30th July 1929 but it operated from 25th September 1928. The water company still allowed the hospital authorities to take 5,000 gallons a day free of charge, but for additional water the charge was to be seven old pence per thousand gallons. This rate was 70 per cent of the current water rate. It was a compromise between ten old pence which was the rate being charged at the time by the water company to ordinary consumers and five or six old pence which would have been the cost to the hospital of getting water from the well. I will return to this agreement later. But the important thing to notice is that it contained clauses which looked as if it was to continue forever. The key words were 'at all times hereafter'. The hospital authorities rely on those words to say that they are entitled to receive water from the mains at seven old pence for 1,000 gallons in perpetuity.

Events since 1929

After the agreement, things went on 'at all times hereafter' for nearly 50 years. The hospital took their whole supply from the water company. During the war years the hospital was greatly enlarged and has doubled in size. They took much more water from the mains. In recent years the hospital authorities have only paid seven old pence per 1,000 gallons. When decimal coinage was introduced, it became 2.9p per 1,000 gallons. The hospital authorities still only pay 2.9p per 1,000 gallons, whereas the ordinary rate has now become 55p per 1,000 gallons. In short the hospital authorities are paying only 1/20th of the current water rate. They say that the agreement was to continue 'at all times hereafter' and cannot be changed ...

The water company feel that the time has come when the hospital authorities should pay a more reasonable rate. In order to accomplish this, they assert that the 1929 agreement is determinable by six months' notice. Accordingly, on 30th September 1975 they gave notice to the hospital authorities to terminate the agreement as from 30th April 1976. They said that they were quite prepared to supply 5,000 gallons a day free of charge, but they would have to charge for the excess at their normal rate. The area health authority refused to accept this notice as valid. So an originating summons was taken out to determine the matter. Foster J held that the agreement of 1929 was to last forever: and that the hospital authorities could take all the water they desired from the mains at the rate of seven old pence (that is 2.9p) per 1,000 gallons in perpetuity. The water company appeal to this court ...

The rule of construction laid down in the 19th century

In 1857 the House of Lords in *Grey v Pearson* ((1857) 6 HL Cas 61) by a majority laid down the so-called 'golden rule' of construction of written instruments. It was said by Lord Cranworth LC (at p 78) that the courts should "adhere as rigidly as possible to the express words that are found and to give those words their natural and ordinary meaning". Lord Wensleydale (at p 106) echoed it by saying that "the grammatical and ordinary sense of the words is to be adhered to".

That golden rule was the rule of the strict constructionists. It had great influence for the next 100 years. It is still very influential over some minds. It was decisive to the mind of Foster J in this case. The words "at all times hereafter" were, he said, a "plain and unambiguous phrase". They could only mean "forever or in perpetuity". He added that "the mere fact that the agreement has proved to be extremely costly to one of the parties cannot lead the court to change the meaning of plain words".

Now I quite agree that, if that rule of construction were in force today, Foster J would be right. There is a great deal to be said for his view that the words "at all times hereafter" are plain and that they mean "forever or in perpetuity". Subtle arguments were adduced before us to limit this meaning. Such as that they meant "at all times during the day and night", or "at all times during the subsistence of the agreement". But I confess that, as a matter of strict construction, I cannot read any such limitation into the words.

The rule has now been changed. But I think that the rule of strict construction is now quite out of date. It has been supplanted by the rule that written instruments are to be construed in relation to the circumstances as they were known to or contemplated by the parties; and that even the plainest words may fall to be modified if events occur which the parties never had in mind and in which they cannot have intended the agreement to operate.

This modern rule was adumbrated by Cardozo J in 1918 in the New York Court of Appeals in *Utica City National Bank v Gunn* ((1918) 222 NY 204 at p 208):

> "To take the primary or strict meaning is to make the whole transaction futile. To take the secondary or loose meaning is to give it efficacy and purpose. In such a situation the genesis and aim of the transaction may rightly guide our choice."

The modern rule has recently been expounded with clarity and authority by Lord Wilberforce in the House of Lords in the case of *Reardon Smith Line Ltd v Hansen-Tangen* ([1976] 1 WLR 989 at pp 996–997) when he said:

> "When one speaks of the intention of the parties to the contract, one is speaking objectively – the parties cannot themselves give direct evidence of what their intention was – and what must be ascertained is what is to be taken as the intention which reasonable people would have had if placed in the situation of the parties. Similarly, when one is speaking of the aim, or object, or commercial purpose, one is speaking objectively of what reasonable persons would have had in mind in the situation of the parties ... what the court must do must be to place itself in thought in the same factual matrix as that in which the parties were."

As I understand this modern rule, we are no longer to go by the strict construction of the words as judges did in the 19th century. We are to put ourselves in the same situation as the parties were in at the time they drew up the instrument, to sit in their chairs with our minds endowed with the same facts as theirs were, and envisage the future with the same degree of foresight as they did. So placed we have to ask ourselves: what were the circumstances in which the contract was made? Does it apply in the least to the new situation which has developed? If events occur for which they have made no provision, and which were outside the realm of their speculations altogether, or of any reasonable persons sitting in their chairs, then the court itself must take a hand and hold that the contract ceases to bind. Such was the rule which I suggested long ago in *British Movietonenews Ltd v London and District Cinemas Ltd* ([1951] 1 KB 190) without success at that time: but which seems to have come into its own now ...

Inflation

From ... five cases it is possible to detect a new principle emerging as to the effect of inflation and the fall in the value of money. In the ordinary way this does not affect the bargain between the parties. As I said in *Treseder-Griffin v Co-operative Insurance Society* ([1956] 2 QB 127 at p 144):

"... in England we have always looked on a pound as a pound whatever its international value ... Creditors and debtors have arranged for payment in our sterling currency in the sure knowledge that the sum they fix will be upheld by the law. A man who stipulates for a pound must take a pound, whenever payment is made, whatever the pound is worth at that time."

But times have changed. We have since had mountainous inflation and the pound dropping to cavernous depths ... The time has come when we may have to revise our views about the principle of nominalism, as it is called. Dr F A Mann in his book, *The Legal Aspect of Money* (3rd edn (1971), p 100), said: "If the trend of inflation which has clouded the last few decades continues some relief in the case of long-term obligations will become unavoidable." That was written in 1971. Inflation has been more rampant than ever since that time. Here we have in the present case a striking instance of a long term obligation entered into 50 years ago. It provided for yearly payments for water supplied at seven old pence a 1,000 gallons. In these 50 years, and especially in the last 10 years, the cost of supplying the water has increased twentyfold. It is likely to increase with every year that passes. Is it right that the hospital should go on forever only paying the old rate of 50 years ago? ...

So here the situation has changed so radically since the contract was made so many years ago that the term of the contract "at all times hereafter" ceases to bind: and it is open to the court to hold that the contract is determined by reasonable notice.

Conclusion

I do not think that the water company could have determined the agreement immediately after it was made. That cannot have been intended by the parties. No rule of construction could sensibly permit such a result. But, in the past 50 years, the whole situation has changed so radically that one can say with confidence: "The parties never intended that the supply should be continued in these days at that price." Rather than force such unequal terms on the parties, the court should hold that the agreement could be and was properly determined in 1975 by the reasonable notice of six months. This does not mean, of course, that on the expiry of the notice the water company can cut off the supply to the hospital. It will be bound to continue it. All that will happen is that the parties will have to negotiate fresh terms of payment. These should take into account the history from the 1909 Act onwards. In the light of that history, it seems to me plain that the 1929 agreement should be up-dated so as to have regard to the effect of inflation. The hospital should be entitled to 5,000 gallons a day free of charge and pay for the excess at a rate which is 70 per cent of the current market rate. I would commend this solution to these two public authorities in the hope that it will settle their difficulties without troubling the courts further.

So I would grant a declaration in respect of the contract being determinable by reasonable notice but I will say nothing about the declaration as to payment. I would allow the appeal accordingly.

Cumming-Bruce LJ: ... I have come to the conclusion that the words do not carry the meaning that the judge decided but that the words "at all times hereafter" mean that the obligations granted and accepted by the agreement were only intended to persist during the continuance of the agreement; and the agreement, in my view, was determinable on reasonable notice ...

I agree with the analysis ... proposed by Goff LJ and cannot usefully add anything. With all respect to Lord Denning MR, I do not found my decision on the existence of an implied term that the agreement should not continue to bind the parties on the emergence of circumstances which the parties did not then foresee ...

Questions

1. If the two parties had been private commercial bodies would the result of this case have been the same?

2. How can a term of a contract 'cease to bind'?

3. Upon what legal authority does Lord Denning base his thesis that the Golden Rule of interpretation has been abandoned? What method of interpretation does Lord Denning replace it with? (Cf Chapter 2.)

4. Does this decision conflict with the *Davis Contractors* case?

5. Is this a decision dealing with the public rather than the private interest? Does the public interest have a role in frustration cases?

6. Just how important is 'the principle of nominalism' to legal reasoning in general? (Cf Chapter 2.)

7. Was Lord Denning getting close to utilising rescission in equity to deal with this contractual problem? Why should this equitable remedy not be available to deal with frustration problems?

Law Reform (Frustrated Contracts) Act 1943 (6 & 7 Geo VI c 40)

1. Adjustment of rights and liabilities of parties to frustrated contracts

(1) Where a contract governed by English law has become impossible of performance or been otherwise frustrated, and the parties thereto have for that reason been discharged from the further performance of the contract, the following provisions of this section shall, subject to the provisions of section two of this Act, have effect in relation thereto.

(2) All sums paid or payable to any party in pursuance of the contract before the time when the parties were so discharged (in this Act referred to as "the time of discharge") shall, in the case of sums so paid, be recoverable from him as money received by him for the use of the party by whom the sums were paid, and, in the case of sums to payable, cease to be so payable.

Provided that, if the party to whom the sums were so paid or payable incurred expenses before the time of discharge in, or for the purpose of, the performance of the contract, the court may, if it considers it just to do so having regard to all the circumstances of the case, allow him to retain or, as the case may be, recover the whole or any part of the sums paid or payable, not being an amount in excess of the expenses so incurred.

(3) Where any party to the contract has, by reason of anything done by any other party thereto in, or for the purpose of, the performance of the contract, obtained a valuable benefit (other than a payment of money to which the last foregoing subsection applies) before the time of discharge, there shall be recoverable from him by the said other party such sum (if any), not exceeding the value of the said benefit to the party obtaining it, as the court considers just, having regard to all the circumstances of the case and, in particular

(a) the amount of any expenses incurred before the time of discharge by the benefitted party in, or for the purpose of, the performance of the contract, including any sums paid or payable by him to any other party in pursuance of the contract and retained or recoverable by that party under the last foregoing subsection, and

(b) the effect, in relation to the said benefit, of the circumstances giving rise to the frustration of the contract.

Questions

1. P contracts with D to paint D's house for £500. When three-quarters of the house is painted, the building is struck by lightning and totally destroyed. Can P claim any money off D?

2. If the central heating system in *Bolton v Mahadeva* (see p 126) had not functioned for some unexplained reason and the engineers had been able to prove that they were not at fault would this Act have been applicable?

3. If the fire in *Reed v Dean* (see p 303) had started for some unexplained reason and the owners of the boat had been able to prove that they were not at fault, would this Act have been applicable?

4. Do you think that the principles laid down in this statute ought sometimes to be available to a court in cases where the non-performance arises out of a breach of contract?

5. Is s 1 based upon the remedy of debt (action for money had and received) or account of profits?

8 CONTRACT: FINAL OBSERVATIONS

It would be idle to think that three chapters on the law of contract could ever possibly be exhaustive in scope. Indeed a whole casebook devoted to the subject would, unless it were very large, be hard-pressed to be comprehensive. Consequently, the purpose of the last three chapters has been to stress method and technique in problem-solving rather than to set out in a coherent and structured fashion all the rules of the English law of contract. These techniques often express themselves through the various remedies available and thus the contract chapters must be read in conjunction with the chapter on remedies (Chapter 3); equally, and obviously, the contract cases should be looked at in terms of actual methods and thus the contract chapters are also, in one sense, simply extensions of the chapter on methodology (Chapter 2). A contract problem is, to borrow and adapt the words of Diplock LJ in *Letang v Cooper* (above p 65), "simply a factual situation the existence of which [might entitle] one person to obtain from the court a remedy against another person". The starting point is, then, always in the analysis of the facts and it is this analysis that should lead one to the remedies and legal relations that could be of relevance.

Where contract is rather special is in its structure. It is a coherent subject in as much as it appears to have a beginning, middle and end and thus it looks like a ready-made model waiting to be applied to sets of facts. If it fits, then there might well be a solution automatically to be deduced. One should not be surprised by this apparent structural coherence since it is a subject trying to determine the future rather than the past, as a case like *Davis Contractors v Fareham UDC* (p 342) so clearly indicates. Nevertheless, this structural coherence can mislead. Certainly it is a subject with many rules and thus when compared with the other law of obligations subjects of tort and restitution (see Chapter 7) it can appear detailed and complex. Yet when viewed from the position of the remedy – ought the plaintiff to get damages from the defendant or ought someone to be able to escape from what they have undertaken to do? –

the problem can often be reduced to some basic issue where the court has to make a qualitative judgment of substance rather than simply apply some formal rule. Ought the court to imply a duty into this agreement? Was the plaintiff the cause of her own damage (cf *Ingham v Emes*, p 305)? What are the responsibilities of one person negotiating with another person? The key to problem-solving is often to identify these substantive issues and to translate them into legal concepts such as the implied term, consideration or condition, not forgetting, of course, the role of quasi-normative notions such as 'expectation' and 'interest' which can aid the translations (see eg, Lord Denning MR in *Beswick v Beswick*, p 86 or Bingham LJ in the *Blackpool & Fylde* case, p 243). The aim, then, of all the previous chapters has been to stress, not the detailed rules of the law of contract, but this problem-solving aspect. This aim will, unsurprisingly, be the guide to the next chapter on non-contractual obligations. However, this next chapter can also be relevant to contract problems as well since factual situations rarely fit neatly into a single legal category.

CHAPTER 7

NON-CONTRACTUAL OBLIGATIONS

1 INTRODUCTION

When viewed from the position of the French *Code civil* the idea that all the non-contractual obligations might be contained in a single chapter is not, at first sight, so bizarre. The whole of the law of tort is contained in just several articles and the law of restitution (or unjust enrichment), such as it is in French law, takes up not much more space. The case law tells a different story of course; and thus in Roman law, a case-based system not dissimilar to the common law,[1] the titles devoted to tort (delict) and restitution are as lengthy as those on contracts. Even so, these titles do not produce as such that many formal rules, save perhaps the title on theft (a tort in Roman law) where, as with the English tort of conversion, property and ownership are in issue. The tort titles are more concerned with illustrating and developing a few basic notions contained in a couple of fundamental principles about wrongfully causing damage. Case law examples about what constitutes fault (*culpa*), damage and cause are what take up the space. One might add that this lack of rules, when combined with the dramatic rise in accidents which the industrial revolution brought in its wake, has tended in recent years to give rise to much literature on theory. Indeed it is now possible to give a whole course on the law of tort simply on the basis of doctrinal writing about theories supposedly underpinning the law of tort.

English law is similar to Roman law in that the law of tort and the law of restitution rest on a few basic principles. What takes up the pages is the application and interpretation of these principles. In fact, because of the importance of method when it comes to analysing the facts of tort and unjust enrichment problems (see, for example, Lord Simon in *FA & AB Ltd v Lupton*, above p 91 and in *Miliangos v George Frank (Textiles) Ltd*, above p 7), many of the cases relevant to this chapter have already been set out in the chapters on remedies and methodology. This present chapter, then, is more concerned with bringing these cases together under the law of obligations heading in the hope of illustrating the institutional structures that underpin these cases. All the same, despite

---

1   See T Weir, Contracts in Rome and England (1992) 66 *Tulane Law Review* 1615; C Kolbert, *Justinian: Digest of Roman Law* (Penguin, 1979).

the development of contract, tort and now restitution as rational categories through which the cases can be understood, it is important to remember that the law of remedies still dominates. It is therefore particularly important to relate tort and restitution, as Lord Goff and others recognise (see below), not just to their historical foundation in the forms of action but to the law of remedies in general (Chapter 3). The starting point for tort is always in the nature of the damage, for this can determine not just the cause of action but also the intensity of the duty, while the starting point for the law of restitution is the notion of benefit or profit. Is this a profit or benefit which ought in justice to be retained? What is the cause of the damage or the profit? A Romanist can certainly appreciate the symmetry between tort and restitution even if the common law cannot always appreciate the differences between its very own remedies of debt and damages.

Henderson v Merrett Syndicates Ltd [1994] 3 WLR 761 House of Lords

Lord Goff: ... The situation in common law countries, including of course England, is exceptional, in that the common law grew up within a procedural framework uninfluenced by Roman law. The law was categorised by reference to the forms of action, and it was not until the abolition of the forms of action by the Common Law Procedure Act 1852 (15 & 16 Vict c 76) that it became necessary to reclassify the law in substantive terms. The result was that common lawyers did at last separate our law of obligations into contract and tort, though in so doing they relegated quasi-contractual claims to the status of an appendix to the law of contract, thereby postponing by a century or so the development of a law of restitution. Even then, there was no systematic reconsideration of the problem of concurrent claims in contract and tort. We can see the courts rather grappling with unpromising material drawn from the old cases in which liability in negligence derived largely from categories based upon the status of the defendant. In a sense, we must not be surprised; for no significant law faculties were established at our universities until the late 19th century, and so until then there was no academic opinion available to guide or stimulate the judges ...

Bryant v Herbert (1877) 3 CPD 389 Court of Appeal

(See p 63).

Notes and questions

1. Given that English law does not easily distinguish between *iura in rem* and *iura in personam* is it really viable for common lawyers to think in terms of a law of obligations? How should one classify the *Lipkin Gorman* case (above p 145) – as a property or an obligations case?

2. We have seen that English law thinks in terms of a law of contract rather than a law of contracts: when it comes to non-contractual

obligations, does the forms of action legacy allow one to think in terms of a law of tort rather than torts and restitution rather than quasi-contracts and remedies?

Esso Petroleum Co Ltd v Southport Corporation [1953] 3 WLR 773 Queen's Bench Division; [1954] 2 QB 182 Court of Appeal; [1956] AC 218 House of Lords

(See p 118).

Rigby v Chief Constable of Northamptonshire [1985] 1 WLR 1242 Queen's Bench Division

(See p 47)

Notes and questions

1. The forms of action legacy is still particularly evident in English legal reasoning. In both *Esso* (in particular the Court of Appeal) and *Rigby* the analysis of the facts was via a set of pre-existing forms of liability which in turn determined the existence or non-existence of a right. The idea that beneath these formal causes of action there might lurk some right waiting to receive its independence was comprehensively rejected by Browne-Wilkinson VC (now a Law Lord) in *Kingdom of Spain v Christie* (see p 112). In fact Denning LJ's judgment in *Esso* is more subtle than it first appears since he uses the forms of liability to achieve procedural objectives which in turn have the effect of giving rise to rights; thus he uses public nuisance to make Esso itself liable for its thing (unseaworthy ship). He uses the same approach in *Mint v Good* (below, p 384) to make an owner liable for damage done by his property (wall). Sometimes, of course, the judges find this approach to liability too restrictive and thus in cases like *Khorasandijian v Bush* (p 74) they struggle to escape from the restrictions of the cause of action approach. However, the lack of a rights and principles tradition usually forces the courts back to what they know best – a formalist approach to liability. To what extent is this English approach an obstacle to harmonisation?

2. The causes (forms) of action approach can present particular difficulties in cases like *Rigby* which raise special public law problems. If public bodies such as the police – or indeed anyone public or private - are successfully to be allowed to raise the defence of necessity, this will mean that the loss must fall on an individual citizen. In an age of property insurance this might not, of course, be such a bad thing. But where personal injury is concerned, even in a country with a National Health Service, it seems cruel that an individual and (or) his or her family should be expected to carry the

burden of injury and loss suffered in the pursuit of the public good. Indeed *Miller v Jackson* (p 22) raises a not dissimilar problem. This is where the French equality principle (see above p 52-3) comes into its own as a legal device; it simply outflanks the defence of necessity. English law has to operate at the level of fact – that is to say the judge usually has to make a finding of negligence – in order for a citizen to get damages in tort and while the judiciary may not these days be unsympathetic, the fault requirement allows insurance companies to bully individuals into settlements that may be well below the extent of their actual damage and losses. Who actually benefits from the fault principle? Is this a question that the judges themselves are prepared to ask?

Lister v Romford Ice & Cold Storage Co Ltd [1957] AC 555 House of Lords

(See p 307)

Notes and questions

1. Another effect of the fault principle is that it can put the burden of the risk of accidents on shoulders least able to bear it. The worker rather than the company insurance policy is the person who must pay according to the House of Lords. Admittedly, the House of Lords have specifically rejected the role of rationalising the law of England (see above p 8) and some of the reasoning looks distinctly dated today; yet the influence of the decision is still to be felt as recent jurisprudence from the Court of Appeal indicates.[2] Why is it that judges seem so sympathetic to insurance companies?

2. It is not just the law of tort that is to blame for the decision in *Lister*. The law of contract (implied terms) and the law of restitution (subrogation) are just as much to blame. Would the worker have been unjustly enriched in *Lister* if the insurance company had been denied the remedy of subrogation? Clearly, the roles of the law of tort, contract and restitution need to be harmonised and this, perhaps, is one of the strongest arguments for developing a law of obligations in English law. Can you think of any other benefits to be obtained from thinking in terms of a law of obligations?

3. All legal systems need an institution which will take on the role of rationalising the law. It is all very well to castigate the logic of Continental systems (see p 8), but to revel in common sense and experience does not always make for a strong system either, since judges and barristers can make no special claim to epistemological

---

2   See eg, *Reid v Rush & Tompkins plc* [1990] 1 WLR 212.

privilege. Academics are now, according to *White v Jones* (above p 56), to be the body to undertake rationalisation. Yet have they really contributed, in England, much more than an intelligent judge? Just how much better would this collection of materials be if, instead of extracts from judgments, it consisted entirely of extracts from doctrine? Certainly there are some fine contributions from academics. But the best of these are usually by comparative lawyers or by jurists trained in the German or South African tradition. One is thus forced back to the civil law if one wants to gain knowledge of models of reasoning. Indeed the great English judges of the 19th century knew their civil law and that is why the judgments of Blackburn J and Lindley LJ are likely to have a longer shelf life than the contributions to be found in some of the law reviews. Of course, judges are little interested in the great questions of theory; but one has to ask if jurisprudence as a subject has really contributed that much to knowledge of law (or at least much more than the great contributions of Aristotle, the Roman jurists, Bartolus and St Thomas Aquinas). Certainly none of the modern jurisprudential theories have proved of much help to Artificial Intelligence which suggests that theorists actually have little insight into the question of what it is to have legal knowledge. Legal history can sometimes seem wanting as well; for example, an essay claiming that there is 'Englishness' in judgments from English judges seems odd in the absence of detailed comparative work on say German, French and (of course) Roman case law. Lord Simon of Glaisdale and Lord Diplock can appear much more thoughtful and reflective on occasions.

Lipkin Gorman v Karpnale Ltd [1991] 2 AC 548 House of Lords

(See p 145)

Notes and questions

1. The law of tort is largely, yet not exclusively, concerned with damage and loss; however, there is, as any Romanist knows, also the question of benefit and profit. Wrongfully causing loss is the great principle of the law of tort, but what is the great principle of wrongfully gaining a profit? The Roman jurists developed the principle of unjust enrichment. All the same, just as wrongfully causing loss is too abstract to solve actual factual problems, so the unjust enrichment principle is of little help to the practical lawyer. What the principle can do is to act both as a rallying point for a range of diverse cases from the common law and from equity and as a counterpoint to the wrongful loss principle. As Lord Goff tries to point out in *Lipkin*, the focal point of discussion is whether the casino ought to be able to

retain the benefit; it is not a question of whether they have acted wrongfully *vis-à-vis* the solicitors. Of course, wrongfully obtaining a benefit can trigger restitution since it amounts to unjust enrichment, but unjust in this context does have a wider meaning than wrongful. Was the casino's benefit unjustly obtained? Or was it simply unjust to retain it? Is this difference of importance?

2. Lord Goff avoided the question of 'wrongful' by basing the plaintiffs' claim on the 'right' of ownership. In the past a quasi-contractual claim was founded on the existence of an implied contract, breach of which would supply the 'wrong'; but it has to be asked if the 'right' approach is any less of a fiction. Moreover, the introduction of property concepts into a category (unjust enrichment) that traditionally belongs to the law of obligations will present harmonisation problems with German law in that the frontier between property and obligations is a fundamental aspect of German legal knowledge. Is the problem one that attaches to the remedy of tracing rather than the remedy of quasi-contractual debt? Or is there just a fundamental mixing up of property and obligation concepts in English law?[3]

2 DAMAGE CAUSED TO ANOTHER

(a) Damage

Best v Samuel Fox & Co Ltd [1952] AC 716 House of Lords

This was an action for damages brought by the wife of an employee injured as a result of the negligence of his employers. The employee recovered damages from his employers, but his injuries rendered him incapable of sexual intercourse and so his wife sued on her own behalf for her mental distress at the loss of both sexual relations and the chance of having children. The House of Lords rejected her claim.

Lord Porter: ... The salient fact, as I see it, is that the wife had herself suffered no physical injury and could only base her claim on the circumstance that she had lost the consortium of her husband by reason of the injury to him. Such a claim was put forward on the analogy of the enticement cases ... In that class of case, however, the wrong is a deliberate action taken with the object of inducing the wife to leave her husband or the husband to leave his wife – malicious because it is their mutual duty to give consortium to one another, and the defendant has persuaded the errant spouse not to fulfil that duty ...

---

3   Cf G Samuel, Property Notions in the Law of Ogligations [1994] CLJ 524.

On behalf of the appellant it is urged that a husband can bring an action for the loss of the consortium of his wife by reason of any tort which deprives him of that consortium and that in the circumstances prevailing today a wife must have a similar right. Even, however, if it be assumed that in enticement cases the husband and wife have equal rights it does not follow that today they have equal rights and liabilities one towards the other in all respects. I do not think it possible to say that a change in the outlook of the public, however great, must inevitably be followed by a change in the law of this country. The common law is a historical development rather than a logical whole, and the fact that a particular doctrine does not logically accord with another or others is no ground for its rejection ...

Lord Goddard: ... Negligence, if it is to give rise to legal liability must result from a breach of duty owed to a person who thereby suffers damage. But what duty was owed here by the employers of the husband to the wife? If she has an action in this case so must the wife of any man run over in the street by a careless driver. The duty there which gives rise to the husband's cause of action arises out of what may for convenience be called proximity; the driver owes a duty not to injure other persons who are using the road on which he is driving. He owes no duty to persons not present except to those whose property may be on or adjoining the road which it is his duty to avoid injuring. It may often happen that an injury to one person may affect another; a servant whose master is killed or permanently injured may lose his employment, it may be of long standing, and the misfortune may come when he is of an age when it would be very difficult for him to obtain other work, but no one would suggest that he thereby acquires a right of action against the wrongdoer. Damages for personal injury can seldom be a perfect compensation, but where injury has been caused to a husband or father it has never been the case that his wife or children whose style of living or education may have radically to be curtailed have on that account a right of action other than that which, in the case of death, the Fatal Accidents Act, 1846, has given ...

Questions

1. Did Mrs Best fail to recover damages because of the type of damage she suffered? If so, is it reasonable to say that this was a form of damage not recognised by the law?

2. What if Mr Best had suffered his injuries as a result of a deliberate assault by a defendant: would Mrs Best have succeeded in her damages claim?

3. Is it right that the plaintiffs in *Attia* (*see* p 299), *Jarvis* (*see* p 180) and *Heywood* (*see* p 334) should recover for their mental distress, but not the plaintiff in *Best*?

4. If these facts had arisen in France or Germany, would Mrs Best have recovered damages?

5. Are the following forms of damage recognised by the English law of obligations: (i) death; (ii) life; (iii) bereavement; (iv) loss of a chance (a) to win a competition or (b) to recover one's health; (v) respect; (vi) dignity?

6. Is financial loss always a form of damage as far as the law is concerned?

7. If a person is killed by the wrongful act of another, will this give rise to any action on behalf of certain others who suffer damage?[4] If so, does this mean that economic loss is a form of damage recognised by the tort of negligence or does it mean that the notion of a legal person is simply given an extended definition?

8. What was the damage suffered by the plaintiff in *Khorasandijian v Bush* (above p 74)?

9. Would Lord Porter's view of equal rights have much validity today?

Spartan Steel & Alloys Ltd v Martin & Co (Contractors) Ltd [1973] 1 QB 27 Court of Appeal

(See p 101)

Questions

1. There are many books and articles in English on damages but little on damage.[5] Why?

2. If the defendants in *Spartan* had been working under contract on the plaintiffs' land when they cut the cable would the plaintiffs have recovered under head (iii)?

3. If the stoppage had been caused, not by the cutting off of the electricity, but by a group of demonstrators blocking the highway outside of the plaintiffs' factory could the plaintiffs sue one or more of the demonstrators for all their economic losses?

(b) Liability for individual acts

Wilkinson v Downton [1897] 2 QB 57 Queen's Bench

Wright J: In this case the defendant, in the execution of what he seems to have regarded as a practical joke, represented to the plaintiff that he was charged by her husband with a message to her to the effect that her husband was smashed up in an accident, and was lying at The Elms at Leytonstone with both legs broken, and that she was to go at once in a cab with two pillows to fetch him home. All this was false. The effect of the statement on the plaintiff was a violent shock to her nervous system, producing vomiting and other more serious and permanent physical consequences at one time threatening her reason, and entailing weeks of suffering and incapacity to her as well as expense to her

---

4 See Fatal Accidents Act 1976.

5 But see T Weir, La notion de dommage en responsabilité civile, in P Legrand (ed), *Common law, d'un siècle l'autre* (Blais, 1992), 1ff.

husband for medical attendance. These consequences were not in any way the result of previous illhealth or weakness of constitution; nor was there any evidence of predisposition to nervous shock or any other idiosyncrasy ...

The defendant has, as I assume for the moment, wilfully done an act calculated to cause physical harm to the plaintiff – that is to say, to infringe her legal right to personal safety, and has in fact thereby caused physical harm to her. That proposition without more appears to me to state a good cause of action, there being no justification alleged for the act. This wilful injuria is in law malicious, although no malicious purpose to cause the harm which was caused nor any motive of spite is imputed to the defendant ...

Questions

1. What was the cause of action in this case?
2. Is this case authority for the proposition that damage indirectly caused can be a trespass? Did the defendant assault the plaintiff?
3. What if the plaintiff had suffered only financial loss?
4. What if the plaintiff had previously played a similar joke (but without harmful consequences) on the defendant?
5. Could this case have been used as an authority for granting an injunction in *Khorasandijian v Bush* (above p 74)?

Donoghue v Stevenson [1932] AC 562 House of Lords

(See p 33)

Notes and questions

1. Article 1382 of the Code civil states: 'Any human act whatsoever which causes damage to another obliges the person by whose fault the damage has occurred to make amends for it'. Does *Donoghue v Stevenson* lay down a similar principle? Or is it more restrictive?[6]
2. How relevant is the law of contract to this decision?
3. What about economic loss deliberately caused? (Cf *Bradford Corporation v Pickles*, see above, p 124.)
4. *Donoghue v Stevenson* in many ways cuts across the old forms of action approach to liability as *Esso v Southport* (p 118) itself goes some way in showing. In introducing fault as the cause of the action it provided the courts with an alternative way of analysing facts. Indeed the full impact of this alternative approach to liability is still

---

6   An elegant and insightful answer to this question can be found in R David & X Blanc-Jouvan, *Le droit anglais* (Presses Universitaires de France, 7th ed, 1994), pp 117-118.

in the process of working its way through the old causes of action as the *Cambridge Water* case will show (below, p 375). Yet the requirement of a duty of care has kept the fault principle closely tied to the facts; the use of the word 'proximity' in an extract from *Heaven v Pender* quoted by Lord Atkin[7] is now a fundamental descriptive notion used to distinguish between duty and no duty factual situations. Indeed attempts to elevate the *ratio decidendi* of *Donoghue* into a principle have been abandoned by the House of Lords[8]; the approach to liability is reasoning by analogy (see Lord Oliver, above p 96 and Lord Woolf p 68). There is no doubt that *Donoghue v Stevenson* was and remains a revolutionary case. The problem is that the full effects of the revolution are still being felt and not just within the idea of a duty of care. Is it still worthwhile searching for causes of action independent of the tort of negligence or has this cause of action infected the whole of the law of tort?

(c) Liability for people

Home Office v Dorset Yacht Co Ltd [1970] AC 1004 House of Lords

This was an action for damages by the owners of a yacht (in truth their insurance company subrogated to their rights) against the Home Office in respect of damage done to the yacht by escaping borstal boys. It was claimed that the three officers supervising the boys had been negligent and that the Home Office was to be vicariously liable for the officers' behaviour. The Home Office, on a preliminary question of law, claimed that the facts disclosed no duty of care. A majority of the House of Lords disagreed with them.

Lord Reid: ... *Donoghue v Stevenson* may be regarded as a milestone, and the well-known passage in Lord Atkin's speech should I think be regarded as a statement of principle. It is not to be treated as if it were a statutory definition. It will require qualification in new circumstances. But I think that the time has come when we can and should say that it ought to apply unless there is some justification or valid explanation for its exclusion ...

It is argued that it would be contrary to public policy to hold the Home Office or its officers liable to a member of the public for this carelessness – or, indeed, any failure of duty on their part. The basic question is: who shall bear the loss caused by that carelessness – the innocent [plaintiff] or the Home Office, who are vicariously liable for the conduct of their careless officers? ... [His Lordship then discussed the American case of *Williams v State of New York* where the state was held not liable for the negligence of prison warders on the ground of public policy] ... It may be that public servants of the State of New York are so apprehensive, easily dissuaded from doing their duty and intent on preserving

---

7 (1883) 11 QBD 503, 509.

8 See *Murphy v Brentwood DC* [1991] 1 AC 398; *Caparo Industries plc v Dickman* [1990] 2 AC 605.

public funds from costly claims that they could be influenced in this way. But my experience leads me to believe that Her Majesty's servants are made of sterner stuff. So I have no hesitation in rejecting this argument. I can see no good ground in public policy for giving this immunity to a government department ...

Lord Pearson: ... The borstal boys were under the control of the Home Office's officers, and control imports responsibility ...

Lord Diplock: ... The method adopted at this stage of the process is analytical and inductive. It starts with an analysis of the characteristics of the conduct and relationship involved in each of the decided cases. But the analyst must know what he is looking for; and this involves his approaching his analysis with some general conception of conduct and relationships which ought to give rise to a duty of care. This analysis leads to a proposition which can be stated in the form: "In all the decisions that have been analysed a duty of care has been held to exist wherever the conduct and the relationship possessed each of the characteristics A, B, C, D etc, and has not so far been found to exist when any of these characteristics were absent."

For the second stage, which is deductive and analytical, that proposition is converted to: "In all cases where the conduct and relationship possess each of the characteristics A, B, C, D etc., a duty of care arises." The conduct and relationship involved in the case for decision is then analysed to ascertain whether they possess each of these characteristics. If they do the conclusion follows that a duty of care does arise in the case for decision.

But since *ex hypothesi* the kind of case which we are now considering offers a choice whether or not to extend the kinds of conduct or relationships which give rise to a duty of care, the conduct or relationship which is involved in it will lack at least one of the characteristics A, B, C, or D etc. And the choice is exercised by making a policy decision ... which ... will be influenced by the same general conception of what ought to give rise to a duty of care as was used in approaching the analysis. The choice to extend is given effect to by redefining the characteristics in more general terms so as to exclude the necessity to conform to limitations imposed by the former definition which are considered to be inessential ...

Inherent in this methodology, however, is a practical limitation which is imposed by the sheer volume of reported cases. The initial selection of previous cases to be analysed will itself eliminate from the analysis those in which the conduct or relationship involved possessed characteristics which are obviously absent in the case for decision. The proposition used in the deductive stage is not a true universal. It needs to be qualified so as to read: 'In all cases where the conduct and relationship possess each of the characteristics A, B, C and D etc, but do not possess any of the characteristics Z, Y or X etc, which were present in the cases eliminated from the analysis, a duty of care arises.' But this qualification, being irrelevant to the decision of the particular case, is generally left unexpressed ...

From the previous decisions of the English courts ... it is possible to arrive by induction at an established proposition of law as respects one of those special-relations: *viz* A is responsible for damage caused to the person or property of B by the tortious act of C (a person responsible in law for his own acts) where the relationship between A and C has the characteristics: (1) that A has the legal right to detain C in penal custody and to control his acts while in custody; (2) that A is actually exercising his legal right of custody of C at the time of C's tortious act; and (3) that A if he had taken reasonable care in the exercise of his right of custody could have prevented C from doing the tortious act which caused damage to the person or property of B; and where also the relationship between A and B has the characteristics; (4) that at the time of C's tortious act A has the legal right to control the situation of B or his property as respects physical proximity to C; and (5) that A can reasonably foresee that B is likely to sustain damage to his person or property if A does not take reasonable care to prevent C from doing tortious acts of the kind which he did ...

Viscount Dilhorne (dissenting) :... I think that it is clear that the *Donoghue v. Stevenson* principle cannot be regarded as an infallible test of the existence of a duty of care, nor do I think that, if that test is satisfied, there arises any presumption of the existence of such a duty ...

I, of course, recognise that the common law develops by the application of well established principles to new circumstances but I cannot accept that the application of Lord Atkin's words, which, though they applied in *Deyong v Shenburn*, and might have applied in *Commissioner for Railways v Quinlan*, were not held to impose a new duty on a master to his servant or on an occupier to a trespasser, suffices to impose a new duty on the Home Office and on others in charge of persons in lawful custody of the kind suggested ...

The absence of authority shows that no such duty now exists. If there should be one, that is, in my view, a matter for the legislature and not for the courts ...

Notes and questions

1. The Criminal Injuries Compensation Scheme provides a state system of compensation for people injured by criminals. However, the system only applies to personal injury, citizens presumably being expected to use the private insurance system when it comes to their property. Ought the courts to have considered this aspect of public law before holding the State liable to an insurance company in respect of property damage?

2. Are borstal boys analogous to defective bottles of ginger-beer?

3. How would this case have been decided in France?

4. Do you think, given Lord Diplock's methodology, that the nature of the damage (eg, property damage as opposed to personal injury) is an important characteristic in establishing whether a duty of care is owed?

5. There are two liability for people aspects to *Dorset Yacht*. First, the direct duty of care owed by the Home Office to property owners up and down the country (or near prisons at any rate) in respect of prisoners under their control. The question here is whether the Home Office as one person is liable for the act of a prisoner, another person, under its control. Secondly, there is the liability of the Home

Office, as a 'principal' (employer?), for acts done by their 'agents' (employees?), namely the prison officers. (It is unlikely that prison warders are ordinary employees employed under a private law contract.) This second kind of liability is quite different from the first in that it arises out of a doctrine known as vicarious liability: a master (employer) will be liable for torts committed by a servant (employee) acting in the course of his employment (see *Keppel* below). If the warders had taken the boys out without any kind of permission or authority, would the Home Office have been liable? What if warders had encouraged some borstal boys to smash up the yacht to bring pressure on the Home Office to settle an industrial dispute?

6. "[C]ontrol imports responsibility". Discuss in relation to English and French law.

Smith v Littlewoods Organisation Ltd [1987] AC 241 House of Lords (Scotland)

This was an action for damages by the owner of a café against a neighbouring owner of a derelict cinema in respect of damage done by a fire deliberately started in the empty cinema by vandals who had broken into the premises. The action failed in the House of Lords.

Lord Brandon: My Lords, it is axiomatic that the question whether there has been negligence in any given case must depend on the particular circumstances of that case. That being so, I do not think that these appeals can in the end be determined by reference to other reported cases in which the particular circumstances were different, even though some degree of analogy between such other cases and the present one can legitimately be drawn. Nor do I think that it is possible, however helpful it might otherwise be, to lay down any general principle designed to apply to all cases in which the negligence alleged against a person involves the unauthorised acts of independent third parties on premises owned or occupied by that person ...

Lord Griffiths: ... Listening to the seductive way in which Mr MacLean developed his argument on the facts step-by-step, as described by Lord Mackay, I was reminded of the fable of the prince who lost his kingdom but for the want of a nail for the shoe of his horse. A series of foreseeable possibilities were added one to another and, hey presto, there emerged at the end the probability of a fire against which Littlewoods should have guarded. But, my Lords, that is not the common sense of this matter.

The fire in this case was caused by the criminal activity of third parties upon Littlewoods' premises. I do not say that there will never be circumstances in which the law will require an occupier of premises to take special precautions against such a contingency but they would surely have to be extreme indeed. It is common ground that only a 24-hour guard on these premises would have been likely to prevent this fire, and even that cannot be certain, such is the determination and ingenuity of young vandals ...

I doubt myself if any search will reveal a touchstone that can be applied as a universal test to decide when an occupier is to be held liable for a danger created on his property by the act of a trespasser for whom he is not responsible. I agree that mere foreseeability of damage is certainly not a sufficient basis to found liability. But with this warning I doubt that more can be done than to leave it to the good sense of the judges to apply realistic standards in conformity with generally accepted patterns of behaviour to determine whether in the particular circumstances of a given case there has been a breach of duty sounding in negligence.

Lord Goff: My Lords, the Lord President founded his judgment on the proposition that the defenders, who were both owners and occupiers of the cinema, were under a general duty to take reasonable care for the safety of premises in the neighbourhood.

Now if this proposition is understood as relating to a general duty to take reasonable care not to cause damage to premises in the neighbourhood (as I believe that the Lord President intended it to be understood) then it is unexceptionable. But it must not be overlooked that a problem arises when the pursuer is seeking to hold the defender responsible for having failed to prevent a third party from causing damage to the pursuer or his property by the third party's own deliberate wrongdoing. In such a case, it is not possible to invoke a general duty of care; for it is well recognised that there is no general duty of care to prevent third parties from causing such damage. The point is expressed very clearly in Hart and Honoré, *Causation in the Law*, 2nd ed (1985), when the authors state, at pp 196-197:

> "The law might acknowledge a general principle that, whenever the harmful conduct of another is reasonably foreseeable, it is our duty to take precautions against it ... But, up to now, no legal system has gone so far as this ..."

The same point is made in Fleming, *The Law of Torts*, 6th ed (1983), where it is said, at p 200: "there is certainly no general duty to protect others against theft or loss". I wish to add that no such general duty exists even between those who are neighbours in the sense of being occupiers of adjoining premises. There is no general duty upon a householder that he should act as a watchdog, or that his house should act as a bastion, to protect his neighbour's house.

Why does the law not recognise a general duty of care to prevent others from suffering loss or damage caused by the deliberate wrongdoing of third parties? The fundamental reason is that the common law does not impose liability for what are called pure omissions. If authority is needed for this proposition, it is to be found in the speech of Lord Diplock in *Dorset Yacht Co Ltd v Home Office* [1970] AC 1004, where he said, at p 1060:

> "The very parable of the good Samaritan (Luke 10, v 30) which was evoked by Lord Atkin in *Donoghue v Stevenson* [1932] AC 562 illustrates, in the conduct of the priest and of the Levite who passed by on the other side, an omission which was likely to have as its reasonable and probable consequence damage to the health of the victim of the thieves, but for which the priest and Levite would have incurred no civil liability in English law."

Lord Diplock then proceeded to give examples which show that, carried to extremes, this proposition may be repugnant to modern thinking. It may therefore require one day to be reconsidered, especially as it is said to provoke an "invidious comparison with affirmative duties of good-neighbourliness in most countries outside the Common Law orbit" (see Fleming, *The Law of Torts*, 6th ed, p 138). But it is of interest to observe that, even if we do follow the example of those countries, in all probability we will, like them, impose strict limits upon any such affirmative duty as may be recognised. In one recent French decision, the condition was imposed that the danger to the claimant must be *"grave, imminent, constant ... nécessitant une intervention immédiate"*, and that such an intervention must not involve any *"risque pour le prévenu ou pour un tiers"*: see Lawson and Markesinis, *Tortious liability for unintentional harm in the Common law and the Civil law* (1982), vol I, pp 74-75. The latter requirement is consistent with our own law, which likewise imposes limits upon steps required to be taken by a person who is under an affirmative duty to prevent harm being caused by a source of danger which has arisen without his fault (see *Goldman v Hargrave* [1967] 1 AC 645) ... But the former requirement indicates that any affirmative duty to prevent deliberate wrongdoing by third parties, if recognised in English law, is likely to be strictly limited. I mention this because I think it important that we should realise that problems like that in the present case are unlikely to be solved by a simple abandonment of the common law's present strict approach to liability for pure omissions.

Another statement of principle, which has been much quoted, is the observation of Lord Sumner in *Weld-Blundell v Stephens* [1920] AC 956, when he said, at p 986: "In general ... even though A is in fault, he is not responsible for injury to C which B, a stranger to him, deliberately chooses to do." This dictum may be read as expressing the general idea that the voluntary act of another, independent of the defender's fault, is regarded as a *novus actus interveniens* which, to use the old metaphor, "breaks the chain of causation". But it also expresses a general perception that we ought not to be held responsible in law for the deliberate wrongdoing of others. Of course, if a duty of care is imposed to guard against deliberate wrongdoing by others, it can hardly be said that the harmful effects of such wrongdoing are not caused by such breach of duty. We are therefore thrown back to the duty of care. But one thing is clear, and that is that liability in negligence for harm caused by the deliberate wrongdoing of others cannot be founded simply upon foreseeability that the pursuer will suffer loss or damage by reason of such wrongdoing. There is no such general principle. We have therefore to identify the circumstances in which such liability may be imposed.

That there are special circumstances in which a defender may be held responsible in law for injuries suffered by the pursuer through a third party's deliberate wrongdoing is not in doubt. For example, a duty of care may arise from a relationship between the parties, which gives rise to an imposition or assumption of responsibility upon or by the defender, as in *Stansbie v Troman* [1948] 2 KB 48, where such responsibility was held to arise from a contract. In that case a decorator, left alone on the premises by the householder's wife, was held liable when he went out leaving the door on the latch, and a thief entered the house and stole property. Such responsibility might well be held to exist in other cases where there is no contract, as, for example, where a person left alone in a house has entered as a licensee of the occupier. Again, the defender may be vicariously liable for the third party's act; or he may be held liable as an occupier to a visitor on his land. Again, as appears from the *dictum* of Dixon J in *Smith v*

Leurs, 70 CLR 256, 262, a duty may arise from a special relationship between the defender and the third party, by virtue of which the defender is responsible for controlling the third party: see, for example, *Dorset Yacht Co Ltd v Home Office* [1970] AC 1004. More pertinently, in a case between adjoining occupiers of land, there may be liability in nuisance if one occupier causes or permits persons to gather on his land, and they impair his neighbour's enjoyment of his land. Indeed, even if such persons come on to his land as trespassers, the occupier may, if they constitute a nuisance, be under an affirmative duty to abate the nuisance. As I pointed out in *P Perl (Exporters) Ltd v Camden London Borough Council* [1984] QB 342, 359, there may well be other cases.

These are all special cases. But there is a more general circumstance in which a defender may be held liable in negligence to the pursuer, although the immediate cause of the damage suffered by the pursuer is the deliberate wrongdoing of another. This may occur where the defender negligently causes or permits to be created a source of danger, and it is reasonably foreseeable that third parties may interfere with it and, sparking off the danger, thereby cause damage to persons in the position of the pursuer. The classic example of such a case is, perhaps, *Haynes v Harwood* [1935] 1 KB 146, where the defendant's carter left a horse-drawn van unattended in a crowded street, and the horses bolted when a boy threw a stone at them. A police officer who suffered injury in stopping the horses before they injured a woman and children was held to be entitled to recover damages from the defendant. There, of course, the defendant's servant had created a source of danger by leaving his horses unattended in a busy street. Many different things might have caused them to bolt – a sudden noise or movement, for example, or, as happened, the deliberate action of a mischievous boy. But all such events were examples of the very sort of thing which the defendant's servant ought reasonably to have foreseen and to have guarded against by taking appropriate precautions. In such a case, Lord Sumner's dictum (*Weld-Blundell v Stephens* [1920] AC 956, 986) can have no application to exclude liability.

Haynes v Harwood was a case concerned with the creation of a source of danger in a public place. We are concerned in the present case with an allegation that the defenders should be held liable for the consequences of deliberate wrongdoing by others who were trespassers on the defenders' property. In such a case it may be said that the defenders are entitled to use their property as their own and so should not be held liable if, for example, trespassers interfere with dangerous things on their land. But this is, I consider, too sweeping a proposition. It is well established that an occupier of land may be liable to a trespasser who has suffered injury on his land; though in *Herrington v British Railways Board* [1972] AC 877, in which the nature and scope of such liability was reconsidered by your Lordships' House, the standard of care so imposed on occupiers was drawn narrowly so as to take proper account of the rights of occupiers to enjoy the use of their land. It is, in my opinion, consistent with the existence of such liability that an occupier who negligently causes or permits a source of danger to be created on his land, and can reasonably foresee that third parties may trespass on his land and, interfering with the source of danger, may spark it off, thereby causing damage to the person or property of those in the vicinity, should be held liable to such a person for damage so caused to him. It is useful to take the example of a fire hazard, not only because that is the relevant hazard which is alleged to have existed in the present case, but also because of the intrinsically dangerous nature of fire hazards as regards neighbouring property. Let me give an example of circumstances in which an occupier of land might be held liable for damage so caused. Suppose that a person is deputed to buy a substantial quantity of fireworks for a village fireworks display on Guy Fawkes night. He stores them, as usual, in an unlocked garden shed abutting onto a neighbouring house. It is well known that he does this. Mischievous boys from the village enter as trespassers and, playing with the fireworks, cause a serious fire which spreads to and burns down the neighbouring house. Liability might well be imposed in such a case; for, having regard to the dangerous and tempting nature of fireworks, interference by naughty children was the very thing which, in the circumstances, the purchaser of the fireworks ought to have guarded against.

But liability should only be imposed under this principle in cases where the defender has negligently caused or permitted the creation of a source of danger on his land, and where it is foreseeable that third parties may trespass on his land and spark it off, thereby damaging the pursuer or his property. Moreover, it is not to be forgotten that, in ordinary households in this country, there are nowadays many things which might be described as possible sources of fire if interfered with by third parties, ranging from matches and firelighters to electric irons and gas cookers and even oil-fired central heating systems. These are commonplaces of modern life; and it would be quite wrong if householders were to be held liable in negligence for acting in a socially acceptable manner. No doubt the question whether liability should be imposed on defenders in a case where a source of danger on his land has been sparked off by the deliberate wrongdoing of a third party is a question to be decided on the facts of each case, and it would, I think, be wrong for your Lordships' House to anticipate the manner in which the law may develop: but I cannot help thinking that cases where liability will be so imposed are likely to be very rare.

There is another basis upon which a defender may be held liable for damage to neighbouring property caused by a fire started on his (the defender's) property by the deliberate wrongdoing of a third party. This arises where he has knowledge or means of knowledge that a third party has created or is creating a risk of fire, or indeed has started a fire, on his premises, and then fails to take such steps as are reasonably open to him (in the limited sense explained by Lord Wilberforce in *Goldman v Hargrave* [1967] 1 AC 645, 663-664) to prevent any such fire from damaging neighbouring property. If, for example, an occupier of property has knowledge, or means of knowledge, that intruders are in the habit of trespassing upon his property and starting fires there, thereby creating a risk that fire may spread to and damage neighbouring property, a duty to take reasonable steps to prevent such damage may be held to fall upon him. He could, for example, take reasonable steps to keep the intruders out. He could also inform the police; or he could warn his neighbours and invite their assistance. If the defender is a person of substantial means, for example, a large public company, he might even be expected to employ some agency to keep a watch on the premises. What is reasonably required would, of course, depend on the particular facts of the case. I observe that, in *Goldman v Hargrave*, such liability was held to sound in nuisance; but it is difficult to believe that, in this respect, there can be any material distinction between liability in nuisance and liability in negligence ...

The present case is, of course, concerned with entry not by thieves but by vandals. Here the point can be made that, whereas an occupier of property can take precautions against thieves, he cannot (apart from insuring his property and its contents) take effective precautions against physical damage caused to his property by a vandal who has gained access to adjacent property and has there created a source of danger which has resulted in damage to his property by, for example, fire or escaping water. Even so, the same difficulty arises. Suppose, taking the example I have given of the family going away on holiday and leaving their front door unlocked, it was not a thief but a vandal who took advantage of that fact; and that the vandal, in wrecking the flat, caused damage to the plumbing which resulted in a water leak and consequent damage to the shop below. Are the occupiers of the flat to be held liable in negligence for such damage? I do not think so, even though it may be well known that vandalism is prevalent in the neighbourhood. The reason is the same, that there is no general duty to prevent third parties from causing damage to others, even though there is a high degree of foresight that this may occur. In the example I have given, it cannot be said that the occupiers of the flat have caused or permitted the creation of a source of danger (as in *Haynes v Harwood* [1935] 1 KB 146, or in the example of the fireworks which I gave earlier) which they ought to have guarded against; nor of course were there any special circumstances giving rise to a duty of care. The practical effect is that it is the owner of the damaged premises (or, in the vast majority of cases, his insurers) who is left with a worthless claim against the vandal, rather than the occupier of the property which the vandal entered (or his insurers) – a conclusion which I find less objectionable than one which may throw an unreasonable burden upon ordinary householders. For these reasons, I consider that both *Lamb v Camden London Borough Council* [1981] QB 625 and *King v Liverpool City Council* [1986] 1 WLR 890 were rightly decided; but I feel bound to say, with all respect, that the principle propounded by Lord Wylie in *Evans v Glasgow District Council*, 1978 SLT 17, *viz* that there is:

> "a general duty on owners or occupiers of property ... to take reasonable care to see that it [is] proof against the kind of vandalism which was calculated to affect adjoining property",

is, in my opinion, too wide.

I wish to emphasise that I do not think that the problem in these cases can be solved simply through the mechanism of foreseeability. When a duty is cast upon a person to take precautions against the wrongdoing of third parties, the ordinary standard of foreseeability applies; and so the possibility of such wrongdoing does not have to be very great before liability is imposed. I do not myself subscribe to the opinion that liability for the wrongdoing of others is limited because of the unpredictability of human conduct ...

I remain of the opinion that to impose a general duty on occupiers to take reasonable care to prevent others from entering their property would impose an unreasonable burden on ordinary householders and an unreasonable curb upon the ordinary enjoyment of their property; and I am also of the opinion that to do so would be contrary to principle. It is very tempting to try to solve all problems of negligence by reference to an all-embracing criterion of foreseeability, thereby effectively reducing all decisions in this field to questions of fact. But this comfortable solution is, alas, not open to us. The law has to accommodate all the untidy complexity of life; and there are circumstances where considerations of practical justice impel us to reject a general imposition of liability for foreseeable damage. An example of this phenomenon is to be found in cases of pure economic loss, where the so-called "floodgates" argument (an argument recognised by Blackburn J as long ago as 1875 in *Cattle v Stockton Waterworks Co* (1875) LR 10 QB 453, 457, the force of which is accepted not only in common law countries but also in civil law countries such as the Federal Republic of Germany) compels us to recognise that to impose a general liability based on a simple criterion of foreseeability would impose an intolerable burden upon defendants. I observe that in *Junior Books Ltd v Veitchi Co Ltd* [1983] 1 AC 520, some members of your Lordships' House succumbed, perhaps too easily, to the temptation to adopt a solution based simply upon "proximity". In truth, in cases such as these, having rejected the generalised principle, we have to search for special cases in which, upon narrower but still identifiable principles, liability can properly be imposed. That is the task which I attempted to perform in *Leigh and Sillavan Ltd v Aliakmon Shipping Co Ltd* [1985] QB 350, by identifying a principle of transferred loss – a principle which has not, so far, achieved recognition by other members of your Lordships' House. As the present case shows, another example of this phenomenon is to be found in cases where the plaintiff has suffered damage through the deliberate wrongdoing of a third party; and it is not surprising that once again we should find the courts seeking to identify specific situations in which liability can properly be imposed. Problems such as these are solved in Scotland, as in England, by means of the mechanism of the duty of care; though we have nowadays to appreciate that the broad general principle of liability for foreseeable damage is so widely applicable that the function of the duty of care is not so much to identify cases where liability is imposed as to identify those where it is not (see *Anns v Merton London Borough Council* [1978] AC 728, 752, by Lord Wilberforce). It is perhaps not surprising that our brother lawyers in France find themselves able to dispense with any such concept, achieving practical justice by means of a simple concept of *"faute"*. But since we all live in the same social and economic environment, and since the judicial function can, I believe, be epitomised as an educated reflex to facts, we find that, in civil law countries as in common law countries, not only are we beset by the same practical problems, but broadly speaking we reach the same practical solutions. Our legal concepts may be different, and may cause us sometimes to diverge; but we have much to learn from each other in our common efforts to achieve practical justice founded upon legal principle.

For these reasons I would dismiss these appeals.

Questions

1. How does this case differ from the *Dorset Yacht* case? What key elements are missing?

2. What kind of reasoning method is Lord Brandon advocating?

3. If the owners had been a local authority would the result of this case have been different?

4. Was the owner not liable because he owed no duty or because he was not in breach of any duty? Can French law (see Lord Goff) help here?

5. In the firework example given by Lord Goff, what if it was interference by a patrolman working for a security company which caused the fire: would the person storing the fireworks be liable? Would the employer of the patrolman be liable?

6. How best would you describe this decision: as one based on 'common sense' (Lord Griffiths), on an 'educated reflex to facts' (Lord Goff), on 'practical justice founded upon legal principle' (Lord Goff) or on an 'analytical', 'inductive' and 'deductive' approach as advocated by Lord Diplock in *Dorset Yacht*? Or what about the 'complex syllogism' of Lord Simon (see above p 91)? Or indeed the painting a picture approach of Mummery J (p 94)? If the answer is to be found in common sense, an educated reflex or by 'instinct' (see p 107), does this mean that the case is not a 'hard case'?

7. Did comparative law prove useful to this decision in *Littlewoods*?

8. Is, as Lord Goff seem to claim, foreseeability a question of fact? Were remoteness of damage and duty of care questions for the jury?

Keppel Bus Co Ltd v Sa'ad bin Ahmad [1974] 2 All ER 700 Privy Council

(See p 310)

Notes and questions

1. Vicarious liability as a legal notion gives rise to a range of problems. First it applies only when the actor is a servant – employee – of the defendant; an act by an independent contractor cannot, then, involve the employer of the contractor in vicarious liability, although it might involve the employer of the contractor in some other kind of liability based upon a direct duty between employer and plaintiff (eg, public nuisance, negligence). One can see now why in *Esso v Southport Corporation* (above p 118) the plaintiffs wanted to add a new cause of action at the appeal stage and why the House of Lords judges were probably failing in their duty in not recognising *ex officio* this direct duty between Esso and plaintiff (*iura novit curia* as the civil lawyers would say: the court should know the law and it is for the parties to plead only the facts). Secondly vicarious liability causes problems because there must be a tort; if the plaintiff cannot point to a cause of action *vis-à-vis* the actor then there will be no liability.[9] Again this seemed to be one of the problems in *Esso*. Thirdly, the servant must have been acting in the course of his employment. If, as in *Keppel*, the servant was on what is sometimes called 'a frolic of his own' then no liability. Why, then, did the House of Lords hold that the patrolman who burnt down the factory in *Photo Production v Securicor* (above p 312) was acting in the course of his employment?

---

9 *Staveley Iron & Chemical Co Ltd v Jones* [1956] AC 627.

2. The course of employment requirement is possibly one of the most difficult questions in vicarious liability problems. One difficulty for practitioners and other problem-solvers is that the vicarious liability issue can blind the lawyers to the existence of other duties, as indeed we have seen with the *Keppel* case itself (see p 310). Is the employer of firemen liable to the owner of a factory burnt down because the firemen were on a go-slow for more money and took hours to get to any fire? The answer is to be found in the law reports,[10] but is it the right answer in the light (one hesitates to say blaze of light) of *Photo Production*? Or put another way, can one really say that all of these cases turn out to be educated reflexes to the facts? Does insurance play a role?

3. Certainly one educated reflex is the judgment of Diplock LJ in *Morris v Martin* (see p 39), even if the *ratio decidendi* of the case turns out to be somewhat irrational (the result depends on luck – which employee actually steals the goods). Diplock LJ saw that the duty problem went beyond that of vicarious liability and into the law of property; the facts, in other words, demanded a reflex that went beyond the law of tort. What role should vicarious liability have outside of the law of tort itself? Does it have any role at all in contract or bailment? Did Diplock LJ, in other words, go far enough?

(d) Liability for things

Rylands v Fletcher (1866) LR 1 Ex 265 Court of Exchequer Chamber; (1868) LR 3 HL 330 House of Lords

This was an action for damages by a landowner against his neighbour in respect of damage done by water escaping from a reservoir on the defendant's land. The escape occurred as a result of negligent work carried out by the contractors who constructed the reservoir. The Court of Exchequer Chamber gave judgment for the plaintiff and an appeal to the House of Lords was dismissed.

Blackburn J (Court of Exchequer Chamber): ... We think that the true rule of law is, that the person who for his own purposes brings on his lands and collects and keeps there anything likely to do mischief if it escapes, must keep it in at his peril, and, if he does not do so, is *prima facie* answerable for all the damage which is the natural consequence of its escape. He can excuse himself by showing that the escape was owing to the plaintiff's default; or perhaps that the escape was the consequences of *vis major*, or the act of God; but as nothing of this sort exists here, it is unnecessary to inquire what excuse would be sufficient. The general rule, as above stated, seems on principle just. The person whose grass or corn is eaten down by the escaping cattle of his neighbour, or whose mine is flooded by the water from his neighbour's reservoir, or whose cellar is invaded by the filth

---

10 *General Engineering Services v Kingston & St Andrews Corp* [1989] 1 WLR 69.

of his neighbour's privy, or whose habitation is made unhealthy by the fumes and noisome vapours of his neighbour's alkali works, is damnified without any fault of his own; and it seems but reasonable and just that the neighbour, who has brought something on his own property which was not naturally there, harmless to others so long as it is confined to his own property, but which he knows to be mischievous if it gets on his neighbour's, should be obliged to make good the damage which ensues if he does not succeed in confining it to his own property ...

Lord Cairns LC (House of Lords): ... My Lords, the principles on which this case must be determined appear to me to be extremely simple. The defendants, treating them as the owners or occupiers of the close on which the reservoir was constructed, might lawfully have used that close for any purpose for which it might in the ordinary course of the enjoyment of land be used; and if, in what I may term the natural user of that land, there had been any accumulation of water, either on the surface or underground, and if, by the operation of the laws of nature, that accumulation of water had passed off into the close occupied by the plaintiff, the plaintiff could not have complained that the result had taken place. If he had desired to guard himself against it, it would have lain upon him to have done so, by leaving, or by interposing, some barrier between his close and the close of the defendants in order to have prevented that operation of the laws of nature ...

On the other hand if the defendants, not stopping at the natural use of their close, had desired to use it for any purpose which I may term a non-natural use, for the purpose of introducing into the close that which in its natural condition was not in or upon it, for the purpose of introducing water either above or below ground in quantities and in a manner not the result of any work or operation on or under the land – and if in consequence of their doing so, or in consequence of any imperfection in the mode of their doing so, the water came to escape and to pass off into the close of the plaintiff, then it appears to me that that which the defendants were doing they were doing at their own peril; and, if in the course of their doing it, the evil arose to which I have referred, the evil, namely, of the escape of the water and its passing away to the close of the plaintiff and injuring the plaintiff, then for the consequence of that, in my opinion, the defendants would be liable ...

Notes and questions

1. This is one of the great cases of the 19th century and there is no 20th century judge who can rival Blackburn J. He knew his Roman and his French law and this case is undoubtedly an educated reflex to the facts (one might note also that at first instance Bramwell J found for the plaintiffs, but on the ground of trespass). It is very sad indeed that the English common lawyers of the 20th century failed to appreciate that here was the English equivalent of article 1384 of the French Code Civil: 'One is liable not only for damage caused by one's own act, but also for damage caused by the act of persons for which one must answer, or for things that one has under one's

control'. Well perhaps the judges in *Read v J Lyons & Co*[11] did appreciate the possibility but not the possibility itself. What if this principle had been applied to *Esso v Southport Corporation*?

2. It is said in the judgment of Lord Goff (below) that Blackburn J never thought he was making new law as such. No doubt. But that is because the answer to the problem seemed obvious to him, as indeed it would to many trained both in the civil law and in the common law. Damage done by things under one's control is a great principle even if it is a principle that can give rise to hard cases on the odd occasion. And it is a principle that can allocate insurance risks. Was there, however, ever any need to treat the rule in *Rylands v Fletcher* as a separate cause of action?

3. "[B]ut which he knows to be mischievous if it gets on his neighbour's" land. Is the rule in *Rylands v Fletcher* based upon foreseeability?

Cambridge Water Co v Eastern Leather Plc [1994] 2 WLR 53 House of Lords

Lord Goff: My Lords, this appeal is concerned with the question whether the appellant company, Eastern Counties Leather Plc (ECL), is liable to the respondent company, Cambridge Water Co (CWC), in damages in respect of damage suffered by reason of the contamination of water available for abstraction at CWC's borehole at Sawston Mill near Cambridge. The contamination was caused by a solvent known as perchloroethene (PCE), used by ECL in the process of degreasing pelts at its tanning works in Sawston, about 1.3 miles away from CWC's borehole, the PCE having seeped into the ground beneath ECL's works and thence having been conveyed in percolating water in the direction of the borehole. CWC's claim against ECL was based on three alternative grounds, *viz* negligence, nuisance and the rule in *Rylands v Fletcher* (1868) LR 3 HL 330. The judge, Ian Kennedy J, dismissed CWC's claim on all three grounds – on the first two grounds, because (as I will explain hereafter) he held that ECL could not reasonably have foreseen that such damage would occur, and on the third ground because he held that the use of a solvent such as PCE in ECL's tanning business constituted, in the circumstances, a natural use of ECL's land. The Court of Appeal, however, allowed CWC's appeal from the decision of the judge, on the ground that ECL was strictly liable for the contamination of the water percolating under CWC's land, on the authority of *Ballard v Tomlinson* (1885) 29 ChD 115, and awarded damages against ECL in the sum assessed by the judge, *viz*, £1,064,886 together with interest totalling £642,885, and costs. It is against that decision that ECL now appeals to your Lordships' House, with leave of this House ...

Nuisance and the rule in Rylands v Fletcher

The question of ECL's liability in nuisance has really only arisen again because the Court of Appeal allowed CWC's appeal on the ground that ECL was liable on the basis of strict liability in nuisance on the principle laid down, as they saw

---

11 [1947] AC 156.

it, in *Ballard v Tomlinson*. Since ... that case does not give rise to any principle of law independent of the ordinary law of nuisance or the rule in *Rylands v Fletcher*, LR 3 HL 330, the strict position now is that CWC, having abandoned its claim in nuisance, can only uphold the decision of the Court of Appeal on the basis of the rule in *Rylands v Fletcher*. However, one important submission advanced by ECL before the Appellate Committee was that strict liability for an escape only arises under that rule where the defendant knows or reasonably ought to have foreseen, when collecting the relevant things on his land, that those things might, if they escaped, cause damage of the relevant kind. Since there is a close relationship between nuisance and the rule in *Rylands v Fletcher*, I myself find it very difficult to form an opinion as to the validity of that submission without first considering whether foreseeability of such damage is an essential element in the law of nuisance. For that reason, therefore, I do not feel able altogether to ignore the latter question simply because it was no longer pursued by CWC before the Court of Appeal.

In order to consider the question in the present case in its proper legal context, it is desirable to look at the nature of liability in a case such as the present in relation both to the law of nuisance and the rule in *Rylands v Fletcher*, and for that purpose to consider the relationship between the two heads of liability.

I begin with the law of nuisance. Our modern understanding of the nature and scope of the law of nuisance was much enhanced by Professor Newark's seminal article on "The Boundaries of Nuisance" (1949) 65 LQR 480. The article is avowedly a historical analysis, in that it traces the nature of the tort of nuisance to its origins, and demonstrates how the original view of nuisance as a tort to land (or more accurately, to accommodate interference with servitudes, a tort directed against the plaintiff's enjoyment of rights over land) became distorted as the tort was extended to embrace claims for personal injuries, even where the plaintiff's injury did not occur while using land in his occupation. In Professor Newark's opinion (p 487), this development produced adverse effects, *viz*, that liability which should have arisen only under the law of negligence was allowed under the law of nuisance which historically was a tort of strict liability; and that there was a tendency for "cross-infection to take place, and notions of negligence began to make an appearance in the realm of nuisance proper". But in addition, Professor Newark considered, at pp 487-488, it contributed to a misappreciation of the decision in *Rylands v Fletcher*:

> "This case is generally regarded as an important landmark – indeed, a turning point – in the law of tort; but an examination of the judgments shows that those who decided it were quite unconscious of any revolutionary or reactionary principles implicit in the decision. They thought of it as calling for no more than a restatement of settled principles, and Lord Cairns went so far as to describe those principles as 'extremely simple'. And in fact the main principle involved was extremely simple, being no more than the principle that negligence is not an element in the tort of nuisance. It is true that Blackburn J in his great judgment in the Exchequer Chamber never once used the word 'nuisance', but three times he cited the case of fumes escaping from an alkali works – a clear case of nuisance – as an instance of liability under the rule which he was laying down. Equally it is true that in 1866 there were a number of cases in the reports suggesting that persons who controlled dangerous things were under a strict duty to take care, but as

none of these cases had anything to do with nuisance Blackburn J did not refer to them.

But the profession as a whole, whose conceptions of the boundaries of nuisance were now becoming fogged, failed to see in *Rylands v Fletcher* a simple case of nuisance. They regarded it as an exceptional case – and the rule in *Rylands v Fletcher* as a generalisation of exceptional cases, where liability was to be strict on account of 'the magnitude of danger, coupled with the difficulty of proving negligence' [Pollock, *Law of Torts*, 14th ed (1939), p 386] rather than on account of the nature of the plaintiff's interest which was invaded. They therefore jumped rashly to two conclusions: firstly, that the rule in *Rylands v Fletcher* could be extended beyond the case of neighbouring occupiers; and secondly, that the rule could be used to afford a remedy in cases of personal injury. Both these conclusions were stoutly denied by Lord Macmillan in *Read v Lyons* [1947] AC 156, but it remains to be seen whether the House of Lords will support his opinion when the precise point comes up for decision."

We are not concerned in the present case with the problem of personal injuries, but we are concerned with the scope of liability in nuisance and in *Rylands v Fletcher*. In my opinion it is right to take as our starting point the fact that, as Professor Newark considered, *Rylands v Fletcher* was indeed not regarded by Blackburn J as a revolutionary decision: see, eg, his observations in *Ross v Fedden* (1872) 26 LT 966, 968. He believed himself not to be creating new law, but to be stating existing law, on the basis of existing authority; and, as is apparent from his judgment, he was concerned in particular with the situation where the defendant collects things upon his land which are likely to do mischief if they escape, in which event the defendant will be strictly liable for damage resulting from any such escape. It follows that the essential basis of liability was the collection by the defendant of such things upon his land; and the consequence was a strict liability in the event of damage caused by their escape, even if the escape was an isolated event. Seen in its context, there is no reason to suppose that Blackburn J intended to create a liability any more strict than that created by the law of nuisance; but even so he must have intended that, in the circumstances specified by him, there should be liability for damage resulting from an isolated escape.

Of course, although liability for nuisance has generally been regarded as strict, at least in the case of a defendant who has been responsible for the creation of a nuisance, even so that liability has been kept under control by the principle of reasonable user – the principle of give and take as between neighbouring occupiers of land, under which "those acts necessary for the common and ordinary use and occupation of land and houses may be done, if conveniently done, without subjecting those who do them to an action": see *Bamford v Turnley* (1862) 3 B & S 62, 83, *per* Bramwell B. The effect is that, if the user is reasonable, the defendant will not be liable for consequent harm to his neighbour's enjoyment of his land; but if the user is not reasonable, the defendant will be liable, even though he may have exercised reasonable care and skill to avoid it. Strikingly, a comparable principle has developed which limits liability under the rule in *Rylands v Fletcher*. This is the principle of natural use of the land. I shall have to consider the principle at a later stage in this judgment. The most authoritative statement of the principle is now to be found in the advice of the Privy Council delivered by Lord Moulton in *Rickards v Lothian* [1913] AC 263, 280, when he said of the rule in *Rylands v Fletcher*:

"It is not every use to which land is put that brings into play that principle. It must be some special use bringing with it increased danger to others, and must not merely be the ordinary use of the land or such a use as is proper for the general benefit of the community."

It is not necessary for me to identify precise differences which may be drawn between this principle, and the principle of reasonable user as applied in the law of nuisance. It is enough for present purposes that I should draw attention to a similarity of function. The effect of this principle is that, where it applies, there will be no liability under the rule in *Rylands v Fletcher*; but that where it does not apply, ie where there is a non-natural use, the defendant will be liable for harm caused to the plaintiff by the escape, notwithstanding that he has exercised all reasonable care and skill to prevent the escape from occurring.

Foreseeability of damage in nuisance

It is against this background that it is necessary to consider the question whether foreseeability of harm of the relevant type is an essential element of liability either in nuisance or under the rule in *Rylands v Fletcher*. I shall take first the case of nuisance In the present case, as I have said, this is not strictly speaking a live issue. Even so, I propose briefly to address it, as part of the analysis of the background to the present case.

It is, of course, axiomatic that in this field we must be on our guard, when considering liability for damages in nuisance, not to draw inapposite conclusions from cases concerned only with a claim for an injunction. This is because, where an injunction is claimed, its purpose is to restrain further action by the defendant which may interfere with the plaintiff's enjoyment of his land, and *ex hypothesi* the defendant must be aware, if and when an injunction is granted, that such interference may be caused by the act which he is restrained from committing. It follows that these cases provide no guidance on the question whether foreseeability of harm of the relevant type is a prerequisite of the recovery of damages for causing such harm to the plaintiff. In the present case, we are not concerned with liability in damages in respect of a nuisance which has arisen through natural causes, or by the act of a person for whose actions the defendant is not responsible, in which cases the applicable principles in nuisance have become closely associated with those applicable in negligence: see *Sedleigh-Denfield v O'Callaghan* [1940] AC 880 and *Goldman v Hargrave* [1967] 1 AC 645. We are concerned with the liability of a person where a nuisance has been created by one for whose actions he is responsible. Here, as I have said, it is still the law that the fact that the defendant has taken all reasonable care will not of itself exonerate him from liability, the relevant control mechanism being found within the principle of reasonable user. But it by no means follows that the defendant should be held liable for damage of a type which he could not reasonably foresee; and the development of the law of negligence in the past 60 years points strongly towards a requirement that such foreseeability should be a prerequisite of liability in damages for nuisance, as it is of liability in negligence. For if a plaintiff is in ordinary circumstances only able to claim damages in respect of personal injuries where he can prove such foreseeability on the part of the defendant, it is difficult to see why, in common justice, he should be in a stronger position to claim damages for interference with the enjoyment of his land where the defendant was unable to foresee such damage. Moreover, this appears to have been the conclusion of the Privy Council in *Overseas Tankship (UK) Ltd v Miller Steamship Co Pty (The Wagon Mound (No 2))* [1967] 1 AC 617. The facts of the case are too well known to require repetition, but they gave rise to a claim for damages arising from a public nuisance caused by a spillage of oil in Sydney Harbour. Lord Reid, who delivered the advice of the Privy Council, considered that, in the class of nuisance which included the case before the Board, foreseeability is an essential element in determining liability. He then continued, at p 640:

> "It could not be right to discriminate between different cases of nuisance so as to make foreseeability a necessary element in determining damages in those cases where it is a necessary element in determining liability, but not in others. So the choice is between it being a necessary element in all cases of nuisance or in none. In their Lordships' judgment the similarities between nuisance and other forms of tort to which *The Wagon Mound (No 1)* applies far outweigh any differences, and they must therefore hold that the judgment appealed from is wrong on this branch of the case. It is not sufficient that the injury suffered by the respondents' vessels was the direct result of the nuisance if that injury was in the relevant sense unforeseeable.

It is widely accepted that this conclusion, although not essential to the decision of the particular case, has nevertheless settled the law to the effect that foreseeability of harm is indeed a prerequisite of the recovery of damages in private nuisance, as in the case of public nuisance. I refer in particular to the opinion expressed by Professor Fleming in Fleming on *The Law of Torts*, 8th ed (1992), pp 443-444. It is unnecessary in the present case to consider the precise nature of this principle; but it appears from Lord Reid's statement of the law that he regarded it essentially as one relating to remoteness of damage.

Foreseeability of damage under the rule in Rylands v Fletcher

It is against this background that I turn to the submission advanced by ECL before your Lordships that there is a similar prerequisite of recovery of damages under the rule in *Rylands v Fletcher*.

I start with the judgment of Blackburn J in *Fletcher v Rylands* (1866) ...

In that passage, Blackburn J spoke of "anything likely to do mischief if it escapes"; and later he spoke of something "which he knows to be mischievous if it gets on his neighbour's [property]", and the liability to "answer for the natural and anticipated consequences". Furthermore, time and again he spoke of the strict liability imposed upon the defendant as being that he must keep the thing in at his peril; and, when referring to liability in actions for damage occasioned by animals, he referred, at p 282, to the established principle that "it is quite immaterial whether the escape is by negligence or not". The general tenor of his statement of principle is therefore that knowledge, or at least foreseeability of the risk, is a prerequisite of the recovery of damages under the principle; but that the principle is one of strict liability in the sense that the defendant may be held liable notwithstanding that he has exercised all due care to prevent the escape from occurring ...

Even so, the question cannot be considered solely as a matter of history. It can be argued that the rule in *Rylands v Fletcher* should not be regarded simply as an extension of the law of nuisance, but should rather be treated as a developing principle of strict liability from which can be derived a general rule of strict liability for damage caused by ultra-hazardous operations on the basis of which persons conducting such operations may properly be held strictly liable for the extraordinary risk to others involved in such operations. As is pointed out in Fleming on *The Law of Torts*, pp 327-328, this would lead to the practical result that the cost of damage resulting from such operations would have to be absorbed as part of the overheads of the relevant business rather than be borne (where there is no negligence) by the injured person or his insurers, or even by the community at large. Such a development appears to have been taking place in the United States, as can be seen from paragraph 519 of the *Restatement of Torts* (2d) vol 3 (1977). The extent to which it has done so is not altogether clear; and I infer from paragraph 519, and the Comment on that paragraph, that the abnormally dangerous activities there referred to are such that their ability to cause harm would be obvious to any reasonable person who carried them on.

I have to say, however, that there are serious obstacles in the way of the development of the rule in *Rylands v Fletcher* in this way. First of all, if it was so to develop, it should logically apply to liability to all persons suffering injury by reason of the ultra-hazardous operations; but the decision of this House in *Read v J Lyons & Co Ltd* [1947] AC 156, which establishes that there can be no liability under the rule except in circumstances where the injury has been caused by an escape from land under the control of the defendant, has effectively precluded any such development. Professor Fleming has observed that "the most damaging effect of the decision in *Read v J Lyons & Co Ltd* is that it prematurely stunted the development of a general theory of strict liability for ultra-hazardous activities" (see Fleming on *Torts*, p 341). Even so, there is much to be said for the view that the courts should not be proceeding down the path of developing such a general theory. In this connection, I refer in particular to the *Report of the Law Commission on Civil Liability for Dangerous Things and Activities* (1970) (Law Com No 32). In paragraphs 14-16 of the Report, the Law Commission expressed serious misgivings about the adoption of any test for the application of strict liability involving a general concept of "especially dangerous" or "ultra-hazardous" activity, having regard to the uncertainties and practical difficulties of its application. If the Law Commission is unwilling to consider statutory reform on this basis, it must follow that judges should if anything be even more reluctant to proceed down that path.

Like the judge in the present case, I incline to the opinion that, as a general rule, it is more appropriate for strict liability in respect of operations of high risk to be imposed by Parliament, than by the courts. If such liability is imposed by statute, the relevant activities can be identified, and those concerned can know where they stand. Furthermore, statute can where appropriate lay down precise criteria establishing the incidence and scope of such liability.

It is of particular relevance that the present case is concerned with environmental pollution. The protection and preservation of the environment is now perceived as being of crucial importance to the future of mankind; and public bodies, both national and international, are taking significant steps towards the establishment of legislation which will promote the protection of the environment, and make the polluter pay for damage to the environment for which he is responsible – as can be seen from the WHO, EEC and national regulations to which I have previously referred. But it does not follow from these developments that a common law principle, such as the rule in *Rylands v Fletcher*, should be developed or rendered more strict to provide for liability in respect of such pollution. On the contrary, given that so much well-informed and carefully structured legislation is now being put in place for this purpose, there is less need for the courts to develop a common law principle to achieve the same end, and indeed it may well be undesirable that they should do so.

Having regard to these considerations, and in particular to the step which this House has already taken in *Read v J Lyons & Co Ltd* [1947] AC 156 to contain the scope of liability under the rule in *Rylands v Fletcher*, it appears to me to be appropriate now to take the view that foreseeability of damage of the relevant type should be regarded as a prerequisite of liability in damages under the rule. Such a conclusion can, as I have already stated, be derived from Blackburn J's original statement of the law; and I can see no good reason why this prerequisite should not be recognised under the rule, as it has been in the case of private nuisance. In particular, I do not regard the two authorities cited to your Lordships, *West v Bristol Tramways Co* [1908] 2 KB 14 and *Rainham Chemical Works Ltd v Belvedere Fish Guano Co Ltd* [1921] 2 AC 465, as providing any strong pointer towards a contrary conclusion. It would moreover lead to a more coherent body of common law principles if the rule were to be regarded essentially as an extension of the law of nuisance to cases of isolated escapes from land, even though the rule as established is not limited to escapes which are in fact isolated. I wish to point out, however, that in truth the escape of the PCE from ECL's land, in the form of trace elements carried in percolating water, has not been an isolated escape, but a continuing escape resulting from a state of affairs which has come into existence at the base of the chalk aquifer underneath ECL's premises. Classically, this would have been regarded as a case of nuisance; and it would seem strange if, by characterising the case as one falling under the rule in *Rylands v Fletcher*, the liability should thereby be rendered more strict in the circumstances of the present case.

The facts of the present case

Turning to the facts of the present case, it is plain that, at the time when the PCE was brought onto ECL's land, and indeed when it was used in the tanning process there, nobody at EC could reasonably have foreseen the resultant damage which occurred at CWC's borehole at Sawston ...

I wish to add that the present case may be regarded as one of what is nowadays called historic pollution, in the sense that the relevant occurrence (the seepage of PCE through the floor of ECL's premises) took place before the relevant legislation came into force; and it appears that, under the current philosophy, it is not envisaged that statutory liability should be imposed for historic pollution (see, eg the Council of Europe's Draft Convention on Civil Liability for Damage Resulting from Activities Dangerous to the Environment (Strasbourg 26 January 1993) article 5.1, and paragraph 48 of the Explanatory Report). If so, it would be strange if liability for such pollution were to arise under a principle of common law.

In the result, since those responsible at ECL could not at the relevant time reasonably have foreseen that the damage in question might occur, the claim of CWC for damages under the rule in *Rylands v Fletcher* must fail.

Natural use of land

I turn to the question whether the use by ECL of its land in the present case constituted a natural use, with the result that ECL cannot be held liable under the rule in *Rylands v Fletcher* ...

It is a commonplace that this particular exception to liability under the rule has developed and changed over the years. It seems clear that, in *Fletcher v Rylands*, LR 1 Ex 265 itself, Blackburn J's statement of the law was limited to things which are brought by the defendant onto his land, and so did not apply to things that were naturally upon the land. Furthermore, it is doubtful whether in the House of Lords in the same case Lord Cairns, to whom we owe the expression "non-natural use" of the land, was intending to expand the concept of natural use beyond that envisaged by Blackburn J. Even so, the law has long since departed from any such simple idea, redolent of a different age; and, at least since the advice of the Privy Council delivered by Lord Moulton in *Rickards v Lothian* [1913] AC 263, 280, natural use has been extended to embrace the ordinary use of land ...

It is obvious that the expression "ordinary use of the land" in Lord Moulton's statement of the law is one which is lacking in precision. There are some writers who welcome the flexibility which has thus been introduced into this branch of the law, on the ground that it enables judges to mould and adapt the principle of strict liability to the changing needs of society; whereas others regret the perceived absence of principle in so vague a concept, and fear that the whole idea of strict liability may as a result be undermined. A particular doubt is introduced by Lord Moulton's alternative criterion – "or such a use as is proper for the general benefit of the community". If these words are understood to refer to a local community, they can be given some content as intended to refer to such matters as, for example, the provision of services; indeed the same idea can, without too much difficulty, be extended to, for example, the provision of services to industrial premises, as in a business park or an industrial estate. But if the words are extended to embrace the wider interests of the local community or the general benefit of the community at large, it is difficult to see how the exception can be kept within reasonable bounds. A notable extension was considered in your Lordships' House in *Read v J Lyons & Co Ltd* [1947] AC 156, 169-170, *per* Viscount Simon, and p 174, *per* Lord Macmillan, where it was suggested that, in time of war, the manufacture of explosives might be held to constitute a natural use of land, apparently on the basis that, in a country in which the greater part of the population was involved in the war effort, many otherwise exceptional uses might become "ordinary" for the duration of the war. It is, however, unnecessary to consider so wide an extension as that in a case such as the present. Even so, we can see the introduction of another extension in the present case, when the judge invoked the creation of employment as clearly for the benefit of the local community, *viz* "the industrial village" at Sawston. I myself, however, do not feel able to accept that the creation of employment as such, even in a small industrial complex, is sufficient of itself to establish a particular use as constituting a natural or ordinary use of land.

Fortunately, I do not think it is necessary for the purposes of the present case to attempt any redefinition of the concept of natural or ordinary use. This is because I am satisfied that the storage of chemicals in substantial quantities, and their use in the manner employed at ECL's premises, cannot fall within the exception. For the purpose of testing the point, let it be assumed that ECL was well aware of the possibility that PCE, if it escaped, could indeed cause damage,, for example, by contaminating any water with which it became mixed so as to render that water undrinkable by human beings. I cannot think that it would be right in such circumstances to exempt ECL from liability under the rule in *Rylands v Fletcher* on the ground that the use was natural or ordinary. The mere fact that the use is common in the tanning industry cannot, in my opinion, be enough to bring the use within the exception, nor the fact that Sawston contains a small industrial community which is worthy of encouragement or support. Indeed I feel bound to say that the storage of substantial quantities of chemicals on industrial premises should be regarded as an almost classic case of non-natural use; and I find it very difficult to think that it should be thought objectionable to impose strict liability for damage caused in the event of their escape. It may well be that, now that it is recognised that foreseeability of harm of the relevant type is a prerequisite of liability in damages under the rule, the courts may feel less pressure to extend the concept of natural use to circumstances such as those in the present case; and in due course it may become easier to control this exception, and to ensure that it has a more recognisable basis of principle. For these reasons, I would not hold that ECL should be exempt from liability on the basis of the exception of natural use.

However, for the reasons I have already given, I would allow ECL's appeal with costs before your Lordships' House and in the courts below.

[The other Lords of Appeal agreed with Lord Goff]

Questions and notes

1. Is this case authority for the proposition that English law refuses to recognise a liability for things similar to the principle to be found in the *Code Civil* Article 1384?

2. Does this case destroy the idea that it is the polluter who should pay?

3. Is fault the basis for all non-contractual compensation claims for physical damage?

4. If the facts of *Read v Lyons* arose again today, would the case be decided in the same way?

5. Lord Goff says that inapposite conclusions must not be drawn from the cases involving injunctions. Does this once again indicate (cf *Miller v Jackson*, above p 22) that it is the remedy and not the right that is the main focal point of English law?

6. Hard cases, it is said, make for bad law. Well *Cambridge* is a hard case in that the plaintiff is hardly the most deserving of people (it might be useful to compare the salaries of the directors of CWC with those of the directors of ECL) and it does seem hard that a defendant should be held liable for something that happened way back in the past. Perhaps, then, the key to the decision is to be found under Lord Goff's heading 'The facts of the present case'. Yet this simply takes us back to the role of a court like the House of Lords (see Chapter 1): is it simply to decide particular cases between particular litigants? Was there not here an opportunity to do for strict liability what *Donoghue v Stevenson* did for fault liability? Lord Goff implied a role for comparative law in his *Littlewoods* judgment (see above p 365 and see

his recent judgment in *White v Jones* [1995] 1 All ER 691), was there not the chance for the common law, perhaps in the spirit of harmonisation, to import the symmetry of the French Code civil? No doubt names at Lloyds might not be so keen on an extension of strict liability, but the ordinary citizen crippled in a road accident and unable to prove fault (see next section) might appreciate the symmetry of the *Jand'heur* case in France[12] which brought car accidents within Article 1384 (now mostly covered by separate legislation: *Loi 5 juillet 1985*). The problem with the *Cambridge Water* case is that it is a case about pollution and the law of tort that tells us not that much about pollution and the law of tort.

7. Using materials to be found in the Chapter on reasoning (Chapter 2), can you construct a judgment arriving at the opposite conclusion to Lord Goff's?

Wringe v Cohen [1940] 1 KB 229 Court of Appeal

Atkinson J: ... In our judgment if, owing to want of repair, premises on a highway become dangerous and, therefore, a nuisance, and a passer-by or an adjoining owner suffers damage by their collapse, the occupier, or the owner if he has undertaken the duty of repair, is answerable whether he knew or ought to have known of the danger or not. The undertaking to repair gives the owner control of the premises, and a right of access thereto for the purpose of maintaining them in a safe condition. On the other hand, if the nuisance is created, not by want of repair, but, for example, by the act of a trespasser, or by a secret and unobservable operation of nature, such as a subsidence under or near the foundations of the premises, neither an occupier nor an owner responsible for repair is answerable, unless with knowledge or means of knowledge he allows the danger to continue. In such a case he has in no sense caused the nuisance by any act or breach of duty. I think that every case decided in the English Courts is consistent with this view.

By common law it is an indictable offence for an occupier of premises on a highway to permit them to get into a dangerous condition owing to non-repair. It was not and is not necessary in an indictment to aver knowledge or means of knowledge ...

Mint v Good [1951] 1 KB 517 Court of Appeal

This was an action for damages by a boy against the owner of premises for injury sustained by the boy on a public highway when a wall on the premises collapsed onto him. The trial judge dismissed the action against the owner on the ground that the owner, who had let the premises to tenants, had not reserved the right of entry to make repairs. An appeal to the Court of Appeal was allowed.

---

12   Ch. réun. 13 févr. 1930; DP 1930.1.57 note Ripert; S.1930.1.121 note Esmein.

Denning LJ: ... The law of England has always taken particular care to protect those who use a highway. It puts on the occupier of adjoining premises a special responsibility for the structures which he keeps beside the highway. So long as those structures are safe, all well and good; but if they fall into disrepair, so as to be a potential danger to passers-by, then they are a nuisance, and, what is more, a public nuisance; and the occupier is liable to anyone using the highway who is injured by reason of the disrepair. It is no answer for him to say that he and his servants took reasonable care; for, even if he has employed a competent independent contractor to repair the structure, and has every reason for supposing it to be safe, the occupier is still liable if the independent contractor did the work badly: see *Tarry v Ashton*.

The occupier's duty to passers-by is to see that the structure is as safe as reasonable care can make it; a duty which is as high as the duty which an occupier owes to people who pay to come on to his premises. He is not liable for latent defects, which could not be discovered by reasonable care on the part of anyone, nor for acts of trespassers of which he neither knew, nor ought to have known: see *Barker v Herbert*; but he is liable when structures fall into dangerous disrepair, because there must be some fault on the part of someone or other for that to happen; and he is responsible for it to persons using the highway, even though he was not actually at fault himself. That principle was laid down in this court in *Wring v Cohen*, where it is to be noted that the principle is confined to "premises on a highway" ...

The question in this case is whether the owner, as well as the occupier, is under a like duty to passers-by. I think he is. The law has shown a remarkable development on this point during the last sixteen years. The three cases of *Wilchick v Marks and Silverstone*, *Wringe v Cohen* and *Heap v Ind Coope and Allsopp Ltd* show that the courts are now taking a realistic view of these matters. They recognise that the occupying tenant of a small dwelling-house does not in practice do the structural repairs, but the owner does; and that if a passer-by is injured by the structure being in dangerous disrepair, the occupier has not the means to pay damages, but the owner has, or, at any rate, he can insure against it. If a passer-by is injured by the structure falling on him, he should be entitled to damages from someone, and the person who ought to pay is the owner, because he is in practice responsible for the repairs ...

That is sufficient for the decision of this case, but I venture to doubt in these days whether a landlord can exempt himself from liability to passers-by by taking a covenant from a tenant to repay the structure adjoining the highway ... The liability of the owner is a liability in tort and cannot be affected by the terms of the agreement between himself and his tenant. Just as a manufacturer who is liable under the principle in *Donoghue v Stevenson* cannot exempt himself from liability to the public by the terms of his contract with the wholesaler, so also I should doubt whether a property owner could exempt himself by the terms of his contract with the tenant ...

Questions

1. Are these cases examples of strict liability (liability without fault)?
2. What if the boy had been injured by a tree on the defendant's land falling on him?

3. Under the Occupiers' Liability Act 1957 an occupier owes a 'common duty of care' to visitors on his property: why should someone off the premises be owed a higher duty? Does the difference mean that compensation can be made to depend upon where a plaintiff was standing when the injury occurred?

4. To what extent is the tort of public nuisance a form of action expressing a principle similar to Article 1384 of the Code Civil?

5. Is the tort of public nuisance conceptually quite different from the tort of private nuisance? Are they, for example, quite separate causes of action?

6. Does Denning LJ use reasoning by analogy?

Consumer Protection Act 1987 (c 43)

(See p 211)

Notes and questions

1. This statute is just one of many dealing with liability for things. Other important statutes to be researched in the library or major tort casebooks are: Occupiers' Liability Act 1957; Employers Liability (Defective Equipment) Act 1969; Animals Act 1971; Defective Premises Act 1972. Is the level of duty the same in all of these statutes?

2. One must not forget the vast amount of statute law in the area of public law which also touches upon liability in respect of things. One question that often occurs is whether breach of a statute will give rise to a claim for damages in tort; this is the tort of breach of statutory duty and it is a tort that often results in case law that could be categorised under liability for things. Equally, of course, such cases can be classified under the heading of liability for unlawful behaviour. Is all unlawful behaviour wrongful behaviour for the purposes of the law of obligations?

3. Is noise a thing?

4. Is *Donoghue v Stevenson* (above p 33) an example of liability for damage done by a thing? What about *Grant v Australian Knitting Mills* (above p 89)?

5. In breach of a statute radiation escapes from a nuclear installation and contaminates local houses. The price of these houses falls dramatically. Can the owners sue the nuclear installation for their losses?[13]

(e) Liability for words

Horrocks v Lowe [1975] AC 135 House of Lords

Lord Diplock: ... My Lords, as a general rule English law gives effect to the ninth commandment that a man shall not speak evil falsely of his neighbour. It supplies a temporal sanction: if he cannot prove that defamatory matter which he published was true, he is liable in damages to whomever he has defamed, except where the publication is oral only, causes no damage and falls outside the categories of slander actionable *per se*. The public interest that the law should provide an effective means whereby a man can vindicate his reputation against calumny has nevertheless to be accommodated to the competing public interest in permitting men to communicate frankly and freely with one another about matters in respect of which the law recognises that they have a duty to perform or an interest to protect in doing so. What is published in good faith on matters of these kinds is published on a privileged occasion. It is not actionable even though it be defamatory and turns out to be untrue. With some exceptions which are irrelevant to the instant appeal, the privilege is not absolute but qualified. It is lost if the occasion which gives rise to it is misused. For in all cases of qualified privilege there is some special reason of public policy why the law accords immunity from suit – the existence of some public or private duty, whether legal or moral, on the part of the maker of the defamatory statement which justifies his communicating it or of some interest of his own which he is entitled to protect by doing so. If he uses the occasion for some other reason he loses the protection of the privilege ...

Notes and questions

1. 'The tort of defamation is in many ways a hangover from a by-gone age. It is concerned with protecting reputation in the eyes of "right thinking" people (as the old judges used to say) and it survives, *inter alia*, because it is a useful weapon to stifle investigative reporting.[14] Admittedly, it is now more difficult for local authorities to use the tort to silence their critics;[15] but it continues to be used by the rich and powerful, together with those MP's with something to hide, and by pop musicians and glamour people. It is a useful means of supplementing the income of those with enough money to use the

---

13 See *Merlin v Britsh Nuclear Fuels* [1990] 2 QB 557.

14 See eg, John Pilger, Letter, *The Guardian* 9 July 1991.

15 *Derbyshire CC v Times Newspapers* [1993] AC 534.

tort (legal aid is not available) and the damages awarded bear no relation to those awarded in personal injury cases.[16] Accordingly, it is a tort that insults the dignity of those who have lost eyes and limbs in factory and car accidents. (One press-hating judge was made a fool of by one plaintiff who obtained thousands in damages and, later, was shown to be a liar and a perjurer: a role here for the law of restitution?) The tort used to consist of quite detailed rules, often procedural because of the continued existence of the jury, but many of these rules seem now to have been abandoned in practice. Libel lawyers seem to be able to get almost any person who criticises another before a jury and if it looks like a jury would find for the defendant, or award 5p damages, the libel lawyers can usually convince some judge or another to abandon the jury. The whole area has become a soap opera and belongs more in a sourcebook on media and entertainment law.' These observations are, of course, deliberately provocative and one-sided; but are they so unfair? What do they overlook?

2. Parliament is unlikely to act because too many MP's have a personal interest in the continued existence of the tort. But, given the way the judges have reinterpreted the tort of *Rylands v Fletcher*, it is possible for change, major change, to be initiated at the level of case law. What kinds of reasons might a judge advance for not making changes at the level of principle? In the light of Hoffmann LJ's brave words in *R v Central Television Plc* (above p 71), has the time not come to rethink this tort?

3. What are the rules of defamation? Do such rules apply mainly to defences? Clearly the rules set out by Lord Diplock in the extract above are very general: what further rules need to be added so as to be able to solve factual situations involving damage to reputation?

4. In American law it is extremely difficult for public officials to sue in defamation which was why the newspapers were able to investigate the Watergate scandal. Ought similar principles to be introduced into UK law?

5. If defamation in its present form were to be abandoned, would there need to be some new tort of privacy? Is the problem actually with defamation itself or with its notion of damage, including the role of the jury in the compensation of this damage?

---

16 For an attempt to justify libel damages in relation to damages awarded for personal injury see *Sutcliffe v Pressdram Ltd* [1991] 1 QB 153.

Spring v Guardian Assurance Plc [1994] 3 WLR 354 House of Lords

(See also p 68).

Lord Slynn: ... I do not for my part consider that to recognise the existence of a duty of care in some situations when a reference is given necessarily means that the law of defamation has to be changed or that a substantial section of the law relating to defamation and malicious falsehood is "emasculated" (Court of Appeal, at p 437). They remain distinct torts. It may be that there will be less resort to these torts because a more realistic approach on the basis of a duty of care is adopted. If to recognise that such a duty of care exists means that there have to be such changes – either by excluding the defence of qualified privilege from the master-servant situation or by withdrawing the privilege where negligence as opposed to malice is shown – then I would in the interests of recognising a fair, just and reasonable result in the master-servant situation accept such change ...

Lord Woolf: ... There would be no purpose in extending the tort of negligence to protect the subject of an inaccurate reference if he was already adequately protected by the law of defamation. However, because of the defence of qualified privilege, before an action for defamation can succeed (or, for that matter, an action for injurious falsehood) it is necessary to establish malice. In my judgment the result of this requirement is that an action for defamation provides a wholly inadequate remedy for an employee who is caused damage by a reference which due to negligence is inaccurate. This is because it places a wholly disproportionate burden on the employee. Malice is extremely difficult to establish. This is demonstrated by the facts of this case. The plaintiff was able to establish that one of his colleagues, who played a part in compiling the information on which the reference was based, had lied about interviewing him, but this was still insufficient to prove malice. Without an action for negligence the employee may, therefore, be left with no practical prospect of redress, even though the reference may have permanently prevented him from obtaining employment in his chosen vocation ...

The historic development of the two actions has been quite separate. Just as it has never been a requirement of an action for defamation to show that the defamatory statement was made negligently, so, if the circumstances establish that it is fair and just that a duty of care should exist, the person who suffers harm in consequence of a breach of that duty should not have to establish malice, merely because that would be a requirement in an action for defamation. I can see no justification for erecting a fence around the whole field to which defamation can apply and treating any other tort, which can beneficially from the point of view of justice enter into part of that field, as a trespasser if it does so ...

Questions

1. Is this case authority for the proposition that there is an English law of torts rather than tort?

2. A newspaper will be liable in damages – often huge damages (half a million pounds in several cases) – if they publish critical statements about individuals or companies and cannot prove that these

statements are true: does this make defamation part of public rather than private law?

3. Can defamation and the interlocutory injunction (see Chapter 3) be used by individuals (eg, Robert Maxwell when he was alive) to suppress publications in the public interest?

4. It is difficult to establish liability in respect of uncritical publications which do actual damage even if they are made negligently but very easy to establish liability in respect of publications which do no obvious damage but whose truth cannot be established in a court of law. Is this logical?

Hedley Byrne & Co v Heller & Partners Ltd [1964] AC 465 House of Lords

(See p 268)

Notes and questions

1. *Hedley Byrne* is a major case of principle in that it is the starting point for non-fraudulent and non-deliberate non-contractual liability for damage done by words. Had the Court of Appeal[17] decision in *Peek v Derry* been upheld by the House of Lords[18] there would have been no need for the 1964 decision since the tort of deceit (on which see *Bradford v Borden*, p 268) would have been adapted, with the help of equity, to deal with negligent misrepresentation. The influence of equity in *Hedley Byrne* itself should not be overlooked either; the idea of a 'special relationship' is an adaption of the equitable notion of a fiduciary relationship.[19]

2. The House of Lords found for the defendant but said, for future reference, that a duty of care would be owed in facts similar to those in the case. Is *Hedley Byrne* an example of prospective overruling (cf p 8)?

3. T contracts with S, a solicitor, for S to draw up a will leaving a substantial legacy to P. S negligently draws up the will with the result that, after T's death, the gift to P is void. Can P sue S? If so, will this be on the basis of *Hedley Byrne*?[20]

4. An auditor of a company negligently certifies a set of accounts for D plc. C, relying on the accounts, invests much money in D plc and loses it all when it fails. Can C sue the auditor?[21]

---

17 (1887) 37 Ch D 541.
18 (1889) 14 App Cas 337.
19 See *White v Jones* [1995] 1 All ER 691.
20 See *White v Jones* [1995] 1 All ER 691.
21 Cf *Caparo Industries plc v Dickman* [1990] 2 AC 605.

5. If the nephew in *Beswick v Beswick* (above p 154) had negligently failed to pay the annuity to the wife and she had suffered damage as a result, could she have sued the nephew for damages under the *Hedley Byrne* principle?

Torquay Hotel Co v Cousins [1969] 2 Ch 106 Court of Appeal

This was an action for an interlocutory injunction brought by a hotel against a trade union that had issued threats to the hotel's oil suppliers not to supply oil to the hotel. The hotel alleged that the union's threats amounted to an attempt to induce a breach of contract between the hotel and the oil suppliers even though this contract contained an exception clause covering labour disputes. The Court of Appeal upheld the grant of the injunction.

Lord Denning MR: ... 2. can the defendants take advantage of the *force majeure* clause?

The Imperial Hotel had a contract with Esso under which the Imperial Hotel agreed to buy their total requirements of fuel-oil from Esso for one year, the quantity being estimated at 120,000 gallons, to be delivered by road tank wagon at a minimum of 3,000 gallons a time. Under that contract there was a course of dealing by which the Imperial Hotel used to order 3,000 gallons every week or 10 days, and Esso used to deliver it the next day. But there was a *force majeure* or exception clause which said that

> "neither party shall be liable for any failure to fulfil any term of this agreement if fulfilment is delayed, hindered or prevented by any circumstance whatever which is not within their immediate control, including ... labour disputes."

It is plain that, if delivery was hindered or prevented by labour disputes, as, for instance, because their drivers would not cross the picket line, Esso could rely on that exception clause as a defence to any claim by Imperial. They would not be liable in damages. And I am prepared to assume that Esso would not be guilty of a breach of contract. But I do not think that would exempt the trade union officials from liability if they unlawfully hindered or prevented Esso from making deliveries. The principle of *Lumley v Gye* extends not only to inducing breach of contract, but also to preventing the performance of it. That can be shown by a simple illustration taken from the books. In *Lumley v Gye*, Miss Wagner, an actress, was engaged by Mr Lumley to sing at Her Majesty's Theatre. Mr Gye, who ran Covent Garden, procured her to break her contract with Mr Lumley by promising to pay her more: see *Lumley v Wagner*. He was held liable to Mr Lumley for inducing a breach of contract. In *Poussard v Spiers & Pond* Madam Poussard was under contract with Spiers to sing in an opera at the Criterion Theatre. She fell sick and was unable to attend rehearsals. Her non-performance, being occasioned by sickness, was not a breach of contract on her part: but it was held to excuse the theatre company from continuing to employ her. Suppose now that an ill-disposed person, knowing of her contract, had given her a potion to make her sick. She would not be guilty of a breach herself. But undoubtedly the person who administered the potion would have done wrong and be liable for the damage suffered by them. So here I think the trade union officials cannot take advantage of the *force majeure* or exception clause in the Esso contract. If they unlawfully prevented or hindered Esso from making deliveries, as ordered by Imperial, they would be liable in damage to Imperial, notwithstanding the exception clause. There is another reason too. They could not rely on an excuse of which they themselves had been "the mean" to use Lord Coke's language: see *New Zealand Shipping Co Ltd v Société des Ateliers et Chantiers de France*.

The principles of law

The principles of *Lumley v Gye* is that each of the parties to a contract has a "right to the performance" of it: and it is wrong for another to procure one of the parties to break it or not to perform it. That principle was extended a step further by Lord Macnaghten in *Quinn v Leathem*, so that each of the parties has a right to have his "contractual relations" with the other duly observed. "It is", he said at p 510, "a violation of legal right to interfere with contractual relations recognised by law if there be no sufficient justification for the interference". That statement was adopted and applied by a strong board of the Privy Council in *Jasperson v Dominion Tobacco Co*. It included Viscount Haldane and Lord Sumner. The time has come when the principle should be further extended to cover deliberate and direct interference with the execution of a contract without that causing any breach". That was a point left open by Lord Reid in *StratJord (JT) & Son Ltd v Lindley*. But the common law would be seriously deficient if it did not condemn such interference. It is this very case. The principle can be subdivided into three elements:

First, there must be interference in the execution of a contract The interference is not confined to the procurement of a breach of contract. It extends to a case where a third person prevents or hinders one party from performing his contract, even though it be not a breach.

Second, the interference must be deliberate. The person must know of the contract or, at any rate, turn a blind eye to it and intend to interfere with it: see *Emerald Construction Co v Lowthian*.

Third, the interference must be direct. Indirect interference will not do. Thus, a man who "corners the market" in a commodity may well know that it may prevent others from performing their contracts, but he is not liable to an action for so doing. A trade union official, who calls a strike on proper notice, may well know that it will prevent the employers from performing their contracts to deliver goods, but he is not liable in damages for calling it. Indirect interference is only unlawful if unlawful means are used. I went too far when I said in *Daily Mirror Newspapers v Gardner* that there was no difference between direct and indirect interference. On reading once again *Thornson (D C) & Co Ltd v Deakin*, with more time, I find there is a difference. Morris LJ, at p 702, there draws the very distinction between "direct persuasion to breach of contract" which is unlawful in itself: and "the intentional bringing about of a breach by indirect methods involving wrongdoing". This distinction must be maintained, else we should take away the right to strike altogether. Nearly every trade union official who calls a strike – even on due notice, as in *Morgan v Fry* – knows that it may prevent the employers from performing their contracts. He may be taken even to intend it. Yet no one has supposed hitherto that it was unlawful: and we should not render it unlawful today. A trade union official is only in the wrong when he procures a contracting party directly to break his contract, or when he does it indirectly by unlawful means. On reconsideration of the *Daily Mirror* case, I think that the defendants there interfered directly by getting the retailers as their agents to approach the wholesalers.

I must say a word about unlawful means, because that brings in another principle. I have always understood that if one person deliberately interferes with the trade or business of another, and does so by unlawful means, that is, by an act which he is not at liberty to commit, then he is acting unlawfully, even though he does not procure or induce any actual breach of contract. If the means are unlawful, that is enough. Thus in *Rookes v Barnard* (as explained by Lord Reid in *Stratford v Lindley and Lord Upjohn*) the defendants interfered with the employment of Rookes – and they did it by unlawful means, namely, by intimidation of his employers – and they were held to be acting unlawfully, even though the employers committed no breach of contract as they gave Rookes proper notice. And in *Stratford v Lindley*, the defendants interfered with the business of Stratford – and they did it by unlawful means, namely, by inducing the men to break their contracts of employment by refusing to handle the barges – and they were held to be acting unlawfully, even in regard to new business of Stratford which was not the subject of contract. Lord Reid said, at p 324:

> "The respondents' action made it practically impossible for the appellants to do any new business with the barge hirers. It was not disputed that such interference is tortious if any unlawful means are employed."

So also on the second point in *Daily Mirror v Gardner*, the defendants interfered with the business of the "Daily Mirror" – and they did it by a collective boycott which was held to be unlawful under the Restrictive Trade Practices Act, 1956 – and they were held to be acting unlawfully.

This point about unlawful means is of particular importance when a place is declared "black". At common law it often involves the use of unlawful means. Take the Imperial Hotel. When it was declared "black," it meant that the drivers of the tankers would not take oil to the hotel. The drivers would thus be induced to break their contracts of employment. That would be unlawful at common law. The only case in which "blacking" of such a kind is lawful is when it is done "in contemplation or furtherance of a trade dispute". It is then protected by section 3 of the Trade Disputes Act, 1906, see *Thomson (D C) & Co Ltd v Deakin* by Upjohn J; for, in that event, the act of inducing a breach of a contract of employment is a lawful act which is not actionable at the suit of anyone: see *Stratford v Lindley* by Salmon LJ, and *Morgan v Fry* by myself. Seeing that the act is lawful, it must, I think, be lawful for the trade union officials to tell the employers and their customers about it. And this is so, even though it does mean that those people are compelled to break their commercial contracts. The interference with the commercial contracts is only indirect, and not direct: see what Lord Upjohn said in *Stratford v Lindley*. So, if there had been a "trade dispute" in this case, I think it would have protected the trade union officials when they informed Esso that the dispute with Imperial was an "official dispute" and said that the hotel was "blacked". It would be like the "blacking" of the barges in *Stratford v Lindley*, where we held, in the Court of Appeal, that, on the basis that there was a "trade dispute", the defendants were not liable.

Applying the principle in this case

Seeing that there was no "trade dispute" this case falls to be determined by the common law. It seems to me that the trade union officials deliberately and directly interfered with the execution of the contract between the Imperial Hotel and Esso. They must have known that there was a contract between the Imperial Hotel and Esso. Why otherwise did they on that very first Saturday afternoon telephone the bulk plant at Plymouth? They may not have known with exactitude all the terms of the contract. But no more did the defendants in *Stratford v Lindley*. They must also have intended to prevent the performance of the contract. That is plain from the telephone message: "Any supplies of fuel-oil will be stopped being made." And the interference was direct. It was as direct as could be – a telephone message from the trade union official to the bulk plant.

Take next the supplies from Alternative Fuels. The first wagon got through. As it happened, there was no need for the Imperial Hotel to order any further supplies from Alternative Fuels. But suppose they had given a further order, it is quite plain that the trade union officials would have done their best to prevent it being delivered. Their telephone messages show that they intended to prevent supplies being made by all means in their power. By threatening "repercussions" they interfered unlawfully with the performance of any future order which Imperial Hotel might give to Alternative Fuels. And the interference was direct again. It was direct to Alternative Fuels. Such interference was sufficient to warrant the grant of an injunction *quia timet* ...

Conclusion

Other wrongs were canvassed, such as conspiracy and intimidation, but I do not think it necessary to go into these. I put my decision on the simple ground that there is evidence that the defendants intended to interfere directly and deliberately with the execution of the existing contracts by Esso and future contracts by Alternative Fuels so as to prevent those companies supplying oil to the Imperial Hotel. This intention was sufficiently manifest to warrant the granting of an injunction. The form of the injunction was criticised by Mr Pain, but it follows the form suggested by Lord Upjohn in *Stratford v Lindsey*, and I think it is in order.

I find myself in substantial agreement with the judge and would dismiss this appeal.

Winn LJ: ... For my part I think that it can at least be said, with confidence, that where a contract between two persons exists which gives one of them an optional extension of time or an optional mode for his performance of it, or of part of it, but, from the normal course of dealing between them, the other person does not anticipate such postponement, or has come to expect a particular mode of performance, a procuring of the exercise of such an option should, in principle, be held actionable if it produces material damage to the other contacting party ...

Notes and questions

1. As a result of the pure economic loss principle in the tort of negligence many unthinking students state that the law of tort does not protect against economic loss. This is nonsense. In addition to misrepresentation cases, which usually lead to economic loss, there are the economic torts which have been fashioned to deal with the problem of strife in the world of business and industrial relations. When will D be liable for deliberately causing economic loss to P?

It might be tempting to say that all deliberately caused loss should be actionable, but this would clash with the ethics of capitalism where competition – that is deliberately causing loss to another since one person's profit is another person's loss – is fundamental. Now if one has the right to open a supermarket even if it ruins all the other local foodshops, does one have the right deliberately to ruin all the local foodshops by opening a supermarket? The common law said yes providing that no wrong was involved.[22] But what is meant by wrong in this context, given that, according to *Bradford v Pickles* (above p 124), malice in itself is not a wrong? The tort of inducing breach of contract was the major starting point. Is there now a tort of economic duress?[23]

2. Do traders have a right to trade free from deliberate interference by others? Do trade unions have any rights at common law?

3. D writes an article urging his readers not to buy goods from P's shop because P makes financial contributions to the Conservative Party: can P sue D for his economic losses? What if D urges people to demonstrate on the pavement outside of P's shop?

4. Is there a right to strike in the English common law?

5. Is a contractual right a property right as far as the English law of tort is concerned?

6. What role has the interlocutory injunction played in the development of the economic torts?

7. Which are the most useful concepts in the area of economic torts: (i) rights; (ii) duties; (iii) wrongs; (iv) directness; (v) intention; (vi) interests; (vii) property?

3 ROAD ACCIDENTS

Phillips v Britannia Hygienic Laundry Co Ltd [1923] 2 KB 832 Court of Appeal

Bankes LJ: This is an appeal from the Divisional Court reversing the county court judge in an action brought by the plaintiff for damage done to his motor van. The axle of the defendants' motor lorry broke and caused the damage. The action in the county court was founded on an alleged breach of a statutory provision contained in the Motor Cars (Use and Construction) Order 1904 and alternatively on the alleged negligence of the defendant. The county court judge absolved the defendant from negligence in relation either to the management of the motor lorry or to the state of its axle, but he found negligence on the part of

---

22 *Mogul SS Co v McGregor, Gow & Co* [1892] AC 25.

23 See *Dimskal Shipping Co v ITWF* [1992] 2 AC 152.

the repairers to whom the motor lorry had been sent, in not having executed the repairs efficiently, and gave judgment for the plaintiff on the ground that the lorry was not in the condition required by cl 6 of art. II of the Order. On an appeal by the defendants the Divisional Court reversed this judgment. The plaintiff appeals to this court.

I agree with the conclusion of the Divisional Court. If the judgment of the county court judge were to stand it would have very far-reaching consequences ...

We have not to consider the case of a person injured on the highway. The injury here was done to the appellant's van; and the appellant, a member of the public, claims a right of action as one of a class for whose benefit cl 6 was introduced. He contends that the public using the highway is the class so favoured. I do not agree. In my view the public using the highway is not a class; it is itself the public and not a class of the public. The clause therefore was not passed for the benefit of a class or section of the public. It applies to the public generally, and it is one among many regulations for breach of which it cannot have been intended that a person aggrieved should have a civil remedy ...

Atkin LJ: ... This is an important question, and I have felt some doubt upon it, because it is clear that these regulations are in part designed to promote the safety of the public using highways. The question is whether they were intended to be enforced only by the special penalty attached to them in the Act. In my opinion, when an Act imposes a duty of commission or omission, the question whether a person aggrieved by a breach of the duty has a right of action depends on the intention of the Act. Was it intended to make the duty one which was owed to the party aggrieved as well as to the State, or was it a public duty only ? That depends on the construction of the Act and the circumstances in which it was made and to which it relates. One question to be considered is, Does the Act contain reference to a remedy for breach of it? *Prima facie* if it does that is the only remedy. But that is not conclusive. The intention as disclosed by its scope and wording must still be regarded, and it may still be that, though the statute creates the duty and provides a penalty, the duty is nevertheless owed to individuals. Instances of this are *Groves v Lord Wimborne* and *Britannic Merthyr Coal Co v David*. To my mind, and in this respect I differ from McCardie J, the question is not to be solved by considering whether or not the person aggrieved can bring himself within some special class of the community or whether he is some designated individual. The duty may be of such paramount importance that it is owed to all the public. It would be strange if a less important duty, which is owed to a section of the public, may be enforced by an action, while a more important duty owed to the public at large cannot. The right of action does not depend on whether a statutory commandment or prohibition is pronounced for the benefit of the public or for the benefit of a class. It may be conferred on anyone who can bring himself within the benefit of the Act, including one who cannot be otherwise specified than as a person using the highway ... I have come to the conclusion that the duty they were intended to impose was not a duty enforceable by individuals injured, but a public duty only, the sole remedy for which is the remedy provided by way of a fine. They impose obligations of various kinds, some are concerned more with the maintenance of the highway than with the safety of passengers; and they are of varying degrees of importance; yet for breach of any regulation a fine not exceeding £10 is the penalty. It is not likely that the legislature, in empowering a department to make regulations for the use and construction of motor cars, permitted the department to impose new duties in favour of individuals and new causes of action for breach of them in addition to the obligations already well provided for and regulated by the common law of those who bring vehicles upon highways. In particular it is not likely that the legislature intended by these means to impose on the owners of vehicles an absolute obligation to have them roadworthy in all events even in the absence of negligence ...

[**Younger LJ** agreed]

Notes and questions

1. If the plaintiff had suffered personal injury would the judges in this case have taken a different view?

2. Does the tort of negligence now view road users as a class or section of the public? If so, ought this to discredit the decision in *Phillips*?

3. Is it important to appreciate that this case was decided before the introduction of compulsory insurance for third party liability?

4. Is this case distinguishing between public and private law?

5. *Read v Lyons* (see *Cambridge Water* case above) has presented an obstacle to the development of strict liability (liability for things) in the area of factory accidents; *Phillips* seems to present an obstacle in respect of the another great source of personal injury litigation, car accidents. Things are different in France where Article 1384, and now a separate statute, has focused more on the activity, or at least on control (*sous sa garde*), than on the existence or non-existence of fault. Is English law behind the rest of Europe in this respect? Does the fault principle give insurance companies a powerful tool to wield against those who try to claim compensation? Is the present tort system the most economically efficient way of providing compensation to those killed, crippled and wounded by vehicles? The literature is enormous and this chapter will give only a very brief insight to the approach of the English judges. Is legislation needed?

Dymond v Pearce and Others [1972] 1 QB 496 Court of Appeal

This was an action for damages by a motor cycle passenger against the employers of a lorry driver (second defendant) in respect of personal injuries suffered by the passenger when the motor cycle ran into the back of the parked lorry. The lorry driver had parked his vehicle with the tail lights on, beneath a street lamp on a dual carriageway, and there was a clear view of the lorry for at least 200 yards. The crash occurred when the driver of the motor cycle (first defendant) was looking behind him at girls on the pavement. The Court of Appeal upheld a judgment that the accident was wholly the fault of the motor cyclist.

Sachs LJ: ... When looking at authorities concerned with highway nuisances it is important to remember that there are these two categories, because otherwise phrases relating to the second – danger – category may be read as necessarily applying to the first – simple obstruction. It is, however, *prima facie* common to both categories – which can in fact overlap – that in neither is it necessary to prove negligence as an ingredient (...); that in both proof of what is *prima facie* a nuisance lays the onus on the defendant to prove justification (compare *Southport Corporation v Esso Petroleum Co Ltd*); and that, of course, neither is actionable – in the sense that a claim for damages can succeed – unless the plaintiff can establish that damage has actually been caused to him by the nuisance.

Leaving on one side those in somewhat special positions, such as frontagers, the common law rights of users of highways are normally confined to use for passage and repassage and for incidents usually associated with such use, such as temporary halts and those emergency stops which often give rise to difficulties ... The leaving of a large vehicle on a highway for any other purpose for a considerable period (it is always a matter of degree) otherwise than in a lay-by *prima facie* results in a nuisance being created, for it narrows the highway. With all respect to the views expressed by the learned trial judge as to the ways of life today, I am unable to accept his conclusion that the parking for many hours for the driver's own convenience of a large lorry on a highway of sufficient importance to have a dual carriageway did not result in the creation of a nuisance ...

But the mere fact that a lorry was a nuisance does not render its driver or owner liable to the plaintiff in damages unless its being in that position was a cause of the accident ...

[The trial judge found] that the sole cause of the accident was the first defendant's negligence ... It entails a parallel conclusion that the nuisance was not a cause of the plaintiff's injuries; that, indeed, in the vast majority of cases is an inevitable conclusion once negligence on the part of a driver of a stationary vehicle is negatived, for only rarely will that which was found not to be a foreseeable cause of an accident also be found to have been in law the actual cause of it ...

It is thus not necessary to decide a further point inherent in much that was canvassed before us as to the ingredients of nuisance of the category under consideration. What would be the position if, even though the third defendant had not been negligent in leaving the lorry as it was in fact left, yet there had occurred some unexpected supervening happening – such as an onset of heavy weather, sea mist or fog, or, for instance, a sudden rear light failure (potent cause of fatalities) – which had so affected the situation that the lorry became the cause of an accident? Should the risk fall entirely on those using the highway properly? Or should some liability attach to the person at fault in creating a nuisance? It may well be that, as I am inclined to think, he who created the nuisance would be under a liability ... If he was thus liable this might be the only class of case in which an action in nuisance by obstruction of the highway could succeed where one in negligence would fail ...

Edmund Davies LJ: ... Where a vehicle has been left parked on the highway for such a length of time or in such other circumstances as constitute it an obstruction amounting to a public nuisance, I remain of the view I expressed in *Parish v Judd* that, in order that a plaintiff who in such proceedings as the present may recover compensation for personal injuries caused by a collision with that obstruction, he must establish that the obstruction constituted a danger ...

[He then cited Denning LJ in *Morton v Wheeler*, as to what constitutes a danger – "whether injury may reasonably be anticipated"] It goes without saying, however, that the person creating a highway obstruction must be alert to such sudden and unpredicted weather changes as those to which we are subject in this country at most seasons, to the possibility that the vehicular or highway lighting may fail or be interfered with in these days of rampant vandalism, and to other circumstances which may convert what was originally a danger-free obstruction into a grave traffic hazard. If he fails to exercise ordinary intelligence in those and similar respects, he can make no proper claim reasonably to have anticipated the probable shape of things to come, and he must expect his conduct to be subjected to the most critical scrutiny in the event of an accident occurring ...

It is true that in the result, as Denning LJ said in *Morton v Wheeler*, "Inasmuch as the test of danger is what may reasonably be foreseen, it is apparent that cases of public nuisance ... have an affinity with negligence." Nevertheless, as he went on to point out: "There is a real distinction between negligence and nuisance. In an action for private damage arising out of a public nuisance, the court does not look at the conduct of the defendant and ask whether he was negligent. It looks at the actual state of affairs as it exists in or adjoining the highway without regard to the merits or demerits of the defendant. If the state of affairs is such as to be a danger ... the person who created it is liable unless he can show sufficient justification or excuse."

Questions

1. If the plaintiff establishes a *prima facie* nuisance does this put the onus of disproving negligence on the defendant?

2. D, suddenly taken ill with a heart attack, creates a dangerous hazard on the road by leaving his lorry in an unsuitable place and the police carelessly fail to deal with the problem with the result that P, a motor cyclist, crashes into the parked lorry. Can P sue anyone?

3. What would be the position if the plaintiff passenger had actually been injured as a result of the motor cycle hitting the lorry because the street lamp had been broken by vandals?

4. What if a thief had stolen the lorry and later parked it in a dangerous position: would the owners of the lorry be liable if there was an accident?

Henderson v HE Jenkins & Sons Ltd [1970] AC 282 House of Lords

This was an action in damages under the Fatal Accidents Act by a widow against the owners of a runaway lorry which had killed her husband. The owners claimed that the lorry's brakes had failed because of a latent defect undiscoverable by the use of reasonable care and this defence was upheld by the trial judge and Court of Appeal; a bare majority of the House of Lords allowed an appeal.

Lord Donovan: ... [The defendants] proved that the pipe in question was visually inspected *in situ* once a week; that the brake pedal was on these occasions depressed to check for leaks from the pipe and none seen; that nothing more than such visual inspection of the pipe was required by Ministry of Transport rules or the maker's advice ...

Yet the kind of load this lorry had been carrying in the past was something which had to be known in order to assess the measure of the duty of reasonable care resting on the [defendants]. For the corrosion of the pipe was caused by some chemical agent. Had the lorry, therefore, been carrying chemicals of any kind? Or had it operated under conditions where salt (also a corrosive agent) might come in contact with the pipe? Or had it at some time been adapted for carrying cattle and done so? If any of these things were the case then clearly visual inspection of the pipe *in situ* would not have been enough. It should have been removed at intervals so that the whole of it, and not merely part of it, could be examined ...

It was, therefore, incumbent on the [defendants], if they were to sustain their plea of latent defect undiscoverable by the exercise of ordinary care, to prove where the vehicle had been and what it had been carrying whilst in their service and in what conditions it had operated. Only then could the standard of reasonable care be ascertained, and their conduct measured against it ...

Questions

1. Did the plaintiff succeed because the defendants were unable to prove that they were not negligent?
2. Is this case like a public nuisance case?
3. Is the approach taken by the House of Lords similar to that taken by the Court of Appeal in *Ward v Tesco* (p 82)?
4. What if the defendant had been a public body rather than a commercial company?
5. Is *Henderson v Jenkins* a case of principle or indeed a principal case?
6. D suffers a heart attack while driving and runs over P, a cyclist. Can P sue D for damages?[24]

Morgans v Launchbury [1973] AC 127 House of Lords

This was an action for damages by passengers injured in a car accident against the owner of the car they were using for their pub-crawl. The owner had lent the car to her husband on condition that he get a friend to drive if he got too drunk. The husband did get too drunk, but the friend he got to drive drove carelessly causing a collision. If the friend was acting as an 'agent' of the owner when the collision occurred the owner's insurance would be liable to the injured passengers for the careless driving. However, the House of Lords, reversing a majority decision of the Court of Appeal, held the owner not liable.

---

24   Cf *Roberts v Ramsbottom* [1980] 1 WLR 823.

Lord Pearson: My Lords, in my opinion, the principle by virtue of which the owner of a car may be held vicariously liable for the negligent driving of the car by another person is the principle *qui facit per alium, facit per se*. If the car is being driven by a servant of the owner in the course of the employment or by an agent of the owner in the course of the agency, the owner is responsible for negligence in the driving. The making of the journey is a delegated duty or task undertaken by the servant or agent in pursuance of an order or instruction or request from the owner and for the purposes of the owner. For the creation of the agency relationship it is not necessary that there should be a legally binding contract of agency, but it is necessary that there should be an instruction or request from the owner and an undertaking of the duty or task by the agent. Also the fact that the journey is undertaken partly for purposes of the agent as well as for the purposes of the owner does not negative the creation of the agency relationship: ... I think there has to be an acceptance by the agent of a mandate from the principal, though neither the acceptance nor the mandate has to be formally expressed or legally binding ...

Lord Denning MR, with the object of ensuring that compensation will be available for injured persons, has sought to extend the liability of a car owner for negligent driving of his car by other persons, because the car owner is the person who has or ought to have a motor insurance policy. Lord Denning MR has done this in ways which, I think, really amount to a departure from the agency principle (*qui facit per alium facit per se*) and the introduction of new bases of a car owner's liability.

First, he says [1971] 2 QB 245, 255:

> "If it is being used wholly or partly on the owner's business or in the owner's interest, the owner is liable for any negligence on the part of the driver."

This would include a case in which some eager or officious person drove the car on the owner's business or in the owner's interest but without any prior authority or subsequent ratification from the owner. There would be no agency in the normal sense of the word, and the owner would not have caused or even permitted the driving of the car by that person. It would be a novelty in the law if the owner were held liable in such a case and some new principle would have to be invented.

Secondly, Lord Denning MR treats permission by the owner for a person to drive his car as being in most cases sufficient to impose upon the owner liability for that person's negligent driving of the car. That is the rule proposed for "most cases" and an exception is stated, at p 255:

> "The owner only escapes liability when he lends it out or hires it out to a third person to be used for purposes in which the owner has no interest or concern."

Apart from that exception the proposed rule is stated broadly. Lord Denning MR says, at p 255:

> "The reason behind this principle is at bottom the principle which lies behind all vicarious liability. It is to put the responsibility on to the person who ought in justice to bear it. Now the owner or hirer of the

vehicle is in most cases the person who ought to bear the responsibility. He is the one who puts it on the road where it is capable of doing damage. He is the one who causes or permits it to be used. He is the one who is, or ought to be, insured in respect of it ... Suffice it that, by himself or by proxy, he allowed the driver to drive it on the fatal occasion. He ought, therefore, at common law to shoulder the responsibility: ... The owner or hirer is at common law responsible for all injury or damage done by his permitted driver in the negligent driving of the car ... But the owner or hirer can, of course, at common law excuse himself from responsibility if it was being used without his permission on an occasion in which he had no interest or concern."

The exact scope of the proposed new principle of owner's liability is not fully explored in this passage, but it seems clear that a new principle is being proposed, whereby permission rather than agency would be the basis of liability.

It seems to me that these innovations, whether or not they may be desirable, are not suitable to be introduced by judicial decision. They raise difficult questions of policy, as well as involving the introduction of new legal principles rather than extension of some principle already recognised and operating. The questions of policy need consideration by the government and Parliament, using the resources at their command for making wide inquiries and gathering evidence and opinions as to the practical effects of the proposed innovations. Apart from the transitional difficulty of current policies of insurance being rendered insufficient by judicial changes in the law, there is the danger of injustice to owners who for one reason or another are not adequately covered by insurance or perhaps not effectively insured at all (for example, if they have forgotten to renew their policies or have taken out policies which are believed by them to be valid but are in fact invalid, or have taken their policies from an insolvent insurance company). Moreover, lack of insurance cover would in some cases defeat the object of the proposed innovation, because uninsured or insufficiently insured owners would often be unable to pay damages awarded against them in favour of injured plaintiffs. Any extension of car owners' liability ought to be accompanied by an extension of effective insurance cover. How would that be brought about? And how would it be paid for? Would the owner of the car be required to take out a policy for the benefit of any person who may drive the car? Would there be an exception for some kinds of unlawful driving? A substantial increase in premiums for motor insurance would be likely to result and to have an inflationary effect on costs and prices. It seems to me that, if the proposed innovations are desirable, they should be introduced not by judicial decision but by legislation after suitable investigation and full consideration of the questions of policy involved.

I would allow the appeal.

Questions

1. Is fear of inflation a good legal reason for not developing new principles of liability? Is it an economically sound reason? Will not such reasoning always act as a bar to judicial innovation?

2. Does the present system of fault liability in traffic accidents encourage litigation?

3. Did the wife (owner) have any interest in the journey? Does a person not have an interest in the well-being of his or her spouse? What if she had asked one of the group to bring her back a bottle of beer?

4. If one is strictly liable for keeping a dangerous animal or an animal with dangerous characteristics,[25] why is one not also liable for keeping a thing which is capable of just as much, if not more, harm? Where is the logic of having an Animals Act but not a Motor Vehicles (Compensation of Injuries) Act?

5. A pub landlord, having served many whiskies to a customer he knew was going to drive home, made no effort at closing time to stop the customer from driving his car out of the pub carpark and home. If the customer killed a cyclist as a result of his drunk condition, can the customer's insurance company, which has paid compensation to the wife of the cyclist, sue the landlord for contribution or an indemnity?

4 QUASI-CONTRACTS

(a) Introduction

United Australia Ltd v Barclays Bank Ltd [1941] AC 1 House of Lords

(See p 130)

Fibrosa Spolka Akcyjna v Fairbairn Lawson Combe Barbour Ltd [1943] AC 32 House of Lords

(See p 130)

Notes and questions

1. The law of quasi-contract deals quite simply with debt claims that fall outside of contract. With regard to debt's now deceased sister,[26] the old action of detinue, this claim finally found itself accommodated within the law of tort on the basis that it was a claim based upon a wrong and seemed to be an action for damages (see *Bryant v Herbert* above p 63); debt, however, could not be so

---

25 Animals Act 1971 s 2.
26 Torts (Interference with Goods) Act 1977 s 2(1).

accommodated since it was an action that by definition was not a claim for damages. The problem with debt, from a classification point of view, was that it was both a remedy in the full sense of the term (like damages) and a form of action (unlike damages). The post-1875 jurists thus placed debt within contract because contract was concerned with rights as well as wrongs. In order to succeed in a non-contractual debt claim one had to establish an implied contract. Was this approach as bad as the doctrine, since 1966, has claimed?

2. One advantage of contrasting debt with damages is that the former can be used to deal with benefit, leaving the latter to compensate for loss. In principle then, the most suitable remedy for depriving someone of a profit wrongfully gained is one of the species of debt (eg, an action for money had and received) or its equitable equivalent, an action in account. This is not to say that damages cannot also be used to deal with wrongful benefits, but, as *Surrey CC v Bredero Homes* (above p 178) shows, it is not always the most subtle of remedies.

Lipkin Gorman v Karpnale Ltd [1991] 2 AC 548 House of Lords

(See p 145)

Notes and questions

1. Can one own debts?
2. Are all debts, to a greater or lesser extent, based upon an undertaking to repay? If so, what is the basis of this undertaking?
3. Is the difference between tort and quasi-contract to be found in the historical difference between trespass and debt?
4. If the formal distinction between common law and equity were to be abolished, would an action in account become a quasi-contractual claim? (Cf *English v Dedham Vale Properties*, p 41.)
5. *Lipkin Gorman* and the *Woolwich* case (see p 54) are of interest from a legal system point of view in that they are cases that are openly influenced by academic writing (doctrine). Admittedly Lord Goff himself is part of this doctrine, but the acceptance of an independent law of restitution appears to be taking English law beyond the position as seen by Lord Diplock in *Orakpo v Manson Investments* (see p 168). In some ways this independence is a good thing, as indeed the Roman lawyers discovered; an independent law of restitution not only allows for an orderly distinction between contractual and non-contractual debt cases but provides a category in which one can class a whole range of common law and equitable remedy cases devoted to the prevention of unjust enrichment. There are, however,

problems. The first is that an English law of restitution can never fully integrate itself into an English law of obligations since it uses the law of property as one of its tools; such an intermixing of property and obligation notions is particularly evident in *Lipkin Gorman* (and see also *Agip (Africa)*, above p 140). Secondly the idea that one can build up a logical model of rules founded upon the 'axiom' that no one should be enriched at another's expense is impractical nonsense; certainly one may wish to take an Occam's razor to the old forms of action, but it must be remembered that people who slash about with razors are likely to cut off their own vital parts. The world of English law is not the world of German law and the remedies approach to problem-solving has its own strengths, as indeed Lord Brown-Wilkinson recognised when he was in Chancery (see *Kingdom of Spain v Christie* above, p 112). The chapter on reasoning and method (Chapter 2) ought to show that ideas of axiomatic precision and logical rationality belong to legal history; *scientia iuris* and *ars judicandi* are now two separate processes each with their own epistemological (theory of knowledge) standpoint. One great strength of approaching unjust enrichment through a law of remedies is that a law of actions provides great flexibility when it comes to analysing and categorising the facts; and thus there is nothing wrong with the idea that tracing or rescission in equity should themselves act as focal points for their own particular rules. Of course, there are drawbacks to a form of liability approach as the *Esso* case perhaps illustrates (above p 118). Yet Denning LJ had little difficulty in this case in finding the just decision, indeed he used the old forms of liability to give expression to underlying legal rights (see above p 355). The problem with the case was a House of Lords insensitive to its own role and the role of judges in the face of facts. Is not a law of remedies more sensitive than a law of axiomatic principles to the nuances of benefit in a society dedicated to the pursuit of profit?

6. This is not to say that one abandons a category of restitutionary rights anymore than one abandons the category of tort; they both are useful for contrasting non-contractual obligations with contractual. But just as tort (and in truth contract) defies theory because it contains a range of cases which have quite different objectives (for example, the protection of constitutional rights as well as loss spreading), so restitution will always be a category with little theoretical cohesion. Indeed one need only look at the case of *Dimskal Shipping Co v ITWF*[27] to see what damage restitution lawyers have done with their ill-thought out theories of economic duress in a

---

27 [1992] 2 AC 152.

capitalist society. An equity lawyer with a sensitive feel to the problems of industrial relations would never have allowed the remedy of rescission to be used in such facts. The law of obligations is about solving problems, admittedly with an eye to the future, and thus the emphasis needs to be on a legal reasoning which can handle social, political and economic complexity within its own model of concepts and relations. The problem with many restitution writers is that they think that their duty is to overcome complexity. Happily, practising common lawyers seem, on the whole, to have known better. Do we need a law of restitution based on rather meaningless abstract propositions? Are different species of debt claims which make various factual distinctions such a bad thing?

(b) The action for money had and received

Rowland v Divall [1923] 2 KB 500 Court of Appeal

(See p 137)

Lipkin Gorman v Karpnale Ltd [1991] 2 AC 548 House of Lords

(See p 145)

Notes and questions

1. One or two judges in the 19th century have observed that the debt action for money had and received is a common law version of the equitable remedy of account (see p 167). Certainly it is a useful claim for depriving those who have benefited through wrongs from retaining their profits, although its scope is wider than this. The action is useful, as *Lipkin Gorman* shows, as a kind of revindication claim for money paid to another by mistake, through duress or as a result of an ineffective or defective transaction. In the last situation the plaintiff must show that the contract is ineffective and thus the requirement of a total failure of consideration.[28] However, has the action suffered through its identification with the notion of tracing? Or has it now become a genuine restitutionary debt claim with its ability to trace an *in rem* relationship with the debt itself?

2. Both *Rowland v Divall* and *Lipkin Gorman* are not without their difficulties. In both cases it could be argued that the plaintiff benefited from the success of each debt claim. One plaintiff got six

---

28 *Rover International Ltd v Canon Films Ltd* [1989] 1 WLR 912.

months free use of a car while the other got most its their money back without too many questions being asked about its own responsibility in the whole sad affair. One may dream of hard and fast principles to govern these kind of cases, but the truth is that they are complex facts where the line between just and unjust benefits is almost impossible to draw. A similar difficulty is to be observed with the claim in *Surrey CC v Bredero Homes* (above p 178), not admittedly a debt claim but a damages action raising similar problems. Could it really have been right to allow a local authority to grab money in respect of a loss they did not suffer simply on the basis that the defendants had committed a wrong? Admittedly a local authority could be said to represent the interests of the local inhabitants of its area[29] and thus it might be the only institution capable of extracting an unjust profit. Yet the law of tort does not allow a damages claim simply on the basis that a defendant has behaved unlawfully, nor perhaps should the law of restitution. Restitution lawyers might think differently of course, but then restitution lawyers thought that the decision in *Bolton v Mahadeva* gave rise to unjustified enrichment.[30] It took a practicing lawyer to point out the nonsense they were talking. Is, then, English law so irrational? Do equitable remedies need to be harmonised with common law debt and damages claims?[31]

(c) The action for money paid

Brook's Wharf & Bull Wharf Ltd v Goodman Brothers [1937] 1 KB 534 Court of Appeal

This was an action in debt by bailees (a firm of bonded warehousemen) against the bailors of a consignment of firs in respect of customs duty that the bailees were compelled by statute to pay when the firs were stolen from their warehouse. The Court of Appeal, rejecting the bailors' counterclaim for the value of the firs, held that the bailees were entitled to recover the money as a debt.

Lord Wright: ... [T]he plaintiffs claim that they are entitled to recover from the defendants the amount which they have paid to the customs in respect of duties due on the defendants' goods. They make their claim as money paid to the defendants' use on the principle stated in Leake on *Contracts*. The passage in question is quoted in the Exchequer Chamber by Cockburn CJ in *Moule v Garrett* (LR 7 Ex 101, 104), and is in these terms: "Where the plaintiff has been compelled

---

29 Local Government Act 1972 s 222.

30 Law Commission, Pecuniary Restitution for Breach of Contract (Report No 121, 1983).

31 For a comparative reflection see W J Swadling, 'Restitution and Unjust Enrichment', in A S Hartkamp *et al* (eds), *Towards a European Civil Code* (Ars Aequi Libri, 1994), pp 267-283.

by law to pay, or, being compellable by law, has paid money which the defendant was ultimately liable to pay, so that the latter obtains the benefit of the payment by the discharge of his liability; under such circumstances the defendant is held indebted to the plaintiff in the amount" ...

The principle has been applied in a great variety of circumstances. Its application does not depend on privity of contract ...

These statements of the principle do not put the obligation on any ground of implied contract or of constructive or notional contract. The obligation is imposed by the Court simply under the circumstances of the case and on what the Court decides is just and reasonable, having regard to the relationship of the parties. It is a debt or obligation constituted by the act of the law, apart from any consent or intention of the parties or any privity of contract.

It is true that in the present case there was a contract of bailment between the plaintiffs and the defendants, but there is no suggestion that the obligation in question had ever been contemplated as between them or that they had ever thought about it. The Court cannot say what they would have agreed if they had considered the matter when the goods were warehoused. All the Court can say is what they ought as just and reasonable men to have decided as between themselves. The defendants would be unjustly benefited at the cost of the plaintiffs if the latter, who had received no extra consideration and had made no express bargain, should be left out of pocket by having to discharge what was the defendants' debt ...

The plaintiffs were no doubt liable to pay the Customs, but, as between themselves and the defendants, the primary liability rested on the defendants. The liability of the plaintiffs as warehousemen was analogous to that of surety. It was imposed in order to facilitate the collection of duties in a case like the present, where there might always be a question as to who stood in the position of importer. The defendants as actual importers have obtained the benefit of the payment made by the plaintiffs and they are thus discharged from the duties which otherwise would have been payable by them. It may also be noted that the goods which were stolen were the defendants' goods and the property remained in them after the theft. If the goods had been recovered, the defendants could have claimed them as their own and would have been free to apply them for home use without further payment of duty.

I think there is every reason in this case for applying the general principle which I have stated. In commercial dealings of this character it is difficult not to think of the case from the point of view of insurance ... I do not, however, lay emphasis on that aspect of the case ...

Notes and questions

1. "If without an antecedent request a person assumes an obligation or makes a payment for the benefit of another, the law will, as a general rule, refuse him a right of indemnity. But if he can show that in the particular circumstances of the case there was some necessity for the obligation to be assumed, then the law will grant him a right of reimbursement if in all the circumstances it is just and reasonable to

do so" (Scarman LJ in *Owen v Tate* [1975] 2 All ER 129). Is an emergency enough to generate the required 'necessity'?

2. If bailees have to expend money to protect, or upkeep, the bailor's goods can this expenditure be recovered by the bailees as a debt from the bailors?[32]

3. P, at considerable expense, patches up the roof of D's house after it has been badly damaged in a gale. Assuming that D has gone away without leaving an address or telephone number with P, his neighbour, and assuming also that, if P had not acted, D's house and contents would have been badly damaged by rain, can P recover his expense from D?

4. Was Lord Wright ahead of his time?

(d) *Quantum meruit*

British Steel Corporation v Cleveland Bridge & Engineering Co Ltd [1984] 1 All ER 504 Queen's Bench Division

(See p 250)

Davis Contractors Ltd v Fareham Urban District Council [1956] AC 696 House of Lords

(See p 342)

Notes and questions

1. The action for money had and received is a remedy which attaches itself so to speak to a specific amount of money in the defendant's patrimony representing the unjust profit. The action for a *quantum meruit* looks to the more intangible benefit arising out of situations where one person confers upon another a service. Clearly, if I cut my neighbour's grass while he is away I have, in principle, conferred upon him a benefit. Should he have to pay for this benefit however? English law takes the view that the mere conferring of a benefit upon another does not of itself give rise to a right to restitution;[33] in order to trigger liability there must have been either a request for the service or some kind of acceptance indicating a willingness to pay for what has been received. Such requests or acceptances can, of course, be implied and this allows the court a degree of latitude when it

---

32 Cf *The Winson* [1982] AC 939.
33 *Falcke v Scottish Imperial Insurance Co* (1886) 34 Ch D 234, 248-249.

comes to interpreting the facts. All the same it is unlikely that the plaintiff in *Bolton v Mahadeva* (above p 126) could have succeeded in a *quantum meruit* debt claim in respect of the benefit (ie, work done) conferred upon the defendant.[34] But what if the contract had been frustrated? Or what if it had turned out to be void or illegal?

2. Quasi-contract is most useful in situations of pre-contractual work undertaken with a view to a formal contract being concluded. However, once such a contract has been concluded it will, in principle, govern the rights and duties; if one of the parties wishes to sue on a *quantum meruit* the contract must be got rid of so to speak either by recourse to frustration or by the court declaring that it is void. Should rescission for breach of contract allow *quantum meruit* to come into play?

3. D hires P to repair his chimney after P had given him an estimate of £400. While P was repairing the chimney he noticed that another one was in equally bad repair and he spends an extra day repairing the second chimney. P did not seek D's permission because D is difficult to contact and, in addition, P assumed that D would want the work done because two thirds of the £400 estimate is taken up with the cost of erecting scaffolding. P sends D a bill for £500. Must D pay this bill or can he insist on paying only £400?

5 UNJUST ENRICHMENT

Orakpo v Manson Investments Ltd [1978] AC 95 House of Lords

(See p 168)

Notes and questions

1. The principle of unjust enrichment comes from Roman law and the *Ius Commune*: 'by natural law it is equitable that no one should be enriched by the loss or injury of another'.[35] It became, during the second life of Roman law, the basis of a category of obligation rights separate from contract and delict (tort). However, even in the civil law the tendency was not to establish a general enrichment action but to give expression to the principle, as in Roman law itself, via a number of specific remedies such as the *condictio* (debt) and

---

34 *Sumpter v Hedges* [1898] 1 QB 673.

35 D.12.6.14; D.50.17.206. See generally D H van Zyl, 'The General Enrichment Action is Alive and Well', in J Lotz & D Visser (eds), *Unjustified Enrichment* (Juta, 1992), pp 115-130.

negotorium gestio (necessitious intervention claim). Nowadays the general enrichment action has become prevalent; indeed the French *Cour de cassation* has outflanked the specific instance approach of the *Code civil* by establishing unjust enrichment as a general principle of law existing independently of *la loi*. Does such a general action really help lawyers solve unjust enrichment problems?

2. When it comes to English law, the traditional position is very clearly stated by Lord Diplock. Nevertheless, once one views the law from the position of the law of actions, including, of course, equitable remedies, the role of the principle of unjust enrichment becomes much more evident. It is the mirror image of the principle of wrongfully causing loss and it invites the court to look, not so much at the plaintiff's loss, but the benefit obtained without just cause. Indeed one French professor once suggested the following principle to act as the mirror image of liability for damage in Article 1382: 'Any human act whatsoever which causes an enrichment to another gives rise to a right on behalf of the person by whose act the enrichment has been procured to recover it'. What problems does such a principle present when analysing factual situations?

3. Ought the court to look at the physical benefit itself (money in a defendant's bank account or property bought with the enrichment money) or should they take an abstract view of benefit (eg, seeing it it terms of value)?[36]

Lipkin Gorman v Karpnale Ltd [1991] 2 AC 548 House of Lords

(See p 145)

Woolwich Equitable Building Society v Inland Revenue Commissioners [1993] AC 70 House of Lords]

(See p 54)

Notes and questions

1. What is the effect of these cases on the status and role of the principle of unjust enrichment? Does English law now recognise the principle of unjust enrichment as a cause of action in itself?

2. Change of position is now recognised as a defence in itself to a claim based on the principle of unjust enrichment. Did not the casino in *Lipkin* change its position when it gave the solicitor who had

---

36 Cf P Birks, 'The Condition of the English Law of Unjust Enrichment', in Lotz & Visser, *op cit* pp 1-22.

embezzled the cash the chance of winning a lot of money off the casino?

3. What does change of position do that the equitable defence of estoppel could not do?

4. Will change of position ever be available as a defence to an action for damages?

5. Is tracing an unjust enrichment claim or a claim belonging to the law of property? If a plaintiff can succeed in a tracing claim on the basis of title (ownership) what is the relevance of unjust enrichment?

6. What, if any, is the role of fault in unjust enrichment?

7. D, a manufacturer of ginger beer, deliberately puts only 98 centilitres of beer in bottles sold as litre bottles. Over several years D makes a profit of £250,000 from this behaviour. Is D entitled to keep this profit? If not, who should have it?

8. D, an employer, deliberately fails to make his workplace safe for his employees. As a result of this behaviour D makes a saving over the years of £1,000,000. No employee is actually injured, but they have all been exposed to much higher risks of injury than employees working in similar, but safer, workplaces elsewhere. Is D entitled to keep the £1,000,000? If not, who should have it? If the employees had threatened to go on strike and the court had given the employer an interlocutory injunction on the basis of threatened breaches of contract, would the employer be able to set off against tax the costs of the injunction against his £1,000,000 profit?

CTN Cash and Carry Ltd v Gallaher Ltd [1994] 4 All ER 714 Court of Appeal

(See also p 290)

Sir Donald Nicholls V-C: ... I confess to being a little troubled at the overall outcome. At a late stage of the trial the defendant's counsel accepted that the risk in the goods had not in law passed to the plaintiff. Hence, and this must follow, the defendant company was not, and never had been, entitled to be paid for the goods. The risk remained throughout on the defendant. What also follows is that the basis on which the defendant had sought and insisted on payment was then shown to be false.

In those circumstances I confess to being a little surprised that a highly reputable tobacco manufacturer has, so far, not reconsidered the position. A claim for restitution based on wrongful retention of the money, once the risk point had been established, was not pursued before us, no doubt for good reasons. But on the sketchy facts before us, and I emphasise that we have heard argument only from the plaintiff, it does seem to me that *prima facie* it would be unconscionable for the defendant company to insist on retaining the money now. It demanded the money when under a mistaken belief as to its legal entitlement to be paid. It only made the demand because of its belief that it was entitled to be paid. The money was then paid to it by a plaintiff which, in practical terms, had no other

412

option. In broad terms, in the end result the defendant may be said to have been unjustly enriched. Whether a new claim for restitution now, on the facts as they have since emerged, would succeed is not a matter I need pursue. I observe, as to that, only that the categories of unjust enrichment are not closed ...

Questions

1. Would an action for money had and received have succeeded?
2. Did the defendants enrich themselves at the plaintiffs' expense? Did they unjustly enrich themselves? Did they abuse their monopoly position?
3. Would an action in account have succeeded?

6 ABUSE OF RIGHTS

Bradford Corporation v Pickles [1895] AC 587 House of Lords

(See p 124)

Notes and questions

1. Alongside the principle of unjust enrichment, the French courts have recognised another general principle outside of the *Code civil*, that of abuse of a right. Those who deliberately use their rights in such a way as intentionally to cause damage to another will be liable in damages under the general fault principle (Article 1382 CC). The key focal points of liability are malice, bad faith or gross error amounting virtually to fraud and, often, an absence of legitimate interest in the exercise of the right. The principle originated in the area of what a common lawyer would call nuisance (*troubles du voisinage*), but now extends into the law of contract and is thus a useful weapon against abusive exclusion clauses. Is *Interfoto v Stiletto* (above) capable of being interpreted as an abuse of rights case?
2. D deliberately practices his trombone playing in order to annoy P, his neighbour. Is P entitled to an injunction and (or) damages?[37]
3. Are the following cases capable of being analysed as abuse of rights cases: (i) *Khorasandijian v Bush* (p 74); (ii) *English v Dedham Vale Properties* (p 41) (iii) *Blackpool & Fylde Aero Club v Blackpool BC* (p 243) (iv) *Beswick v Beswick* (p 154) (v) *High Trees* (p 257).

---

37 Cf *Hollywood Silver Fox Farm v Emmett* [1936] 2 KB 468.

4. Does *Bradford v Pickles* act as a barrier to the recognition of a principle of an abuse of a right in English law?

5. Does English law think in terms of rights? Does it think in terms of abuses?

White & Carter (Councils) Ltd v McGregor [1962] AC 413 House of Lords (Scotland)

(See p 133)

Questions

1. Does equity recognise a principle of abuse of rights?

2. When will a contractor have no legitimate interest in suing in debt?

3. When does an interest become illegitimate?

4. Has English law now reached the position where a principle of abuse of rights could be induced out of a range of contract, tort and remedy cases?

5. Is a contractor entitled to exercise his rights under a contract for good reason, bad reason or no reason at all?[38]

7 FINAL OBSERVATIONS

This collection of materials will not have provided anything more than an introduction to the law of obligations and the law of remedies. Hopefully, however, it will have provided a more thorough grounding in legal method and legal reasoning, at least in respect of problem-solving in the law of obligations. Cases have been selected with this purpose in mind and all of them are worth re-reading many times. For example, the factual problem in a modest decision like that of *Poole v Smith's Car Sales* (above p 306) or *Reed v Dean* (above p 303) can prove richer than the facts of some of the major cases. Equally, some of the overturned Court of Appeal judgments can sometimes prove richer than the speeches in the House of Lords (see eg, Lord Denning's judgment in *Beswick*, above, p 37). These cases and judgments are worth returning to from time to time and the facts of all cases in this collection should be reflected upon, changed a little and mixed with facts from other cases (how else are exam questions compiled?). No judgment is ever valueless from a legal method and legal reasoning point of view (see eg, *Thomas v Countryside Council for Wales*, p 200) and the student who spends time

---

38   Cf *Chapman v Honig* [1963] 2 QB 502.

reading, if only very quickly, all the reported cases in every weekly part of the All England or Weekly law reports will soon have a rich knowledge of the *ars judicandi*, if not of the *scientia iuris*.

This collection of materials has also been compiled with Europe in mind. It must never be forgotten that many of the great judges of the second half of the 19th century – the judges who laid the main foundations for the modern law of contract and tort – had an excellent knowledge of Roman law and the *Code civil* (see eg, *Taylor v Caldwell*, p 338). They may not have been faced with demands for harmonisation,[39] but many of them recognised that legal knowledge was not strictly a common law phenomenom. What comparative law can bring to problem-solving is the application of alternative models of analysis which in turn can stimulate alternative approaches to problems within the common law itself.[40] In addition there is of course the question of harmonisation: is English law capable of developing a law of obligations that can be harmonised with the structured systems of the codes? This present work is deliberately ambiguous, for it is the student who must investigate the *mentalité* of the common lawyer so as to place it in the context of European law. Nevertheless, the collection ought to be used alongside copies of one or more of the great civil codes: legal knowledge is not equivalent to knowledge of a legal system.

The whole question of legal knowledge is another theme that is underlying this collection of materials. Is knowledge of law knowledge of rules and principles? Or is it something more? This collection has been designed to suggest that something more is required: law may express itself primarily, and not surprisingly, through the written proposition but, as the Romans recognised, the law is not to be found in the rules.[41] *Ex facto ius oritur* (law arises out of facts), as a famous medieval commentator on Roman law put it. Is such a maxim not the guiding principle of this collection? Certainly, when it comes to analysing factual situations the syllogism is not enough, as this collection has hopefully indicated; an ability to understand the relationship between institutional focal points (persons, things and actions), legal relations (contract, duty of care, possession and ownership), quasi-normative notions (damage, statements, fault, interest and expectations) and legal concepts (rights

---

39 On which see A S Hartkamp *et al* (eds), *Towards a European Civil Code* (Ars Aequi/Nijhoff, 1994).

40 With great respect to Professor Jolowicz one might ask whether he took a rather narrow view of the importance of comparative law to the legal profession: J A Jolowicz, Les professions juridiques et le droit comparé: Angleterre [1994] *Revue Internationale de Droit Comparé* 747. Are there not a whole range of indirect influences? Do not practitioners, if only unconsciously, use arguments rooted in comparative law? Is not unjust enrichment an example?

41 D.50.17.1.

and duties) is the key to analysing factual problems. An exam question in the University of Cambridge's Contract & Tort Paper II once invited candidates to discuss, in relation to an action for damages, the following statement: 'Before the law can be applied to the facts the facts must be categorised, but before the facts can be categorised the law must be applied.' Modern developments in epistemology (theory of scientific knowledge)[42] and cognitive science[43] have given us a major insight into answering this question: science constructs its own models which act as both the science and the object of science and thus when it comes to law and legal science what is required is the building of a model within the facts which will act at one and the same time as the means of understanding both the facts and the law (cf Diplock LJ in *Letang v Cooper*, p 65). In saying that all law is about persons, things and actions the Romans, perhaps unconsciously, recognised this (see above pp 13-27). At any rate they certainly provided the tools and the insights for categorising the facts and applying the law.

---

42 R Blanché, *L'épistémologie* (Presses Universitaires de France, 3rd ed, 1983); G-G Granger, *La science et les sciences* (Presses Universitaires de France, 1993); C Atias, *Épistémologie du droit* (Presses Universitaires de France, 1994). And see generally G Samuel, *The Foundations of Legal Reasoning* (Maklu/Blackstone, 1994).

43 J-P Dupuy, *Aux origines des sciences cognitives* (Éditions La Découverte, 1994).

APPENDIX

The cases extracted in this section were reported too late to be incorporated into the main part of the book. The headings, notes and questions will attempt, however, to relate them to the relevant parts of the book.

1 THE STRUCTURE OF THE COMMON LAW

White v Jones [1995] 1 All ER 691 House of Lords

Lord Mustill (dissenting): ... My Lords, I have two final observations. The first concerns the marked contrast between the scores of authorities cited in argument, and the very few reported cases which I have called up. This may seem discouraging to those who with great skill and labour have gathered together and analysed all this diverse material. Such a feeling would be understandable but mistaken. The extensive citation has been indispensable as a means of placing before your Lordships the interplay of ideas so copiously developed by jurists here and abroad. The whole of the landscape has been exposed. Yet when it comes to reaching a decision and explaining the grounds for it there is a possibility of surfeit. The construction of an intelligible mosaic becomes impossible if there are too many pieces. Many of them will not fit. A full account of all the previous decisions would be endless and useless. Ultimately it is the broad shape of the principles which matters, and to obscure them in a fog of citation would not in my opinion advance the development of the law of negligence, so important to everyday life.

Secondly, the judgment of Steyn LJ remarked on the sparseness of reference to academic writings in the argument before the Court of Appeal. No such complaint could be made of the proceedings in this House. There can be few branches of contemporary law on which the commentators have had so much to say. Citation has been copious, and of great value. If I refer to none of the writings it is only because, as with the reported cases, the volume is too large to permit accurate and economical exposition; and the selection of some in preference to others would be invidious. It is the practice in official law reports to record not only the cases referred to in the judgments, but also those brought forward in argument. This is an invaluable feature for those who follow behind. A similar record of the doctrinal materials brought forth in argument would, I believe, greatly help to place in perspective the views which your Lordships have expressed ...

Lord Goff: ... Strongly though I support the study of comparative law, I hesitate to embark in an opinion such as this upon a comparison, however brief, with a civil law system; because experience has taught me how very difficult, and indeed potentially misleading, such an exercise can be. Exceptionally however, in the present case, thanks to material published in our language by distinguished comparatists, German as well as English, we have direct access to publications which should sufficiently dispel our ignorance of German law and so by comparison illuminate our understanding of our own ...

Questions

1. Is the precedent system breaking down?

2. Is the role of the House of Lords now to develop broad principles rather than merely to decide particular cases between particular litigants? (Cf above pp 5-9.)

3. Is academic doctrine now a formal source of law? (Cf above pp 56-57.)

4. Is civil law becoming a formal source of law? Should UK law schools now be teaching the law of obligations in a comparative context? Are judges like Lord Goff, and indeed Lord Mustill, expecting academic lawyers to provide them with something more than just an analysis of the English caselaw?

5. Is there too much law?

2 LEGAL METHOD AND THE COMMON LAW

White v Jones [1995] 1 All ER 691 House of Lords

(For facts see further extracts below p 424)

Lord Brown-Wilkinson: ... In my view, although the present case is not directly covered by the decided cases, it is legitimate to extend the law to the limited extent proposed using the incremental approach by way of analogy advocated in *Carparo Industries plc v Dickman* [1990] 2 AC 605 ...

... In my judgment, this is a case where such development should take place since there is a close analogy with existing categories of special relationship giving rise to a duty of care to prevent economic loss ...

Lord Mustill (dissenting): ... A broad new type of claim may properly be met by a broad new type of rationalisation, as happened in *Hedley Byrne*; but rationalisation there must be, and it does not conduce to the orderly development of the law, or to the certainty which practical convenience demands, if duties are simply conjured up as a matter of positive law, to answer the apparent justice of an individual case. Be that as it may, the present case does not as it seems to me concern a unique and limited situation, where a remedy might be granted on an *ad hoc* basis without causing serious harm to the general structure of the law; for I cannot see anything sufficiently special about the calling of a solicitor to distinguish him from others in a much broader category. If the claim in the present case is sound, for any reasons other than those given by my noble and learned friends, it must be sound in every instance of the general situation which I have already identified, namely: where A promises B for reward to perform a service for B, in circumstances where it is foreseeable that performance of the service with care will cause C to receive a benefit, and that failure to perform it may cause C not to receive that benefit. To hold that a duty exists, even *prima facie*, in such a situation would be to go far beyond anything so far contemplated by the law of negligence ...

Questions

1. In *Donoghue v Stevenson* (above p 33) the House of Lords held that a manufacturer owes a duty of care to his consumers. Is it really 'to go far beyond anything so far contemplated by the law of negligence' to say that a provider of services (a solicitor) owes a duty of care to his consumers? There is, of course, an important difference: what is it?

2. Ought not a family solicitor to owe a duty of care to the family that has employed him?

3. Why must it 'be sound in every instance of the general situation'?

4. Is Lord Brown-Wilkinson thinking in terms of images rather than rules? (Cf Chapter 2.)

3 REMEDIES

Jaggard v Sawyer [1995] 2 All ER 189 Court of Appeal

Sir Thomas Bingham MR: On 26 January 1993 Judge Jack QC ([1993] 1 EGLR 197), sitting in the Weymouth County Court, refused the plaintiff, Mrs Jaggard, injunctions to restrain continuing acts of trespass and breaches of covenant and awarded damages in lieu. The plaintiff says the judge should have granted injunctions. This appeal requires the court to consider the principles on which judges should act when deciding whether to grant injunctions or to award damages in lieu ...

The law

In considering the legal issues in this case, I should acknowledge at the outset my debt to an illuminating article by Professor Jolowicz 'Damages in Equity – A Study of Lord Cairns' Act' [1975] CLJ 224.

Historically, the remedy given by courts of common law was damages. These afforded retrospective compensation for past wrongs. If the wrongs were repeated or continued, a fresh action was needed. Courts of equity, in contrast, were able to give prospective relief by way of injunction or specific performance. A mandatory injunction would require the defendant to observe a legal obligation or undo the effects of a past breach of legal obligation. A negative injunction would restrain a defendant from committing breaches of legal obligation in future. But these courts could not award damages. This anomaly was mitigated by the Common Law Procedure Act 1854, which gave courts of common law a limited power to grant equitable relief as well as damages. It was further mitigated by the Chancery Amendment Act 1858 (Lord Cairns' Act), which gave the Court of Chancery the power to award damages.

Section 2 of Lord Cairns' Act provided:

'In all cases in which the Court of Chancery has jurisdiction to entertain an application for an injunction against a breach of any covenant, contract, or agreement, or against the commission or continuance of any wrongful act, or for the specific performance of any covenant, contract, or agreement, it shall be lawful for the same Court, if it shall think fit, to award damages to the party injured, either in addition to or in substitution for such injunction or specific performance; and such damages may be assessed in such manner as the Court shall direct.'

This enabled the Chancery Court on appropriate facts to award damages for unlawful conduct in the past as well as an injunction to restrain unlawful conduct in the future. It also enabled the Chancery Court to award damages instead of granting an injunction to restrain unlawful conduct in the future. Such damages can only have been intended to compensate the plaintiff for future unlawful conduct, the commission of which, in the absence of any injunction, the court must have contemplated as likely to occur. Despite the repeal of Lord Cairns' Act, it has never been doubted that the jurisdiction thereby conferred on the Court of Chancery is exercisable by the High Court and by county courts.

The authorities show that there were, not surprisingly, differing approaches to the exercise of this new jurisdiction. [The Master of the Rolls discussed the authorities] ...

Mention should finally be made of *Surrey CC v Bredero Homes Ltd* [1993] 1 WLR 1361 ...

The court's approach to restitutionary damages in this case has provoked some regretful comment (see Professor Birks 'Profits of Breach of Contract' (1993) 109 LQR 518), and it may be (as suggested at 520) that these judgments will not be the last word on that subject. But the court plainly treated the case as one not falling under the principles derived from Lord Cairns' Act. I cannot, however, accept that Brightman J's assessment of damages in *Wrotham Park* was based on other than compensatory principles. The defendants had committed a breach of covenant, the effects of which continued. The judge was not willing to order the defendants to undo the continuing effects of that breach. He had therefore to assess the damages necessary to compensate the plaintiffs for this continuing invasion of their right. He paid attention to the profits earned by the defendants, as it seems to me, not in order to strip the defendants of their unjust gains, but because of the obvious relationship between the profits earned by the defendants and the sum which the defendants would reasonably have been willing to pay to secure release from the covenant ...

The present case

The judge recognised that a plaintiff who can show that his legal right will be violated by the defendant's conduct is *prima facie* entitled to the grant of an injunction. He accepted that the court will only rarely and reluctantly permit such a violation to occur or continue. But he held that this case fulfilled the four tests laid down by AL Smith LJ in *Shelfer v City of London Electric Lighting Co* [1895] 1 Ch 287 to bring this case within the exception ...

(1) He regarded the injury to the plaintiff's right as small ...

(2) The judge considered the value of the injury to the plaintiff's right as capable of being estimated in money ...

(3) The judge held that the injury to the plaintiff's legal right was one which could be adequately compensated by a small money payment ...

(4) The judge concluded that in all the circumstances it would be oppressive to the defendants to grant the injunction sought ...

It is important to bear in mind that the test is one of oppression, and the court should not slide into application of a general balance of convenience test. But oppression must be judged as at the date the court is asked to grant an injunction, and (as Brightman J recognised in *Wrotham Park*) the court cannot ignore the reality with which it is then confronted ... As s 84 of the Law of Property Act 1925 makes clear, restrictive covenants cannot be regarded as absolute and inviolable for all time. The judge was, in my view, entitled to hold on all the facts before the court at the trial that the grant of an injunction would be oppressive to the defendants, and I share that view ...

Kennedy LJ: I agree

Millett LJ: This appeal raises yet again the questions: what approach should the court adopt when invited to exercise its statutory jurisdiction to award damages instead of granting an injunction to restrain a threatened or continuing trespass or breach of a restrictive covenant? And if the court accedes to the invitation, on what basis should damages be assessed?

Before considering these questions, it is desirable to state some general propositions which are established by the authorities and which are, or at least ought to be, uncontroversial.

(1) The jurisdiction was originally conferred by s 2 of the Chancery Amendment Act 1858, commonly known as Lord Cairns' Act. It is now to be found in s 50 of the Supreme Court Act 1981. It is a jurisdiction to award damages 'in addition to, or in substitution for, an injunction or specific performance'.

(2) The principal object of Lord Cairns' Act is well known ... It was to enable the Court of Chancery, when declining to grant equitable relief and leaving the plaintiff to his remedy at law, to award the plaintiff damages itself instead of sending him to the common law courts to obtain them. From the very first, however, it was recognised that the Act did more than this. The jurisdiction of the Court of Chancery was wider than that of the common law courts, for it could give relief where there was no cause of action at law ... Damages at common law are recoverable only in respect of causes of action which are complete at the date of the writ; damages for future or repeated wrongs must be made the subject of fresh proceedings. Damages in substitution for an injunction, however, relate to the future, not the past. They inevitably extend beyond the damages to which the plaintiff may be entitled at law ...

(3) The nature of the cause of action is immaterial; it may be in contract or tort.

Lord Cairns' Act referred in terms to 'a breach of any covenant, contract, or agreement, or against the commission or continuance of any wrongful act' ... Equitable relief, whether by way of injunction or damages under Lord Cairns' Act, is available because the common law remedy is inadequate; but the common law remedy of damages in cases of continuing trespass is inadequate not because the damages are likely to be small or nominal but because they cover the past only and not the future.

(4) The power to award damages under Lord Cairns' Act arises whenever the court 'has jurisdiction to entertain an application' for an injunction or specific performance ... When the court comes to consider whether to grant an injunction or award damages instead, of course, it must do so by reference to the circumstances as they exist at the date of the hearing.

(5) The former question is effectively one of jurisdiction. The question is whether, at the date of the writ, the court could have granted an injunction, not whether it would have done ...

(6) It is not necessary for the plaintiff to include a claim for damages in his writ ... By a parity of reasoning it is not in my opinion necessary for a plaintiff to include a claim for an injunction in order to found a claim for damages under the Act. It would be absurd to require him to include a claim for an injunction if he is sufficiently realistic to recognise that in the circumstances he is unlikely to obtain one and intends from the first to ask the court for damages instead. But he ought to make it clear whether he is claiming damages for past injury at common law or under the Act in substitution for an injunction.

(7) ... The court can in my judgment properly award damages 'once and for all' in respect of future wrongs because it awards them in substitution for an injunction and to compensate for those future wrongs which an injunction would have prevented. The doctrine of *res judicata* operates to prevent the plaintiff and his successors in title from bringing proceedings thereafter to recover even nominal damages in respect of further wrongs for which the plaintiff has been fully compensated.

It has always been recognised that the practical consequence of withholding injunctive relief is to authorise the continuance of an unlawful state of affairs ... After the passing of Lord Cairns' Act many of the judges warned that the jurisdiction to award damages instead of an injunction should not be exercised as a matter of course so as to legalise the commission of a tort by any defendant who was willing and able to pay compensation ... What does need to be stressed, however, is that ... Lord Cairns' Act did not worsen the plaintiff's position but improved it. Thenceforth, if injunctive relief was withheld, the plaintiff was not compelled to wait until further wrongs were committed and then bring successive actions for damages; he could be compensated by a once and for all payment to cover future as well as past wrongs ...

Nevertheless, references to the 'expropriation' of the plaintiff's property are somewhat overdone, not because that is not the practical effect of withholding an injunction, but because the grant of an injunction, like all equitable remedies, is discretionary. Many property rights cannot be protected at all by the common law. The owner must submit to unlawful interference with his rights and be content with damages. If he wants to be protected he must seek equitable relief, and he has no absolute right to that. In many cases, it is true, an injunction will be granted almost as of course, but this is not always the case, and it will never be granted if this would cause injustice to the defendant ...

When the plaintiff claims and injunction and the defendant asks the court to award damages instead, the proper approach for the court to adopt cannot be in doubt. Clearly the plaintiff must first establish a case for equitable relief, not only by proving his legal right and an actual or threatened infringement by the defendant, but also by overcoming all equitable defences such as laches, acquiescence or estoppel. If he succeeds in doing this, he is *prima facie* entitled to an injunction. The court may nevertheless in its discretion withhold injunctive relief and award damages instead. How is this discretion to be exercised? [Millett LJ then referred to AL Smith's checklist in the *Shelfer* case] ...

Reported cases are merely illustrations of circumstances in which particular judges have exercised their discretion ... Since they are all cases on the exercise of a discretion, none of them is a binding authority on how the discretion should be exercised ...

In the present case, the defendants acted openly and in good faith and in the not unreasonable belief that they were entitled to ... access to the house that they were building. At the same time, they had been warned by the plaintiff and her solicitors ... that they were not entitled to use it for access ... They went ahead, not with their eyes open, but at their own risk. On the other hand, the plaintiff did not seek interlocutory relief at a time when she would almost certainly have obtained it. She should not be criticised for that, but it follows that she also took a risk, *viz* that by the time her case came for trial the court would be presented with a *fait accompli*. The case was a difficult one, but in an exemplary judgment the judge took into account all the relevant considerations, both those which told in favour of granting an injunction and those which told against, and in the exercise of his discretion he decided to refuse it. In my judgment his conclusion cannot be faulted ...

Questions

1. Must a plaintiff specifically claim equitable relief before a court can award damages in equity?
2. Does the statutory power to award damages in equity effectively allow defendants an opportunity to purchase the right to commit a nuisance? What implications might this have for environmental law?
3. Does a court of equity have the power to make and unmake property and obligational rights?
4. Is *Miller v Jackson* (above p 22) a precedent?
5. How can the defendants have acted in good faith if they knew they were taking a risk with respect to the legal situation?

4 NON-CONTRACTUAL OBLIGATIONS

White v Jones [1995] 1 All ER 691 House of Lords

Lord Goff: My Lords, in this appeal, your Lordships' House has to consider for the first time the much discussed question whether an intended beneficiary under a will is entitled to recover damages from the testator's solicitors by reason of whose negligence the testator's intention to benefit him under the will has failed to be carried into effect. In *Ross v Caunters (a firm)* [1980] Ch 297, a case in which the will failed because, through the negligence of the testator's solicitors, the will was not duly attested, Megarry V-C held that the disappointed beneficiary under the ineffective will was entitled to recover damages from the solicitors in negligence. In the present case, the testator's solicitors negligently delayed the preparation of a fresh will in place of a previous will which the testator had decided to revoke, and the testator died before the new will was prepared. The plaintiffs were the two daughters of the testator who would have benefited under the fresh will but received nothing under the previous will which, by reason of the solicitors' delay, remained unrevoked. It was held by the Court of Appeal ([1993] 3 All ER 481, [1993] 3 WLR 730), reversing the decision of Turner J, that the plaintiffs were entitled to recover damages from the solicitors in negligence. The question which your Lordships have to decide is whether, in cases such as these, the solicitors are liable to the intended beneficiaries who, as a result of their negligence, have failed to receive the benefit which the testator intended they should receive ...

... [T]he question is one which has been much discussed, not only in this country and other common law countries, but also in some civil law countries, notably Germany. There can be no doubt that *Ross v Caunters* has been generally welcomed by academic writers (...). Furthermore, it does not appear to have been the subject of adverse comment in the higher courts in this country, though it has not been approved except by the Court of Appeal in the present case. Indeed, as far as I am aware, *Ross v Caunters* has created no serious problems in practice since it was decided nearly 15 years ago. A similar conclusion has been reached in the courts of New Zealand (...), and the law appears to be developing in the same direction in Canada (...). The position in Australia (...), is at present less clear. In the United States, following two earlier decisions in California ..., the trend now appears to be moving strongly in favour of liability... In Germany a disappointed beneficiary may be entitled to claim damages from the testator's negligent solicitor under the principle known as contract with protective effect for third parties (Vertrag mit Schutzwirkung für Dritte). I shall discuss the relevant German law on the subject in greater detail at a later stage in this opinion. It also appears that a similar conclusion would be reached in France: ..., which appears to be based on the broad principle that a notary is responsible, even as against third parties, for all fault causing damage committed by him in the exercise of his functions. On facts very similar to those of the present case, the Court of Appeal of Amsterdam has held a notary liable in negligence to the intended beneficiary ...

The conceptual difficulties

Even so, it has been recognised on all hands that *Ross v Caunters* raises difficulties of a conceptual nature, and that as a result it is not altogether easy to accommodate the decision within the ordinary principles of our law of obligations ...

It is right however that I should immediately summarise these conceptual difficulties. They are as follows.

(1) First, the general rule is well established that a solicitor acting on behalf of a client owes a duty of care only to his client. The relationship between a solicitor and his client is nearly always contractual, and the scope of the solicitor's duties will be set by the terms of his retainer; but a duty of care owed by a solicitor to his client will arise concurrently in contract and in tort (see *Midland Bank Trust Co Ltd v Hett, Stubbs & Kemp (a firm)* [1979] Ch 384, recently approved by your Lordships' House in *Henderson v Merrett Syndicates Ltd* [1994] 3 All ER 506, [1994] 3 WLR 761). But, when a solicitor is performing his duties to his client, he will generally owe no duty of care to third parties ...

In these circumstances, it is said, there can be no liability of the solicitor to a beneficiary under a will ... There can be no liability in contract, because there is no contract between the solicitor and the disappointed beneficiary; if any contractual claim was to be recognised, it could only be by way of a *ius quaesitum tertio*, and no such claim is recognised in English law. Nor could there be liability in tort, because in the performance of his duties to his client a solicitor owes no duty of care in tort to a third party such as a disappointed beneficiary under his client's will.

(2) A further reason is given which is said to reinforce the conclusion that no duty of care is owed by the solicitor to the beneficiary in tort. Here, it is suggested, is one of those situations in which a plaintiff is entitled to damages if, and only if, he can establish a breach of contract by the defendant. First, the plaintiff's claim is one for purely financial loss; and as a general rule, apart from cases of assumption of responsibility arising under the principle in *Hedley Byrne & Co Ltd v Heller & Partners Ltd* [1964] AC 465, no action will lie in respect of such loss in the tort of negligence. Furthermore, in particular, no claim will lie in tort for damages in respect of a mere loss of expectation, as opposed to damages in respect of damage to an existing right or interest of the plaintiff. Such a claim falls within the exclusive zone of contractual liability; and it is contrary to principle that the law of tort should be allowed to invade that zone ...

(3) A third, and distinct, objection is that, if liability in tort was recognised in cases such as *Ross v Caunters*, it would be impossible to place any sensible bounds to cases in which such recovery was allowed ...

(4) Other miscellaneous objections were taken, though in my opinion they were without substance ...

(5) There is however another objection of a conceptual nature, which was not adumbrated in argument before the Appellate Committee. In the present case, unlike *Ross v Caunters* itself, there was no act of the defendant solicitor which could be characterised as negligent. All that happened was that the solicitor did nothing at all for a period of time ... As a general rule, however, there is no liability in tortious negligence for an omission, unless the defendant is under some pre-existing duty. Once again, therefore, the question arises how liability can arise in the present case in the absence of a contract ...

The impulse to do practical justice

Before addressing the legal questions which lie at the heart of the present case, it is, I consider, desirable to identify the reasons of justice which prompt judges and academic writers to conclude ... that a duty should be owed ... to a disappointed beneficiary. The principal reasons are, I believe, as follows.

(1) In the forefront stands the extraordinary fact that, if such a duty is not recognised, the only persons who might have a valid claim (ie the testator and his estate) have suffered no loss, and the only person who has suffered a loss (ie the disappointed beneficiary) has no claim ... It can therefore be said that, if the solicitor owes no duty to the intended beneficiaries, there is a lacuna in the law which needs to be filled. This I regard as being a point of cardinal importance in the present case.

(2) The injustice of denying such a remedy is reinforced if one considers the importance of legacies in a society which recognises (...) the right of citizens to leave their assets to whom they please, and in which, as a result, legacies can be of great importance to individual citizens, providing very often the only opportunity for a citizen to acquire a significant capital sum; or to inherit a house, so providing a secure roof over the heads of himself and his family; or to make special provision for his or her old age ... [Evidence presented by counsel] perhaps indicates that it is where a testator instructs a small firm of solicitors that mistakes of this kind are most likely to occur, with the result that it tends to be people of modest means, who need the money so badly, who suffer.

(3) There is a sense in which the solicitors' profession cannot complain if such a liability may be imposed upon their members. If one of them has been negligent in such a way as to defeat his client's testamentary intentions, he must regard himself as very lucky indeed if the effect of the law is that he is not liable to pay damages in the ordinary way. It can involve no injustice to render him subject to such a liability, even if the damages are payable not to his client's estate for distribution to the disappointed beneficiary (which might have been the preferred solution) but direct to the disappointed beneficiary.

(4) That such a conclusion is required as a matter of justice is reinforced by consideration of the role played by solicitors in society ...

The German experience

The fact that the problems which arise in cases such as the present have troubled the courts in many jurisdictions, both common law and civil law, and have prompted a variety of reactions, indicates that they are of their very nature difficult to accommodate within the ordinary principles of the law of obligations. It is true that our law of contract is widely seen as deficient in the sense that it is perceived to be hampered by the presence of an unnecessary doctrine of consideration and (through a strict doctrine of privity of contract) stunted through a failure to recognise a *jus quaesitum tertio*. But even if we lacked the former and possessed the latter, the ordinary law could not provide a simple answer to the problems which arise in the present case, which appear at first sight to require the imposition of something like a contractual liability which is beyond the scope of the ordinary *jus quasitum tertio*. In these circumstances, the effect of the special characteristics of any particular system of law is likely to be, as indeed appears from the authorities I have cited, not so much that no remedy is recognised, but rather that the system in question will choose its own special means for granting a remedy notwithstanding the doctrinal difficulties involved.

We can, I believe, see this most clearly if we compare the English and German reactions to problems of this kind ...

I have already referred to problems created in the English law of contract by the doctrines of consideration and of privity of contract. These, of course, encourage us to seek a solution to problems of this kind within our law of tortious negligence. In German law, on the other hand, in which the law of delict does not allow for the recovery of damages for pure economic loss in negligence, it is natural that the judges should extend the law of contract to meet the justice of the case. In a case such as the present, which is concerned with a breach of duty owed by a professional man, A, to his client, B, in circumstances in which practical justice requires that a third party, C, should have a remedy against the professional man, A, in respect of damage which he has suffered by reason of the breach, German law may have recourse to a doctrine called Vertrag mit Schutzwirkung für Dritte (contract with protective effect for third parties), the scope of which extends beyond that of an ordinary contract for the benefit of a third party ... In these cases, it appears that the court will examine whether the contracting parties intended to create a duty of care in favour of the third person ..., or whether there is to be inferred a protective obligation based on good faith ... But any such inference of intention would, in English law, be beyond the scope of our doctrine of implied terms; and it is legitimate to infer that the German judges, in creating this special doctrine, were extending the law of contract beyond orthodox contractual principles.

I wish next to refer to another German doctrine known as Drittschadensliquidation, which is available in cases of transferred loss (Schadensverlagerung) ...

Under this doctrine, to take one example, the defendant, A, typically a carrier, may be held liable to the seller of goods, B, for the loss suffered by the buyer, C, to whom the risk but not the property in the goods has passed. In such circumstances the seller is held to have a contractual claim against the carrier in respect of the damage suffered by the buyer. This claim can be pursued by the seller against the carrier; but it can also be assigned by him to the buyer. If, exceptionally, the seller refuses either to exercise his right for the benefit of the buyer or to assign his claim to him, the seller can be compelled to make the assignment ... At all events both doctrines have the effect of extending to the plaintiff the benefit of what is, in substance, a contractual cause of action; though, at least as seen through English eyes, this result is achieved not by orthodox contractual reasoning, but by the contractual remedy being made available by law in order to achieve practical justice.

Transferred loss in English law

I can deal with this topic briefly. The problem of transferred loss has arisen in particular in maritime law, when a buyer of goods seeks to enforce against a shipowner a remedy in tort in respect of loss of or damage to goods at his risk when neither the rights under the contract nor the property in the goods has passed to him (see *Leigh & Sillavan Ltd v Aliakmon Shipping Co Ltd, The Aliakmon* [1985] QB 350 at 399 *per* Robert Goff LJ and [1986] AC 785 at 820 *per* Lord Brandon). In cases such as these (...) there was a serious lacuna in the law, as was revealed when all relevant interests in the City of London called for reform to make a remedy available to the buyers who under the existing law were without a direct remedy against the shipowners. The problem was solved, as a matter of urgency, by the Carriage of Goods by Sea Act 1992 ... see s 2(1) of the 1992 Act. Here is a sweeping statutory reform, powered by the needs of commerce, which has the effect of enlarging the circumstances in which contractual rights may be transferred by virtue of the transfer of certain documents. For present purposes, however, an important consequence is the solution in this context of a problem of transferred loss, the lacuna being filled by statute rather than by the common law. Moreover, this result has been achieved, as in German law, by vesting in the plaintiff, who has suffered the relevant loss, the contractual rights of the person who has stipulated for the carrier's obligation but has suffered no loss.

I turn next to English law in relation to cases such as the present. Here there is a lacuna in the law, in the sense that practical justice requires that the disappointed beneficiary should have a remedy against the testator's solicitor in circumstances in which neither the testator nor his estate has in law suffered a loss ...

A contractual approach

It may be suggested that, in cases such as the present, the simplest course would be to solve the problem by making available to the disappointed beneficiary, by some means or another, the benefit of the contractual rights (such as they are) of the testator or his estate against the negligent solicitor, as is for example done under the German principle of Vertrag mit Schutzwirkung für Dritte. Indeed that course has been urged upon us by Professor Markesinis in 'An Expanding Tort Law' (1987) 103 LQR 354 at 396-397, echoing a view expressed by Professor Fleming in 'Comparative Law of Torts' (1986) 4 OJLS 235 at 241. Attractive though this solution is, there is unfortunately a serious difficulty in its way. The doctrine of consideration still forms part of our law of contract, as does the doctrine of privity of contract which is considered to exclude the recognition of a *jus quaesitum tertio*. To proceed as Professor Markesinis has suggested may be acceptable in German law, but in this country could be open to criticism as an illegitimate circumvention of these long-established doctrines; and this criticism could be reinforced by reference to the fact that, in the case of carriage of goods by sea, a contractual solution to a particular of transferred loss, and to other cognate problems, was provided only by recourse to Parliament. Furthermore, I myself do not consider that the present case provides a suitable occasion for reconsideration of doctrines so fundamental as these ...

The Albazero principle

Even so, I have considered whether the present problem might be solved by adding cases such as the present to the group of cases referred to by Lord Diplock in *The Albazero, Albacruz (cargo owners) v Albazero (owners)* [1977] AC 774 at 846-847. In these cases, a person may exceptionally sue in his own name to recover a loss which he has not in fact suffered, being personally accountable for any damages so recovered to the person who has in fact suffered the loss ...

Furthermore, in *Linden Gardens Trust Ltd v Lenesta Sludge Disposals Ltd* [1994] 1 AC 85 your Lordships' House extended this group of cases to include a case in which work was done by the defendants under a contract with the first plaintiffs who, despite a contractual bar against assignment of their contractual rights without the consent of the defendants, had without consent assigned them to the second plaintiffs who suffered damage by reason of defective work carried out by the defendants. It was held that, by analogy with the cases referred to in *The Albazero* the first plaintiffs could recover the damages from the defendants for the benefit of the second plaintiffs ...

Even so, the result was only to enable a person to recover damages in respect of loss which he himself had not suffered, for the benefit of a third party. In the present case, there is the difficulty that the third party (the intended beneficiary) is seeking to recover damages for a loss (expectation loss) which the contracting party (the testator) would not himself have suffered ... In the last analysis ... any such right would be contrary to the doctrine of privity of contract ...

The tortious solution

I therefore return to the law of tort for a solution to the problem. For the reasons I have already given, an ordinary action in tortious negligence on the lines proposed by Megarry V-C in *Ross v Caunters* [1980] Ch 297 must, with the greatest respect, be regarded as inappropriate, because it does not meet any of the conceptual problems which have been raised. Furthermore, for the reasons I have previously given, the *Hedley Byrne* principle cannot, in the absence of special circumstances, give rise on ordinary principles to an assumption of responsibility by the testator's solicitor towards an intended beneficiary. Even so, it seems to me that it is open to your Lordships' House, as in *Linden Gardens Trust Ltd v Lenesta Sludge Disposals Ltd* [1994] 1 AC 85, to fashion a remedy to fill a lacuna in the law and so prevent the injustice which would otherwise occur on the facts of cases such as the present. In the *Lenesta Sludge* case, as I have said, the House made available a remedy as a matter of law to solve the problem of transferred loss in the case before them. The present case is, if anything, *a fortiori*, since the nature of the transaction was such that, if the solicitors were negligent and their negligence did not come to light until after the death of the testator, there would be no remedy for the ensuing loss unless the intended beneficiary could claim. In my opinion, therefore, your Lordships' House should in cases such as these extend to the intended beneficiary a remedy under the *Hedley Byrne* principle by holding that the assumption of responsibility by the solicitors towards his client should be held in law to extend to the intended beneficiary who (as the solicitor can reasonably foresee) may, as a result of the solicitor's negligence, be deprived of his intended legacy in circumstances in which neither the testator nor his estate will have a remedy against the solicitor ... I only wish to add that, with the benefit of experience during the 15 years in which *Ross v Caunters* has been regularly applied, we can say with some confidence that a direct remedy by the intended beneficiary against the solicitor appears to create no problems in practice. That is therefore the solution which I would recommend to your Lordships.

As I see it, not only does this conclusion produce practical justice as far as all parties are concerned, but it also has the following beneficial consequences.

(1) There is no unacceptable circumvention of established principles of the law of contract.

(2) No problem arises by reason of the loss being of a purely economic character.

(3) Such assumption of responsibility will of course be subject to any term of the contract between the solicitor and the testator which may exclude or restrict the solicitor's liability to the testator under the principle in *Hedley Byrne* ...

(4) Since the *Hedley Byrne* principle is founded upon an assumption of responsibility, the solicitor may be liable for negligent omissions as well as negligent acts of commission ...

(5) I do not consider that damages for loss of an expectation are excluded in cases of negligence arising under the principle in *Hedley Byrne*, simply because the cause of action is classified as tortious. Such damages may in principle be recoverable in cases of contractual negligence; and I cannot see that, for present purposes, any relevant distinction can be drawn between the two forms of action. In particular, an expectation loss may well occur in cases where a professional man, such as a solicitor, has assumed responsibility for the affairs of another; and I for my part can see no reason in principle why the professional man should not, in an appropriate case, be liable for such loss under the *Hedley Byrne* principle ...

Conclusion

For these reasons I would dismiss the appeal with costs.

Lord Brown-Wilkinson: My Lords, I have read the speech of my noble and learned friend, Lord Goff of Chieveley, and agree with him that this appeal should be dismissed. In particular, I agree that your Lordships should hold that the defendant solicitors were under a duty of care to the plaintiffs arising from an extension of the principle of assumption of responsibility explored in *Hedley Byrne & Co Ltd v Heller & Partners Ltd* [1964] AC 465. In my view, although the present case is not directly covered by the decided cases, it is legitimate to extend the law to the limited extent proposed using the incremental approach by way of analogy advocated in *Caparo Industries plc v Dickman* [1990] 2 AC 605 ...

Lord Nolan: My Lords, I would dismiss this appeal. I would do so because ... the respondents' claim appears to me to satisfy the criteria laid down by the decisions of your Lordships' House in *Caparo Industries plc v Dickman* [1990] 2 AC 605 and *Murphy v Brentwood DC* [1991] 1 AC 398.

I reach this conclusion the more readily because.... [t]o reverse the decision in *Ross v Caunters* at this stage would be, in my judgment, a disservice to the law. I agree with the views expressed in the unanimous judgments of the Court of Appeal ...

Lord Keith of Kinkel (dissenting): ... To admit the plaintiffs' claim in the present case would in substance, in my opinion, be to give them the benefit of a contract to which they were not parties.

Further, there is, in my opinion, no decided case the grounds of decision in which are capable of being extended incrementally and by way of analogy so as to admit of a remedy in tort being made available to the plaintiffs ...

Upon the whole matter I have found the conceptual difficulties involved in the plaintiffs' claim, which are fully recognised by all your Lordships, to be too formidable to be resolved by any process of reasoning compatible with existing principles of law ...

I would therefore allow the appeal.

Lord Mustill (dissenting): ... At first sight it might seem that an approach somewhat similar to the concept of 'transferred loss', to which reference is made in some of the notable commentaries on foreign legal systems which have been placed before the House, might yield a solution on these lines. On reflection, however, I am satisfied that this is not so. As I understand it, the nature of a 'transferred loss' is revealed by its name. In situations where party A has a cause of action for a breach of duty by the defendant, but the loss resulting from the breach is suffered not by A himself but by B, the loss is 'transferred', or attributed, to A so as to enable him to recover damages for the breach. Essentially this is a fiction. There have been many such in English law over the centuries, in the main to its enrichment: always provided that they are recognised for what they are. It may be that some instances of an equivalent principle, albeit so far very isolated, are already to be found in English law: for example, the exceptional situations recorded by Lord Diplock in *The Albazero, Albacruz (cargo owners) v Albazero (owners)* [1977] AC 774 at 846, and perhaps also *Linden Gardens Trust Ltd v Lenestra Sludge Disposals Ltd* [1994] 1 AC 85. These are however far distant from the present case, for they concerned situations where there was a single loss which might have been suffered indifferently by the obligee or by someone else, and which the courts were content to attribute to the obligee. Here, by contrast, to enable the estate, in title of the deceased testator, to recover a sum equivalent to the disappointed expectations of the beneficiaries would be to compensate it for a loss which it not only had not, but could not have, suffered. The plaintiffs' complaint and the consequent damage are quite different from the complaint and the damage to which the estate succeeded on the death of the testator. To allow them to be treated as if they were the same would extend the boundaries of a contractual obligation far further than has ever been previously contemplated; and, I suspect further than has been contemplated even in the majority of those jurisdictions where concepts of privity are less rigorous than in our own.

Furthermore, even if the doctrine were to be fully received into English law I am unable to visualise how it could help the plaintiffs here. As its name denotes it is concerned with the transfer of loss to the claimant from someone else. In the present case the intended beneficiaries do not need such a transfer, for they already have a loss. Their problem is to find a cause of action, and to achieve this a quite different kind of transfer would be required ...

Notes and Questions

1. To what extent was Donoghue v Stevenson (above p 33) and example of (i) Vertrag mit Schutzwirkung für Dritte; (ii) Drittschadensliquidation; (iii) a contractual remedy being made available to a third party?

2. Was *Beswick v Beswick* (above pp 37, 86, 154) a problem of transferred loss? What about *Jackson v Horizon Holidays* (p 121)? Could someone in Mrs Beswick's position now sue, in her personal capacity, the nephew in damages under the *Hedley Byrne* principle? What about the family in *Jackson*?

3. What does Lord Goff mean by 'practical justice'? Why does the word 'justice' need the qualification?

4. Did comparative law play a role in arriving at the solution in this case? If so, how?

5. Does *White v Jones* in effect extend s 13 of the Supply of Goods and Services Act 1992 (above p 210) to a third parties?

6. When a person dies most causes of action (defamation remains an exception) vest in a new legal *persona* called the 'estate' (Law Reform (Miscellaneous Provisions) Act 1934 s 1). Is this an example, as one tort specialist once suggested, of the law allowing a ghost to sue and be sued? If so, what 'damage' can ghosts suffer? Why should ghosts not be allowed to sue in defamation? In allowing Mrs Beswick and Mrs White and her sister to sue, is not the law transferring a loss from the spiritual to the real world? Is this kind of fiction any less rational than the fiction discussed in *Tesco v Nattrass* (above p 17)?

7. Could not *White v Jones* have been decided in equity: for example, would it not have been possible to say that the solicitors, *vis-à-vis* the beneficiaries, were estopped by their negligence from denying the validity of the new will?

8. Does *White v Jones* put the decision of the majority in *Spartan Steel* (above p 101) in doubt? If not, why not?

Regalian Properties plc v London Dockland Development Corpn [1995] 1 All ER 1005 Chancery Division

Rattee J: ... I can well understand why Goff J [in *British Steel Corp v Cleveland Bridge and Engineering Co Ltd* [1984] 1 All ER 504] concluded that where one party to an expected contract expressly requests the other to perform services or supply goods that would have been performable or suppliable under the expected contract when concluded in advance of the contract, that party should have to pay a *quantum meruit* if the contract does not materialise. The present case is not analogous. The costs for which Regalian seeks reimbursement were incurred by it not by way of accelerated performance of the anticipated contract at the request of LDDC, but for the purpose of putting itself in a position to obtain and then perform the contract ...

I appreciate that the English law of restitution should be flexible and capable of continuous development. However, I see no good reason to extend it to apply some ... principle ... to facts such as those of the present case, where, however much the parties expect a contract between them to materialise, both enter negotiations expressly (whether by use of the words 'subject to contract' or otherwise) on terms that each party is free to withdraw from the negotiations at any time. Each party to such negotiations must be taken to know (as in my judgment Regalian did in the present case) that pending the conclusion of a binding contract any cost incurred by him in preparation for the intended contract will be incurred at his own risk in the sense that he will have no recompense for those costs if no contract results. In other words ... each accepted that in the event of no contract being entered into, any resultant loss should lie where it fell ...

Questions

1. Discuss the role that risk plays in the law of restitution. Is it a helpful concept in the law of obligations? Is it a normative, quasi-normative or descriptive concept (Cf Chapter 2)?

2 If the result of *Regalian* had been different, would this have altered in any way the legal situation described by Sir Thomas Bingham MR in *Pitt v PHH* (above p 249)?

5 FINAL NOTE

1. Remedies: (i) Rectification: see *Commission for the New Towns v Cooper* [1995] 2 All ER 929; (ii) Damages: *Banque Bruxelles Lambert SA v Eagle Star Insurance Co* [1995] 2 All ER 769; *Page v Smith* [1995] 2 All ER 736.

2. Contractual Obligations: *Commission for the New Towns*, above.

3. Non-Contractual Obligations: *Page v Smith*, above.

INDEX

Acceptance 235-52
  advertisement 237-8
  communication
    of acceptance 238, 241-2
  fact and law 235
  French law and 236-7
    international uniformity,and 242
  methods 241-2
  mistake 264
  objective mutuality 233, 241
  offer essential 233, 243
  performance as 238
  pre-contractual liability 241-2
  strict interpretation of 219-20
  tenders 243-6
  unilateral contract, and 206

Accord and satisfaction 257

Account 167-8

Actions, law of
  actiones 14
  chose in action 17
  civil and Roman law 123
  in personam 16, 17-19
  in rem 16, 22-6
  procedure 26
  remedy 26-7, 111, 405

Agency
  appointment 287, 401-2
  consultants 213
  duties under 39-41, 365
  revocation 279

Agreement
  see also promise
  civil law 203-4, 297, 302
  contract, and 204, 219
  negotiate, to 248
  promise, and 203-4, 216-20,
    234, 264, 297
  suspension of rights 256

Bailment 38-41, 198, 407-9

Breach of contact 320-7
  care 321, 323-4
  causation 198, 306
  condition 230, 329
  consequences 328, 329, 331, 332
  damage as cause 306
  fault 210-11, 227, 302
  frustration 304, 328, 331
  inducing 391-3, 395
  interference with contact 391-5
  interpretation 322
  loss, need to minimise 136
  lump sum and performance 126
  mistake 264, 265
  non-performance 127, 297, 337
  obligations, other 329
  penalties 224, 335-8
  promise 227, 297, 302-3, 322
  remedies, choice of 32, 134, 136, 155
  repudiation 127, 133-6, 229-30, 231
  root, going to the 298
  specific performance 32, 136, 154-7
  specific terms of 198, 306, 331-2
  third person's benefit 121-2, 154-6
  unilateral contract 206

Carriage, contracts of 320, 321, 323

Case law, use 2, 8, 9-11, 57, 234

Case, striking out of 112

Causation, rules and principles 198-9

Causes of action
  see also forms of
    action 63-6
  fault and 361
  limited to pleadings 67, 78, 120
  nature of 65, 66
  public law and 355
  remedies and rights in
    modern law 65-6
  rights and 66, 107, 112, 113

Collateral contracts 238-9, 247,
    261, 265

Common law
  see also legal method,
    legal reasoning

causes of action   63-6
contract, central role   203
courts, role of   1-9
equity and   42
facts, role of   57-8, 81-8
general principles of law   69-70, 104
institutions and   13-27
law and fact   81-8
legal categories   27-43
legal concepts   58-9, 70-81
legal rule   68-9
parliament and   9-11
precedent and   9-11
property and   38
public and private law   28-9, 43-56
remedies and   38
structure of   1-59
system, as   8-9, 42
text books   56-7

Comparative law, role   367, 383

Conditions
  see also contract   229-31
  business efficacy   209, 226
  contracts, importance in   239
  consumer goods   316-17
  covenants and   218, 219
  minimum payment clause   336, 337
  non-performance on   207
  onerous, unfair   222-6
  penalty   224, 335-8
  performance,on   207
  precondition   230
  primary and secondary   313, 314
  printed   223-5
  quality, as to   274
  reasonable   221
  terms, usual   225
  terms, written standard   316

Conditions precedent   204-5, 233,
                                264, 281-2, 298

Consideration   252-61
  abuse of rights, and   255-60
  additional   252-4, 256-7
  breach, acting in own   254
  contract, essential in   234, 253
  definition   254-5
  failure of   130, 282, 406
  good   205

legal rights suspended   256
lesser sum, agreement to pay   255-9
moving from promisee   238, 261
third parties, and   260-1
unilateral contract, in   205
validity of   218, 252-5
variation deed   254, 258

Construction of written
  instruments   226-31, 346-7

Consumer   221-2, 225, 226, 314, 316-17

Contract
  see also breach of contract,
  consideration, formation of
  contract, sale of goods
  agreement and   204, 219
  contracts, or   206-8, 354
  duty, level of   209-14
  French law compared   203, 204, 210
  good faith   224, 225
  historical background   v, 203,
                                206-7, 219, 261
  inequality of bargaining power   291
  intention   209, 220, 226-7, 230
  interpretation of   226-31, 346-7
  law and structure of   350
  mutuality in   135, 205, 207
  reasonable expectations
    of parties   280
  remedy, role of   204
  terms, standard written   316
  third parties and   86, 260-1
  void and voidable   234, 265, 289

Contract, bilateral   204, 205-6, 328

Contract of employment
  see also vicarious liability
  delegation   19
  duties under   18, 19, 213, 308-9, 315
  implied terms   227-8, 308, 310-12
  insurance   227-8, 308, 309
  management   311
  subrogation, and   308-9, 310

Contract, executory   251

Contract law, use of Criminal law   12

Contract, lump sum   126, 298

Contract, synallagmatic   204,
                          205-6, 328

Contract, unilateral   205-6, 251, 297

Contractual obligations
  see also formation of contract,
  sale of goods
  duty, level of   209-14
  fault and liability   210
  freedom of contract   220-6
  French law and   210
  interpretation   226-31
  persons   214-16
  promise and agreement   216-20
  property   214-16

Contributory negligence
  defence as   48, 51-2, 210, 306
  implied consent   48
  misrepresentation in   164
  mitigation, and   199
  statutory provisions   201-2, 228-9

Conversion
  assumpsit to debt, and   130
  bailment, and   40
  hire purchase and   214
  mistake, and   265, 288-9
  nature of   27, 191-2
  profit earning and non-profit
    earning chattels   192, 200

Council of Europe's Draft
  Convention on Civil Liability 381

Courts
  abuse of process   115-16
  county courts   75, 78

Court of Appeal   4-7
  divisional court   7, 75, 78
  House of Lords   7-9, 68
  injunctions, power to grant   75, 78
  law reports, use by   5-6

limitations on law   226
personal injuries guidelines   189-90
role   1-9, 383
scientific truth distinguished   2-3
trial judge's factual findings   84

Criminal Injuries Compensation
  Scheme   364

Damage, classification of   79

Damage caused to another   358-95
  actionability   198
  causation   183, 197, 198-9
  cosortium, loss of   358-9
  danger, by   368-9
  death   183, 359
  foreseeability   366, 367, 369, 370
  French law compared   361, 367,
                      371, 374, 383-4
  individual acts by   360-2
  intervening act   367
  nature, operation of   384
  novus actus interveniens   367
  omissions, no common
    law liability   366
  people, liability for   362-73
  statutory duties   386
  things, liability for   373-87, 397
  third parties by   365-71
  trade dispute   393
  'transferred loss principle'   371
  unlawful behaviour   386

Damages   177-202, 332-5
  action and proof of damage   33, 297
  action in and interest   139
  compensatory nature   32, 139,
                        177, 179, 188
  consent vitiates claim   199
  conspiracy   190-1
  contributory negligence   199, 201-2
  defendant's behaviour   188, 190-1
  definitions   177, 178, 185, 190
  exemplary   30-1, 188-9
  government employees   188-9
  insurance, and   187, 308
  interest   127, 138
  judicial review, and   28
  land   186-7, 194-6
  loss, genuine   186
  mistake   265

negative interest of plaintiff 179
non-performance 297
nominal 179
punitive elements 30-1 36
reasonableness 184, 185,
187, 198, 201
role of 177-8
single sum payment 177, 189
special 138, 190
statutory misrepresentation 271-2

Damages in contract 30
benefit, loss of 180, 187
breach for 32, 136-7, 182,
189, 190, 297
exemplary 189
Hadley v Baxendale rule 179, 193-6
interests protected by 121, 332
profits 179, 180, 194-6, 200, 406
warranty, breach of 181, 183, 274

Damages, difference
with debt 132, 136, 138-40, 204, 307

Damages measure of 185, 191,
197-9, 193-202
assessment 177, 179, 181, 201, 202
bargain, loss of 179
economic and
non-economic loss 189, 200
French Code civil, and 194
general rules 178-9, 191, 193-6
Hadley v Baxendale rule 179, 193-6
land 186-7
natural consequences 193, 333-4
personal injury guidelines 189-90
practical reasons 196
psychiatric damage 181, 334-5
profits 194-6, 200
special circumstances 193

Damages and
misrepresentation 30-1, 181, 183,
265, 271-2

Damages in tort 30
consent vitiates claim 199
conversion 191, 192, 200
deceit 191
defamation 177, 190, 387-8
defendant's gain 179

fraud 190-1
general principle 191
negligence 33
nuisance 187
patent infringement 179
reasonable foreseeability 196
personal injury 187, 189-90
trespass 179, 192
wrongful interference 191-2

Death, liability 212, 221

Debt
see also tracing, *quantum meruit*,
quasi-contract 130-40, 335-8
account, action in 167-8, 404, 406
assumpsit, action in 130, 132, 219
consideration failed 130-1,
137-8, 406
contractual debt 130, 133-8, 404, 405
damages contrasted 136, 404
deceit 130
historical background 16-17, 130-3
implied contract 133
money had and received 130, 132,
137, 404, 406-7
money paid 130, 131, 140, 406, 407-9
non-contractual 133, 140, 243, 403-10
non-performance and 335-8
property in 37, 38, 145-6, 151, 206
repudiation 133-6
salvage, and 140

Deceit 219, 233, 265, 268, 287

Declaration 112-17, 118, 265, 345-8

Defamation 113, 190, 387-8, 389-91

Detinue 179, 191, 192, 214, 403

Distress 128-9
Donoghue v Stevenson rule 33-4,
362, 364

Duress 54-5, 125, 290-4, 406

Economic duress   253, 290-1,
    395, 405-6

Economic loss assessment   101-2,
    189, 200
   foreseeability, and   370
   negligence   243, 394-5

Economic torts   394-5

Equity   41-3, 104, 259, 260

Error
   see also mistake   275-85, 286-89, 291

Estoppel   27, 218-19, 243,
    253, 258-60

Exclusion and limitation
   clauses   312-20
   bargaining strength, and   319
   breach of contract and   391-3
   consent and   199
   considered   313-14
   hire purchase agreements and   224
   negligence and   221, 269,
    316, 319-20
   onerous clauses and   223
   reasonableness test   318-19, 320
   statutory regulations   221, 224, 314,
    316-7, 319
   trade disputes and   391-3

Fault   302-12
   agreement and promise   302
   burden of proof   303, 304, 356
   fault principle   35, 361, 362
   French law compared   210, 361, 397
   insurance   356

Formation of contract
   see also acceptance,
   consideration, offer   233-294
   bilateral contracts   204-5
   condition precedent   204, 205, 206
   conduct during negotiations   207-8
   inequality of bargaining power   291
   pre-contractual liability   241-52
   unilateral contracts   205-6

Forms of action   63-5
   abolition   65, 354
   legal reasoning, and   355
   public law, and   355
   rights and remedies   132, 354,
    355, 405

Fraud   190-1, 289-90
   consent   233, 234, 290
   damages   190-1, 234
   deceit   265, 268, 287
   nature and effect   233, 234, 290

Freedom of contract   69, 207, 220-6,
    280, 313

Frustration of contract
   adjustment of rights and
   considered   262-3, 282-3, 343, 344
   damages, and   304

Fault of neither party   328

Failure of consideration   130
   implied term
    contemplating   339, 343
   liabilities, and   349

Gaius and institutional system   14-15,
    16, 216

Gaming and wagering   146, 147, 148

Good faith   224, 225, 240, 249

Government officers, employees   120,
    188

Hire purchase
   agreements   214-16, 224,
    279-80, 335-8

Implied contract   84, 133, 358, 404

Implied terms
   business, course of   209, 210, 228-9
   business efficacy   209-10, 226, 281
   care, due (carriage)   321, 322, 323

care and skill (goods) 302-3, 323
care and skill (professional) 209,
    212-14, 325-7, 334-5
care and skill (services) 210, 221,
    303, 313, 315
common intention
    of the parties 207-8
conditions 329-31
defence, statutory 211
disclosure 306
fitness for the purposes 209, 228-9,
    303, 306, 321
food 304-5
goods 209, 210-11, 216, 279, 316-17
habitation, fit for 209
hiring 303-4, 322-4
intentions, presumed 226-7
level of duty 209-14
management 311
manufacturer, and 33-4, 362,
    364, 385
nature of 207, 229
objective rules 229
'obvious' terms 281-2
performance and
    non-performance 207
quality, as to 209, 228-9, 274, 302-3
reject, right to 275, 298
statutory 207, 209-12,
    221, 228-9, 315-17
unfair terms 221, 225
warranties 209, 226-7, 327, 329-31

Impossibility of performance
    see also frustration
of contract 335-50
conditions contemplating 339, 340
delay, effect of 344
inflation, and 347
interpretation of 343, 346-7
performance and
    non-performance 339, 340
subject matter, non-existent
    or changed 341-3

Injunction 170-7
    Anton Piller order 172-4
    county courts and 75, 78

Interlocutory 78, 116, 171-5, 391

Mareva injunction 172
nature of 170, 175-7, 378, 383
negative covenants 175-6
restraint 114, 171, 174,
    175-6, 378

Insurance
    see also subrogation
employment contract, and 227-8,
    307-9

Influence of 35, 187, 314, 328, 375

Intention to create legal
    relations 234, 245, 246

Interference with contract 70, 391-4

Judges cases and legislation,
    binding 2
development of law by 7-8, 11,
    178, 189-90, 357
role of 2, 7-8, 10, 68, 178
trial 2-4, 84

Judicial review 28

Land, sale of contracts 250
    damages and 186-7, 194-6
    negotiations 247, 249-50

Law and fact 81-88
analysis of facts and remedy 81, 85,
    86, 350, 415-16
categorisation of facts 84-5
determination of 82-4, 85, 87, 87-8

'Law arises out of facts' 111, 415

Legal reasoning and 97-8
    response to 85-6, 87-8

Law reports 5-6, 414-15

Legal categories,
    see also public and
    private categories 27-43, 43-56
    bailment 38-41

civil and criminal law 30-1
classification 27-8, 29-43, 85
contract 32, 354
equity 41-3
forms of action and 354
logic and 92-3
real and personal property 37-8
restitution 36, 354
Roman law 27-8, 29
tort 33-6, 354
legal concepts 70-81, 415-16
descriptive 80-1
interests 74, 79-80
institutions of law and 415-16
natural law 70, 71
normative 70-3, 227, 302
quasi-normative 74-80, 415

Legal institutions
see also legal concepts 13-27
actions *in personam* 16, 28, 216, 415
actions *in rem* 16, 21-26, 28, 216, 415
classification 27-43
common law and equity 42-3
definitional problems 13-14
institutional system 13-16

Legal object (*res*) 19-22, 415

Legal relations 15, 16, 415-16

Legal subject (*persona*) 17-19, 27-8, 415
quasi-normative rules 415
Roman law 13-17, 27-8, 29
role of 13-27, 356
subrogation 169

Legal method
See also legal institution,
legal reasoning 61-109, 414
analysis 353, 363, 415-16
case law 8, 9-11, 57, 234, 363
facts from 246, 363
general principles of law and 69-70
importance of 350-353

Legal rule, the 68
Roman and civil law 61, 74, 416
technique 350

Legal reasoning
See also legal method 88-109, 414
academics, and 357
analysis 14, 350, 363, 415-16
analogy 91, 95-6, 103, 108
argumentation 93, 107
certainty, need for 105
commercial reality 104-5
common sense 104, 365, 372
deduction 88, 91, 363, 372
definitions, uniform 92
educated reflex to facts 371, 372, 373, 374
elimination 94
facts 57-8, 97-8, 246
hard and clear cases 91, 102-3
hypotheses 94, 97-8
induction 88, 91, 96, 363, 372
interpretation of rights 101-3
logic and categorisation 92-3, 94
mental imagery 94-5, 97, 372
metaphor 97
painting a picture 94-5, 97, 372
policy 100, 101-2, 106, 363
practical 103-8, 372
principle 102-3
public confidence 105
Roman law 98, 415
syllogism 68, 91-2, 372, 415
symmetry 108-9
values 98-9

Legislation 11, 12, 56

Mental distress
See psychiatric damage

Misrepresentation
see also damages

Mistake
consent, vitiates 282
contributory negligence 164
fraudulent 30, 233-4
identity 288, 289
innocent 30, 31, 233, 269, 271-2
innocent, and damages 181, 266, 267, 271-2
nature of 266, 269, 272-3, 277, 278
negligent 269, 310

notice   160, 161, 162, 164
remedies   233, 265
rescission   157-165, 233-4,
                                265, 271-3, 275
sureties, and   157, 160, 161, 163

Mistake,
    see also misrepresentation 261-89
    abuse of power or rights   266
    common   282-4
    common law and   262-3, 264,
                                265, 282-4
    consent, and   277, 282
    consideration, substance of and 283
    contract liability   233, 262,
                                266-7, 284, 289
    deceit   268
    equity, in   263, 266, 284, 285
    error *in corpore*   275-85
    error *in negotio*   286-8
    error *in persona*   288-9
    fraud   268
    fundamental   262, 263, 274, 282
    identity   277, 288-9
    misrepresentation, and   265
    money paid under   130,131, 406
    nature of   165, 166, 264,
                                265-6, 282-4
    non est factum   265, 286, 287
    quality of goods   274, 277-8,
                                282, 284
    remedies   233, 264-6
    reasonable grounds, lack of 284
    specific performance   265
    subject matter changed   281, 284
    tort   268-72
    unjustified enrichment, and 266

Mitigation of damages
    duty   136, 199-200, 201
    reasonableness, and   184, 185,
                                198, 201

Necessity   48-9, 50, 355-6

Negligence   48, 49, 50-2, 118
    care, absence of   83, 324
    care, duty of   89, 268-71, 363
    care, reasonable   69, 89
    care, standard of   69, 268-71
    causing or permitting danger 368-9
    considered   213-14

defences   48-52
definition, statutory   315
employment and   227-8, 372
escape of mischief   373-4, 375
establishing   82-3, 119, 198,
                                323, 356
foreseeability and   370, 375, 399
highway   398
manufacturer   33-4, 89-91
privity, and doctrine of   261
public interest in   47
remedy   23-4
road accidents   395-403
special relationships   270
Unfair Contract Terms Act   221
wrongdoing of others, and   367-8

Nervous shock
    see psychiatric damage

Non-contractual obligations
    see also damage caused
    to another, torts   353-416
    background   353-4, 356, 367, 374
    damage caused to another   358-95
    Donoghue v Stevenson rule 362
    occupiers liability   368-9, 370,
                                384-5, 386
    road accidents   395-403
    Ryland v Fletcher, rule   373-4
    vicarious liability   362-65,
                                372-3, 400-2

Non-performance of contract
    see also breach of contract
    frustration   295-351
    analysis, and   296
    breach and
        non-performance   296-301
    contract providing for   207
    fault, role of   302-12
    French law and   297, 340

Non-liability, and   340
    remedies prompting
        substantive consideration 295-6
    unilateral contract   297

Nuisance,
    See also occupiers liability,
        Rylands v Fletcher rule 375-87

considered   69, 118-20, 376-7
defences   48-52
foreseeability   376, 378-9, 383, 399
highways, and   384-5, 397-9
interest in land   76-7, 79
natural and non-natural
   use of land   374, 377-8, 382, 384
negligence, and   23-4, 369, 376, 399
new categories   76, 77
private, considered   119, 123
public   119, 120, 123, 372, 386
reasonable care, and   378, 385
remedy   23-4
statutory   386

Obligations, law of
   breach must cause damage   306
   contract and   32, 203-294, 356
   damage, classifications   79
   legal method   61-109
   legal reasoning   88-109
   non-contractual   353-416
   personum, actio in   16, 19
   rem, actio in   16, 22-26
   Roman and civil law   13-16
   subrogation   169

Occupiers liability   368-9, 370, 386

Offer
   see also acceptance   219-20, 235-51
   commerce, and   239-40
   communication, and   241-2
   consideration and
      advertisement   238
   consumers   236-9
   fact and law   235
   French law and   236-7
   mistake   264
   'puff' and   237
   revocation of   240-1
   shop, goods for sale in   236-7
   tender   243-6
   variation of clause   239-40
   world at large, to   238

Performance of contract
   failure is breach   313
   liability   339
   lump sum contracts   126, 298
   substantial performance   126-7

time of   135, 394

Personal injury   79
   Criminal Injuries
      Compensation Scheme   364
   damages, guidelines for   189-90
   negligence and   221
   Rylands v Fletcher rule   377
   sale of goods and   212, 221

Persons (persona) law of
   see obligations law of

Pleadings   66-7
   actions limited to   67, 78, 120
   amendment of   75
   court and questions of law   226
   negligence   67
   substance not form   64, 66-7

Pollution   121, 380, 381, 383, 384

Pre-contractual liability
   see also collateral contracts,
   quantum meruit,
   quasi-contract   241-52, 410
   good faith in civil law   249
   land and   247, 249-50
   lockout agreements   247, 248-9, 250
   negotiations   247, 248-50

Promise   216-20
   agreement and   216-20, 234,
                                    264, 297, 302
   classification   208
   contract law and   203-4, 216-20,
                                    234, 297, 302
   errors, and risk of   219
   foundation of liability   238

Promissory estoppel, doctrine of 253,
                                           258-60

Property
   damage to   212, 365-6, 370
   extinguishment   259
   goods, in   208, 289, 307
   interference with use
      and enjoyment   79

Property (*rem*)
  see obligations law of

Proximity   80-1, 359, 362, 371

Psychiatric damage   79, 121, 181-2,
                    299-301, 358-61

Public and private law
  categories   28-9, 43-56
  causes of action, and   355
  civil law compared 28, 29, 46, 47, 53
  considered   28, 45, 120
  constitutional function   47
  contracts   44-6
  defences   48-52
  government, and   52, 53, 54, 55-6
  institutions, and role of   310
  ownership   38
  public body and rights   247
  public law, duty   45
  remedies   44
  restitution   54-6
  tort   24, 46-53

Quasi contract
  see also collateral contracts debt
  pre-contract liabilities   358, 403-4

Quantum meruit   409-10
  considered   140, 222,
             224-5, 250-1, 409-10
  rectification   165-7
  references   268-71, 389-90
  remedies   111-202, 327-8
  account   167-8, 404, 406
  damages   177-202, 332-5
  debt   130-40, 335-8, 404
  declaration   112-17, 265, 345-8
  forms of action, link   26-7
  injunction   170-7
  justification   119
  legal institutions, and   1, 111
  nature of   117-18, 120
  non-performance of
    condition, for   337
  penalties, relief against   335-8
  rectification   165-7
  release   328, 331
  repudiation   331
  rescission   157-65, 331

restitution   354
rights and   65-6, 111-21, 354, 383
self-help   124-9, 327-32
specific performance   136, 154-7
subrogation   168-70
tracing   140-54

Remoteness causation, and 183, 197-8
  damages and   101-2, 183,
               196, 198, 333
  economic loss   101-2
  nervous shock   299
  psychiatric damage   299
  test   193, 196, 197-8, 300, 333-4

Representations   217-18, 219,
                    266, 272-3

Repudiation   133-6, 229-30, 330, 331

Rescission   157-65
  avoidance by creditors 162-3, 163-4
  damages in lieu   265
  deceit and   233
  equity   157-65, 272-5, 294
  fraud and   233-4
  misrepresentation   157-65
  mistake   263, 264, 265, 272-5
  notice   160, 161, 162, 164
  nature of   234, 272-5
  third parties 157, 161, 163-4, 234
  unconscionable transactions   165

Restitution
  see also unjust enrichment   404-6
  account of profits   168
  bailment   39, 407-8
  benefit/profit basis   354
  change in position   149, 411
  development   131, 355, 404-5
  frustrated contract   130-1
  mistake and   266
  non-contractual obligation   405
  quantum meruit   251, 409-10
  wrongful obtaining
    of a benefit   412-13

Rights abuse of   255-60, 266,
                 336, 413-14
  combined with other
    elements   113-14

definition 71
duty 71, 73
estoppel 259
French law 413
natural 71
new rights under proprietory
  normative concept, as 70-80
social aspects 73

Road accidents 395-403

Rylands v Fletcher rule 373-4, 380
considered 49-50, 379-82
defences 49-50, 373, 377-8, 382
foreseeability 376, 379-81, 383
natural and non-natural
  use of land 374, 377-8, 381-3
nuisance, as extension to 381
strict liability 49, 375-7, 379-81, 383

Sale of goods
see also contract, implied terms
action for the price 135
acceptance 274-5, 298
contractual rules 20, 206-8
description 267
fault 21, 302-3, 327
faulty goods 303, 327
fitness 20, 21, 209, 228-9, 305-6
guarantee of consumer
  goods 316-17
property in 135-6, 208, 234
quality 21, 209, 228-9, 274, 303
quality and mistake 274, 277-8,
  282, 284
reject, right to 274-5, 298
sale and return basis 307
standard written terms 316
warranties 329

Self-help 124-9, 327-32
defaulting party 328
discharge 328, 330-1
distress 128-9
frustration 328
innocent party 328, 329, 331
liens 129
motives 124
personal justice 124-5

refusal to pay 126-9
repudiation 127, 133-6,
  229-30, 231, 331
rescission 330-1
self-protection 125-6
set-off 128, 129

Services
see also contracts of
employment fault 303
hirer 323
professional skill and care 209,
  213-14,
  325-7, 334-5
reasonable expectations of 326-7

Statutory 210

Specific performance 136-7, 154-7, 265

Statutory compensation 79, 396

Strict liability 210, 211, 212, 227, 397

Subrogation 129, 168-70, 309, 310, 356

Surety 157, 160-5, 281, 287

Tender 243-7

Tort
see also individual torts 33-6
breach of trust, aiding 143
care, general duty of 33-4, 69, 83
compensation 35-6
consent (*volenti
  non fit injuria*) 48, 199
conversion 200
damage caused to another 358-95
damage, nature of 354, 357, 358-60
deceit 233, 265, 268, 287
defamation 387-8, 389-91
detinue 403
economic 394-5
foreseeability 33, 378-9
harassment 76-9
individual acts, for 360-2
insurance and 35, 402
nature of 35-6, 357

people and liability for 362-73
road accidents 395-403
statutory duty, breach 384

Things, liability for 373-87
misrepresentation and 265
new 74-9
non-contractual
  obligations and 353-416
nuisance and 375-87
personal injury 79
plaintiffs, discrimination
  between 34-5
property damage and 35, 79
privacy, and 76
words, liability for 387-95

Tracing 140-54, 405, 406
change in position 149-50, 151
chose in action 141, 146
development of 140-2, 143, 144, 145
money 141, 142, 145-6, 151
nature of 140-1, 142, 143, 144
tangible goods 151-4
trespass considered 48-50
damage caused by 366, 368, 369
defence 125, 176
land 48, 118-19, 120, 365-9
person, to 125

Trust 38, 42, 143

Unconscionable transaction 165, 224, 337-8

Undue influence 157-64, 165, 282, 287

Unjust enrichment 233-4, 357-8, 404-5, 407, 410-13

Vicarious liability 310-12, 362-3, 365, 372-3, 401-2

Warranties breach 181, 183, 274
considered 206, 216-18, 219, 266-7
implied 20, 84, 228, 274

Wrongful interference 191-2

Wrongfully gaining a benefit 357-8, 407, 412